KT-504-547

DAVID KYNASTON

THE FINANCIAL TIMES

A CENTENARY HISTORY

VIKING

VIKING

Published by the Penguin Group
27 Wrights Lane, London W8 5TZ England
Viking Penguin Inc., 40 West 23rd Street, New York, New York 10010, USA
Penguin Books Australia Ltd, Ringwood, Victoria, Australia
Penguin Books Canada Ltd, 2801 John Street, Markham, Ontario, Canada L3R 1B4
Penguin Books (NZ) Ltd, 182–190 Wairau Road, Auckland 10, New Zealand

Penguin Books Ltd, Registered Offices; Harmondsworth, Middlesex, England

First published 1988
Reprinted 1988

Filmset in Bembo
Printed in Great Britain by Richard Clay, Bungay, Suffolk

British Library Cataloguing in Publication Data

Kynaston, David
The Financial Times: a centenary history.
1. Financial times——History
I. Title
330.9'005 PN5129.L7F5

ISBN 0-670-81295-1

Library of Congress Catalog Card No. 87-51089

CONTENTS

PREFACE

The history of the *Financial Times* is the history of how two newspapers became one and in so doing began to attain a breadth and stature previously undreamt of in financial journalism. For almost sixty years the *Financial News* (founded in 1884) and the *Financial Times* (founded in 1888) were rivals; they were the leading daily financial papers, and their parish was firmly the City of London. In 1945 the *Financial News* bought the *Financial Times*, and the two papers became one, taking the name of the higher-circulation *Financial Times*. The chairman, the managing director and the editor of the combined paper all came from the *FN* stable, and not surprisingly the new paper derived at least as much of its character from the old *FN* as from the old *FT*. Accordingly, the early chapters of this book are in the nature of a 'double' history, recording the respective origins and fortunes of the *FN* and the *FT*, culminating in their merger at the end of the Second World War.

It was a merger that proved brilliantly successful. By the 1950s the 'new' *Financial Times* was branching out into full-scale industrial coverage to complement its traditional financial coverage, as well as starting an arts page. By the 1960s it had indisputably 'arrived' as an established national quality paper. By the 1970s it was becoming an international paper of the first order. In 1979 it began to print in Frankfurt, in 1985 in New York. By the mid-1980s the *FT* was the pre-eminent British daily newspaper and one of the best known in the world, recognized as authoritative, non-partisan and of sustained analytical quality. In the space of less than forty years it had undergone a remarkable transformation.

Starting from the standpoint that it is a story worth telling, I have tried to tell it sympathetically but critically. It was made clear to me at the outset, when I was offered the commission in 1984, that above all the *FT* wanted a vigorous, independent and honest book; that I would have access to all company records and personnel; and that I was to have complete freedom to exercise my historical judgement. These criteria have been upheld, without question or demur, and I must express my fullest thanks for this liberal-minded attitude. I have tried to write a history worthy of the high standards of the paper. If I have failed, the fault lies solely with myself.

London, February 1987

ACKNOWLEDGEMENTS

The following kindly gave me permission to consult and reproduce material in their possession: the British Library of Political and Economic Science (Dalton diaries): Vivian Brooks (Brooks diaries); Churchill College, Cambridge, and Ruth Einzig (Einzig papers); the House of Lords Record Office and the Clerk of the Records (Bracken/Beaverbrook correspondence); the Institute of Economic Affairs; Nuffield College, Oxford, and the English-Speaking Union (Cherwell papers); the Royal Society (Simon papers); and the University Library, Cambridge, and Lord Kennet (Kennet papers). In addition, extracts from Lord Drogheda's memoirs, *Double Harness*, are reproduced by kind permission of Weidenfeld & Nicolson.

Much of my research was conducted in Bracken House, where I encountered great friendliness and co-operation. I would particularly like to thank not only Terry Damer and his department for their hospitality, but also Non Morgan in the picture library for her help in gathering the illustrations. I tried to interview as many current members of staff as possible, and would like to apologize to those whom time precluded me from seeing.

This book could not have been written without the help of many former members of staff. I would like to thank the following people, who are in no way responsible for any errors of fact or interpretation: Gertrude Bannister, Paul Bareau, A. G. Bennett, Leslie Bentley, Basil Bicknell, Sheila Black, B. T. Bradberry, Lord Bruce-Gardyne, George Bull, Ronald Butt, Peter Cartwright, Alan Chalkley, Sir Geoffrey Chandler, Archie Chisholm, Victor Clark, Dorothy Cohen, Nicholas Colchester, Patrick Coldstream, Norman Courtman-Davies, Alan Cox, George Cyriax, Lord Drogheda, Justin Dukes, A. L. Emerick, James Ensor, Fredy Fisher, Alfie Fonseca, Peter Galliner, John Gardiner, Ken Gomm, Derek Granger, Maurice Green, Christopher Gwinner, Alan Hare, Lord Hartwell, John Hay, Robert Heller, John Higgins, John Horam, Joe Hutton, Hammond Innes, Christopher Johnson, James Joll, William Keegan, Kerry Kerrigan, Nigel Lawson, Hilda Levy, John Lloyd,

Alistair Macdonald, Fred Marshall, Kenneth Marston, Tony Martin, Len Miller, John Murray, Kelsey van Musschenbroek, Sir Gordon Newton, Robert Oakeshott, Murrough O'Brien, Hugh O'Shaughnessy, S. W. Parkinson, Len Pearce, Andrew Porter, Jack Prosser, Sir William Rees-Mogg, Victor Sandelson, Adrian Secker, A. L. W. Shillady, Nicholas Stacey, Allan Todd, Ian Trafford, Christopher Tugendhat, Peter Tumiati, Cyril Ubsdell, Anthony Vice, John White, Dick Wilson, Rex Winsbury, Dorothy Woods, Peggy Yeo, Doug York.

I would also like to thank the following people for the help they gave me: Barry Atkinson, Roland Bird, Lord Blakenham, Ian Brocklesby, Vivian Brooks, John Brumwell, Linda Christmas, Harold Cowen, Louise Craven, Glenda Davies, Courtenay Edwards, Ruth Dudley Edwards, Richard Fry, Lord Gibson, David Gordon, Harry Hake, Lillian Henschel, Graham Hutton, Peter Jay, Simon Jenkins, Mrs Arthur Knock, Philip Landells, James Lee, David Linton, Roderick Martin, Christopher Powell-Cotton, Ronald Prentice, Alan Rodford, W. Howard Saunders, John Williams, Joyce Wincott.

I owe a considerable debt to Dilwyn Porter, who with great generosity put at my disposal his unrivalled knowledge of the life and career of Harry Marks, founder of the *Financial News*.

Finally, my thanks go to my wife Lucy for her forbearance; my daughter Laurie for her help with the typing; and my Brother 900, whose swan-song this was.

[ONE]

BEGINNINGS

1884–95

The 1880s saw the foundation of the two newspapers – the *Financial News* and the *Financial Times* – that were to come together some sixty years later to form the modern *Financial Times*. The City of London had been a powerful financial centre long before the 1880s, long indeed before the Industrial Revolution, from which it was quite separate. One thinks of the growth of Lloyd's and the Bank of England, of the Royal Exchange and the Stock Exchange. But now, in the last quarter of the nineteenth century, as Britain's purely *industrial* supremacy started to be challenged by both the United States and Germany, the City by contrast found itself assuming an unprecedented importance in both the British and the world economies.

This dominance of the late-Victorian City took three main forms. First, the development, very much on the back of Britain's immense trading muscle during the half-century after the Napoleonic Wars, of an international money market capable of providing short-term finance for trade not only involving Britain but also between trading partners all round the world. Secondly, the concurrent development, largely through the merchant banks and the Stock Exchange, of an international capital market capable of providing long-term finance for governments, railway contractors, mining entrepreneurs and so on. And thirdly, intimately related to both these developments, the increasing adoption after 1870 by the rest of the world of the gold standard. The result was that London, where sterling had been ordained to be as good as gold since 1717 (apart from during the Napoleonic Wars) and where gold knew its largest and freest market, came to act as a kind of universal switchboard in the settling of trading and financial matters. One commentator tried to encapsulate what the City was:

> It is the greatest shop, the greatest store, the freest market for commodities, gold and securities, the greatest disposer of capital, the greatest dispenser of credit, but above and beyond, as well as by reason of all these marks of financial and commercial supremacy, it is the world's clearing house.[1]

Written shortly before the First World War, this bucolic description was equally applicable to the 1880s.

From the point of view of a prospective financial paper, in search of readership and advertising, the alluring word in such a description was 'securities' – in other words, the London Stock Exchange and that murky but populous world of touts and half-commission men, outside brokers and speculators, spinning off from it. By 1884 the Stock Exchange had been in existence in Capel Court for almost a century; its membership comprised more than two and a half thousand brokers and jobbers who traded in rather fewer than two thousand quoted securities; and a major new extension to its premises was on the verge of completion. The main markets within it were the consol market (dealing in British government stock), the foreign market, the home rails market and above all at this time the American or 'Yankee' market, which dealt primarily in railroads and for over a decade had been in a state of almost constant speculative excitement. At this stage the mining market was still fairly small, though in the early 1880s a number of mining companies had been floated in India, America and West Africa; and in 1884 gold was discovered on the South African Rand, one of the momentous events of the century. British domestic industry was but thinly represented on the Stock Exchange; the great majority of large concerns stuck to the self-financing tradition of raising capital established since the Industrial Revolution, while even new enterprises preferred to take advantage of the Joint Stock Companies Act of 1856 by going to their local provincial stock exchange for a flotation rather than coming to London. Clubbish, boisterous and often febrile, Capel Court had the rest of the world for its stage and bothered little about the cotton mills of Lancashire.

Who were the investors and speculators (contemporaries agonized about the difference between them, but never quite resolved it) who kept the brokers and jobbers in business? By the 1880s the typical private investor was, as he had always been, a person of some wealth, certainly a payer of income tax. Nevertheless, the investing class as a whole was now considerably broader than it had been some twenty or thirty years earlier, as a result partly of the introduction of limited liability as an encouragement to share ownership, partly also of the growth of lower-denomination £1 shares, beginning to supplant the traditional £5 shares. At the same time, Britain was in general becoming an ever wealthier country, and the Empire was creating a *rentier* class – the legendary widows of Kensington and Cheltenham – whose principal income derived from Stock Exchange securities. But whoever the average late-Victorian punter was, and for whatever reason he or she held shares, it would be fair to say that the amount of investor protection on offer was nugatory, with the underlying assumption of the market remaining the bracing *caveat emptor*, 'let the buyer beware'. Nor at this time was there much point looking to a stockbroker for informed and disinterested guidance, since one was unlikely to get anything more from him than a stale retailing of the tips and rumours of the particular day. In this sense a *Punch* cartoon of the 1890s, showing a dean being importuned for alms by a beggar, said it all: 'Ah, my good woman, it is not the poor only who have their troubles; you, for instance, have probably never experienced the difficulty of finding investments combining adequate security with a remunerative rate of interest.'

If that troubled eminent had been around in January 1884, he would have found only limited succour and advice from the Fourth Estate. In the main daily newspapers there was the well-established 'money article', but this was an arid affair, consisting of little more than the flattest of reviews, usually in the smallest of types, of the principal price movements in the more traditional markets. As for weeklies, there were some well-respected journals like the *Economist* and the more recent *Statist*, but these and other specialist publications tended to be fairly staid, adopting a respectful rather than critical attitude towards the Stock Exchange and keeping a certain distance; in any case they were by definition usually out of date as far as the active player of the market was concerned. In fact, in January 1884 the only London financial daily already in existence was the *Financier*, established in 1870, costing twopence and published from Monday to Friday. Its subtitle was 'A Daily Record of the Money Market, Investments and Trade', and that was really what it was, providing minimal editorial comment and little in the way of genuine reportage. Moreover, even as a plain record it was deficient: its five or so pages of Stock Exchange prices were merely the misleadingly wide official ones, while its Wall Street coverage came from circulars issued by a London firm of American brokers rather than being cabled from New York direct. In short, though a perfectly respectable organ, the *Financier* was not all that much help to the average investor, and above all it was desperately dull.

It was a situation that prior to 1884 left deans, widows and others badly placed, and considerably mitigated against the natural attraction of holding shares. In 1904 an interested historian of nineteenth-century financial journalism described in more detail the problems they had had to face:

Investors had great difficulty in obtaining trustworthy information about the securities in which their money was embarked. The Money Articles of the general newspapers were chiefly taken up with the bare records of movements in the Funds, foreign stocks, and English railway securities. About the various American railways – Erie, Wabash, Central Pacific – in which millions of English capital were invested they had no information except that which was contained in the inspired memoranda sent to them from time to time by the London agents of the American directors, which was frequently stale and sometimes misleading. Of the operations of the syndicates, formed to manipulate stocks, nothing was known outside the inner rings of Stock Exchange speculators. Mine shareholders were at an equal disadvantage, having to wait for news from their properties until it suited the directors, in their own good time, to communicate so much of the intelligence to hand as they saw fit to publish. Many of them were even kept from week to week in ignorance of the price of their shares, for in those days the few daily papers which condescended to quote any mining shares paid no attention to those that were not included on the Official List. They dealt with quotations generally in the same perfunctory manner, omitting to record any prices made after official hours in the Exchange, although the changes made by late dealings were sometimes very important and gave the operator on the spot a considerable advantage over the investor at a distance.[2]

This was a harsh verdict but it commands respect, for the writer was Harry Marks. No one in the early 1880s had studied the subject more assiduously, more objectively and with a keener eye for the potentialities of the situation.

Harry Hananel Marks, the originator of modern British financial journalism and, as founder of the *Financial News*, ultimate founder of the modern *Financial Times*, was born in London in 1855. His father was the head of the Reformed Congregation of British Jews. His formal education, at University College School and the Athenée Royale in Brussels, ended early, for at the age of fifteen he went out to New Orleans, where his father had friends. There he worked in various clerical capacities before moving on a couple of years later to Texas, where, he later recalled, 'my first employment was as canvasser for sewing machines and a driver of a mule team for the agent'. The young Harry was not long in the saddle, for by dint of lying about journalistic experience in London he soon secured a post on the *San Antonio Express* and then, as managing editor, on the *San Antonio Daily Press*. It proved a literal blooding as a newspaperman: to the end of his life he bore two Texan scars, on the face and hand, 'which the maintenance of the right of free criticism had obtained for him from those who objected to it'.[3] In 1873, at the ripe age of eighteen, he settled in New York, where he fairly rapidly advanced himself. For five years he was on the *New York World*, becoming assistant night editor; in 1880 he became editor of the *Daily Mining News*, the first daily mining paper anywhere; and the following year he started and ran a new edition of the paper and called it the *Financial and Mining News*, which he later described as 'chiefly a price-list, with reports from the mines and small paragraphs'. He was also a member at various times of the Mining Exchange and the Oil Exchange, both based in New York. In 1883 the American apprenticeship came to an end, and Harry Marks returned home. He had not only learned a lot and made a host of contacts, but he had also dreamed a dream, and now he wanted the pay-off.

I dreamed of a journal that should treat of financial subjects as the most thorough and the most enterprising newspapers deal with political and general news topics, aiming to give the earliest, completest, and surest information upon all matters of public interest, even 'premature' information when its prematurity would enhance its value to my readers. My dream contemplated a journal doing bold and seasonable service in the interests of the community.[4]

Thus Marks writing many years later in the autumnal glow of success, but during the last weeks of 1883 he was a more or less unknown journalist of slender means, living in lodgings in Regent Street and in search of a backer. Not perhaps surprisingly, the man he found was an American, Colonel Edward McMurdo, who had been in London in connection with the launching of a United States railroad issue and now agreed to put £1,000 into the new paper and guarantee all expenses in return for having half-interest with Marks. McMurdo was a widely travelled engineer-cum-financier who during his career initiated mining ventures in Portugal and Honduras as well as in the USA, was one of the mining pioneers in the Transvaal, involved himself in Italian tramways, obtained the concession for and built the Delagoa Bay Railway and introduced the Gardner gun to Europe. In the words of an obituary, 'he was a most energetic man, and one of a most sanguine temperament'.[5] He was also a good man to have in one's corner, as Marks prepared to turn dream into reality.

The first London edition of the *Financial and Mining News*, subtitled 'A Daily Journal Devoted to the Interests of Investors', appeared on Wednesday 23 January 1884, price one penny and consisting of four pages of smallish size. The main item on page one was 'The Stock Market', beginning with the following snappy assessment:

Business as a whole was far from active in the Stock Exchange yesterday, but the features were somewhat of a more favourable character than on the previous

Financial & Mining News

VOL. I.—No. 1. LONDON, WEDNESDAY, JANUARY 23, 1884. PRICE ONE PENNY.

THE STOCK MARKET.

FOREIGN SHARES FIRMER—BETTER TONE IN AMERICANS—HOME RAILS IRREGULAR.

Business as a whole was far from active in the Stock Exchange yesterday, but the features were somewhat of a more favourable character than on the previous day; though it cannot be doubted the general public evince a strong disinclination to venture into new engagements of a speculative nature, which is not surprising considering the heavy losses incurred during the past year or two. The Funds have been steady. Foreign Government Securities were mostly sustained by the firmness on the Paris Bourse, from which centre buying orders were received to a small extent—sufficient, however, to show the tendency of the market there. A feature was a sharp advance in Peruvian Five per Cents., and a decline in the Six per Cents., on a report that the two stocks are to rank the same. An improvement occurred in Egyptians, French Rentes, Italian, and several others. Spanish was easier on realisations. In the American market there was an absence of rumours, and there was some indication of recovery in prices, due to better prices in New York; but, considering the extent of the fall, the improvement was comparatively insignificant, while confidence is still very far from restored. There were comparatively few sales on the part of Dutch holders, which in itself is a satisfactory feature, for a pressure of sales was expected from Amsterdam. There is no doubt many of the stocks are considerably under their real value, but in times of excitement nothing is taken into account. Canadian Railways are steadier. Home Railways were somewhat irregular; but, beyond an advance in Brighton Deferred and Great Northern A, the changes were unimportant, while the dealings were on a comparatively small scale. Mexican …

AMERICAN SECURITIES.

FOREIGN RAILWAYS.

BANKS.

FINANCIAL, LAND, AND INVESTMENT.

MINES.

TELEGRAPHS.

Money Market.

THE BERLIN BOURSE.

FOREIGN EXCHANGES.

CLOSING QUOTATIONS.

BRITISH FUNDS, &c.

FOREIGN STOCKS.

RAILWAYS.

CANADIAN RAILWAYS.

A BLOW TO CALIFORNIA.

HYDRAULIC MINING PRACTICALLY PROHIBITED UNTIL ITS METHODS ARE REFORMED.

La Plata of Colorado.

Little Pittsburg of Colorado.

Three Thousand Feet down in a Mine.

The United Mexican.

The Potosi Mine.

The Richmond Consolidated.

A Plea for a Public Nuisance.

The Samoan Islands Again.

Bear Rumours Denied.

In Vino Veritas.

Tramway Traffic Receipts.

The P. and O. Service.

Victoria Four per Cent. Loan.

London, Tilbury, and Southend.

The Long Island R.R.

A Paying Business.

Submarine Telegraph Dividend.

The Mercantile Bank of Sydney.

Liebig Extracts a Dividend.

Railway Debenture Trust Company.

Railway Share Trust Company.

The Suez Canal.

THE AMERICAN MARKETS.

AN IMPROVEMENT IN PRICES—THE GOULD STOCKS HIGHER—CONTINUED BEARISH FEELING.

STOCKS AND SHARES.

PRODUCE, &c.

American Securities.

Electric Light in Trains.

23 January 1884: first issue of the *FN*

day; though it cannot be doubted the general public evince a strong disinclination to venture into new engagements of a speculative nature, which is not surprising considering the heavy losses incurred during the past year or two.

Also featuring on page one were some of the stock-market prices, information about the money market, the Berlin bourse and the foreign exchanges, the report of a meeting of the shareholders of the United Telephone Company (held at the Cannon Street Hotel), tramway traffic receipts and a column about movements on the New York Stock Exchange. The main editorial matter was left to page two, including a leader on Mexico and its rapid development since the introduction of railways (a theme dear to the Colonel's heart) and an outlining of 'Our Programme', in which great stress was laid on the paper's unique supply of early and reliable news from the United States, especially in relation to its mines. The rest of the page was given over to various snippets about 'Personalities' ('The report that the insanity of the late Charles Delmonico was due to losses on the Stock Exchange is utterly without foundation. Delmonico died a millionaire'), the musings of 'Amodeus' (*sic*) on 'Change' ('The steadiness of Mexican Rails astonishes all the members, and operators seem timid for the moment. In my opinion this seems ominous, and looks like a calm before a storm') and almost a column of 'Points' ('What has become of the proposed steamship line between Milford Haven and New York?' 'The value of the silver and copper product of the mines of Arizona for 1883 is estimated at 15,000,000 dols.' '"Serious railroad accident" is a common head-line in the newspapers. Did anyone ever see a comic railroad accident?'). Page three under the heading 'Guide for Investors' provided various information about securities quoted on the London Stock Exchange, such as number of shares, dividends and traffic returns. And page four, besides carrying advertisements in connection with the issues of two new waterworks companies, together with a number of smaller, miscellaneous notices, also reported the meeting held in New York more than a fortnight previously of the board of directors of the Northern Pacific Railway.

The first issue out of the way, the *Financial and Mining News* quickly settled down to a confident tone displaying much Yankee-style 'bounce' and a considerable relish for the cut and thrust of financial controversy. An editorial comment in the paper's third issue was typical: 'The swindling operations of a certain class of money-lenders and loan-officers seem to engage the attention of everyone except the police. If the police could spare a little time from the engrossing occupation of unearthing imaginary dynamite plots, they might do something to curtail their operations.' The first week also included interviews with the American railway magnates William H. Vanderbilt and Jay Gould, while at the beginning of February a story about the failure of a Stock Exchange firm was not slow to play up the 'human interest', especially in connection with the firm's major partner:

Mr Blakeway, it is said, cashed a cheque for £500 a couple of days ago, and since that time has not been seen in the City. He is described as a dapper-looking person of about forty, who devotes considerable attention to the curl of his moustache . . . He lived in elegant style at Hampstead, drove a handsome drag, and was every inch a 'City swell'.

Soon afterwards the paper's political leaning was made clear by the presumably facetious assertion that 'Cetewayo [the Zulu King] is believed to have died of congestion of the brain, brought on by over study, in a vain attempt to comprehend the foreign policy (!) of the Gladstone Government.'

By early March, though still just the four pages and appearing only from Tuesday to Saturday, the paper had adopted the larger size usual for the period and had started a letters section ('The Voice of the Public') as well as an 'Answers to Correspondents' column for readers with investment queries. April saw the proud citation of the *Fish Trades Gazette*'s opinion of the new paper ('Truly a marvellous penny's worth . . . promises to be a gigantic success'), the introduction of a 'Some Things We'd Like to Know' column (for example, whether 'the Mr Bentley who occupies the high position of Brazilian Consul in Canada is the Mr Bentley who, some years ago, was caught "short" of Erie on the London Stock Exchange') and on the 30th a resolute self-defence:

We have been more or less severely criticised in Stock Exchange circles for publishing in our issue of yesterday the names of buyers and sellers of Mexican rails, together with the amounts of their respective purchases and sales. This, we are told, is personal journalism . . . We are distinctly of opinion that the matter which we published yesterday very much concerns the public, since the public supplies the money for the operations in Mexican rails as it does for operations in other securities publicly dealt in.

The editorial added darkly: 'As to the way in which we get our news, that is our business. We do get it, and we pay for it, and we find that it pays us to pay for it, and to print it.'

Over the next few months the *News* continued to develop a nice line in ironic criticism, as in these remarks about the large claims made by the

East Florida Land & Produce Company in its prospectus: 'We are at a loss to understand why, in the estimates of profit, no account is taken of the luscious yellow pineapples that would grow under the tall yellow pine trees. Where are the profits from the fragrant and graceful banana; from the early strawberry and the toothsome green pea?' Of more immediate import, however, was a major coup in May, in the context of an American financial crisis caused by the collapse of the Marine National Bank and the failure of the leading New York brokerage firm of Grant & Ward. Marks twenty years later recalled the triumph:

Day by day we had given warnings of an impending crash, and night by night our New York correspondent had cabled news of the increasing embarrassments of the stock-jobbing combinations which controlled the market. While the other daily papers, in complete ignorance of the situation, were discoursing of the great improvement in American business, the *Financial and Mining News* alone saw and told the truth about the situation and urged investors to sell their holdings in American railways. It predicted the panic almost to a day, and when the collapse came, when Eries and Central Pacific, Lake Shores, and New York Centrals were tumbling down 5 dols and 10 dols at a time, those who had followed the *Financial and Mining News* reaped large profits, the accuracy of our information was established, and the reputation of the paper made.[6]

Or, as Marks in person told a court in 1890, 'I made a good deal by bearing the stocks, and by warning the public in the paper of what was pending eight days before the panic came.' Clearly the paper had now arrived and was a source of intelligence to be reckoned with.

This sense of permanence was confirmed by the decision at the beginning of July 1884 to drop the words 'and Mining' from the title and call the paper simply the *Financial News*, subtitled 'A Daily Journal Devoted to the Interests of Investors'. Why was the change made? According to Marks himself, writing in 1909, it had always been part of the paper's programme 'to give to the Mining Market an amount of space and attention which it received from no existing daily paper', and as far as the original title was concerned he 'was only induced to change it because it was found to be cumbrous and inconvenient'.[7] In 1895, however, the paper's Stock Exchange gossip columnist, 'Midas', gave a rather different version of why Marks had been persuaded that the word 'Mining' had to go:

As I have heard him relate, his friends assured him that it was in such bad odour that it would prejudice the prospects of the paper. No respectable banking firm, said they, would have a mining paper in its office; no member of the Stock Exchange of any standing would have any dealings in mining shares; the whole business was disreputable and discredited.[8]

The new title was undoubtedly less 'cumbrous'; but, granted the general (and not unjustified) contemporary belief that 'a mine is a hole in the ground owned by a liar', as the adage went, then probably the 'Midas' version of the change is the truer one.

The new nomenclature did not herald any drastic change of character. On 13 August, for instance, the *FN* took a fairly typical swipe: 'This being the "big gooseberry" season, the *Pall Mall Gazette* treats its readers to a very amusing interview with Captain Eads on "the projected ship railway from the Atlantic to the Pacific", which reads like a page from Mark Twain.' Various campaigns filled the paper's pages: in August against the dodges of circularizing brokers, in October against the management of the Grand Trunk Railway Company of Canada and in December against company directors whose social prestige (and thus influence on investors) was matched only by their incompetence. An increasingly popular part of the paper was the 'Answers to Correspondents' column, so much so that, on 2 December, Marks stated that 'by yesterday's mails we received 43 letters from readers of the *Financial News*, all requesting information in regard to investments of various kinds', of whom 22 wanted a reply in an enclosed envelope and 21 were content with a public reply. The item went on to say that in future only subscribers to the paper would have their queries answered by mail, unless a 5*s*. fee was paid, and added: 'We are not working for glory; the labourer is worthy of his hire, and the laborious editor of the *Financial News* is no exception to the rule.'

On 23 January 1885 the paper celebrated its first birthday. That day's issue showed the extent to which it was becoming a solid and authoritative organ of record as well as opinion. On page one the stock-market and Wall Street reports included perceptive commentaries in addition to the latest price changes, and there was also various legal news, but the main item was a lengthy report, filling almost two closely printed columns, of the shareholders' meeting of the South-Eastern Railway Company. In the chair was the combative Sir Edward Watkin, who looked ahead to the building of a Channel tunnel within four or five years and asserted that 'if the tunnel was made the South-Eastern Railway would be the best property in the world, carrying goods without breaking bulk, and conveying passengers without making them sick'. Page two included five main leaders: 'Our Anniversary' (predictably self-congratulatory); 'Eighteen Hundred Brokers in Default' (i.e. who had failed to pay their annual licence fee to the City authorities); 'One Hope for Canadian Pacific' (very critical about a guarantee scheme being arranged by the Canadian government that meant ill-gotten gains for 'the Canadian

Pacific syndicate'); 'Land Titles in America' (expressing anxiety about a House of Representatives proposal to bar Britons from holding land in the USA); and a not unprophetic disquisition on 'The Prosperity of Germany': 'Twenty years ago, when her industries were insignificant, Germany was undoubtedly a poor country. She is, perhaps, not yet a rich one in the sense that England and America are rich; but she is rapidly becoming so, and her wealth increases visibly.' Also on page two was detailed news about the Transvaal gold fields received from the *Cape Argus*, a report on the produce markets and an altogether more sober collection of 'Points' than had featured a year previously, being really small news items about such things as the falling due of the debenture coupons of the Land & Loan Company of New Zealand and the monthly statement of the Schwab's Gully Diamond Mining Company. Page three was mostly taken up with a fairly full record of the previous day's Stock Exchange business, Reuters telegrams from the European bourses and a detailed list of recent American, English, foreign and colonial railway traffic returns. The paper signed off on page four with a couple of substantial company-meeting reports, a list of forthcoming meetings and a lengthy, immensely factual historical survey of 'Transatlantic Travel', concluding that 'the passenger traffic is, in fact, likely to increase considerably in the future, the effect of swift, well-appointed vessels of the present day being to induce travellers to journey to and from America for purely holiday purposes'.

Over the next three years the Marksian dream continued to flourish, especially with the publication in October 1885 for the first time of the much more accurate 'tape' prices collected through the Stock Exchange day by the Exchange Telegraph Company. As the paper put it: 'By printing this record we place all our readers upon an equal footing with the favoured few in London who always have the tape under their eyes, and we enable them to check the transactions reported to them by their brokers.'

Coverage further expanded. By 1886 the *FN* included a regular column on real estate, taking the form of reports of the mart in Tokenhouse Yard; and that spring it ran a series of articles from provincial centres about 'The Industrial Crisis'. In October, Marks appeared for the first time at the Mansion House police court, accused by John Barr, manager of the London & Leeds Bank, of having launched a series of vicious, libellous attacks on the now defunct bank because it had declined to advertise its prospectus in the paper. The *FN* had certainly laid in hard to 'Barr's Bogus Bank', but the court decided that the articles had been published as a public benefit, without any malice, and the editorial the next day gloated, 'Exit Mr John Barr'.[9] That same month the paper started its long series of articles, going through into 1887, about the corrupt practices of the Metropolitan Board of Works, articles described by the historian of that institution as being, 'within the limits of the genre, a brilliant piece of muck-raking journalism'.[10] Other newspapers then took up the attack, and the days of the Board of Works were numbered, leading to the establishment in 1889 of the London County Council.

Another, more personalized *FN* campaign started in July 1887 and continued to the following March. This was a series of articles called the 'Spider's Web' and the 'Wasp's Nest', of which one in September 1887 was fairly typical: 'The late secretary of the bogus Northern Transvaal Gold Mining Company, the *chef d'oeuvre* of Mr C. W. Perryman, *alias* Burchell, *alias* Morris, Stewart & Co., has started in business as Fagge & Co., stockbrokers. From what we know of Mr Fagge's previous financial operations, we should be inclined to think that Mr Fagge is just the sort of stockbroker to avoid.' Fagge eventually sued for libel, but the jury accepted that the Northern Transvaal had been a bogus company, though Fagge did get £50 for unfounded accusations in the *FN* that some years previously he had misappropriated church money.[11] Marks's finest courtroom hour, however, came in November 1887 when he successfully sued W. R. Grenfell, a director of the Bank of England, for slander. Grenfell had been involved in the promotion of the Harney Peak Tin Company, which had sought to obtain capital of £2 million and had been attacked so vigorously by the *FN* as to cause withdrawal of the prospectus. A bitter exchange then followed, but in court Grenfell apologized and agreed to pay 50 guineas damages and £300 costs. Magnanimously, the victor stated that he did not wish to recover damages and that the 50 guineas were to go to the Newspaper Press Fund.[12]

The internal history of the paper during these first four years is, as with the beginnings of most ventures, fairly obscure. We know that the original editorial offices were at 6 St Swithin's Lane, EC, and that the first printers were Judd & Company of Doctors' Commons, EC. During the trying early months of 1884 considerable recourse was made to the pocket of Colonel McMurdo, but gradually the advertising revenue built up, especially through the publication on Saturdays of prospectuses for new issues. A certain editorial fillip could help: on 16 July 1884, for example, a large prospectus for the Western Australia Mortgage & Mercantile Agency Company was complemented on another page by a glowing article about that company's prospects, a technique repeated on 1 August in connection with an issue of preference shares in the North Harbour Smelting Works. Walter Skinner, the subsequent founder of the annual *Mining Manual*, played an important early part in obtaining advertisements (especially from 'outside' brokers, who, unlike members of the Stock Exchange, were allowed to advertise) and pushing the paper's circulation. Marks himself seems to have pioneered two forms of advertising revenue, persuading companies to pay not only for extended reports of their meetings but also, unless their shares were particularly active, for the space occupied by a share price quotation. As for circulation figures, these were to remain a mystery for many years, as indeed for some years were profit figures, but in July 1884 the *FN* did announce to advertisers that it guaranteed a circulation 'greater than that of all the other Financial Journals in England combined'. Some clue is given by the lists the paper published of newsvendors from whom the *FN* could be ordered: thus by January 1885 it was available all over London and in eleven provincial centres, including from no less than a dozen vendors in Bradford alone. It is hard to believe that the *FN*'s circulation at this stage can have been more than a few thousand, but pending the audited figures of a later era one simply does not know for certain.

There then followed a series of steps that paved the way towards a long-term future. In March 1885 the Financial News Ltd was formed to control the affairs of the paper, with at its disposal a nominal capital of 50,000 shares of £1 each, though by July that year only 32,296 had been taken up. The initial directorate comprised Aden Beresford, P. H. Bagenal and James Head, who had known Marks in New York, lodged with him in London and was in later years to claim that he and his brother sank £30,000 into the paper. Early shareholders included Patrick O'Sullivan and Timothy Creedon, both members of the Royal Irish Constabulary in County Tipperary, with five shares each. Marks himself held over 12,000 shares – acquired largely through selling the paper's copyright, goodwill, subscription lists and so on to the company – and was also deemed by the company's memorandum of association to be editor of the *FN* at a salary of £520 a year, enjoying 'absolute discretion' over editorial control, 'subject only to the power of the Board of Directors to examine into and check expenditure'. McMurdo seems to have receded as a presence from about this time, though his connection with the *FN* cannot have done him permanent harm, in that when he died in 1889 he left almost £400,000. The next stage in the paper's progress came with the move to larger offices, at 11 Abchurch Lane, in February 1886. The key step, however, was the decision reached early in 1887 to establish printing works, in the form of the Argus Printing Company in Bouverie Street, which would be under the effective control of the *FN*'s management, be custom-built for printing the *FN* and in general provide a greater continuity and quality of printing than had hitherto been the case. In the event, though not without some squalls and grumbles, the Argus would continue to print the *FN* for the rest of the paper's life.

It was as well that this decision was made when it was, for not only was the *FN* by now being published on Mondays as well, but it was also becoming quite common for six-page issues of the paper to appear and occasionally even eight pages. The main reason for this was the first of the major 'Kaffir' booms on the Stock Exchange. South African mining securities, which flourished during 1887 and 1888, provided the financial press with much-needed additional readership and, above all, advertising, and inevitably provoked a spate of hopeful rivals. The *Statist* in February 1888 pronounced sternly on the myriad ranks of 'so-called financial journals' being sold in Throgmorton Street, especially of a Saturday morning:

In the course of a few weeks many of them disappear, and another swarm takes their place. The promoter of financial newspapers seems to be not only ubiquitous but inexhaustible. He will do anything to catch the wayward taste of the public – from cheating his printer to libelling his mother-in-law. If Throgmorton Street will not have him under one spicey title he will try it with a spicier one still . . . The one end and aim of his vagabond industry is to be seen about the street, so that he may be able to bully advertising agents and tradespeople into giving him a few advertisements.[13]

One such seemingly ephemeral publication, though from the start with rather higher pretensions than most of the other newcomers, was the *London Financial Guide*, which appeared for the first time on 9 January 1888. The subtitle under the masthead was the ringing declaration 'Without Fear and Without Favour'; it anticipated coming out thrice weekly; and on page two was laid out the programme of 'Ourselves':

In this Journal it is proposed to deal as little in personalities as possible, always having a due regard to the interests of the public.

We start upon the plain straightforward mission of conveying to our readers the latest news from all parts of the world upon questions of Finance and Market prices with now and then a word of caution and advice.

We have not the interests of any particular clique under our special charge, nor do we propose to start as private detectives. As facts present themselves so shall we record them.

We do not appoint to ourselves the clearing out of any particular Augean stable, either railway or otherwise. We simply propose to take our share of the good thing that may be going as our reward for endeavouring to serve a generous and discriminating public faithfully and honestly.

In January, 1788, was started a paper [*The Times*, formerly the *London Daily Universal Register*] which grew to be one of the wonders of the world – not bound down by any hard and fast line it went with the current of events, serving one master – the public, and today stands unrivalled in its greatness and power.

At an immeasurable distance from this great luminary, but borrowing a portion of its light, the *London Financial Guide* commences its career in January 1888, and hopes by adopting a similar line of action, and by a constant and strict adherence to truth and a watchfulness of the best interests of its readers, to merit and win a small portion of the public favour and support.

The fare in this first issue was motley enough: on page one reports of various company meetings, an article attacking the Stock Exchange's 'old-fashioned mode of secrecy and closed doors', an article arguing that the company promoter was often unfairly blamed by the press when things went wrong, and a column of 'Latest Home and Foreign News' ('The Notts Murder' and 'Fatal Accident to a Nun' jostling with 'Foreign Orders for the Welsh Steel Trade'); on page two 'Our Letter Box', with 'A Broker' querying some detail in a letter recently published in the *Financial News*; prices, including Stock Exchange tape prices and a wide range of commodity prices, on page three; and finally a full-page prospectus of the Upper Trent Navigation Company. It was a reasonable start, though the bold statement on the second page that 'the *London Financial Guide* will contain a greater amount and variety of Commercial, Financial, and Shipping information than any similar publication, besides the General News of the day', was one still to be taken on trust.

Over the next month the *Guide* remained a fairly scrappy publication, though on 23 January it was able to promise that 'in our next issue we shall give the latest financial news from America, as well as the closing prices of the American markets by cable'. Editorially the paper trained its guns on two main targets: the Stock Exchange with its 'Closed Doors' and 'Guarded Secrets', or as another headline put it, '"Now Barrabas Was – A Jobber"'; and the *FN*, which was criticized in virtually every issue for getting something or other wrong. The *Guide*'s level of advertising was quite healthy, helped by the familiar technique (as with the Hull Brewery Company on 11 January and the Manchester Brewery Company on 6 February) of printing a prospectus on one page and 'puffing' the prospects of the flotation on another. As for circulation, an appeal 'To our Readers' on 18 January betrayed a certain anxiety: 'If already a subscriber, please show the paper to others. If you cannot obtain it where

The Friend of
THE HONEST FINANCIER.
THE BONA FIDE INVESTOR.
THE RESPECTABLE BROKER.
THE GENUINE DIRECTOR.
THE LEGITIMATE SPECULATOR.

The Financial Times.

"Without Fear and Without Favour."

DAILY.

With which is Incorporated the "LONDON FINANCIAL GUIDE."

The Enemy of
THE CLOSED STOCK EXCHANGE.
THE UNPRINCIPLED PROMOTER.
THE COMPANY WRECKER.
THE "GUINEA PIG."
THE "BULL." THE "BEAR."
THE GAMBLING OPERATOR.

New Series.—No. 1.] [REGISTERED FOR TRANSMISSION ABROAD.] LONDON, MONDAY, FEBRUARY 13, 1888. [ONE PENNY.

13 February 1888: first issue of the *FT*

you get your other papers, buy your other papers where you can get this.' Five days later the claim was made that 'the *London Financial Guide* has been so well received that, next week, we shall print 30,000 copies', but it is hard to believe that at this stage the circulation really could have been running at 10,000 an issue. The paper was probably not doing too badly, at least to judge by the fact that the issue of 10 February featured as many as twenty-four 'Answers to Correspondents'. In that same issue the announcement was made that from the following Monday the paper was going to be published under a new title; the *London Financial Guide* was about to give birth to a famous scion.

The *Financial Times* appeared for the first time on 13 February 1888 and from the outset was a Monday-to-Saturday daily. To the left of the masthead it declared itself to be 'the friend of the honest financier, the bona fide investor, the respectable broker, the genuine director, the legitimate speculator'; and on the other side its enemies were stated to be 'the closed Stock Exchange, the unprincipled promoter, the company wrecker, the "guinea pig", the "bull", the "bear", the gambling operator'. The first article on the front page told the reader a bit more about 'Ourselves':

> The *London Financial Guide* has so far justified its existence that today – under the more concise and dignified title of the *Financial Times* – it makes its appearance in the character of a daily morning financial paper. This change is to some extent the result of natural development, whilst in a still larger degree it is the outcome of a widely expressed desire that the arena into which we have stepped should be permanently occupied. As in the case of every other publication, we came to supply a long-felt want, the only difference being that, in this particular instance, such want has been found not only to have a real existence, but to abound in a much greater degree than even we ourselves imagined. The congratulations we have received since the first appearance of the *London Financial Guide*; the good wishes; the earnest and liberal offers of assistance; the promises of active support; the eager curiosity to discover our personal identity; the consternation already caused in various financial camps; the astounding revelations which are being daily confided to us; the angry threats; the cautious overtures – these and numerous other evidences have satisfied us, more conclusively than ever, that a financial paper for the City of London carrying the banner of WITHOUT FEAR AND WITHOUT FAVOUR will not fail for lack of a *raison d'être*. It is not our intention to draw, or even to suggest, any invidious comparison between our own methods and policy and those of any of our contemporaries. Today we are concerned only with ourselves. Our attitude, our principles and our programme are summed up in the motto we have quoted, whilst they are

elaborated more in detail in the corners of our title-page. This is the field we have entered – and our arrangements have been made with a view to permanent occupation.

The notion of permanence was not so fanciful. The first issue of the *FT* was quite an impressive effort, certainly superior to its precursor the *Guide*. Thus on the middle two pages there was solid up-to-date market information, together with an enterprising collection of company reports, company-meeting reports, law reports bearing on finance and general financial matters, including a list of the day's auction sales. There was also an advertisement for Messrs Fagge & Company (telegraphic address: 'Faggio, London') which would not have appeared in a certain other paper. The entire back page, for the next two issues as well as this one, was taken up by the prospectus of the European & American Machine Made Bottle Company. On the front page, in addition to 'Ourselves', there were two main leaders (one about negotiations between the Brighton and South-Eastern railway companies and attacking the *FN*'s coverage of them, the other a rather confused assessment of the European diplomatic chessboard in the light of Russia's Balkans policy) and no less than nine so-called 'leaderettes', including a highly optimistic one about the prospects for machine-made bottling. Also on this crowded page were 'Our Letter Box', 'Latest Shipping News' and an impeccably stolid collection of miscellaneous financial news items under the heading 'Scraps'. It may or may not have thrilled the reader to know that 'the Kursk–Charkow–Azow Railway Company has issued a circular with reference to the conversion of the £1,760,000 Five per Cent bonds issued by them in 1872 into Four per Cent bonds', but the inclusion of such a piece of information was precisely the sort of thing that from the first distinguished the *FT* from all the fly-by-night papers also now springing up.

For the rest of 1888 the *FT* continued to run at four pages long, though from April it had smaller print and an altogether tighter layout, really packing the information in. The editorial tone adopted was in general fairly heavyweight. On 27 February, for instance, there were substantial leaders on 'Mr Goschen's Conversion', 'The European Outlook' and 'The Utilisation of Niagara Falls'; while on 2 October 'A Protection Craze' saw the paper coming out strongly against the first emerging notions of imperial protection. Various campaigns were launched during the year, including one against certain outside brokers (i.e. not members of the Stock Exchange) and another against guinea-pig or 'ornamental' directors, aristocrats elected to boards of new companies on account of their social rather than financial attractiveness to would-be-investors. The real abuse, however, was reserved for the *FN*, which was clearly seen as *the* paper that had to be somehow cut down to size if the *FT* was to survive. As early as 20 February an editorial fiercely attacked the *FN* for simultaneously criticizing 'bucket-shops' (i.e. the businesses run by the more disreputable outside brokers, where the coils of tape showing the latest Stock Exchange prices would eventually fall into a conveniently placed bucket) and including advertisements for them, concluding: 'Our advice to all our readers is to leave this class of business alone; but if they *will* try their luck, then let them be careful to deal only with houses of known respectability, whose code of honour – at any rate in this matter – is not that of the *Financial News*.' Other such attacks and aspersions followed, including in March an intriguing letter from 'Enquirer', wondering whether the Henry Marks mentioned in the *FT* was the same Harry Marks about whom he had heard some strange tales in New York, especially in connection 'with a poor widow named Annie Koppel'. Just once in this first year, on 13 December, the tone was different:

> We much regret to hear that Mr H. H. Marks, the editor of our contemporary, the *Financial News*, is lying seriously ill. Mr Marks only recently returned from the Continent, where he was ordered by his doctors, but the change has apparently not had the desired effect. Many of his friends in the City will, we are sure, join us in wishing him a speedy recovery.

Who were the people behind the *London Financial Guide* and then the *FT*? In terms of official records, the early internal history is almost as elusive and ill-documented as that of the *FN*, but fortunately we have at our disposal two sets of remarkable memoirs – by the company promoter H. Osborne O'Hagan and the man of letters Frank Harris – that add some flesh to the bare bones. For most of 1888 the editorial offices were at 28 Budge Row (second floor), Cannon Street, and the paper was printed and published for the proprietors by MacRae, Curtice & Company of Clement's House, Clement's Inn Passage, Strand. It is clear from board minutes that within a few weeks of the paper's name being changed in February, a journalist called Reginald Brinsley Coe, who seems to have been the founder of the *Guide*, sold his interest in that and the *FT* for £5,000 to a new company calling itself the Financial Times Ltd. The company's meagre minutes for 1888 reveal further snippets of detail. On 10 March two directors were elected, in the persons of Horatio Bottomley and Jas Sheridan. On 13 July two new directors were elected, George Foster and D. G. MacRae, and Bottomley was appointed chairman. Three days later Leopold Graham was appointed editor for six months at

£6 per week. It is O'Hagan, however, who provides the key evidence about these first six months:

When the *Financial News* was becoming a success, the brothers Sheridan, minor lights in the financial world, conceived the idea of starting a rival paper, and calling it the *Financial Times*. They did the thing in a slipshod way, and soon they could not pay their printer's bills, and Horatio Bottomley of MacRae, Curtice and Co, the printers, took the paper over.[14]

Nothing is known about those 'brothers Sheridan' who were to the fore in the original syndicate that bought out Coe. Jas Sheridan faded early from the official record; by the time that board minutes were resumed in 1889 after a gap of several months, he had become an unperson. As for the journalist, Leopold Graham, who became the first designated editor of the *FT*, Harris has left a brief description: 'He had no notion of writing and was poorly educated, but he had a smattering of common French phrases and a real understanding of company promoting and speculative City business. He interested me at once and we became friendly, if not friends.'[15]

What of the man who in July 1888 became chairman of the *FT*? Horatio Bottomley was then twenty-eight years old, having been born in Bethnal Green in 1860, the son of a tailor's cutter. After a series of office-boy jobs, and then joining and becoming a partner in a firm of legal shorthand writers, he had founded his first paper in 1884. This was the *Hackney Hansard*, which recorded the proceedings of one of the local 'parliaments', or debating societies, that were then very popular. The paper did well, and other local *Hansards* followed, along with one or two other magazines, all published by his Catherine Publishing Company from Catherine Street off the Strand. In about 1887 Bottomley approached the company promoter O'Hagan, saying that he wanted to expand his business, and introduced to him a Douglas MacRae, proprietor of a large but unprofitable printing works. O'Hagan duly undertook to form a company to take over the Catherine Publishing Company, MacRae's printing works and another firm, Curtice & Company, advertising agents and newspaper publishers. The new company was called MacRae, Curtice & Company, with Bottomley as chairman – and this was the company that began by printing the *FT* and within a few months took over its control. Harris later described the financier, whom he got to know at about this time:

Bottomly was a trifle shorter even than I was, perhaps five feet four or five, but very broad and even then threatened to become stout. He had a very large head, well-balanced, too, with good forehead and heavy jaws; the eyes small and grey; the peculiarity of the face a prodigiously long upper lip . . . He was greedy of all the sensual pleasures, intensely greedy; even at thirty he ate too much and habitually drank too much. To see him lunching at Romano's with two or three of his intimates, usually subordinates, with a pretty chorus girl on one side and another siren opposite, while the waiter uncorked the fourth or fifth bottle of champagne, was to see the man as he was.[16]

Yet, as Harris also said, almost no one whom he ever met had the same 'invincible good humour' as Bottomley. It was a quality that was to stand him in good stead over the years.

Bottomley's connection with the *FT* proved to be brief. O'Hagan tells the story of the parting of ways between Bottomley and MacRae, Curtice & Company, which probably took place during the autumn of 1888:

A company of £120,000 was small fry to a man of Bottomley's ambition; he figured on managing a concern with £500,000 or £1,000,000 capital. He tried to interest me in a scheme he had in mind, but was unsuccessful. He went about getting options on a whole lot of printing and publishing concerns, many of them of first-rate importance, such as Hansards, the printers of the Parliamentary Debates. Bottomley then proceeded to register a new company called the Hansard Union, with a couple of million capital, to take over the business of MacRae, Curtice & Co. and the various concerns he had obtained options upon . . . Bottomley again tried to interest me, but failed, so took his goods elsewhere. Douglas MacRae liked not the new venture any more than I did, and he retired from the combination, taking with him the *Financial Times* and a valuable paper called the *Draper's Record*.[17]

Bottomley's Hansard Union was duly launched in 1889, but within two years it had crashed to the ground amidst justifiable charges of swindling and gross over-capitalization. Bottomley, however, put up a superb defence in the resulting lawsuit and lived to fight another day. During the 1890s he floated a series of fraudulent companies on the back of the West Australian gold boom. In the First World War he ran the infamous mass-circulation paper *John Bull*, fairly described by A. J. P. Taylor as a 'cheap organ of hate'.[18] In 1922 he was at last convicted of fraud and went to prison. There he was visited one day by an acquaintance, who found him stitching mail-bags and said:

'Ah, Bottomley, sewing?'

To which Bottomley replied: 'No, reaping.'[19]

The year 1888 had been an eventful one for the *FT*. Coe, the Sheridans and Bottomley had all briefly held the baton of control, but by the end it was firmly in the hands of Douglas Gordon MacRae. On Christmas Eve the paper moved its offices from the tiny premises in Budge Row to the rather more spacious White House in Telegraph Street, EC, further signifying the break with the past. It was an apt name, for under MacRae the control of the paper now took on a presidential quality: 'Our Chief was a man in a thousand – a man of the finest business faculties, of the most intense energy, of the most indomitable pluck and of the most unswerving loyalty towards those who worked with him or who enjoyed the privilege of his friendship.'[20] So ran the eventual *FT* obituary of the man who, if not technically, was in spirit and deed the real founding father of the pre-1945 paper. The shrewd O'Hagan had much to do at this time with both Bottomley and MacRae: 'The former I soon came to regard as one who was unsuited to the paths of finance, and wanting in ballast, while, on the other hand, I took a considerable fancy to Douglas MacRae, whom I came to know as a rather rough but a downright honest and capable man.'[21]

Not much is known about MacRae's early life. He was born in 1861, the son of John Gordon MacRae of Fyvie, Aberdeenshire, and attended Shoreham Grammar School before being apprenticed to the printing trade. His first journalistic efforts were cricket notes, and he later wrote weekly letters to the *Eastern Province Herald* and five other Cape papers. After his apprenticeship he set up as a full-time printer, eventually at Clement's House in Clement's Inn Passage, until in his mid-twenties there took place that fateful conjunction between himself, Bottomley and O'Hagan. MacRae was surely right in 1888 not to allow the *FT* and the highly profitable *Draper's Record* to be subsumed in Bottomley's grandiose schemes. Both papers, but especially the *FT*, needed careful individual attention if they were to fulfil their potential, and this attention MacRae proceeded to lavish, becoming during 1889 the managing director of the Financial Times Ltd (embracing the *FT* itself, the *Draper's Record*, in time other trade magazines, and the printing works at Clement's House), the dominant shareholder in the company and, as far as one can tell, the ultimate repository of editorial control. It had been a remarkable rise, but as the racing phrase goes, he still had it all to do.

Harry Marks, meanwhile, was by the late 1880s becoming an increasingly prosperous, high-profile figure. In 1888 there took place a reconstruction of the Financial News Ltd, which raised the capital to £100,000 and left him with a controlling interest in the company's affairs. The following summer he was the subject of the weekly portrait in *Vanity Fair*, with the accompanying pen picture by 'Jehu Junior' concluding:

He lives in anything but Grub Street style at Loudoun Hall, in St John's Wood. He is fond of horses, and owns a promising colt, which lately began to carry his colours at Newmarket. He has a fine picture gallery, wears tight boots, suffers from the gout, and is fond of music. He cannot sing, although he sometimes tries to do so. He abolished the Metropolitan Board of Works.[22]

That same year he was elected for Marylebone on the newly created London County Council, soon afterwards beginning to seek adoption as a Conservative parliamentary candidate. And in 1890 he acquired a country seat at Callis Court, near Broadstairs, a handsome property situated, in the words of one admiring local reporter, 'at a beautiful, invigorating spot overlooking the sea at the North Foreland'. There is no doubt that at this time, in his mid-thirties, Marks was an immensely capable, energetic operator. As someone who briefly worked under him on the *FN* later recalled: 'No soldier in journalism could have an officer so concise and dependable in command, so diplomatic and charming in personal contact, so deft and simple in instruction, so cynically humorous in criticism, so studiously and generously appreciative.'[23] He too was known to his staff as 'the Chief' (though sometimes apparently as 'H.H.M.'). Not surprisingly, riding the crest of a wave, his initial attitude towards the upstart rival in Budge Row and then Telegraph Street was a mixture of the sanguine and the contemptuous.

As hard as the *FT* slung mud at the *FN* during 1888, the *FN* slung it back. Apart from the reciprocal theme of attacking each other's bucket-shop advertisements, the main focus of the obloquy concerned Colonel J. T. North, the so-called 'Nitrate King', whose group was responsible for developing the Nitrate Railway and various nitrate companies in South America. 'The Coming Crash in Nitrate Rails' was the headline of a typical editorial comment in the *FN*: 'Colonel North is a Pactolus among promoters. Whatever he touches turns, if not to gold, at least to premiums. In the end there is often a considerable difference between gold and premiums, but at the outset they may be easily mistaken for each other.' The *FT* by contrast offered the warmest of support to the Colonel, especially in early 1889 when, amidst a fanfare of publicity, he prepared to leave for a trip to Chile. On 22 January the previous evening's banquet to North at the Cannon Street Hotel, at which MacRae had been present, was given a full front-page report, including detailed lists of wine, menu and music; four days later there was an equally lengthy report about 'The Nitrate King at Leeds', where North was presented with the freedom of the borough; and on 5 February the *FT* reproduced a letter that had been sent by the editor to the principal daily and financial journals to the effect that Montague Vizetelly, the 'well-known correspondent', who was to accompany the Colonel on his journey, had indeed been commissioned by the *FT* to report on the nitrate deposits of the western coast of South America, but that 'he will neither be biassed nor influenced in any way by Colonel North's courtesy'. That same day O'Hagan decided that the time had come for a cessation of overt hostilities between the two papers, and he called on the chiefs in turn:

Having first talked MacRae into leaving himself in my hands, I saw Harry Marks and told him he was on the wrong tack. He assumed the high hand, and said it was a case of the survival of the fittest, and he knew which paper was going to the wall . . . I replied, 'You do not know MacRae. There is room for you both, and money will go on being found until the *Times* becomes a paying proposition.' I so impressed this on Marks, and I think he gathered that my money was behind the *Times*, that he consented to a truce, and it was agreed between these two newspaper proprietors that for the future neither of them should allow into his columns anything offensive to the other.[24]

To all appearances the truce lasted less than twenty-four hours, for on the evening of the 5th, the day before the Colonel sailed, there was a banquet given at Liverpool's Adelphi Hotel in honour of North, who spoke feelingly about his harshest critic. The next morning the *FT* printed the text of his speech:

I am going out to improve the output of Nitrate works, or rather Nitrate railways, in which you are interested, but I warn you against what you may hear from pessimist papers such as the *Financial News* . . . I say in connection with the *Financial News* that I do not stand blackmailing. I will recall a few facts to you. When the Primitiva Company was started you were told by the *Financial News* what they thought of it as an advertisement. You know what it is, and I tell you that I shall not be satisfied this year unless it pays cent per cent. The same paper sneered at Nitrate Rails, saying that the Nitrate Railway was a tramway going over bogs and swamps. Yet over £70,000 was made by it last month.

What had happened to the agreement? The overworked mediator tells the story:

MacRae, feeling sure that the report would contain matter which, owing to the truce, it would be undesirable to print in his paper, arranged to be on the printing premises, to go through the report and delete any offensive matter. He had a bedroom on the premises, where he arranged to stay the night. The paper was set up by the compositors, leaving space for the report of the Liverpool speech, which did not come. Two o'clock, 3 o'clock, and 3.30 – and no report.

MacRae came to the conclusion that it could not now come. He gave directions that the space reserved was to be filled with other matter, and the paper go to press, and then turned in for the night. It took twenty minutes to fill in the empty space, and just then the belated report arrived. It had been delivered by mistake at the printing works of the *Financial News*, and the manager of that paper had kept it back until he thought the *Financial Times* had gone to press. On its arrival at MacRae's printing works, the energetic manager removed the new matter he had set up, and put the full report in its place . . .

The fat was in the fire. MacRae was greatly distressed, as he was a man of honourable instincts, while Harry Marks was furious, and wrote me a stinging letter and asked me what I meant by pledging MacRae to a truce. I had great trouble with these two men during the next few days, but eventually I got Marks to see that the trouble had come about through the overzeal of his own subordinates, and the truce was again patched up, and lasted.[25]

So peace broke out between the two papers and was never again seriously threatened, keen though the competition between them continued to be. When MacRae died, it was with sincerity that the *FN* in its warm obituary referred to how he had been 'as a rival the most courteous'.

As for the main lieutenants of the respective chiefs during these formative years, the records leave one with little more than names. The impression, though, is that both Marks and MacRae possessed the crucial knack of talent-spotting. On the *FN* side, early recruits included the capable J. W. Clark, who remained as sub-editor until 1910; C. A. Reeve, subsequently City editor of the *Daily Telegraph* for many years; and D. O. Croal, incisive and pungent chief leader writer until after the First World War. In the administrative sphere, the two people who seem to have carried the paper in these years were E. A. O'Brien, the business manager, and C. F. Tombs, who in 1884 was based in Lombard Street as secretary to a number of Indian gold-mining companies, started as a sideline to keep the *FN*'s books and was soon appointed company secretary, holding that position until 1902, when he became a director. Over in MacRae's domain, much of the journalistic donkey-work was done by George Springfield, up to 1905 successively reporter, chief sub-editor and night editor, and the three Murray brothers (S. J., A. E. and R.), who as a trio reputedly wrote the entire editorial matter, including market reports, in one of the fairly early issues. Sydney Murray, who had originally been in banking, was in fact editor (though strictly under the supervision of MacRae as managing director) from about 1892 to 1895, while his brother Arthur also later took up the reins of editorship. The *FT*'s company secretary was C. Layton, who also became a director in 1890.

If all these are merely names, the same does not apply to one of the early journalists, the redoubtable and astonishingly prolific William Ramage Lawson, who after a variegated past, mostly on newspapers in Scotland and Australia, arrived in London in 1886 in his mid-forties and was taken on to the strength of the *FN* by Marks. Lawson researched and wrote the articles about the Metropolitan Board of Works, but in 1889, angry about the lack of both public and private recognition he was getting from Marks about the true authorship of these and other pieces, he left the *FN*. During 1890 he published a book on *Spain of To-day*, personally investigated the state of American railroads and Argentine finance for MacRae, and in December 1890 became editor of the *FT*, holding the post for two years. Subsequently, he travelled widely in the interests of Sir Ernest Cassel and in 1895 joined the Stock Exchange, making a small fortune through mainly 'bear' operations, while all the time continuing his financial journalism and authorship. His writings may have 'displayed a spirit of cocksureness which was sometimes in excess of the facts', as one obituary was to put it in 1922, and socially he may have 'shown that slight strain of brusqueness not uncommon in men of such unbounding physical and mental verve', but as a long-lived controversialist of great versatility he was to go on figuring largely in the history of both papers.[26]

What of respective reputations and strength during these early years of rivalry? *Sell's Dictionary of the World's Press* had no doubt in 1890 of the *FN*'s position of leadership, describing it as 'now the recognised authority upon financial affairs, domestic and foreign'. That same year the *FN*'s standing and potential were further enhanced by the move of the Argus Press to larger, better-equipped premises, at the corner of Temple Avenue and Tudor Street. Indeed, the move worked so well that in 1897 the business manager O'Brien was able to claim that 'for eight years past the *Financial News* has never been ten minutes late in the time of publication'.[27] Issue sizes also tell a story. For instance, in the week beginning 6 October 1890 the *FT* totalled 42 pages, the *FN* 46 pages; while for the week beginning 6 April the following year the respective figures were 36 and 46. Moreover, from the spring of 1891 the size of the *FT*'s pages was often smaller, varying from issue to issue. Circulation comparisons are of course impossible, though both papers were not shy of making bold, unspecified claims. Thus the *FN* daily guaranteed to advertisers 'a circulation greater than that of all the other Financial Journals in England combined', to which the *FT* during 1892 riposted by quoting a firm of chartered accountants to the effect that the books of the *FT* showed an increase in the paper's sales in 1891 of 73 per cent over those of 1890, adding off its own bat that 'the manager of the *Financial News*, in a letter dated 28 January 1892, "makes no claim that the circulation of the *Financial News* has increased during the past twelve months"'. Yet all this seems to have been whistling in the dark; for though it may have been some comfort for the *FT* to know that it was probably on about a level with the *Financier* and that even the *FN* had its problems, the fundamental fact was that during the early 1890s, as the Stock Exchange slumped in the wake of the near collapse of Barings Bank in November 1890, it was a desperate struggle for MacRae to keep the *FT* going. Indeed, he could not have done so without a mixture of enormous will-power and the profits (several thousand pounds a year) of the *Draper's Record*. In the words of MacRae's successor, F. M. Bridgewater, who became a director of the company in 1893: 'To speak of the career of the *Financial Times* for the first few years as chequered would be to describe it in too favourable terms, because there were not even occasional patches of sunshine.' He added that the obstinate MacRae persevered during these years 'in spite, not only of the advice of his best friends, but in flagrant disregard of their entreaties'.[28]

There are other ways of comparing the two papers. When Pooter's son Lupin in *The Diary of a Nobody* (published in 1892) was 'riveted to the *Financial News*, as if he had been a born capitalist', one wonders whether he would have got a better pennyworth reading the *FT*. Would he, for example, have had more of the 'dirt' uncovered before his eyes? The *FT* over the years certainly thought so, referring with pride in its tenth anniversary issue in 1898 to how 'we have steadfastly adhered to the principle of protecting the public', notwithstanding the 'many furious assaults on account of our independent attitude'.[29] One of these assaults was literal, in September 1889, when the company promoter Alfred Green, repeatedly criticized in the columns of the *FT* under the editorship of Leopold Graham and then MacRae, launched a physical attack on MacRae and hurled him down a flight of stairs, leaving him with cuts, bruises, a strained wrist and a swollen thumb.[30] The editor-proprietor was perhaps not the only injured party, for according to his friend O'Hagan, 'MacRae's judgement was not always sound, and in his desire to clear the Augean stables he struck recklessly and sometimes a little unfairly.' But O'Hagan added: 'Many are the times when, having read my day's *Financial Times*, I would send for MacRae, who, when entering my room, would say, 'I know, I know – you don't like my attack on —?' He would at once modify it.'[31] Perhaps the principal victim of MacRae's stable-cleansing was the Equitable Life Assurance Society of the United States, which in a series of investigatory articles was severely taken to task over its methods of selling to prospective English policy-holders, eventually leading to legal proceedings and judgement against the Equitable.[32] Nevertheless, reading through the early years of the *FT*, one's overall impression is that, despite O'Hagan's remarks (which were perhaps more applicable to later in the 1890s), the paper was a relatively restrained organ, preferring to record the facts and doings of the financial world rather than comment outspokenly on them. For the more forthright exposure, no doubt beloved by Lupin, it was usually necessary to look elsewhere.

'The bugbear of dishonest promoters' and 'the trusted guide of the investing public' were further tributes paid by *Sell's Dictionary* in 1890 to the *FN*. Certainly there were plenty of examples around this time of the *FN* feeling able to indulge in shameless trumpet-blowing on account of its investigative efficacy. Thus in April 1891 readers were informed that 'Mr Alexander Brown, who was yesterday sentenced to five years penal servitude for conspiring to steal £200, is the same Mr Alexander Brown who endeavoured three years ago to float the Commercial Bank of London scheme, which the *Financial News* exposed and defeated.' Similarly a few days later the announcement was made that 'Samuel Victor Morley, well known to readers of the *Financial News* in conjunction with the Hornchurch Brewery Co., and the Bristol & Midlands Colliery Co. against which we warned the public when they were brought out, was yesterday sentenced to five years penal servitude for conspiracy.' Again, in March 1894, this time in connection with an outside broker, the paper was able to express satisfaction that 'W. H. Scott, *alias* Dawson, whose fraudulent methods have been exposed time and again in the *Financial News*, has at last met with his deserts, and goes to hard labour for eighteen months.' All these revelations were no doubt in the public interest, but it is worth quoting what an earlier historian of the *FN* related about Marks in this context:

> He had in him a sadistic strain. It is told of him that he once launched an attack on a certain personage who came in daily from an outlying suburb. At that suburban station the contents bills of the *Financial News* displayed only the startling line, 'Exposure of So-and-so'. Before the arrival of the victim for his usual train, an emissary of Marks had brought up the available supply of the paper. The emissary entered the same carriage as the victim and read tantalisingly one of the copies, allowing his fellow passenger merely to whet his curiosity and rage on an occasional glimpse of a headline. Only when within a few minutes of their destination did the assiduous reader ask blandly, 'Would you care to see the *Financial News*, sir?'[33]

Marks perhaps expected his victims to show the same resilience that he himself had learned to acquire. Writing in 1904 of 'the false and rancorous charges which were brought against us and pressed with passionate and malignant persistence' during the paper's first decade by those whom the paper had attacked, he reckoned that these charges 'at least served to show that reiterated calumnies and reiterated mendacities are powerless against those who, hardened to the wounds of public conflict, have the sense and fortitude to despise them'. He added: 'The *Financial News* lives; the schemes it attacked are dead.'[34]

There was, however, another altogether murkier side to the picture, as a series of three court cases in fairly rapid succession made embarrassingly obvious. First, in November 1888, Albert Myers, promoter of the Ashley Bottle Company, won a libel case against the *FN*, after the paper had stated that Myers had lied in claiming that Marks and the *FN* had sought to obtain a large sum of money, up to £50,000, through ensuring the successful flotation of the company, though in the event this failed to happen. The outcome was a blow to the good name of Marks, while in the course of evidence unfavourable light was also thrown on Graham of the *FT*.[35] Then there was the case heard in January 1890 in which the Crystal Reef Gold Mining Company charged Claude Marks (brother of Harry), James Woolfe and James Marix (an advertising agent employed by the *FT*, but also connected with the *FN*, being a long-time associate of Harry Marks) with having started a new paper, the *Mining Record*, for the express purpose of blackmailing the company. The case did not directly concern the *FN* or *FT*, but much came out of the evidence: in general, a vivid evocation of the unscrupulous atmosphere in which the new, entwined worlds of financial journalism and company promoting operated; in particular, details of how George Grant, editor of the *FT*'s 'Money and Stock Market' columns, had underwritten £4,000 of the Crystal Reef shares and been intimately involved in the company's flotation.[36]

It was the third case, however, which pulled no punches. It began in June 1890 when George Washington Butterfield, an American who had come to England in the mid-1880s to raise capital for a Californian gold-mining company, unsuccessfully sued the *FN* for libel over a series of derogatory articles published in 1886–7. The paper the next day duly congratulated itself that 'but for our unaided efforts British investors might today have been saddled with Butterfield's million of worthless chromos', adding that 'he may return to California and to honest mining work – in the mines, or he may, like some other victims of the *Financial News* exposures, remain in London, and revenge himself by issuing weekly leaflets abusing the editor'. Butterfield in fact did just that, accusing Marks of having 'robbed, ill-used and deserted' a woman whom he had lived with in the USA and stating that he was now 'exploiting London . . . after overdoing New York'. Marks sued Butterfield for libel, and the case was heard at the Old Bailey in December 1890. The ensuing evidence revealed not only that Marks in New York in the late 1870s had had an affair with a Mrs Koppel that may have produced a child (whom Marks disowned) and certainly resulted in Marks booking a passage to England as 'Mr Henry', but also that in 1886 Marks had secretly promoted a worthless concern called the Rae (Transvaal) Gold Mining Company before proceeding over the next year to advise readers to buy its shares while more or less simultaneously selling off his own shares through a variety of 'dummy' vendors. A glance at the *FN*'s back files showed how systematic the 'puffing' had been: 'a very safe and remunerative investment', said the paper on 15 January 1887; 'a good mining investment' on 18 January; 'we think very well of the Rae Transvaal Gold Mine' on 26 January. The jury duly found for Butterfield – 'A Perverse Verdict', according to the *FN* – and the press at large, even the Tory press, came down heavily against Marks, typified by the opinion of the *Morning Advertiser* that 'a man who has failed to clear his character of charges such as those made by Mr Butterfield is wholly unfitted to conduct the business of the Empire or the City'. According to James Head in later years, a contrite Marks apologized to him for having done such a thing and said it would not happen again.[37]

In terms of editorial attitudes, the two papers over the years did not usually differ all that much, apart from on a few specific issues. Granted that they were appealing to the same constituency – the City and those who lived off it – this was hardly surprising. There tended, though, to be a rather more populist tone to the *FN*'s leaders, whereas almost from the first the *FT*'s approach was cooler and more pragmatic. Thus in January 1889 the *FT* argued of the previous year's companies legislation that, in its futile and too narrow attempt to define fraud, 'honest directors, already too few, will be driven away, while rogues will not be deterred'. Instead, what was needed was much more specific company legislation, with the aim of 'finally determining and setting at rest a number of questions of great practical importance', such as 'the legality of the issue of shares at a discount', 'the power of directors to pay interest during the construction of works' and 'the power of a company to purchase its own shares'. All this was manifestly sound and sensible, stated in a low-key way. By contrast, there was a much more fervent feel to the *FN*'s campaign the following year for some sort of licensing system to govern the myriad outside brokers and bucket-shops, culminating in the publication of its own draft bill, 'Legislation for Touting Brokers', formally drafted in parliamentary style. The 'bill' aroused considerable interest, but was upstaged later that month, November 1890, by the high drama of the Baring crisis, which proved a severe test for the nascent craft of financial journalism.

As markets plunged and Bank Rate rose, neither paper doubted the depth or intensity of the crisis, but equally neither paper was able to reveal, at least in public, the true cause of the crisis until it was over. On Saturday the 15th, as the situation reached its climax, the *FT* sought to describe 'The Agony':

> The City is becoming enveloped deeper and deeper in a baleful, mysterious crisis. Day by day thick clouds gather over the Stock Markets, and where they come from, or who is responsible for them, no one has a definite opinion. All who have financial interests at stake feel as if they were standing on the brink of a volcano which at any moment may open up and swallow them. This slow-killing agony has been going on now for about two months without coming to a head. The worst kind of fever would reach its climax in less time.

It was, the *FT* believed, 'high time to try to shake off this depressing enervating nightmare, or, failing that, to find out what it really means'. There were various causes, according to the paper, to which the total collapse of confidence could *not* be ascribed. 'It can no longer be fairly charged to over-speculation in stocks.' Nor was it the result of 'underwriting and syndicate mongering'. Nor also was it caused by the tumbling price of American stocks. Therefore: 'The root of it is evidently not in the Stock Market at all. Nor is it in the Money Market pure and simple.' Instead, the key lay in 'the portfolios of the high finance houses', though in terms of detail the *FT* could refer only to how 'a certain class of paper originating at the River Plate has been under severe discussion lately'. However, as the editorial rather abjectly concluded: 'But as yet all is merely surmise. The public from whom such delicate secrets must be rigidly concealed can only stand trembling before the advancing cloud.'

Readers of the *FT* and *FN* would not have known it, but succour was at hand even as these words appeared. Partly through the columns of *The Times*, it became public knowledge over the weekend that the Bank of England had arranged a guarantee fund to bail out if necessary the big merchant bank Barings, which had found itself badly over-committed in the Argentine. The relief of the City, above all the inhabitants of Capel Court, was profound. In the words of the *FT*'s leader on the Monday, entitled simply 'Saved':

What might have happened on the Stock Exchange is a prospect too fearful to contemplate. If the mere indefinable dread of there being a screw loose in Bishopsgate Street [home of Barings] could spread terror through every market, and cause twenty, thirty or forty per cent declines even in sound securities, what might not have followed the collapse itself? Not a living man in the House has witnessed anything approaching the catastrophe which would have been inevitable.

Praise for the Bank's 'judicious action' (*FN*) and the guarantors' 'patriotic and courageous intervention' (*FT*) abounded, but the *FN* gave it hard to the original culprits:

If Messrs Baring did not know about the existence of these concealed and growing liabilities, why did they not? We do not recall these facts for the purpose of exulting over Messrs Baring's downfall, but for the purpose of proving our contention that their system of business has been so loose and so reckless that they have themselves to blame for the consequences of it . . . The investors who through Messrs Baring's recklessness have sustained heavy, and in some cases ruinous, losses, have at least some claim to the public sympathy which has been by our contemporaries [including to some extent the *FT*] so thoughtlessly lavished upon the involved firm.

The *FN* did well to berate Barings, for the loss of confidence caused by the crisis resulted for several years in a sharp downturn of investment abroad, while the home field continued stagnant until the second half of the decade and inevitably the Stock Exchange and in turn the financial press were among the worst hit.

The equally characteristic voice of the *FT* was heard the following May, as the Chancellor of the Exchequer faced a dilemma:

Mr Goschen seems still uncertain in his mind about one-pound notes. He has received urgent requests from the North of England to issue them at once, and he has been told that if he ventures to do so he will make an enemy of every Club man in London. A Chancellor of the Exchequer should hardly condescend to place against one another such opinions. The North of England demand is the fruit of experience, though somewhat indirect, of the utility and convenience of the Scottish paper currency, while the Club man's views are simply the outcome of childish prejudice. This question has to be fought out independently of the barbaric attachment to gold which exists in England, and must be settled on purely scientific lines.

Other monetary matters in the early 1890s pointed up the difference in approach between the two papers. In April 1892 an *FT* leader on 'Provincial Banks' was a model of micro caution. It included a detailed examination of a batch of recent bankers' balance sheets, asserted that 'in many instances the proportion of advances to deposits is abnormally and dangerously high' and asked a series of pertinent questions:

Will bankers contend that they are justified in lending up to the hilt? Will not each and every one of them admit that 75 per cent of the deposits is quite enough to use by way of loans and discounts? Will they not further admit that taking deposits, capital and reserve into consideration, 50 to 60 per cent of this total is a fair proportion to thus utilise?

As for the more macro *FN* approach, a leader of October 1893 on 'Three Per Cent' is worth quoting at some length, for both style (one senses the hand of Croal) and content:

The Bank of England is trying to serve two masters. One of these masters is the body of its own shareholders, whose dividends depend upon the amount of discount business done by the Bank, and who do not like to see their prospects injured by the successful competition of the open market; and the other is the vast interest of British credit, represented in the City mind by the amount of gold in the Bank's vaults. The policy of the directors, as exemplified in their latest exploit of reducing the minimum official rate to 3 per cent, is too obviously the policy that animated Mr Facing-both-ways in Bunyan's allegory. They want to get some of the business which now drifts into other channels, and they do not want to encourage withdrawals of bullion by foreign customers. As usual in similar attempts, they have adopted a compromise course which is not at all certain to achieve either of the desired ends. A 3 per cent rate is ineffective when competing with a market rate for fine three months paper of 1¼ per cent. It is, on the other hand, anything but calculated to strengthen the Bank's position as the custodian of the national reserve of bullion . . . This 'letting I dare not wait upon I would' sort of action serves to show once more what an anomalous position the Bank holds in attempting to sustain its dual capacity of a private banking institution, borrowing and lending for profit, like other banks, and a quasi-national State department whose business is to regulate things so as to avert every influence that could make for a crisis.

The leader then went on to analyse the Bank's conflicting relationships with the government and its own shareholders ('No doubt, the Bank would say, with Captain Macheath, "How happy could I be with either were t'other dear charmer away"'), painted in grim terms the consequences of the Bank failing to fulfil its wider duties ('A depleted gold reserve has a terrifying effect on the City, shakes credit, and leads to that disposition to hoard which results in runs on banks, panics, suspensions of the Bank Charter Act, and widespread calamity') and concluded by calling in strong terms for the Bank's responsibilities to be more clearly defined.

Inevitably the editorial comment of both papers tended to reflect the concerns and prejudices of their largely City readerships. Thus in January 1889, in an attack on 'American Railway Methods', the *FT* took the line that 'it is notorious to everyone familiar with the market for American Rails that the ordinary stocks of the majority of the lines have become mere gambling counters, which are manipulated by the leading officials for their own profit, utterly regardless of the interests of the shareholders or the convenience of the public'. Three years later a leader in the same paper, perhaps penned by Lawson, allowed itself a certain jocosity on the theme of 'Venezuelan Spoilation':

When Mr W. S. Gilbert is in want of a really good subject for a new comic opera he might turn his attention to the Venezuelan Government, under the presidency of Dr Raimundo Andueza Palacio. There he will find everything already turned topsy-turvy in the best Gilbertian style, and practically all he will have to do is to turn the actual incidents into verse, requesting his collaborator to put a pathetic *motif* in the score to represent the tangible injustice which British investors have suffered at the hands of the operatic President and his chorus.[38]

It was the *FN*, though, that had the real cutting edge when it chose to exercise it. For instance, when in October 1888 the Home Secretary returned a cheque for £300 sent by the paper on behalf of its readers, following the government's refusal to offer a reward in connection with the recent 'Jack the Ripper' killings, the ensuing editorial tore into the minister. 'Murder may hold high carnival in the East End for all that Mr Henry Matthews will do to check it', was one of the kinder remarks. Or again, four years later, there was no doubt where the *FN* stood first on the subject of having a Catholic as Lord Mayor ('a triumph of intelligence and fairness over bigotry and prejudice') and then, soon after, on the question of foreign immigration ('It seems useless to expect the initiative to come from the legislature. Unless English working men bestir themselves, and demand that a check shall be put to the ceaseless flood of impecunious foreigners, with its inevitable consequence of lower labour market, the evil will go on').[39]

There was one matter, however, on which both papers spoke as with a single voice, and this was the Liberal government of 1892 to 1895: it had to go. In March 1894, with Gladstone resigning and the ministry starting to totter, the *FN* spoke of 'the waste, the official jobbery, the spending of taxpayers' money on foreign manufactured goods', the *FT* of how 'from a financial point of view' the advent of a Conservative government 'will be heartily welcomed, for it will doubtless help to hasten the long delayed revival of public confidence'. The *FT* would always be less overtly political than the *FN*, but when it came to it, it usually supported the party most of its readers voted for.

By St Valentine's Day 1893, a Tuesday, the *FT* was into the sixth year of its existence, the *FN* its tenth. The respective issues of that fairly typical day were six and eight pages long, though the *FT* did have an extra column to each page. The similarities were considerable: money-market, stock-market and Wall Street reports on page one; two or three columns of tape prices; half a column or just under of answers to investment queries; and between one and two pages of company-meeting reports, with the *FT* doing rather better. Where the *FN* scored in terms of revenue was in the formal advertising, both small ads (especially for outside brokers) and bigger ones announcing new issues. In particular, the Olympic Music Hall Ltd prospectus filled half a page, whereas all that the *FT* secured was a truncated version filling less than half a column. As far as 'features' went, the main extra in the *FT* was a 'Synopsis of General News' and a parliamentary report, between them filling almost a page; while the *FN*'s readers enjoyed fuller legal reports, more information about the produce markets and the continental bourses and a 'special' in the form of a half-page of 'English and Welsh Railway Statistics', summarizing the accounts of the companies for the second half of 1892. On the main editorial page (page two in the *FT*, page four in the *FN*) each paper had two principal leaders and some eight or nine leaderettes. One of the latter in the *FN* propounded the dictum that 'this is essentially the age of music halls' and considered in a fairly sanguine spirit the prospects of the new Olympic venture. The major *FN* leaders both had a self-publicizing streak to them: one on 'The Railway Accounts' that made much of the fact that 'no attempt has hitherto been made, so far as we are aware, to bring the chief features of these half-yearly accounts into one uniform table'; while the other leader, 'A D.D. on the Defensive', employed the best house style to demolish a New York ecclesiastic who had materialized in England as a company promoter and, following an earlier *FN* attack, written an unconvincing letter to the paper published in this issue on the opposite page. The *FT*'s leaders were stolid indeed: almost 2,000 words of measured assessement of the 'The Chatham Outlook' (i.e. that of the London, Chatham & Dover Railway following the publication of half-year results) and 'Austrian Currency', a detailed survey by the paper's Paris correspondent of the monetary situation in Austria–Hungary. There was not much spin off the pitch in either piece, but then increasingly that was not what the *FT* was seeking to provide.

★

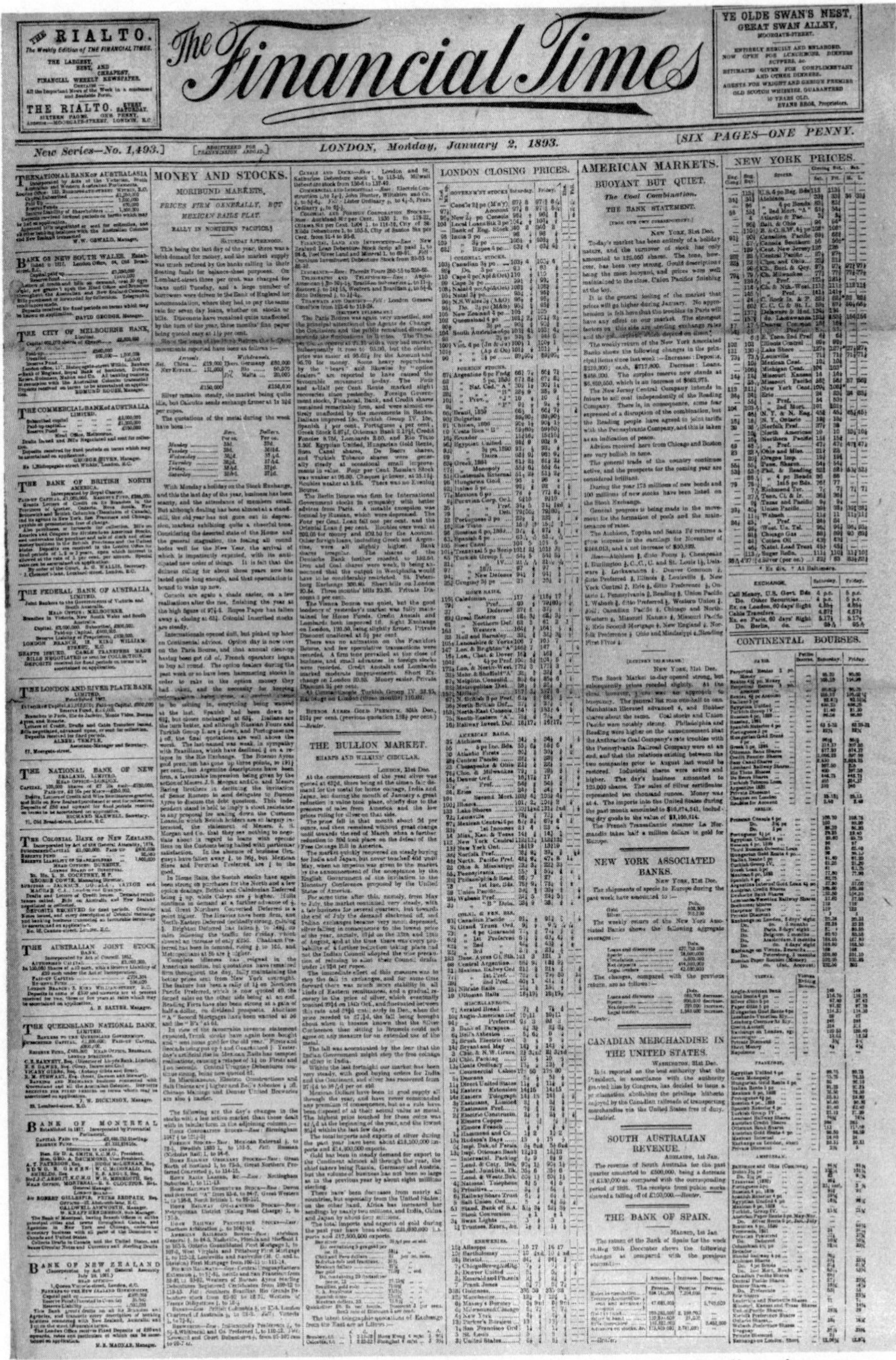

THE RIALTO. The Weekly Edition of THE FINANCIAL TIMES.

The Financial Times

YE OLDE SWAN'S NEST, GREAT SWAN ALLEY, MOORGATE-STREET.

New Series—No. 1,493. LONDON, Monday, January 2, 1893. [SIX PAGES—ONE PENNY.

MONEY AND STOCKS.

MORIBUND MARKETS.

LONDON CLOSING PRICES.

AMERICAN MARKETS.

BUOYANT BUT QUIET.

The Coal Combination.

THE BANK STATEMENT.

NEW YORK PRICES.

CONTINENTAL BOURSES.

THE BULLION MARKET.

NEW YORK ASSOCIATED BANKS.

CANADIAN MERCHANDISE IN THE UNITED STATES.

SOUTH AUSTRALIAN REVENUE.

THE BANK OF SPAIN.

2 January 1893: the *FT* with a new masthead and printed for the first time on pink paper

At about this time, the winter of 1892–3, one has a distinct sense of MacRae gathering together his resources and making possibly one final effort to establish the *FT* as a serious rival – above all serious – to the *FN*. In December the company reached an agreement with Reuters concerning the supply from the New Year, at £400 a year, of 'every telegram of their general service, including the New York commercial and financial service'. In the last few days of the year the editorial and business offices were moved to larger premises at 52 Coleman Street, EC. And from the first issue of the New Year, Monday 2 January 1893, there were three striking new aspects to the *FT*. One was the provision of a 'Synopsis of General News', the rationale for which had been carefully thought out:

A City man cannot afford to ignore political events when he attempts to gauge the markets, and even such apparently trifling matters as a snowstorm or a landslip are often of high significance to particular stocks. Hitherto it has been the necessary practice for business men to take the *Financial Times* and one of the other daily papers giving general news, and to this course we can have no objection. But many of our readers have. In these busy times the opportunity for gathering news is only to be found in the railway journey to town, and this does not suffice for the careful study of a financial newspaper, and a search through the columns of a general newspaper in addition. Our present object is to search the general newspaper, or rather to search the sources from which the general newspaper draws its information, and to give in a short and quickly readable form all the news which can be of interest financially or otherwise to the intelligent business man. We shall not attempt to compete with the ordinary newspapers in tales of sea serpents, or in discovering what to do with our girls. That sort of old maid's gossip has nothing of interest for business men; but, on the other hand, we shall endeavour to omit nothing which can be of interest to them.

Within a couple of days the paper was publishing a congratulatory letter from 'Suburban' of Leytonstone: 'Personally, I always treat myself to an ordinary daily besides the *Financial Times*, but I do not always find time to read it, except on foggy days, when my train takes an hour and a quarter to cover five miles.'

The other innovations to mark the New Year were even more striking, but received little in the way of public explanation and no mention in the board minutes. An announcement at the end of December put the matter baldly: 'In order to provide outward features which will distinguish the *Financial Times* from other journals of similar appearance, a new heading and distinctive headlines will be introduced, and the paper will be slightly tinted.' The new masthead was indeed bolder and more flowing than its predecessor; as for those momentous words 'slightly tinted', it is difficult almost a century later to know how much colour has faded from original copies, but as far as one can tell the *FT* for quite a long time from 1893 had a slight pinkish tint to its pages rather than rejoicing in that bold salmon pink with which we are now familiar. Yet whatever the precise colouring involved, it was a typically bold stroke by MacRae, marking out the *FT* as a very special paper at a time when almost the only other coloured publication was the *Sporting Times*, popularly known as the 'Pink 'Un'. It was a marketing decision that over the years must have been responsible for selling many millions of extra copies of the paper.

There was no immediate reward for these changes; 1893 was a year of still deepening depression on the Stock Exchange. The words of 'Midas' (the *FN*'s new Saturday gossip columnist from the floor of the Stock Exchange) in March would have been applicable at any time in 1893 and well into 1894: 'The absence of business is having a most depressing effect upon the members. There are no longer any practical jokes or good stories to relieve the monotony of existence in the "House", and even Mr Gloag's world-famed conundrums fall flat, and fail to mitigate the general gloom.' In these discouraging cirumstances it was a further tribute to MacRae's self-belief, and faith in the long-term future of an alternative financial daily, that towards the end of 1893 the *FT* became the first London morning paper to be composed on the revolutionary Linotype machine, which was much faster than the old style of hand composition, saved enormously on production costs and within a few years was being employed by virtually all the metropolitan dailies.

Even the *FN* was suffering quite badly by this time, as the company's board minutes, which survive from 1894, reveal. The board for most of that year comprised James Head in the chair, Aden Beresford and Percy Marks (another brother of Harry), and the talk was of 'cuts'. Thus on 21 February: 'The letter of February 1st inst, terminating the engagement with Mr C. A. Reeve at three months date unless Mr Reeve consents to a reduction in salary of one guinea per week from 1st May next was confirmed.' And: 'It was reported that Mr Ribbons had consented to a reduction of £1 per week from 29th January last. Resolved to confirm this arrangement.' Eventually Reeve agreed to follow the Ribbons example, but the atmosphere in Abchurch Lane cannot have been a happy one. Money remained tight for the rest of 1894, as on 22 October: 'The terms for advertising on the outside boards on road car omnibuses were discussed, and it was resolved to decline same for the present.' The editor himself was not in the best of financial health, probably through having been an optimistic 'bull' while markets continued to fall. During the autumn protracted negotiations took place between the company, Marks and George Gregory & Company (a large firm of outside brokers) about how the large debt that Marks had incurred was to be paid off. By January the company had virtually become his bankers: 'A letter from Mr Marks of November 29th, 1894, was read authorising the retention of his salary from 1st January 1895 in reduction of his loan, and stipulating that no interest be charged. Resolved to forgo interest on the loan under the special circumstances.' Though he could still 'stipulate', it must have been a painful position for the Chief to find himself in.

Yet for both papers the tide was at last turning. O'Hagan recalled more than thirty years later how MacRae continued to battle on into 1894:

> He consulted with me frequently, and it was painful to see everything he had fast disappearing. He asked no help, but I thought much of his abilities and his doggedness, and I said to him, 'Let the thing go, and I will lend you ten thousand pounds to start a new line of business. I don't care to see my money go down your sink, but I do believe that if you start in a new line you will be successful.'
>
> He then pleaded very hard that I should stand behind him with ten thousand pounds, and long before that was exhausted he was sure he would have the paper on its legs. He was so much in earnest that I gave way. I made no bargain with him, as I might have done. He would no doubt have sold me one-half interest in the paper for less than £10,000 and I see from recent reports that the paper is making over £150,000 a year, one-half of which would have been mine. It was not a business arrangement, but an act of friendship for a man I admired and wanted to help; but as he came weekly for £200 or £300 and sometimes more, I felt it was only a matter of time when my £10,000 would have followed what had already been lost.
>
> But he was right – the change came when he had taken two thousand pounds only. The boom in South African mining set in, and with it success to the *Financial Times*, from which success it never went back.[40]

O'Hagan's memory did not play him false. The second and by far the greater 'Kaffir' boom got under way in December 1894 and, amidst feverish speculation on almost continuously rising markets, lasted until October 1895. Mining magnates like Barney Barnato became household names and built houses for themselves in Park Lane. The leading firms on the Stock Exchange almost doubled their staffs in order to cope with the volume of speculative business. And the *FN* and *FT* milked this remarkable turn of events for all it was worth. By May almost the whole of the right-hand centre page of a typical day's *FT* was taken up with mining matters, including a dense array of news cabled from South Africa, yields of South African mines and mining closing prices (the 'Kaffir circus' would continue on the pavement of Throgmorton Street after the Stock Exchange had closed for the day). In July a typical Saturday *FN*, the issue of 6 July, featured a rash of mining prospectuses, including new issues by the British Exploration Company Ltd (half-page), Rhodesia Ltd (full page), the Gresham Gold Exploring Syndicate Ltd (half-page) and Rights & Exploring of Rhodesia Ltd (half-page). That same day the 'Midas' column, almost exculsively concerned with 'Kaffirs', well reflected the ever-upward tone that characterized the atmosphere of the boom: 'New African have kept firm at £6; but I expect to see them considerably higher before very long. The company's assets were daily increasing in value, and I hear of some fresh business which has been concluded during the last day or two that promises to bring huge profits to the company.' All booms must end, and disenchantment eventually set in on the part of the speculating public, but not before the future of two deserving financial dailies was at last assured. 'Golden Africa,' sang Ada Blanche at the Empire, and Marks and MacRae would have concurred.

[TWO]

THE RIVALS

1895–1914

'That motor-cars are to be the vehicles of the future there is, of course, absolutely no doubt. But before the invention becomes popular as well as useful, science will have to find a way for minimising smell, sound and vibration.' So concluded the *FT*'s 'Special Correspondent' on 16 November 1896 in a fairly jocular two-column report on 'The Advent of the Motor Car: Saturday's Journey to Brighton'. He had seen the cars leave the Hotel Métropole, then taken a train to Croydon, from there cycled ahead of the cars to Reigate, and finally given up. The trip to Brighton was essentially a publicity stunt organized by Harry J. Lawson in connection with the flotation of the British Motor Syndicate Ltd and as such was part of the wider boom in domestic industrial promotions (cycles, textiles, breweries, multiple shops and so on) which, together with a sizeable number of West Australian mining flotations, took up most of the speculative slack after 'Kaffirs' had slumped (though still remaining a large market) and continued to do so almost up to the outbreak of the Boer War in 1899.

These were generally good years for the Stock Exchange and therefore for the financial press also. In the week beginning 10 May 1897, for example, the *FN* totalled 58 pages and the *FT* 54 (of which 22 were of the slightly smaller size). Three other financial dailies were currently in existence, but none was a serious threat. The *Financier* continued on its stolid, old-fashioned, factual way, without a hint of the 'new' financial journalism; *Financial Truth* (1889–1904) was a thin paper and surprisingly long-lived; while the *Financial Post* (1895–8) was more solid and reputable in feel but lacked the advertising of the *FN* or *FT*. Meanwhile, 1897 also witnessed Queen Victoria's Diamond Jubilee, giving the *FN* the chance to produce a very handsome 34-page special number, printed in blue ink and enclosed in a cover of red, blue and gold. Most of the articles reviewed the history of finance during the Victorian era, while the array of accompanying advertising more than vindicated the extra effort and cost involved. To prove that he no longer bore a grudge, even W. R. Lawson contributed a piece on 'English Capital in America'.

The Financial News Ltd's board minute of 19 November 1896 was eloquent testimony to these happy times: 'In view of the large amount of money at the bank, and on deposit, it was resolved to advance to Mr James Head £6,000 upon the security of the company's shares.' About a year later the mood at Abchurch Lane remained munificent: 'A letter to Mr S. Lamert was read appointing him special commissioner to proceed to Rhodesia for three months @ 6.6.0 salary per week, with allowance of £20 outfit, and £15 prem. life assurance with "Sun" office. A credit at Standard Bank of £100 at Cape Town and £50 at Bulawayo to provide incidental expenses was confirmed.' The figures offer substantiation. Net profits of the FN Ltd in the years 1895 to 1897 inclusive averaged more than £31,000 a year, with in 1897 the dividend paid on the ordinary shares reaching the dizzy height of 35 per cent. Significant consequences followed. In 1897 a flotation was arranged to enable the Argus Printing Company (already printing twenty-one weekly and monthly papers, and a good deal of prospectuses and other work, as well as the *FN* itself) to extend its premises and thereby double its capacity. In 1898 a major reconstruction took place of the FN Ltd itself, with the result that the company's capital was increased to £200,000 in £1 shares, of which 150,000 were 5 per cent cumulative preference shares. Existing shareholders enjoyed first refusal of these new shares, prompting the leading shareholder, Harry Marks, to remark at the following February's AGM, after praising Head for his work in carrying the arrangements through:

> It will be remembered that the reconstruction enabled them not only to put the company on a footing in accordance with what was regarded – and he thought fairly regarded – as its market value, but it enabled them, without any disparagement to the value of their property, to receive a substantial bonus of £1 on the top of every £1 they held in the company. That was a result which was gratifying to all of them.[1]

Indeed it was, but especially to Marks himself.

A similar expansiveness permeated the Financial Times Ltd, with reconstruction taking place in 1896 and likewise increasing the capital to £200,000. There was an equal division into preference shares, of which MacRae held the overwhelming majority, and rather more widely distributed ordinary shares, of which MacRae had about a third. Also in 1896 George Grant and G. E. Hart became directors (Sydney Murray having dropped out the previous year), while an agreement was reached by which MacRae became 'managing director for life and editor of the *Financial Times* at a salary equal to 10% of the profits made by the company in respect of the *Financial Times*'. With one exception, the figures do not exist to show what profits the paper (as opposed to the company) made over the years. The exception is the very prosperous second half of 1896, when, according to company secretary Layton's report to the board in January 1897, the *FT* made a handsome £14,300. At the AGM in April 1897 MacRae announced a dividend on the company's ordinary shares of 25 per cent, carrying forward more than £14,000 in order 'to keep ourselves in a thoroughly sound and strong position', and then went on to suggest a change of premises for the Clements Printing Works, soon to be known as the St Clements Press:

> Our present works have sufficed for our needs up to the present, but it is literally packed with the regular works we have in hand for ourselves, and we are frequently obliged to refuse work for other newspapers which do not own their own plant . . . The factory, which I personally erected, has been designed for printing works, and is eminently suited for our business. It adjoins the present works . . . I have built it as a private enterprise, and there is no necessity for you to take it unless you are so inclined, nor will any advantage accrue to me by letting the premises to you upon the terms I have offered, as I am perfectly sure that in the open market it will not lack tenants whose rents would yield a higher return than 5 per cent . . . As regards the purchase price, you may rely that in building the premises for myself I have taken every precaution to have the best material and workmanship at the minimum cost, and I offer them to you at the prime cost.[2]

The grateful shareholders accepted the offer, and a few weeks later the company paid to MacRae, in cash, a total purchase price of £9,058.15*s*.

The new works – situated in Portugal Street on the site of the old Clare Market and lying just off what was soon to be Kingsway – began printing the *FT* in 1898 and were indeed, as one would have expected from MacRae, an impressive affair, consisting of a basement and six lofty storeys and being equipped with the most modern machinery. G. E. Hart had the day-to-day running of the place, and, in the admiring words of *Linotype Notes*, 'a visit to this well-equipped, well-managed office is like ozone to a practical man'.[3] Business continued to flourish. In February 1899 MacRae was able to tell his fellow-shareholders that total profits since the reconstruction three years previously came to £105,000 and that 'we are in as strong a financial position as any company could wish to be'.[4] Later in 1899 the final step took place in this phase of what one may truthfully call 'planning for growth', with the purchase of the lease, and conversion to newspaper purposes, of offices at 72 Coleman Street, which in the course of 1900 became the new and rather more commodious home of the *FT*. In every way, the paper was now ready to face the new century.

During the second half of the 1890s Marks and MacRae remained very much the respective boss men. Though brother Percy was no longer on the *FN* board after 1898, Harry Marks continued as editor and principal shareholder, with Head as chairman and managing director, apparently subservient. That was at least what Head was to tell a court of law in 1903: 'Witness had no authority or control over Mr Marks and could not dismiss him from his position or censure him. Mr Marks held a controlling interest in the company.'[5] In his editorial capacity Marks drew an annual salary of £2,000, though one senses that in the more narrow day-to-day running of the paper he was increasingly relying on his seasoned editorial staff and instead turning much of his attention to politics. He had been elected as Conservative MP for St George's-in-the-East in 1895 and in Parliament emerged as a prominent supporter of the Salisbury government. He was also reputed to have introduced to the House of Commons the joys of the double-breasted cream silk dress waistcoat.

MacRae, too, though without political or sartorial ambitions, was also becoming a more worldly figure, with the result that at some point A. E. Murray took over the day-to-day editorship of the *FT*, also becoming a director in 1899, being commended by MacRae to the shareholders as 'not only a practical editor, but a thorough business man'. MacRae himself travelled a lot, building up his formidable grasp of the world's commerce, and generally lived life with plenty of gusto. A pen portrait by a friend after his death caught the man well:

> In the hunting field, on his yacht or launch, at a game of billiards or chess, or when enjoying any other form of recreation he was more like a big schoolboy home for the holidays and bent on pure enjoyment than the active brainworker whose success in life was entirely due to his wide knowledge of men and matters, perseverence, originality, tenacious temperament and, last but not least, his honourable dealing and entertaining, even fascinating manners.[6]

By the late 1890s he was perhaps not quite the man he had been, having almost been killed in a riding accident near his home in Norbiton. One effect may have been to develop in him rather a perverse streak, typified by an episode in 1899 when he appealed against the decision of the local bench to fine him for 'allowing' his dog to be at large unmuzzled. The law report showed MacRae vigorously taking the line to an unconvinced court that the original summons was bad because the dog had escaped from the house without his knowledge or consent:

> *Mr Justice Day*: It is the nature of dogs to wander about. If it had been strapped up in a room it could not have got out.

Appellant said that even then it might bite through the strap.
Mr Justice Day: If you had kept the door shut the dog would not have got out.
Appellant answered that he did not know, there were gates to be jumped and windows to be jumped through (*Laughter*).[7]

MacRae lost his appeal, but then, he was not one to muzzle or be muzzled.

It was a reflection of the increased confidence of the *FT* during the second half of the 1890s that its investigative teeth seem at this time to have been particularly sharp. In 1896 a former journalist called Wicks advertised in *The Times* a rotary machine for newspaper printing that he had patented, with a view eventually to bringing out a company. The project was savaged in the *FT*, in an article headed 'Smouldering Wicks' that asserted that the machine had previously been reported impracticable, that there were no contemporary independent reports and that the patents had run out. Wicks sued for libel, and MacRae gave evidence: 'He dictated parts of the article and gave particulars of other parts to Mr Irons, who wrote the article, and brought it to him for revision . . . He knew the machine had been offered to the *Financial News* and refused.' The jury found for the *FT*.[8] The following year it was the turn of C. D. Rudd of the Consolidated Gold Fields of South Africa Company to complain about a 'vindictive attack' made on him by the *FT*, which had had the temerity to state that Rudd had disposed of shares in the company given to him in commutation of his managing director's position.[9] The next year, 1898, the *FT* indulged itself in a real old-style attack, in a leader headed 'Another Blind Pool Parallel':

> Several times we have succeeded by our persistent exposures in stamping out these pernicious syndicate touts, who swindle country people, working men and unsophisticated women into joining their so-called 'Stock Exchange operations', and then disappear with their subscriptions; but the pestilent nuisances have a habit of poking their heads out again from their dens unless a vigilant eye is kept on them. To act as a detective in watching the gang has therefore become one of the pet recreations of the *Financial Times*. When the City Solicitor took up the crusade with energy, and, availing himself of the numerous documents in our possession, secured the conviction of Thomas Tarrant and his satellites, and also of the Krahn group, while Harrison Ainsworth and Bernard Love have also been convicted, it made us almost sad to think that our sport with that type of gentry was over.

But in fact in recent months there had sprung up a fresh operation, and this the rest of the leader proceeded to document fully.[10]

Two exposures in 1899 both led to court cases the following year.

Thomas Fenwick was a company promoter who had registered twenty-four companies in the previous twelve years, none of which had paid a dividend. The complained-of articles, one headed 'Fenwick and the Pulpit', concentrated on his fraudulent plan for the establishment of a new Christian newspaper, involving the duping of no less than 184 Nonconformist ministers in the North of England. After the first day's evidence Fenwick decided not to proceed with the case.[11] The other exposure was of George Jerome Hornsby, a man with a mixed past, being formerly a seaman, a professional boxer and a picture dealer, and now operating as a commission and inquiry agent, in this case on behalf of shareholders of the Westralian, London & Johannesburg Company who were seeking to have the company's affairs investigated. In 'Another Company Undertaker: Cash Strictly Payable in Advance', the *FT* asserted of Hornsby that 'surely an undischarged bankrupt is hardly the ideal individual to invite subscriptions for the purpose of agitating about other people's affairs'. Hornsby told the court of the aftermath to the publication of the article: 'He went to see the editor of the paper [i.e. MacRae] and asked him to publish a letter which he had written defending himself against the attack made upon him. The editor replied that the letter would be placed in the waste-paper basket and that before long he [Hornsby] would be in gaol. He was arrested soon afterwards.' Giving evidence for the *FT* was A. E. Murray, billed as 'assistant editor' and author of the article in question. He stated that 'it was usual for his paper to receive inquiries from subscribers with respect to circulars similar to that issued by the plaintiff' and that 'it was a very old game to send out circulars asking for subscriptions from shareholders of companies', being 'often used as a means for obtaining money by false pretences'. In fact the jury found for Hornsby, and the *FT* was unsuccessful in its attempt to secure a new trial, but almost certainly it had provided valuable (if expensive to itself) information in the course of the exposure.[12]

All such court-room revelations, however, paled beside the remarkable Hooley outpourings of the summer and autumn of 1898. Ernest Terah Hooley was originally a Nottingham lace manufacturer who during 1896 turned himself into the most famous company promoter of the age. Basing himself in a luxurious suite at the Midland Grand Hotel, St Pancras, and employing a mixture of skilful publicity and sheer audacity, he floated company after company (including Bovril, Schweppes and the Humber Cycle Company) and in the process acquired an almost instant fortune of several million pounds. Some of the companies were legitimate ventures and prospered, others were worthless, but what they all had in common was that they were sold to the public for grossly inflated sums, involving a high proportion of 'watered' capital. This was certainly true of Hooley's first major coup, the Dunlop Tyre Company, for which he paid £3 million before refloating it with a capital of £5 million. A full-page prospectus appeared in both the *FN* and the *FT* on 9 May 1896, and that day the *FT* duly contained a leader on 'A Gigantic Promotion'. It reached a not unfavourable conclusion about the company's prospects, including pointing out that cycling had been a popular pastime for at least twenty years before the current craze. The general tone, however, was very cautious.

The same could not be said for the *FN*'s leader on the subject, which had already appeared the previous day and was typified in understatement by the modest assertion that

> rarely has a company been started under more favourable auspices, or with such commanding credentials . . . Not only does the company come before the investing public with the very strong support and co-operation of the leading men connected with the cycle industry, but it can boast of a Board of Directors which, for a combination of social influence and practical acquaintance with the tyre-manufacturing business, is almost, if not quite, unique.

Over the rest of the summer other favourable assessments of Hooley or Hooley-related ventures popped up at regular intervals in the *FN*. 'There is every indication that before long it will be impossible to obtain the shares at anything like their present value', it was reckoned of Simpson's Lever Chain Company later that month; in June the New Beeston Cycle Company received an optimistic leader; while in August, in connection with the flotation of the French Dunlop Company, it was graphically stated that 'not only at Lyons, Marseilles, Bordeaux, and scores of other cities, but in every hamlet, in every remote village, the cyclist puts himself or herself in evidence', with the consequence, very favourable to all premium-hunters, that 'we should not be in the least surprised to see the whole capital subscribed in France alone many times over'. When it came to pedalling the Dunlop issues, the *FN* consistently wore the leader's yellow jersey.

Hooley of course went the way of all such great men and crashed, filing his petition in bankruptcy in 1898. The ensuing proceedings, with Hooley being examined at the London Bankruptcy Court, included some choice passages of considerable interest in the history of the financial press. The general impression conveyed was one of Hooley being forced to pay large sums of money, directly or indirectly, in order to ensure favourable treatment. Many journalistic names were mentioned in the course of his evidence, but none more frequently than that of Harry Marks, who seems to have received from Hooley, in cash and shares, a grand total of £31,110, which must have paid for the winter's coal. Hooley at one point was pressed to explain one of the larger payments, in connection with Harry Lawson's New Beeston flotation, which for £25,000, of which a third went to Marks, he had agreed not to oppose:

He did not give the money to Mr Marks to abstain from writing in the *Financial News*. He would not say whether the payment was in virtue of a preconcerted arrangement. As a fact Mr Marks did about this time cease to publish unfavourable comments. The only reason why he gave Mr Marks this money was that Mr Marks was a friend of his (*Laughter*).

Another beneficiary was one of the *FN*'s leader writers, H. J. Jennings, about whom Hooley told the court: 'The articles I saw in the *Financial News* I thought the celeverest I had ever seen in my life. I found out who the writer was and told him what I thought of him, and gave him £500 and got him to leave the *Financial News* and come to me.' Even MacRae's name was mentioned, though according to Hooley the cheque for £1,970 paid to him 'represented a legitimate transaction in shares', Hooley adding of MacRae that he was 'the honestest man of the lot (*laughter*)' and 'never had a penny from him'. Still, there was the question of the nag Northallerton. This was a racehorse which Hooley had bought for £2,000 and proceeded to give one-third interest in to the editor of the financial weekly the *Rialto* (which had once been in the *FT* stable) and another third to MacRae's wife. 'There was,' Hooley insisted, 'no other reason than friendship for these gifts.'[13] Such revelations were undeniably embarrassing; but in the prevailing rough-and-tumble, *caveat emptor* ethos of the Stock Exchange and its attendant world, they had no serious long-term consequences for either paper.

Of much greater tangible import to the financial press was the fatefully deteriorating situation in South Africa, with the final phase that led to war beginning with the ill-conceived, worse-executed Jameson raid of 1895–6. Neither paper was sympathetic to the Boers and their leaders ('men boorish in manner and hostile and lethargic in disposition', according to the *FT*), nor to the Boer refusal to yield to the desire of the majority Uitlanders to be given the vote ('a simple demand for bare justice', stated the *FN*), but both, against the popular mood of the day, condemned the raid. 'This irresponsible movement of an irregular armed force', was what the *FN* called it, while the *FT* talked of 'this deplorable attack', more mildly of how 'as the farmer said when he saw his prize bull preparing to meet an express train, we "admire his pluck, but d—n his discretion"'. By early October 1899, however, with war seemingly inevitable, both papers had taken part in the general (though not uniform) closing of ranks behind the aggressive stance of the Colonial Secretary Joseph Chamberlain, whose name will always be linked with the Boer War. The Boer leader was the particular target of abuse. According to the *FN* on the 6th: 'Mr Kruger seems to have improved upon Cromwell's old motto, "Trust in God, but keep your powder dry." His motto is, "Trust in God, but grab all the gold you can lay your hands on."' Four days later the *FT* included a hostile feature (with drawings) of Kruger on the occasion of his seventy-fourth birthday, with the heading 'Old Enough to Know Better'. Ultimatums were now being delivered and repudiated, and in effect war had begun. The *FN*'s leader on the 12th was especially strong: 'Despite the false and fatuous pretences of Boer sympathisers, it is plain that the one object of the Pretorian oligarchy has been to throw off British supremacy and, in conjunction with the Free State and Afrikander traitors in the Cape Colony, to set up a Dutch Federation in South Africa.' It added ominously: 'We must be on our guard against traitors both at home and in South Africa.'

The *FN* the previous year had covered fully the war between Spain and the United States, earning criticism that this was not appropriate to a financial newspaper, but according to Head putting several thousands on the circulation. Now, in October 1899, the board agreed to sanction the arrangement that Marks had made with a war correspondent in South Africa to cover the impending events there for a monthly salary of 30 guineas. The *FT* preferred to rely on Reuters and Dalziels news agencies for its war coverage, but made good capital from the innovative and splendid four-coloured map, 'The Seat of War', published on 23 October as a supplement at no extra price and later reprinted and sold at a penny. The paper also started a Stock Exchange Clerks' War Fund (i.e. for clerks who had joined up), though it was not stunningly successful and was wound up in December at £759.17*s*. December was an anxious month, and news of the 'Transvaal War' dominated the headlines, especially in the *FN*. 'General Buller Tries to Force the Tugula River, and Is Repulsed with Loss' (16 December) was fairly typical. Two days later the leader on 'A Grave Situation' ended: 'We have a great effort to make, and in spite of everything we mean to make it, in the full assurance of ultimate success.' The *FT* saw out the year in similarly stirring tones: 'We enter 1900 with the most unfaltering confidence that the outcome of the struggle will be a conclusive victory for the cause of our Empire, which is the cause of civilisation, of peace, and of equality of rights.'

By May 1900 victory was beckoning, or at least the prospect of humiliating defeat had been averted. The briefest of *FT* leaderettes on the 8th reflected the lightening mood: 'Why is Lord Roberts now able to keep the Boers on the run? – Because his cavalry has just passed the Vet.' Nine days later Mafeking was relieved, and London went wild. And on the 26th the *FT* printed one of the stanzas and the chorus of the new patriotic song, 'Khaki Here, Khaki There!', published, written and composed by Percy M. Costello of the Stock Exchange. There was still, however, a long way to go and much frustration before the war ended in 1902. On 3 August 1900 an *FN* leader on 'The Handling of Treason-Mongers' sounded a note that in the next war would turn into the paper's theme tune:

Readers of the *Financial News* will remember that, time and again, we have pointed out the real behind-the-scene character of the Stop-the-War, the Conciliation, and the Peace Committees in this country. We are ready to grant – nay, insist – that many of the orators, figure-heads, and others concerned in this agitation, were misguided dupes, who allowed the Little England principle of loving every country but one's own to run away with what judgment they possessed; but these puppets were put in motion by wire-pullers, for whom heavier condemnation is necessary, and to whom, we trust, heavy punishment will be meted out.

The *FT* for its part was less concerned with enemies within, more with the inefficiencies of officialdom, as in the tart headline of 22 December 1900, 'War Office Waking Up', reporting the belated decision to send reinforcements of mounted troops. Meanwhile, long before the war did end, the financial press and the Stock Exchange were starting to count the cost.

According to Hirst of the *Economist*, the Boer War was the most disastrous event for the City since the failure of the discount house Overend, Gurney & Company in 1866 and the ensuing financial panic. Thus he described the aftermath of war:

When the Milner policy of unconditional surrender was at last abandoned, and the peace of Vereeniging signed, Consols and Kaffirs rallied. But it was only a short and feverish flicker of speculative purchases, which collapsed under heavy liquidation. The mining industry had been temporarily ruined [i.e. in the Transvaal, having been almost completely closed down during the war], the cost of living had risen, the native labour had dispersed . . . Many of the promoters and speculators who had been most eager for the war were ruined. All the mining houses connected with the Rand suffered severely.[14]

The once rumbustuous 'Kaffir circus' was but a pale shadow during the early 1900s. In general, after a brief burst of promotional activity in West

African mining at the start of the century, the unvarying plaint of Stock Exchange members until at least the mid-1900s was that there was too little business to make ends meet. Both papers suffered, but the annual general meetings of the FT Ltd were particularly eloquent. In 1901 MacRae referred to 'adverse conditions' leading to a drop in profits; in 1902 Bridgewater talked of the depressing influence of the continuing war, with consols in 1901 twice going lower than at any time since the Franco-Prussian War; in 1903 Bridgewater said that the lack of prospectuses the previous year had been 'absolutely without parallel in the history of financial journalism'; and in 1904 Murray observed that the year just past had been 'so blank and so unremunerative that it reminds one of the Desert of Sahara', except that 'it is worse even than the desert of Sahara, where there is an occasional oasis'.[15] On 7 November 1904 a letter appeared in the *FN* about the disastrous human and economic effects of the South African war, from a correspondent calling himself 'Peace Means Good Trade'. The heading given to the letter was suitably ironic, 'A Rather Late Protest', but it was hard to deny the truth of the point.

It was fortunate that both papers had built for the future while the going was good during the late 1890s, because from the turn of the century they found themselves facing other problems apart from the Boer War and its dismal legacy. One was the Companies Act of 1900 which, in the wake of Hooleyism and other scandals of the 1890s, sought tighter regulation over such matters as the wording and issuing of prospectuses and the allotment and underwriting of shares. The *FN* generally welcomed the legislation (not surprisingly, in that Marks was involved in the committee stages), whereas the *FT* in outspoken attacks in July and August 1900 described the bill as 'that excessively feeble embodiment of the joint wisdom of our legislators' and 'a half-baked measure which will positively do more harm than good', being likely 'to hamper the movements of the honest promoter, while carefully setting up danger signals to warn the rascal where his hazard lies'. What, however, both papers soon united in deploring about the Bill was that the more stringent requirements in the matter of disclosure in prospectuses, allied to stiff punishments for incorrect statements, had the natural consequence of making promoters shy away from issuing prospectuses altogether. Thus whereas prior to 1900 some two-thirds of new concerns were introduced to the public by prospectus, by 1903 the proportion was down to less than one-third. According to one account, the only reason why Parliament in 1900 declined to make the issuing of a prospectus or its equivalent compulsory was because that provision was proposed by Marks, who for some mysterious reason was suspected of thereby seeking to line his own pocket.[16] If that was so, the mistrusters of Marks were well rewarded over the next few years, as the advertising revenue of the *FN* (and its contemporaries) slumped alarmingly.

The new Companies Act became law on New Year's Day 1901. Barely three months later the *FT* had a much more personal blow to announce:

For some time past he had been ailing and had planned a yacht trip to South and West Africa, his insatiable desire for work impelling him to avoid any holiday which did not lead towards some sphere of labour; but he postponed his departure in order to preside at our annual meeting of shareholders on 28 February, which was virtually his last appearance in the City. Abandoning the African trip, he sailed on his yacht for the Mediterranean, and after cruising there for some weeks, proceeded to Switzerland for the benefits of the mountain air.[17]

Restless to the last, MacRae died by the banks of Lake Constance on 2 April 1901, four days before his fortieth birthday. He was buried in Norbiton Cemetery on the 14th and left an estate of no less than £394,295.

As far as the control and running of the *FT* was concerned, the two main developments took place after MacRae's death. One was the purchase by the company, largely through O'Hagan's mediation as a friend of the family, of MacRae's interest in it; the other was the election of F. M. Bridgewater as chairman and managing director of the company, with A. E. Murray retaining the day-to-day editorship of the *FT* itself. Francis Bridgewater, who was born in Cheltenham in 1851 and educated there, had come up on the *Draper's Record* side of the company and had been much involved in that paper's founding. He does not emerge from the sources as a particularly distinct character – there are no 'stories' about him – but one has the impression, largely from his annual address to shareholders, of the old-fashioned qualities of solidity, industry and commonsensical business acumen. In short, he seems to have been precisely the right sort of person to consolidate the pioneering achievements of MacRae.

Change was also brewing at the *FN*, but of a more discordant nature. It is not certain why Marks and Head fell out, though Head later claimed that he had been dissatisfied at the way things were being managed. But for whatever reason the upshot was that on 29 December 1902 Head resigned from the company and was replaced as chairman by Ernest Flower, who is almost as shadowy a figure as Bridgewater. The bare outline facts of his life have come down to us: he was born in 1865, became Conservative MP for one of the Bradford constituencies in 1895 (losing his seat in 1906), and a year after assuming the *FN* chairmanship was knighted in honour of his philanthropic work in the East End of London, having been among other things one of the founders and honorary secretaries of the People's Palace (a highly moral cultural centre for the working class) and the East London Horticultural Society. He was also at various times a member of the London School Board, honorary treasurer of Queen Mary's Royal Naval Hospital at Southend-on-Sea, chairman of the Blue Cross Fund, JP for the County of London, a Lieutenant for the City, and so on – in short, if not one of the great, certainly one of the good. It is hard to resist the impression that he was brought by Marks into the *FN* scheme of things as someone of impeccable reputation who would give the minimum of trouble to the editor-founder. There was, however, an unhappy sequel for Marks to the departure of Head. This was in May 1903, when Head sued the *Morning Post* for having described him as a man with a 'financial past' and therefore unsuited to be a director of the Royal Mail Steam Packet Company. Counsel for the defence made much of Head's lengthy association with Marks and recapitulated in some detail the Rae and Hooley episodes. Head lost his case, while Marks himself was described by Justice Bigham as 'a dishonest rogue' and 'a scoundrel'. [18] A few days later Marks sent the judge a lengthy open letter of virtuous self-defence, but by then the continuing damage to his good name had been done.

Part of the evidence in the Head case concerned the relationship between Marks and Whitaker Wright, whose intricate but colourful dealings were at the time one of the most dominant and talked-about features of the financial world. In 1897 Wright had formed (to favourable notices from the *FN*) the drastically over-capitalized London & Globe Finance Corporation, which over the next three years proceeded to float and manipulate the stocks of a variety of companies, most of them West Australian mining concerns. By 1900 the Globe's inherently unsound finances were showing the strain, and at the end of the year it defaulted, bringing down in its trail more than a dozen firms on the Stock Exchange. 'The very hand of Barker, the waiter [i.e. Stock Exchange attendant], shook like an aspen leaf as, amid death-like silence, he announced failure after failure.' [19] Wright was not exactly the flavour of the month, but the *FT* on 2 January 1901 deplored the vindictive attacks on him, while not denying that his financing had been 'reckless, indiscreet and blameworthy'. A year later the winding-up proceedings of the London & Globe included a public examination of Wright, during which he made the following assertion:

It is well known in the City that all the financial daily press and those who publish the reports of transactions on the Stock Exchange and call attention to them, put in the official lists and the transactions of the tape and everything of that kind, will not do it, will not assist companies in any shape or form unless they have consideration in some form or other.

Wright then explained how he had been obliged 'for market purposes' to set aside shares that were sold at an artificially low price to the press and then, by pre-arrangement, rebought by the company at a higher price. Pressed by the Official Receiver as to whether Marks had had a large portion of these cheap shares, he replied, to laughter, 'I should think so.'[20] A few months later the Committee of the Stock Exchange investigated these 'press calls', as they were known, and discovered that brokers acting on Wright's behalf had sweetened at least ten financial journalists, including not only Marks but also three employed by the *FN*, one by the *FT* and, last but not least, the great MacRae himself, who in July 1900 had picked up some 6,500 shares at a bargain price.[21]

Eventually, after a dramatic arrest in New York in March 1903, and a letter sent from there to Marks thanking him for his loyal friendship and declaring that 'if people were all built on your lines it would be better for the City of London', Wright appeared at the Old Bailey in January 1904 accused of large-scale fraud. The trial lasted twelve days, and at the end Wright was sentenced to seven years' penal servitude. Half an hour later he was dead, having swallowed a tablet of cyanide of potassium. The *FN* the next day praised Wright for his courage as a financier and argued that he had falsified balance sheets only in order 'to tide over appalling difficulties, in the hope of saving the shareholders' money'. The post-MacRae *FT*, however, was implacable:

The climax is only the grim logical outcome of a course of life deliberately planned. For many a year Whitaker Wright had devoted himself to the work of dishonestly using the public as a tool for the advancement of his own financial interests, and he brought to the task a degree of ingenuity and cunning that it would be hard to parallel . . . He was a Fregoli of finance, a quick-change artist of exceptional ability. In the result he produced such a tangle that he fancied himself safe.

The watching crowd may have doffed its hats in silent admiration as the body was taken out, recognizing that whatever his sins a giant had passed, but in the unromantic eyes of the *FT*, looking ahead to an era of cleaner finance, 'a pestilent influence has been removed from the City'.[22]

What of the newspapers themselves by this time? The fifteenth anniversary of the *FT*, 13 February 1903, fell on a Friday, and in these difficult times both papers turned out issues of only six pages each (the *FN* from 1900 had followed the *FT*'s example in having seven columns per page). The similarities were even more obvious than they had been ten years previously: main market reports and prices on the front page, leaders and leaderettes on page two, a virtually undifferentiated array of company meetings, company reports, dividend announcements, law reports, tape prices and so on, and an almost entire absence of general non-financial news (the *FT*'s 'Synopsis' had disappeared several years earlier). Both journals addressed themselves squarely to their City and City-related audiences: no more, no less. On this particular day the *FN*'s leaders comprised a hard-headed assessment of the prospects for American railroad stock and a fairly fierce attack on Sir Alexander Henderson, who in the chair at Wednesday's half-yearly meeting of the Great Central Railway had displayed 'a cynicism not often matched'. The *FT* concentrated on 'The Underground Railway Half-year', complementing company results presented in tabular form on the opposite page, and on a euphemistic prospectus sent out by a Glasgow concern calling itself the Mutual Property Investment & Accident Company, the leader being entitled 'Assurance or Impudence?'. Outside the leader page, the only real commentary on financial matters, faintly previewing the 'Lex' of a later day, was an incisive 'Mining Topics' column in the *FT*, including a critique of Lord Ernest Hamilton's 'able, if somewhat superficial, handling of the disputed questions' at the previous day's meeting of Le Roi No. 2 Ltd, an old Whitaker Wright mine. By now the *FT* also included, modelled on *The Times*, a list of its contents and a summary of the main news contained in the paper, though also like *The Times* tucked away inside. As for the respective amounts of advertising, it is hard to be sure, though the *FN* thoughtfully sought to clarify matters in its daily announcement:

> The managers of the *Financial News* print all the financial intelligence of general public interest for which they can afford the requisite space, but reserve the right to charge, at current rates, for inserting in their news columns, official reports of company meetings, descriptions of railway, mining, and other properties, and such other matters as do not come into the category of news. Paragraphs in solid nonpareil at the foot of a column are inserted as advertisements.

On 13 February 1903 the *FN* had a total (including company-meeting reports) of just over two pages of advertising, the *FT* just over one page. Where the *FN* scored here was in the weekly circular on the state of the markets issued by the prominent outside brokers Lockwood & Company, a regular Friday feature that took up almost half a page and was full of punch and information, generally of a bullish colouring. Taken as a whole, there was now not much to choose between the papers. The *FN* was perhaps rather more outward-looking, typified by an item sent from St Petersburg on the state of limited-liability enterprise in Russia, whereas the *FT* contained fuller produce, commodities and trade reports.

If no longer outright leaders of the pack, the *FN* and Harry Marks were about to enjoy a day of glory and immense self-satisfaction. It took place on 23 January 1904 when, in addition to a normal eight-page issue, the paper produced free of charge a remarkable forty-page supplement to commemorate its twentieth anniversary. The cover, printed in gold and colours, featured a painting of a winged figure with a scroll in each outstretched hand, standing on a globe and against a background of St Paul's and the City. On the scrolls were written a series of sonorous verses by Lewis Morris, entitled 'Gaudeamus':

'Tis twenty years! With what swift change
  Sunshine and storm succeed in life.
What new adventurous fortunes strange,
  Vicissitudes of calm and strife!

Since first our bold bark's sails were spread
  To seek – and caught – the favouring breeze,
England her bravest blood has shed
  By shores unknown, o'er far-off seas.

After celebrating the ever-waxing extent and power of the British Empire, the poet asked:

Have we no part in all, because
  Our sole work is the work of peace?
Who, armed with economic laws,
  Would fain the nation's store increase.

He concluded strongly:

Whate'er thy Fate, great Realm, indeed,
  Our humble part we claim to bear,
Strong in the faith of Honour's creed
  Prudent to keep, yet bold to dare!

Inside the supplement, each page was surrounded by a coloured border and included designs by Walter Crane; while an array of articles by *FN* writers and others surveyed the world's financial progress over the previous twenty years.

That evening, a Saturday, Sir Ernest Flower hosted a large banquet at the Carlton Hotel, with those present including Sir Arthur Conan Doyle. On the Monday the *FN* reprinted various compliments paid to Saturday's issue. According to the *Pall Mall Gazette*, 'if anything, it is too sumptuous, and we are so little accustomed to financial articles in such a setting that the effect is rather staggering'; the sober *Morning Post* reckoned it 'the most magnificent pennyworth ever published'; while even the Liberal *Daily News*, notoriously hostile to Marks, described it as 'one of the most remarkable "pennyworths" modern journalism has produced'. Notwithstanding a past distinctly imperfect, it was a deserved moment of acclaim for Marks. In the course of two decades he had initiated and then sustained nothing less than a revolution, so that by 1901 Duguid reckoned that only four of the main morning and evening papers still subscribed to what he called 'the older form of financial journalism', in the sense of merely providing 'the bare record' and 'seldom indulging in any outspoken comment or venturing any opinion'.[23] Or as Marks himself put it without false modesty in his anniversary retrospective, 'the advent of the *Financial News* marked an era in English journalism'.

The *FT* did not deign to notice its rival's celebrations, but quietly continued its efficient, anonymous and (truth be told) rather dull course. Financially, the paper was underpinned by the emergence from the mid-1900s of the phenomenally rich, legendarily secretive shipowner Sir John Ellerman as an increasingly major shareholder in the company. He does not seem to have interfered with the board before the war, nor attempted to influence editorial policy. It was a rather piquant development, in that in the 1890s he had had a major row with MacRae, who, according to the inevitable O'Hagan, 'hated Ellerman like poison, though for no good reason'.[24] Few formal changes took place among the *FT*'s leading personnel. A. E. Murray resigned (for reasons unknown) as director and editor in July 1909; C. H. Palmer, an *FT* veteran, became acting editor, with F. M. Bridgewater now the editor as well as chairman and managing director; and Bridgewater's son, Frank, became a director in 1910 and assistant managing director two years later. The only real guide to life at the top in the *FT* during these years is Murray's address to shareholders in February 1908, explaining the company's good results in recent difficult years:

> We are asked, 'How do you do it?' Well, I answer that we did it by working like a cricket team. We are not a theoretical board. There have been times, although I am a man of somewhat cheerful temperament, when I have been depressed, but all I had to do was to go down to Mr Bridgewater, who told me that the other

departments of the business were doing well, and I had only to ring up Mr Hart on the telephone and he would tell me that the printing works were doing splendid business, and then I went back with fresh heart to my own work. It has been like a 'test match' during the past few years; it has been a case where each man has had to 'keep up his end', and I must say that each member of the board has made his 'century' during the past three years.

Nor were the board just good batsmen, for as G. E. Hart at the same meeting said of the secret of success: 'Your directors are all practical in their particular business. They know their business, they mind their own business, and instead of being a case of pull baker pull devil, we pull with a strong pull and pull all together (Hear, hear).'[25]

Matters were somewhat less anonymous and constant in the world of the *FN*, though the composition of the board itself remained unchanged from 1902 almost up to the war, in the form of Flower as chairman and Beresford and Tombs as directors. Having decided not to stand in the 1900 general election because of ill-health, Marks in the autumn of 1904 won a highly controversial by-election in his home seat of Thanet, despite the vigorous opposition of many local Conservatives, who were dismayed by his 'financial past'. During the campaign a leader in *The Times* argued strongly that Marks was unfit to stand unless he could disprove the various charges against his personal history and character, but Marks preferred, through a range of methods extending from free drinks and parcels of groceries to donations paid to local benefit clubs and friendly societies, to concentrate on the minds and hearts of the good people of Thanet. He later boasted to a journalist that he could win Thanet 'as a Radical if need be' and even, 'between ourselves, I believe could win it as a Socialist'.[26] In 1906 Marks was returned at the general election, but three years later he suffered a stroke, which for him was the beginning of a tortuous end. He decided not to stand at the next election and also gave up his editorship of the *FN*, though as editor-in-chief, a largely nominal position, retained his annual salary of £3,000.

The new editor was Ellis Thomas Powell, who had been born at Ludlow in Shropshire in 1868. After attending the local grammar school, he was apprenticed to the town's principal draper:

Even at that early age, however, he had ambition, and was by no means content to spend his years behind the counter. While his fellow-apprentices wasted their time he spent all his leisure in studying and in the art of illustrating, and at the expiry of his indentures he made his long-cherished move to London. Here his first engagement was with the Church Army, during which period he perfected himself in Pitman's Shorthand. Realising that even the Church Army had its limitations, at least so far as a restless and ambitious spirit was concerned, Powell applied for the position of shorthand writer on the *Financial News*.[27]

This was probably in 1889. He soon attracted the personal attention of his Chief, especially when, 'by intense application', he learnt in a short period of time six or seven foreign languages. Marks employed him as his election agent at St George's-in-the-East and then Thanet, while on the *FN*'s editorial staff Powell rose quickly through the ranks, employing to the full what was aptly described as 'an acquisitive brain and a powerful pen'.[28] He was a prolific writer of books as well as journalism, his pre-war publications including a manual of election law as a result of his activities on behalf of Marks and a major survey entitled *The Mechanism of the City*. In addition to all this, his memory was elephantine and his manner of public speaking magnetic.

Yet Powell it was who, for all his considerable qualities, eventually undid the paper that he loved and to which he gave the best part of his life. The trouble, put simply, was that he was a fanatic who, to an increasing degree, lacked the crucial qualities for any editor of balance and judgement. It was typical of the man that at the age of thirty-eight he took not just one but two London University degree examinations – simultaneously, in the course of two consecutive weeks. Apart from acquiring and then reproducing knowledge, his ruling passions in life were imperialism of the most lofty kind, propagating the tenets of social Darwinism, uncovering conspiracies, studying the microscope and telescope, and furthering the cause of psychic research. In 1915, after he had been editor for several years, the *FN* published on his behalf a 700-page-long treatise on *The Evolution of the Money Market (1385–1915)*. It was subtitled 'An Historical and Analytical Study of the Rise and Development of Finance as a Centralised, Co-ordinated Force' and included in its foreword the following sentence: 'Long before the German war crisis of 1914, the present writer had formulated for himself the theory that the ever-increasing stability and potency of modern finance were attributable to something in the nature of organic development, operating by means of Natural Selection, and therefore completely in accordance with the main postulate of the Darwinian theory.' It was not the sentence of a man in tune with the traditional City mentality of immediate horizons, quick gains and 'ask no questions', above all no questions of the intellect. It was not, in fine, the sentence of a man who should have been editing what was still essentially a Stock Exchange organ.

For it was the Stock Exchange and the state of speculative business on it that continued, as ever, to hold the key to the papers' prosperity or otherwise. In February 1905 Bridgewater attributed the reduced dividend for the previous year to jitters in the stock market caused by the Russo-Japanese War and the prospect of an unfavourable general election; two years later he reiterated to shareholders that the *FT* 'accurately reflects the condition of business in the City' and that 'when there is activity', of which in 1906 there had been little, 'and new companies are being formed, we get the prospectuses'; and in 1909, the year of Lloyd George's 'People's Budget', Flower for the *FN* talked gloomily on the company's behalf of 'the nervousness which has pervaded alike the financial world and the investing classes'.[29] Not that the papers' profits can have been wholly nugatory during these years. In the case of the *FT* it was still impossible to know how much the paper itself contributed to the company's earnings, though in 1905 Bridgewater did tell the shareholders that 'the part of our enterprise to which we look for providing by far the greater portion of the profits of this company is, and will always be, the newspaper from which this company takes its name'. But from whatever source, and despite the continuing dullness on the Stock Exchange through most of the 1900s, Bridgewater was able, to applause, to inform shareholders in 1909 that since the company's conception in its existing form in 1896, 'dividends on the ordinary shares to the amount of no less than 188½ per cent have been paid, giving an average of about 14½ per cent per annum'; while that same year, Flower told his troops that 'in the 24 completed years of its existence, the ordinary shareholders of the *Financial News* have received in bonuses and dividends 344 per cent, equal to an average of over 17 per cent per annum for the past 20 years, or, if we include the first four years of the existence of the paper, an average of over 14 per cent'.[30]

Within months of these respective figures being trotted out, the Stock Exchange entered a two-year period of sustained boom, taking its tone mainly from home industrials (including cinema companies for the first time, together with a veritable craze in ice rinks), the oil market and, far and away most spectacularly, rubber. Stimulated by the belief that there would be an ever-expanding demand for rubber, especially on the part of the rapidly growing motor and electricity industries, the public during the first five months of 1910 subscribed to more than £16 million of new rubber shares, as well as speculating prodigiously on existing concerns. The scenes on the floor of the Stock Exchange were akin to a rugby scrum – so much so that a member one day fainted at eleven o'clock and was not picked up until four, when the crowd that had been unwittingly supporting him all day started to leave. Also swept off his feet by the joy of it all was Bridgewater, who in March 1911 announced to great applause that the previous year's profit of £60,500, producing a dividend including bonuses of 30 per cent on the ordinary shares, was almost £20,000 more than the company's previous record.[31] Unfortunately for the financial press, though booms were marvellous while they lasted, they came all too rarely and lasted too short a time. Already by 1914 Flower was characterizing the previous year as 'an exceptionally difficult one from the newspaper point of view', being marked by industrial conflict at home and war in the Balkans abroad.[32] Perceptibly, the shadows were again lengthening.

During most of these Edwardian years the *FN* made the daily claim that it 'has, from its establishment in 1884, continuously had, and still has, the largest circulation of any financial newspaper in the world'. The *FT* more succinctly described itself each day as having 'the largest circulation of any financial newspaper in the world'. It is impossible to know which of the papers really could lay a genuine claim to the distinction, but one feels there was a ring of conviction about Bridgewater's almost annual assertions to shareholders about the *FT*'s rising circulation. What we do know, though, is that between 1903 and 1911 various agreements were signed between the *FN* and the Argus on the assumption that the regular print run of the paper would be in the order of twelve to fifteen thousand copies. It is unlikely, though unprovable, that during this period the *FT*'s circulation would have been dramatically higher or lower than those sort of figures. Yet numbers alone were not everything, as a shareholder reminded the *FT*'s AGM in March 1911:

> Mr E. T. Thornton said that it might be of interest to the directors to learn that last year, when he made a trip through Siberia, China, and the East, he found the *Financial Times* in all the clubs, and there was quite a run on it. In fact, in Shanghai there were two motions on the notice board in favour of securing further copies of the paper. He also went through Turkey about six weeks ago, and found the *Financial Times* in all the clubs there.[33]

To this sort of talk, though, the *FN* had a more than adequate riposte, in the form of the Continental edition of the paper, which was published daily in Paris, in French, from 1907 to 1914. Despite justly claiming to be 'the only paper on the Continent which prints full daily reports of the South African and other Mining Markets', it does not seem to have been an enormous success, and the English parent company lost a fair amount of money on it. Still, for 'Investors Wintering Abroad', as another advertising pitch ran, it must have been a pleasantly exotic bonus to find on the luncheon table at Aix-les-Bains.

As far as advertising in general was concerned, the *FN* at this stage tended to attract more than the *FT*, though the rates were virtually identical. On New Year's Day 1906, in a characteristically pointed statement 'To Advertisers', the *FN* claimed that for 1905 the total number of paid advertising columns in its pages was 1,384 in excess of the number for the same period of 'any other daily financial newspaper'. Specifically financial advertising remained the backbone for both papers, never more so than during the rubber boom of 1910, when prospectuses littered the pages, or for the *FN* on 12 December that year, when no less than ten whole pages were filled with numbers of Mexican government bonds. Gradually, however, the range of advertising attracted to the papers was broadening. For example, in different issues of the *FN* in December 1905 there were full pages of advertisements for hotels abroad, gramophones and, as desirable Christmas gifts, the various silver products of Boots Cash Chemists Ltd; while a glance at the *FT* for 14 December 1907 reveals a striking collection of automobile advertisements to tie in with the Olympia Motor Exhibition, including ones for Sunbeam, Argyll, Darracq and of course, symbol of an age, Hispano-Suiza. It was not presumably to this high-class 'trade' advertising (a tacit recognition of the relative wealth of the average *FN* or *FT* reader) that Bridgewater was referring in an important passage of his 1909 address to *FT* shareholders:

> I may tell you that if we accepted all the advertisements which are offered to us our receipts would be considerably greater than they are. But we do not take everything that comes along. Advertisements which are apparently specially designed to entrap the unwary, to induce poor persons to part with hard-earned savings, and to tempt necessitous debtors to take almost the only step which could possibly make their financial troubles greater are declined by the *Financial Times*. The business of newspaper publishing is not, in my judgement, one which is free from proprietorial responsibility.[34]

It is unclear what this moral censorship amounted to in practice (apart from the continuing *FT* notice that 'Advertisements of Blind Pool or Syndicate Touts cannot be inserted'). But the very fact of Bridgewater's remarks was a sign that times were changing and that higher ethical standards were being demanded than those of the epoch of Hooley and Whitaker Wright.

Two years later Flower's speech to the *FN*'s AGM – almost certainly written for him by Powell – confirmed the trend of the daily financial press towards a greater professionalism, in the acceptable sense of the term:

> The various members of the staff are encouraged to specialise in prominent departments of financial activity . . . For instance, American market affairs are dealt with by members of the staff who have themselves been sent over from our head office to serve an apprenticeship as workers on the New York financial

press. The same system is applied, *mutatis mutandi*, in the chief financial centres of the world. Its working has endowed the *Financial News* with an authority which, in scientific language, is both extensive and intensive.[35]

One such specialist, highly respected for his column signed 'W.A.D.' on mining matters, was W. A. Doman, who had joined the *FN* in 1890, during the 1900s spent some years on the staff of A. Goerz & Company (later to become the Union Corporation) and in 1911 was formally appointed the paper's first mining editor, at a salary of £600. Someone else now on the scene, who also was to be of long-term significance in the *FN*'s history, was H. A. Woodcock, who joined the staff in 1905 on a weekly 'screw' of three guineas, exclusive of £40 a year for contributing theatrical notes, and by 1908 had been appointed manager of City news. Like Doman, he and all the others moved desks in 1910, when the paper, having decided that it had outgrown its Abchurch Lane offices, moved to new premises at 111 Queen Victoria Street, becoming a tenant in the Salvation Army buildings there.

Both the *FN* and the *FT* probably had at this time about fifty to sixty people on their respective strengths, divided equally into editorial and commercial staff, but the *FT* in 1911, with its larger resources, was able to do something which the *FN* would not have contemplated, namely, to initiate a staff pension fund. This was something of an innovation in the newspaper world, but by 1912 it seems to have been well in train. We do not know, however, what life was really like for the members of the staff on the two papers. One small clue lies in this extract from a brief history of the *FN* compiled in 1934, much of it based on Doman's manuscript memoirs:

The backbone of a newspaper is its sub-editors' room . . . The tradition of hard work in that department was, perhaps, best exemplified by F. A. Hanson, who was reputed to return home for sleep only at the week-ends. He had invented a special script-writing of his own that served him better than short-hand, and would call at the office at eleven each morning to be assigned to a [company] meeting. This engagement fulfilled, and his 'copy' transcribed, he would write up the produce markets – no light task in those days of easy space – before going down to his real night's duty at five in the afternoon. Having seen the paper to bed in the small hours of the morning, he would snatch a few hours' sleep in a chair, take breakfast at a restaurant in which he was wickedly reputed to have some financial interest, and begin the routine again.[36]

Specialization was increasing, but for a long time yet it would perforce be a versatile life being on the staff of either of the papers.

'Dealings Are Accounted Fair for a Fine Boat-Race Saturday', proclaimed a front-page headline in the *FN* on the first Monday of April 1912. The Stock Exchange and its way of life remained a well-defined world, of 'core' concern, but in fact the coverage as a whole of both papers expanded more or less continuously during the Edwardian period, especially with the increase of revenue from 1909. In the pages of the *FN* one could mention almost at random, from a host of possible examples: by 1903 a weekly column of 'Trade Notes' on 'matters of interest to English manufacturers and men of business'; in 1904 a series of six articles, complete with charts and diagrams, on 'The Finances of Japan'; in December 1905 a long interview with General Booth of the Salvation Army on his 'Back to the Land' scheme; by 1907 the inclusion of 'Yesterday's Parliament' and 'Up-to-Date Motor Notes' as regular features; on 12 February 1908 a sparkling feature entitled 'New Telephone Numbers: A List of Subscribers Who Have Lately Been Connected'; from 1909 a series of major articles, with accompanying line drawings, on 'Great British Business Institutions'; and by August 1911 the paper was able to boast that it had printed, in the course of one week, no less than forty-one 'specials', including ones on British capital in the Dutch East Indies, Austro-Hungarian trade, the London to Ostend line, the Denver & Rio Grande Railway, Canadian grain trade, Romanian crude oil production, loan banks for British Guiana and Germany's gold movement – articles which, in Powellite phrase, 'enable the reader to keep in close touch with all phases of thought and experience in current financial, economic, and commercial matters, and to add to his, or her, mental equipment in the perpetual struggle in the world of money'.

The pattern was the same in the *FT*, though typically billed in less sonorous terms. 'I think I am right in saying that the paper, from the reader's point of view, is a more valuable one now than it has ever been before,' remarked Bridgewater to the AGM in April 1910.[37] One of the relatively recent improvements he was referring to was a series that was to run for a long time called 'Chairmen of Public Companies', which about once a fortnight provided a profile of an Edwardian captain of industry, together with a one-page photo supplement. The visual element was becoming increasingly important. Not only did the *FT*, like the *FN*, become more proficient at publishing features of several pages that very much anticipated the modern *FT* supplements (for example, on 30 April 1912 there were five pages of articles, photographs and advertisements about Australia); but by 1910 the *FT* also introduced something each Friday called the 'Magazine Page'. This tended to treat of rather narrow, worthy themes like 'Alluvial Tin Mining in Cornwall' and 'Hydro-

Electric Power Development', but undoubtedly brought in the advertising and, through a generous spread of photographs, increased the visual appeal of the paper. The editorial independence may not yet have been high in what were essentially advertising features, but the features themselves denoted a significant shift away from concentrating purely on finance itself.

Nevertheless, what strikes one about the Edwardian *FT* is the extent to which it now began to establish itself in a cultural as well as factual sense as *the* paper of the Stock Exchange, preparing the way for the reputation it was to enjoy between the wars as the 'stockbroker's bible'. Indicative of this was the comprehensive coverage it provided in May 1903, including a full-page supplement of marvellous photos, of the celebrated Stock Exchange walk from London to Brighton, which reputedly set the nation itself walking and was to become an annual event. By 1909 the paper included a regular Saturday feature on 'House and Sport', i.e. about the Stock Exchange at play; while at the time of the general election the following January it was characteristically the *FT* which provided a photographic supplement featuring portraits of eight Stock Exchange members who were parliamentary candidates. It would not forget where its first and most abiding constituency lay.

From a perspective of three-quarters of a century later, it was the pre-war *FN* under the still more or less stable Powell that, in two major respects, made the real running as a 'modern' outward-looking newspaper of finance. Firstly, there was the 'Empire Section', published each Thursday from April 1910 and usually comprising three or four pages. This section was under the direction of Ben Morgan, an engineer who, as honorary secretary of the British Manufacturers' Association, had spent the best part of the 1900s zealously touring the Dominions in an effort to further trade with the 'mother country'; and undoubtedly the section had to it a strongly proselytizing flavour of tariff reform and imperial unity. From a journalistic point of view, it provided a considerable source of weekly information on the colonies at a time when British capital was flowing to them, especially to the Dominions, at an unprecedented rate. The articles themselves tended to toe the offical line, and indeed were often written by actual colonial leaders, but purely at the level of factual matter something like the seven-page section of 25 April 1912, including a well-illustrated four-page 'Hong Kong Special', met a definite gap.

The other distinctive contribution made by Powell was equally timely, and rather further-reaching in its implications – namely, his perception that as industry increasingly turned to the joint-stock form of organization, and as the average share denomination was steadily reduced from the £5 of the 1870s or thereabouts to the 2*s.* of the rubber boom of 1910, so the social base of the investing class was broadening, requiring from the financial press a rather different kind of treatment. It was in fact the rubber boom which gave Powell the chance he had been looking for to stamp his mark upon the paper. Whereas the *FT* tended to adopt a faintly negative tone towards the whole phenomenon ('We are afraid that when the boom is over many rash investors who have been tempted into Rubber will be left contemplating bundles of doubtful scrip'), Powell from the first grasped the social significance of what was afoot, to such effect that by the first week of April 1910 the *FN* was averaging fourteen pages a day, two more than the *FT*. Powell's devices to attract new readers and advertising were many, including extremely full reports of the rubber share markets in both the Stock Exchange and Mincing Lane, but his master-stroke was the 'Voice of the Rubber Public' column, subtitled 'Further opinions, gleaned from a wide area, with regard to the absolute and comparative merits of rubber securities now before the investor'.

Thus on 22 April, for example, an array of rubber-fanciers added their opinions to the debate on which shares to choose, including 'Bon Accord' of Canonbury, North London, on the prospects for Chersonese and Malang: 'I beg to second your correspondent "Suburbanite's" opinion with regard to these two sound companies, whose shares, as a lock-up, have a very promising outlook and may go to 25*s.* or 35*s.* in the not very distant future, while Anglo-Johores, comparatively speaking, should be £3 instead of 25*s.* premium.'

'Japhet' of West Norwood saw things differently: 'May I endorse the views of your correspondents, "G.C.", "Para", and "Albert Leonard", as to Diamantino Rubbers? I look upon them as the pick of the bunch at present. The company has already got some rubber here, and I understand regular shipments will be coming along very soon.'

'Northerner' of Holmlands Park, Sunderland, wanted to know why the Telogoredjos Company had been overlooked in previous columns of the 'Voice': 'Situated in the fertile Malang district of Java, it should this year produce enough to pay 10 per cent, and steadily rising as the 7,000 acres are planted out with rubber. There are already 160,000 trees planted, many being nine years old, and these are being rapidly added to.'

In the cloistered world of *haute finance*, Dr Powell could pride himself on running an open university, admission fee a penny a day.

Both papers retained a certain critical-cum-investigative flavour. The *FT*, for instance, in May 1903 lambasted the prospectus of the South-Western Vacuum Cleaner Company, under the heading 'A Vacuous

Prospectus'; while in November 1904 'Hot Curry' was the title for a leader exposing the dubious methods of the outside brokers Currie & Crisp. On 30 December 1911 the review of the year in the mining market emphasized the significance of certain revelations in the pages of the *FT*:

For months before the cable which came from our Johannesburg correspondent at the end of August, and which forced the management to admit that something was wrong, East Rands [i.e. East Rand Proprietary Mines Ltd] were a bad market, but the news that irregularities had been practised for eighteen months with the cognisance of more than one of the directors came as a shock, not only to the shareholders of the East Rand, but to market men and others interested in Kaffirs. Then there were the discloures in regard to Rhodesian financial methods, which rendered futile the efforts made by the shops [i.e. the jobbers closely linked with the particular companies] to engineer another upward movement in that market. The discovery that the Amalgamated Properties directors had doubled the capital of that concern without notifying the shareholders and had issued a large number of shares in exchange for a very mixed collection of assets of doubtful value, led to other investigations, which resulted in the feeling of distrust being accentuated.

For their part the companies retaliated with what Bridgewater in February 1912 described as the 'somewhat childish' tactic of boycotting the *FT* in terms of providing information and advertising, but in due course the squall blew over.

The overall impression, though, is that the *FT* under Bridgewater's direction was becoming rather more cautious in these matters than it had been during the MacRae era. 'We do not go about inviting people to tread on the tail of our coat', was how Bridgewater himself put it to his shareholders in 1907 about the ever-present danger of libel actions – a danger especially great because, as happened to the *FT* in 1909, even if the paper won the case it would still have to pay its own costs if the plaintiff was unable to meet them.[38] With the odd notable exception (such as the exposure of some of the flotations in the Nigerian tin boom of the spring and early summer of 1912) the *FT* tended to adopt a fairly neutral tone towards new issues, merely summarizing the main aspects of the particular prospectus. Nor was the *FN* all that much more forthright in this respect, though, taking at random a week in January 1907, the only real criticism of the week's new issues was made by the *FN* rather than the *FT*, upbraiding a Grimsby company, William Sharpe & Son, for employing unwarrantable accounting methods in its prospectus.

As one would expect, it was the *FN* that generally showed a bolder commitment to the pioneer investigative tradition, typified by a case that

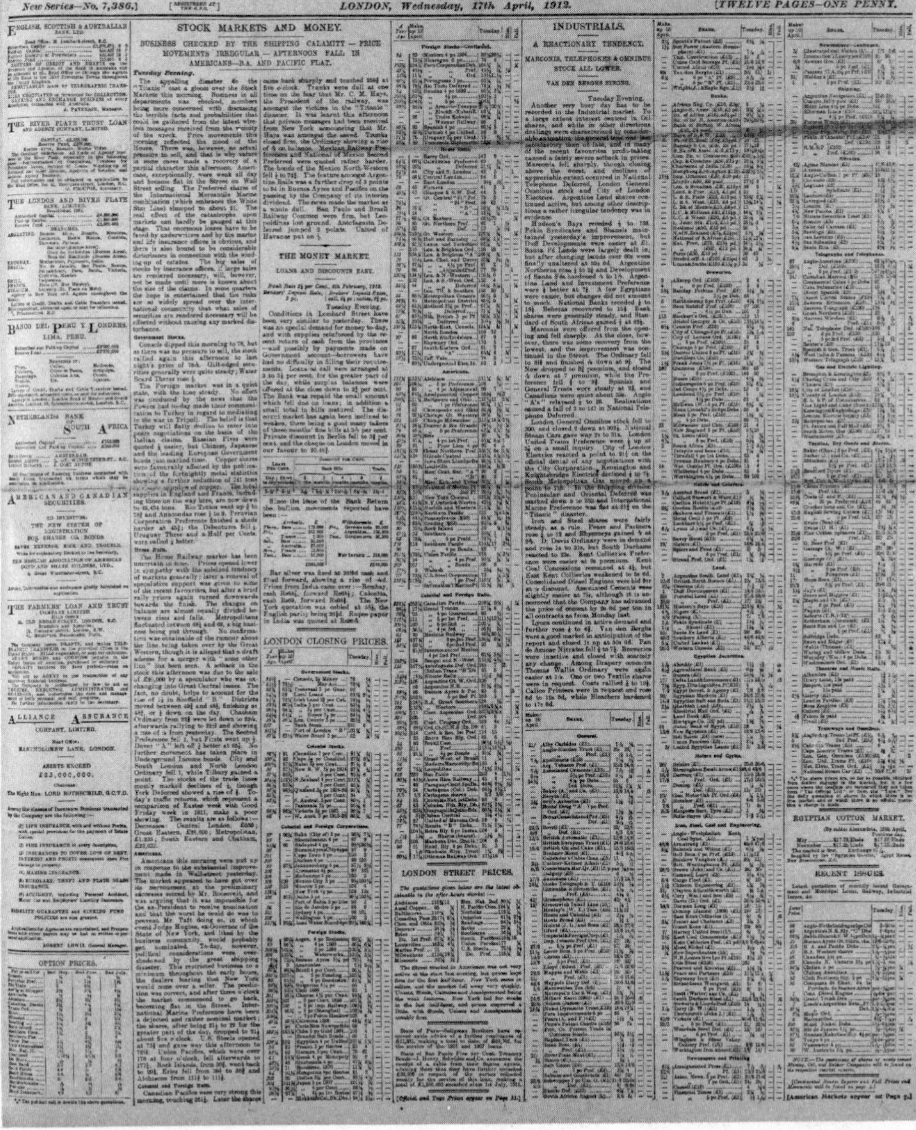

The Financial Times.

New Series—No. 7,386.] [REGISTERED AT THE G.P.O.] LONDON, Wednesday, 17th April, 1912. [TWELVE PAGES—ONE PENNY.

STOCK MARKETS AND MONEY.

BUSINESS CHECKED BY THE SHIPPING CALAMITY — PRICE MOVEMENTS IRREGULAR — AFTERNOON FALL IN AMERICANS—B.A. AND PACIFIC FLAT.

Tuesday Evening.

The appalling disaster to the "Titanic" cast a gloom over the Stock Markets this morning. Business in all departments was checked, members being more concerned with discussing the terrible facts and probabilities that could be gathered from the latest wireless messages received from the vicinity of the wreck. Price movements this morning reflected the mood of the House. There was, however, no actual pressure to sell, and that is why values in some cases made a recovery of a partial character this afternoon. Americans, exceptionally, were weak all day and became flat in the Street on Wall Street selling. The Preferred shares of the International Mercantile Marine combination (which embraces the White Star Line) slumped to about 11. The real effect of the catastrophe upon markets can hardly be gauged at this stage. That enormous losses have to be faced by underwriters and by the marine and life insurance offices is obvious, and there is also bound to be considerable disturbance in connection with the winding-up of estates. The big sales of stocks by insurance offices, if large sales are rendered necessary, will, however, not be made until more is known about the size of the claims. In some quarters the hope is entertained that the risks are so widely spread over the international community that what sales of securities are rendered necessary will be effected without causing any marked disturbance.

Government Stocks.

Consols dipped this morning to 78, but [illegible]

[illegible] came back sharply and touched 28¾ at five o'clock. Trunks were dull at one time on the fear that Mr. C. M. Hays, the President of the railway, was amongst the victims in the "Titanic" disaster. It was learnt this afternoon that private messages had been received from New York announcing that Mr. Hays was amongst the saved. Trunks closed firm, the Ordinary showing a rise of ¼ on balance. Mexican Railway Preferences and National of Mexico Second Preferred were quoted rather harder. The bonds of the Mexico North-Western fell ½ to 74½. The feature amongst Argentine Rails was a further drop of 3 points to 94 in Buenos Ayres and Pacifics on the passing by the Company of its interim dividend. The news made the market as a whole dull. San Paulo and Brazil Railway Common were firm, but Leopoldinas lost ground. Antofagasta Deferred jumped 2 points. United of Havana put on ½.

THE MONEY MARKET.

LOANS AND DISCOUNTS EASY.

Bank Rate 3½ per Cent., 8th February, 1912.
Bankers' Deposit Rate, 2 pc. | *Brokers' Deposit Rates, call, 2¼ pc.; notice, 2½ pc.*

Tuesday Evening.

Conditions in Lombard Street have been very similar to yesterday. There was no special demand for money to-day, and with supplies reinforced by the recent return of cash from the provinces [illegible]

LONDON CLOSING PRICES.

INDUSTRIALS.

A REACTIONARY TENDENCY.

MARCONIS, TELEPHONES & OMNIBUS STOCK ALL LOWER.

VAN DEN BERGHS STRONG.

Tuesday Evening.

Another very busy day has to be recorded in the Industrial market. To a large extent interest centred in Oil shares, and while in other directions dealings were characterised by considerable animation, the general tone was less satisfactory than of late, and in many of the recent favourites profit-taking caused a fairly severe setback in prices. Marconis fell sharply, though closing above the worst, and declines of appreciable extent occurred in National Telephone Deferred, London General Omnibus stock and City of London Electrics. Argentine Land shares continued active, but among other descriptions a rather irregular tendency was in evidence.

Hudson's Bays receded ¼ to 138. Pekin Syndicates and Shansis maintained yesterday's improvement, but Duff Developments were easier at £1. Santa Fé Lands were largely dealt in, but after changing hands over 60s were finally unaltered at 50s 6d. Argentine Northerns rose ⅛ to 2¾ and Development of Santa Fés hardened ⅛ to 1⅛. Argentine Land and Investment Preference were ⅛ better at 7½. A few Egyptians were easier, but changes did not amount to much. National Banks receded ⅛ to 18½. Beheras recovered to 15¼. Bank shares were generally steady, and Standard of South Africas gained ⅛ at 6¾.

Marconis were offered from the opening and fell sharply. At the close, however, there was some recovery from the [illegible]

LONDON STREET PRICES.

EGYPTIAN COTTON MARKET.

RECENT ISSUES.

OPTION PRICES.

[Official and Tape Prices appear on Page 11.]

[American Markets appear on Page 3.]

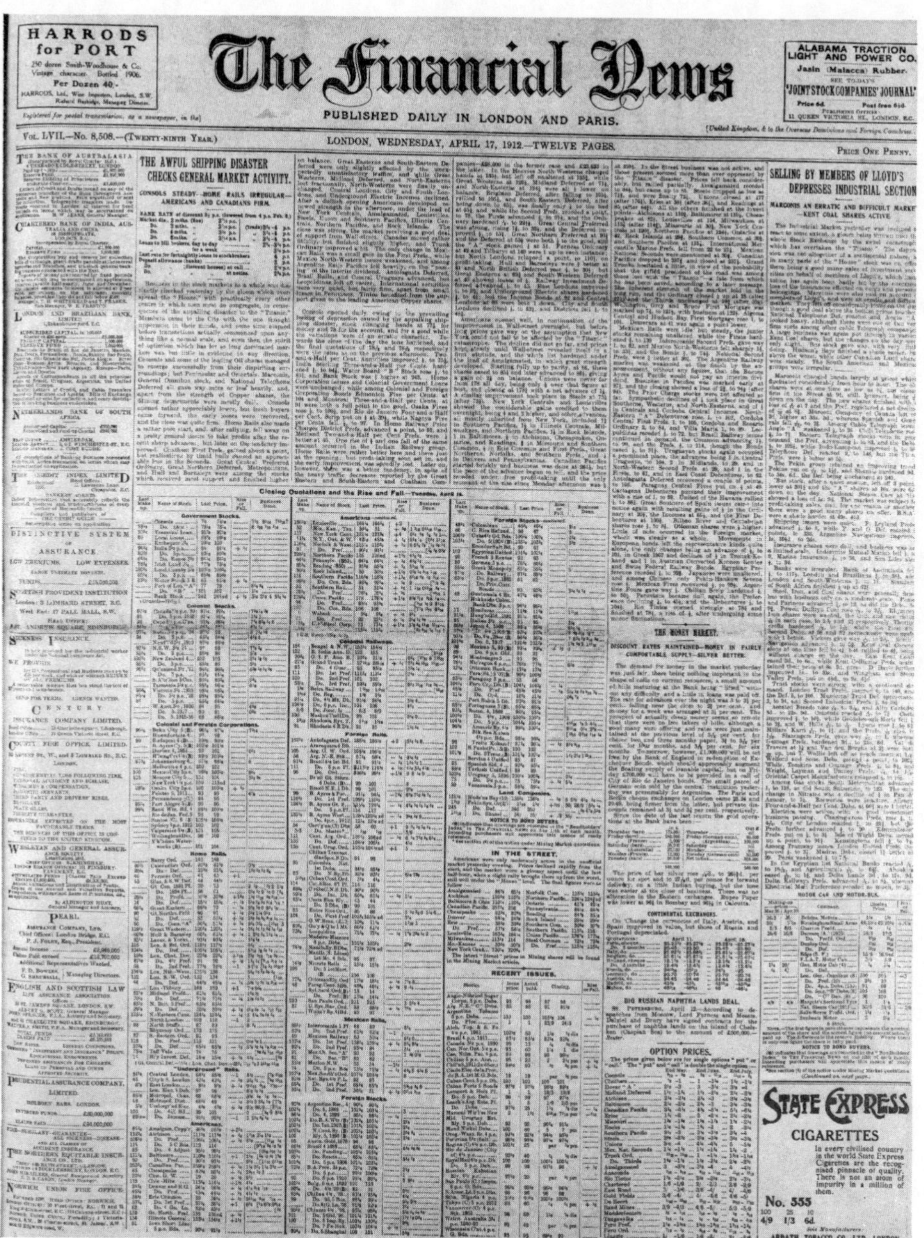

HARRODS for PORT
250 dozen Smith-Woodhouse & Co. Vintage character. Bottled 1906.
Per Dozen 40/-
HARRODS, Ltd., Wine Importers, London, S.W. Richard Burbidge, Managing Director.

The Financial News

PUBLISHED DAILY IN LONDON AND PARIS.

ALABAMA TRACTION LIGHT AND POWER CO.
Jasin (Malacca) Rubber.
SEE TO-DAY'S 'JOINT STOCK COMPANIES' JOURNAL'
Price 6d. Post free 6½d.
Publishing Offices: 11 QUEEN VICTORIA ST., LONDON, E.C.

Registered for postal transmission, as a newspaper, in the (United Kingdom, & to the Overseas Dominions and Foreign Countries.)

VOL. LVII.—No. 8,508.—(TWENTY-NINTH YEAR.) LONDON, WEDNESDAY, APRIL 17, 1912.—TWELVE PAGES. PRICE ONE PENNY.

THE AWFUL SHIPPING DISASTER CHECKS GENERAL MARKET ACTIVITY.

CONSOLS STEADY—HOME RAILS IRREGULAR—AMERICANS AND CANADIANS FIRM.

SELLING BY MEMBERS OF LLOYD'S DEPRESSES INDUSTRIAL SECTION

MARCONIS AN ERRATIC AND DIFFICULT MARKET—KENT COAL SHARES ACTIVE

Closing Quotations and the Rise and Fall—Tuesday, April 16.

THE MONEY MARKET.

IN THE STREET.

RECENT ISSUES.

CONTINENTAL EXCHANGES.

BIG RUSSIAN NAPHTHA LANDS DEAL.

OPTION PRICES.

STATE EXPRESS CIGARETTES
In every civilised country in the world State Express Cigarettes are the recognised pinnacle of quality. There is not an atom of impurity in a million of them.
No. 555
ARDATH TOBACCO CO. LTD., LONDON.

17 April 1912: sinking of the *Titanic*

came to court in January 1908, when Arthur Digby, a solicitor-cum-promoter, sued for libel following a piece in the *FN* under the heading, 'Colliery business is moving in Lady Godiva's old home'. It transpired Digby had advertised in the *Daily Telegraph* for a partner with a capital of £250 in order to develop certain collieries in the Coventry area; that the advertisement had been answered by one Carruthers, 'who gave as his address the name of a house to the owner of which he paid 5*s.* a month for receiving letters', but who was in fact on the staff of the *FN*; and that after Digby sent the relevant reports and suchlike to Curruthers, there appeared the complained-of piece, described by Digby in court as 'undoubtedly a clever article which threw ridicule on his scheme and imputed that he was obtaining money by false pretences'. Powell, in the absence of Marks, denied Digby's suggestion 'that his paper endeavoured to seek out private promoters who advertise in other papers' and, under questioning from Mr Justice Darling, defended his sleuth:

What are Mr Carruthers' duties? – His duties are those of a ledger clerk.
Is it part of his business to do the kind of thing which is alleged here? – He does it in the evenings after he has left the office.
This is not the only occasion on which he has done it? – No, we do it in the public interest to find out what is going on.
It that what is called philanthropy? – No, my Lord, we call it journalism.

A fine reply, but the jury found for Digby, with damages of £500, which perhaps served as a lesson in discretion to Powell and his ledger clerk.[39]

As for the editorial policy and attitudes of the two papers during these years, it would be wrong to imagine either that they played as yet a significant part in shaping opinion on the wider questions of the day or that they were considerate enough to address themselves to the themes that now preoccupy economic historians. An *FT* leader of 2 June 1905 on 'Channels of Investment' was an illustration of the latter point, describing in plain factual terms the quickening pace of investment going abroad, especially to Egypt and the Argentine during the first half of the year, and offering not the faintest hint of regret that more capital was not being directed instead towards Britain's own industries. When, however, the papers did raise their heads above the immediate parapets of the markets, it was almost invariably the *FN* that led the way in providing the sharp, contentious perspective. Thus when Joseph Chamberlain in 1903 launched his campaign for tariff reform, of which Marks had been a strong advocate for some time, the *FN* gave it its vigorous support, leaving the *FT* to follow the example of the Conservative leader Balfour in timidly sitting on the fence. Six years later, when Lloyd George initiated one of the great political rows of the century with his 'People's Budget', the contrast was even more marked. The *FT* was of course critical – 'It is obvious that the Budget has been introduced without that previous careful study of the probable incidence and effect of new taxation which such legislation imperatively demands in the interests of the community' – but adopted a fairly mild tone and concentrated on the details rather than the broad thrust of the proposals. The *FN*, however, regarded the raising of death duties and the introduction of land-value duties as part of something altogether deeper-dyed: 'We find in Mr Lloyd George's first Budget a patent and deliberate determination to use the machinery of finance to establish schemes and systems which, for want of a more specific term, may be called Socialistic.' W. R. Lawson added his weight to the attack and wrote a series of articles that were subsequently reprinted as a pamphlet. The collective title was graphic enough: 'Lloyd George Finance; or, the Gentle Art of Robbing Hen-Roosts'.

The general election of January 1910 confirmed the *FN*'s new tone of barely concealed hysteria. On the 14th an article 'By an Old Election Hand', almost certainly Powell, made the paper's electoral preferences fairly clear: 'YOUR VOTE may turn the day in the constituency where you live. Make sure you record it. If the Liberal-Socialist goes in by a handful of votes, what a reflection, for you, that you were one of the apathetics who let him do so!' Three days later, early Conservative successes inspired the following headlines: 'The Nation Wins the First Round of the Fight against Dictatorship, Bureaucracy, and Reaction, Arrayed in Giant Phalanx to Destroy its Liberties'. By the 21st, with Conservative successes continuing, the paper was placing itself at the hub of events: 'As yesterday's declarations were made in the daytime, we showed them, as they came in on the "tape", in the windows of the *Financial News* offices in Queen Victoria Street, where huge crowds assembled and cheered to the echo the successive announcements.' Three days later the paper declared: 'Animated crowds again gathered on Saturday outside the *Financial News* offices and indulged in plenty of cheering. It was not the office-boy crowd, but was composed of solid, sensible, well-dressed men, with papers and pencils, working out the results, making comparisons, and eagerly discussing the new aspect of events.' They were heady days (though in the event the Liberals remained in office), and the educative sentiments were classic Powell, but whether this partisan obsession with the political arena, in such contrast to the *FT*'s semi-indifference, was beneficial to a specialist financial paper is surely doubtful.

★

On Tuesday 13 February 1913 the *FT* celebrated its twenty-fifth birthday with not only a sixteen-page mining supplement but also a twenty-page issue including a host of special features on such subjects as the humour of the City, famous legal cases and the meaning and history of the signs of Lombard Street. It was time for a bit of *FN*-style fancy prose: 'If a morning train running into the City could be unroofed and viewed from above a drift of pink would be noted running through the white stretch of open newspapers, and that distinct note of delicate colour would represent the *Financial Times*.' The next day it was back to business as usual, and the *FT* and *FN* both clocked in with twelve-page issues, each impressively dense in terms of financial figures, information and reportage, with little to choose between them. The *FN* perhaps had the edge in classy advertising – a small advert on page one for 'Liberty's Furnishing and Colour Schemes' being more *bon ton* than a large one on page three for 'unrivalled' industrial facilities at Barrow-in-Furness – but the *FT* scored for erudition with a lengthy review of a new translation of Georgius Agricola's sixteenth-century treatise *De Re Metallica*, which must have gone down well in the 'Kaffir circus'. Certain defining characteristics were present: in the *FT* a full column of 'House and City Sport', in the *FN* that hardiest of perennials, 'Points', with perhaps the choice item this particular day being that the King had sent a gift of pheasants to the Queen's Hospital for Children in Hackney Road. In terms of news coverage outside the strictly financial sphere, the *FT*'s was superior on the two major stories, the war in the Balkans and the revolution in Mexico, but the two papers were heavily reliant on what came from the agencies. At this stage each had a full-time correspondent in New York, and at times also Paris and Johannesburg, but almost certainly nowhere else. The main editorial matter was on page six, the *FN*'s principal leader being on the history and prospects of the Imperial Tobacco Company, the *FT*'s on the report just issued of the Great Western Railway, with the final paragraph of the latter editorial reading as follows:

The Company's capital expenditure during the half-year amounted to £173,200, of which £45,000 was on the Snow Hill Station, Birmingham, £21,900 on the enlargements at Paddington and £25,300 on the South Lambeth goods depot. Good progress has been made with all these works, and the warehouse at South Lambeth has been completed and brought into use. A contract has also been let for the construction of the Ealing and Shepherd's Bush railway, which will swell the capital outlay for the current year, the total being put at £300,000, and as the debt balance at capital account is now £1,086,600, it is not improbable that the Company may come on the market for further funds before very long. Its available capital powers are, however, ample, the unissued stock and share capital amounting to £3,649,250, in addition to borrowing powers for £2,747,600.

Conrad or Kipling it was not, but for that thin pink line of commuters it was the right stuff.

During the last eighteen months before the war, the *FN* was, as usual, more to the fore than the *FT*. This was particularly so with the 'Marconi scandal', which followed rumours (first propagated in print by W. R. Lawson in a weekly, the *Outlook*) that Lloyd George and the Attorney-General Sir Rufus Isaacs had corruptly influenced a government contract with the Marconi Company in order to make personal gain for themselves through buying Marconi shares. They were rumours hardened by the fact that Isaacs was the brother of the company's managing director. The upshot was the appointment of a parliamentary select committee to examine the whole affair. The *FN*'s coverage of the proceedings reached saturation level, especially when on 15 April 1913 it achieved a genuine 'scoop', and gained enormous publicity, by printing the terms of a key agreement which Godfrey Isaacs had declined to divulge to the committee the previous day. The following week Powell himself gave evidence and at one point said that he had heard that a third minister was implicated. Under pressure he gave the name: Winston Churchill. Whereupon Churchill was summoned and, arriving in a furious, disdainful mood ('Am I to understand that it is simply upon the statement of the editor of the *Financial News*? I did not catch his name'), proceeded to deny the rumour.[40] The Liberal majority on the committee eventually produced a whitewashing report, but the conspiracy-minded Powell ensured that the episode continued to live for several years in the pages of the *FN*.

The Stock Exchange fared poorly during the rest of 1913 and into 1914, adding to an already unharmonious atmosphere at Queen Victoria Street. In February 1914 Beresford was compelled by Flower to resign his directorship. This was because he had beome chairman of the Northampton Cinema Company; and according to Flower, their shares 'were being hawked for sale by Mr J. Henry Iredale, whose proceedings as a notorious tout have been frequently animadverted upon in the columns of our paper'. That same month Morgan was given notice, apparently on the grounds of expense. And in April a worried Marks, still editor-in-chief, wrote to Flower urging further reductions in the paper's expenses. The *FN* itself still looked healthy enough – by early July, a 36-page supplement on Canada celebrated Dominion Day, 'Finance in the Courts' was subtitled 'Cases of City Interest Bovrilised for the Busy Man', and Powell had reached his forty-seventh article on 'The Evolution of Finance'

– but the management side was in poor shape for the events about to overtake it.

During the last week of July 1914 the City of London watched helplessly as Europe moved towards the brink of its first major war for almost a century. On Wednesday 29 July the *FN* allowed itself a moment of mordant humour: 'No company was ever issued with a more timely title than this morning's "J.M." Shock Absorbers. The market ought to have a large supply.' That day seven firms were 'hammered' and went under, mainly because of defaulting clients on the Continent; but according to the paper's market report, 'the calm and dignity with which the Stock Exchange comported itself will probably become historic'. In the more candid words of the *FT*'s 'Stock Markets and Money' front-page headline: 'A Day of Doubt and Dread'. On Friday the 31st the Stock Exchange was closed until further notice, and the next day both papers approved of the Committee's action. As the *FT* put it: 'It was impossible to allow London to remain the only "dumping ground" for all Continental holders of securities. London had stood the brunt of the storm, and it was necessary that protection should be given for dealers who must otherwise have been overwhelmed.' The question remained: would Britain itself be dragged into war? Already on the 29th the *FT* had declared its belief that 'whatever otherwise may be thought of the Government, it may at least be trusted to keep this country out of the area of conflict unless forced by some extreme and improbable contingency'. Now, on 1 August, the *FN* provisionally agreed: 'How far the conflict may spread is incalculable, but it should be possible for this country to hold aloof, at least until there is danger of a complete overturn of the European equilibrium, in which event the intervention of an unscathed Power should be effective.'

Much happened over the bank holiday weekend, so that by the time the *FN* appeared next, on Tuesday the 4th, its tone was very different. The paper sought to show where 'The Duty of England' lay:

> Where we were free a few days ago we now appear to be involved, for the challenge has been thrown out by the wanton invasion of Belgium. This warlike act, in defiance of treaty obligation, cannot be tolerated, for if we ignore it it may be the beginning of the end, so far as the British Empire is concerned. It is a menace to our very existence.

The *FN*'s main headline the next day marked the end of an era: 'German Reply to the British Ultimatum Is Unsatisfactory and War Is Declared'. It took the *FT* a further day to redefine its attitude, but 'A Word in Season' on the 6th revealed the paper's full backing for the government's action, on the grounds of both 'honour' and 'intelligent self-interest', above all showing France that Britain was not merely a fair-weather friend. The City's patriotic fervour could not have been more intense, but even amidst jingoistic euphoria it was realized that something was going to have to be done about the complete breakdown in the machinery of credit that had occurred since the end of July. Neither paper, however, debated possible remedies, preferring to wait for the official announcement. It came on the 12th and was to the effect that the government had agreed to guarantee the Bank of England for any loss it might incur in discounting bills of exchange – whether home or foreign, bank or trade – accepted prior to the 4th. The reaction of both papers was highly favourable. 'The Chancellor of the Exchequer has grasped the position in a most remarkable manner,' declared the *FN*, while the *FT* indulged in a rare passage of grandiloquence: 'While our Fleet keeps the trade routes clear the London Money Market, thanks to wise statesmanship, has been enabled to resume its accustomed function of granting credits, which is as indispensable as a safe sea passage to the smooth carrying on of our commerce.' Such praise from the usually grudging *FT* perhaps justified the title of the relevant chapter in Lloyd George's *War Memoirs*: 'How We Saved the City'.

Yet to the *FN*'s Ellis Powell, supreme patriot and imperialist though he was, the guns of August must have been a bitter personal blow. Some two years earlier, through his chairman mouthpiece, he had expressed to the paper's shareholders his most profound belief:

> We have, up to now, been accustomed to think that the destinies of the world were, in the main, entrusted to the hands of politicians . . . But within the last few years it has dawned upon the most competent observers that this progress and contentment depend very much more upon financial than upon political factors . . . The financial and economic forces have become the predominant factors in our twentieth-century life, while the political elements have receded into the second place . . . This is a distinct gain for humanity as a whole, since political forces are capable of being distorted, minimised, and outwitted, while economic power is the absolute and inexorable auxiliary of every effort to advance the prosperity of the world.[41]

Surrounded by frightened monarchies and restless masses, Powell's was the 'great illusion' of the age on the part of the commercial middle classes, whether merchants in Lübeck, stock jobbers in Capel Court or humble scribes in Queen Victoria Street.

[THREE]

FT IN THE ASCENDANT: 1914–28

'We must make the Germans and their very High-up War Lord a present of the acknowledgement that we are temporarily inconvenienced,' Frank Bridgewater (in the absence of his ill father) wryly admitted to the *FT*'s shareholders in February 1915.[1] For both the *FT* and the *FN*, 'inconvenienced' was one way of putting it. The Stock Exchange had remained closed throughout the previous autumn, and the newspapers had been but four-page shadows of their former selves, being able to do little more than print nominal prices for the benefit of those seeking to make private bargains. And even when the Exchange reopened on 4 January 1915, following lengthy negotiations with the Bank of England, the clearing banks and the Treasury, the difficulties facing the financial press were still formidable. A system of minimum prices remained in force on the Exchange for eighteen months, severely constraining speculative enthusiasm. Increasingly tight Treasury control over new issues had the effect of drastically reducing revenue from prospectuses. As wartime austerity became the norm, company-meeting reports were more and more condensed. A high proportion of the staffs of both papers joined up, leaving skeleton operations behind them. Perhaps as serious as any of these factors, an often acute shortage of paper led to rationing of the available supply, the discontinuing of the daily contents bills and the inevitably trying system by which newsagents were compelled to make exact orders and no longer allowed to return unsold copies.

Not surprisingly, for these parochial reasons alone, there was little in the way of a chivalrous attitude towards the German foe, especially in May 1915 when the sinking of the *Lusitania* brought the Stock Exchange's campaign against German-born members to a pitch of hysteria. 'The average naturalised German is as much German now as he was before he was naturalised. His darling hope is the smashing of the British Empire.' This editorial opinion of the *FN* on 11 May was echoed in its pages the following day in a piece from W. R. Lawson headed: 'Out with every German from the Stock Exchange'. Even the more temperate *FT* joined the agitation, arguing on the 12th that, whatever the injustices involved to individual German-born members, 'in plain truth, the country has at last come to the limit of its endurance, and is roused to righteous wrath'. Or, in equally plain truth, the 'House' had turned savage, and its faithful financial press could not afford not to follow – with relish on the part of the *FN*, if a certain reluctance on the *FT*'s.

A month later, in June 1915, F. M. Bridgewater, architect of the second major phase of the *FT*'s history, died after a long illness. If he had not already been before, Sir John Ellerman, worth at this time some £55 million, now became chief proprietor; Frank Bridgewater succeeded his father as managing director; C. H. Palmer continued to edit the paper; and the prominent City solicitor William Graham, renowned for his knowledge of company law, was elected chairman. H. A. Randall, hard-working company secretary since 1903, joined the board in 1916; while G. E. Hart remained a director and continued to run the St Clements Press. Between them this team provided the soundest and most prudent of management, steering the *FT* through three and a half more difficult years. From the admittedly patchy evidence that survives, the only episode of palpable managerial inefficiency occurred in December 1916, when 'with regard to paper stock the secretary intimated to the board that the stock of paper stored at St Pauls Wharf consisting of ninety-three reels had been destroyed by fire, and unfortunately was not covered by insurance as the premium on policy had inadvertently been overlooked and not paid'.

Otherwise, all was the familiar and well-oiled *FT* machine, if under strain. Salaries were reduced by a third, but according to Graham in his address to shareholders in March 1916, 'the members of your staff have accepted these reductions without murmur, and have not reduced, but rather increased their efforts on behalf of the company'.[2] The usual contributions continued to be made to the staff pension fund, while by 1917 dividend payments were resumed to ordinary shareholders. The paper shortage reduced the average issue size for most of the war to six pages, but as Graham explained in May 1918, this did not have to mean a decline in standards:

> Every effort has been made to save space without injury to the efficiency of the paper. Non-essential features have been eliminated, superfluous quotations have been weeded out, condensation has been the order of the day, and even the types and headlines have been subjected to vigorous censorship. The maximum of information, with the minimum of space, has been the watchword of the staff, and I think we can claim that this ideal has been very nearly reached.

The result was not a beautiful paper, but it was undoubtedly a functional one, more than justifying Graham's boast of the *FT* in the same speech that 'its prestige never stood higher' and that 'it will get the benefit of all financial advertising going when the war is over, and there will be plenty of it'.[3] Graham himself would have been the last to deny that the *FT*'s emergence from the war in good shape was much due to the company's profitable ownership of sound trade papers and the well-equipped St Clements Press. Yet nor would he have denied that the existence of a dedicated management, working harmoniously towards one end, was as great a boon.

By contrast to this happy if dull story, the internal history of the *FN* during the First World War was immensely complicated, incorrigibly factious and, for the long-term health and standing of the paper, well-nigh catastrophic. The labyrinthine saga must be reduced to a short horror story. Ellis Powell continued to preside over the paper's fortunes, finally and formally becoming editor in 1915 when Marks, with the utmost reluctance but increasingly ill, agreed to be known as 'consulting editor' at a third of his former salary of £3,000. The books still flowed from Powell's pen; *The Practical Affairs of Life*, published by the *FN* in 1916, was subtitled 'An Utterly Unconventional Guide to Spiritual "Poise" and to Intellectual and Physical Efficiency', contained sections with headings like 'Don't Do Business in Bed', 'No Brooding', 'Don't Lend to Relatives', 'Try to Inspire Confidence' and 'Post-Nuptial Prudence', and was dedicated 'To "Buds", May, Ellis, "Girlie", "Buster", and Agnes, who, either by their mortal presence or their immortal influence from behind the veil, have surrounded me with all the domestic happiness that a man could desire'. But the *FN* itself was in a flat spin. Figures given to a court of law in 1918 revealed that within weeks of the war beginning circulation was down to 9,500 and that by September 1916 barely 7,000 copies were being printed each day. Staff salaries were cut by half for most of the war, causing considerable rancour and the eventual issuing by the company of certificates of indebtedness. The Argus Printing Company provided easy terms and generous credit, but even so at the end of the war the company had failed to pay a preference dividend, let alone an ordinary one, for four years, and the accumulated deficiency stood at £37,497. Still more importantly, the very *way* in which the paper had conducted its affairs meant that by 1918 the financial community as a whole no longer reposed its former confidence in it. Once forfeited, that confidence would be hard indeed to regain.

Much of the problem lay with Powell himself, whose penchant for uncovering conspiracies reached its apogee during the war with the campaign which he helped to lead in print and on public platforms against the so-called 'Unseen Hand', a term he coined himself. 'The time has come when a sustained effort should be made to track this treacherous disturber, this unsurpassable master of vicious derangement, to the lair where he (or she) lurks,' cried the *FN* in January 1917 in the first of a series of six articles on the menace. At the same time the following notice was inserted each day in the paper.

Watch This German Move. Readers will do us a service if they will report to us (a post card is sufficient) any efforts to induce them to purchase some other newspaper in preference to the *Financial News*. There is quite a German campaign going on in that direction, and numerous instances are being reported to us. Those who watch these moves, and report to us, will be doing a patriotic duty.

In April the paper even linked its removal from the stand in the Brighton Public Library to pro-German influence, though subsequently accepted this had been an honest error by the library. By July the Chancellor of the Exchequer, Bonar Law, was having his attention called in the Commons 'to articles in a London financial paper to the effect that a man of very high position in this country had been for three years systematically playing the traitor', while another member asked him if he was aware 'that it is an open secret that the *Financial News*, rightly or wrongly, on three or four days a week, contains articles of a most extraordinary character'. In reply, Bonar Law professed ignorance of the articles and added of newspapers in general: 'I read a good many of them myself, but the *Financial News* is not one of them.'[4] The campaign climaxed in October 1917 with a series of articles against the dangers of 'Boloism'. The term was coined by the journalist Arnold White (author of a book on *The Hidden Hand*), who in an article reprinted in the *FN* stated that 'to "bolo" is to work towards an end unseen by an innocent helper' and that 'what petrol is to a Boche submarine Bolo is to the pacifist and cosmopolitan financial movements against England'. Finally, in November, the board unequivocally told Powell to lay off the whole subject, a move reinforced the following July when H. A. Woodcock was appointed managing director 'in order to carry out and enforce the policy of the board upon editorial and managerial questions'. But by then it was a case of shutting the stable door after the horse had boloed.

Entwined with this frenzied and unworthy hunt for the enemy within was the other principal motif of the war years: the fierce and often public battle for control of the *FN*. Much of it revolved around the dying and dead Harry Marks, who, after severe bouts of gout and at least one more stroke, died on 22 December 1916. Powell in the obituary notice justly noted that Marks had 'founded a school as well as a newspaper' and that 'every City article today bears unconscious witness to the revolution he worked'. There was, however, a less favourable side to his legacy. In the long term, the stain of Rae, Hooley and Whitaker Wright did not readily fade away. Lord Hartwell, who served part of his apprenticeship in financial journalism in the 1930s, remembers that it was still then the received historical wisdom that when Marks went round to brokers canvassing for prospectuses, he would produce three potential critiques of the prospectus: one for the full prospectus, another for the abridged and a third for nothing at all.

As for the short-term legacy, Powell made an oblique, tactful reference in the obituary, describing the difficult period after July 1915 when Marks at last surrendered all editorial responsibilities:

> It would be affectation to pretend that the cessation of lifelong activities and the termination of a personal predominance were accepted in a spirit of resignation by so dauntless a temperament as that of Marks. So much must be said in explanation of certain incidents in Marks's later life which otherwise might remain an insoluble problem to a wide circle of old friends. But in the presence of the austere and ultimate Visitant this hint must suffice. Over the details let oblivion fall like the mantling snow, as befits the season amid which the inexorable summons came.[5]

Unfortunately, the snow descended too late, for already, in the first week of December 1916, a case had been heard in court that cast an unwelcome light on the affairs of the paper. It was a complicated case, with considerable ramifications. In essence, a commission agent called Thomas Jackson was found guilty of attempting to extort money by menaces from Godfrey Isaacs of the Marconi Company, by attempting to induce him to buy 30,000 ordinary shares in the FN Ltd owned by Marks, on the representation that if he bought them he would be able to control the editorial policy of the paper, which was notoriously hostile to Isaacs and the company.[6] The *FN* after the case carried a daily announcement stating that the 30,000 Marks shares did not carry control of the paper, but in an accompanying article Powell revealed that for most of 1916 he and Flower had been much concerned about signs that Marks was seeking to 'hawk' his shares about, as if they were 'a piece of merchandise instead of a public trust'. Marks died a fortnight later and, by a will dated 29 November 1916, left the bulk of his estate to his nephew, 'at present in Salonica', spelling out to him what he wanted to be done:

> It is my desire and beilef that my nephew Julian David Marks being the only Journalist left in my family with the complex ability of an Englishman and American should drag the *Financial News* out of the depths. I beseech and beg

him to do for that paper what he knows I in my time have done for it. Nothing is impossible for any one man if he means to do it and sticks to his determination. Experience has taught me that I made the *Financial News* a great power in my hands and it returned me an income of some thousands a year for many years. There is no reason why it cannot do so again if only Julian sticks to it with a powerful English and American Journalistic Arm.

Over the next three years Julian Marks and a trio of associates, including W. R. Lawson, sought to gain control over the paper, but the existing board, ably marshalled by Woodcock (on behalf of the rather ineffectual Flower) and idiosyncratically abetted by Powell, just about managed to fend them off, amid a damaging array of reconstruction schemes designed to alter voting rights, circulars and counter-circulars to shareholders, extraordinary meetings breaking up in bitter scenes, and protracted injunctions and lawsuits. At one point, in October 1917, Powell in a most graphic article stated that Marks in 1915 ('in a state of intellectual and physical degeneracy, of such a nature that he was only at intervals capable of properly understanding and appreciating what he was about') had actually agreed to sell his 30,000 ordinary shares to the infamous German agent 'Bolo Pasha' and had been prevented only by the swift intervention of Powell himself. How much this was really true, and how much it made *Greenmantle* look like historical fact, it is impossible to say. The point rather, as with the whole lengthy conflict, is that the dirty washing was hung up for all to see, with the inevitable consequences. At last, in 1919, the Marks estate was sold, and it became theoretically possible to start to rebuild the tattered reputation of the *FN*.

Neither paper dealt with the war itself in any great detail, though if anything there was rather more news from the front in the *FT*. At home, each in typical fashion welcomed the advent to power of Lloyd George in December 1916. The *FT* congratulated him on forming a government 'which is to be run on business as distinguished from party lines' and had the grace to note that 'it is not so many years ago since Mr George's name was absolute anathema within the sound of Bow bells'. The *FN* declared that 'at last the nation realises that the ship of Empire is drifting fast towards the rocks of defeat and German domination', described Lloyd George as possessing 'the combination of the practical and the romantic which has always characterised our great leaders' and warned that 'a thousand sordid and unpatriotic influences, some of them confessedly Teuton in aim and inspiration, will endeavour to deflect his policy and paralyse his efforts'. The next day W. R. Lawson contributed a piece demanding a three-man Executive Council of War to replace the Cabinet, universal military service and the declaration of martial law, all under the headline, 'Real, Not Sham, Dictators'. The following month the government issued its third and biggest war loan, to a fanfare of patriotic publicity to which the financial press contributed its full share. 'Every Cheque Is a She££ Fired at the German Trenches', ran an *FN* headline. Powell, aware that the loan was attracting a host of financially inexperienced members of the public, published in the paper a 'War Loan Dictionary' to mark the event. On March 1917 the *FN* celebrated its 10,000th issue, in which Powell, after referring to 'the colossal total of self-sacrificing and exacting labour which goes to the production of a penny financial newspaper', looked forward to the 20,000th number in 1951, but made no attempt to forecast: 'We are in the vortex of a great world-change. Not even the most prescient of us has the remotest idea of its ultimate outcome in spiritual, social, constitutional, and economic readjustments.' Twenty months and one Russian Revolution later, there was further cause to celebrate, as the guns at last fell silent and the papers prepared to report a world fit for financiers to live in.

What sort of a world? The *FN* in greeting the sweeping victory of Lloyd George's coalition in the 'coupon' election of December 1918 eloquently argued that 'between the England of today and that which waited for the polls in 1910 there rolls a gulf wider than that which separates us from Oliver Cromwell':

> A wholly new line of social and political cleavage has suddenly become discernible. On the one side is the electoral endorsement of the policy of ordered but pauseless social advance which is the peremptory need of the hour; on the other, a pitiless repudiation of various survivals from old-time political creeds, which have been thrust into oblivion, together with such propagandas as Bolshevism, the whole-sale confiscation of savings, government by 'flappers', and, generally, the ideals which flourish under the Red Flag.

For a while it did seem a wonderful new world for the financial press, especially once Treasury control over domestic new issues was lifted in March 1919, leading to a Stock Exchange boom that lasted about a year and featured the floating of up to £400 million of new company issues. These ranged from the raising of additional capital for firms like Lever Brothers and Armstrong Whitworth to the launching of entirely new undertakings in the burgeoning entertainments sector. Almost all of these flotations were domestic, with wartime restrictions on lending abroad still in force. The *FT* did particularly well out of this boom, carrying 444 prospectuses during 1920, with a peak of 76 in March. It was still behind *The Times* (556 prospectuses in 1920), but it is unlikely that anyone in Coleman Street was complaining.

However, by the second half of 1920, as the boom petered out, Stock Exchange prices fell, and Bank Rate stood at a discouraging (for those days) 7 per cent, so the City began to contemplate the long-run consequences of 'the world crisis' of the previous decade. There were, from the vantage-point of the square mile, several causes of concern. The war had increased Britain's National Debt tenfold, which meant that merely servicing the debt would be a heavy burden on the state's finance. The war had also resulted in the liquidation of about a quarter of that large income from investment abroad that had traditionally paid for Britain's trade deficit. There was also the bitter truth that Wall Street had taken advantage of the United States' three years of neutrality to supplant many of London's functions as a centre of international finance. It was in the face of these unfavourable developments that the City now nurtured the deeply felt conviction, based as much on psychological as strictly economic grounds, that not until Britain's return to the gold standard, which the war had forced it to abandon, would London be restored to its former place in the sun, however arduous the return to and maintenance of the standard might be. Nor was this all, for in the context of the Stock Exchange becoming an increasingly important *domestic* capital market, the City at last was no longer impervious to the state of the British economy as a whole. In 1920 the condition of this economy could only be described as poor; above all, the classic nineteenth-century export industries – coal, iron and steel, textiles and shipbuilding – had lost many of their markets and showed few signs in the post-war world of being able to regain them. It would take a long, long time for new forms of economic activity to emerge and satisfactorily replace the once dominant role of the traditional staples.

Yet all was not gloom and doom for the financial press. For one thing, the way in which the government had helped to finance the war – through war loans and war-savings certificates – had had the important side-effect of making the smaller investor and would-be investor lose much of what was fairly described as his or her fear of paper.[7] More importantly, it would now be one of the basic facts of inter-war life, not only in Britain, that economic questions dominated politics and political discourse to a far greater extent than had been the case before the war. Whether in terms of currency policy or budgetary deficits, price levels or trade balances, there was a host of more or less recondite themes that increasingly demanded accessible, readily digestible presentation and explanation. Entering the 1920s, the challenge was clearly there to be met.

★

Appropriately, both papers prepared to meet this challenge under new management. In October 1919 the brothers William and Gomer Berry made an offer for the *FT* and St Clements Press that was rumoured to be in the order of £225,000, but anyway was sufficient to persuade Ellerman to sell at what was almost certainly a handsome profit. The Berry brothers (known to their staff as the 'Busy Bees', which they quite liked, or as 'Beri-Beri', which they did not) were in their way as remarkable as any of the more publicized press lords of the twentieth century. They were born in 1879 and 1883, the sons of Alderman Berry, an estate agent of Gwaelodygarth in South Wales. William, the elder brother, after a time as an apprentice journalist went to London in 1898 and, after various reporting jobs, started up on his own account in 1901 with *Advertising World*. Gomer joined him, and there began a 35-year partnership in which William tended to control the editorial side, Gomer the advertising and business management, though the lines were never hard and fast. They proceeded to acquire other periodicals, including *Boxing*, before making their first big purchase in 1915 in the form of the *Sunday Times*. After the war they forged ahead, acquiring among other papers the *Financier*. It is impossible to be sure, but the purchase of the *FT* was probably prompted at least as much by the fair prospect of St Clements Press as by the attractions of the paper itself.

The real driving force was William Berry, who was an utterly capable operator, dedicated equally to the craft of journalism and the business of newspapers. He is described by one biographer as 'a tall, handsome, elegant man with a distinguished bearing and a quietly genial, but decisive manner'; according to a rival proprietor, 'he was that rare being: an imaginative Celt without nerves'.[8] Now, in charge of the *FT*, William Berry became chairman, Gomer Berry vice-chairman, and for the day-to-day running of the paper they brought in the experienced R. J. ('Bob') Barrett as managing director and managing editor, though C. H. Palmer remained acting editor. Barrett had worked for the *FT* as a young reporter as well as travelling extensively and acting as special correspondent in several countries for other papers. In 1900 he became editor of the *Financier*, at about the time of its merger with the weekly *Bullionist*, and did much to revitalize that pioneer financial daily. Though now in his late fifties, Barrett dominated the life of the *FT* over most of the next two decades and ensured that the considerable inheritance bequeathed by MacRae and the Bridgewaters was not squandered. A man of great energy, whose head undoubtedly ruled his heart, he could be trusted by the brothers to do a sound, professional job.

At the *FN* the change of ownership seems, at the last, to have been surprisingly smooth for that paper. As far as one can tell, what happened was that when the Marks estate was sold in 1919 a large number of ordinary and preference shares in the company were bought cheap by John Jarvis, who at this point or soon afterwards attained a position of numerical 'control' and in July 1920 took a seat on the board. Flower remained chairman until his death in 1926, but from 1920 the ultimate say-so appears to have rested with Jarvis. Irritatingly little is known about him, apart from the bare facts that he was born in 1876, was obviously wealthy and was associated with other business interests apart from the *FN*; during the war he had enjoyed 'a fairly wide reputation as a financial expert', so that 'the government continued to seek his advice on financial problems after the war'.[9] In later life, after ending his connection with the paper, he became Conservative MP for Guildford in 1935 and was the initiator of the Surrey Scheme to Help the Distressed Area of Jarrow. He was an able, conscientious proprietor of the *FN* and took a fairly close interest in its affairs.

The question of the editorship was an altogether bumpier matter. In May 1920 the board decided that enough was enough and unanimously carried the resoultion 'that the directors are not prepared to renew the agreement between the company and Dr Powell, in view of the continued introduction of political criticisms and comments which are inconsistent with the interests of a financial newspaper'. Powell received 500 guineas, and the hope was expressed that he would continue to contribute to the paper, though he seems to have declined to do so. He lived only to 1922. On 22 May that year he chaired a meeting at the Queen's Hall on psychic phenomena, expressing the hope that at the next meeting, in the autumn, he would be able 'to offer to those present a direct address, audible throughout the hall, from one or more spirit voices'; but on the 30th he was taken ill while addressing a meeting of the National Citizens' Union at Cirencester and died two days later.

The new editor of the *FN* from December 1920 was H. C. O'Neill, who had been on the staff of the *Daily Mail* before the war, but only for two years, before becoming editor and literary adviser to the publishers Messrs Jack in 1910. For them he 'projected and edited *The People's Books, The New Encyclopaedia, The Nations' Histories*, etc.', as his *Who's Who* entry put it; while from 1916 to 1918 he 'projected and wrote the *History of the War* for the Foreign Office Department of Information, published month by month in French, German, Dutch, Danish, Norwegian, and Swedish'. After the war he worked as a clerk in the Foreign Office, until he was enticed to Queen Victoria Street. Though obviously a fluent writer and possessing wide general knowledge, he was not a trained newspaperman, least of all in the realm of financial journalism, and it was not a happy appointment. But to judge by O'Neill's hurt letter to Flower after the board had decided as early as March 1921 to end his engagement, it cannot have been an easy post to take up:

When I took control you suggested that the assistant editor [Doman] should take a fortnight's leave. This would, of course, have been a prudent course if there had been an adequate staff without him. Unfortunately, there was not. Mr Roberts had given notice to terminate his engagement, and Mr Pritchard actually left two nights after I arrived. Mr Culmer came on the following Monday and as he could not do the stock markets I had to ask Mr Roberts to do that work while Mr Culmer acted in the position for which he had been selected. Pray notice that for the fortnight Mr Doman was absent I had to depend on Mr Culmer whom I speedily found to be quite unreliable, and Mr Kelley a comparative beginner.

When Mr Doman returned, Mr Green had to stay away for a fortnight. Thus I was for a further fortnight thrown upon Mr Culmer's services without any help from Mr Doman.

Towards the end of January I heard that 'Midas Minor' was unwilling to continue his work and I was thus compelled to seek for two substitutes. Mr Roberts who was leaving with a grievance bacame openly recalcitrant and I had to put Mr Culmer on to the stock markets. For three weeks this meant endless care and I had then to teach Mr Kelley the same work for another two weeks. Mr Roberts only left ten days before the board came to its decision, so that for ten days only have I had the staff I should have to work with, and for a week of this time I had to supervise the work of still another new man, Dollman.

But you have decided . . .

Clearly the paper was falling apart – a sorry state typified by the decision of the veteran leader writer Croal, even before O'Neill became editor, to leave and go to work for the *FT*.

At this critical juncture the *FN* was more or less saved by the two men who from 1921 acted as joint editors for the next seven years. On 'days' was the experienced and good-natured Doman, remembered by Gertrude Bannister, who became his secretary in 1922, as 'a grave, elderly man, with a slight moustache . . . a real fixture'. In charge of night duty was a recruit in his thirties, the Scotsman William Lang, who was trained in law, had worked on a variety of provincial papers and had published in 1919 a highly praised book (*A Sea Lawyer's Log*) about his wartime experiences, besides being the author of various political and economic monographs. He had a good sense of humour beneath his Presbyterian front and was both liked and respected. Together Doman and Lang pulled the *FN* round, helped by the indomitable Woodcock as managing director, but there was much, much ground to make up.

In purely financial terms, neither paper was doing too badly at this time, largely as a result of the considerable profits reaped from the immediate post-war Stock Exchange boom. The ensuing slump of the early 1920s naturally caused a drop in revenue, but from 1923 markets and new issues began steadily to pick up again. Money remained tight through most of the 1920s, especially at the *FN*, but survival was not in doubt. From 1920 both papers sold at twopence, following steep post-war rises in the cost of labour and paper that caused the newspaper industry as a whole to raise its cover prices. One of the things that readers now got for their money was a daily front-page column written by a Stock Exchange member ('Midas' in the *FN*, 'Autolycus' in the *FT*) that, in bright, chatty form, summarized the main market happenings of the day, retailed odd titbits of House gossip and as often as not passed on a tip or two. 'Autolycus' began picking up his unconsidered trifles in April 1921 and was in fact the *nom de plume* of Walter Landells, a broker who had contributed before the war to the *Quarterly Review* and, more recently, to the *FN*. A fellow-member of the Stock Exchange recalls him as 'a birdlike little man, scuttling abstractedly about the floor, a great sheaf of papers invariably clutched beneath his arm'.[10] In his long-running column for the *FT*, he maintained a cheery outlook, talked often of 'the nimble ninepence' and firmly eschewed the scientific or analytical approach. He soon commanded a loyal and sizeable following.

The rising star in the *FN* firmament was of a quite different order. Paul Einzig was born in Transylvania in 1897, graduated from the Oriental Academy of Budapest, and arrived in London in 1919 almost penniless and completely friendless. His goal was to become a financial journalist, having briefly been one in Budapest. Despite in his first week getting an article accepted by the *Economist*, his early difficulties were acute, until in 1921 he was asked by the *FN* to be the paper's correspondent in Paris. Einzig gratefully accepted, though offered only half the salary of his predecessor, and while there completed a doctorate on French price movements since 1914. Making the most of his knowledge of foreign languages, he then successfully suggested himself for the new post of foreign editor and returned to London in 1923. Over the next few years he, in his own words, 'combined the functions of a City journalist with those of a diplomatic correspondent'; and his first big 'scoop' (forerunner of many more) came in October 1923 when he revealed Schroeders' intended acquisition of the financial control of the Anatolian Railway Company, which led to him being wrongly accused by Schroeders of having 'published a document that was practically stolen'.[11] Einzig loved ferreting out the secrets of the money world, and there was usually a solid core of truth to his findings. He also had a formidable knowledge of European monetary conditions, which in the context of the financial turbulence of inter-war Europe was invaluable to his paper. He was not an easy man to get to know, and he continued to make enemies throughout his career, but it is hard to underestimate his importance in the revival of the *FN*.

In his autobiography, Einzig recalled his early colleagues:

> When I first joined the London staff it consisted mostly of middle-aged men grown up in the service of the paper. Some of them started their careers as junior clerks on the business staff, or even as office boys, and worked their way up to comparatively senior posts, in the editorial department. They were hard-working journalists, with a thorough specialised knowledge of the routine work in their respective sections, and they were excellent fellows. But imagination was not their strong point.[12]

The same was no doubt true of the *FT*'s staff at this time – but in the case of the *FT* there existed a tried and tested formula that had won the assured allegiance of the broad middlebrow readership of the City. For the *FN*, seeking to regain a following, something new was needed.

The truth of this was shown by the respective issues of 13 February 1923. The *FN* of the day (by now merely 'the world's leading authority on finance', having been forced to drop its circulation claim) was not dissimilar to the *FT*'s issue, each being eight pages long (reflecting the continuing doldrums of the Stock Exchange) and each having plenty of facts, figures and general financial coverage. Both papers still religiously stuck to the stock markets on page one and gave very thin treatment to the non-financial world. Indeed, the *FN* possessed certain attractive features of its own: on page one a rather finely designed 'Market Barometer' showing the day's main changes, together with a full summary of contents down the left-hand side; and elsewhere a notably lively correspondence column, a detailed report from the paper's New York correspondent on 'America's Labour Shortage', and from Paris a provocative, somewhat sarcastic piece by Einzig on the French finance minister's frantic efforts to balance his budget. What the *FN* lacked by this stage, though, was not only the weight and quality of the *FT*'s advertising, but also its air of quiet confidence, of almost taking pride in producing a rather dull and worthy, albeit indispensable, paper. The main *FT* features of that day – a survey by the paper's correspondent in Montreal of 'New Canadian Water Power Developments', the report of a speech by Sir Lynden

Macassey, KC, on unemployment insurance by industries, and tabulated Australasian and miscellaneous mining returns for the second half of 1922 – were all impeccably stolid; and the principal leader offered a distinctly more thorough assessment of the Board of Trade returns for January than the *FN*'s essay on the same theme. Moreover, the *FT* now had 'Autolycus' up its sleeve, as a trump-card to appeal especially to investors who might otherwise have found the paper wholly unreadable. In addition to his regular 'Round the Markets' column, he also fielded, as he did two or three times a week, queries from correspondents:

Ucello. – 1. Keep the bonds. 2. Good stuff. 3. Think you can do better.

W.C.D., Belfast. – 1. Rather a long shot. 2. Shouldn't pick them out.

Warrior. – 1. A sporting chance. 2. Not bad; it's a gamble. 3. Camp Birds are a good speculation.

In Doubt. – Which is more than I am. Have nothing whatever to do with the outsiders whose circulars you send me.

Huile. – Keep your shares, dear sir, as you don't worry over them.

Mart. – Fully understand your frame of mind. I should cut it, feeling, however, that this would probably prove wrong.

Blue John. – Should keep the Mexicans for the time being until you see something in my column which will appeal to you more strongly.

F.H.O. – Sorry if you think I am brusque. As I said before, I find it no easy matter to combine politeness with brevity.

It was all fairly harmless and, like any good problems page, combined the qualities of being mildly therapeutic and mildly enjoyable.

A month later, in search of a fresh ploy, the *FN* board considered 'the question of substituting a tinted paper for that at present used', but the matter 'was left over for future consideration' and in the event not raised again. Instead, the board early in 1924 decided to pin its hopes on bringing in from the outside world a public personality to be editor-in-chief, someone who would add lustre and a sense of importance to the *FN* while Doman and Lang continued as joint editors to do the daily spade-work. The board's first choice, however, was at best a qualified success. Sir Laming Worthington-Evans had made his name before the war as an expert on company law, before going into politics as a Conservative. He had been Secretary of State for War from 1921 to 1922 and Postmaster-General from 1923 to 1924. Now, temporarily out of office, he accepted a salary of £2,500 in order to, in Flower's inviting words, 'undertake the general direction of the editorial management of the paper, contribute to its columns under your own name, and otherwise as the occasion warrants, and with the joint editors, arrange daily for the production of the editorial matter and news'. Flower referred tactfully to 'the claims of your Parliamentary duties', adding that 'the actual preparation of editorial matter for the press must be undertaken by the joint editors under your instructions'. Worthington-Evans was a tall and impressive figure, with a fair knowledge of finance and a particular fondness for the tea share market, but as a newspaper editor his habit of delegating almost everything was summed up in his favourite phrase, 'Oh, oh – I'll leave that for the butler.' Einzig was not impressed:

> Actually he spent very little time at the *Financial News*. The occasional articles that appeared under his signature were written by Lang. Even when the editor-in-chief put in his appearance at Queen Victoria Street he spent most of his time on his political work. One day when I entered his room I found him dictating his speech to his private secretary. He was facing the big mirror over the mantelpiece and was addressing himself as his own audience. We got on reasonably well, but I did not care for his sarcasm and was not sorry when he rejoined the government after the Conservative victory in [October] 1924.[13]

Meanwhile, the *FT* in 1924 was appointing a distinctly 'efficient' (as opposed to 'dignified') editor in place of the retiring Palmer. This was 'an old-fashioned Scottish journalist', as his successor was to call him, in the person of D. S. T. ('Dusty') Hunter. As a young man he had been briefly on the staff before returning in 1920 as news editor. He was now in his fifties and had spent half a lifetime in financial journalism, but his place was strictly below Barrett, and he was not a member of the board. The *FT* also at this time took over and incorporated the *Financier*, the other less successful financial daily in the Berry stable. In a speech to *FT* shareholders in May 1924, Sir William Berry spoke of 'the great advantages of thus removing a competitor and thus being able to substantially advance advertising rates'.[14] In its final issue the *Financier* bravely claimed that within the *FT* there would be retained for its loyal readers 'the exceptionally complete service of rubber information, the exposition of company law and practice appearing under our "Secretaries' Column", and the well-informed supply of Empire intelligence', but basically what happened was that the *FT* swallowed the older paper up and in so doing ominously reduced the field of financial dailies to two.[15]

Undeterred by the brief duration and patchy performance of the Worthington-Evans experiment, the *FN* board early in 1925 recruited as its new editor-in-chief someone who had proposed marriage to Virginia Woolf, enjoyed regular correspondence with E. M. Forster and was now the husband of the widow of Scott of the Antarctic. A prominent figure in his day, if now almost entirely forgotten, Edward Hilton Young had been City editor of the *Morning Post* before the war and wrote a study of *The System of National Finance* (1915) that remained the standard text until 1939. His war service had been immensely distinguished, culminating in 1918 when he lost his right arm during the blocking of Zeebrugge. Since 1915 he had been, with a brief interruption, Liberal MP for Norwich and from 1921 to 1922 he was Financial Secretary to the Treasury. The First World War had converted Hilton Young to Spinozan pantheism, and by temperament he was, according to his son, 'quizzical and rather reserved'.[16] Desmond MacCarthy, in a famous phrase, called him 'the sphinx without a secret'.[17] The journalist Collin Brooks met him at Leeds in 1927 and found him to be like 'some actor-manager's conception of Nelson': 'He wears the empty sleeve pinned to his breast and his figure is small and slight. Speaking he wears a gold-rimmed monocle, and his manner is clipped, and even a little stilted. He gives the impression of enormous self-conceit and superiority, but improves after a few minutes of acquaintance.' Brooks subsequently joined the staff of the *FN* and, though still finding Hilton Young 'reserved and "quarter-deck"', grew increasingly attached to him, so that by 1929 he was confiding in his diary: 'Dear man! He has been faithful and just to me, and a great inspiration.'[18]

The hard-to-please Einzig was another fan of the new editor-in-chief:

> He always encouraged all of us to make suggestions. The way he received them made us feel that we were collaborating in running the paper, instead of merely working on one section of it in a subordinate capacity. Under the stimulating effect of his attitude I was very fertile in ideas during that period. I went to see him in his room every morning and he usually greeted me with these words: 'Hallo, Einstein, what is today's crop of ideas?'
>
> He arrived very early every morning – I always found his chauffeur-driven Austen Seven parked in front of the office when I arrived. His first task was to send out chits to members of the staff who had contributed something of interest to the current issue. In a very few words he conveyed a great deal – criticism, suggestions, praise, encouragement. This system enabled us to know from day to day exactly how we stood with him. When he was dissatisfied he said so in no uncertain terms, and that was the end of the matter. He never brought up the subject again.[19]

The one big snag with Hilton Young's reign was that he was constantly going abroad on lengthy trips, whether as British delegate to the League of Nations, or chairing a royal commission to inquire into the condition of the finances of India, or leading a mission at the Prime Minister's request to prepare a scheme for the federation of the East African colonies.

He also had his commitment to domestic politics, which seems to have increased after 1926 when he crossed the floor to join the Conservative ranks. Yet the fact was that, on the basis of half a day's work whenever he was in town, he, in Einzig's words, 'improved the *Financial News* beyond recognition and greatly increased its standing and influence in the City'.[20] Hilton Young himself, in an unpublished autobiography mostly written in 1959, explained his secret, apart from the man management testified to by Brooks and Einzig:

The *Financial News* was free [i.e. of particular interests], and it had an able and strenuous staff of assistant editors, of specialists for the markets, and of market reporters. So it was a pleasure to work for it. With their skilled knowledge we gave the paper a more readable form. When that was done, and the services of news amplified, it seemed that the chief thing left to do was to increase the interest and utility of all the information which we provided by articles summarising and analysing the economic tendencies of the day. To write these I recruited a series of young economists from the universities. It is pleasant to recall their names, and present occupations: Geoffrey Eley, chairman of Richard Thomas and Baldwin (*inter alia*), and a director of the Bank of England; C. I. Carr Bosenquet, rector of King's College, Newcastle, and vice-chancellor of Durham University; Lucius Thompson-McCausland, adviser to the governor of the Bank of England; Francis Whitmore, City editor of the *Daily Telegraph*; and, later, Maurice Green, assistant editor of *The Times*.[21]

The systematic recruitment of bright young things was to be a key to the latter-day success and expansion of the modern, post-merger *FT*. In a very real sense the pattern began with the man whom Miss Stephen rejected.

Through the 1920s the financial press treated questions of how to revive the British economy and how to restore (and keep restored) the pre-1914 financial system as one and the same, with rarely if ever a suggestion that there might be a conflict between the two. Parsimony and still more parsimony on the part of government was the reiterated theme, with just the occasional variation. Thus in December 1920 the *FT* gave its full backing to what it called 'the movement for a rigid and relentless economy', reinforced a few days later by a major article entitled 'The Orgy of National Extravagance'. In January 1922 the *FN* poured scorn on the trade-union remedy for unemployment, that the government should employ labour at times when trade requirements were low; but in October that year an *FN* leader on 'The Alternative to the Dole' did argue in connection with road-building programmes that 'it is cheaper to pay wages in return for useful work than to pay doles in return for nothing'. A few weeks later Lloyd George's coalition fell, and the *FN* elucidated 'What the City Wants' from the Bonar Law ministry: 'The great responsibility of the new government is to effect drastic, yet sound, economy, the conservation of national and imperial resources, and the diminution of our international commitments.' It went on: 'As we have said on many previous occasions, the greatest social reform this country could seek is a policy of national economy which would render possible a substantial reduction of taxation.' After referring to the 'crushing burden' laid by taxation upon industry, the leader concluded by asserting that 'the City expects that the new government will waste no time upon specious and ill-founded proposals for the reduction of the war debt by means of a capital levy'.

All the time the deflationary policy of successive governments in the early 1920s, including the brief Labour minority of 1924, was working towards the long-awaited return to the gold standard. For almost everyone in the City and the Treasury the question was not whether Britain should return but simply when. At last, in April 1925, in Churchill's first Budget, it happened. 'A real stride towards world recovery', was the verdict of the *FN*, while the *FT* described the decision to return and thereby restore the free gold market as 'the best thing that could have happened in the interests of British credit and prestige'. In neither optimistic assessment was there a hint that the return to gold, epecially at the old pre-war parity of $4.86 to the pound, might further damage Britain's already battered export industries, above all coal. Hilton Young himself was in increasingly close and sympathetic contact with the governor of the Bank of England, the legendary Montagu Norman. On 1 October 1925 he asked to see him: 'I am puzzled by the BR [Bank Rate] decision: and I want to keep public opinion straight about it, as far as the *FN* can.' Norman's diary for that day had the entry for 1.30: 'Hilton Young – as *Financial News* Editor – enquires as to BR & conditions wh. I explain privately but fully.'[22] Meanwhile, for the rest of the decade the chorus continued. 'It is gratifying to the City to note that the Chancellor of the Exchequer has been making public economy the text of his speeches,' began an *FN* leader in October 1927, and so it went on. Einzig in his memoirs recalled how 'during the twenties and early thirties, when hardly any financial editor had a good word for Keynes or for the policies he was advocating, he probably received more support from me than from the rest of the financial press put together', adding that 'having been allowed a fairly free hand in my column, I managed from time to time to get in a word of support for his ideas, even though this was not in accordance with the editorial policy of the *Financial News*'.[23] The exaggeration was probably only slight; deflation was the ruling orthodoxy of the day, and to its crushing weight the *FN* and *FT* lent their full share of support.

Towards the bitter industrial relations of this period, the natural instincts of both papers were predictable. 'Lawless "Labour" on Top' was the *FN* headline for a strong attack by W. R. Lawson in 1919 on the syndicalists of South Wales. The widespread strife and unrest, above all in the coal-fields, culminated in the General Strike of May 1926, when the TUC supported the miners in their resistance against a further reduction of wages. On the last day of peace, the 3rd, the *FT*'s leader, 'An Assault on the Community', accused the coal-miners of 'attempting to hold the nation to ransom' and being 'completely indifferent on whose shoulders the burden is thrown, and what the toll of monetary loss, physical suffering, and industrial stagnation may be'. In the *FN* there was a signed piece on 'The Crisis' by Hilton Young:

> Law and order must be supported with the whole force of public opinion. There are constitutional methods of redress for grievances, by negotiation and in Parliament. The sympathetic strike with which the country is now threatened is an unconstitutional method . . . At the last hour saner counsels may prevail. But if a season of great trouble comes, it is well to remember that men of good will need not, and should not, accept the issue of a class-war, which it is the object of the anti-social forces to promote. To approach the struggle as if it necessarily involved a fight between classes would be to play into the hands of the followers of Karl Marx. The issue is between the whole community and a misguided minority . . . The public interest has to be maintained; and ultimately it cannot be maintained by any settlement that leaves the coalmines on an uneconomic footing, and a charge upon the public purse.

Doman of the *FN* later recalled what happened next:

> The printers 'played the game' right well up to the minute at which they were under orders to quit. They did their work as usual in the production of the paper in the time available to them. Inside the printing works the hum of machinery went on, and outside the newspaper motor vans were carrying on as usual. And then the clocks chimed, or pointed the hour of midnight; the noise and bustle ceased as if by magic; in their place there came a silence, grim and impressive – a silence that anyone who experienced it will never forget. Conversation was carried on in whispers; everyone seemed stunned at the dramatic change that had suddenly sapped the energy and good will of men. The Great Strike had begun.[24]

The next morning, the 4th, saw a normal, eight-page *FN*, including another signed letter by Hilton Young, entitled 'Hold Fast, John Bull!'

But from the 5th to the 11th the *FN* was reduced to a duplicated circular of a few pages that was sent out to subscribers and summarized the main strike and market news. The management then discovered a small printing office where, according to Doman, 'the typesetting and reading were done entirely by women'; and from there, from the 12th to the 17th, small printed issues were produced, though still without any advertisements. Finally, on the 18th, six days after the strike had ended, it was back to normal with a sixteen-page issue printed at the Argus Press.

Over the same period the *FT* was similarly reduced to smaller-format four-page issues, but its claim to fame was that it was, in its own words, 'the only newspaper produced in something resembling normal form daily throughout the great strike', albeit on white paper up to the 13th. The man primarily responsible for this achievement was Barrett, who as the strike began reached an arrangement with a non-unionized printing firm in the suburbs to produce the paper. Copy was taken from Coleman Street to the print works by a corps of motor-cyclists, including members of the editorial staff, while distribution relied heavily on a fleet of fast motor cars hired by Barrett. The managing director's triumph was particularly great on the 5th, when the *FT* appeared in printed form by breakfast, hours before any other paper, most of which were in typescript when they did come out. 'A great epitaph for any journalist,' remarked the *FT* after Barrett's death in 1942.[25] For a just and considered epitaph by the financial press on the strike itself, one has to look to 'Midas' of the *FN*: 'When the TUC and NUR got a reverse they CUT and RUN.'

Shortly before the balloon went up, Hilton Young wrote to his wife in April 1926: 'I am at the House, getting through the division lobby. This has been just a normal day's work: many letters, newspaper, which is very good just now, and lastly House.' The *FN* was indeed picking up at this time, helped by a lighter, more attractive layout. Now and over the next year or two, several new features were added: on Mondays, a column of 'Amusement Notes'; on Tuesdays, 'Company Law Notes'; on Wednesdays, a humorous miscellany by 'Gog McGog'; on Thursdays, 'Scottish Affairs'; on Fridays, 'Industrial Securities', focusing each week on a particular type; and on Saturdays, not only a 'Small Investor's Guide' but also a rather fine weekly 'Portrait Gallery' from the skilful hand of 'Ginsbury'. General coverage of the economy improved greatly, with at least one major series investigating the state of the country's trade and industry. The new Oxbridge recruits gradually added a more penetrating quality to the paper's analysis. Above all, there was Einzig, who on 23 June 1926 initiated his famous 'Lombard Street' column, complete with phone number (City: 6830) at the top of it. There was apparently much agonized discussion as to what the column should be called, but in the end the name of Walter Bagehot's renowed study of the City was deemed worthy. It was run by Einzig at first in collaboration with other members of the staff, but after a few years became his sole responsibility. Each day he surveyed the money markets of London and abroad, revealed what secrets he had been able to uncover and rode his particular hobby-horses for all they were worth and more. In the early years of the column, he waged two especially forceful campaigns – one against allowing further German flotations abroad until the reparations issue was settled, the other attacking the Bank of France for using its large sterling balances to apply political pressure on Britain. Soon, whatever City people and others thought of him and his causes, he had to be read. When he fell ill early in 1927, Hilton Young, aware of what an asset he had, wrote to Einzig most solicitously (and characteristically):

> Take a good holiday with a clear mind and no worries. You have been overworking and doing without a holiday too long. You needn't worry the least about your work lately. There has been nothing the matter with it.
>
> Tell me if Brighton is too noisy for you at first and if you want a quiet place; I could put you in the way of one.[26]

One should not exaggerate the progress of the *FN* under Hilton Young's stewardship. Though much less venal than it had been during the Marks era and indeed thereafter, it still retained an unhealthily strong 'tipster' element, epitomized by the column 'On Swings and Roundabouts' by 'El Dorado' on Tuesdays, or the Saturday column by 'Denarius'. The latter's contribution on 1 October 1927 included a humorous interjection: 'I had a real bit of bad luck last week in that a par. on Phillips Rubber Soles got squeezed out. (Unfortunately, our columns are not elastic. – ED) It was a strong recommendation to buy around 39*s*. Of course, in the very cussedness of things they went up and have been 46*s*.' Nor in other respects had the paper advanced so much. On 24 May 1928 the leader on 'Empire Day' concluded in tones redolent of none so much as Powell and Morgan:

> The people of this country, the founders of Empire, possess qualities of character, powers of organisation, that are necessary to the world's progress, and that we cannot refuse without being untrue to ourselves to accept the task which has been entrusted to us guiding those still in relatively early stages of mental and social development towards true civilisation.

Meanwhile, the paper that according to an eyewitness was always on the *FN* editor's desk continued to evolve very slowly, but always within a well-defined, unshakable pattern. Various features strike the eye from a sampling of the *FT* during the second half of the 1920s: at least once a week a column entitled 'Analyses of Potential Investments', examining a handful of specific companies, though usually in a rather bland way; in 1925 a series of Saturday crossword puzzles, offering for the first six correct solutions 'the choice of either a Dunhill Standard £1.1*s*. pipe or a cabinet of 300 Abdulla No. 75 superb Virginia cigarettes', with in addition 'two special prizes for Eve, consisting of 6-lb. boxes of Cadbury's chocolates'; a long-running column by John Phillimore on 'Motoring for the Owner-Driver'; in October 1927 a lengthy report on the London Stock Exchange's 3–2 win at soccer over the Liverpool Stock Exchange; and on the same day, in 'Round the Theatres', a brief review of Noël Coward's *Home Chat*, including the crisp comment that 'when the curtain fell at 10.30 p.m. the hour seemed later'. 'Autolycus' continued to dispense advice, as in, again, October 1927 to 'Boswell': 'If you sold 100 of your shares, the remainder would stand you in at about 9*s*. and put you very much on velvet. Nevertheless, I should feel inclined to tempt financial providence and run the whole profit still further.' In February 1928 the paper began a long series of 'Appreciations of Modern Architecture' (such as the new Carreras factory at Mornington Crescent) that over the years brought in a lot of accompanying advertising. The series, later called 'Architecture To-Day', was the brain-child of a schoolmaster called Charles Pughe Morgan. He had had the idea walking down Regent Street one day, sold it to the *FT* and forthwith gave up his profession. Thereafter he was responsible for choosing the subjects and securing the advertising; up to the war an ecclesiastical friend supplied the editorial matter.

Two *FT* contributors were becoming particularly important. One was Norman Crump, who had been the paper's statistical correspondent since 1921, in which year he had successfully started the *FT*'s commodity price index. Now, in January 1927, he began the *Financial Times* Weekly Index of Industrial Stocks, whose special feature was that 'the calculations are confined to the most active shares of each week, and so an attempt is made to measure that elusive entity, Stock Exchange sentiment'. In fact, Einzig four years earlier had begun an 'Index Number of Stock Exchange Prices' for the *FN*, but 'it was discontinued, after a while, because there was nobody else to do the routine work and I was too busy with other matters'.[27] Crump's statistics, however, were a permanent feature, and by 1928 he was publishing in the *FT* weekly stock indices for no less than seven categories, of which home industrials was only one. Altogether his work represented an important development, though the ancestor of the modern *FT* Index awaited the *FN* in the 1930s. The other emerging contributor was the portly D. Wylie King, who had joined the *FT* in 1899, become mining editor in 1920 and from 1928 was 'The Diarist' on page one, writing 'An Investor's Note-Book', which, in addition to the usual formula of market chat and tips, offered a fair amount of genuine objective analysis, especially in the way of dissecting company reports and balance sheets.

Whether in terms of commenting on new issues (usually favourably), or of general editorializing, the *FT* at this stage was still a critical match for the *FN*. The day of the official opening of Lloyd's new building in Leadenhall Street – 24 March 1928, after more than a century and a half at the Royal Exchange – was not untypical. The *FN*'s leader to mark the occasion was anodyne in the extreme ('Everywhere its name stands for security and integrity . . . Wherever it is housed, Lloyd's will carry with it noble traditions'), whereas the *FT*, while not denying that 'Lloyd's performs functions indispensable to the functions of oversea trade', argued forcibly that in recent years underwriters had 'exhibited hesitancy in condemning the opening for fraud inseparable from the use of letters of indemnity in conjunction with inaccurate bills of lading' and had also 'failed to secure the lead in international action'. The real gap in editorial quality had yet to open up between the two papers.

These were prosperous years for the *FT*, as the stock market gathered momentum and headed towards another boom. In July 1926 the company paid a dividend on its ordinary shares of 12½ per cent, in July 1927 20 per cent. The Berry brothers took advantage of the situation to liquidate the existing company and establish in its place the Financial Times (1928) Ltd, in the process issuing for cash one million 7 per cent cumulative preference shares of £1 each. The issue was made in January 1928 and was considerably oversubscribed, leading to more than 8,000 new *FT* shareholders. In terms of voting, however, the Berry brothers maintained through the ordinary shares a controlling interest in the new company. At the statutory meeting in May 1928, Sir William Berry (he had been knighted in 1921 and was to become First Baron Camrose of Long Cross, Surrey, in 1929) was in confident vein. He stated that the *FT* enjoyed a circulation 'far more than double that of any other financial daily newspaper in this country'; he provided figures to show that in the first four months of the year the *FT* had outstripped all papers in volume of prospectus and company-meeting advertising; and he referred proudly to the *FT*'s 'large staff of experts in all the various markets' who in the course of a year were accustomed to answering by post more than 50,000 separate investment inquiries.[28]

As to what life was like in 72 Coleman Street at this time – the flesh behind the bare bones of Berry's speech – there are enough survivors from the late 1920s and soon after to give some idea. The total strength on the pay-roll was just under a hundred (of whom only a handful were women), ranging from Barrett as managing director on a salary of £5,000 a year through to Hunter the editor on £1,650 plus £100 for expenses down to the messenger boys on appreciably less than a pound a week. Barrett, who ran 'a tight ship', is remembered not particularly fondly as someone who was conscious of his small height, somewhat pompous and rather short-tempered. He had a private secretary, C. J. Newland, whom he treated fairly roughly, and Newland in turn employed an assistant who was responsible, among other things, for making sure that Barrett's fire was kept alight, helping him to dress before going out to functions and typing the copy for the City article that appeared under Barrett's name in the *Sunday Times*. Barrett and the 'hard-swearing, hard-cursing' Hunter felt little love for each other and were often at loggerheads, constantly going backwards and forwards to and from each other's offices, which were on the second floor and separated by a partition. Barrett arranged the telephone booth in his room in such a way that Hunter would be unable to hear what he was saying. Even more omnipresent than these two was the veteran company secretary, the bushy-moustached H. A. Randall, who dominated the first floor (advertising and accounts) and was an old-fashioned martinet, especially about noise, coming down particularly hard on Fridays when the cashier paid out the wages to the weekly staff. Of the advertising men, the one who is remembered best is F. S. ('Klondyke') Clark, who was the company-meetings canvasser, dressed in a frock coat and always wore gold about his person. Upstairs, where the editorial staff resided, Wylie King was a stimulating presence, as was the charming Graham Hill, the news editor, but perhaps the man who increasingly held things together there was the solid and dependable A. G. Cole, who had joined the paper in 1912 and had a wooden leg as a result of the war. In many ways, he embodied the abiding *FT* virtues of continuity and anonymity.

Coleman Street, however, was not the only place where the *FT* was assembled daily. John Hay joined the staff in 1934, and his description of working at the cavernous St Clements Press is probably broadly applicable to a few years earlier:

Our night sub-editorial office was on the first floor, along a corridor which we christened the 'submarine', as at ceiling level there were innumerable pipes and wires festooned along it. In those days there was no night editor and the man of last resort was the chief sub-editor. Philip Capon [who already held the post in the late twenties] was a portly man, capable, and he wrote with a dip pen and a large inkwell. The scratch of the nib was clearly heard above the hubbub, and it was said there was only one 'comp' who could decipher it and put it into hot metal. He spoke to the editor by telephone after the first edition was sent by motor-cycle messenger from St Clements to the editor's house, and the Owl and Waverley nib would scratch again all over the front page at instructions to move this story, add to that one, and who did column four? Change the heading!

We had a wonderful copy-carrying contraption, an endless rope winding its way along above our desks and going up through a hole in the ceiling to the floor above. If you wanted a proof you wrote 'Proof, please, of . . .' and put the piece of paper in the machine in front of you, which snapped it up as one of the 'hands' went past you and delivered it to the printer. Eventually a proof would come down and as the claw of the hand opened in front of you you got your proof. Each claw (there were about four) was slightly different so that it opened at the appropriate place.

There were about ten of us as subs and juniors, and in those days we had two PA machines, one Reuter, one parliamentary. I was a verbatim shorthand writer, and one of my jobs was to take fixed-time telephone calls each evening from three continental centres – Amsterdam, Paris, and Berlin. We had short news stories dictated to us which had to be transcribed quickly, and were orientated towards the *FT*'s financial news requirements as distinct from the general service of Reuters. One recurring theme at very short intervals was the almost weekly collapse of the French government and the interminable wranglings to get a new one.

It is a long way from inkwells to direct input, but the painstaking essence of daily journalism remains the same and is well caught in Hay's account,

During the second half of the 1920s, however, it was at the *FN* that momentous stirrings were taking place. In 1926 control of the paper changed hands once again, when the Trireme Trust, owners of the *Morning Post*, bought the *FN* from Jarvis primarily in order to acquire its printing subsidiary, the Argus Press. Jarvis (who had succeeded Flower earlier in 1926) remained chairman of the FN Ltd, while Lieutenant -Colonel Ivor Fraser, general manager of the *Morning Post*, took a seat on the board. The Trireme Trust felt little commitment to the *FN* itself and had nothing to do with the editorial side of the paper. By early 1928, as the losses of the *Morning Post* continued to drain capital, the Trust decided to sell the *FN*, while holding on to the Argus Press. For a time it seemed that the financier Colonel Grant-Morden, MP, was going to buy the paper, but negotiations hung fire. At this point, with the future ownership of the *FN* in the balance, Einzig intervened decisively. For the previous year or so, in addition to his zealous work for the *FN*, he had been acting as foreign editor of the *Banker*. This was a magazine recently founded by Brendan Bracken, the rapidly emerging entrepreneur, on behalf of the printers and publishers Eyre & Spottiswoode. Now, unhappy about the prospect of Grant-Morden taking over the *FN*, Einzig told Bracken that the paper was for sale and urged him to persuade the board of Eyre & Spottiswoode to buy it. This Bracken managed to do with some difficulty, thanks largely to the enthusiasm expressed for the venture by Major Simon Crosthwaite-Eyre's wife, Dorothy. Einzig himself tells the rest of the story:

> There followed a period of protracted negotiations during the course of which I acted as adviser to Bracken. He discussed with me at great length every phase of the bargaining. Unfortunately he was quite obviously even keener to buy than the proprietors were to sell. As a result the Trireme Trust raised its selling price in stages week after week. It was a period of Stock Exchange boom when a financial newspaper was bound to be coining money. Both prospective vendor and prospective purchaser were inclined to judge the value of the property from the figures of current profits without regard to the fact that in the not so distant past the *Financial News* went through very lean periods – an experience that was liable to repeat itself sooner or later. The price asked for was becoming increasingly unrealistic, but by then Bracken became so keen on it that he simply could not back out. So the deal was concluded.[29]

The eventual price (without the Argus Press) was £280,000. On 11 June 1928 Bracken was elected to the *FN* board and on 5 July he replaced Jarvis as chairman. The winds of change had arrived.

[FOUR]

THE BRACKEN YEARS 1928–45

'The impression that remains is of a gross Philistine with a buttonholing hail-fellow-well-met manner who might have been effective as a tough guy on the stage or screen.'[1] The person who laid the foundations of the modern, post-war *FT* was never everyone's cup of tea, least of all the aesthete Harold Acton's. Nor, in his complex and often contradictory character, has Brendan Bracken proved an easy subject for the historian or biographer, especially since he instructed all his papers to be burnt after his death. The main outline, however, is now reasonably clear, as (deliberately) it never was in his lifetime. He was born in North Tipperary in 1901, the son of a well-to-do sculptor and builder, and after a turbulent childhood was sent to Australia at the age of fifteen to make good. There he travelled around, took all sorts of temporary jobs and returned to Ireland after three years. He soon crossed the Irish Sea and, after saving some money, took the remarkable step of going for a term, at the age of nineteen and a half, to the public school Sedbergh. There followed, after a brief spell as a (possibly sadistic) teacher at a prep school, an equally astonishing sequence of events. In the summer of 1922 he got to know J. L. Garvin, celebrated editor of the *Observer*, and at Garvin's the following January for the first time met Churchill, whose wholly devoted subordinate he became almost at once, much to the irritation of Clemmie Churchill. Also in 1923 he was introduced to Major J. S. Crosthwaite-Eyre, who, seeking to inject fresh talent and energy into the rather moribund activities of the family firm, asked Bracken to take over the editorship of the monthly *Illustrated Review*, soon afterwards renamed *English Life*. Over the next three years Bracken ran the magazine with great verve and gusto (though at a loss) until it was sold in 1926; founded the *Banker* after discovering that banking was the only trade or profession without its own specialist organ; and was elected to the Eyre & Spottiswoode board. He acquired a house in North Street (later Lord North Street), a wide circle of acquaintances and a buff-coloured Hispano-Suiza with blue carriage-lamps. In 1928 he also acquired, on behalf of Eyre & Spottiswoode, a by now rather venerable financial daily.

The new proprietor of the *FN* made a striking figure: twenty-seven years old, tall, well built, spectacled, with a pale complexion, blackened teeth (the result of sepsis), rather simian features and a shock of flaming-red hair. He had already accumulated a mass of information about many diverse subjects, ranging from English poetry to memorized lists of bishops and public-school headmasters, but curiously one area where he remained somewhat ignorant, at least for a long time, was finance itself. Above all he seems to have been possessed as a young man of enormous drive and energy, the gift of eloquence and a limitless self-belief in his worldly capacities. Oscar Hobson, City editor of the *Manchester Guardian* at the time, came into Bracken's orbit from 1926 and later recalled him as someone who was 'then "on the make", employing all his talents, his charm, his brilliance, his persistence, his ingenuity in seeking the acquaintance of the notabilities of the political and newspaper worlds'.[2] The best portrait of the Bracken of this formative period comes, however, from Einzig, who was in close contact with him on first the *Banker* and then the *FN* and was a perceptive if sometimes sentimental witness. After referring to Bracken's 'enviable overdose of self-assurance', his 'talent for infuriating and antagonising people', his 'brilliant' conversation, his 'flair for eliciting from people the information he was interested in' and his 'amazingly quick brain', Einzig went on:

> His basic quality was his immense kindness and his desire to help, not only his friends but even people whom he had only known casually. It was my impression that he derived great satisfaction from the feeling of possessing the brains and influence that made it possible to help others. But it would be much less than fair to suggest that this feeling of power was the only reason, or even the main reason, why he often went out of his way to help others. His kindness was very genuine.
>
> On the other hand, when he was annoyed his sarcasm could be absolutely devastating. He seldom lost his temper – at any rate during the early phase when I was in close contact with him – but when he did the target of his scorn was anything but enviable. And even what he said in a deliberately quiet tone could pulverise his victim very effectively. Quite unexpectedly he would do one a good turn, some major favour that was liable to affect the course of one's whole life. But anybody who felt rightly or wrongly that Bracken was under some obligation to do something for him and claimed it as his right was apt to get very little satisfaction out of him.[3]

Bracken's character has amply realized its potential for being the subject of endless psychological analysis, but two particular biographical snippets are immensely suggestive. One is the fact that, of the few books he brought back with him from Australia, one was a copy of J. A. Froude's life of Benjamin Disraeli. It is hard not to feel that there was a strong adolescent identity with the outsider who rose to the top in Victorian England. The other occurred later, in 1937, when he was on holiday in France with Lady Diana Cooper and others. One afternoon everyone in the party went bathing except Bracken, who declined to. Very early the next morning, before anyone would normally have been up, he was spotted bathing on his own. It is this sort of story that Lysaght (the pick of his biographers) has in mind when he writes of 'the coming man' and his lack of close friends:

> He had no desire to allow anyone into his confidence, to see beyond the façade he chose to present to the world. Beneath his confident and reckless manner, he concealed a sensitive and vulnerable inner self. He was plainly very conscious of the impression of ugliness made by his bizarre colouring and found it difficult to come to terms with such an imperfection. Eventually, as if from habit, an inescapable inner reticence and reserve became ingrained at the very core of his nature and grew to encase him. Perhaps for this reason rather than any other, he shied away from the prospect of marriage or even female companionship.[4]

It has often been claimed that Bracken was the original for the character of Rex Mottram in Evelyn Waugh's *Brideshead Revisited*. It is unlikely that Waugh knew Bracken well, but certainly the prototype was far more interesting, far more 'rounded' than that ultimate hollow man of twentieth-century fiction.

The new regime began at the *FN* at a time when the Stock Exchange boom of 1928 in industrial shares and new issues, continuing through into 1929, was at its height. The financial press prospered accordingly, as reflected by the value of shares in the *FN*. Soon after the war Jarvis had acquired his controlling interest through buying them at 6*s*. a share; in 1926 he had sold out to the Trireme Trust at £5 a share; and now, by the time Bracken concluded negotiations, they were worth £9 each. In October 1928 the company paid on its ordinary shares an interim dividend of 25 per cent and a special dividend of 50 per cent; and for the first half of 1929 the paper's profits of £56,000 were even more than the previous year's handsome returns. The *FT* did equally well. On 1 November 1928 the paper announced that a record number of prospectuses (eighty-nine) had appeared in its pages during the previous month; and for 1928 as a whole a record profit of £191,000 was announced – though, significantly in these intoxicating times, a much more conservative dividends policy was pursued by Berry than by Bracken. For both papers it was advertising that primarily provided this influx of riches, but at last for the *FT* we have audited circulation figures, showing that in both 1928 and 1929 its average daily net sale was more than 31,000 copies.

Issue sizes naturally expanded – in the week beginning 5 November 1928 the *FT* totalled eighty-two pages, the *FN* eight less – and new features bloomed. To complement the continuing international banking supplements, the *FT*'s main innovation, from 1927, was a half-yearly 32-page supplement on the resources of Canada, which, according to Camrose in 1930, did much to provide 'a clearer perception than there was of the Dominion's assured greatness'.[5] As for the *FN*, a glance at its pages by the autumn of 1929 shows the extent to which new management was shaking things up: a full page was now devoted to American markets, including a more comprehensive list of share prices on Wall Street, and there was a new correspondent in New York in the person of Professor H. Parker Willis, former Secretary of the Federal Reserve Board; each Saturday there were photographs of three selected 'Men of the Week'; a Saturday series on 'Notable London Buildings' and a Monday series on 'Progress in Modern Architecture' probably reflected Bracken's keen personal interest in the subject; from 21 October the *FN* was printed on better paper and with new clearer typefaces; and finally, most profound of changes, general news, and not just market news, was appearing daily on the front page. This last development was typified by a headline and story on 3 October, 'Abolition of War the Aim', about Henderson's speech on foreign policy to the Labour Party conference, that would have been unthinkable a few years earlier. In fact:

> We strive to produce a paper which is not only indispensable to the financier, the banker, the stockbroker and the investor, but also appeals to the man of business and to the general reader. Nearly every subject of popular interest, whether it be foreign politics or home affairs, has a financial basis, and it is our object to treat finance from the broadest standpoint and to show how deeply it enters into all business and into all the various activities of national life.[6]

Thus Major J. W. Hills in October 1929, in a speech almost certainly written for him by Bracken, outlining the *FN* creed that would in due course become that of the merged *FT*.

Hills was speaking to shareholders in his capacity as chairman of Financial Newspaper Proprietors Ltd, the company formed by Eyre & Spottiswoode to manage the group of papers acquired by Bracken in an astonishing burst of entrepreneurial optimism in the months immediately following his purchase of the *FN*. The papers acquired were the *Investors Chronicle*, the Liverpool *Journal of Commerce* and the *Practitioner* (a popular medical journal), together with a half-interest in the most eminent of weeklies, the *Economist*; but throughout it was the *FN* that dominated the group and, for better or worse, determined its fortunes. Hills himself was a well-respected Conservative MP of independent mind, a former Financial Secretary to the Treasury and author of a book on *The Finance of Government*. He also followed a certain local tradition through being connected with Virginia Woolf, who in 1918 described her half-brother-in-law as somehow always reminding her of 'an excellent highly polished well seasoned brown boot'.[7] As chairman of FNP and a director of the *FN*, Hills does not seem to have been a particularly dynamic figure and was always subservient to Bracken. The same was perhaps less true of another member of the respective boards, Major-General Guy Payan Dawnay, who was now a merchant banker and appears to have undertaken the complex financial arrangements involved in forming the group. Compton Mackenzie in *Gallipoli Memories* described him as 'a fragile figure with something of an exquisitely fashioned porcelain in the finely chiselled features of his small face'; while to T. E. Lawrence he was 'the least professional of soldiers, a banker who read Greek history'.[8] But over the next two decades he and his new firm of Dawnay Day would prove their worth to Bracken in advice and expertise.

At the *FN* itself, all was change. Early in 1929 Herbert Hill was recruited from the *FT* to be advertising manager, and he soon afterwards became general manager, to the discontent of Woodcock, who resigned, expressing himself 'unsettled and depressed' by 'the recent reorganisation'. Pressure was put on the now separate Argus Press to provide a better, cheaper service. New premises were acquired for the group, at 20 Bishopsgate, into which the *FN* moved from Queen Victoria Street in March 1929. It was a tall building, though not going back very far, with a bright yellow frontage on the ground floor and windows like big portholes. It made a striking contrast to its sober Victorian neighbours and was welcomed by the staff for providing pleasanter, more roomy offices. There was even talk of creating a pension fund for the *FN* staff, until the rude interruption of events. A new presence at this time was Collin Brooks, who had worked his way up through the provincial press, was an immensely prolific writer of novels, thrillers and guides to finance, and in the autumn of 1928 had become the new assistant editor, following the death of Lang earlier that year and the promotion of Doman to the position of editor under Hilton Young. Brooks also kept a fairly full diary, in which in July 1929 he described Bracken as 'a likeable, erratic fellow', referring to his habit of forgetting to turn up at meetings. He added: 'One can affect this casual style when one has the Bracken personality – backed by the Bracken power and money.' Bracken in fact had no great personal fortune (being on an annual salary of £3,000 as chairman of the *FN* and possessing 500 shares in FNP) but was certainly generating considerable sums of money through his papers. In the words of the script delivered by Hills in October 1929: 'Do not for one moment imagine that we mean to stand still. The future possibilities are great, and we mean to do our best to obtain our share of them.'[9]

There was yet one other major change at the *FN* during these stirring eighteen or so months. In January 1929 Hilton Young resigned after almost four years as editor-in-chief. This was possibly because he was unable to give the paper a firm promise that he would stay on if he did not take office after the impending general election; possibly because he was not prepared to work other than as a part-time journalist; and possibly also because, as Bracken wrote to a friend almost thirty years later, the new management found that it had 'inherited an editor of the highest character whose energies were below freezing point, if not zero'.[10] The new editor from May, on a five-year contract of £2,500 per annum, was Oscar Hobson, who since 1920 had been financial editor of the *Manchester Guardian*. He was not the most imaginative of men, as Brooks was to note in his diary in 1932: 'O.R.H. hasn't really any idea of the artistry of leader writing. His method – probably a good one – is merely to write a pedestrian statement of a point of view. The technique of creating an idea which develops to a destined conclusion, the use of Arnold's iteration – all wasted.' The qualities, however, that Hobson did bring to his job included considerable journalistic competence and experience, a large degree of dedication, great knowledge of finance, a ready entrée to Norman at the Bank of England, the clearest of minds and above all an intense rectitude of outlook and tone. The biographical details are telling. He was born in 1886 into a strongly Protestant family, his mother being a Swiss German; at Cambridge he took a first in the classical tripos; in 1910 he married a daughter of the stipendiary magistrate at Leeds; and that same year he entered the office of the London Joint-Stock Bank, where he worked until the war.

The decision to make Hobson, rather than another more public figure, the new editor-in-chief was a notable one, showing clearly Bracken's determination to raise the standing of financial journalism as a profession in its own right and, through the particular person of Hobson, to erase any lingering doubts about the *FN*'s integrity. It was, to begin with, the happiest of choices. 'A good fellow, very quiet', was the initial response of Brooks, who appreciated Hobson as a man of learning and high standards and did not mind his rather austere manner. 'Before we ended the day,' he noted on 4 October, 'Hobson and I began to swap bits of Calverley, arising from a disputed tag raised by Hamilton.' Towards the end of 1929 he wrote of how 'Hobson's advent has made life at the office singularly happy.' The transplant of the *Manchester Guardian* ethos to 20 Bishopsgate had, it seemed, taken.

But even while Brooks was writing of harmony in the ranks, and Hills was proclaiming the Bracken message of mutually expanding profits and horizons, the larger world on which the fianancial press depended was falling to pieces. In September 1929 the collapse of the various schemes forged by the most ambitious company promoter of the 1920s, Clarence Hatry, marked the end of the Stock Exchange boom in company shares. 'The harvest of figs has turned to thistles', declared the *FN*, in a Hobsonian leader of gloomy, told-you-so triumph; while the *FT* insisted, as usual, on the 'Need of Calmness', asserting that 'it is desirable in the highest degree to realise that the ramifications and consequences of an isolated breakdown justify no general adverse reflection upon the business of the City as a whole'. Bad, however, soon went to worse.

On 22 October, in a leader on 'Pros and Cons of Wall Street', the *FT* argued that too much should not be read into recent heavy price falls and stated that, in terms of the US economy as a whole, 'there is little evidence of any all-round falling off in prosperity'. The headlines of the two papers over the next week told their own story: 'Heaviest Selling This Year', 'Black Day on Wall Street', 'Feverish Rally after Huge Fall', 'New Wall Street Debacle', 'Huge Losses in All Leaders'. The *FN* greeted the Wall Street crash in its Hobsonian vein of grim, almost puritanical satisfaction:

> It sets at rest the doubt (which at times it has proved difficult for the most clear-sighted observer from afar to resist) that Providence had created some new law of perpetual motion by which American material prosperity might be safe-guarded against even temporary setbacks and the share prices by which material prosperity is measured be imbued with the power of uninterrupted and limitless growth . . . It requires no great powers of memory to recall how extraordinarily widespread and infectious was the conviction that this Wall Street 'boom' now ended was in some subtle way different from any boom which had ever preceded it.

Equally characteristic was the response of the *FT*, which by early November attempted, on behalf of London-based investors, to find 'Signs of Strength' in the overall situation: 'Once Wall Street has assessed its losses – and the Hatry tangle has been sorted out – and established a new basis of trading the period of tension should come to an end, and the sane investor should have scope to display his enterprise. Optimism and pessimism each have their innings, and the latter's wicket is now due to fall.'

Pessimism proved a dismayingly obdurate customer, for the famous crash turned out to be merely the harbinger of the deep financial and industrial depression that over the next four years was to devastate the Western world. The slump was not immediate, but even by October 1930 Hills, reviewing the past year, was stating to FNP shareholders that 'our journals, being mainly financial, felt, of course, the full effect of the depression through which we are passing, a depression of unexampled severity'.[11] The number of prospectuses appearing in the *FN* reflected the darkening economic backcloth: 646 in 1928, 381 in 1929 and 186 in 1930. The following year proved still worse, being described by Hills in December as one 'throughout the course of which conditions prevailed which approached financial paralysis'.[12] And so it went on, with the situation specifically from the point of view of the British financial press not being at all helped by first the banning of foreign flotations in London from August 1931 (in order to keep capital at home) and then, during the summer of 1932 while the war loan of 1917 was being converted to a lower interest level, the banning of all new issues. By December 1932 Hills was referring wearily to 'the unprecendented difficulties which confronted all financial newspapers during the last twelve months'.[13] Camrose concurred, saying soon afterwards to *FT* shareholders that he had been 'assured by those with the requisite length of experience to know' that the second half of 1932 had been 'the worst from the standpoint of financial activity within unusually long memories'.[14]

Average issue sizes inevitably shrank, so that for both papers eight or ten pages was the norm during these years. The *FT*'s circulation also declined (as presumably did the *FN*'s), going down to 25,000 in 1930 and 20,000 by 1931, where it more or less stayed until the City began to pick up again during 1933. Separate figures were not divulged for the *FN*, but the FNP as a group lost around £25,000 each year during the early 1930s, and the situation would have been much worse but for the sale of the *Journal of Commerce* and the steadily increasing profits of the *Practitioner*. FT Ltd profits (including, as usual, St Clements Press) were down – to £65,691 in 1930, £12,094 in 1931, £16,886 in 1932 and £40,509 in 1933. 'Political derangements, economic depression, and a persistent fall of the price level provide as few opportunities for the financial newspaper to prosper as they do to trade generally.'[15] These words of Camrose in June 1932 were none the less true for being obvious, granted especially the fundamental dependence of the financial press on advertising, above all financial advertising, in order to survive.

The major British event during these dismal years was, of course, the financial crisis of 1931, which led to the downfall of the minority Labour government under Ramsay MacDonald, the formation of the Conservative-dominated National government and the decision soon afterwards to go off the gold standard, permanently as it transpired. Neither paper had warmed to Labour in office, even though Snowden as Chancellor for the most part pursued impeccably Gladstonian old-fashioned policies, and the *FT* leader of 25 August on the formation of the National government was full of predictable nostrums: an assertion that 'it is to economy more than to fresh taxation that we must look for a cure'; a reference to the 'dole' as having been 'poured out as though the supply were limitless'; and, with sterling in a parlous state, a concluding statement that 'the strongest efforts of the new government, and of all whose objective is the true welfare of the whole country and not the seeming benefit merely of a section of the people, should be such as to uphold the confidence of the foreigner in our currency, as well as to assist the recovery of our industry'. But less than a month later the *FT* was shaping its sad leader on 'Gold Exports Stopped': 'Stated bluntly, the main reason is that foreigners for no cause associated with our own internal conditions have not only prevented gold from fulfilling its proper function in the settlement of international trade balances but have also drawn largely upon our supplies for reasons peculiar to their own territories.' The *FN* agreed and contrasted the 'panic-stricken scramble for gold' abroad with the situation at home, where 'the development of the crisis has been faced with our characteristic coolness and good humour'. Almost two years later the *FT* at least would still be looking forward to a return to the good old days – 'Restoration of the gold standard will once more make people think of sound currency, deflation and falling prices,' it asserted wistfully in June 1933 – but to all intents and purposes an era had ended in September 1931, forcing the City back on its wits in order to remain an international financial centre.

The old days were coming to an end in another fundamental respect. Britain's nineteenth-century prosperity had owed much to the worldwide system of free trade, which other countries had moved away from towards the end of the century, but Britain had not. Now, in 1932, culminating at the Ottawa conference during the summer, the National government adopted something like the system of imperial tariffs that Joseph Chamberlain had advocated in vain some thirty years earlier. The *FT* welcomed the development, as Camrose told shareholders in June:

'We may hope for some benefit from the change of the fiscal system of this country. Some of the industries, at least, should be stimulated by protection and exert a generally helpful influence upon the earning capacity of others.' Rather different was the attitude of the *FN*, where Hobson, with his strongly *laissez-faire*, *Manchester Guardian* background, was a convinced believer in the continuing merits of free trade. The Brooks diary has a particularly graphic entry for 22 January that year:

> At the office we were bombshelled by the Cabinet announcement that on tariffs the Cabinet is to speak and vote by sections. Hobson said, 'The only title for a leader is "The Gutless Buggers"', but when I wrote a hot leader he spent quite a long time toning it down. At the end he said, 'There, I don't think there is anything offensive in it now.' I said: 'I'm sorry about that.' He said, 'Oh, it was all right.' I said: 'I don't mean I'm sorry you've had to cut it down, I mean I'm sorry there's nothing offensive left in it.' It is terribly hard to find an editor with courage, I find.

Over the succeeding months, however, Hobson did increasingly display the courage of his convictions. On 12 May a leader entitled 'A World in Fetters' made a loud call for freer trade; and assessing the Ottawa conference in August, with its 'vexing' tariffs, the *FN* was especially hard on the 'quota schemes' for beef, mutton and bacon, describing their introduction as a 'real horror'.

There was also a significant difference between the two papers in their treatment of the National government's economic policy generally. The *FT* gave its whole-hearted support to Neville Chamberlain's cautious approach at the Treasury, epitomized by an editorial of 30 Janaury 1933, 'The Chancellor and National Finance', that applauded a recent speech of his opposing any notions of an imbalanced budget and asserted that he had been 'wise to lose no time in stating clearly this country will indulge in no financial chicanery'. The *FN* was altogether more critical, as in its leader of 4 May 1932 on 'The Lack of a Policy', which began categorically: 'There is a widespread feeling that the government has no effective policy that will rescue the country from the economic depression.' It then continued about the need to go beyond merely balancing budgets and creating cheap money: '*Now* is evidently the time to undertake the large plans of the reorganisation and re-equipment of such industries as cotton and iron and steel. Yet nothing is being done.' Five days later the *FN* renewed its attack on the government's deflationary policies: 'The most pronounced quality of the government's attitudes is a lack of grip and a failure of courage consequent upon the absence of conviction.'

This is not to say that the *FN* at this stage was anything like Keynesian in its approach. A leader of 7 January 1933 on what was needed on the government's part for industrial revival was typical, calling for 'a bold, healthy rate of spending wherever it can be financially justified on its merits – neither a timid parsimony nor a spending mania'. Moreover, though giving it far more attention than the *FT* (which had hardly anything to say on the subject), the *FN* was also distinctly sceptical at this time about the desirability of Roosevelt's 'New Deal' programme, above all as a possible exemplar to European countries. On 24 June 1933 a leader on 'Prosperity Legislation' began startlingly enough: 'The full text of Roosevelt's National Industrial Recovery Act, which we publish today on another page, will be readily admitted to be an excellent exposition of economic Fascism.' Ten days later the *FN* set out more fully where it stood and what lessons should and should not be drawn:

> The position is clear. Roosevelt desires to make what he can out of letting the dollar rip. From our point of view, we can only sit back and hope that his policy succeeds in accelerating business revival in the USA without giving too much momentum to the inflationary boomerang, in which case there should be some kind of a rake-off for other countries without there being too much to pay for it later. But let us not delude ourselves with the idea that we can follow America and the dollar. We cannot afford it. And our circumstances differ materially. As a country to which export trade is of fundamental importance, the policy of indefinitely increasing costs, wages and prices in isolation is no good to us.

A residual caution persisted, but the *FN* in its editorial columns of the early 1930s still showed a much greater consciousness than its contemporary did of the acute plight of industrial Britain, of the human suffering that went with it and of the need for something to be done.

Not surprisingly, in the face of a fairly grim situation, both papers tried their hardest to reduce expenditure to a minimum. Thus in May 1931 the *FT* staff took a 10 per cent cut in wages that seems to have stayed in force for several years; while at the *FN*, permanent reductions took effect from August 1931, with the amount varying according to individual members of the staff, but in some cases being as much as 33 per cent cuts. The *FN* board led by example, with directors taking a 50 per cent cut in their fees from November 1930, and Bracken's salary going down from £3,000 to £2,000. Some staff were sacked and older members retired, including Doman in 1930.

On the more positive side, both papers attempted to broaden the basis of their advertising, especially through the systematic development of handsomely designed supplements, in order to attract new sources of revenue. The most famous of the *FT*'s efforts was a 36-page China supplement that appeared on 27 June 1932 and was primarily the work of E. R. Skipwith, who had gone out to China especially and is remembered as an elderly, quite flamboyant, Bob Hope type of figure. Unfortunately, as Camrose told his shareholders three days later, 'the arrival of our special representative in the Far East coincided with the outbreak of troubles, with the nature and extent of which you are familiar'. Camrose was presumably referring to the Shanghai crisis of January that year when an assault on Japanese priests by a Chinese mob led to Japanese forces landing on the Chinese mainland. He added: 'The exceedingly difficult situation which ensued in Shanghai turned people's minds away from thoughts of advantageous publicity, while floods and the devastation they caused were other unlooked-for handicaps.'[16]

As for the *FN*, it produced, under the auspices of S. R. Chaloner, with advertisements garnered by Martin Turner, a whole series of profitable supplements, most of them with memorably beautiful coloured covers and featuring subjects as diverse as the Irish Free State, diesel traction and transport, and Palestine. In June 1932 a 32-page survey of the Russian economy, full of photographs on themes like 'Furnaces and Coke Batteries at Kuznetz' and 'Loading Tractors at Stalingrad', began apologetically: 'We are well aware that we run the risk – in publishing a special number on Russia – that some of our readers will find themselves temperamentally unable even to scan these few lines of introduction.' But, as the prefatory remarks then went on, 'we desire no truck with those who hit below the belt; and hold that it is unsportsmanlike to hang a dog because of his name'. The following month it was the turn of the British film industry, which supplement included an article by that rising young talent, Alfred Hitchcock, on 'Secrets of a Film Producer'. In truth, however, most of the matter in these and the *FT* supplements was rather tamer stuff, usually written by local worthies and seeking in distinctly uncritical fashion to show the subject under review in the best possible light. The point of them was the advertising they brought in, never more needed than in the early 1930s.

All this helped to provide an affirmative answer to the very real question posed by the *World's Press News* in October 1931, 'Can the Financial Press Survive?' There was never much chance of the *FT* going under, but such was not the case with the *FN*, where the pervasive atmosphere of anxiety, shading sometimes into desperation, emerges strongly from the diary kept by Brooks. By July 1931 the warning lights were flashing: 'The European crisis has led to the German collapse which has so accentuated the slump that the *Financial News* may not weather the storm.' The next entry was five months later: 'It has been a queer time.

The world slump has smitten London badly and the *Financial News* has been an adventure of hard work in the face of growing difficulties, men sacked, equipment cut down.' Soon the situation approached its apparent climactic:

9.2.32. Attempts to fuse *FN* and *FT* not going too smoothly. O.R.H. [Hobson] very anxious as to survival.

10.2.32. O.R.H. still more worried and B.B. [Bracken] talking of printing the paper in Liverpool as a last resort.

12.2.32. At office there was a board meeting to which Oscar was summoned to discuss the proposed Liverpool experiment . . . Oscar returned and he and Chaloner and Hill and I had an informal conference – quite exciting but taken very calmly. O.R.H. thinks that if Liverpool doesn't come off the paper is doomed and dead.

15.2.32. Office as usual, where all is on the hazard about the transition to L'pool or nonentity. B.B. has apparently made himself very objectionable to O.R.H. and Chaloner during the morning, and adversity gave us all a chummy feeling.

16.2.32. B.B. bubbling with the idea of the amalgamation of the *FN* and the *JOC* and wanted quick action taken. The [Liverpool] *Journal of Commerce*, he insisted with great excitement, would save us all . . . I left the Press soon after 11.30 and taxied with C. to his flat where over a whiskey we resumed the sorry tale. He will not believe that the *FN* will bust – if it does he declares himself 'done'. I was sorry for him – he was so different from the old cocksure, aggressive Chaloner.

19.2.32. O.R.H., Chaloner, Birchall [of the *JOC*] and I made a dummy of the new combined paper. B.B. has already bought a new rotary and we are committed to the experiment.

21.2.32. Liverpool is off, and the latest scheme is for the Birchalls to buy back the Financial Newspaper Proprietors' share of their journal. Bracken is now busy looking for printing works nearer London where we would get the advantage of the T A [Typographical Association] minimum as against the London society minimum.

22.2.32. The scheme now is to print the *FN* at St Albans.

24.2.32. Things at office as normal as can be nowadays.

26.2.32. B.B. now wanting to cut down more staff.

29.2.32. The office is still astir with the impending dissolution of the paper and Bracken's rat-like rushings from one expedient to another. He has quite lost his nerve, Hobson says, and last night summoned Hill to his house for an emergency consultation, drank himself asleep and snored the bout off on a sofa.

1.3.32. Chaloner rang to see if I could lunch with O.R.H. and him at the Reform. I did – and we were a conspiratorial three discussing how to rid the paper of Bracken. I was all for a brutal frontal attack by O.R.H., but Bracken is such a lovable boy as well as such a dangerous bloody fool that we went to the office still without having our resolutions screwed up . . . The worry is the fate of all the subordinate ranks – for them to be flung into the street by the death of the paper would mean a terrible weight and tragedy on O.R.H. and us. We have simply to humour B.B. and try to save the sheet.

2.3.32. At the office the news was that Birchall has bought the *JOC* out of the group and that the storm has for a while abated.

3.3.32. The *FN* now seems safe for a year.

The judgements may be individual and subjective, but the bunker atmosphere is authentic enough. The *FT* reference of 9 February is particularly tantalizing and completely undocumented in the official records. Just over a year later, on 23 February 1933, the theme was picked up again by Brooks: 'Lunched at the Savoy with all the financial editors to discuss a fixed trust for Kaffir shares, and gave Barrett of the *FT* a lift back to the City in my taxi to hear him talk of his desire to merge the *FN* and the *FT*.' By then the crisis point was past for the *FN*, and the desire for an independent existence strong on the part of Bracken, but it had undoubtedly been a close-run thing.

The real miracle, according to Einzig amongst others, was how Hobson 'managed to produce such a good newspaper on so little money'. After all, Einzig pointed out, 'even Caligula's immortal quadruped could have produced a good paper on an unlimited editorial budget', but 'it takes a really first-rate editor to achieve and maintain high quality with his staff reduced to a minimum for lack of funds and with practically no money available for outside contributors'.[17] An important element in Hobson's success was his ability, despite or perhaps because of his personal remoteness, somehow to create a certain heightening of moral tone and purpose, in the process inspiring his staff to greater efforts. This was particularly so in the case of his various young recruits, often taken straight from the universities and known in later years as 'Hobson's boys'. Brooks, the experienced provincial journalist, cast a rather jaundiced eye on this aspect of Hobson's editorship at one point during the trials of February 1932:

O.R.H.'s personality and general decency and one own's sense of sheer duty compel a vast amount of effort, but not the burning interest I used to have in my Leeds days. Also – the sweating of the staff by the *FN*, defensible as it may be, is repugnant. I do not mean by this that I am sweated, but the employment of boys to do men's responsible work, and the slating and kicking of sub-editors – who have to work in crowded conditions at low pay – for not being Double Firsts makes the game less attractive.

In fact, however, Hobson's most notable recruit, at least in terms of the future of the *FN*, was already a trained financial journalist. 'Took Lex to lunch at the Café Royal,' wrote Brooks in August 1933, adding that 'we talked chiefly of foreign affairs and Dickens'. The 'Lex' in question was the original one, Hargreaves Parkinson, who had started writing his column, entitled 'Notes for Investors' and initially placed on the left-hand centre page, soon after Hobson became editor-in-chief. Parkinson was in his mid-thirties and had been educated at Blackpool Grammar School, King's College, London, and the London School of Economics. After the war he had worked at the Department of Overseas Trade and for the National Savings Committee (as assistant press officer) before joining the staff of the *Economist* in 1923, becoming City editor five years later. He was a ready writer on everything relating to investment, and his first two publications were *The ABC of Stocks and Shares* (1925) and *The Small Investor* (1930). He remained on the *Economist* through most of the 1930s, but as 'Lex' for the *FN* his column was an immediate success, offering objective analysis of market values and underlying causes of change, as well as increasingly tackling general investment questions in addition to specific securities, company reports and so on. Soon Parkinson was complemented by a new tenant of the 'Midas' column, a member of the Stock Exchange called Harold Cowen, whose survey of day-to-day events in the stock market was far acuter than that provided by 'Autolycus' in the *FT* and also much less 'tipping'.

Inevitably, it was not easy at this time for a financial paper, desperate for advertising and support generally, to maintain complete objectivity of attitude; the implicit (and occasionally explicit) pressures were always there. Einzig in his memoirs recalled with gratitude how, when his column in the early 1930s was so critical of Lloyds Bank that the bank demanded his dismissal, Bracken flatly refused, in spite of the paper's heavy reliance on Lloyds for a long-running overdraft. Similarly, there was a famous occasion in 1931 when Anglo-Foreign Newspapers made a large issue, placed a big advertisement in the *FN* and on that same day were roundly attacked in the *FN* (though nowhere else), in a piece written by Bracken himself that compared the flotation to the South Sea Bubble, when money was raised from the public for a 'purpose to be made known subsequently'.[18] The paper was much criticized for its hostile attitude, but Bracken was unrepentant. Yet even the highly moral Hobson could occasionally succumb, to judge by a rather bitter Brooks entry for March 1933:

I made an epigram, after reviewing the effect upon him of four years with Bracken, thus:

> Hobson, still swearing honour must direct us,
> Sells all our souls to gain one dud prospectus.

This was because he restrained Lex from an attack on the Decca flotation.

To which one might add that Hobson at least had, largely by dint of his own efforts, the soul of his paper available to sell.

Hobson's period as *FN* editor was indeed the reverse of easy, for in addition to (and compounding) all his other problems there was the dominant fact of his increasingly bitter relations with Bracken. When at the FNP meeting of December 1931 a shareholder laid into Hobson ('It is no good flouting the people from whom he expects business as he has done continuously for the past two or three years . . . The only thing for the *Financial News* is to put it in a museum . . . It is *Manchester Guardian* from A to Z'), Bracken defended his man staunchly enough, describing Hobson as 'the best financial editor in the City of London'. Over the next year, however, the question of tariffs laid a permanent, deeply damaging wedge between them. Bracken was well aware that the City was almost wholly in favour of some form of protection, while Hobson stuck to his nineteenth-century guns and on one occasion (according to Einzig, who was present) said to Bracken: 'The *Financial News* is a free-trade paper. I am the editor and I have a five years' contract. So what are you going to do about it?' Soon Bracken was referring to his editor as 'that incorrigible Calvinist' and worse.[19]

The situation was further exacerbated during 1932 by an almost continuous dispute over economy measures. Hobson fought hard to maintain at least semi-adequate editorial resources at both Bishopsgate and the Argus Press. Brooks recorded matters coming to a head towards the end of the year:

3.11.32. This afternoon the famous memorandum to O.R.H. from Bracken was delivered. It was a slashing, cruel attack on every feature of O.R.H.'s editorship – from 'dull political leaders which nobody reads' to 'a paper like an uninteresting scrapbook'. O.R.H. cut up, but determined not to resign but to fight Bracken.

9.11.32. O.R.H. stays put, and we are in a lull, waiting for the next shot in the war.

23.11.32. Oscar is determined he can't go on under the Bracken regime.

2.12.32. Hobson was rowing for nearly two and a half hours with Bracken yesterday . . . Both sides are right in the quarrel. Hobson has killed the paper by preaching bitter Cobdenism when the country was Protectionist, but Bracken and Hill by ineptitude have failed to get business. After all, the job of the salesman is to sell the product as he has it, not, because he finds the work hard, to damn the product to the very people to whom he is trying to sell it.

6.12.32. When I reached the office Oscar told me that the board had met and that Major Hills had come down to him and said that he (Hills) had told the board that Hobson couldn't see his way to going on after the expiry of this contract and the board thought there was no more to be said . . . The position now is awkward. Hobson stays on until May 1934, openly at war with his directors who feel (and with justice) that he has ruined the paper by his stiff-necked policy on free trade and his highbrowism . . .

30.12.32. At the office all normal – and less of the 'happy new year' spirit than I ever remember.

There would have been even less of that spirit if it had been realized that an article published by the *FN* on Christmas Eve, attacking C. W. Goff, a member of the Stock Exchange, as 'a company meeting agitator', would eventually lead to a libel action in April 1934, resulting in the *FN* paying costs and £2,500 damages. Hobson, who had passed the article, described it in court as 'written in a jocular form', but 'appreciated now that Mr Goff did not take the joke'.[20] The final sixteen months cannot have been comfortable as Hobson obdurately played out time. Bracken honourably continued to allow his editor full editorial control – as in the case of the tin quota scheme, when Bracken came under pressure from his powerful friend Oliver Lyttelton to get Hobson to withdraw his opposition to the scheme, but in the end bowed to the editor's prerogative. It was presumably a great relief to all when May Day 1934 at last dawned, and Hobson took up his new post as City editor of the *News Chronicle*, where he remained until 1959.

Brooks had already moved on, becoming City editor of the *Sunday Dispatch* in October 1933 and subsequently editor of that paper and also of *Truth*. When he died in 1959, the address at his memorial service was given by T. S. Eliot. His *FN* diary stands not only as a first-rate primary source on the Hobson phase of the paper and its various troubles, but also as a marvellous narrative record of the perennial problems attached to the arduous task of bringing out a financial daily. It serves as a salutary reminder that behind the crises, the personality clashes and the 'big' questions of the day – the themes in fact that attract the historian's attention –

Harry Marks, founder of the *FN*

Douglas MacRae, founding father of the *FT*

Ellis Powell, editor of the *FN*

Linotype operators at St Clements Press, *c.* 1900

72 Coleman Street, *c.* 1910

Edward Hilton Young, editor-in-chief of the *FN*

R. J. Barrett, managing director of the *FT*, drawn by Sidney Perrin, a member of the *FT* staff

Walter Landells ('Autolycus'), drawn by a fellow member of the Stock Exchange

Paul Einzig

FN annual dinner, *c.* 1938

Brendan Bracken with Churchill in 1939

there always lies the mundane, unceasing occupation of getting the paper ready for the next morning. As in the following selection from June to August 1932, it also gives one something of the texture of one particular financial journalist's life during trying times:

17.6.32. Usual routine – 3 o'c. bus for the station, district train [from Chiswick] to Monument, iced coffee at 3.40 in the Court rooms, office at 4 – tray of bad tea at 4.30 – china and a cream bun at a Mecca at 6.30 – to Fleet Street at 8 o'c. – drink with Machreay at one Red Lion, to plant my [Liverpool] *Daily Post* paragraph – food and ale at the other Red Lion with Baxter – Argus Press at about 9.15 – home [to Chiswick] by the 11.45 train from Blackfriars – all these points being linked by work, by the incoming of various people – Bracken to say that Lloyd George had made his 'come back' on the Irish issue – the messenger from 'Midas' with his Stock Exchange column, de Pallons with his news of the metal market – Bittles worrying about company meetings that demand comment – Hobson talking high politics and occasionally, as today, blowing some poor devil, like Brocklebank, sky high, or, as today, laying down the law about the Argus weakness on headlines, or treatment of news. On the whole, very happy days, despite the crisis in the paper's affairs, and the feeling that with reduced staffs and a divided high command the game is not really worth the candle.

22.6.32. Hobson in quite a little tantrum about the copy basket being neglected, but, I turning savage, he became extra-polite. He and I stayed at the Bishopsgate end till nearly nine doing a leader on the Hoover disarmament offer. Actually he dictated the leader while I typed it.

1.7.32. Last night was very strenuous at the Press. The fall in the Bank Rate to 2 per cent following a little gilt-edged boom and Neville Chamberlain's return from Lausanne [where he had been attending a conference on reparations] caused us all to expect a conversion of sorts, but most people thought it would be Treasuries. At nine thirty I had a call from Shaw to say it was the big thing – war loan. Our stuff didn't reach us till twenty past ten, and last copy down first edition is nominally 10.30. However Shaw's tip had given us time to prepare, and I raked Hobson from a dinner to bear an expert hand, I in the meantime contriving to alter a leader to fit the new event – having, also, to alter the Lausanne leader. At midnight Valance came over from the *Economist* to talk it over, before doing his hurried comments. It was all very strenuous for a hot sultry night, but enjoyable.

3.7.32. The Press was rather a nuisance, the paper going early to bed and Dell very late with his stuff from Lausanne . . . Home by midnight, feeling that we had produced a thoroughly bad paper for the third night in succession, but as good as could be contrived.

12.7.32. The paper was a bit difficult at the Press, and when I was in the tube I happened to look at a late *Star* and found that our first edition had missed 'the news of the night for us' – Chamberlain's reassurance about returning to a gold standard. This meant agitated 'phoning when I got home – but it was all right for the City edition.

25.7.32. Grave trouble at the office. The 'splash' should have carried a large table inside – and it was not given! There was no defence for anybody, although I had asked the chief-sub if a table was not necessary. It was due to a combination of faults – Thompson who did the story and table did not mark the table for Sunday night and did not indicate on copy that the table was attached. Hobson in charge on Saturday did not note it on the menue. The sub who handled the story saw the par. saying 'elsewhere we give a table' but did not check the cross reference. I read down the splash in galley and assumed that the table mentioned was given, but was some small table . . . Altogether a bad business from a technical viewpoint. A factor inviting such a disaster was the arrival of the Ottawa cable at 11, just when the page was in proof, which distracted Lyon and Reynolds and me from the splash. This is the second blunder in a week by the Press and I actually offered Hobson my resignation. He said 'For God's sake don't talk about resignations or they'll be asking for mine!' Just to cheer us up tonight as the page was being made up in forme the third section of the page one stock indicator (most important thing on the page from some viewpoints) was hopelessly pied, and we had to fill with misc and get away. Altogether, a bad day.

19.8.32. At the office all normal except the heat.

21.8.32. The publication of the full texts of the Ottawa agreements gave us a busy night.

22.8.32. At the office things normal but busy, with the Post Office report the main news.

23.8.32.At the office things quiet: B.B. back but did not see him. A silly error in this morning's paper annoyed me – one can stop the big mistakes but the small things slip past.

They did then, do now and always will.

By the time of the decennial viewing-point, Monday 13 February 1933, both papers were still in a rather depressed state, managing ten pages each, with barely a page and a half of advertising between them (the majority going to the *FT*). It was, as it happened, exactly a week since the *FN* had made some major changes in its format, including moving 'Lex' and 'Midas' to the front page (arguably an implicit acceptance that it would be unwise to move too far away from the Stock Exchange basis of the paper, but also a tribute to the high quality of the two columnists) and adopting a new, less cluttered layout on the leader page inside. In addition, what Hobson in an explanatory article called 'the ornate conventionality of the existing Gothic title block' was replaced by the Perpetua type designed by Eric Gill in 1925 and representing the forms he had used in his inscriptional lettering, 'generally adjudged to be the finest work of its kind in our time'. The same type was also now used in the headings of Stock Exchange and investment comment; while elsewhere in the *FN* the new heading type employed was 'a modern rendering of the type first cast by Giambattista Bodoni, the world-famous printer, of Parma, in the early years of the nineteenth century', and chosen 'under expert advice for its qualities of boldness and straightforwardness'. In a word, wrote Hobson, 'functionalism is applicable no less to journalism than to architecture; and if that be true, a financial newspaper of all newspapers needs artistic type and arrangement – artistic in this modern sense of suitability to purpose – for a financial newspaper has few idle and dilettante readers'.

The night of the change-over at the Argus was, Brooks recorded, pretty good hell: 'O.R.H. – looking a drule in a suit of stale-dung coloured "plus fours" that was too big for him and grey stockings that concertinaed about his short legs – came in about nine, rather ill tempered. We fratched about a sentence in Einzig which O.R.H. declared was not English and which I defended, but later achieved a reasonable harmony.' The following night Hobson again looked in, causing Brooks to comment that 'a man should either take command for the whole of an action, or keep out of the way'. And by the night of the 7th 'everyone seemed oppressed by the fact that we had bitten off more than we can chew in the new make up . . . The night run was pretty terrible.'

On the 13th, though, the signs were that things had settled down, allowing a reasonable comparison between the *FN* and its rival. The usual daily similarities of information and coverage obtained, while a feature in the *FN* like 'Quarterly Analysis of Rand Mining Companies', supplied by Moodys–*Economist* Services (a subsidiary of the *Economist*) and taking up half a page of dense tabulation, was matched by the same amount of space being filled in the *FT* with details of investment trust companies' results for the third quarter of 1932. Each paper had, as ever, its distinctive, characteristic aspects. The *FT*'s page seven, for instance, included a column and a half (much more than in the *FN*) of densely printed 'Answers to Correspondents', about taxation as well as investment matters, together with a report of the annual dinner of the South London Harriers at the Criterion Restaurant ('the attendance was large . . . the tone of the evening was excellent'); while in the *FN*, 'Ginsbury' pressed on with portrait number CCCXXVI (General The Hon. Sir H. A. Lawrence, Chairman of Vickers-Armstong), and on the back page there was a large item about a new, free investment service for *FN* readers being provided by the paper in conjunction with Moodys–*Economist* Services, taking the form of sheets of information about companies (up to ten per person) chosen by the readers themselves. In general, the by now well-established contrast also obtained on this particular day: on the *FT*'s part a more thorough coverage of the markets (twice the number of reports on provincial stock exchanges, for example), on the *FN*'s a more analytical approach and a greater willingness to look outwards. The contrast between the papers' respective front-page Stock Exchange columnists, 'Autolycus' and 'Midas', was particularly stark. Whereas the *FN*'s 'Midas' kept the personal 'House' element to a minimum and concentrated on such stern themes as the state of investment demand for fixed-interest stocks and the prospects for the British canning industry, 'Autolycus' of the *FT* devoted his column mainly to puffing Hovis preference shares ('Well Bred' was the subheading), praising the work of the Stock Exchange Clearing House and describing the annual dinner of the Stock Exchange Staffs Sports Club, all rounded off with a story ('Are you going to the International?' 'No, I generally go to Sainsbury's') about the two ladies who met on Saturday in Twickenham while out shopping. 'Midas' was a glimpse of the future of financial journalism, while 'Autolycus' faithfully reflected the mores of his day. There are no prizes for guessing (and it can only be a guess) who had the greater following.

Over the next few years the good times returned for the financial press, though not to the same halcyon extent as immediately after the war and during the late 1920s. In particular, severe restrictions remained on the international capital market. By November 1935, in its election leader successfully advocating the return of the National government, the *FT* felt able to claim that since 1931 Britain had made 'so rapid and marked a recovery from her previous ills that she has become the envy of the world'. And in January 1937, writing to his friend Lord Beaverbrook in the USA, Bracken described almost euphorically the continuing Stock Exchange revival: 'Everything booms here. Fortunes are being piled up & there is hardly a sign of apprehension about another slump. The City has had one of the best years in its history.'[21] There was even another financial daily on the market during these years, namely the *Financial Digest*, though it folded in 1937. For the *FT*, Camrose was able each summer to announce for the previous year a steadily increasing profit: £40,509 for 1933, £70,400 (and a resumption of dividends on ordinary shares) for 1934, £81,918 for 1935 and £102,543 for 1936. Circulation likewise rose, from an average daily net sale of 21,867 in 1933 to one of 30,380 by 1937, which was almost back to the 1928–9 level. In the pages of the paper itself, nothing much changed under the well-entrenched regime of the veterans Barrett and Hunter; thus by the time of the 1935 election, the series of supplements was up to number 136 with a one-page feature on the industrial growth and prospects of Acton, 'Architecture To-Day' had reached number 168, and the daddy of them all, 'Potential Investments', focusing on a particular company, was on number 1,678.

The *FN* manfully tried to compete with the *FT* formula and in so doing offered a visually more attractive (apart from the pink-coloured paper) as well as intellectually more stimulating product, but simply could not catch up. It still declined to reveal its sales figures, but Leonard Shapland, appointed circulation manager in March 1933, later recalled of these years that 'we had reason to believe that the sales of the *Financial Times* were at least three times and probably nearer four times that of ours'. He added that it was not until the spring of 1937 that the paper passed – and then only briefly – the 10,000 mark.[22] Not surprisingly, advertisers continued to look first to the *FT* and only to the *FN* as a possible optional extra. There was a particular story that Beaverbrook enjoyed telling:

> Once at a dinner party given by Lord Rothermere, someone came in with news that interested everyone present, including Lloyd George, Winston Churchill, Oswald Mosley and Brendan Bracken. Messengers were despatched from the room for fuller details, so Rothermere sent for the *Daily Mail* and Bracken for the *Financial News*. When the messengers returned, they brought one copy of the *Mail* and six of the *Financial News*. 'That shows', said Brendan, 'how much more generous my organisation is.' To which Rothermere retorted: 'Nothing of the sort, it merely shows you bought the whole edition.'[23]

In such company, it was a galling moment for a proprietor who was also, having represented North Paddington since 1929, emerging as an important dissident Conservative politician, firmly in the Churchill camp. His principal paper may have been respected, even admired, *as* a paper; but with a four-figure circulation it undeniably lacked clout.

Nevertheless, there was plenty about the *FN* in the mid-1930s from which Bracken could derive satisfaction. By the second half of 1933 the paper seems to have been breaking even again and in November that year it published a highly successful supplement devoted to the Stock Exchange, including a superb 'zoological' map of the House specially drawn by Rex Whistler. The following January the *FN* celebrated its fiftieth anniversary with a supplement on the City, a string of congratulatory messages (including one from Mussolini) and a 3½-page history of the paper written by Brooks for a fee of 50 guineas, making use of material provided by Doman. One of the articles in the City supplement asked the question 'What Would Wren Have Built Today?' and, in the context of the increasingly overcrowded square mile, provided a confident, uncompromising answer:

> We must give up the building rule which restricts the height of buildings, and we must not only do that, but we must build office blocks twice as high as St Paul's, and have green spaces and wide roads in between the blocks . . . Two dozen skyscrapers, though they would obviously dwarf St Paul's, would not take away from its beauty if they were beautiful themselves. They would alter the sky-line, certainly, yet we should not sacrifice health, time, and comfort to one skyline because we have not the courage to create another.

The writer was John Betjeman. There was also at this time a jubilee dinner, 'with Bracken in the chair and a most devilishly strained atmosphere', according to Brooks, 'because most of us knew that Hobson and Chaloner and Thompson were all leaving the ship'.

The ship, however, did not sink. Later in 1934 a major and complex reorganization took place by which the shares held by FNP in the *FN* were distributed to FNP shareholders, and FNP's other assets (principally the *Banker*, the *Investors Chronicle*, the *Practitioner* and the half-interest in the *Economist*) were taken over by Financial News Ltd, of which Bracken remained chairman. Eyre & Spottiswoode, in the form of the Eyre Trust, continued to hold the controlling interest in the group. Visible signs of progress rapidly followed between 1935 and 1937: annual profits of £21,597, £52,094 and £62,244 (with the *FN* itself contributing heavily); dividends on the ordinary shares conservatively steady (a lesson learnt from the late 1920s) at ten per cent; an issue of £50,000 successfully made to existing shareholders; Bracken's salary up to £5,000; and advertising rates increased to match those of *The Times* and the *FT*.

The two people who take prime credit for this improving state of affairs are Bracken himself and the man who replaced Hobson as editor, Maurice Green. Only twenty-eight years old when he succeeded, Green had been recruited to the *FN* in Hilton Young's time, apparently after his Oxford contemporary Randolph Churchill had given his name to Bracken as someone who had got a double first despite being drunk every evening. The drinking was exaggerated, but the intellect and the ability to perform under pressure, without ever seeming to be in a hurry, were not. Under Hobson he earned a high reputation as chief leader writer, and by January 1934 Brooks was describing him in his history of the paper as 'more Balfourian than was Balfour... his foible is languid omniscience'. Possessing this formidable equipment, he was an altogether more urbane and subtle operator than Hobson, less liable to antagonize Bracken, but at the same time quite capable of standing up to him. Bracken respected the man he had chosen and particularly valued Green's qualities of mediation, especially when it came to dealing with the difficult, but invaluable and irreplaceable, Einzig.

In terms of energy and drive, increasingly allied to sense and sound judgement, Bracken himself was now at his zenith as a newspaper proprietor. The faults did not vanish, and some new ones even emerged; he could be ridiculously parsimonious (and, one should add, ridiculously generous), while such was his occasional hyper-attention to minutiae that he was capable of dispatching a blast from the north of Scotland to Bishopsgate about the unobtainability of the *FN* at Nairn and the lack of a poster on Inverness station. Yet at the same time he displayed an intense commitment to the *FN*'s cause and, as his biographer Lysaght well puts it, was able to fire his mainly young team with enthusiam for his fundamental belief that the only long-term future for a specialist paper like the *FN* lay in achieving and then maintaining the best possible quality, in all senses of the word and whatever the temptations to the contrary.[24] 'Above all, and despite superficial appearances, a man of high standards and high ideals': the judgement on Bracken was particularly significant, coming as it did after his death from none other than Oscar Hobson, who had certainly had enough intimate dealings with his old sparring partner to be able to know.[25]

'Few newspaper companies have a more intelligent and energetic personnel,' Bracken told his shareholders in 1935.[26] This appreciation, however, did not take a monetary form, even after Bracken at about this time was persuaded by Green to pay National Union of Journalists rates – which, up to the Second World War, accorded a guinea less a week to financial journalists than to others. There remained something of the 'sweated' element that Brooks had complained of so eloquently, while even in the higher editorial ranks pay was distinctly on the poor side. Consequently, a high proportion of the *FN* editorial staff of the 1930s was young, with several of them using the paper as a stepping-stone to greater things. Paul Bareau, who replaced Brooks as deputy editor and then joined Hobson at the *News Chronicle* in 1935, subsequently became the last editor of the *Statist*. His successor on the *FN* was the intensely hard-working and able Wilfred King, who by 1936 was established as the world's leading authority on the London discount market past and present. Ten years later King became editor of the *Banker*, in which capacity he took over from another old *FN* man, W. Manning Dacey, who now took up the post of economic adviser to Lloyds Bank. Also on the *FN* staff in the mid-1930s, in fairly lowly positions, were Harry Fischer, co-founder after the war of the Marlborough Fine Art Gallery; J. P. W. ('Curly') Mallalieu, a future Labour minister; and Ralph Hammond Innes, the celebrated thriller writer.

Three subsequent high-flyers were particularly interesting. One was Harold Wincott, who as a young man, working as a statistician in a stockbroker's office, was recruited by his friend Wilfred King in 1930 to be a sub-editor at six guineas a week. Wincott patiently worked his way up, in due course becoming chief sub-editor, and in 1938 was appointed editor of the *Investors Chronicle*, from which platform he emerged after the war as probably the leading financial journalist of the day. 'I wish I could have written that story myself,' he was often heard to say while subbing at the *FN*, and perhaps a more glittering educational past than Hornsey County School would have helped. Another young editorial newcomer with a great journalistic future was Gordon Newton, who, soon after Green became editor, was employed at £4 a week to look after press cuttings for Green's secretary, Miss Bannister. After a while Newton started to write on company topics, then became commodity editor and in 1939 was made news editor. Few would have guessed that a great editor was in the making. Altogether more manifestly brilliant was Richard ('Otto') Clarke, who under Green was both chief leader writer and in overall charge of the 'Lex' column. Douglas Jay (City editor of the *Daily Herald* in the late 1930s) dined weekly with him at Pimms Red House in Bishopsgate and recalled Clarke as not only 'a Fabian, author of a New Fabian Research Bureau pamphlet signed "Ingot", advocating nationalisation of iron and steel' but also 'a first-class Cambridge mathematician' and 'a brilliant chess player'.[27] After leaving the paper in 1939, he became the most incisive and distinguished of civil servants. He could, Keynes once remarked, 'do anything with figures'.[28]

Nor in these days was future distinction absent on the business side, especially in the person of the youthful Lord Moore, later Eleventh Earl of Drogheda, who started on the *FN* early in 1933 selling advertising space. 'Moore seems too sensitive to be on the business side of a financial journal, but he does it well,' thought Brooks, and indeed Moore now began to establish his firm reputation as the most charming but also obdurate of salesmen. He was very much Bracken's man and as early as 1934 was elected a director. One way and another it was an impressive new line-up, operating at 20 Bishopsgate in a generally happy, family atmosphere despite the indifferent conditions and poor pay. From almost everyone who survives from those pre-war days the chorus is that 'there was no paper like it'.

The *FN* also, though never attaining the same status as a paper of record as the *FT*, exhibited under Green considerable flair and courage. The first of July 1935 was the date for a particularly pioneering innovation: the start of the *FN* Thirty-Share Index, which supplanted the daily share index that the paper had begun five years earlier and which would in due course become the famous *FT* Ordinary Share Index. The thirty shares chosen were solely industrial equities, thereby reflecting the steep growth since the war of domestic manufacturing and distribution securities quoted on the London Stock Exchange; while the decision to concentrate on a relatively narrow band of the most actively traded shares of the day, irrespective of their market capitalization and employing a geometric rather than arithmetic mean, gave the index its long-lived qualities of sensitivity and continuity. The creator of the index was the 24-year-old Clarke, in close collaboration with Green himself, and it was soon welcomed by the *Economist* as likely to give 'a very fair representation of the changes of market temper'. Three months later the *FN* published a notable 56-page supplement on 'American Finance and Industry', the first such survey in an English paper since 1929 and featuring a plentiful supply of advertisements collected in New York that summer by Turner and Moore, including a dramatic one for Cable & Wireless on the front cover.

Things were also moving on the investigative-cum-campaigning front. Einzig, in the intervals between his phenomenal production of books on all manner of monetary subjects, continued to dig deep and propagandize, in particular about the need for the 'gold bloc' countries of Western Europe, above all France, to devalue their currencies, earning him much opprobrium abroad. Events, however, proved him right. 'Midas' too was causing a stir. In November 1935 Cowen wrote in his column in a detailed, highly critical way about a semi-fraudulent concern called Coal & Allied Industries Ltd, which was supposed to convert coal into oil. The company's shares fell rapidly, and the *FN* was warned that it would be sued for damages if there was another such article, which in fact Cowen had already prepared. On 2 December, the eve of intended publication, Cowen, Green and Bracken conferred. 'I leave it to you, Maurice,' said Bracken; Green decided to publish; and no writ was issued. The following September something similar happened when Cowen was able to uncover enough information and suspicious circumstances to 'pull the plug' on a big speculative gamble in the Commonwealth Mining & Finance Group, run by a financier called de Bernales. He specialized in giving big lunches at the Great Eastern Hotel, floated various subdivisions on the strength of specious reports about new fields being found in Australia and had even persuaded the *FN* itself to run at least one not unfavourable 'leader page special' on its prospects.

'We hold that the financial press can have no real goodwill or security unless it is vigilant and independent,' Bracken told his shareholders next month, and broadly speaking the *FN* of this period lived up to that lofty ideal.[29] This is not to deny that the libel laws retained their constraining influence; nor that there was considerable truth in Hobson's assertion of 1934 that 'the system under which a large part of the costs of newspaper production is provided not by selling news but by selling advertising space to some extent restricts freedom of criticism in matters of finance'; nor indeed that Beaverbrook was essentially right in his late judgement on Bracken that he 'never challenged directly the powerful interests of the City, preferring to fall in with them', and in particular 'refused to quarrel with the banks'.[30] Hands that feed cannot be bitten; exceptions to the rule would always be precisely that. Yet, all things considered, there was about the pre-war *FN* a candour, a willingness to come clean, somewhat lacking in the pages of its more successful rival.

In the *FN* on 31 January 1933 there were two main front-page headlines: in the top left-hand corner 'Kaffirs Higher Still', in the top right 'Herr Hitler – Chancellor of Germany'. The main leader of the day was entitled 'Heil Hitler!' and began: 'If ever man had a right to chuckle, the little Austrian pocket-Mussolini has some justification for chuckling today.' But the leader then went on to argue that Hitler would be the prisoner of the non-Nazi majority in the new government, even asserting that 'it is, to say the least of it, highly unlikely that the Nazis would attempt to base their power on armed force'. The *FT* was similarly reassuring, drawing particular comfort from the fact that 'finance is left in the capable hands of Count Schwerin von Krosigle, whose views were placed before readers of the *Financial Times* on 1 September last year'. Later that year the *FT* published an eight-page supplement which it called 'The Renaissance of Italy: Fascism's Gift of Order and Progress'. The front page featured a signed photograph of a studious-looking Mussolini, while in the main body of the paper an editorial commented admiringly on the way Italy had weathered the world storms of recent years.[31]

Over the next few years, as Hitler gained total power and the Axis began to be formed, the *FT*'s sympathies were with the appeasers. Thus when Hitler occupied the Rhineland in March 1936, the paper confined its disapproval to a comment on Hitler having 'acted with his customary precipitancy' and took the line that out of the episode there might 'well emerge in the end a clearer prospect of European peace than has existed for a generation past'. The *FN* now adopted an altogether different stance:

> We must face the clear fact of Germany's all-embracing policy of expansion, which is not altered by occasional olive branches. Now may or may not be the right time for the firm front – much must inevitably depend on Mussolini – but it is difficult to believe that a stand will not have to be taken one day unless Germany's maximum demands are to be conceded.

The next day, after a résumé of the aims of *Mein Kampf* ('the original German edition, not the version presented for English readers'), the paper called for greater solidarity with France.

There was, however, a piquant financial coda to such a call. It occurred in April 1937 when Chamberlain, in his first Budget, proposed a new tax on business profits, the National Defence Contribution, in order to help pay for rearmament. The *FT*'s initial response was that the Budget contained 'nothing threatening any diminution of the activity or profitability of industry' and that 'the NDC is acceptable in principle and doubtful only in application'. But over the next few weeks City opposition to the new tax mounted, including from the *FT*, and at the beginning of June the scheme was withdrawn. By contrast, the *FN* was out of the blocks with a vengeance against the proposed imposition. Green wanted to call its initial attack (the day after the Budget) 'Soak the Rich', but on Bracken's suggestion changed it to the much more effective 'Soak the Enterprising'. Over the next few days a series of hostile articles followed, with headlines like 'Mr Chamberlain – Robin Hood Reversed', and by the end of May the paper was referring to Chamberlain as 'our Iron (or corrugated iron?) Chancellor'. The *FN* had, in fact, led the way in effectively moulding City opinion – a striking tribute to its new qualitative, if not quantitative, influence.

By this time significant high-level changes had taken place at the *FT*. At the beginning of 1937 the long partnership between Camrose and his brother was broken up, with Camrose taking as his chunk of the empire the *Daily Telegraph*, the *FT* and the many periodicals published by the Amalgamated Press. The reasons for the split are uncertain, but the likeliest explanation is that Kemsley felt that the time had come to move out of the shadow of his older brother and at last become a powerful press proprietor in his own right. Nor was this all. Camrose had for several years been anxious about the increasingly thin top layer at the *FT*, with Barrett no longer the man he had been, Hunter still sharp but getting on in years, and things more or less held together by A. G. Cole. He decided therefore early in 1937 to ease out Barrett and Hunter (though Barrett became a director, and Hunter was briefly managing editor), appoint his son Michael Berry as managing director and find a new editor. In effect, the choice lay between Cole – the utter professional, with no great social graces and now in his late forties – and a relatively new face in Coleman Street in the person of Archie Chisholm, who was in his mid-thirties and had been educated at Westminster and Oxford. Chisholm had spent some time in the London office of the *Wall Street Journal* before going out to Persia as an executive with the Anglo-Persian Oil Company. He returned in 1936, when he soon got a job as a leader writer on the *FT*. Conscious of the *FN*'s brilliant young staff and generally up-market image, Camrose chose Chisholm, who, with his impressively slim, tall figure, his monocle and his ability to hit it off quickly with people, had just the right manner and appearance for being an editor and acting as the paper's front man in the City. Chisholm was no fool, but his knowledge of the mechanism of the City and of financial journalism was not at this stage very extensive. However, he learnt quickly; working closely with Berry and Murrough O'Brien (advertising manager since 1934), and receiving loyal support from Cole as associate editor, he was soon leading a good new team.

In the face of the threatening, confidence-sapping international situation, they were not the easiest of years, with the Stock Exchange on the slide by the second half of 1937. *FT* profits fell, down to a miserable £8,496 for 1938, and in June 1939 the board was forced to suspend payment of the half-yearly preference dividend. Circulation also fell, down in 1938 to an average sale of just under 25,000. There was therefore little room for manoeuvre, but Chisholm did try in one or two respects to brighten the paper. 'Potential Investments' was at last sent out to grass, and the left-hand centre page was redesigned. In particular, there now appeared each day on that page a chatty, anecdotal column 'City Men and Matters', which Chisholm wrote most of and was consciously modelled on 'Peterborough' in the *Daily Telegraph*. Chisholm also became, when the *FT* celebrated its fiftieth anniversary in February 1938 with a special issue, the first national editor to appear on television, being interviewed by Leslie Mitchell on *Picture Page*. Chisholm was reluctant, but Camrose pointed out to him the value of the free advertising. Camrose also had his way when Chisholm, soon after he became editor, wanted to change the colour of the paper back to white, on technical grounds and because of associations with the 'Pink 'Un'. Camrose gave the firmest of vetoes, pointing out that young fellows travelling into the City by tube liked to be seen with the distinctive paper, thereby indentifying them as 'something in the City'. Once more, the thin pink line held.

There was also a change of editorship at Bishopsgate. Green in the summer of 1938 moved on and up to become City editor of *The Times* and was succeeded by Hargreaves Parkinson, who, in addition to writing many 'Lex' columns for the *FN*, had been since 1935 associate editor of the *Economist*. It was an uncontentious choice on Bracken's part, for Parkinson had by this time established a considerable reputation as an expert on investment – was indeed very much regarded as the investor's friend, especially the small investor – and no one could doubt his commitment to enhancing the cause of financial journalism. 'H.P.', as he was almost invariably known, was in many ways an old-fashioned Lancastrian in manner and character: ruddy-faced, always dressed in tweeds, something of an autodidact. A diary entry by Brooks in 1932 catches a little the flavour of the man:

> Lunched Lex at the Press Club. We talked mostly of R.L.S. [Robert Louis Stevenson]. Lex is not only a profound student of R.L.S. but brings to him that same detached balance that he brings to finance, which sounds bloodless but isn't. It was a little odd to find him, with his pleasant, solid manner, advancing the theory that too little research had been done on R.L.S.'s youth and that almost certainly something happened to him not yet revealed – some venereal disease.

Parkinson was also a man of great probity. On one occasion, after paying a visit to the Royal Danish Brewery and writing a friendly, chit-chat sort of article about it, he received from the brewery a case of lager, which he felt impelled to return, saying it was impossible in the circumstances to accept it. Drogheda later summed him up: 'H.P. was a man of exceptional goodness, willing to undertake any task allotted to him, and he was I fear somewhat exploited by Brendan, who could be a bully to those who did not stand up to him.'[32] This was true, though most of the bullying was still to come.

In the late 1930s, under the shadow of war and the Stock Exchange slump, with the *FN* suffering at least as much as the *FT*, Parkinson did not do all that much to the paper, though there was perhaps a tendency for it to be rather more strictly markets-orientated than it had been under Hobson and Green. Parkinson had invented a character called Cyrus Q. Hatch, who expounded and demonstrated the merits of Parkinson's 'Hatch' theory of investment (basically, sell if shares fall by more than 10 per cent, buy if they rise by more than 10 per cent, i.e. in each case representing a secular trend), and the exploits of Cyrus filled quite a few pages. Parkinson also allowed Einzig to affix his initials to his 'Lombard Street' column, which was not inappropriate, for the European dimension that Einzig specialized in was now becoming the omnipresent focus of everyone's thoughts.

The Financial Times

3.45 a.m. EDITION

LARGEST CIRCULATION OF ANY FINANCIAL JOURNAL IN THE EMPIRE

No. 15,473 LONDON, Friday, 30th September, 1938 [Twopence

Money & Exchanges

GOLD SALES REDUCED

NOTE CIRCULATION EXPANSION

THURSDAY Evening.

Relief brought by the calling of the Four-Power Conference in Munich had a reflection in nearly all sections of the Money markets to-day. The exodus of nervous capital from London abated and there was a rush to sell dollars.

DOLLAR CHEAPENS

Forward Premiums Also Run Down

BIG RECOVERY IN BRITISH GOVERNMENT FUNDS

HOME RAILS HIGHER

STRONG ADVANCE IN GERMAN AND OTHER EUROPEAN STOCKS

Stock Exchange Settling Days

	October			November		
Contango	*Mon.*	10	24	*Mon.*	7	21
Ticket	*Tues.*	11	25	*Tues.*	8	22
Intermediate	*Wed.*	12	26	*Wed.*	9	23
Account	*Thurs.*	13	27	*Thurs.*	10	24

THURSDAY Evening.

The full effect of the Prime Minister's dramatic statement on the international political situation in the House of Commons on Wednesday afternoon was felt in the Stock Exchange to-day.

The upswing in prices which started in the Street last night gained in momentum, and in practically all markets recent falls consequent on the crisis were to a large extent regained.

Actually, the volume of business transacted was quite moderate. At the last a little hesitation was noticeable in some directions, the view being expressed that the recovery had been too fast.

From the start dealers raised prices substantially, and on the whole the improvement was well maintained.

Minimum prices for gilt-edged securities went into cold storage and British Funds closed with advances ranging up to 5 points in extent.

Higher prices also were quoted for other investment stocks.

Advances were even more marked in the Foreign market, and ranged up to 20 points in the case of Czech 8 per cents.

Quotations were, of course, very nominal, and dealings a matter of negotiation.

Home Railway stocks participated in the recovery, as also did Foreign Railway issues.

Industrials closed with a long series of rises, although the volume of business transacted was moderate.

Rubber, Tea and Oil shares all participated in the recovery, and in the Mining markets numerous strong advances occurred.

WAR LOAN DEALT IN AT 100

Quite a considerable volume of business was transacted in the gilt-edged market. Prices of British Funds were raised by several points from the start ...

... market. Great Western rose 1 to 33. Midland and Scottish also was 1 up at 13. The 4 per cent. Preference moved up $3\frac{1}{2}$ to 53 and the 4 per cent. Preference ...

FRENCH RAILS RALLY

GERMAN LOANS BUOYANT

OPTIONS IN GOOD DEMAND

An Investor's Note Book

HOPEFULNESS RESTRAINED

LUCKY DEALS

BURMAH OIL INTERIM

Restrained optimism was, to a greater extent than might be inferred from the general advance in prices, the keynote of the Stock Markets yesterday. As one member observed, it is still a case of "Trust in Chamberlain and keep your powder dry."

Brokers were unanimous in discouraging short-term speculation—clients were given a tactful hint that they must be prepared to pay cash at the mid-October Settlement for any new purchases. During the afternoon business fell off markedly. Operators were evidently envisaging the risk of another worrying week-end should no definitely reassuring news come from Munich to-day.

A travelled House man uneasily recalled that owing to the birthplace of the Nazi party standing on a hill and being in proximity to the Alps, Munich is very subject to violent changes of temperature.

"F.T." Index Readings

The readings of THE FINANCIAL TIMES security indices (which will be found as usual in the south-west corner of this page) were all 4 to 6 per cent. up yesterday. In many cases quotations had recovered by the close to their making-up prices on Monday week, 19th September, and some were even higher.

Luck Rewards Pluck

Kaffirs and Oils

Burmah Interim

Flower and Sons

The Diarist

WOOL FIRM AT SYDNEY

WIDESPREAD IMPROVEMENT IN INDUSTRIAL SHARES

BUSINESS EXPANDS

BANKING, INSURANCE AND STORES GROUPS PROMINENT

THURSDAY Evening.

Yesterday's late improvement in Industrial shares was reflected more widely in prices to-day. Values advanced rapidly in the morning, under the influence of the more favourable political outlook, and generally retained their rises to the close.

Groups showing substantial rises included Bank, Insurance and Stores shares. Some fairly large transactions were reported to have been put through in the leading Tobaccos and in Dunlops and Imperial Chemicals.

Although still a matter of negotiation, business increased in volume. The number of bargains recorded in all markets was 3,848, or more than double yesterday's figure of 2,007.

The rapidity of the rise was reflected in THE FINANCIAL TIMES Industrial index, which rose to 97.2, compared with 91.2 yesterday.

Business in the Street market was idle and price changes small. U.S. Steels were easier and Nickels unaltered, while Radio Corporations were firmer.

BANK SHARES SPURT

Quotations Recover Rapidly From Previous Depression

ELECTRICALS BETTER

FORD MOTORS GOOD

STEELS HIGHER

Good Improvement in Wm. Cory Shares

United Steels were 2s 9d up at 24s and Vickers gained 1s 9d at 20s 3d. Indian Irons were put up ⅛ to 2⅟₁₆, but Halesowens, with a loss of 1s 6d to 19s, were a dull exception to the general trend of the market.

Richard Thomas Ordinary at 5s and the Preference at 9s were both unaltered. Announcement of the passing of the Preference dividend was not received during business hours.

A jump in Wm. Cory shares was the most striking movement among Coal shares. ...

RAYONS FIRMER

Big Recoveries in the Stores Group

TOBACCOS ADVANCE

RECENT ISSUES

Higher Preferences

STREET DEALINGS

Quietly Firm

Round the Markets

A CHEERY SLOGAN

INQUIRIES POUR IN

"The war is over!"

With this cheery slogan, Stock Exchange markets set up a fresh structure of strength, the effect of which was felt in every part of the House. Some of the price-fluctuations look astonishing. German Sevens (5 per cent.) marked 19 on Wednesday, and yesterday were quoted 41½. The Five and a-Half per Cent. Bonds (4½ per cent.), which changed hands at 15, recovered to 33.

To take a very different stock, Lever Sevens, which were 29s. left off last night at 29s. Stock Exchange shares hardly moved, remaining at 100. Central Argentine Railway stocks refused to be downcast by the absence of a dividend on the Four and a-Half per Cent. and the Six per Cent. Preference. Optimists had looked for a small distribution on the former.

More Inquiries Than Orders?

Entering the Stock Exchange soon after half-past nine yesterday morning, one found a few dealers in the Kaffir market, none in the Consol market, and two or three in the Yankee market. The Kaffir prices were being quoted nominally the same as those of Wednesday evening in the Street.

Everyone was agog to hear what the first price might be. As the market filled up, so the curiosity increased, the first price being awaited with undisguised interest. A shout of laughter arose when somebody made 1½ to 2 in Ventersport.

Prices Marked Up

The Lurking Doubt

Bank Rate

Police War Reserve

Autolycus

INDEX AND NEWS SUMMARY

SALIENT POINTS

COMPANY RESULTS

MARKET NOTES

"Financial Times" Stock Indices

U.K. Commodity Index

London Stock Exchange Markings

THE

FINANCIAL NEWS

LATE LONDON EDITION

No. 16,594 [ESTABLISHED 1884] LONDON, FRIDAY, SEPTEMBER 30, 1938 PRICE 2d.

AGREEMENT AT MUNICH

NEW PLAN SENT TO CZECHS

PACT SIGNED AT 1.30 A.M.

ON TERMS OF CESSION OF SUDETEN AREAS

ALL-ROUND RECOVERY IN MARKETS

After sessions lasting six hours the Four-Power talks at Munich were suspended at 8.30 p.m. for dinner. The Conference was resumed at 10 p.m. and sat until early this morning.

Before the talks were resumed, however, messages from Berlin, Munich and Rome. announced that agreement had been reached in principle and that the plan was being communicated to Prague.

This was later confirmed by a Munich wireless announcement as follows:—

"The Fuehrer, the Duce, Mr. Chamberlain and M. Daladier at 1.30 this morning signed an agreement regarding the terms of the methods of the cession of the Sudeten German areas."

M. Masaryk, the Czech representative in Munich, is believed to have already flown to Prague with the outline of the proposed plan of the occupation together with military maps. These show how Czech troops may be withdrawn without there being any danger of their clashing with the occupying German forces.

Signor Gayda, the "Giornale d'Italia" writer known as Mussolini's mouthpiece, announced last night that the agreement included recognition for the rights of Slovaks, Magyars and Poles in Czechoslovakia.

UNOFFICIAL OUTLINE OF PLAN

Unofficial reports declared that the plan envisaged the immediate occupation by Germany of "token" areas with the appointment of an international commission to draw the new frontier and to supervise the transfer of populations.

It was also stated that an international force, including British troops, would take over the areas to be ceded to Germany pending their occupation by German troops on given dates during October.

Finally, plebiscites would be held in areas with a considerable percentage of Sudeten Germans in Hungarian and Polish areas, the ultimate settlement being backed by an international guarantee for the new Czechoslovakia.

Modifications in the Czech attitude, according to a statement in official circles in Prague, were conveyed to the British representatives before the Munich conference.

The Czech Government agreed to cede territory where the inhabitants were more than half German and to ask only for frontiers which would make the Czech State capable of existence and defence.

A plebiscite in Czech areas or in those with a large Czech majority was declined.

All these arrangements are to be carried out by December 15, but a settlement is possible by October 31.

The Czech Government agreed also to the supervision by an international commission and by the British Legion, as well as to an occupation by British troops before the territory is handed to the Germans.

STOCK MARKETS' SHARP RECOVERY

The recovery in Stock markets which began in the "Street" on Wednesday evening made rapid headway yesterday. Closing prices were virtually at the day's highest and business was the largest for some days. Gilt-edged showed gains of up to 4 points, and "The Financial News" Industrial share index jumped 6.2, to 79.9. The downward trend on the Paris Bourse was completely reversed. In Berlin and Amsterdam "boom" conditions prevailed.

Wall Street began with a further substantial gain on Wednesday's closing levels, but thereafter moved within narrow limits until the last hour, when reports of an agreement in Munich caused a sharp advance. The Dow Industrial average rose on the day from 133.68 to 137.16.

Sterling and francs were heavily bought against dollars. The New York rate closed with a rise of 4⅛c. at 4.75¼. No change was made in the Bank rate despite the recent sharp rise in discounts.

The reaction of Commodity markets was mainly limited to a further sharp fall in Liverpool wheat. There was some heavy selling of copper, which closed 17s. 6d. down, at £42 0s. 3d.

The Bank of England note issue showed a striking increase of £21,700,000 in the week to Wednesday last. The demand for notes was mainly from banks anxious to build up "till money" reserves of provincial branches.

FROM OUR POLITICAL CORRESPONDENT

FURTHER ADVANCE IN STERLING

SMALLER GOLD TURNOVER

BIG RISES IN MARKETS

PRICES CLOSE AT HIGHEST

GILTS GOOD RECOVERY

CHINA SUSPENDS TWO SINKING FUNDS

BUT LOAN INTEREST TO BE PAID

WHEAT ADVISORY COMMITTEE

WALL ST. AGAIN STRONG

DOW GAINS FURTHER 3½ POINTS

NEW U.S. GOLD MOVE

IMPORTS NOT TO BE PLACED IN GENERAL FUND

SHARP FALL IN WHEAT

HEAVY SELLING OF COPPER

The Stock Exchange

Complete Volte-face by Markets Economics of Crisis

A Minor Caveat

What a Market!

Traffics

Shipping & Textile Shares

Sandbags in the "House"?

MART.

Notes for Investors

War Preparations

The Effects at Home

Economics of Sandbags

LEX.

Financial News Contents Summary

THE MORNING'S NEWS

INDEX TO PAGES

YESTERDAY'S MARKETS

CHIEF CHANGES

30 September 1938: Munich

In March 1938 Hitler annexed Austria and during September steadily turned the screws on Czechoslovakia, leading to the Munich agreement at the end of the month that more or less gave him everything he wanted. 'Mr Chamberlain's efforts to preserve the peace have assumed heroic proportions,' declared the *FT* on the day the Prime Minister met Hitler at Munich, adding: 'Today's meeting gives Reason a last chance, with Peace at stake and four resolute men [i.e. including Daladier and Mussolini] bent on striking a just balance on great issues.' The next day, with 'Peace Coming Into View', the *FT* reflected general City opinion and relief (soon to take the form of a congratulatory message from the Stock Exchange to Chamberlain) when it asserted that, though 'dismemberment is a painful thing for a proud country to contemplate', nevertheless 'it possesses the one virtue, that it will have spared countless millions of horrors of a war more intense and destructive even than that of 1914–18'.

More surprisingly, the *FN* during the Munich crisis, under the editorship of Parkinson and despite Bracken's allegiance to Churchill, displayed similar appeasing tendencies, above all in the editor's Monday column 'This Week and Last' on 3 October:

> If the period which follows last week's agreement is to be more than a brief interlude of concentrated British rearmament activity, before the occurrence of the next crisis, it will be necessary to assume that there is, after all, something in Herr Hitler's profession that his territorial ambitions in Europe are satisfied. No one will, of course, dream for one moment of taking this assertion literally. But if the British Government puts upon it the construction that, given some accommodation on Colonies (which, clearly, is not impossible and is probably not regarded as outside the borders of ratiocination by important members of the British Government), then the Fuehrer may believe he has reached the point at which he can cease belabouring the democracies and ask them to come in with him and Italy in some sort of Concert of Europe. It is difficult to say what the basis of such an unethical deal might be, beyond a suggestion that the world was big enough to allow different international rackets to operate without getting mixed up with each other.

That particular vision was not to be. Over the rest of the winter Germany gradually whittled away the remaining economic independence of central and south-eastern Europe, to an aggrieved but unavailing almost daily chorus from Einzig, who on 6 February 1939 was reminded by Bracken that 'the *Financial News* is a newspaper – not a propagandist sheet'.[33]

The following month Hitler occupied Prague, and at last the worm turned, to general support. The *FT* declared on 20 March: 'There can be no doubt now that Mr Chamberlain's sweeping condemnation of Herr

Hitler involves a major reorientation of British foreign policy. It could not have been otherwise.' The *FN* agreed: 'Nazi policy menaces certain principles which are fundamental to all trading – no less than political – relations.' In April the guarantee to Poland was given, and that same month the *FN*'s company secretary, Arthur Knock, was instructed by his board 'to make enquiries regarding the suitability of basement accommodation at No. 16 Bishopsgate as an air raid shelter in an emergency'. Appeasement was not yet dead; during the summer a brilliant, relentlessly sustained exposure by Einzig of how the Bank for International Settlements (with British and French directors) had successfully instructed the Bank of England to hand over to the Reichsbank a gold deposit of some £6 million belonging to the Czechoslovak National Bank caused considerable embarrassment to the government. But when Hitler invaded Poland at the beginning of September there was only one course open. 'It was inevitable that sooner or later', said the *FN*, 'we should have to fight to check Germany's drive to world supremacy.' The *FT*'s leader, 'Our War for Peace', expressed belief in the justness of the cause and confidence in victory. At the last there was no whining, no snivelling about markets in a state of collapse, but instead a shared resolve.

Inevitably, the financial press died a death, metaphorically if not literally. 'The City is depressing beyond description. I go there for about an hour a day and I depart feeling like Job in the depth of his woes.'[34] Bracken's private words to Moore early in November 1939 were echoed in public a few weeks later, when he told shareholders that 'war makes the worst of slumps seem a matter of small consequence'.[35] This time the Stock Exchange closed for a few days only, but it was soon suffering from familiar restrictions: all bargains to be done for cash, no bargains to be 'carried over' from one account to another and no new issues to be dealt in unless sanctioned by both the Stock Exchange Committee and the Treasury. As a result, prospectus revenue virtually dried up, while in addition there was soon a tendency on the part of companies to pay only for shortened reports of their meetings. There was also the usual crop of other difficulties to deal with: editorial, business and production staff all severely denuded; less than half the customary time allowed for typesetting, in order to meet the demands of a wartime railway timetable; newsprint in short supply, especially after the German invasion of Norway in April 1940; and the threat, far more acute than in the previous war, of bombardment from the air. Hardly surprisingly, there emerged out of all this newspapers of only four or six pages an issue, produced with great difficulty, carrying little advertising and earning at best slender profits. Circulation fell predictably, with the *FT* being on about 12,000 during 1940 and 1941 and the *FN* reputedly but a quarter to a third of that.

At Coleman Street, with Berry leaving for the war in the autumn of 1939 and Chisholm a year later, the man who held the fort until 1945 was Cole as acting editor. Newland the company secretary was killed in November 1940 when an enemy bomb fell on his home. The *FT* at the outset of hostilities cut salaries by about a third. At Bishopsgate there was an almost immediate full-scale purge, though after a few weeks most people who had not joined up were reinstated to their jobs at reduced salaries. The two people there who bore most of the day-to-day brunt and kept the *FN* going in the most adverse of circumstances were Parkinson, whose secretary kept a typewriter down in the basement where the editor could dictate away regardless of air raids, and the company secretary Knock, who in the early days had to put up with a good deal of needless vituperation by phone and memorandum from his chairman. Bracken himself became Minister of Information in July 1941 and accordingly resigned from the board, with General Dawnay being elected chairman and most of the real decision-making devolving on Moore as managing director. Slowly, however, the darkest days of the war passed, and a certain semi-normality returned to City life, symbolized in the case of the *FN* by the return to Bishopsgate in April 1942 of the accounts department, which since late 1940 had been going about its business in the unfamiliar surroundings of Knock's home in rural Hampshire.

'The paper continues to publish the maximum of up-to-date news, and in the past year has published more company reports, meetings and dividends, and Stock Exchange prices than any other newspaper, together with a full editorial and feature service.'[36] Camrose's brave words of June 1940 about his truncated paper were justified. Eschewing (like the *FN*) formal coverage of the war itself, the *FT* managed to preserve intact most of its regular features, concentrating heavily, as in the previous war, on concision and compression rather than readability. Also in accordance with the paper's traditions, it tended to be uncritical of the government's methods of financing and generally running the war, though it did wage certain specific campaigns on behalf of the City, as against Treasury proposals in 1940 for a system of dividend limitation and the following year against the workings of the Excess Profits Tax. Moreover, even after the *FT* took the bold step in March 1940 of at last moving the main news on to the front page, the paper continued to remain less outward-looking than the *FN*. Thus, on Saturday 13 February 1943, the *FT* devoted two out of its four pages to comprehensive lists of Stock Exchange prices and marked bargains, covering the whole of the week as well as the previous day; while of the other two pages, most of page one was given over to the dividend announcement of the London Midland & Scottish Railway Company, a factual review of the markets, 'The Diarist' column for investors that Wylie King continued to write almost up to his death in April 1945, and a column of 'Market Notes and Views' by 'Veritas', who on Saturdays subbed for 'Autolycus' Landells. The *FN* that day was also four pages and had rather less (but not much less) Stock Exchange detail, but arguably more than made up for the relative lack with a variety of quite substantial items on such subjects as the response of Conservative MPs to the recent Beveridge Report, measures to control spending power in Australia and the grandiose claims of Dr Funk, German Minister of Economics, at the annual meeting of the Reichsbank. On the front page, where the LMS dividend was the main story in the *FN* too, 'Midas' had departed the scene, but the 'Lex' column (in the custody of Wincott for most of the war) was its usual cogent self, offering a clear-sighted analysis of the financial aspects of Lord Nuffield's latest £10 million gift to charity.

The *FN* was also in general much more critical of government policy – and not only during the pre-Churchill phase of the war, when it called for 'an Economic General Staff' with 'supreme power' and talked of 'the regrettable affinity between the appeasement mentality and the business-as-usual mentality which has stultified so much of our war effort'.[37] Einzig in particular, who at the start of the war had become political correspondent in addition to continuing his 'Lombard Street' column, proved a constant thorn in the government's side, despite Bracken's ministerial status. 'The first thing I do every morning is to read Einzig's column in the *Financial News*, and it always makes me sick,' remarked Kingsley Wood, the Chancellor of the Exchequer, to Montagu Norman on one occasion; while his successor at the Treasury, Sir John Anderson, became so annoyed by Einzig's constant harping on the government's folly in allowing sterling balances to pile up in countries like India and Egypt where British forces were stationed, together with his revelations about Anglo-American currency negotiations, that he tried to have him arrested. That failed, thanks to Bracken's good offices, but early in 1944 Anderson was able to induce the *FN* board to tell Parkinson that unless he was able to restrain his headstrong columnist Einzig would have to go. Parkinson duly delivered the ultimatum, forbidding the publication of anything likely to displease the Treasury, and Einzig reluctantly complied, 'muzzled' for the first time in his long journalistic career.[38]

By this time the war was going well. Newsprint supplies had been picking up since September 1943, and Stock Exchange prices similarly from about two months later. As had been the case since 1940, the *FT* was still printed more often than not on white rather than pink paper and indeed did not return to full-time pink paper until after the war; but the paper's circulation rose significantly, to an average net sale of 20,272 in 1943 and 25,898 in 1944. Both companies resumed the payment of dividends. At the *FN* the editor even found time to write his long-nurtured treatise on *Ordinary Shares* (1944), which, anticipating the post-war 'cult of equity', sold very well and was described by *The Times* in later years as 'a study of the fortunes of risk-bearing investment' and 'something of a standard work'.[39] Issue sizes increased very gradually, so that by the week of D-Day in June 1944 the *FT* was running at a total of 32 pages for its six issues and the *FN* (for once ahead) at 34.

During these last two years of hostilities the *FT* presumably began to plan ahead for the post-war period, but the *FN* certainly did, with a fair amount of documentation surviving. In particular, Parkinson in September 1943 produced for Moore's benefit a detailed fifteen-page memorandum on post-war editorial policy, containing much food for thought:

> The peace-time selling opportunities for a daily financial newspaper, with a purely *general* appeal, are extremely limited. The readership is specialised, its interest is concentrated on the stock market, and no paper with our circulation, staff and resources can hope to compete with the big dailies in giving its readers a first-rate foreign or political news service.

With this basic assumption in mind, Parkinson made a series of proposals for strengthening the post-war *FN*'s markets coverage, of which the key one was having the chief market man and two assistants out in the City all day, 'following up stories and continually testing contacts', trying to pin down 'the real market news': that is, the news that 'comes from behind the Stock Exchange – from what members say to each other, from "shops" and finance houses, from the insurance and investment trust people, etc.'. This type of news, Parkinson added, went beyond merely market prices and reports:

> It is readers' *pabulum*, and the paper that can get hold of it will sell whatever its colour, views or approach. Apart from what Autolycus picks up in the House, the *FT* does not get a tithe of it. But the reputation Autolycus has built up even on the slender amount he has caught hold of, shows how important it is.

In accordance with this priority, Parkinson stated that though there might be a long-term case for 'a planned campaign to bring in industrial readers', in the immediate post-war period 'we should lay down the principle that industry interests us chiefly for its Stock Exchange bearing'. He concluded:

I believe that the *FT* gets its readers, not because it is bad (it would be libelling them to say that they do not deserve a better paper) but because it gives them, as far as it can, what they want. If we can give it, and give it so much better that they cannot fail to see how much better it is, our problem is on its way to being solved.

Following this course it might yet be possible, Parkinson believed, for the *FN* 'once for all to clear ourselves from the thankless position of being the number two paper in a market which is not over-wide anyhow'.

Yet the really interesting thing is that only a year after producing this major policy statement, which in a fundamental sense ran counter to the whole 'broadening' thrust of the pre-war *FN*, Parkinson had changed his tack. By the autumn of 1944, in the course of a major set-piece correspondence, it was Shapland the circulation manager who believed that the *FN*'s post-war chances 'of becoming the premier financial daily . . . lie in our producing precisely what you [now] say we should not produce, viz. a bigger and better *FT*', Parkinson, who wanted something different, going well beyond the traditional remit of financial journalism. On 9 October he replied to Shapland:

There is no suggestion whatever that private enterprise, as we have known it, will disappear in any post-war regime. What is clear is that public and private enterprise will exist side by side, with rather less private and more public than before. The Stock Exchange will remain an essential institution in the post-war economy, but its field will contract, relatively and perhaps absolutely. If the railways, for example, are nationalised or placed under some public board, £1,100 millions of capital stock are removed from the Stock Exchange area, and over a million stock holdings are affected. Add whatever else you wish – electricity, say – and what have you? A smaller market, where booms are regarded as against public policy and speculation is frowned on, but vast numbers of people are interested in production, employment, wages, the state of trade, prices, exports, taxation, overseas balances, etc., who never thought about such things before.

You suggest that, in such an environment, 20 Bishopsgate had better put up the shutters. Here I completely disagree. There will still be a wide demand for investment advice (though less for speculative hints), and to give the finest investment service ever known must be the first foundation of our effort. But much more will be wanted – and this is where the policy followed by the *Financial News*, in the teeth of every kind of discouragement, for the last sixteen years, may at last be seen to have been strictly realist. The new readership, you say, will be difficult to get at. So it will, but it will be a bigger numerical readership than the other ever would have been. And there are certain pressing reasons why we should go out to find it.

In the first place, it seems clear that, if Stock Exchange booms and large (though intermittent) totals of prospectuses are far less frequent, a circulation of 15,000 to 20,000 is far too small for the effort that has to be put into any *daily* paper and the overheads it has to carry. Nothing less than 50,000 is economic and, ultimately, 100,000 should be the minimum target. What is 15,000 for a *daily*, trade or otherwise, when advertisers are comparing us with competitors like the *Times* and *Telegraph*?

Secondly, if we do start taking many readers from the *FT* (and if that is the beginning and end of things), we shall have the full weight of the Camrose organisation, the Camrose energy and the Camrose purse down on us in no time. They will not stand by; and their purse is longer than ours.

In any case, from the *Daily Mail* onwards, the big circulations have come from tapping new markets.

It was a brilliant vision and a cardinal document, for in it Parkinson showed how a post-war financial daily – as it unexpectedly happened calling itself the *FT*, but drawing heavily on its *FN* antecedents – would be able to transform itself from a small-scale 'City rag', of however high a calibre, into something far more national and ambitious, with infinitely greater commercial potential. As Brooks had long before noted, there was more to the solid, pragmatic Lancastrian than met the eye.

Parkinson's fundamental change of mind was played out against the background of a world much preoccupied with the post-war order, how it would work and who would control it. As early as April 1941 the *FN* had asked the question, '*Quis custodiet ipsos custodes?* – who shall plan the planners?' The following year the famous Beveridge Report was published, laying the intellectual foundations of the post-war Welfare State. The *FN* adopted a fairly favourable tone towards it, but not so the *FT*, according to whom 'the Beveridge plan, in its main outlines, is that of the Trades Union Congress'.[40] In June 1944 a further pillar of the coming domestic dispensation was erected with the publication of the government's White Paper on *Employment Policy*, declaring full employment to be the indispensable goal of post-war administrations. Again, the *FT* accorded a less than warm welcome, whereas the *FN*'s new Saturday cartoonist, 'Marchant', drew a sympathetic sketch entitled 'Never Again!', showing long queues outside an employment exchange.

Meanwhile, the allied nations continued to debate at enormous length the post-war monetary and trading order, culminating in the United Nations conference at Bretton Woods in July 1944, when the basic principles were established of an International Monetary Fund designed to stabilize exchange rates and a Bank for Reconstruction and Development designed to provide long-term loans. The *FT* was generally favourable to the conference's efforts, 'a noble measure of success in formulating plans for the most far-reaching monetary measures ever attempted'. Characteristically, it nevertheless expressed some anxiety about whether the Bank would make its loans selectively, pointing out that 'the creditworthiness of the borrower as well as the nature of the work helps to determine the ultimate fate of the loan and of the lenders' money'. The *FN* was much more critical, especially about the system of IMF quotas, giving the United States 'such a figure as will make her attitude, at any future moment, decisive to all intents and purposes'. But at the end of the conference it acknowledged that 'this is the first constructive essay in – and probably the world's last chance of – rebuilding trade and prosperity on liberal international lines' and that therefore for Britain to refuse co-operation 'would be a heavy responsibility indeed'. The paper concluded: 'If anyone has earned a hearty vote of thanks, it is Lord Keynes.'

Increasingly, though, the City's eyes were firmly if parochially fixed on the general election that would follow the end of the war. 'That Mr Churchill and his party will be returned is practically taken for granted,' affirmed 'Autolycus' on 19 July 1945. Five days later: 'Certain it is that no sign exists in the Stock Exchange of apprehension in regard to the outcome of the general election.' At the last, however, Landells had got it wrong; results were declared on the 26th, and Labour was in by a landslide. 'It must be hoped,' said the *FT*, 'the victors will not allow their great majority to persuade them to extremist courses such as would aggravate world anxiety.' According to the *FN*, 'the responsibility of office is a sobering thing, and Mr Attlee's general conduct of affairs is hardly likely to be irresponsible and revolutionary'. The City was whistling in the dark.

[FIVE]

MERGER

In the course of the war a warm friendship developed between Bracken and Camrose, fuelled in part by their mutual admiration and support for Churchill. Bracken seems to have regarded Camrose as something of a father-figure and always spoke of him with the greatest respect. Early in the war they came to an agreement that their two financial dailies should both raise their advertising rates in order to protect themselves; and it appears that at some point thereafter they reached a private understanding by which the other would have the first option on purchase if either decided to sell.[1] It was a pact that soon came into play, for towards the end of the war Camrose made the crucial decision that he would indeed sell the *FT*. Why he did so is not at all documented, but one may plausibly put forward three specific reasons: indifferent personal health; the 'dynastic' motive that the post-war energies of his son Michael (the future Lord Hartwell) would best be devoted to ensuring the future prosperity of the jewel in Camrose's crown, the *Daily Telegraph*; and a generally rather pessimistic vision of the future of the City and financial journalism in post-war Britain, especially if, as Camrose believed was likely, a Labour government was elected. Subsequently he came to regret the decision, even telling O'Brien, the *FT*'s pre-war advertising manager, that it was the greatest mistake he had ever made. His brother Gomer (by this time Lord Kemsley) always insisted in later years that he rather than Bracken should have been given the first option to buy.

Moore as managing director now received his marching orders from his spiritual if not actual chairman: 'Garrett, the *Financial Times* is for sale, why don't you go out and buy it?'[2] Bracken thereafter had his doubts about whether they could afford to pay the price asked, but Moore did not. His editor and circulation manager may have been laying their various plans for the post-war to catch up or even outflank the *FT*, but Moore, at least according to his later account, did not believe it to be possible:

The habit of preferring the *FT* was ingrained in conservative City readers. To overtake its sale would have meant the expenditure of much money, which we did not have, with no guarantee of success; whereas the *FT* had considerable resources, as well as its own printing works, while the *FN* was printed outside under contract. There was no doubt that despite the excellence of some of the *FN*'s writers, the *FT* was regarded as the leading City paper for its stock market comment and greater volume of straightforward financial information; and, because of its greater sale, it attracted more financial advertising, which was itself news, at any rate for readers of financial papers, and this in turn attracted more readers, so that success bred success.

In short, 'with newspapers the important thing is not the absolute level of sale, but to be the leader in one's own particular field'.[3] There was also the important question of newsprint. Restrictions were likely to continue in peacetime for some considerable time, and it was a major attraction that, if the two publications became one, then it would be possible to combine their newsprint quotas and produce a more substantial paper. This duly happened and was later described by Bracken as the principal motive for the merger.[4]

Moore went to his task of buying the *FT* with considerable enthusiasm and determination – qualities that he needed much of during June and early July 1945, as the announcement of handsome profits in 1944 for the *FT* drove up Camrose's asking price, and Bracken from the side started to make noises of apprehensive dissent. At this critical juncture, Moore was greatly helped by Camrose himself, who did everything that he could to ease the *FN*'s path and ensure that the sale went through. A great man, with a large, disinterested mind and deeply committed to the well-being of the press as a whole as well as his own particular ventures, he must have known that one combined paper would ensure the future of daily financial journalism, whereas the continuing existence of two might not.

The ensuing deal was a complex one, but may be summarized as follows. Camrose sold to the Financial News Ltd his controlling interest in the Financial Times Ltd, amounting to 368,000 ordinary shares, for a sum of £743,000. The FN Ltd raised this formidable total partly by selling its Bishopsgate offices; partly by selling investments; partly by getting its brokers to arrange a syndicate to take up some 115,000 of the shares; partly by the willingness of the Eyre Trustees to take up a further 25,000; and partly (most crucially) by selling to the *FT* the copyright and goodwill of the *FN* for the sum of £280,000. To this latter arrangement in particular Camrose made two important contributions: buying the bulk of the *FT* investments that then financed the purchase of the *FN*'s copyright and goodwill; and second, because for legal reasons this purchase could not be made until after the the basic take-over had taken place, agreeing to provide a three-month bridging loan to the *FN* until the copyright and goodwill were bought. As part of the overall deal, Camrose insisted that the outside holders of the remaining 132,000 ordinary shares in the *FT* be given the chance to sell their shares at the same price as Camrose had sold his. Most of these shareholders proceeded to take what seemed the main chance and duly sold, but again Camrose helped the *FN* by agreeing to buy most of them himself. Indeed, since Camrose even bought from the *FN* £50,000 of *FN* shares, in order further to help the *FN* reach the asking price, he ensured that he had a significant minority interest in the new venture. Both companies remained in formal existence, but the Financial News Ltd was the holding company, continuing to have a half-interest in the *Economist* and to be responsible for the *Banker*, *Investors Chronicle* and *Practitioner* as well as the new combined paper and, going with the purchase of a controlling interest in the *FT*, St Clements Press. The two papers announced the take-over on 26 July, the morning of the counting of general election votes. One day later and the *FN* might have had to pay rather less for what was still an exceedingly good bargain.

Thus the *FN* as a company took over the *FT*, but as a paper was taken over by it and ceased separate existence. It was a logical enough decision. The *FT* had the greater circulation, the greater commercial muscle power and of course the pinkness of its paper. It was, however, an undeniable wound to certain *FN* loyalists. Einzig for one, typically hearing the buzz several days before the announcement, wrote in aggrieved tones to Bracken:

> Having devoted more than half my life to an effort to increase the influence of the *Financial News*, I may perhaps be forgiven if I feel bitter about the impending destruction of my life's work. A newspaper is not like an ordinary business firm. It has its traditions and individuality. We have every reason to be proud of having been associated with the *Financial News* as its name commands respect over five continents . . . Now all the good will for its reputation for honest and frank criticism will be destroyed.
>
> I fail to see why the absorbing paper should be discontinued instead of the absorbed paper. It is as if after Germany's defeat the British Empire had changed its name to Grossdeutschland.[5]

With a certain latitude from the strictest truth, Bracken replied on 20 July from the Admiralty, where he was now First Lord in the caretaker government following VE day:

> I have heard indirectly about the proposed amalgamation between the *FN* and

the *FT*, but you will understand that my political responsibilities make it impossible for me to have anything to do with the arrangements you mention in your letter.

I don't expect ever to go back to the newspaper work in which you and I worked so happily together, but I should be more depressed than you are if one financial paper does not continue the *FN*'s policy of fearless criticism, and of the ventilation of all sorts of ideas however painful to some of the troglodytes of the City. There is no hope for any newspaper unless it is independent and lively.

I haven't heard any details about the proposed amalgamation. I am not even certain if a firm agreement has been made, nor can I say anything to the parties concerned while they are negotiating. If they ever do me the honour of asking my opinion you can rely upon me to press them to stick to the old courageous policy that gave the *FN* such a good reputation.[6]

It soon became clear that Einzig's worst fears about a pink anschluss would not be realized. The three top jobs in the new venture all went to *FN* men: Parkinson as editor (with Cole as his deputy, Chisholm preferring to return to the oil business); Moore as managing director; and, most piquantly of all, Bracken as chairman, with Dawnay agreeing to stand down. The chances are that Moore's was the crucial voice in enabling his former chief to return to the fold. For Bracken personally, having at the election lost not only office but also his seat, it was an offer gratefully accepted.

On the ground, the task of fusing the two papers was, in human terms, an immensely complicated one, but in the event went relatively smoothly. Much of the credit for this was due to Parkinson, who between July and September devoted himself with great industry and punctiliousness to the merger, though working in close collaboration with Cole and always looking to Moore for ultimate sanction of his actions. Early in July he scribbled down his thoughts in a private notebook. He began with a statement of intent about the new combined paper:

Ultimate Policy – To build up readership – 50,000 first goal, anything up to 100,000 eventual goal – and at all times to have such a head start that no rival paper, ever started, can keep up with us.

Features bring the readers, if we want a really *big* readership, *plus* the best news and market service for our specialist readers.

Parkinson then considered the inevitable problem of overstaffing – inevitable because the *FT* had insisted that any member of its staff of pre-retirement age and at least five years' standing must be given a minimum of one year's notice before dismissal. But he asked of the overstaffing:

Is this necessarily bad? a) The Americans have much bigger staffs than ours, and produce better papers. b) The men will be trained and experienced men – hard to get again if we lose them and then require to expand – as we shall do as soon as paper rationing is lifted. c) Labour in all trades is going to be in short supply for next three years, probably four. d) Many *FT* people are older men; some of ours are. We can let out by pensioning some at once and others on certain age.

The immediate crux, however, was the character of the paper: how much was it to have of the old *FN* and how much of the old *FT*? Parkinson was clear in his own mind. After noting that he would try to retain as many as possible of the *FN*'s special features, such as the market indices and 'Lex', he instructed himself as follows:

Impress on everyone that we are publishing the *FT*, not the *FN*, and they must adjust their ideas to that – *FT* readers will be up to four-fifths of our combined circulation. Presumably, the *FT* gave them what they want, because they bought it. So, at the start, the format, contents, style and approach of the *FT* must be left unaltered, or changed only in a few respects (e.g. pepping up leaders), which keep the loyalty of *FN* readers who change over, without upsetting existing *FT* readers. Allow certain period (? two to three months) for shaking down and running in of new arrangements on this basis, and overcoming all the inevitable snags. Meanwhile, work out a) improved new features that can be introduced successively, without increased cost, to tone up the paper generally; b) larger issues of editorial policy and aims, under board's directives, for the entire undertaking.

The larger aims thus remained, as outlined in Parkinson's memorandum of the previous year, but for the time being 'permeation' was the name of the *FN*'s game, allied to the semi-helpful fact of the *FT*'s older age profile.

One *FT* veteran (though not on the staff) at last on his way out was the inimitable Landells, who had been due to retire as 'Autolycus' in 1939, but had then been pressed back into service for the duration of the war. An even more senior *FT* contributor, however, still had his uses. This was Frank Layton, nephew of the *FT*'s company secretary back in the MacRae era. He was now sixty-eight years old, had been with the paper since 1894 and for the last forty years had been doing what Parkinson, writing to Moore, called 'that indispensable *FT* feature, "Answers to Correspondents"'. Parkinson added that the *FN*'s people had always made a 'poor fist' of their equivalent column and that therefore 'I want to see how he does it, before letting him go.' Someone with rather longer-term prospects on the new venture was T. S. G. ('Jim') Hunter, who was the son of the former editor and had been on the *FT* since 1928. He had worked his way up from company-meetings reporter to news editor and was now returning from five years in the RAF. His former position was offered to him, for as Parkinson put it to Moore, 'the *FT* News side was the one part of their editorial outfit I have always had (and still have) a healthy respect for'. More often, though, Parkinson found himself offering jobs to old *FT* men with a certain reluctance. Another passage in his explanatory letter to his managing director was fairly typical, this time about a stalwart who had been at Coleman Street since 1919:

> 'Chief Leader Writer' is [H. M.] Muggeridge's present title on the *FT*. My idea was that it should mean much or little, according to my estimate of the man when I had had the chance to try him out. Cole's report on him is: 'Good utility man, a thinker, stable, reliable, accurate, but rather slow and pedestrian in style.' Not very encouraging, but we are paying him £850 with a three year contract, and I should like to get something for our money.

Parkinson's hands were tied, but Moore had already made the wider point tartly enough: 'Is it wise to call Muggeridge *Chief* Leader Writer? I thought we regarded the quality of the *FT* leaders as being pretty poor.'

Making the dispositions for the future was especially invidious for Parkinson when it came to deciding what to do with his *FN* colleagues. Thus, for example, he justified to Moore his choice for assistant editor:

> Dacey definitely wants to work for the new *FT* and would be rather hurt if he was dropped. Actually, his title was meant to be chiefly honorific [Dacey still being editor of the *Banker*], but I want his leaders, and I should like him to be sufficiently 'in' on the paper to be a potential balance-weight in daily conferences if Cole turns out (as I rather suspect) to be a tremendous worker, with a genius for detail but limited vision.

Somewhat similar considerations applied to Wincott, who according to Parkinson was 'willing to drop Lex, but in his own heart would much like to be asked to go on with it'. Parkinson added: 'I should like him to. He is the best Lex since Clarke's day, though he has taken on a lot of outside work which, Lex-wise, is a nuisance.' In the event, the main *FN* person who seems to have come the closest to being left out in the cold was Einzig. 'I cannot agree to Einzig being Political Correspondent,' Moore wrote to Parkinson on 31 July, adding in the same letter: '"Lombard St" I take it will be dropped.' In his reply, Parkinson agreed that the column itself should go and that J. Grahame-Parker – who since the 1930s had done the equivalent *FT* column – should be the new City editor. But as he then asked: 'Query? What do we do with Einzig if he is neither Lom. Street nor political correspondent? He does good, non-controversial foreign leaders, but can hardly pay his way on those alone.' In the end, Moore, who had always had limited patience with Einzig's campaigning tendencies, yielded to the extent of making him political correspondent, but keeping Idris Thomas, an old *FT* man, in the parliamentary lobby. Cole expressed his satisfaction to Parkinson: 'I know some people find him awkward, but I have always thought his service good for the paper with the public.' Einzig himself was resentful – not without justification – about the ending of his column, which for almost twenty years had been his personal platform and would have been a considerable asset in the new paper. But he later came to feel that Moore had been 'perfectly right', in that 'even though it was the *Financial News* that had acquired the *Financial Times*, the latter's circulation was much larger, and this fact alone was more conclusive than any conceivable Gallup Poll in making it clear that my campaigns only appealed to a minority of City men'.[7]

One former *FN* hand who might easily have played a significant part in the new set-up was Hammond Innes. During the war he had been employed by the British Army Newspaper Unit and on 12 August, awaiting demobilization, he wrote to Parkinson from its headquarters in Rome. It was a letter of considerable prophetic interest:

> I have been following the London dailies out here very closely and almost without exception I find them way wide of the mark on European affairs in the case of the countries where I do know what is going on. This particularly applies to the economic side. The reason of course is that in general articles written for British newspapers on foreign affairs are produced by journalists re-writing from the files. It is a great weakness, and the British press has always suffered from it. And the result is that people, even those who should be informed, do *not* know what is really going on outside their own country. Further, I have talked to many business men out here – men who are at the moment still in the services – and they are unanimous in their view that what they will want after the war is detailed European information, not only about what is happening politically and economically, but what each country is in need of and what it has to offer, down to even the smaller factories.
>
> Now that the FN Group is such a large factor in the City it would, in my opinion, be far-sighted policy to begin immediately after the war to build up a foreign news service. It would take at least six months to complete the necessary contacts in the more important countries and the service would then be able to operate as soon as newsprint was available for papers of a reasonable size. Later the same service, apart from supplying bulletins and material to all the papers in

the Group, could be used as the foundation for a new weekly called something like *European Business* and appealing to a wide range of company managements . . .

My own interest in the matter is this. I have been offered by my publishers a three-year salary guarantee to enable me to be a free agent if I wish to be. This is very satisfactory, but to do two thrillers a year is not going to take up all that much of my time. In any case, to get the necessary background for good thrillers I need to be knocking around Europe – because that is where the thrills are. But to knock around Europe requires money and if I am to continue thriller writing (and it would be foolish not to maintain this sideline) I would prefer either a foreign correspondent's job or something in the nature of the idea I have outlined.

It was an exciting bait, anticipating the whole European dimension of post-war financial journalism, but Parkinson, who anyway seems to have believed that Canada and South Africa were where the exciting future international action lay, declined to nibble. 'I am not quite sure how the suggestions you put up would dovetail in with such arrangements as we have provisionally in contemplation,' he replied on the 20th:

One difficulty frankly is that a good deal of Europe – particularly Eastern and South-Eastern Europe – from which the financial dailies drew revenue in the past and might have expected to draw it again after the war, seems likely on present indicators to be a closed area.

Otherwise, we should be offering you the post of leader writer at a salary which would, in fact, be based on pre-war plus allowances for increased cost of living, etc. I don't know how attractive you would consider that to be. The merger seems likely to have the dual result of offering better and firmer prospects to the really 'live' members of the staff but at the same time giving us a much larger staff (and consequently a much larger total pay bill) than before.

Perhaps Parkinson needed Bracken around (he had not yet returned as chairman) to fire him with even larger possibilities than he already had in mind. Or perhaps he simply believed that the *FT* and 'thrills' were inappropriate bedmates. In any case, for whatever reason, nothing immediately was to come of the Innes blueprint. When its author returned to London a few months later, Parkinson declined to up the ante, and Innes decided that the life of a financial journalist was no longer for him.

In his letter to Parkinson, Innes mentioned that he had recently run into a former colleague also now in the services, Gordon Newton: 'I understand he is likely to return to you as Assistant Editor. I am glad, as I had a high opinion of his drive.' Others shared his opinion. Though all members of the *FN* staff who had joined up had their service wages supplemented by regular payments from the company (as did the *FT* staff), none fared as well as Newton, who for almost the entire duration of the war received a £5 weekly retainer, with five £1 notes arriving by registered letter wherever he was stationed. The hand of Bracken was almost certainly behind this and it is likely that he had marked out Newton as a coming man whose future loyalty must be ensured. Parkinson agreed, describing him to Moore as 'one of the men we want most'. In fact, the position he now offered Newton, who was expected back in the autumn, was not the assistant editorship, but that of features editor, which in Parkinson's eyes held the key to the future expansion of the paper. In September he drew up a draft letter, offering 'a salary of £1,000 and attractive future prospects', asking Newton to read carefully his *FN* memorandum of the previous October and setting the job in context:

We want to develop, broadly, along two special lines:

1) to provide, for the first time, a daily paper which will successfully cater for the industrialist and trader
2) to bring in non-specialist people of all classes who find that, under the conditions we shall have after this war, questions of employment, manpower, production, prices, exports, taxation, etc. are playing a major part in their daily lives, and want a first-class but easily assimilated daily 'service' on these questions . . .

We should never *play down*. Even our most 'elementary' articles must maintain a minimum standard of style, content and presentation. But our *range* of subjects must be catholic. Our objectives – increased readership, improved investment services, development on the industrial side and 'economics in daily life' – these determine the range and subject matter of our articles.

Moore (on holiday in Wales) sent back his response to Parkinson's draft: 'I liked your letter to Newton, except that you must explain that anything very ambitious is debarred at the moment by shortage of newsprint. Also should you say "*specially* attractive future prospects"?' Parkinson added the extra enticement, and Newton became features editor. The pieces on the chess-board were slipping into place.

At a more mundane level than grand editorial strategy, Parkinson had much on his mind during the last few weeks before the consummation of merger. One matter of pressing concern, despite the future combining of quotas, was the continuing newsprint rationing. Towards the end of August he was informed by Leslie Dearlove, general manager of the *FT* since 1941, that for the first four weeks of the combined paper there would be forty-two pages available each week, in other words three issues of six pages and three of eight. This was on the basis of a projected sale of 36,000 copies from Monday to Friday and 54,000 on Saturday. Interestingly, Dearlove mentioned in his note that 'our present average daily sale is about 33,000, which figure includes a Saturday's sale of about 47,000' – the first formal record of the *FT*'s 'weekends only' readership. About the same time Parkinson issued a memorandum on the subject of 'Seating of *FN* Men at *FT*', stating that '*FT* seating arrangements remain' and that as a result of the proposed allocation of office space on the editorial third floor '*FN* men are thoroughly "mixed" with *FT* men'. The *FN* men, however, were less than enchanted by the prospect, for on 5 September the paper's NUJ chapel submitted to Parkinson a highly critical memorandum about 'working conditions at Coleman Street', arguing that there would be 'three, and even four, persons, each doing his own specialised work and with his own contacts, crowded into one small room with (at present) only one telephone and insufficiently lighted'. According to the chapel, the inevitable result would be work 'subject to constant interruption, difficulties over telephoning, communication with individual contacts, personal antipathies, and so on'. The memo also went to Cole, whom Parkinson hastened to mollify: 'Leave it to me to talk to our Chapel. Though they express themselves with force and precision, they are good people and I shall assure them that everything will be done that can be . . . I am sure they will understand and make the best of what I am afraid in the circumstances cannot be ideal conditions.' What the chapel did not know was that the ground floor at 74 Coleman Street had been taken in order to house the new paper's (and indeed group's) publishing and circulation staffs. But certainly, working conditions at number 72 would never be, as Parkinson put it, 'ideal'.

The final issue of the *FN* was six pages long and appeared on Saturday 29 September 1945. An announcement on the front page stated that, as a result of the paper's editorial staff joining that of the *FT*, the new *FT* 'will thus have at its disposal a larger personnel, richer in skill and specialised knowledge than any financial newspaper has ever possessed'. The announcement also referred encouragingly to 'further new features' whenever 'the newsprint shortage is alleviated'. That weekend much of the Bishopsgate furniture was moved to Coleman Street, ranging from desks and filing-cabinets to correspondence trays and memo pads. The *FN* staff now took stock of their new home. According to legend, the immediate reaction of Wincott was the one-word comment, 'Belsen'. On Monday 1 October the new *FT* made its bow, and, in characteristically lucid terms, Parkinson outlined what he saw as the paper's future role:

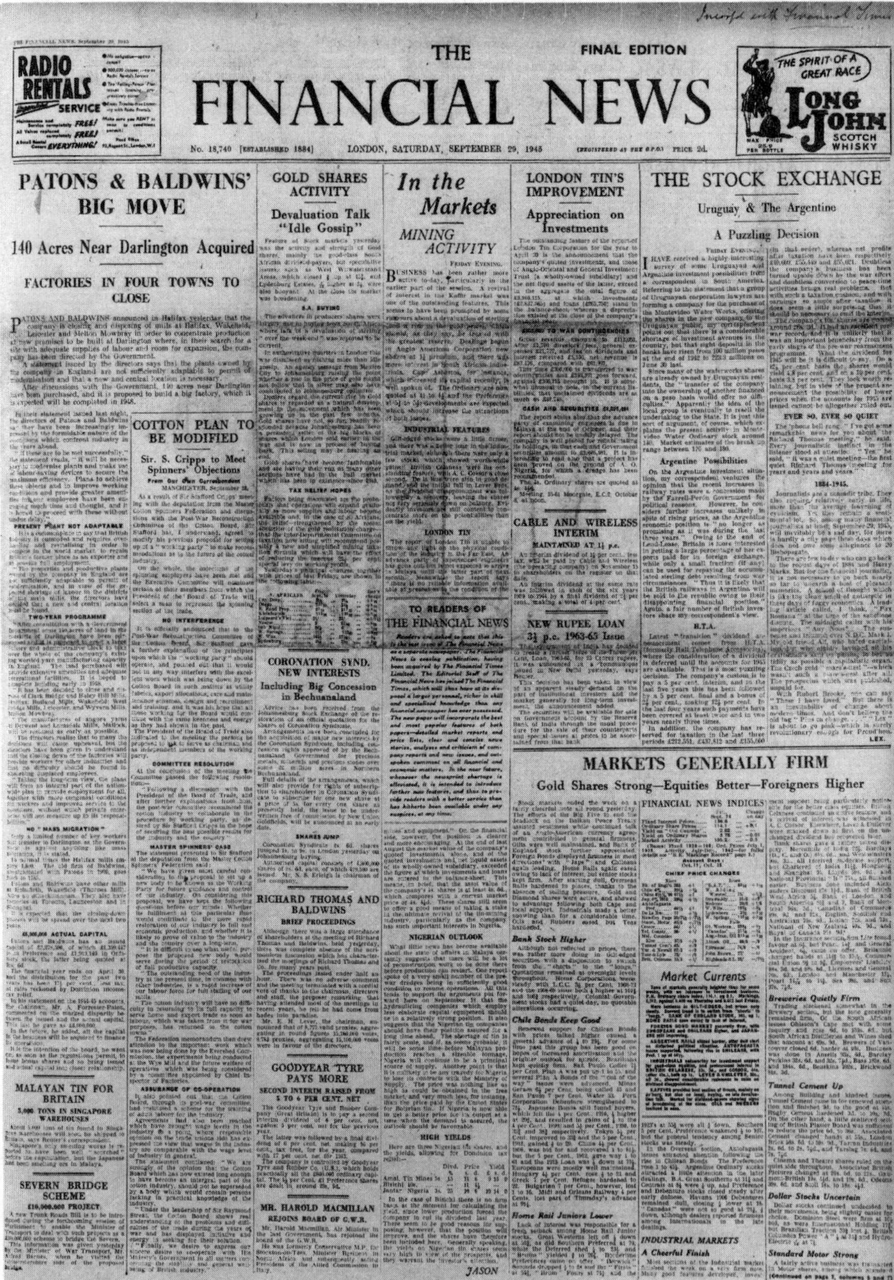

FINAL EDITION

THE FINANCIAL NEWS

No. 18,740 [ESTABLISHED 1884] LONDON, SATURDAY, SEPTEMBER 29, 1945 PRICE 2d.

PATONS & BALDWINS' BIG MOVE

140 Acres Near Darlington Acquired

FACTORIES IN FOUR TOWNS TO CLOSE

PATONS AND BALDWINS announced in Halifax yesterday that the company is closing and disposing of mills at Halifax, Wakefield, Leicester and Melton Mowbray in order to concentrate production at new premises to be built at Darlington where, in their search for a site with adequate supplies of labour and room for expansion, the company has been directed by the Government.

A statement issued by the directors says that the plants owned by the company in England are not sufficiently adaptable to permit of modernisation and that a new and central location is necessary.

After discussions with the Government, 140 acres near Darlington have been purchased, and it is proposed to build a big factory, which it is expected will be completed in 1948.

COTTON PLAN TO BE MODIFIED

Sir. S. Cripps to Meet Spinners' Objections

From Our Own Correspondent

MANCHESTER, September 28.

MALAYAN TIN FOR BRITAIN

SEVERN BRIDGE SCHEME

£10,000,000 PROJECT

GOLD SHARES ACTIVITY

Devaluation Talk "Idle Gossip"

CORONATION SYND. NEW INTERESTS

Including Big Concession in Bechuanaland

RICHARD THOMAS AND BALDWINS

BRIEF PROCEEDINGS

GOODYEAR TYRE PAYS MORE

SECOND INTERIM RAISED FROM 5 TO 6 PER CENT. NET

MR. HAROLD MACMILLAN REJOINS BOARD OF G.W.R.

In the Markets

MINING ACTIVITY

FRIDAY EVENING.

BUSINESS has been rather more active to-day, particularly in the earlier part of the session.

NIGERIAN OUTLOOK

HIGH YIELDS

JASON

TO READERS OF THE FINANCIAL NEWS

LONDON TIN'S IMPROVEMENT

Appreciation on Investments

CABLE AND WIRELESS INTERIM

MAINTAINED AT $1\frac{1}{2}$ p.c.

NEW RUPEE LOAN

$3\frac{1}{4}$ p.c. 1963-65 Issue

THE STOCK EXCHANGE

Uruguay & The Argentine

A Puzzling Decision

FRIDAY EVENING.

Argentine Possibilities

EVER SO, EVER SO QUIET

1884-1945.

LEX.

MARKETS GENERALLY FIRM

Gold Shares Strong—Equities Better—Foreigners Higher

FINANCIAL NEWS INDICES

Bank Stock Higher

Chile Bonds Keep Good

Home Rail Juniors Lower

INDUSTRIAL MARKETS

A Cheerful Finish

Market Currents

Breweries Quietly Firm

Tunnel Cement Up

Dollar Stocks Uncertain

Standard Motor Strong

29 September 1945: last issue of the *FN*

The dynamic of events, the growing complexity of daily life after two great wars, changed relations between the State and the individual – these are among the many forces which necessitate a new approach and open up fresh fields for a modern financial newspaper. Its readers and their requirements are changing also. The investor himself is no longer a member of a relatively small 'moneyed class', which taxation is fast driving out of existence. He is Everyman – one of the holders of less than £300 of shares who make up 75 per cent of the ownership of every big industrial company. Or he is a high executive of some financial institution. He is interested no longer merely in the published profits of the companies whose shares he holds; he demands, in addition, all available information on conditions and prospects in the industries where the profits are earned, and on industry in general, on employment, exports, and much else.

Nor is the readership of the daily financial newspaper now confined to investors and 'the City'. The growing class of business managers and professional advisers whose function is destined to be decisive in every branch of industry and trade, under any form of capital ownership, calls for increasingly specialised service on matters bearing directly on the daily conduct of its affairs. Above all, a great body of readers, men and women in every walk of life, find that, in this difficult mid-twentieth century world, questions which used to be the exclusive concern of the economist and the business man exert a profound influence on their daily work and happiness. Never have readers been so avid for guidance on everything bearing on full employment, inflation, taxation, the future of Government controls and similar problems. To satisfy demands like these is a worthy ambition for any newspaper. It is the objective to which the *Financial Times* proposes to devote its energy, experience and authority, as its contribution to the task of national reconstruction.

[SIX]

TOWARDS A NATIONAL PAPER: 1945–9

In true circumspect *FT* fashion, and in accordance with Parkinson's avowed intent, the first 'merged' issue betrayed few signs that the paper was on the verge of entering the most profound and sustained transformation of its life. It was eight pages long and included lengthy, rather stolid articles on the City's place in the national economy, the case for option dealing, and the plastics industry, as well as a feature by Parkinson himself on 'Sixty Years of Financial Journalism', in which he tactfully concealed his real feelings about the rather mediocre quality of the old *FT*. On page one 'Lex' from the *FN* and 'Diarist' from the *FT* jostled alongside each other, while to their left the main headline of the day – 'National Outgo But Slightly Down', referring to the latest Exchequer returns on ordinary expenditure – had a thoroughly reassuring *FT* feel to it. There was, however, one eye-catching innovation. This was the handiwork of the famous typographical consultant Stanley Morison, who, having already restyled the title pieces of the *Daily Worker*, *Reynolds News*, the *Daily Herald* and *The Times*, now did so for the *FT*. Out went the old 'written' masthead, and in came classical and dignified roman caps, not all that dissimilar to the old *FN*, though rather spoilt by the reduced 'The' that would now hover awkwardly above the larger words 'Financial Times' for the next twenty-two years. Beneath ran the rubric 'Incorporating The Financial News'. This too would run and run, ungainly but instructive reminder of the true origins of the modern *FT*.

It was not an altogether cheerful world that the new order at Coleman Street prepared to record, analyse and perhaps influence. The course of the war had wrought devastation upon the British economic position. Almost a third of overseas investments had been liquidated; the export trade was in shreds; the industrial base was no stronger than that of Central Europe; and debts, largely to the United States, the Dominions and the colonies, were enormous. In sum, it is generally reckoned that as a result of the war Britian lost about a quarter of its pre-war national

THE FINANCIAL TIMES, 1st October, 1945

CITY EDITION

THE FINANCIAL TIMES

Incorporating THE FINANCIAL NEWS

No. 17,619 — *LONDON, Monday, 1st October, 1945* — Twopence

NATIONAL OUTGO BUT SLIGHTLY DOWN

LAST QUARTER 5% LESS THAN YEAR AGO

SIX MONTHS' REVENUE UP AGAIN BUT E.P.T. RECEIPTS DROP

The level of national expenditure so far shows little fall despite the end of the war and the cancellation of Supply contracts. The half-year Exchequer Returns show total Ordinary expenditure for the six months £193¼ millions less than for the first half of the previous financial year.

Only £79.7 millions of this decline, however, occurred in the last quarter. In other words, expenditure during the last three months was only 5.2 per cent. less than for the corresponding period of 1944.

Ordinary revenue at £1,363.2 millions for the six months is £27.7 millions up on the year, though a slightly smaller proportion of the Budget estimate than at this time last year. Income-tax, Excise and motor duties are buoyant, but there has been a heavy fall in excess profits tax receipts.

The current deficit for the six months amounted to £1,387.9 millions—slightly more than the revenue. "Savings" in the technical sense accounted for 47 per cent. of borrowings, against 49 per cent. in the previous year and 77 per cent. for the first half of the financial year 1943-44.

POSITION SUMMARISED

REVENUE & EXPENDITURE

MILITARY CONTRACTS

REVENUE PROSPECTS

COMMITTEE TO ADVISE ON INDUSTRY

EXAMINATION OF CAPITAL NEEDS

SIR NIGEL CAMPBELL AS CHAIRMAN

CAPITAL APPLICATIONS

ANNUAL GRANTS

ON OTHER PAGES

MIDLAND BANK JOINT GENERAL MANAGER

MR. H. WHEELER APPTD.

LONDON & STRATHCLYDE TRUST

Company Meetings in this Issue

LORD WOOLTON'S NEW DIRECTORSHIP

JOINS L.M.S. BOARD

THIS WEEK'S MEETINGS

GOLD COAST SELECTION—TRIPLEX

BOARD MEETING DATES

IMPL. BANK OF IRAN

An Investor's Note Book

A TRIO FOR SAFETY

CALCUTTA TRAMS —CAMP BIRD

Relevant Factors

Calcutta Trams

Camp Bird

Price Below Value

Spotlight

The Diarist

"Financial Times" Stock Indices

"Financial News" Indices

CANADA PLANS LOAN TO U.K.

TO PURCHASE SUPPLIES

OTTAWA, 29th Sept.

WAR EXPENDITURE

TRADE TALKS IN LONDON

WESTMINSTER BANK NEW DIRECTORS

LORD LEATHERS AND MR. EDEN

JOINT GENERAL MANAGERS

THE STOCK EXCHANGE

Buying for Transition Period

Rezende Mines

TRANSITION—AND BEYOND

Murex Prospects

REZENDE

VISITORS' GALLERY?

LEX

INTERESTING AND ACTIVE WEEK

Rally in Rails—Bright Equity Shares

INDUSTRIALS MAINLY FIRM

RALLY IN JAPS

OIL SHARES

Continued on Page 4 Col. 5

1 October 1945: first issue of the new *FT*

wealth. Not surprisingly, there ensued a general climate of austerity and rationing, in the context of a determined attempt by the Labour government to rectify the disastrous balance of payments position. Nor on the face of it was the situation in the immediate post-war period any happier from the specific vantage-point of the City of London. The foreign exchange market, the gold market and the majority of commodity markets remained closed until the 1950s. The wartime Capital Issues Committee (under the chairmanship of Lord Kennet, the former Hilton Young) continued afterwards severely to restrict the floating of foreign issues in London. And on the Stock Exchange generally, the Labour government not only considerably narrowed the equity market through its policy of nationalization, but also had an adverse impact through its taxation of profits, limitation of dividends and indeed its fiscal policy as a whole. To those of an apocalyptic cast of mind, George Orwell's 1941 prophecy of the post-war social revolution still rang ominously true: 'The Stock Exchange will be pulled down, the horse plough will give way to the tractor, the country houses will be turned into children's holiday camps, the Eton and Harrow match will be forgotten.'[1]

Tractors apart, it was not to be. The City never came to love Attlee and his ministers, but its shrewder operators quite quickly conceded that Labour had neither the will nor the imagination to kill off the denizens of Throgmorton Street; while the measures imposed by Chancellors Dalton and Cripps, though mildly damaging to the investing class, were nevertheless distinctly unpunitive. Indeed, it is probable that Dalton's celebrated 'cheap money' policy of 1945–7 positively stimulated activity in the stock market. The *FT* Ordinary Share Index (continuing on from the *FN*'s) remained steady almost throughout the government's tenure; and when devaluation of sterling did come in 1949 it was caused by a loss of confidence outside the country rather than inside the City. In other ways, moreover, the City showed its traditional resilience. In particular, it re-established itself with impressive speed and assurance as both the primary centre of foreign trade financing and the largest international insurance market, thereby contributing handsomely to the country's so-called 'invisibles'. London was undoubtedly helped, at this potentially difficult stage, by the surprising failure of New York as a rival international financial centre to capitalize on the almost total dominance of the dollar in these post-war years. Various explanations have been put forward – including the excessive diverting of funds into government agencies, the essentially domestic orientation of Wall Street and the almost obsessive hoarding of gold – but whatever their respective truth, the striking fact was that even by the early 1960s the New York market was exporting barely a third of the capital that London had done on the eve of the First World War. As a result the post-1945 City remained one of the two big players on the world financial stage, which might easily not have been the case. And if it had not been, then the future for its parish paper would have been bleak indeed.

In fact, the first issue of the *FT*, merging together the Monday circulations of the two old papers and arriving at a print order of 38,415 copies, was a sell out. By mid-November 1945 the average daily net sale was more than 44,000, but on 15 December an announcement on the front page informed readers: 'Since the *Financial Times* and the *Financial News* were merged on 1 October, the demand for copies of the combined paper has steadily grown. Until a few days ago it was just possible, by making every economy, to satisfy this demand, but we are now compelled to prevent the circulation rising any further.' The fundamental decision was made, in other words, that in the context of continuing newsprint rationing, and despite the newsprint quotas of the two old papers being added together, there was an irreducible core of content below which the paper could not go, even at the cost of sacrificing would-be readers. Significantly, this core included the daily record of Stock Exchange dealings, which the more mainstream quality papers, similarly truncated, were unable to provide for several more years. Whatever the nation's larger balance of payments considerations, it was a thoroughly frustrating situation, preventing editorial as well as circulation growth and prompting later in December a bitter leader: 'The effects of the present position are insidious and regrettable. If indefinitely prolonged, they could become dangerous and evil. The nation has as much right to be well informed as to be adequately supplied with foreign films and Virginian tobacco.' Or as Bracken told the paper's shareholders the following April, 'the only complaint of the *Financial Times* comes from people in all parts of Britain who cannot get it', even though 'we have restricted the size of the paper to the smallest practicable size', usually six pages and occasionally eight.[2]

In September 1946 the clouds temporarily lifted; newsprint rationing was eased. By December the AGM of the FN Ltd was being informed by Bracken that 'there is certainly no reason to regret the results of the amalgamation' and that 'our sales monotonously increase and far exceed the total pre-war combined circulation'.[3] There is unfortunately no exact figure for the daily sales reached by the end of the year, but it was probably more than 70,000. Then, however, came what Dalton himself called the *annus horrendus*. In February 1947 the fuel crisis resulted in a fresh bout of newsprint restrictions, so much so that for two weeks the *Economist* and the *Investors Chronicle* were entirely unable to appear and were kindly lent editorial space in the already cribbed and confined *FT*; over the spring and early summer the paper stabilized at eight tight-fitting pages a day; and then in July came the 'convertibility crisis', when sterling was made freely convertible and an immediate drastic run on the pound ensued, together with swingeing import cuts, including newsprint consumption. 'What *is* the true reason for a decision which can impart only bitterness and justified resentment?' asked the *FT* in a predictably angry leader on 'The Clipped Press'. True to policy, the paper maintained its eight pages but cut back circulation to a daily average of a little over 60,000. Bracken in November was once again duly apologetic to those unable to obtain copies: 'We share their grievances, for the *Financial Times*, despite its austere contents, steadily grows in popularity. We could increase our circulation by more than one-third if newsprint were available.'[4] In the event, it was to be seven rather depressing years before newsprint rationing was substantially lifted and circulation was able to find its natural level.

For the first time, however, the historian has some clear statistical idea of who, or at least where, these privileged readers were. Thus for the week ending 10 November 1945, with an average daily net sale of 44,107, the breakdown was as follows:

London	19,817
Northern England and North Wales	7,859
Home Counties (Bedford to Bournemouth)	3,834
Midlands	3,521
West Country	2,961
Foreign	1,568
Scotland	1,421
East Anglia	802
South Wales	796
Country subscriptions (i.e. by post)	660
Eire	454
Northern Ireland	310
Channel Islands	104

The metropolis inevitably dominates, but one is struck by the strength of readership in the industrial North and the relative weakness amongst the Home Counties *rentier* class. By November 1948, when the next such breakdown was undertaken, foreign sales had been boosted by much improved facilities for flying copies of the paper to Europe, Africa and North America. Otherwise, London sales had gone up by about a quarter,

Northern by almost a half and Home Counties almost doubled. Beyond that one cannot definitely go, apart from one small anecdote suggesting a broadening (if perforce not deepening) readership. It concerns the young Lester Piggott, entering his teens at about this time. The story goes that when a bank manager called on his parents and was unable to find in the *FT* a financial report he wished to discuss with them, the watching Piggott eventually lost patience, snatched the paper from the manager's hands and turned immediately to the right page.[5]

Traditionally, however, it was not from sales but from advertising that the financial press made its real money, and this remained very much the case with the post-war *FT*. It was a truth that Moore above all never forgot during these years of newsprint shortage and naturally insistent editorial demands for more space. A memorandum he sent to Parkinson and others in May 1946 set the tone for the future:

> I think we must have a meeting to discuss the newsprint position. Even if we get an increase it will only be a small one and it is not beyond the bounds of possibility that we shall not get an increase at all, for six months. In the meantime, the back log of unpublished Company meeting reports may increase and trade advertising has been almost completely pushed out of the paper in the last few weeks. Henschel [the advertisement director] has made representations that in order not to lose the goodwill of all trade advertisers, he should have allocated to him no less than one column a day for trade display in addition to the special positions. We must do something to meet him.

In fact, despite newsprint restrictions and the general economic climate, the advertising picture was really quite encouraging. In 1946 the advertisement columnage in the paper totalled 3,984, rising to 5,262 in 1947 and 5,873 in 1948, figures that compared well (even allowing for the merger) with the *FT*'s best 1930s tally of 4,149 columns in 1936.

There were, moreover, certain significant portents for the future. In terms of foreign advertising, there was the appointment as the paper's first foreign manager of Robin Bruce-Lockhart, son of Bracken's friend Sir Robert, the well-known intelligence agent. Although in the event only a short-term appointment, it did produce certain results, especially in the United States, culminating in November 1947 in a forty-page 'North America Supplement', the first such venture since the war. In the sphere of financial advertising, though the adverse trend was now under way for chairmen's speeches at annual meetings to be replaced by chairmen's statements before them, this was compensated for by the Stock Exchange's policy of tightening up its new-issue requirements, resulting in longer, more complex prospectuses. Moreover, the first signs now became apparent of what was to become the standard practice of companies paying an annual charge to have their shares quoted in the paper. Hitherto, as far as one can tell on the basis of rather patchy and conflicting evidence, the *FN* and *FT* had charged only for share prices that either were inactive or lacked an official Stock Exchange quotation, often those of South African gold-mining companies. In each case it had been only a sporadic, haphazard practice. Now, soon after the merger, a business man named Arthur Whitehead persuaded the *FT* to accept payment for quoting the shares of the various small businesses that operated under the auspices of the Whitehead Industrial Trust. As a result, in Moore's subsequent words, 'soon other companies approached us, asking us to quote their shares, and there was no logical reason for refusing'.[6]

These years also saw the first seeds of what was to become large-scale and extremely lucrative trade or display advertising, again of relatively little consequence before the war. Here the key figure, setting an example that others followed, was the builder Bernard Sunley, who was cultivated by Henschel, became friendly with Bracken himself and adopted a policy of advertising his company, Blackwood Hodge, exclusively in the *FT*. One way and another, the advertisement side of the paper, from which all else in a certain basic sense derived, was preparing for great things. Or as Henschel put it many years later on the eve of retirement, looking back on it all: 'I stopped the men chasing cigar ads and we went for the big stuff.'[7]

Against this hopeful if constricted background, profits steadily increased. It is impossible to know exactly how much money the paper itself made, but there are figures for the FT Ltd – embracing the *FT*, St Clements Press and a subsidiary printing venture – which show a profit on trading of £293,336 for 1946 rising to £470,298 for 1947 and £526,922 for 1948. Granted that the FN Ltd had, in effect, spent barely £200,000 in acquiring its controlling interest in the paper and print works, these were highly satisfactory figures, even though almost half those trading profits went to the Inland Revenue. In a sense the money made itself, in that the newsprint rationing had the triple effect of keeping down costs, discouraging any potential competitor from starting a rival financial publication and creating a seller's market for advertising space. Indeed, the major flaw in the commercial situation was arguably the price of the newsprint itself, which before the war had been £11.10*s.* a ton and by 1948 had risen to £45 a ton, resulting in the price of the paper going up at the start of that year from 2*d.* to 3*d.* It was the *FT*'s first increase for almost thirty years; the frequency would soon accelerate.

Benefiting more than anyone from these profits was of course the Crosthwaite-Eyre family, which in the course of the war had bought out the Spottiswoode interest. Major J. S. Crosthwaite-Eyre, the youthful Bracken's great benefactor, did not stay on the scene much longer, emigrating to South Africa in about 1946. He left behind him his eldest son, Oliver, who in effect became the *FT*'s owner and sat on the boards of both the FT Ltd and the FN Ltd, the latter of which was responsible for the *Banker*, *Investors Chronicle* and so on, while also enjoying an effective controlling interest in the *FT*. It was a rather anomalous situation, especially as at any one time both boards had an identical composition, and remained so until the 1960s, when a corporate reconstruction enabled the FN Ltd to be wound up and its group interests absorbed in the FT Ltd. Oliver Crosthwaite-Eyre was not perhaps the ideal proprietor, living as he did almost entirely on nerves, nicotine and gin, possessing a tendency to fly off at a tangent and much preferring the world of parliamentary intrigue (he was a Conservative MP from 1945) to that of sober business. He was, however, knowledgeable about the printing side and, like his father before him, conscientiously abstained from interfering in editorial matters. If not ideal, he was not a negligible figure, and should not have been treated by Bracken for all the world as if he was an errant schoolboy. Common courtesy apart, it was a tactical mistake, and one that was to have profound consequences for the future of the *FT*.

Bracken himself was, by comparison with his pre-war commitment to the *FN*, only a part-time chairman of the new paper. He did not have his own office in Coleman Street and was there only once or at most twice a week, which had the important effect of allowing Moore as managing director to begin to start doing things his own way without having Bracken breathing down his neck the whole time. Instead, still full of enthusiasm at this stage for life and its battles, Bracken based himself in the City at the offices a few hundred yards away of the Union Corporation. This was the South African mining company of which he had recently become chairman, an appointment that before long had the profitable (and permanent) side-effect for the *FT* of leading to the publication of the quarterly results of almost all the leading South African mining houses. Otherwise he spent much of his energies at Westminster (having been elected to a seat early in the Parliament), where he waged a doughty and verbose campaign against the government's nationalization programme.

Nevertheless, Bracken remained a distinct presence in the life of the *FT*, above all through the medium of the Tuesday lunches, which he instigated. On these occasions he would stride into the dining-room rather late, help himself to a gin and Martini and start abusing someone from the assembled company, which usually consisted of the rest of the board, the editor and one or two journalists, with perhaps also a distinguished guest. The bullying was blatant and of a mental rather than physical nature. Indeed, it would be fair to say that the staff as a whole of the post-war *FT*, in as much as it came into contact with Bracken, loathed and feared him in about equal proportions. He did not have his own permanent secretary in the building, and it was ever the dread of the editor's secretary that she would be called upon to assist the chairman. The very fact of his presence may have stimulated activity and ideas, at least for those who were able to stand up to him, but it did not make for harmony and good feeling.

This was particularly so in the case of poor Hargreaves Parkinson, who found himself the especial target of Bracken's Tuesday tongue. 'H.P.' was the nicest of men, but had already worked himself into the ground on behalf of the *FN*, remained constitutionally almost incapable of delegating and was unable to exert an editor's authority over most of his senior journalists, let alone his chairman. These failings were a great shame, for in many ways he was extremely well qualified to take the *FT* into a new, more ambitious age. His City knowledge and contacts were excellent, but he also had a sure grasp of the economy at large; he was infinitely patient in bringing on young writers; and his devotion to duty and what he saw (usually correctly) as the paper's best interests was positively Victorian. It is no defence of Bracken's treatment to say that Parkinson was not tough enough for the job and should not have been given it. In the context of the merger, he was the right and only man to be editor; and as such he should have been supported to the hilt by management rather than, as was the case, consistently undermined.

Interestingly, although almost certainly not specifically related to the treatment he was receiving, Parkinson not long after the merger suggested the creation of an *FT* editorial trust (comprising up to five heads of City institutions) to act as arbiter between editor and owner over any differences concerning editorial policy. He did so in February 1947, as the first of the post-war Royal Commissions on the Press was going about its work. Moore in his counter-memorandum summarized Parkinson's arguments:

> He thinks hostile witnesses may base their attack on the grounds of 'improper influence', members of our Board being identified with particular City interests, and argue that any influence they chose to exert could not be withstood by editorial policy. (He points out that Dalton always asserts that B.B. writes or

inspires everything in the paper.) He thinks denial by itself might be unconvincing, and argues that the one complete answer would be an Editorial Trust.

Expediency alone, however, is not his only ground for urging this. The thing most likely in his view to change the 'personality' of a paper is a change of proprietorship. As the circulation and reputation of the *FT* increase, its market value, he says, will increase, and likewise its attractions for an outside purchaser. It is the duty of the *FT*'s Board to promote the Company's best interests and he recognises that the Board could not undertake that they would in no circumstances part with control of the *FT*. Furthermore, our present Board may not always remain unchanged.

Therefore he argues that whoever has or obtains control of the paper should accept with it its 'settled policy', and the only way yet devised of securing this is by means of an impartial Editorial Trust.

Parkinson obviously had in mind the example of the *Economist*'s trustee arrangements, but Moore was not persuaded:

It seems doubtful whether Parkinson's conditions for an *FT* Trust would in fact achieve the desired objective. If, for instance, there were to be a change of ownership, and the Editor were to resign or die, appointment of the new Editor would rest with the new Board, and they would surely appoint someone whom they expected to give the paper the character they wished, and any change in character or policy would therefore be unlikely to be referred to the Trustees. It would seem, therefore, as though the Trustees might have initiating powers: and if so should these powers go beyond the appointment of an Editor? Even if they did not go beyond his appointment, it is not inconceivable that in the future a majority of the Trustees would be, as is already the Governor of the Bank, public officials, and in that event, might not the Editor nominated be a Whitehall stooge? Would it be better therefore if the Trustees were not ex-officio members?

Who in that case would have the job of nominating them? Perhaps the Board and Editor jointly, subsequent Trustees to be appointed by themselves. There might be an argument in favour of this, but it would scarcely commend itself to the chief advocates of the Royal Commission. And there would still be the fundamental dilemma that if the Trustees had no initiating powers, they would not necessarily be able to discharge their duty, and, if they had, then the Board might not be able to discharge theirs.

It is hard to legislate for every possible set of circumstances, and on the question of appointing Trustees for the *FT*, I think the cure might well prove to be worse than the illness, particularly when so far as I am aware there is no present illness, that is, improper influence, and if there were, I am sure that the Editor would not hesitate to say so.

Moore's negative arguments won the day, the Royal Commission barely touched on the *FT*, and the matter was dropped, though in his regretful response Parkinson observed wistfully that 'it is really the two enemies of mortality – Time and Change – that we are proposing to circumvent'.

Meanwhile, in the here and now at 72 Coleman Street, day-to-day life on the new paper was gradually sorting itself out. As early as January 1946 Parkinson sent his managing director a progress report that, in addition to various individual assessments, considered as a whole the manpower at his disposal and its potential:

> The staff is ample in numbers, but not really excessive to carry the work we shall have to do with a paper of normal length and scope. It is a united staff and on the whole, apart from inevitable safety-valve grumbling about physical congestion of accommodation and the failure of heating in some parts of the building during cold spells, a happy staff . . .
>
> I think it is fair to say that the *FT*'s pre-merger staff was sound, capable, knowledgeable and hard-working, but rather much of a muchness. The *FN* members who joined them supplied what I should consider the minimum of more specialised knowledge and the added element of brilliance, personality in style, independence of mind and vigour in expression, which were absolutely necessary if a paper is to make its mark intellectually and not merely on the sales side . . .
>
> This is the amalgam out of which we make the *Financial Times* of the future. It is good raw material and diversified enough to enable us to put on, when reasonably free conditions arrive, the best paper financial journalism has ever turned out. We need people who will do the bread and butter work well, in addition to the brilliant ones.

Parkinson perhaps overstated the happiness theme. According to those who were there at the time, for at least a year or two there was a fair amount of tension not only between the ex-*FT* and ex-*FN* people, but also between those (mostly very young or very old) who had kept the papers going during the war and those now returning from the armed forces. It was also, because of the merger and then the continuing newsprint restrictions, a badly overstaffed paper in most areas, with Parkinson being too kind a man to dispose of the dross. Indeed, those who did leave soon after the merger tended to be talented people, like Manning Dacey, who felt frustrated by the lack of immediate opportunity to stretch themselves.

Nevertheless, for those who stayed the material situation was an improving one. Salary increases in May 1946 more than matched inflation;

that same month the board gave approval 'to the expenditure of not more than £6,000 on the establishment of a staff canteen'; and two years later, with the new paper clearly an assured financial success, Bracken wryly informed his friend Beaverbrook that 'the hard-bitten Tory who runs the *Financial Times* has handed over his nice fat fee arranged by his predecessor, Lord Camrose, to the staff in order that they may have a Pension Fund'.[8] The reference was to the FT Ltd's 1928 articles of association, by which the chairman was entitled to a 6 per cent share of the profits. Although there had been an *FT* pension scheme in earlier days, this was something altogether more ambitious, and pioneering in Fleet Street terms, by which members of staff would in retirement receive two-thirds of their salaries. The initiative for it seems to have come entirely from Bracken, that strange and unfathomable mixture of cruelty and goodness.

In general editorial terms, the dominant fact of life was of course the intense pressure on space imposed by the newsprint rationing. Running for the most part during these early post-war years on eight pages a day, the print was usually small, the pages cramped and cluttered, and coverage patchy. This particularly applied to company news. As the deputy editor Cole noted in a memo to Parkinson, probably in 1946, 'it is almost unique for the results of even the most important Companies to be dealt with other than in "Dividends and Reports", and the space given to the average Company in Dividends and Reports is quite inadequate and frequently results in important matters arising in particular reports receiving scant and summary attention'. It was a similar case with market reports, where the newsprint restrictions ruled out a return to the pre-war system of a separate report for each market. There was little that Parkinson or anyone else could do about this fundamental constraint, though in August 1946, again under the influence of Stanley Morison, the paper did move over almost throughout to Times New Roman type. 'Typonym' of the *Newspaper World* (a trade weekly) welcomed the change:

> One particular advantage the new type gives: the advertised company meeting reports appear, in their headlines, more distinct from the news and features. Even to a City man it must be useful to have this distinction clearer . . . Another great advantage is that each line of the back-page 'To-day's Closing Prices' is infinitesimally clearer, and the improved clarity is considerable when one reads carefully down the tabulated columns . . . The leader-page is certainly improved by the change; the new-type headlines give a more determined appearance than the old style . . . The 'Dividends and Reports' column, that feature of close and compressed reading, is also clearer . . . The *Financial Times* is to be congratulated

on being (I believe) the first national to follow the example of *The Times*; and in its new dress it is not only an excellent and indeed outstanding financial newspaper; it is also an extremely successful essay in typography.[9]

Times New Roman alone did not work miracles; a quart was still being crammed into a pint size. But it did give the *FT* a much more modern appearance, appropriate to the era of innovation and expansion that lay ahead.

During these early years of concision and excision, two writers were notable exceptions to the rule and spread themselves more or less freely across the pages of the paper. One was Einzig, who had been shunted off permanently to Westminster and away from his Lombard Street beat. For the moment he revelled in it, building up a range of impressively powerful contacts. By January 1946 Parkinson was telling a probably sceptical Moore that 'he has, as Political Correspondent, turned in first-rate stuff and we are better served there than any financial paper has ever been'. He was certainly getting plenty of material printed, including a series of stories about the government's steel nationalization plans that were so accurate that – according to official records and not just Einzig's rather self-important imagination – the Secretary of the Cabinet successfully applied to Attlee to allow MI5 to have Einzig's phone tapped.[10] The trouble was that the veteran journalist's love of intrigue was matched only by that of the novice parliamentarian Crosthwaite-Eyre, with the result that the two became absolutely cahoots, Einzig spending much of his time devising questions for the MP to ask, and his objectivity and detachment began to suffer in consequence. Indeed, from the point of view of the news room he started to become a positive menace, hatching and then producing scoops that were usually inappropriate and sometimes inaccurate. He could still come up with the goods on occasion – his nose was almost never less than keen – but the simple truth was that it had been a bad mistake to move him out of the City, which was what he knew best and where his reputation stood deservedly high. Indeed, even his nose could betray him: on 12 May 1948, when without any fanfare the first announcement was made in Parliament that Britain was building an atomic bomb, the *FT* the next day completely failed to mention the fact and instead devoted its Westminster story to 'Government and the Gas Bill'.

The other great consumer of space was the chairman. In January 1946 Bracken took over the writing of the 'Men and Matters' column, dropping the 'City' prefix but continuing to use the 'Observer' by-line. The column still appeared on Mondays only, having been written by

Bracken the previous afternoon with the aid of Alan Hodge, who had been his private secretary at the Ministry of Information. Hodge later described the process:

The scribe [i.e. Hodge himself] was asked to produce a list of targets for attack. Invariably these were shot down by Bracken in withering terms. This was part of a process of warming up by which he got into his stride. He would then pace about, talking explosively, jumping from one subject to another, from the problems of the coal mines to Impressionist painters, from technological education to the needs of St Paul's Cathedral, from politics and business in the United States, about which he was deeply informed, to the beauty of Georgian country houses, on which he was no less expert. 'Polymath' was a word that he liked to apply to men of far-ranging interests and varied knowledge. The word fits him.[11]

Hodge's judgement may be valid, and those Sunday afternoons may have been wonderful experiences, but what emerged the following morning was on the whole pretty poor stuff. Bracken's biographer puts it fairly: 'In fact there was little of the polymath about the political tirades and personal tittle-tattle that made up most of Bracken's column in its early years. Although sometimes highly spiced and entertaining, it suffered from the twin vices of verbosity and repetitiveness, and would have benefited from the editorial pruning that Bracken forbade under pain of dismissal.'[12] A typical enough column was that of 11 November 1946. It began with a lengthy disquisition on President Truman (in the context of recent British press attacks on him) and recent American political figures; had an item on Lord Brand, who was just finishing as the Treasury's representative in Washington and was described as being 'gifted with none of the back-slapping proclivities that appeal to Americans'; mentioned that the Board of Trade was looking for a site for a 1951 rival to the New York World Fair and suggested Whipsnade; and ended by criticizing the government for refusing to spend more on repairing Dr Johnson's house: 'The Government solemnly announce that they intend to develop tourist traffic, aiming at a yield of £100 millions a year. But judging by the high standards of vandalism they maintain, I doubt if there will be any historic houses left in Britain for tourists to see.' The column had a certain vitality and no doubt a certain following, but on a weekly basis it became wearisome and, taken in the round, cannot have helped the paper's reputation.

Otherwise Bracken stayed clear of editorial matters, apart from just occasionally playing an active role in whipping up a campaign. One such took place, to tangible effect, late in 1947. On 25 November he wrote to Beaverbrook enclosing an article from that day's *FT*, explaining that 'it deals with Rank's impudent attempt to sell his General Cinema Finance Corporation to Odeon'; he added:

Rank does not condescend to give any information about his Finance Company. No Balance-Sheet or Profit and Loss Account is to be given to the shareholders of Odeon. Rank and his deferential colleagues on the Board of Odeon are going to pay out a large sum of shareholders' money for Rank's private investment in a highly speculative Finance Company.

That day's *FT* certainly gave the man with the gong the full treatment. In addition to the page-one 'splash' sent to Beaverbrook, there was a leader on the subject full of pertinent questions, while the 'Lex' column was headed: 'This Odeon Deal: Facts Wanted'. Bracken's cohorts then kept up the pressure, so much so that by 5 December he was writing again to his fellow press lord:

When the *Financial Times* first started to oppose this deal, Rank issued a statement declaring that our criticism was mischievous and ill-informed. And he added that he did not intend to make any statement about the deal. It was going through. A fortnight's reading of the *Financial Times*, which was mightily aided by the *Daily Express* and the *Evening Standard*, has unsealed the film magnate's lips. Last night he issued a statement to say that he was willing to publish a Balance-sheet and give full information about the profits and the liabilities of his General Film Finance Corporation.[13]

As the paper itself put it in a leader on the same day, the *FT* had been 'in the vanguard of Mr Rank's critics in this matter'. Nevertheless, as an episode it was a rare example not only of Bracken's personal intervention in such a specific matter, but also of trenchant and investigative reporting by the paper as a whole. The laws of libel remained unfavourable, the culture of caution ran deep after the harrowing experiences of the early 1930s, and over succeeding decades the *FT* would rarely go out on a limb to expose crooked or even dubious dealings. It was a culture passed on by Bracken through Moore, Parkinson and their successors, and was essentially unstated, unquestioned and of immense significance in determining the character of the modern *FT*.

Two areas where there was virtually no growth during the second half of the 1940s were features and foreign affairs. At the time of the merger Parkinson had laid ambitious plans for Newton's role as features editor, but in practice there was simply not the space available to print more than one fairly small feature article each day, and even that sometimes had to go. The six features for the week beginning 21 October 1946 give a fair impression of what sort of articles they tended to be: 'The Reaction in

US Commodity Prices' from 'An American Correspondent'; 'Planning for Industry' by I. A. R. Stediford, chairman of Tube Investments; 'Raw Cotton at the Cross Roads' from 'A Trade Correspondent'; 'Sweden Today' from 'a Correspondent recently returned from Sweden'; 'Linoleum: Why Is It Scarce?' from 'A Trade Correspondent' again; and finally, on Saturday, 'Tractors on the Farm', an uncredited piece on the state of tractor manufacturing. There were occasional features by outside distinguished contributors, such as the economist Roy Harrold, while Einzig sometimes returned to his old themes. In general, however, it was unambitious writing on unambitious subjects, with as yet no systematic development of a feature-writing team based in Coleman Street.

As for the coverage of foreign affairs outside a fairly narrow financial or economic sphere, it more or less did not happen. The civil war in Greece, the Palestine question, the rise of Mao – these all received minimal or no attention. By 1948 the *FT*'s only full-time correspondents were in Paris and Johannesburg (the latter choice entirely a reflection of Bracken's South African mining interests), while there were journalists being paid a retaining fee in New York, Washington and Rome. The man in Rome, Peter Tumiati, tells a nice story of these days:

> Other London papers looked down on the *FT*, which they considered little more than a Stock Exchange bulletin, not a newspaper. I owned a war-weary jeep on which I had written 'British Press' to render moving about a little easier. Once, while driving from Rome to Milan, I stopped at a closed level crossing. There was another car waiting there. A lady got out (later I got to know her name. It was Sylvia Sprigge of the *Manchester Guardian*) and approached me. She said: 'What paper do you work for?' When I said the *FT* she answered: 'Do you call the *FT* a newspaper?'

From a European point of view it was still a fair gibe, even though there was the extenuating circumstance of the newsprint shortage.

By contrast, and despite the space problem, significant developments were starting to take place in terms of Parkinson's underlying aim of transforming the *FT* into an industrial as well as strictly a financial paper. As early as April 1946, looking ahead to larger newsprint rations later in the year, he told senior editorial staff of his hopes of being able 'to make a start with the building up of a strong commercial and industrial section', adding pointedly that 'this is a matter which deserves all the attention we can give it, because the field itself holds out very great possibilities and it is one which we may not be allowed to occupy without outside competition'. Later that month he typically used the Easter break to prepare the methodological ground for the *Financial Times* Index of Productivity, using statistics by now coming out of the Central Statistical Office. The index, to be monthly, appeared for the first time in July, was geometric and based on the consumption of the most important raw materials used in industry, and justly claimed that it would fill a gap and in so doing 'help not only the body of investors but trade generally to obtain a quick over-all picture of what is happening in industry as a whole'. It indeed filled a gap, for it was not until almost two years later that there appeared from the government an official index of production.

The autumn of 1946 proved to be a false dawn on the newsprint front, but even in its wake Parkinson was able during the first half of 1947 to launch a major 'industrial' initiative. Doug York became industrial correspondent in the news room; permanent provincial offices were established at Glasgow, Manchester and Birmingham, each with its own business representative to generate regional advertising and circulation, and the first two each having an editorial representative, Birmingham getting its the following year. To co-ordinate the correspondents in the provinces, the leader writer H. M. Muggeridge was seconded as liaison man. Parkinson in his letter to Muggeridge put the appointment in context:

> Broadly, this is part of the general policy of developing the industry and economic side *pari passu* with the market and investment side of the paper. It is a policy which, so far as we can discover, has so far paid us good dividends, and we are anxious that the *Financial Times* shall earn and maintain a reputation for giving, of all the *daily* papers, the best coverage on industrial matters.

In practice, room for proper industrial coverage remained limited for a while yet, though even by the summer of 1947 a lengthy series of feature articles was under way 'on leading industrial concerns in which large numbers of investors are interested, setting out their problems, traditions, aims and difficulties, not in financial but in "human" terms, and written by special correspondents who have personally visited the works and headquarters of the companies concerned'. When the paper celebrated its diamond jubilee in February 1948, it proudly proclaimed: 'No longer is the *Financial Times* preoccupied with events in the Square Mile. The whole world has become its oyster.'

This was not all. By September 1947 that well-established *FT* revenue-earner 'Architecture To-Day' had returned from its enforced break along with its progenitor Pughe Morgan, who during the interim had gone back to schoolmastering. Morgan continued to garner the advertising and in effect decide the subject-matter, while the accompanying text was now in the hands of a former *FN* contributor, A. Trystan Edwards, who not only was a noted architectural historian but also had founded the Hundred New Towns Association in the 1930s. He was a suitably versatile writer for the column and continued to do it until the 1960s. Meanwhile, in a more orthodox sphere of the paper, the *FT* from November 1947 started to publish each Monday, in its London closing prices table, the latest annual dividends and estimated gross yields on all the industrial securities quoted there, amounting to more than 600 stocks. It was a major new departure in financial journalism, for as Parkinson explained in an accompanying leader: 'Yields provide a rough-and-ready common denominator for Stock Exchange prices, and have become one of the prime influences in establishing share values. As such, they are indispensable to toilers in the investment field.' North-country caution, however, impelled him to go on: 'In commending the figures to readers, the *Financial Times* must add a warning. Yields are a measure of a risk. Broadly speaking (there are some exceptions), high yields imply doubt as to the maintenance of dividends.'

There was one other thrust of significant long-term implications. By March 1948 it was decided to employ a scientific correspondent, and Bracken wrote to his friend Lord Cherwell to ask if he could suggest anyone. Cherwell in reply suggested Professor Francis Simon, who in Berlin in the 1920s had established his reputation as the outstanding low-temperature physicist of his generation and had fled Hitler's Germany as a Jew to come to work in Oxford at the invitation of Cherwell. The letter of recommendation mentioned Simon's early involvement in atomic energy development, his numerous contacts on the Continent and in the United States and, what probably clinched it from the *FT*'s point of view, the fact that 'he always keeps in touch with industrial developments at home and abroad and has a better knowledge of the relation between pure physics and industry than anyone in Oxford'.[14] Simon was duly approached, agreed to accept the post and quickly struck up a cordial relationship with Parkinson. Writing anonymously, Simon undoubtedly rode his hobby-horses pretty hard – the need for an integrated power and fuel policy, the poorness of technological education and the waste of fuel in open grates were perhaps the big three – but he also performed a useful service for the paper. To start with he confined himself to 'think-piece' articles at roughly monthly intervals, usually choosing the subject-matter on his own initiative. 'Your articles on the neglect of science appear to have made an impression on quite a number of readers,' Parkinson wrote to him in July after a three-part feature.[15] By November 1948, however, Simon was not only writing full-length peices but also sending in on a weekly basis three or four news stories on scientific subjects, such as 'Streptomycin in Pulmonary Tuberculosis'. These aroused considerable reader interest and in due course became integrated in a regular Monday column on 'Science and Industry', forerunner of what is now the technology page. Coming from one of the half-dozen most eminent scientists in the world, it was quite a contribution on behalf of what was still, for all its aspirations, a small-time City paper.

What, then, of editorial policy during these years of a first Labour government with real power? Bracken was in no doubt what that policy should be, telling shareholders in July 1947 that it was his task to 'try to produce a paper which never falters in the fight for free enterprise', a theme he reiterated the following year. In the course of his Monday column he himself never faltered in that fight, whatever the price to be paid in good taste or measured objectivity. His first column set the tone:

> What a vast power of patronage the Government is building up! I understand it is proposed to pay £6,000 a year to ordinary members of the National Coal Board, and considerably more to its chairman. This is only a small measure of the growing store of gifts the Government will have at its disposal as its plans of nationalisation progress. No such gilded prospect has opened since the days when Charles James Fox proposed to abolish the East India Company in order to hand over its powers of patronage to the Government of the day.

Thereafter the abuse followed thick and fast. Of Dalton, 'there was nothing oily in the Budget speech except its manner of delivery'. Of Shinwell, he was 'the Minister of Plentiful Power and No Fuel'. Of 'the job of teaching economics to the 395 Socialist MPs', it was 'the largest missionary endeavour in Britain since Saint Augustine arrived at Canterbury'. When 'the slippery Schacht', former President of the Reichsbank, was acquitted at Nuremberg, the obvious new job for him was with the British government, which 'have set up so many contraptions of a totalitarian kind that our lop-sided economy cannot possibly work unless some wizards are found to co-ordinate and guide it'. Bracken reserved his special contempt for 'the City gentlemen who have been prostrating themselves before the Socialists ever since the summer of 1945'. By April 1947, in the wake of the fuel crisis caused by Shinwell's belief that 'Socialist Britain would be spared the usual winter quota of ice and snow', he saw things as going his way:

> The fact is that there has been far too much defeatism about resisting crackpot Socialist schemes, dating from the time when the Socialists arrogantly behaved as if they were to be in office for half a generation. But in the last two years the

Socialists have proved themselves to be a Cabinet of all the Incompetents. I never doubted that these puppets of Transport House would lose their nerve when they came up against real difficulties.

It was to be another four years before Labour lost office, but during that time the clarion call from 'Observer' remained loud and insistent: 'The future of this country does not lie with the bloated monopolies. It lies in the hands of the thousands of energetic smaller companies that are capable of thrusting expansion.'

'Men and Matters' was purely Bracken's demesne. On the other hand, there is no evidence to suggest that he exercised any tangible influence over the general writing of *FT* leaders. Both he and Moore might have something to say afterwards, but not before. Thus in September 1946, after Einzig had written a leader arguing that 'there is everything to be said for taking trade with Russia out of the hands of the United Kingdom Commercial Corporation and restoring it to normal pre-war channels', Parkinson sent him a brief memo: 'Lord Moore has asked me to say that he thought your leader this morning on Russia was excellent and so did B.B.' He went on: 'I thought the same – particularly since I knew the conditions in which you had to write it', probably a reference to one of Einzig's many post-war illnesses.[16] In practice, as was only right and proper, it was very much Parkinson himself who was responsible for shaping and formulating the *FT*'s editorial policy during these years. A passage from the 1949 edition of his book on *Ordinary Shares*, in which he looked back on the situation at the end of the war, gives a helpful insight into his inner thinking:

It was a tacit assumption, among all who gave the matter serious thought, that the post-war period would have as its objective a progressive reversion, as opportunity permitted, to something basically like the old system in Britain (though not necessarily identical with it in all respects), and, as its indispensable accompaniment, a steady and deliberate relinquishing of controls. As a matter of fact, that did not happen. *That* was the real revolution.[17]

Parkinson, in other words, saw during these years the Labour government as presiding over a fundamental shift in the order of things, and furthermore saw it as a shift against which it was his duty to protest with all the strength at his disposal. The result was a shrillness in the *FT*'s leader columns that, to someone familiar with the modern *FT*, reads strangely. It was not always there, but for at least two or three years it was barely below the surface. Nor was the tone confined to the leader pages. In April 1946 the headline for the report of a speech by Shinwell ran simply:

'Venomous Attack on Industrialists'. From the chairman down, feelings ran high during these unprecedented years when the *FT*'s natural readers were, on the face of it, no longer the 'masters'.

This was particularly so over the subject of nationalization, about which Parkinson felt passionately. Indeed, his last book, *Ownership of Industry* (1951), though basically a statistical investigation, ended with a strong plea against nationalization and a call to the country's 1¼ million investors to unite to fight the evil. In fact, the first thing to be nationalized by Labour was the Bank of England, but it was done in such a half-cocked way that even the *FT* had to admit in its leader of 11 October 1945 that 'so far as status – apart from ownership – is concerned, the Bank's unique and responsible position is maintained', adding that 'given the present Government's policy, it is hard to see what better arrangements could have been made'.

Altogether less sanguine was the response to the complete nationalization package unveiled the following month. The paper laid out its full position on the issue as a whole:

> The motive of the 'programme' which Mr Morrison announced on Monday is not, at bottom, economic – it is political. It is not practical, but dangerously theorist. The inclusion or exclusion of particular industries, clearly, has nothing to do with their own condition, but has been determined entirely on doctrinal grounds. It is all the same whether an industry is 'old', like the railways, or has future potentialities hardly yet explored, like civil aviation; whether it is monopolistic or as fiercely competitive as long-distance road haulage; whether it is as inefficient as some coal mines or, like Cable and Wireless, has a world-wide reputation for its enterprises. Merely to be dubbed a 'utility' is enough.

Above all, the *FT* argued, nationalization was *irrelevant* to the country's needs:

> It is not the substitution of one owner, public or private, for another that can put British industry, or any part of it, on its feet again. That is a matter of organisation, of the infusion of large doses of new physical capital, of enterprise and planning in the widest sense. When nationalisation has been carried out, all the essential reorganisations will remain to do, and meanwhile the Labour programme will have delayed it.

As for the immediate future, the next few years while the programme was being implemented, 'What industrialist can be expected to devise and carry out large-scale, and very costly, projects, while the sword of Damocles hangs over him?'

The leader concluded: 'All in all, a more unfortunate time and a more unfortunate programme could hardly have been chosen by any Government. The present administration must be pressed by every constitutional means to postpone a large part of the programme, and, in carrying out its mandate to revive national prosperity, to put first things first.'[18]

The 'pressing', mostly to little avail, duly continued in the *FT*'s leader columns. 'Political mysticism – or is it purely political opportunism? – has prevailed over all realistic arguments', was the reaction to the news in April 1946 that Labour was also going to nationalize the iron and steel industry. The following January a leader on the Electricity Bill began with the blunt statement that 'the Government pursues its nationalisation programme heedless of the lessons of experience, and careless of the inequities its proposals create'. Fiercely protective of existing shareholders' interests, Parkinson fought the measures all the way.

The other major preoccupation during the early months of the new *FT* was the question of the acceptance or not of the United States loan, which was vast and seemed necessary to keep the British economy going, but was couched in ungenerous terms and was also contingent on the Bretton Woods agreement coming into operation. Along with the government and, when it came to it, the Conservative Party, the basic position was one of reluctant acceptance. Thus on 22 November 1945, with agreement impending in Washington, a leader firmly rejected romantic notions of instead going it alone in the sterling area and relying on purely bilateral barter dealing: 'The primary purpose of the negotiations, in fact, is to open the way for a return to the multilateral trading system that has always prevailed in the past and alone offers hope of an expanding world economy.' A fortnight later reluctance about accepting the loan was more apparent:

> It would imply the eventual abandonment of Imperial Preference; and it would imply the acceptance of at least a provisional parity for Sterling, though with safeguards to ensure that we should never be forced to follow a deflationary policy to protect that parity. Parliament must decide whether these limitations are too great a price to pay for the avoidance of an economic war with America and the hope of a new era of international co-operation in world trade.

Parliament duly accepted the loan and with it Bretton Woods, the Conservatives mostly abstaining, and on 14 December there was a tinge of bitterness in 'Washington – The Moral':

> We had hoped, at the outset, that our approach to America could be that of a friend and comrade in arms. Whatever one may say about the present 'business

deal', it remains something far removed from that. Besides, we believed we had a good case. What was the capitalised dollar value, to America, of the Battle of Britain, which we won, alone, when we were still buying from America on a cash-and-carry basis?

But overall, the *FT* for once did not disagree with the Chancellor: 'Mr Dalton put the case clearly enough when he suggested that, even if the escape doors proved less effective than he made them out to be, the consequences of present refusal of American aid would be more grievous than the possibility of subsequent failure to live up to its conditions.' Even more sceptical, though not influencing the *FT*'s line, was Bracken, who wrote to Einzig a few days later about the failure of most MPs to understand what was involved in acceptance of the Bretton Woods system: 'Many of them sincerely believe that it is a return to the Gold Standard. But, in fact, it is much more like a return to the Dollar Standard. And nobody who has any knowledge of America will welcome such a development.'[19]

In the more parochial sphere of purely domestic politics, the *FT* by the spring of 1946 was laying heavily into the government over its fiscal, welfare and planning policies as well as its nationalization programme. 'Soaking the Rich Again' was the self-explanatory title of the leader following Dalton's Budget in April; while soon afterwards an anxious leader on the heavy cost of the social services programme ('High Taxation for Ever?') declared that 'the choice is not between these services and no service at all, but between pledging ourselves to services of this magnitude, at this particular time, and waiting for an enhanced national income which will enable us to carry them without an over-burden'. Finally, on 23 April, 'Politics and Prosperity' examined the government's record and rhetoric to date:

> At the same time as the Government has been appealing to industrialists to put their utmost into increasing productivity, Ministers have indulged in a series of threats, jeers, and menaces against a well-trained financial and industrial machinery whose complexity they do not understand . . . No one need be amazed – though he may rightly be indignant – when Ministers play to the galleries of the Left by threatening the motor industry, issuing warnings of possible Government action against trusts and combines, sneering at mythical 'City rackets', recklessly abolishing commodity markets, and the like. All these signs of ebullience arise out of a confident majority. They are to be expected, and greeted more in sorrow than in anger.

This particular editorial ended with the theme that future generations of *FT* leader writers would find themselves reiterating almost in their sleep:

Britain is piling up a large burden of social services in outlays on health, education, national insurance, family allowances and subsidies for housing and for food. We are a nation of producers with an ever-increasing overhead of social charges, and with an ever-expanding realm of doubtful experimentation in State-control. With these extensive commitments, we shall have to meet the competition of the United States for the markets of the world, once the immediate famine for goods of all kinds has abated. When we have topped our potential wave of prosperity, how shall we deal with the potential challenge of reviving German and Japanese exporting industries, now temporarily out of commission?

Such were the paper's long-term 'macro' musings. In the more micro field of monetary matters, the *FT* naturally devoted close attention to Dalton's celebrated or notorious (according to taste) cheap money policy. No judgement was made for a time, but by May 1946, following a new 'tap' issue in the form of 2½ per cent savings bonds, a leader argued that 'it is surely moving toward the extreme of orthodoxy to rush out a new tap issue a bare month after the Chancellor's Budget speech' and wondered whether the announcement might be 'construed as an admission of partial failure in the move towards ever-cheaper money'. Dalton himself, who spent much of his time in the Commons engaging in robust exchanges with Bracken, noted in his diary that day: 'Yesterday I announced a new Savings Bond issue . . . and the poor *Financial Times*, which I have been publicly ragging, tried hard this morning to pretend that I could have "got better terms" and perhaps I could, just a little.'[20] In November the paper carried a powerful anonymous two-part feature – headed 'Has the Rise in Gilt-Edged Gone Too Far? Doubtful Benefits of Cheap Money Policy' – which argued that the effect of cheap money in stimulating recovery in the 1930s had been exaggerated, viewed the policy as 'an encouragement to wasteful spending' and 'a powerful discouragement to thrift', and asserted near the end that 'Mr Dalton is now in a position to rest on his laurels, and he would be well-advised to do so.'

But despite increasingly great problems in getting the co-operation of the City and of investors generally, Dalton pressed on with his policy, which by April 1947 the *FT* was criticizing above all on account of its inflationary implications: 'It is true of the Chancellor's attitude generally that, while he inveighs against inflation's dangers in the abstract, he has been unwilling to take major effective action against them.' In July, in a leader on 'Problems of Inflation', there was a positive call for 'a measure of "disinflation", or at least an orderly retreat from the forward lines of cheap money'. Yet from Dalton's point of view this campaign against him (which was mild compared to that waged by the *Economist* under Geoffrey Crowther's editorship) was not altogether to be regretted; for according to Einzig in his memoirs, 'in Socialist circles the *Financial Times* became nicknamed *Dalton's Daily Advertiser*, owing to its frequent attacks against the Chancellor, attacks which tended to strengthen his position in the Party'.[21]

As Dalton's cheap money policy started to run into difficulties, so too, during the harshest of winters, did Britain's coal production. As early as September 1946 an *FT* leader was demanding 'an entirely new approach to the coal problem' and prophesying that 'little but a miracle can prevent a hold-up to national recovery this winter, through lack of fuel'. By mid-January 1947 a leader on 'Economic Outlook' was stating baldly that 'without more coal all attempts to solve Britain's economic problem are doomed to fail', adding: 'The solution is obvious. We must import labour for the mines. Is there any alternative? Facts impose it and "politics" cannot alter them.' This drastic advice was not heeded. On 7 February, Shinwell announced severe power cuts. The *FT* (like *The Times*) was pitiless:

> To attempt to throw the blame on earlier Governments, or on the weather, is quite unconvincing. Have we never had ice and snow in January and February? . . . As the signs of danger have become plainer, the Minister has veered like a weather-cock in his public pronouncements, first declaring that winter power cuts were sheer nonsense, then calling on industry to reduce all round.
>
> Essentially, the Government's policy has been defeatist. Cut on cut means an increasingly vicious spiral of depression. Before we can do anything else, as the *Financial Times* has asserted time and again, we must have more coal production. On that, our whole post-war recovery and future prosperity depends. We cannot indefinitely go on cutting down production in a hundred industries because one has a marginal shortage of labour. This is suicidal.
>
> There should be no minimisation of the crisis on us now. It is as serious a threat to prosperity, in peace time, as the events which brought down Mr Neville Chamberlain's Government were to victory in war time.

It was pungent stuff, far more incisive than the old *FT* could have managed. In the event, the crisis was just about surmounted, after a dreadful few weeks; but for Attlee's government it would never be glad confident morning again.

The balance of political power was changing, but not in an entirely predictable way. Under the strong influence of 'Rab' Butler and the bright young men working under him, the Conservative Party in May 1947 published its 'Industrial Charter'. It received from the

FT a significantly appreciative leader, headed 'Freedom for Enterprise':

One most important question the Charter tackles at the outset. It is the problem how freedom for industrial enterprise can exist in the midst of the vast machinery of State-planning built up during the war and since complicated beyond reason by the Socialists. Do the Conservatives propose to liberate initiative by abolishing all planning? No, they are not such Bourbons. Their aim is a system 'which reconciles the need for central direction with the encouragement of individual effort'.

Especial keenness was expressed about the Conservative commitment to reopen the commodity markets, before going on: 'Nowhere is common sense more evident than in the Conservative proposals for dealing with Socialist enactments. There is to be no orgy of tit for tat. The coal industry, the Bank of England and, apparently, the railways will remain in national ownership. But freedom will be restored to road transport and to some sectors of civil aviation.' In general, the leader applauded the charter's 'practical aims, designed to achieve and guard over the middle way of life between *laissez-faire* capitalism, which would mean anarchy in modern Britain, and the dictatorship of the corporate State to which Socialism threatens to lead us'. The way was beckoning for post-war consensual government under the 'middle-way' Conservatives; it was not a vision of a desirable future that the *FT*'s chairman shared.

For the time being, however, this all seemed mildly academic, as attention focused for the rest of 1947 on the death throes of Dalton's chancellorship. The obligatory leader on 'Convertibility Day' appeared on 15 July beginning: 'Today the curtain rises on the second act in the drama of the Bartered Bride, or Sold for Gold. The first act opened when a reluctant Britain signed the Anglo-American Loan Agreement in Washington, nineteen months ago.' The piece ended: 'If the dollar blizzard descends, then indeed we shall see a case of *sauve qui peut*.' The blizzard did descend, and five weeks later the paper was having to comment on the enforced suspension of convertibility: 'It is in fact a default . . . Such a misjudgement of the situation and such precipitate abandonment of the position taken up so recently cannot fail to bring the gravest discredit upon this Government of self-styled planners.' The *FT* also had something to say about the mode of announcement of suspension: 'Mr Dalton will astonish the country by having elected to use the easy, but totally unsuitable, medium of the wireless so soon after the adjournment of Parliament. There can be no justification for bringing a matter of such profound significance before the country, and indeed the world, in this way.' The final scene in Dalton's personal drama occurred in November when he inadvertently leaked a Budget secret to the *Star*'s lobby correspondent and resigned the next day. An old adversary was generous at the last, as it could now afford to be: 'The *Financial Times*, which claims to have disagreed with Mr Dalton on more subjects than any other newspaper, has nothing but sympathy to offer him now. He was indiscreet, and he traversed an inviolable Parliamentary convention. But, as a man, his reputation stands; he nothing common did or mean.' The paper remarked that the late Chancellor 'called financial journalists hard names sometimes, but he paid them the unusual compliment of reading them'.

The *FT* welcomed 'the carrot-crunching Cripps' (Bracken's phrase) as Dalton's successor: 'The new Chancellor is fundamentally no lover of capitalism. But he is well aware of the value, in the present crisis, of full and willing co-operation from industry.' Over the next few months the paper responded with approbation to Cripps's emphasis on the primacy of production and his 'disinflationary' phasing out of the cheap money policy. His Budget of April 1948, however, earned strong criticism, partly because of its once-for-all levy on investment income and partly because of its failure to cut expenditure. In the words of a leader a few weeks earlier: 'Why should wage-earners, business men and investors be required to draw in when the biggest spender of all – the State itself – goes merrily on?' But on the whole there was a mood of optimism in 1948, generated above all by the Marshall Plan, which at the time of its inception the previous year had been described by the *FT* as 'a magnificent gesture' and by April 1948 began to take fruition with the signing in Paris by sixteen countries of the Charter of the Permanent Organization for European Recovery (the OECC).The leader on this event was only third of the day – below 'On Guard!' about the latest govenment attack on ordinary shareholders and 'Funds to Australia' about the flow of money from Britain – but it was significantly entitled 'European Co-operation' and included this stirring passage: 'Thus begins a unique episode in European history. The fate of this great co-operative effort, underwritten on a prodigiously generous scale by America, will determine whether Europe is to move forward decisively to peace and prosperity under democratic forms of government, or to sink back into poverty and despair.' It concluded of the sixteen nations: 'They surely cannot fail to write a new and more glorious page in European history.' Again, here was a tone, in this case a perceptibly pro-European one, with which Bracken, a mixture of little Englander and great supporter of the Dominions, would have felt remarkably little sympathy.

By the autumn of 1948 the new *FT* was three years old. Bracken continued to lay about him and was not afraid of making bold predictions, as in a paragraph in his column on 27 September entitled 'Hands Off!':

'The time may come when the Egyptian Government will be imploring the French and ourselves to stay in the Canal Zone in order to protect them from the grasping hands of Moscow. In the meantime, the Egyptians will be well advised to keep their paws off the Suez Canal company so long as the lease lasts.' If that was an old tune, a new and altogether more auspicious motif in the paper's development was the start of industrial surveys. Each was of eight pages, appeared at roughly monthly intervals, and the first three were on commerce and industry in the Midlands, the British iron and steel industry and the British motor industry. Advertising filled roughly half the pages, and the editorial content was anonymous, apart from an introductory article by a 'name' like Sir Ellis Hunter, President of the British Iron and Steel Federation. Taken together the surveys showed that the 'industrial' gleam in the respective eyes of Parkinson and Henschel was starting to become reality, to the mutual dovetailing benefit of the editorial and advertising departments. That November the chairman talked in glowing terms to the FN Ltd's shareholders about their flagship publication:

> It is now reaping the reward of years of strenuous efforts to increase the services it offers to readers. Great are the benefits that come from those efforts. Today the *Financial Times* is much more than a financial newspaper. Industrialists and traders now regard it as an essential paper. And it is read by many who are more interested in public affairs than in the technicalities of finance or industry.[22]

As ever with a Bracken pronouncement, there was an element of hyperbole. A look at a 'random' issue of the *FT* at this time perhaps gives one a more precise idea of how far the paper really had broadened its character by this stage.

The last Wednesday of October 1948 fell on the 27th, and the news in that day's *FT* was dominated by the government's decision to go ahead with its plans to nationalize the iron and steel industry, with the text of its Bill to be published on the Friday. The issue was eight pages long, and the only photographs were in the seven small display ads, of which three were for motor cars and the others were for Blackwood Hodge, Vickers-Armstrong, Shell Chemicals and Clubland White Finest Old Port. There were plenty of traditional elements on view: a page of home and foreign market reports and analysis, including 'Lex' and 'Diarist' on the front page; a page and a half of Stock Exchange dealings and prices; a page and a half of prospectuses; and a page of company-meeting reports. There were also two columns of dividends and reports, a column about impending new issues, some fairly critical comments about actual new issues, and 'Money Market Notes' dealing with the latest anti-inflationary measures in Argentina. The feature of the day was about the latest trends in motor-car design, in the context of the Motor Show about to open at Earls Court, and the main leader examined the state of the motor industry, calling on the government to increase its steel allocation. Of the other three leaders, one argued that the iron and steel industry 'cannot be torn apart without grave injury', while another employed three annual reports published the previous day as 'a triple example of the way an unsympathetic (and extremely short-sighted) Treasury is steadily denuding industry of liquid resources'. This day as any other, there were two recent if small innovations on the centre pages: a list of 'To-Day's Events', which had been started at Moore's instigation in September 1946; and 'Sixty Years Ago', being a brief extract from the appropriate old *FT*, which had been introduced at the time of the paper's diamond jubilee.

On this particular day, however, there was little that could not have been in the paper before 1939. Perhaps a story from Melbourne on page one about the industrial situation in Australia, perhaps also the impressively full reportage and analysis of the coming political battle over the Steel Bill; but as far as coverage from the domestic industrial heartlands was concerned, this particular issue drew a virtual blank, apart from the briefest of items about the new Remington typewriter factory at Glasgow and a production campaign about to be launched by the main cotton-weaving firms in Skipton, Yorkshire. The conclusion is inescapable that at this stage the *FT* was still an 'industrial' paper in aspiration only. How much this was because of the newsprint restrictions it is impossible to say, but granted Parkinson's clear intentions they must have played a part.

Certain figures were now coming to the fore who would have an important role in the paper's future. One such was Jim Hunter, who as news editor proved to be the absolute rock in the post-war news room. Emerging under his tutelage were Doug York and John Hay. Of York, Hunter justly wrote to Parkinson in January 1947 that he had 'every confidence in his ability and, what is more important, in his conscientiousness and his loyalty'; while of Hay, Parkinson himself told Moore soon afterwards that he could not 'possibly be drawn from the news room without the present system there breaking down' and that 'there is not one single field of daily news coverage and presentation that Hay does not now cover'. On the markets side of the paper, the kingpin was undoubtedly A. L. W. Shillady, who had come from the *FN*, was the hardest of workers and thoroughly understood the Stock Exchange. 'Shill' ran the prices operation single-handed and stood no nonsense from the many youngsters who were in his charge in the prices room, sometimes giving them impossibly long jobs just to keep them quiet. These youngsters, mostly straight from secondary school, included one Norman Tebbit, as well as the trio of Kenneth Marston, James McDonald and Michael Donne, each of whom subsequently became specialist journalists on the paper. Already making a name for himself was Bill Roger, who had started as a messenger boy on the *FN* and was now writing the 'Diarist' column, having been marked out by Parkinson for his 'youth and ambition plus post-war market experience'. Then there was Gordon Newton, of whom Parkinson wrote to Moore soon after Newton's return from the forces that 'even under the cramped conditions of ultra-short "feature"-less papers which might have driven a less resourceful man to despair, he has already distinguished himself'.

Coming into a category of their own at this stage among the upwardly mobile were the two emerging leader writers, John Applebey and Andrew Shonfield. Applebey was the son of the research director of ICI, was educated at Oundle and Oxford and had been in the Royal Artillery during the war, winning the DFC as an air reconnaissance pilot. He came to the *FT* in July 1946 and after a training in the paper's various departments was soon making an impact. By 1948 he was first leader writer, and in July that year Parkinson managed to persuade Moore to pay him more in order to resist the counter-attractions of the Brewers Society, who wanted Applebey as their economic adviser. Parkinson in his memo to Moore put the situation squarely:

> The problem always arises with gifted young men, who after one has trained them, become attractive to outsiders. In four cases out of five, one has to let them go, engage someone else and go through the round. Applebey, I feel, is the fifth case. His going would definitely be a loss, and he is young enough at 30 to have a good many years' useful work for the paper before him.

Applebey's new salary of £1,000 was still £250 less than that being offered by the brewers, but fortunately for the paper he decided to stay in Coleman Street. He was a highly intelligent, self-contained man, of the moderate right in his political views and with an ability to write lengthy, analytical and very logical leading articles. His was almost certainly the typewriter behind the leader so firmly supporting the Conservative Party's 'Industrial Charter'. Altogether, his was an influence, raising the intellectual stakes and cooling the political tempers, that the inner counsels of the paper badly needed by the late 1940s.

Complementing Applebey, and acting as the perfect foil, was Shonfield, who was two years older, had likewise been at Oxford before the war and then served with distinction in it, and was taken on by the *FT* in December 1946. Within weeks Parkinson was commenting favourably on him; soon he was writing leaders and in 1949 he became foreign editor. He was in many ways the archetypal European intellectual (his own background was Polish) and was at his happiest in discursive, penetrating conversation, which during his decade on the paper became his hallmark in Coleman Street. He believed deeply that it was a person's duty to take a view about things and once remarked to a colleague that he could not understand how people could read Jane Austen. Politically Shonfield was a socialist, but in a sufficiently moderate way not to alarm his masters. Indeed, increasingly over the years there was a bipartisan character to his work, as he sought to elucidate and then propound – at the *FT*, in books and on radio and television – what Britain's economic and foreign policies should be in the changed circumstances of the post-war world. His great influence on the paper, apart from the personal one on those around him, was to get it to ask questions it had not thought of asking before. This was epitomized by a leader of December 1947 called 'Sterling Area – Why?' which it is hard to believe was not written by Shonfield. It was still almost taboo at this time to question the desirability of maintaining the sterling area, but now he raised the question, making much of the fact that drawings from the dollar pool by sterling-area countries were accounting for between a third and a half of Britain's total dollar drain. The leader, though not calling for the dismemberment of the sterling area, did emphatically make the point that 'the foolish belief that the sterling area system would function satisfactorily so long as it boasted no principles and shrouded all its operations in complete secrecy has been proved false'. With Shonfield writing leaders like these, and Applebey concentrating more on the domestic economy, the *FT* was on the way to becoming compulsory reading not only for politicians but also for mandarins.

As the new order rose, so the old started to falter. Parkinson was forced to spend the first few weeks of 1949 in hospital, for what he described to Professor Simon as 'observation and treatment of the bloodstream'. On 20 January he wrote optimistically to Einzig from the Royal Free Hospital in Islington that 'they have thoroughly examined me here, and say that, with reasonable care, I should have many years still of active service before me'. After a fortnight's convalescence in Bournemouth, the message to Simon was that 'I am back in harness again now, and very glad to be, because it is amazing how dull life seems when one is away.' The sad truth, however, was that he was probably suffering from Parkinson's disease and was a sick man. The immediate effect on the paper was a significant loss of coherence and vitality during what proved to be a difficult year, as share values fell, prospectuses disappointed and circulation declined by several thousand. By the autumn of 1949 morale was so low that the noon editorial conferences had become strife-ridden and virtually out of control. The ship was in danger of becoming rudderless, and the captain should probably not have been at the bridge.

Nevertheless, in a day-to-day sense life went on. Further fortified by the opening of a business office in Leeds, the industrial surveys continued through 1949 on more or less a monthly basis, though still without any of the splendour or colour of the pre-war supplements. Subjects included non-ferrous metals, commercial vehicles, and aluminium and light alloys, and according to Bracken in June, addressing perhaps doubtful shareholders, 'these surveys are widely appreciated'.[23] The paper was able to publish the surveys in the context of a slight easing of the newsprint situation, first at the beginning of the year and then in April. Given this room for manoeuvre, the Monday yield figures were from now also given 'for British Government and kindred securities, Dominion, Corporation and Foreign Bonds, and Overseas Railways'; while to the doubtless relief of many, the 'Business Done' dealings page and the majority of company results were henceforth printed in appreciably larger and more legible type. In addition, Parkinson in a flurry of memos during March began to lay plans for applying the extra newsprint to Saturday editions of the *FT*:

They already have the largest circulation of the week, though rather a different one from other days. The Saturday reader is of a wider, less-specialist type, who is presumed to buy the paper to check up on his (or her) investments at the week-end, and, while catholic in taste, is mainly non-expert. In fact, the Saturday *FT* is much like a Sunday Financial Paper published on Saturday. We propose to make a special appeal to the week-end reader, on that basis.

Moore, however, was unconvinced about the merits of this particular form of expansion and in April replied to his editor:

The more I think about it the more I feel we should not have any set rule about a Saturday 10 [i.e. ten pages]. Revenue is already proving harder to get, and more and more of its sources are threatened by the Comrades. Also, I am against turning the whole staff onto the writing of *weekly* features when their job is to get out the best possible *daily* paper. And I would not like the *FT* to go out of its way to make things more difficult for the *IC* [*Investors Chronicle*].

Parkinson was forced to give way, and for the time being the Saturday edition remained a fairly threadbare affair.

The paper's underlying attitude towards the government did not change fundamentally during this time. Thus of Cripps's Budget in April it asserted that 'to the taxpayer groaning under the burdens implied by the passing of no less than 40 per cent of the national income through the hands of the authorities, Sir Stafford offers the prospect of penal servitude for life'. But the same leader did note with pleasure that 'Sir Stafford seemed to keep his most schoolmasterly admonitions for those of his own Party who had the wild idea that they could have *increased* Social Services and lower taxation (and presumably lower cost of living) at one and the same time'. As for Bracken, neither his range of targets nor his brand of arrows altered: 'I am a cautious man. But I think I am right in saying that Mr Creech Jones is the worst Colonial Secretary in British history.' Or of the newly published plans for what would be the Royal Festival Hall:

> In appearance the new hall will be like a Zeppelin on stilts. Its façade might not look out of place among the gas-holders of Beckton or the factories that line the Great West Road. Concert-goers will have to try to concentrate on their music amidst the roar of trains on Charing Cross Bridge, which is only a few yards away.

There was also an interesting exchange between the editor and his scientific correspondent during 1949. In March, Parkinson told Simon that 'I always feel that I could take any amount of articles from you, because they always provoke a great deal of interest among readers.' Three months later, however, he felt compelled to return an article called 'Can the World's Population Be Fed?' and to ask for changes. In particular, Parkinson wrote, 'the reference to a World State brings us to a political issue on which, frankly, I do not want to commit the paper'. Simon declined to make any changes and argued that the issue in question was no longer a political one, that indeed 'nearly everyone now realises that a World State is inevitable in the long run'. To which Parkinson's response was entirely typical: 'Let us agree to differ in unbroken amity.'

All paled, however, beside the devaluation of the pound, which was the big financial and political news story of 1949. As speculative pressure against sterling built up and Britain's gold and dollar reserves began to disappear, so during June and July the Cabinet's Economic Policy Committee held a series of highly secret meetings to discuss not only the hitherto great unmentionable of devaluation but even the possibility of floating the pound. Rumours abounded in Washington and to a lesser extent in London, but during these weeks the British press provided virtually no enlightenment to its readers about what the government was thinking of doing.[24] Almost the only partial exception was the *FT*, which at times got somewhere near to sniffing the truth, but whose leads were continuously not followed by the other papers. Thus on 13 June, as ministers considered Cripps's 'top secret' paper on the dollar drain, it was 'Money Market Notes' which quoted the latest information sheet by Messrs Godsell & Company, in which they analysed the possible benefits of a free exchange market. On the 16th the same column flatly stated that 'the recent attempt to counter devaluation rumours with the aid of a string of pronouncements by various British officials, from the Chancellor of the Exchequer downwards, pointing out that readjustment of the sterling–dollar rate was not under consideration in London, appears to have had no more than a limited success'. That same day there appeared a leader called 'Freeing the Pound', but no conclusion was reached: 'The effect of sterling participation in a free and fluctuating exchange market would be all but incalculable. The question is whether we can afford such an experiment, as things are now.' As for the devaluation option, the same leader noted that, though some were in favour, 'considered opinion here seems on the whole to hold that sterling devaluation in terms of the dollar would not help to break down the hard core of the dollar problem and that sterling devaluation in terms of other currencies would quite unnecessarily turn the terms of trade against this country'. By 5 July, as government denials of any crisis continued, an *FT* leader was referring to 'what is beginning to look suspiciously like a loss of confidence in the present sterling rate all over the world'. The following day the paper strongly attacked government secrecy over the whole question of sterling: 'The British people are already far too dependent on outside sources for information vital to themselves. They are entitled to an outline of the immediate steps the Government proposes.'

But in fact the British people got nothing from Cripps, who reiterated to the Commons on the 7th that 'the government have not the slightest intention of devaluing the pound'. The *FT* bought the line, stating in a leader on the 15th that 'sterling devaluation is as far from the Government's mind as ever'. Over the next month Cripps was in Switzerland convalescing; but by 26 August an impatient Einzig, himself about to go on holiday and with Cripps soon to attend the International Monetary Fund meeting in Washington, was writing to Parkinson (who has probably just returned from holiday) to put him on red alert:

> My news stories during the last ten days or so disclosed the fact that in Cripps's absence the Government's policy has undergone a fundamental change. While six weeks ago the Cabinet agreed with Cripps not to discuss devaluation [at the IMF meeting], now the brief for the British delegation to Washington contains instructions to use it as a bargaining counter. I did not say so, for obvious reasons

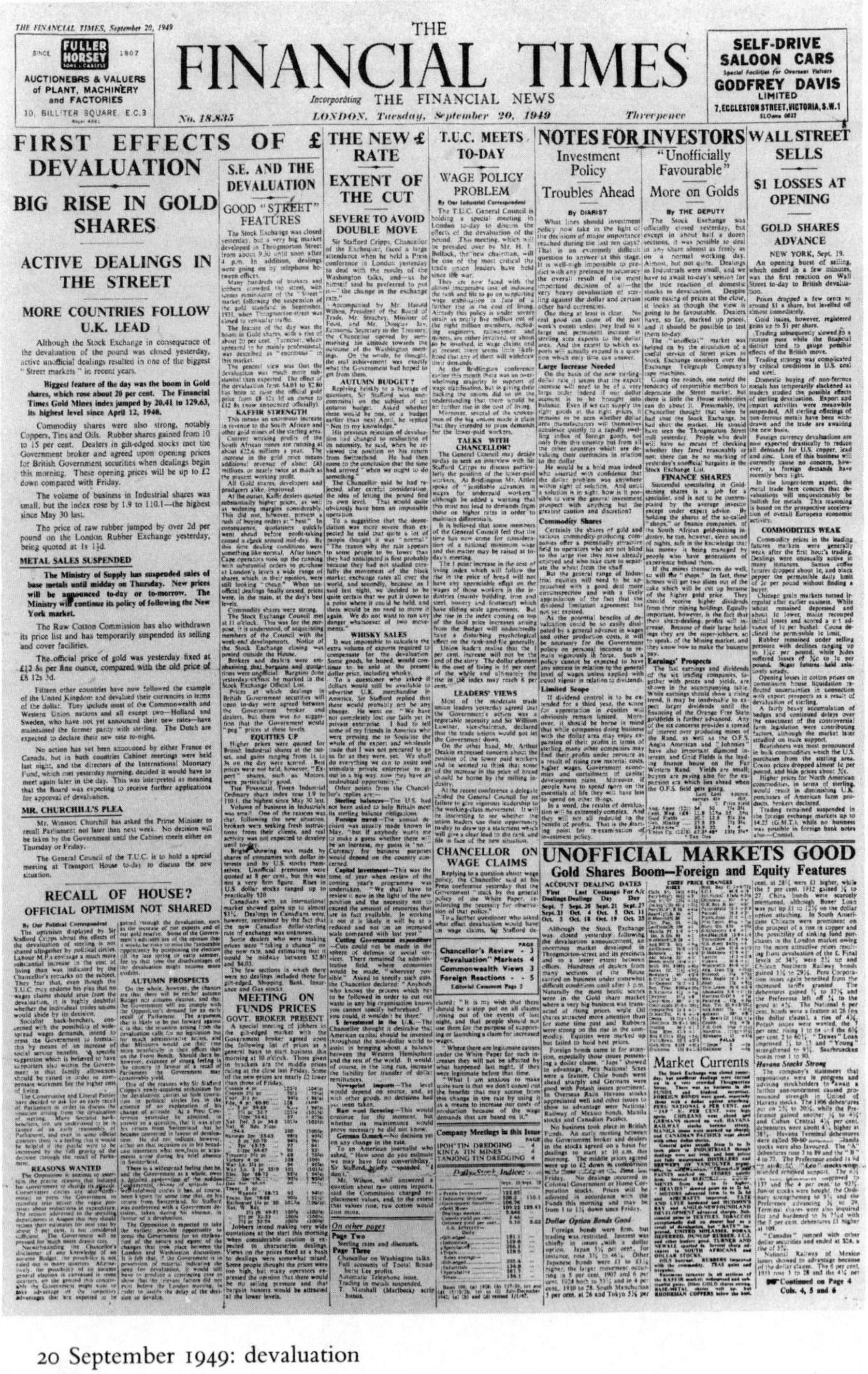

THE FINANCIAL TIMES, September 20, 1949

THE FINANCIAL TIMES

Incorporating THE FINANCIAL NEWS

No. 18,835 — *LONDON, Tuesday, September 20, 1949* — *Threepence*

FIRST EFFECTS OF £ DEVALUATION

BIG RISE IN GOLD SHARES

ACTIVE DEALINGS IN THE STREET

MORE COUNTRIES FOLLOW U.K. LEAD

Although the Stock Exchange in consequence of the devaluation of the pound was closed yesterday, active unofficial dealings resulted in one of the biggest "Street markets" in recent years.

Biggest feature of the day was the boom in Gold shares, which rose about 20 per cent. The Financial Times Gold Mines index jumped by 20.41 to 129.63, its highest level since April 12, 1948.

Commodity shares were also strong, notably Coppers, Tins and Oils. Rubber shares gained from 10 to 15 per cent. Dealers in gilt-edged stocks met the Government broker and agreed upon opening prices for British Government securities when dealings begin this morning. These opening prices will be up to £2 down compared with Friday.

The volume of business in Industrial shares was small, but the index rose by 1.9 to 110.1—the highest since May 30 last.

The price of raw rubber jumped by over 2d per pound on the London Rubber Exchange yesterday, being quoted at 1s 1½d.

METAL SALES SUSPENDED

The Ministry of Supply has suspended sales of base metals until midday on Thursday. New prices will be announced to-day or to-morrow. The Ministry will continue its policy of following the New York market.

The Raw Cotton Commission has also withdrawn its price list and has temporarily suspended its selling and cover facilities.

The official price of gold was yesterday fixed at £12 8s per fine ounce, compared with the old price of £8 12s 3d.

Fifteen other countries have now followed the example of the United Kingdom and devalued their currencies in terms of the dollar. They include most of the Commonwealth and Western Union nations and all except two—Holland and Sweden, who have not yet announced their new rates—have maintained the former parity with sterling. The Dutch are expected to declare their new rate to-night.

No action has yet been announced by either France or Canada, but in both countries Cabinet meetings were held last night, and the directors of the International Monetary Fund, which met yesterday morning, decided it would have to meet again later in the day. This was interpreted as meaning that the Board was expecting to receive further applications for approval of devaluation.

MR. CHURCHILL'S PLEA

Mr. Winston Churchill has asked the Prime Minister to recall Parliament not later than next week. No decision will be taken by the Government until the Cabinet meets either on Thursday or Friday.

The General Council of the T.U.C. is to hold a special meeting at Transport House to-day to discuss the new situation.

RECALL OF HOUSE?

OFFICIAL OPTIMISM NOT SHARED

By Our Political Correspondent

S.E. AND THE DEVALUATION

GOOD "STREET" FEATURES

MEETING ON FUNDS PRICES

GOVT. BROKER PRESENT

THE NEW £ RATE

EXTENT OF THE CUT

SEVERE TO AVOID DOUBLE MOVE

T.U.C. MEETS TO-DAY

WAGE POLICY PROBLEM

By Our Industrial Correspondent

CHANCELLOR ON WAGE CLAIMS

NOTES FOR INVESTORS

Investment Policy

Troubles Ahead

By DIARIST

"Unofficially Favourable"

More on Golds

By THE DEPUTY

WALL STREET SELLS

$1 LOSSES AT OPENING

GOLD SHARES ADVANCE

NEW YORK, Sept. 19.

UNOFFICIAL MARKETS GOOD

Gold Shares Boom—Foreign and Equity Features

Market Currents

20 September 1949: devaluation

[presumably the danger of causing further pressure on sterling, a constraint familiar to Einzig from 1931], but merely stated that if substantial American aid is conditional upon devaluation, the Government is prepared to consider it.

What matters is that we should be well covered in Washington, because all the leaks will come from that side. I understand our arrangement with Wells will come to an end on August 31, and in any case he was most unsatisfactory in recent weeks when other papers carried incomparably better stories from their Washington Correspondents.[25]

Parkinson responded quickly to Einzig's warning and got hold of Newton, on holiday climbing in Chamonix, to ask him to fly to Washington to cover the IMF meeting. There, on 18 September, it was duly announced that sterling was to be devalued, not just from $4.03 to the $3 that was this time generally expected, but to a seemingly panic-struck $2.80. The Chancellor's denials had been shown for what they were worth.

The *FT*'s immediate reaction was to criticize the government for having so expensively 'dithered on the devaluation brink' over previous months and to argue forcibly that, in the context of devaluation inevitably increasing the cost of living, 'if personal incomes are to be allowed to rise in proportion to the rise in living costs, the benefits of devaluation will be rapidly eliminated and the country will be speedily returned to a condition of chronic dollar crisis'. The tone remained stern on the 20th: 'Until it becomes clear where this shot in the dark is leading us, official enthusiasm over the virtues of devaluation is a case of counting chickens before they are hatched. By diverting attention from the real issues facing the country it does it a grave disservice.' As Parliament prepared to debate devaluation a week later, the *FT* outlined what these 'real issues' were:

What, in sober fact, can be done if the Government persists in the illusion that current levels of national expenditure are in no way responsible for the domestic inflation which has priced our goods out of certain critical overseas markets and forced a drastic currency devaluation? Unless this illusion can be dispelled, any improvement in our competitive position in the world economy must surely be transient. Another expedient will have been exhausted and we shall stagger on to another crisis . . .

No one is suggesting that the apparatus of the Welfare State should be dismantled, nor is there any necessity for such action even at this critical juncture in our affairs. But there are many who believe that unless the apparatus is operated with much greater restraint and with a proper regard for our straitened circumstances, the foundations of the Welfare State will inevitably crumble and decay.

But Cripps that same day provided cold comfort, ruling out the possibility of any substantial drop in government expenditure, raising the distributed profits tax and threatening to make dividend limitation compulsory. It was like the proverbial red rag: 'He has once again struck at the investor, at the young and ambitious, at all who would exercise foresight and daring in the use of their funds and their talent. Even some Socialists may foresee the evil consequences of that.' At the end of the debate the *FT* flatly and unequivocally concluded: 'The country can look for no constructive measures from the present Administration.'

The devaluation saga had a sad epilogue from the paper's point of view, for by the time Newton had returned from Washington his chief had suffered a stroke while talking to Moore in the office one day. It was the end; on 25 October, Bracken reported to the rest of the board that 'Mr Hargreaves Parkinson, the editor, had been advised by his doctors that his health would not permit of his returning to full-time service with the paper.' The board elected him a director. Writing to Simon on 22 November from his home in Esher, Parkinson expressed his feelings:

> It was indeed a wrench to relinquish a post which has been the breath of life to me. But thanks to the inexhaustible kindness of the Board of the *Financial Times*, I have been appointed to another sphere which, whether or not it be more exalted, is certainly less exacting. I am now having very encouraging medical reports, and if all goes well I hope to be back again in the City after Christmas, and, I hope, still to do useful work for the paper.

In fact, he never properly recovered and died the following May, aged fifty-four. His long-time chairman paid warm public tribute, saying what was undeniably true, that 'few men have done more than he did to heighten the standards of financial journalism'. Bracken went on to refer to Parkinson's legacy, to how as editor of first the *FN* and then the *FT* he 'took great pains to create and retain a staff of first-rate young men who have every reason to remember him with thanksgiving for all he taught them as well as for his invariable kindness and steady encouragement'. Bracken added: 'In a newspaper business, men are far more important than money.'[26] All this fairly said, yet there was truth also in the verdict of the journalist and economist Nicholas Davenport, who knew both men. Writing many years later of how Parkinson 'wore himself out to an untimely death', he said: 'His heart could not stand the pace of Brendan Bracken.'[27]

Whose could? The deputy editor A. G. Cole was sanguine enough in the autumn of 1949, and in Parkinson's absence after his stroke he became temporary editor. He moved into Parkinson's office and, once it became clear that Parkinson would not return, anticipated formal appointment as editor in due course. Meanwhile, Newton, now filling the job of being Cole's deputy, was starting to have hints dropped to him by Moore that he rather than Cole was in line for becoming editor, a position that Newton neither expected nor coveted. Newton was then summoned to see Bracken and Moore. Bracken's speech to Newton could hardly have been briefer – 'Congratulations, you're the editor. Don't tell anyone' – and he strode out of the room, leaving Moore to tell a doubtless bemused Newton that the appointment would take formal effect from the New Year. For the next four or five days, however, poor Cole still expected to be made editor, until Newton told Moore that the situation was impossible; and on 19 November a brief announcement was made on the front page of the paper about Newton's appointment, adding that Hunter would become deputy editor. From the start of December the appointments took practical effect. It had been a classic exercise in man management.

Who were the realistic alternatives to Newton? Cole himself was by now in his late fifties and, although a highly reliable and professional financial journalist who had done much to smooth Parkinson's path after the merger, he could not have been more than a capable caretaker, with little long-term potential as editor. As for Hunter, he was on paper probably better qualified than Newton, and of course his father had been editor between the wars. But whatever his abilities, which were considerable rather than perhaps outstanding, his fatal flaw in this particular contest was that he had come up on the *FT* side. He was still in his forties, might expect to edit the paper for at least ten to fifteen years and was in no sense 'Bracken's man'. It would, in short, have been going against the human grain for him to have been appointed, though Hunter himself felt bitterly let down. The other plausible candidate, equally disappointed in the event, was Harold Wincott. Since 1938 he had been editor of the *Investors Chronicle*, while continuing during the war and for some time afterwards to write many of the 'Lex' columns in the *FN* and then *FT*. No one could have doubted his talents, but there was probably some truth in Moore's subsequent judgement that he would have been too much of a worrier to have withstood easily the manifold strains and stresses of editing a daily newspaper. It is also arguable that Wincott's orientation towards the stock market – a natural consequence of his years on the *IC* – would have hindered the *FT* in its continuing expansion away from being primarily a City paper. But whatever the arguments, Wincott himself came to accept after a year or so that the best man for the particular post had in fact got it.

Newton was by no means the obvious choice. Although he had worked industriously on the paper's behalf since returning from the Army – for two or three years combining being features editor with writing leaders and then for a year or so being the sole 'Lex' before going to Washington to cover devaluation – no one in the autumn of 1949 would have called him a gifted as opposed to a highly efficient journalist. Three things probably got him the job. One was the fact that he was at this time being, in his own subsequent term, 'courted' by the Beaverbrook press, which caused a realization, probably on Moore's part, that unless he became editor he might well be lost to the paper. Secondly, it is clear that Parkinson after his disabling stroke expressed himself emphatically that Newton was the right successor. Thirdly, and most crucially, he was Bracken's choice, quite possibly having been marked out by him since wartime days as a probable future editor. Newton himself came to believe, on the basis of what Bracken later told him, that it was a wartime incident that had led to his appointment. He was at Liverpool Docks with his men, and coming under heavy bombardment, when he was told to report to 10 Downing Street if he spoke German. There he was assigned a special mission, but one that meant his leaving the Army. In his own words: 'I refused. Having just done a tough OCTU course and got my 2nd lieutenant's pips, leaving wasn't on.' So he returned to the docks, but not without having greatly impressed the Minister of Information. Now, several years on, Bracken made his decision, a characteristically intuitive one, and it carried the day. The new editor was forty-two years old and about to enter his own.

[SEVEN]

THE TRIUMVIRATE

Bracken was right. People *are* more important than money in the making (or breaking) of a newspaper business. In the case of the *FT* over the next twenty years, going virtually through the 1950s and 1960s, three people dominated the day-to-day life of the paper and presided over its astonishing transformation from a smallish, City-focused 'rag' into a major and highly respected national and international organ. In 1950 the *FT*'s circulation was about 57,000 and its advertisement columnage for the year was 5,845. In 1969 the respective figures were 171,000 and 26,360. The figures do not lie: these were decades of phenomenal growth for the paper and undoubtedly represent one of the two or three great success stories of post-war Fleet Street. The three men who oversaw this expansion were the editor Gordon Newton, the managing director Lord Drogheda (as Moore became on the death of his father in 1957) and the advertisement director Sidney Henschel. This is not to deny that others played an important part – after all, the 'triumvirate' hardly wrote a word between them in the paper. But no one who was present during these years would question that they were the three who lay, unrivalled and almost beyond criticism, at the heart of the whole operation.

Sidney Henschel was not the sort of person given to reminiscence, and apart from the bare bones not much is known about the first half of his life. He was born in 1893 and grew up in Camden Road, North London, the son of richly contrasting parents. His father was a Pole, in life-style something of a Bohemian, who at some stage lost all his money in business and had to go to Germany; his mother was the daughter of a suffragan bishop and very English. As a young man Henschel went to a technical college attached to London University and trained to be an analytical chemist. But then came the war, which resulted in his being invalided out of the Army in 1918 with a 100 per cent pension for shell shock. A scientific career was out of the question, and so instead, through the help of a friend in hospital, he got a job on the *Manchester Guardian* as an advertising representative. Subsequently he became advertisement manager of the *Yorkshire Post*, before taking up a similar position with the *FN* in 1936. After the merger of the two papers he became advertisement director. He was the type of man who would have given his utmost to his company anyway, but he now had every financial reason to broaden and maximize the revenue potential of the new *FT*, following a board decision in 1947 'to continue the remuneration of Mr S. Henschel on the basis of a salary plus a percentage on advertisement revenue over a datum figure and not, at the present time, to fix an inclusive salary'. That datum figure was apparently £100,000 and would soon look puny.

By this time of the merger Henschel was in his fifties, but for at least another twenty years he would continue to show the energy and vitality of someone half his age. He had been a great cyclist when young, loved walking and for nine months of the year would take a morning bathe at Brighton, where he lived until moving to Cadogan Square in 1955. He was a man of certain marked habits and enthusiasms, entirely consistent with each other. These included doing *The Times* crossword first thing each day; looking at car number-plates and making up words from the three letters; drinking wine in a knowledgeable way, though on the train back to Brighton it would be a gin and tonic with a game of bridge; regularly going to the theatre, including the Royal Court, as well as being a member of the Savage Club; and, perhaps the keenest enthusiasm, being greatly interested in motor cars. Indeed, he was a founder member of the Guild of Motoring Writers, having become the *FN*'s temporary motoring correspondent during the war, which he then continued to be on the *FT* for some time afterwards. Yet the surprising thing is that Henschel himself did not drive. The story goes that, some time between the wars, he was in a car with a friend who had an accident that would have meant losing his licence, and with it his livelihood, so Henschel instead took the rap and apparently never drove again. The truth of the story is uncertain, but all who knew him agree that it is wholly in character.

In appearance he was conventional: tallish, thinnish, silver-haired, spectacled, distinguished-looking. He was always immaculately dressed and would wear a brown trilby and highly polished brogue shoes. Although in some ways a curiously shy man, his manner was charming, and he always found time for people. In instructive contrast with that other doyen of the post-war Fleet Street advertising world, 'Bill' Needham of the *Daily Express*, he never pushed himself forward and preferred to let his achievements speak for themselves. The fact was that, behind the modest façade, he had qualities which made him perfect for the job, as he himself, rightly, never doubted. He was devoted to the cause of the paper; had a host of friends and acquaintances in the business world; was the most brilliant and persuasive of letter-writers; and, above all, possessed powers of mind, both analytical and intuitive, that gave him a vision of where the future of the *FT* lay and how he should go about fulfilling that vision. It was not a vision that he ever formally expressed in words at the time, but as he put it many years later when recalling the situation after the merger and the subsequent expansion, 'there was an obvious group of advertisers – particularly on the industrial side – who needed us'.[1]

Henschel made it his job to ensure that they fully appreciated that need and then never forgot it. To this task he devoted himself, building up in the process a happy, purposeful advertisement department that came to feel a great sense of loyalty towards him and the paper. In particular, he got on well with the young people whom he recruited and was not afraid to give them their head. His approach was the best sort of old-fashioned paternalism, nicely illustrated by a note he sent in February 1955 to one of his older hands, Len Miller:

> I went to a party last night to meet Sir John Elliot – head of London Transport. The party was to mark the opening of a new advertising campaign and as you know we figure on this for the first time. Clarkson was there, representing S. H. Benson Ltd, and I thought I would let you know he spoke very highly of the way you look after that agency. I was very pleased to hear this because I am quite sure you do the same with every agency.
>
> He also spoke extremely highly of the ability and the character of your daughter, Joyce, and I thought it would please you also to hear this.

After the war Henschel had quickly discerned the new importance of the advertising agencies. With Miller as a willing helpmate, he had begun the practice, probably by 1946, of writing regular letters to the media directors of every agency in the country telling them what the *FT* was doing in the way of its coverage, industrial and otherwise, and what it was proposing to do in the future. The tone of these letters, and indeed of his whole approach to selling advertising space in the *FT*, was distinctive and in keeping with his personality. There was nothing of the hard-sell, buttonholing manner about it, but rather a quietly authoritative insistence on the high and undiluted *quality* of the *FT*'s readership, making a virtue of the highness of the rates and more or less implying that it was a positive privilege to be able to advertise in such a unique medium. Along with this went a complete honesty of approach, making it a rule always to give an immediate and unquestioning rebate to the advertiser if there had been a shortfall of copies or below-par reproduction. But he could be tough enough when it mattered. It is said that on one occasion in the 1950s, after the paper had been consistently criticizing issues made by Arthur Whitehead's issuing house, Whitehead finally rang Henschel and said:

'I am not going to go on paying to have my arse kicked. We're going to give you no more advertising.'

Henschel replied: 'All right, but you must remember if your advertisement doesn't appear in the *Financial Times*, people won't know that you have withheld it, they will think we have refused to accept it.'

Whereupon Whitehead said, 'You're absolutely right', and forthwith told his agents to put the *FT* back on the advertising schedule.[2] It is always a help as a salesman to have faith in the indispensable nature of the product, and this faith Henschel had in abundance.

In all these activities he found a close ally in his managing director. It is easy to fashion a two-dimensional picture of the Eleventh Earl of Drogheda: the languid, drooping aristocrat, with the long cigarette-holder, the keen interest in the arts, the best possible social connections and a certain almost obligatory *hauteur*. He did not really divide the world into earls and others, but at times it seemed so. The anecdotes abound. When Professor Simon invited him one November up to Christ Church, he replied: 'Would you think it awful of me if I asked to be allowed to defer my visit to Oxford until the short winter nights are past?' When the paper moved to new premises over an Easter weekend, he turned up in green plus-fours to supervise proceedings. When welcoming a young journalist on to the paper, he remarked that the difference between the City and the West End was that in the City 'one can't just wander out at lunchtime and buy a picture'. It was not a deliberate disguise, but there is no doubt that over the years many outsiders were deceived into seeing Drogheda as something of a dilettante, meddling in an amateurish way in a world to which he did not truly belong. The truth could not have been more different; as all who knew him as the *FT*'s managing director (and later chairman) would testify, he was always one of the first to arrive at the office, extremely hard-working and conscientious and a newspaperman to his fingertips, however elegant. There was perhaps a paradox, but it was altogether more apparent than real.

The early background explains much. He was born in 1910 on St George's Day – appropriately enough for the heir to an Irish peerage who would later have nothing to do with Ireland and say that the only Irish thing about him was his name. His parents were divorced in 1921, and his father in consequence resigned from the Diplomatic Service. Much of his childhood was spent being shuttled between parents. He went to Eton and then Cambridge, but left early, having revealed no great academic distinction. He was already mixing freely in society and enjoying himself to the full, but as to the future there was no major family wealth at his disposal and no traditional family career for him to follow. Moreover, from the point of view of employment, the economic climate of the early 1930s was of the chilliest. After two dull years of book-keeping on behalf of the Mining Trust, his great personal turning-point came in 1932 when he met Bracken at Brooks's Club, clearly made an impression on him and went to the *FN* the following year. He began by selling advertising space and during the rest of the pre-war period applied himself to learning the nuts and bolts of the newspaper business. During the war, with Bracken for the most part otherwise engaged, he began to emerge as a force in his own right; and the process continued after the merger and above all in the 1950s, as Bracken lost his vitality and Drogheda, though only seven years younger, entered his prime. It had been a full, indeed exhaustive apprenticeship, in which it had taken him more than two decades wholly to move out of his master's shadow.

It was against this background – of having risen from the ranks almost despite his birth – that Drogheda in later years liked to call himself 'a humble canvasser'. This was of course an affectation, but it contained an important core of truth; for all are agreed that in the causes to which he was attached (which during the 1950s and 1960s were primarily the *FT* and the Royal Opera House at Covent Garden, of which he was secretary and then chairman) he would stop at nothing on their commercial behalf. Newton subsequently described this aspect of Drogheda rather well:

> He was a supreme and quite shameless salesman. Many a chairman or managing director has arrived for lunch little knowing that he was soon to arrange more advertising in one of the group's publications and heaven help a chairman who thought that he would save money by cutting down the space occupied in the *FT* by his annual speech. Garrett would trounce him, either to his face or on the phone. There may have been a few who held out to the end but the fingers on your hand would count them.[3]

Drogheda was especially fearless at tackling the big boys. When the BBC started using the Extel share price index rather than the *FT*'s, he was at once at them with all verbal guns blazing, and the corporation soon reverted to the *FT*. Or if the paper looked as if it was going to be short of advertising in the coming weeks, he simply rang round a dozen or so company chairmen whom he knew and, literally, never took 'no' for an answer. His early years on the struggling *FN* had taught him that there was no such thing as a free lunch, and he now felt no qualms about teaching that lesson to everyone else. The *FT* could not render its indispensable service to business men unless it secured an adequate income from advertising; it was, he sincerely argued to the utmost of his formidable ability, as simple as that.

Within the paper, Drogheda's style as managing director was, as he later wrote, very much his own:

I was never one for management techniques. I used to read the books, but instinct always guided me. My ways were thoroughly unorthodox, something which I inherited I suppose less from my father than from my mother, who was always fearfully impulsive. I had a habit of wandering round the office, and dropping in on people in a completely haphazard way, trying quietly to sense the atmosphere. From these chance encounters developed chance ideas, and as often as not they proved fruitful.[4]

Underwriting this approach were his marvellous human qualities. He was witty and companionable, was usually relaxed and possessed the gift of intimacy; he had a lovely sense of fun and mischief (to which his memoirs fail to do justice); he tried his hardest to be just, especially once away from the influence of Bracken, and of all things hated to be called unfair; he was keenly interested in people and their problems and was a good listener; perhaps above all, he had what one might call an inherent curiosity, which meant that there were extraordinarily few subjects from which he 'switched off'. It was in many ways a very old-fashioned style of management, by which he kept people up to the mark often without their realizing that he was doing so. It relied entirely on his flair, his attention to detail and a certain personal magnetism. With his finger so close to the pulse, it was a style that worked brilliantly in an age still willing to accept paternalism more or less on its own terms.

In addition to the ubiquitous physical presence, there was a further weapon in Drogheda's armoury, equally distinctive and equally effective. This was the memo or letter, sometimes known as the 'Droghedagram', which poured out from him in profusion on all manner of subjects, at times coming to their particular recipient at the rate of half a dozen or more a day. The only way to stop them was to go and see him; trying to ignore them merely quickened the flow. No one received more of these Droghedagrams than Newton, who towards the end of his editorship paid tribute to their constructive aspect:

He has nagged, often to good effect. Those streams of memos from upstairs have made me step outside my own paper and look at it. At first, I wouldn't answer them. Then, more in sorrow than in anger, I would get a memo asking why I hadn't answered the memos. And I would look at our coverage of American affairs or whatever was under fire. I would often agree and do something about it.[5]

Or as Newton put it on another occasion about these memos, 'they had a purpose, for they brought a state of creative tension'.[6] Often, however, Drogheda's memos were simply to keep the human wheels of the paper well oiled, something he did superbly. Typical in tone as well as content was a note he sent to Miller in April 1953: 'I should like to congratulate you for the excellent advertising in the Banking Survey which your hard work obtained. It was a splendid effort and we are most grateful to you.' He may, in other words, have been a patrician, but he cared deeply about the well-being of the paper and its staff. Nothing was too small or too trivial for his quizzical, even whimsical attention. Thus when he received a memo himself, whose points were numbered in Latin, his only response to the document was to ask: 'Why have we got classical scholarship here?' It was an approach learnt in the school of Bracken, but carried with an infinitely lighter, more generous touch.

At the same time, it is impossible to deny that there were flaws in Drogheda's make-up. He was thin-skinned and capable of displays of extreme pique if he felt that he or one of his concerns was being unfairly criticized. He could be a snob and had the embarrassing habit at *FT* lunches of reading aloud to all present the *Who's Who* entry of the guest of the day. His humour could be of the waspish rather than pleasant variety. He could treat people with unthinking condescension and had the unfortunate habit of addressing eminent but younger acquaintances as 'Master This' or 'Master That'. These were faults, however, that were many times outweighed by his life-enhancing qualities, his relentless and genuinely disinterested pursuit of excellence and his ability to create in a working environment like the *FT* a thoroughly healthy atmosphere of trust and confidence. He was a person to whom a member of staff could go with an idea or problem, receive a fair hearing and be given a response that was the product of a flexible, positive and essentially forward-looking mind; such a capacity inspired boundless loyalty and affection. From the point of view of the few who worked above him, the depiction of his character by Lionel Robbins (chairman of the *FT* in the 1960s) as 'audacious, percipient, quick in action, dedicated and essentially self-deprecatory' fairly hits the mark.[7] The words are conventional enough, like all tributes, but behind them lay a remarkable day-to-day, memo-to-memo reality, helping to take the paper into spheres of which his master and mentor had not even dreamt.

One person, however, went through the *FT* and its competitors with an even finer toothcomb than Drogheda did. Leslie Gordon Newton (never using the first name, but often referred to in the office as 'L.G.', to Drogheda's 'L.M.' and then 'L.D.') was one of the most extraordinary editors in post-war Fleet Street and arguably the most successful. Certainly he was the most important single person in the first hundred years of the *Financial Times*. As he has become a legend in his own lifetime, so myths have grown about him that tend to mask the reality of the man who, rather against the odds, was chosen by Bracken in 1949 to succeed Hargreaves Parkinson. Neither he nor those who worked with him had any idea then of the future greatness that awaited him and his paper. Fortunately, however, in addition to a profusion of oral evidence, which because of its subject is not wholly reliable, there exists a certain amount of written documentation from the 1950s. Together they give one a fairly good idea of what Newton was like during the formative first decade of his editorship. One needs to know: for though in some ways different, the *FT* of the 1980s is still fundamentally imbued with Newtonian values and a Newtonian outlook.

In appearance he was not unlike a carved Red Indian, with a glacial, rather hatchet face, tight lips, straight jaw and skin drawn tight over it. The effect was daunting and, until the 1960s, seldom transformed by a smile. His physical stamina was extraordinary (in his youth he had been a notable athlete, both long distance and sprint), and he possessed the rare gift in an editor of being able to accelerate his pace in the evening. During the early years he seldom left the office before the small hours. He was in no sense an intellectual, nor was he even particularly interested in the City or the Stock Exchange as such. Rather, not unlike Drogheda, he was full of practical curiosity, in his case perhaps related to the fact that at school he had been a science scholar and for a time had cherished the idea of becoming a surgeon. Quite unlike Drogheda, however, he was no aesthete, even though, again in his youth, he had been a budding violinist. He had no interest in things sartorial; while as for being a gourmet, he was taken out once by his Paris correspondent to one of the finest restaurants in the city and chose sardines followed by liver and bacon, all washed down with beer. He was a keen follower of all kinds of sport, was a lifelong fisherman, played golf, did the crossword and enjoyed going to an occasional musical. He was, in short, on precisely the same wavelength as the average *FT* reader of those days, that celebrated commuter on the 8.10 from Surbiton. And granted that affinity, he was able as editor to rely to the full on his instincts and his hunches, knowing that they would rarely betray him.

Two particular traits, both now central parts of the Newton mythology, reflected his intuitive rather than cerebral approach. One was his habit, when he was trying to reach a decision, of insistently tapping his teeth – probably with his forefinger nail, though according to others with his thumb or his pencil. But by whatever means, the tooth-tapping would ensue and a decision be reached, which was always final and unequivocal. His other foible, likewise presumably unconscious, was the string of marvellous linguistic creations that have passed into *FT* folklore. Often they were highly creative, as when he instructed a leader writer to 'keep it tert', or described someone as being 'nonpulsed', or referred to an 'insinnuendo'. He would say of having a first leader on the subject of the press: 'We shall grind our own horse.' Or of the amount of work being supplied by a foreign correspondent: 'It wouldn't get through the eye of a camel.' Or of sending someone on a particular assignment: 'You must do it – it's right up your pigeon.' Sometimes the effect was merely comic, as when he called a Tintoretto a 'Rio Tinto', but usually it was something more. Perhaps the best of all was his description of an acid, humorous book review, which he called 'a superb little vinaigrette'. One should not make too much of these slips of the tongue, but they do give a good clue to how, in a completely instinctive and spontaneous way, Newton (in the subsequent words of one of his journalists) 'put across his thought, and made his point, in a manner that was more personal and more compellingly alive than the most gifted of his writers could have achieved by deliberation'.

The man himself was the strangest of amalgams. He was never an easy person to get close to, possessed no small talk and seemingly little sense of humour, and was prone to long silences that had the effect of virtually freezing people out. He could be intensely suspicious. When he looked ill one day and a colleague said, 'Bad luck,' he replied, 'Why bad luck?' Or when invited to one of the frequent impromptu parties in the basement of Coleman Street: 'Gordon, have a drink' – 'Why?' There was also at some level a prudish streak to him. Early on he refused to publish a review of a biography of Lawrence of Arabia because of a reference to its subject's illegitimacy, even after the reviewer said he would take it out; for some years, features on baby foods were too near the knuckle to be allowed; while later on, inspecting a review of Hitchcock's *Psycho*, he came across the term 'transvestite', proceeded to look it up in the dictionary and said firmly that that was not the sort of thing he wanted discussed in the *FT*. During the 1960s – attended by worldly success and recognition, including a knighthood in 1966 – he gradually mellowed and became somewhat more relaxed. Before that, however, 'tert' was the word.

Two particular pieces of correspondence with Simon help to bring out the Newton of the early, testing years as editor. In May 1950 he received a letter from the professor expressing shock at the death of Parkinson, referring warmly to 'his wide vision, his grasp of essentials and his outstanding personality', and asking the new editor to pass on condolences to his colleagues. Newton's reply was as follows: 'Thank you very much for your letter of the 24th instant and the sentiments expressed therein.' No more, no less. The following spring Simon invited Newton to Christ Church, where he dined and spent the night. His subsequent letter of thanks captures rather well certain elements of the man, with his literal-mindedness, his enthusiasm for practical things and what one might almost call his naïveté:

> It was a most delightful evening I spent with you on Friday. I did enjoy it immensely. You were quite right about the Fellows' Garden. I went there on Saturday morning and spent half an hour sitting on one of the seats. You do get a good view. The one disappointing feature of the whole trip, indeed, was the fact that the speedometer of the car broke almost as soon as I left Oxford so that I could not tell whether the car could do 75 m.p.h. after all.

Someone who knew him best, though more in the 1960s than the 1950s, has described Newton as having the gut instincts of a French peasant, and in some basic sense it is an apt analogy. The cash may not have been hidden under the mattress, but it was certainly never freely on display. Again, even more than with Drogheda, the early life holds the key. In his case, there was a family business – J. M. Newton & Sons, glass merchants and mirror manufacturers – and he went to public school at Blundells. But even before he left there, his hopes of entering the medical profession were dashed by the fact that his elder brother chose to be a doctor rather than going into the family firm. So Newton was sent to Cambridge to read economics, with a view to the business, although increasingly he dreamt of becoming a concert violinist instead. The crash of 1929 put paid to all that. His father soon afterwards lost everything on the Stock Exchange, and the firm went under; the Stradivarius was sold; and the young Newton, with £500 borrowed against a family reversionary trust, began his own glass business in Bethnal Green. For two or three years it proved a desperate and rough struggle, until he was eventually bought out. 'I had every dirty trick in trade hurled at me and had to learn how to hit back,' he later recalled. He then sunk his capital into a business that specialized in retailing car accessories. It folded after six months, leaving Newton almost penniless. Two elderly landladies in Pimlico took pity on him, believing in the honesty of his face, and gave him a room while he searched for a job. He was taken on briefly by a firm called O. W. Roskill, which specialized in writing reports on industries, including for the *Financial News*, but even they made him redundant. Eventually, late in 1934, he went to see Maurice Green at the *FN* and (with the words 'I suppose you will do') was hired by him to cut out and file articles marked by his secretary. Newton was now twenty-seven and over the previous five years had experienced the sharp end of life: the mark was indelible.

Yet the French peasant analogy has its limitations, for there was far more to Newton than that. His human qualities were many and considerable. He was a man of innate modesty and honesty, utterly straightforward and truthful. He was in no way a snob and was bereft of personal ambition, whether social or financial, seeing himself simply as a technician in the service of his paper. He was fundamentally unprejudiced, had no axes of his own to grind and had the adaptability to be receptive to new ideas. He listened and he cared. His judgement of people became legendary for its accuracy. Above all, perhaps, he was an enthusiast, in love with his job as editor and all, or almost all, that it entailed. He had no grand visions, either for himself or for the *FT*, but instead lived from day to day. He was the ultimate round peg in the round hole, performing a function at which all his particular qualities were placed at a premium. As the editor of, say, the *Economist* he would have been a disaster; as the editor of a daily paper, whose bedrock was fact and information, he was almost perfect. The remark of Oliver Cromwell, that there is no man so great who knows not where he is going, could hardly be more appropriate than when applied to Newton and his paper in the 1950s.

There could not have been a more 'hands-on' editor. Apart from two obituary pieces (both remarkably good), he hardly ever spent time writing himself. Asked once if he wrote leaders, he replied: 'No, of course I don't. What's the point of having a dog and barking yourself?' Nor was he remotely Parkinsonian in his memo-writing, though he did circulate the occasional one, epitomized by the curt directive that 'There will be no question marks in headlines in future.' Instead, he kept his desk clear and spent much of the day 'on the beat', going from office to office (with a chair reserved for him in each one) and asking what became the time-honoured question, 'What are you on?', as he peered over the journalist's shoulder. Sometimes he would look at the piece that was being typed and say something like, 'I wouldn't bother about that introduction.' Characteristically, he once observed that he preferred to see people outside rather than inside his office, because he could then end the conversation when he wanted to, simply by leaving the room. And indeed in general, a lengthy meeting was not something that he relished. Nor did his 'hands-on' editorship end at keeping tabs on what his journalists were doing and reading every line that they wrote. He was interested in all aspects of production, concerned himself greatly with questions of layout and at least once a month (certainly after the printing moved to the same premises as the editorial) would go down to the 'stone' to see the front page coming off. His commitment to the next day's paper, followed by the next, and the one after that, was absolute. And although he gradually extended his range of contacts with important people in the outside world, befitting the paper's enhanced status, he never forsook that commitment, which he believed to be the prime duty of an editor.

What was Newton like towards his staff? It is impossible to deny that he could be extremely tough, even brutal, in both his manner and treatment. Perhaps it was because of an inner shyness, perhaps because of the need to establish and then retain his authority, but for whatever reason he presented himself, especially during the 1950s, as something of an ogre, smiling rarely, seldom bestowing praise and quick to find fault. He tended in these early years to be particularly severe towards the older generation, several of whom had come up with him from the old *FN*. They were usually on the news or markets side of the paper and some of them never really forgave him in their hearts for the rough treatment they received. Towards newcomers he could be kinder, though often for those in a new post there was an extremely tense learning period of several weeks or even months while he hypercritically took the novice through his paces before at last, usually suddenly, deciding that he was 'all right' and more or less leaving him alone. He was not the sort of person one would want to go to at seven in the evening and say that one was unhappy about the leader one had written. 'What's the use of saying you're not happy with it at this hour?' would be the response, with barely disguised anger. There were other telling manifestations of the quasi-despot. He had a phone that rang at double speed for internal calls; he received carbon copies of all correspondence done on *FT* paper; and he imposed an unwritten rule that journalists were not to grow beards, to the extent of once telling a junior journalist to shave his off. He also took on to himself what would now be regarded as management functions. Thus it was necessary to get specific permission from him for trips abroad, entertaining people at lunches and so on, almost certainly resulting in smaller expenses than under the modern-day system of planned budgets. No successor, however, could have carried it off. It was typical that after a labour reporter had been attending a TUC conference in Folkestone, Newton quizzed him why he had stayed at the Grand Hotel and not somewhere cheaper. He himself lived in Folkestone at the time and it would not have been like him to let that sort of thing pass by without scrutiny.

Yet in many ways Newton could be an extraordinarily good and liberating person to work for. He was always accessible and always decisive; one knew where one stood with him. He might show anger or irritation, but he bore no grudges, and the next day the incident was forgotten, at least by him. Within the context of the iron discipline that he imposed, he gave great personal freedom to his journalists, never making them write something against their will. He did not encourage favouritism or cliques. He liked people to switch jobs and not to become possessive or jealous, which in practice meant that his journalists, especially the younger ones, picked up a lot of experience in a relatively short time. Above all, if one was a writer whom he trusted, then one's opportunities under Newton were almost limitless, at least once the paper was expanding physically from the mid-1950s. This was partly because of the very nature of the paper's growth, but also partly because it was a conscious axiom on his part that the paper should be about 10 per cent understaffed, which, apart from costing less, had the effect of giving the journalists plenty of writing to do, thereby, he more or less rightly believed, keeping them busy and happy. The old *FN* ethos had been that everyone should pitch in, and he saw no reason to alter it now.

Most of the journalists soon came to respect and admire him deeply, even if they were slower to love him. They knew, increasingly, that he would bear the brunt of any criticism against them from management or outsiders or even shareholders. They also knew that, beards and ethical misconduct apart, he would tolerate, perhaps barely even notice, their personal eccentricities or peccadilloes. Most importantly of all, they respected his judgement and knew that, in the long if not always in the short run, they would get their just deserts from him. It was no doubt frustrating that he was *never* able to give a reason why he thought a piece was unsatisfactory – 'Take it away, you know it's not right,' he might say, or 'It's only 70 per cent there', or he might simply call it 'punk' (a favourite expression) – but almost certainly the journalist would then do it better and accept that it was right that he had been told to do so. 'I knew you'd get the point,' Newton might say, and perhaps give a disarming grin. He had, as Otto Clarke on the *FN* had observed many years before and Drogheda to his great credit never forgot, the maddening but also fortifying habit of nearly always being right about things, based on a quite incalculable sixth sense. But if a journalist denied that sense and argued the toss, he would simply say, 'Who's editing this paper, you or me?' and there was an end to the matter.

Usually inarticulate, sometimes laconic, occasionally Pickwickian in turn of phrase, what *did* Newton want, indeed demand, from his staff? The short answer would probably be accuracy, freshness and lucidity – and of that holy trinity, accuracy always came first. In an article he wrote for *Punch* in 1965 about editing the *FT*, he described this overriding preoccupation:

> There is no point in having the most learned article on this or that or the most brilliant theatre review if the price of, say, New York cotton is wrong or the price of ICI is *6d.* out. We live on facts. They may seem mundane facts. But somewhere someone is relying on us to print just one accurate figure each day. Now multiply that by thousands.[8]

In pursuit of this unfailing accuracy he was prepared, especially in the early 1950s, to bully and harass his journalists to an almost unbelievable degree. Nearly all of his relentless pressure was applied orally, but a curt note he sent to Einzig in November 1952 faintly gives something of the effect: 'I was rather disturbed to see that we made an error about Lord Lloyd and Lloyds Bank. We must do our utmost to avoid mistakes like this because if we don't know who the directors of Lloyds Bank are, then no one else should. We look such idiots.'[9]

As for the qualities of freshness and lucidity, these particularly applied in his eyes to features and leaders. Thus a feature might be erudite and well written, but if its subject-matter seemed in any way 'stale' – and, characteristically, Newton could not usually define what he meant by this – then it was out. In practice, he liked his features to have some sort of topicality or 'angle'; he disliked equally abstract speculation and wodges of undigested facts; he preferred anecdotes to be short; he disliked 'fine' writing; he was easily bored; and he never forgot that he was editing not an academic journal but a practical paper for practical people. The same values informed his attitude to leaders, whose function he believed was essentially expository, setting out the main issues as lucidly as possible and, for the most part, allowing the reader to make up his or her mind. Taken as a whole, they were workmanlike criteria that he imposed upon his journalists but, underwritten by his brilliant hiring policy and his own superb news sense, they produced something rather special.

Newton's ultra-empirical style of editorship could not have worked without the existence of a tacit assumption of consensus, whatever the divergence of opinion amongst journalists on individual questions. After all, with only the occasional exception, leader conferences under his chairmanship lasted less than five minutes and merely consisted of what the subjects of the day should be and who would write them. There was rarely any agonized discussion over what 'line' to take. Later in the day

Newton might question the line that had been taken ('Or perhaps not?' he once famously pencilled at the foot of an editorial that he was going through), but again this was very much the exception. What, then, was that unstated consensus? By definition the answer is not easy. Inevitably it took much from Newton himself and also, lying behind him, the old *FN* tradition of the 1930s – a tradition that subscribed to the values of liberal capitalism, sought objectivity and detachment, was fundamentally patriotic and avoided muck-raking or any suggestion of knocking for its own sake. Newton implicitly consolidated that tradition. He tried if possible to lend support to the government of the day, though felt entirely free to criticize it. He usually endorsed the Conservative Party at general elections. He eschewed controversy and disliked going out on a limb. He avoided rigid doctrinal attitudes or remedies, which in practice meant that the paper tended to be susceptible to the latest fashionable economic nostrum, whether French-style planning or Chicago-style monetarism. It was in sum a supremely pragmatic consensus, allowing a certain room for individual manoeuvre, but never deviating far from those traditional English standards of decency, moderation and above all caution. The editor's authority was such that no one strayed off limits for long.

A further question remains: what sort of paper, when he took over from Parkinson late in 1949, did Newton hope to fashion? The answer is perhaps threefold. He wanted it to be a useful, serious and disciplined paper. He also, with that streak of puritanism in him, wanted it to be a morally pure and respectable paper, free of any taint of the tipping and puffing that had marred the old financial journalism. Thirdly, he wanted it, though he did not yet quite know how, to broaden out from its narrow City base on which it still fundamentally rested. All this, it must be stressed, was *felt* by the new editor rather than articulated at the time and was the product of instinct rather than any systematic rational thought. He never did evolve a master-plan and over the years felt his way carefully, painstakingly into each new development. Typically, he never allowed the publicity people to herald new features with any fanfare of trumpets. 'We may drop it next week,' he would explain; and if indeed reader response was unfavourable, which usually was not the case, he would simply say, 'It didn't go.' He knew, or soon came to know, that he had a good hand. The *FT* was in an essentially monopolistic position; the British economy was entering its period of the long boom; and the new professional classes, in management and elsewhere, were starting to boom with it. Like any astute bridge-player with a good hand, he was determined not to overplay it.

★

Such was the 'triumvirate' that guided the paper through the 1950s and 1960s. Inevitably there existed certain internal strains among the three. Probably the most harmonious relationship was between Drogheda and Henschel; both were business men at heart, dedicated to the cause of increasing the *FT*'s revenue. If Drogheda did find something rather droll about the contrast between Henschel's rather conventional middle-class habits and his ability to get on well with 'buccaneers' like Bernard Sunley, then that was not unusual, for Drogheda found something amusing about most people. As for Henschel and Newton, they got on well enough when they saw each other, but on the whole Newton seems to have preferred to keep his distance. He was determined that the paper should be whiter than white, and under his regime a person from the advertising department found wandering on the editorial floor was usually given a roasting. This is not to say that Newton and Henschel did not respect each other, for they did, greatly. Rather, they tended to develop their respective spheres of the paper along similar but parallel lines, rarely touching but to enormous and mutually beneficial effect. To modern eyes, nourished on inter-departmental committees and corporate strategy reviews, this 'never the twain' approach may seem strange, but it really was how things happened, certainly in the 1950s.

The truly piquant relationship, however, was that between Newton and Drogheda. Each in later years tried in print to describe it:

There is no doubt that at first we were quite good at getting on one another's nerves. In this respect I was the active and Gordon the passive agent. I made myself a great nuisance because if I felt a certain line of development was desirable I kept on pressing for action. (I do not mean the taking of a particular editorial line – I was always at pains not to interfere in editorial policy, although it was not unusual for me to criticise the line taken *after* an article had appeared.) Gordon once referred to me as his goad, a charge to which I admit. His skill at resisting my goading was brilliant. However, I was very persistent, and fortunately we managed far more often than not to see eye to eye. We had the same basic values, and we both knew instinctively where we wanted the *FT* to go.[10]

As Garrett nicely puts it, our relationship had its ups and downs. We had different temperaments; we had few common interests outside the office; we inevitably touched each other's nerves. But we had a common objective, the paper, and as that developed over the years, so I formed a deep attachment to him. He is a remarkable man. Whatever our differences, we never left the office other than as friends.[11]

Nerves were touched, and in Newton's case they were often raw nerves.

Dedicating his life absolutely to the paper, he could not help but resent at some level the worldly, cultured aristocrat, with his many-sided interests and host of friends and acquaintances. Drogheda for his part, it is hard not to feel, was intolerant of what he saw as Newton's philistinism, as well as resenting the glamour attached to the role of editor, as opposed to prosaic managing director. Certainly, on the surface one could hardly imagine two more different types.

Yet in truth they worked well together, complementing each other and each coming to appreciate the other's merits. There were rows, but they did not fester. And as time went on, and the paper prospered and grew, so they came to relish the fact that they were both survivors from the old *FN*, founding influence on the new *FT*. Moreover, quite apart from, as Drogheda says, certain shared basic values, it is arguable that at root they were never such chalk and cheese as they appeared to be. They were both masters of detail and fundamentally uninterested in ideas, indeed mistrustful of them; it was a crucial similarity in the context of running a daily newspaper, where there simply is not time to accommodate major philosophical differences. Resilient and obdurate, with feet firmly on the ground and eyes seldom raised to the stars, they were equipped to meet the most challenging, stressful, unpredictable and wholly fascinating era yet in the history of the paper.

[EIGHT]

'INDUSTRY, COMMERCE AND PUBLIC AFFAIRS': 1950–56

Life gradually returned to capitalist veins during the first half of the 1950s. Early in 1951 London's cocoa and tea markets reopened. That autumn the Conservatives returned to power, promising to 'set the people free'. In December the foreign exchange market reopened on a limited basis, before going ahead properly from May 1953 with the introduction of arbitrage dealings within the European Payments Union. During 1953 most of the remaining commodity markets reopened, followed in March 1954 by the gold market. In the country at large, food controls were removed between the spring of 1953 and the middle of 1954, starting with eggs and ending with meat. Building licences were abolished towards the end of 1954. On the Stock Exchange, traditional focus of all things capitalist, the mood of confidence was such that, despite continuing restrictions on new issues, the *FT* Thirty-Share Index rose from 103 in June 1952 to 224 by July 1955. Sterling was not yet convertible, but to most intents and purposes, outside as well as inside the City, the money-go-round was back by the mid-1950s to something like full swing.

Ironically enough from the point of view of an organ of business news, one of the more lingering captives was the newspaper industry. For almost a year from the autumn of 1950, in the context of the Korean War, the newsprint situation was almost as bad as it had ever been. Bracken in May 1951 recited a familiar dirge to the company's shareholders:

> We receive an ever-rolling stream of complaints from people who cannot obtain copies of the *Financial Times*. In a vain endeavour to meet their needs we have reduced the size of the paper. We have also tried through reducing the size of types to save every inch of space so that we may partly provide for the clamant demand for the *Financial Times*. I regret to say that our efforts are no more effective than the use of Mrs. Partington's broom.[1]

One victim of this particular round of cuts was the *FT*'s 'Continental Edition', which had been started early in 1950 in order to provide European readers with later news, including Wall Street closing prices, than that hitherto available to them. By 1952 the situation had slightly improved, but even so newsprint supplies were still running at only 51 per cent of their pre-war level. It remained a thoroughly irksome constraint, prompting Bracken to write to Beaverbrook in December 1953: 'I reckon if we could get some more paper for the *Financial Times* we could not only increase circulation, but we could probably increase our revenue by 25%.'[2] In fact newsprint supplies had eased significantly during 1953, but until they became effectively free, which was not the case until the end of 1956, the potential growth and expansion of the paper continued to be limited.

The lack of newsprint, together with rising labour and newsprint costs, explained the lacklustre profit figures of the early 1950s. They stayed fairly constant at about £400,000 and now included, in addition to the paper itself and St Clements Press, the monthly magazine *History Today*, which was never a great money-spinner and was once described by Bracken as the *FT*'s 'contribution to culture'. Circulation likewise stagnated, at about 60,000, though a significant effort on the promotional front began. In September 1951 the *FT* sponsored the City Charity Festival Year's athletics meeting, which was held at the White City Stadium and has a small place in history as the first floodlit athletics meeting in London. The following month the paper was responsible for displaying a large election results board near the Royal Exchange, and crowds of City workers thronged the street to cheer Churchill home. Above all, there was the 'Games man'. The graphic designer Abram Games had been responsible for the 1951 Festival of Britain symbol and thereby came to the attention of Moore (as he still was). To Moore's surprise and pleasure, Games accepted a commission to design a poster for the *FT* and produced the famous 'walking newspaper', with pin-striped trousers, rolled-up umbrella and briefcase. The design was a hit from the start, and six of these symbolic figures were soon on display on the giant poster site on the railway bridge of London Bridge Station. In a sense the figure was inappropriate, given that the *FT* was trying to broaden its appeal away from being purely a City paper, but the design itself was so instantly pleasing – and recognizable – that it must have done much more good than harm.

Meanwhile, in the advertising department, hampered by the newsprint rationing but conscious that the economy was starting to expand, Henschel began to put significant flesh on the 'industrial' vision that in some sense he, Bracken and Parkinson had first nurtured from soon after the war, or in Parkinson's case even earlier. From January 1951 a series of full-page advertisements appeared in the trade press proclaiming the theme of 'Industrial Advertising in the *Financial Times*', which 'reaches Top Management certainly'. After referring to how 'a realisation grows that the coverage of industrial advertising must include the men who authorise capital expenditure – which purchases of machinery and equipment involve', the accompanying text went on: 'At the top of the small list of the right channels is the *Financial Times*, read for business reasons by the men who sign the minute, "Agree to place the order".'[3]

In terms of implementing his campaign – one of fundamental importance in the history of the paper – Henschel was much helped by the existence of the provincial offices established in the late 1940s. Thus in the Midlands, arguably the single key area, John Redman had his finger on the pulse of all the major companies and knew exactly whom to approach for advertising and also when. At the London end, Henschel both built up a youthful selling team (who received their initial training in the provincial offices) and recruited from the *News Chronicle* an experienced salesman of the old school in the person of Wilfrid Gabriel, who worked closely under him, also had close ties with the motor industry and was unashamedly capable of crocodile tears when selling half a page. Between them, together with Peter Yeo as a seasoned campaigner from the old *FN*, they made a formidable team. So much so that by the end of 1953 Bracken was telling Beaverbrook that 'last year we carried a little more trade and prestige advertising than we did financial advertising and we certainly cannot complain about the supply of the latter as we had more meetings than we have ever known in the paper's history'.[4]

What had happened was nothing less than a revolution in the financing of the *FT* – and in the event absolutely critical, for without the 'industrial' dimension to its advertising the paper would have been hard pressed to surmount the ensuing years of ferociously rising costs. Pivotal to the revolution was not so much the editorial expansion of industrial coverage, which, despite Parkinson's intentions and Newton's similar instincts in succession to him, was prevented by the newsprint shortage from getting going properly until about 1953. Rather, it was Henschel's perception some years earlier that, on the basis of what the paper *already* was, he would be able to sell the *FT* to industry as a prime medium for its advertising. And this, virtually without any facts and figures to substantiate his bold claims about the unique quality of the paper's readership, he conclusively and brilliantly succeeded in doing – a remarkable tribute to a remarkable man.

There were two other significant components of this drive for advertising revenue in the early 1950s. One was the continuing expansion of surveys dealing with particular subjects, often industrial. Between 1950 and 1953 twenty-nine were published as separate supplements in tabloid 'magazine' form, ranging from British plastics and British rubber to a revival of the pre-war banking and insurance survey, and culminating rather imaginatively in June 1953 with a 24-page survey on British Central Africa, to commemorate the centenary of the birth of not only Cecil Rhodes but also Alfred Beit and Leander Starr Jameson. More often they were insets within the main body of the paper, tending to cover fairly narrow but not unprofitable areas such as office equipment, locomotive and carriage makers and even drop forgings. These surveys were still generally written by outsiders rather than members of staff, and their editorial value was variable, but there is no doubt that they fulfilled their main purpose, which was to bring in the advertising.

The other component was the creation in 1951 of what was known as the foreign department, which had responsibility for the business affairs of the paper relating to Europe and other parts of the world not coloured pink on the map. The key figure in building it up was Bruce-Lockhart's successor as foreign manager, Peter Galliner, who was German by origin and had spent several years in the *FT*'s library. He now had the acuity to realize the potential of persuading foreign companies, starting with West German, to advertise their reports and meetings in the *FT*, the foreign department providing the translations. Galliner proved a dedicated and imaginative empire-builder, was not interfered with by Henschel and within a few years was obtaining considerable foreign revenue: not only from this form of financial advertising, but also through surveys on foreign countries and supplying foreign newspapers with a comprehensive syndication service of financial and economic news, both culled from the *FT* and specially written. Spending some five years in Galliner's foreign department was the young Shirley Williams (as she was to become). She tried to persuade Newton to let her write, but to no avail; in journalistic terms at least, 72 Coleman Street remained, like ancient Greece, a world untroubled by gods or by women.

It was a world which Bracken was increasingly less part of, though he was to remain chairman until his death in 1958. A change seems to have come over him during the weeks and months after the general election of October 1951, when he declined the possibility of office, resigned his seat in the Commons and accepted a viscountcy. He never attended Parliament again; it was as if he had lost all appetite for the centres of power. When he wrote to Einzig in December 1951, marking a quarter-century of their association, there was an unmistakably valedictory tinge to the letter:

Financial newspapers have changed a good deal since we first met. I may be wrong but I think they have improved out of all knowledge. But that may be a partisan point of view! No one, however, can deny that they have become absolutely independent and are willing to stand up to the successors of the old City Moguls and to hit hard at the bumptious promoters who in the past were much too kindly dealt with by financial newspapers.[5]

They had fought their battles; others would have to fight them in the future.

The process of Bracken withdrawing from the *FT* fray had been going on since the war, but it was now much accelerated, involving increasingly lengthy absences, months at a time, when no one in London seemed to know where he was. Inevitably this created an enormous vacuum at the heart of the paper, which of necessity it was left to Moore to fill. Newton subsequently described this aspect of the early years of his editorship:

What kind of man did Bracken become? He kept until near the end that commanding presence and that ability to talk in company on almost any subject. But the ebullience gradually left him. He became withdrawn and even morose. He lived increasingly in the past to such an extent that some of those close to him must have known the inner history of the war by heart. And most important so far as the paper was concerned, he became fearful of the future. As the confidence ebbed so it became more difficult to obtain a decision from him, so it became practically impossible if as a result money had to be spent.

But the paper had to be run and it had to progress. There was a head of steam building up in the staff which had to find its outlet somewhere. Garrett seemed to sense this and more and more the decisions came from him. Two examples of this come to mind. After the Chairman had refused to give a decision for about six weeks whether the first tentative step [under Newton's editorship] should be taken to develop the Price Information Service, Garrett said when asked what could be done: 'You can resign, or you can forget it or you can just do it and if you do it I will back you.' So it happened. On another occasion when Bracken had cut the suggested salary increases by half, Garrett signed the original list without hesitation because he thought it was right to do that.

He was naturally rather diffident about all this at first. His major role had been to act as a buffer between the Chairman and the staff. If you wanted a decision about some development you discussed it with Garrett who then discussed it with Bracken. The latter seldom discussed the paper with the staff direct. But with the Chairman increasingly absent, Garrett was increasingly in control.[6]

This is not to say that Bracken was no longer a powerful presence – and arguably one best avoided – when he pitched up in Coleman Street.

For instance, the story goes that on one occasion he spotted a secretary getting into the lift with a cup of coffee and a bun. A brief dialogue ensued:

'Who's that for?'

'For Mr Henschel.'

'Tell Mr Henschel to have his breakfast before he gets into the office.'

Or there were the Tuesday lunches, which he still often attended. For one of them, Moore had arranged with the paper's labour correspondent of the early 1950s, S. W. ('Bill') Parkinson, that the special guests should be Sir Godfrey Ince, then Permanent Secretary at the Ministry of Labour, and Sir Robert Gould, the ministry's head of conciliation. Parkinson explains what happened:

> That morning Bracken telephoned to say he would lunch at Coleman Street and bring Walter Elliott, a Tory ex-minister of health and labour. How we all got round the table remains a mystery and Bracken's control of the conversation left the men from the Ministry silent and confused. They were also nettled by Bracken's constant reference to them as 'our Christian Science friends'. Eventually Sir Godfrey asked what he meant, to which Bracken replied: 'Conciliators, great healers, Christian Science.' This was not well received.

Bracken remained mostly feared by those of the staff who came into contact with him, though he could still be kind and thoughtful about their welfare. Thus when a young journalist was being sent to Washington for a few days to cover a story, he took the trouble to write to a friend there to make sure that he would be well looked after. Moreover, apart from occasional bursts of uncontrolled vexation about particular leaders or misprints, his attitude towards Newton, when Newton could get hold of him, was constructive rather than otherwise. 'Science, my boy, science,' he might say, proclaiming the virtue of having a leader every day on a scientific subject. Newton would not take the advice literally, but these periodic shafts of guidance were still valuable. Bracken also staunchly upheld the editorial independence of the paper, on one occasion sending his friend Lord Chandos away with a flea in his ear after Chandos had complained about criticism of his company, AEI, in the 'Lex' column and even threatened to take away advertising. Newton for his part stood up to Bracken far more than Hargreaves Parkinson had done and thereby earned his chairman's respect. Occasionally Bracken would invite him to lunch at his offices at the Union Corporation. There he would talk and talk about the war and Cabinet meetings, never about the *FT*, until finally he would say, 'You're doing a good job, Gordon', and send him back to the paper.

The job facing Newton during these years of almost unremitting endeavour was a tough one. He had to strive to tighten up the accuracy of the paper, first in its City coverage (to ensure that the square mile was the *FT*'s impregnable base) and then its industrial. He had to try to achieve a consensus through the paper, which had been lacking before, and also to stop the staff fighting amongst themselves, which again had been the case under Parkinson. Perhaps most important of all, he had to seek out (and often train) new journalists, in order to provide for the paper's future expansion. All the time during these early years he was handicapped not only by the continuing newsprint shortage, but also by the quantity of what one has to call sheer deadwood among the paper's employees, many of whom were either survivors of the pre-war *FT* or had been recruited on to the old *FN* or *FT* owing to the exigencies of war. The *FT* under Bracken and Moore was the most paternalist, non-sacking of papers, and in practice there was little alternative for Newton but to put them into sidings while they played out time until retirement, sometimes taken early. Some were competent enough in their way, while one or two were good only for doing *The Times* crossword; either way, there was no valid role by the 1950s for, say, an old *FT* leader writer whose idea of a suitable subject for a first leader was probably a broker's circular on P&O.

Cautiously, empirically, but also resolutely, Newton went about his daunting task. An early letter to Simon in Oxford throws light on an important strand of his approach as editor:

> I am receiving a number of letters about your last scientific note. This dealt with a new type of clutch. All the enquirers want to be put in touch with the Dutch and French company you mention. Could you let me know their address? The reader reaction to your note is most gratifying and shows how a note which deals with a practical subject such as this does arouse interest.

It was a conscious research ploy on Newton's part, repeated over the years with new columns until they were properly established, not to give the details of where new products that the paper discussed could be obtained. This prompted readers to write to him, or to ring the library, which was under instructions to log every call, and so by this means Newton would be able to evaluate what sort of response a new column was getting. Slowly the sixth sense would get to work, the teeth might be tapped, and out of seemingly insignificant acorns there would grow lasting trees. A further letter to Simon, in March 1952, catches the process in the still inchoate stage:

There is one point I do want to talk to you about. We have always had quite a considerable reader-interest in that little Monday feature of yours, 'Science in Industry', and I have been wondering for some time whether we should not develop this in some way or another. With certain of our readers it seems to hit a bell, and it is something which, so far as I know, is not done by anyone else. It is only a vague idea I have which has not been developed in any way.

The eventual 'Technical' (now 'Technology') page was still a fair way off, but Newton was starting to see what he wanted and – encouraged, perhaps even inspired, by Bracken – would not let go of it.

That was one side of Newton's early editorship. Less pleasurable aspects are revealed in his exchanges with Einzig: above all, the imposition of authority and the primacy of accuracy. As early as February 1950, in the context of the general election campaign, Einzig was writing to Moore to complain about 'the increasingly hostile and malevolent way in which my contributions have come to be treated', typically adding that 'there seems to be a systematic effort to keep my contributions out of the *Financial Times*'. Equally characteristically, Newton responded to the complaint, once it had been passed on to him, by seeing Einzig in person and securing a promise that in future, if he had a grievance, he would submit it directly to himself rather than to Moore or any of the other directors. It was an uneasy concordat but lasted for several years. During that time Einzig was out of action quite often because of illness, including during September 1952. His editor's letter of sympathy was to the point: 'So sorry to hear that you are unwell. Don't worry about us – just get well.' By October, Einzig was back in harness, but perhaps would rather not have been, receiving the following missive from Newton:

We must make every effort to be as accurate as possible, and this is especially true of any story we carry which affects industry. Today, for example, we have been inundated with messages about your story on softwood imports, which contained an unfortunate mistake. You stated in your first sentence that 'imports of softwood next year will be subject to a limit of one million standards'. The truth is that imports of softwood next year will not be less than one million standards. Others have the story correct, and as a result the timber trade as a whole is up in arms against us. It does take a long time to live this sort of thing down with the industry concerned.

The following month poor Einzig put his foot in it about Lord Lloyd and Lloyds Bank, so altogether it was not a happy autumn for the former doyen of Lombard Street.[7]

Newton was an unpopular and, partly by choice, rather isolated figure during these years. His deputy, Jim Hunter, remained for some time resentful of having been passed over; most of the rest of the old guard inevitably disliked the rough (but never devious or malicious) treatment he handed out to them; and the younger, brighter intake, headed by Shonfield and Applebey, tended to look down on him because of his lack of intellectuality, unaware as yet of his instinctive journalistic genius. Nevertheless, Newton *wanted* to be the father-figure and was genuinely upset when one of his young journalists, seeking time off because his father-in-law was dying, approached the features editor, Allan Todd, rather than himself. This was disloyal, according to Newton, but the truth was that at this stage he simply did not have the qualities, the human responsiveness, to be a father-figure while also fulfilling his manifold other duties. How much did it all weigh on him as an oppressive burden? It is impossible to be sure, but certainly he did worry long, hard and anxiously about the paper that had been entrusted to him and the problem of improving it. Nevertheless, he never allowed himself to worry to an extent that might have proved counter-productive – a strength of mind perhaps typified by the story of the young feature writer going into Newton's office the morning after George VI had unexpectedly died in the night, expecting to find him racked by the problem of how the paper should cover it, and instead seeing him, to the young journalist's immense admiration, reading a detective story. Arguably, it was that laconic quality, a supreme matter-of-factness, which over the years was the single great Newtonian saving grace.

Through most of the 1950s and 1960s there existed a hard core of six or seven journalists, in addition to Newton, who maintained the basic day-to-day framework of the *FT*. Each deserves an honourable mention in the history of the paper. Deputy editor for seven years, until he moved to management, was Jim Hunter, who was a highly experienced and capable newspaperman, red-cheeked and plumpish in appearance. Not everyone warmed to him, but to many young recruits he was a reassuring figure from whom one could seek solace after being scolded by Newton. He also had the gift of emollience, which served him particularly well in his dealings with Einzig and probably delayed the eventual rift between the editor and his touchy political correspondent. An equally safe pair of hands belonged to Bill Roger, assistant editor from 1950. A handsome, charming man, he was in many ways the arch-practitioner, capable of writing about almost anything, and has been aptly described as a person 'under-educated for his intelligence'. In addition to the Saturday paper, his main editorial responsibility by the mid-1950s was for surveys, which he gradually improved in quality. His particular forte was the stock market, and for several years he wrote each Saturday a faintly Damon-Runyonesque review as 'Onlooker'. No one, however, knew the markets better than A. L. W. Shillady, who not only ran the Stock Exchange part of the paper for more than twenty years but also wrote many of the 'Lex' columns during the 1950s. Although a stern disciplinarian, Shillady was a thoroughly nice, honest and patient person, who demanded accuracy and high ethical standards from his subordinates in the prices room. If he thought a share issue was dubious, he was quite capable of refusing to have it quoted in the paper. If he thought jobbers were trying to get prices quoted with too wide a 'spread', he would never give them a free ride. For much of the post-war period he was a significant force in the Stock Exchange, and it was one of the sights of the City to see 'Shill' standing in Throgmorton Street at about half-past three, holes in his coat and trousers at half-mast, waiting for the big jobbers to come out of the House. He was not a great writer, but he had the markets in his bones and was, in the best possible sense, a true disciple of his mentor Hargreaves Parkinson.

The other enduring figures, gluing it all together, resided in the news room. On the night side, the two key people during most of Newton's editorship were Ben Kipling and Cyril Ubsdell. Both had worked their way up on the old *FN* and both were utterly reliable. Newton kept a private line to Kipling and reposed entire trust in him. On the day side, the number-two man during these years was John Hay, an altogether more extrovert and colourful character. His speed at typing and taking shorthand notes was phenomenal; his bark was worse than his bite, but still loud enough; and he saw it almost as his duty to 'break' young recruits and rid them of any arrogance that they might have. In many ways he was a perfect foil to the number one, Doug York, whose tenure as news editor coincided almost exactly with that of Newton as editor, and who was quiet almost to the point of ghostliness. York and Newton were never personally close, but what they did share was a highly cautious temperament, so that it did not unduly worry Newton that under York the *FT* acquired the reputation of being the paper that got everything right, the day after everyone else got it wrong. Indeed, the oft-told story goes that a young journalist rushed up to York one day with an exclusive piece of news and that York looked at it extremely doubtfully before finally saying, 'I haven't seen this in any of the other papers.' Yet in truth his abiding scepticism was wholly justified, for both he and Newton knew that, in a paper that was aimed at decision-makers, one serious error would do far more damage than almost any number of scoops could do good. Taken together with his unflappability and his superb organization of the news flow, this quality of absolute insistence on accuracy made York the ideal news editor for a paper seeking the stamp of national and international respectability.

At a less senior level on the staff there was also emerging to the fore in the early to mid-1950s a group of fairly specialist journalists whose contribution to the development of the *FT* during these formative years has perhaps been underestimated. One would, for instance, include in this group Brian Bromwich and Bill Parkinson, industrial and labour correspondents respectively. Neither was on the paper for long and both had left by the mid-1950s, but they were respected for their previous journalistic experience (Parkinson came from the *Manchester Guardian*) and they each covered their field with notable objectivity. Somewhat similar was the youthful and highly talented Derek Wragge-Morley, who had been science correspondent for *Picture Post*, was a world authority on ants and arrived at Coleman Street in 1952 when it became clear that Simon did not have the time to provide the paper with the comprehensive scientific coverage it was starting to seek. Then there were the emerging industry specialists, providing news rather than features, of whom by the mid-1950s the three most notable were perhaps Leslie Parker on mining, James McDonald on shipping and Michael Donne on aviation. Each got to know his industry backwards and each was thoroughly trusted by everyone in that industry, perhaps at the expense of a certain critical penetration in their writing. The case of Donne was in its way classic. He was working as usual in the news room when Newton, aware of the expanding aircraft industry, came up to him one day in 1953 and said, 'I understand you do this flying at weekends.' Donne admitted the fact and was given six months' probation as air correspondent. Helped by a series of Comet disasters, he made good and never looked back.

There were two other main specialist writers on the staff by the early to mid-1950s, each very distinctive and each adding much to the authority and also to the 'attack' of the paper. One was C. Gordon Tether, who had joined the *FN* library as a boy and was by now primarily responsible for the 'Lombard' column on the money markets. In many ways he inherited Einzig's mantle: both wrote in a workmanlike rather than literary style, both were extremely knowledgeable and industrious, and both liked nothing better than trying to get under the rather thin skin of the Bank of England. Tether, like Einzig, had his bees in his bonnet, particularly at this stage about gold and the United States; but he did have the capacity not only to provide an acute running commentary on monetary events but also to ask the pertinent questions that no one else was asking, such as in the 1950s questioning the very desirability, let alone feasibility, of making sterling convertible. He had a considerable following amongst central bankers abroad and was usually staunchly defended by Newton whenever bankers at home sought to have him muffled.

The other specialist writer was Arthur Winspear, who was recruited from the *Investors Chronicle* to help Shillady with the 'Lex' column. He undoubtedly benefited from Shillady's rapport with the jobbers and transmission of market intelligence, but it is to Winspear that the prime credit must go for raising 'Lex' by the end of the 1950s to a level of sustained analysis that it had not previously attained. He was a Yorkshireman, possessed of a compulsion to explain, and in terms of outlook and mental capacity might as easily have become a don as a journalist. He worked in an office with files up to the ceiling, but the basis of his writing was sheer brain-power, getting to the heart of the issue (often literally) and laying it bare. Stringent in his assessments of company results, Winspear was also highly critical of how companies conducted themselves and pounced on what he saw as any malpractices. Altogether he evolved a new style for the column, setting the highest of standards for his successors to emulate, though none would ever be such a notoriously late provider of copy as he was.

There was one more aspect of Newton's recruitment policy and it was one with extraordinarily fruitful consequences, especially in the long run. The paper had already employed a few graduates direct from Oxbridge (Applebey and Shonfield most notably), but it was Newton who from 1951 made this a systematic practice, involving a direct intake each year of some two or three. From his point of view, it meant that he was not only sowing the seeds for the future but also taking on cheap labour at several hundred pounds below the NUJ minimum; while from the graduates' point of view, the blessings were equally great. Coming to Coleman Street meant avoiding a two-year stint in the provinces (which all other national papers insisted on as a prerequisite), and even *FT* pay was usually better than that on offer as, for example, an industrial trainee. Newton usually insisted on a first-class degree from his Oxbridge recruits, but he was not particularly concerned which school it was in, perhaps because he had read economics himself. Otherwise, he would hold one or two interviews and then make up his mind almost wholly on the basis of whether he thought he could get on with the person concerned. The policy all hinged on his judgement of character, and it did not usually let him down, as testified to by the remarkably high proportion of his youthful recruits (though hardened until the late 1950s by two years of National Service) who achieved great distinction in later life, whether on the *FT* itself, on other papers or in other powerful walks of life.

Of the early 1950s direct intake, the names that arguably stand out are Ronald Butt, Ian Trafford, Robert Collin, William Rees-Mogg, George Bull, Anthony Vice and Michael Shanks. Most of them applied to the *FT* via their university appointments board, but Rees-Mogg was an exception. The paper at that time subscribed to a cuttings service, which one day included a piece from *Isis* featuring him as an 'Isis Idol' (being president of the Oxford Union), in which he declared that he read the *FT* every morning in bed before getting up. He arrived in 1952, old before his time with a Churchill hard hat and a silver-topped cane, and became in due course the most fluent of leader writers. Many of the intake over the years came to the paper knowing little of finance and less of economics, exemplified by Collin, who sat down at lunch on his first day to read Keynes's *General Theory*, reckoning to have it and Marshall's *Principles* mastered by the end of a fortnight. Such was his formidable intelligence that he probably succeeded. Almost all the graduates started in features, where they sank or swam by their ability to digest information quickly and transcribe it into readable prose – the same qualities, in fact, that had gained them their degrees. They might then branch out, like Butt to commodities or Trafford to industrial or Shanks to labour, but it was the initial training that counted, with Newton making it a firm policy that a newcomer should get a feature printed within the first month, however painfully doctored or adapted it had to be. Once that hurdle was surmounted, the rest usually followed quite easily, though it could take up to eighteen months, Newton reckoned, to have them trained properly.

How did they view Newton? A fairly common process seems to have been initial bafflement, followed by amused tolerance-cum-irritation (taking something of its tone from Applebey and Shonfield, the senior graduates in residence), followed by sneaking respect and culminating in most cases in open admiration. But the Newton of the early 1950s was such that inevitably other people played a significant part in the training operation, until the time, certainly reached by the end of that decade, when the kindergarten became more or less self-propelling. In addition to Hunter, the ultimate shoulder to cry on, two people should perhaps be mentioned, both slightly older than this first generation of Newtonian direct intake. One was Applebey, who consciously saw himself as a tutor and, before leaving for the *Daily Telegraph* in 1955, did much to bring on sympathetic spirits like Rees-Mogg; the other was Geoffrey Chandler, features editor in the mid-1950s and himself a graduate, in tune with his charges, but who had come to the *FT* in 1951 via the *Economist* and the BBC.

Once they had settled in, life on the paper was great fun for these young Turks, with work, play, gossip and erudite discussion mixed in roughly equal proportions, much of it going on in the canteen and bar downstairs. It was, as more than one of them has recalled, rather like a university extension course, in which they generally learnt far more than they had done at university. After all, there were not many newspapers where one would go into the office and find two journalists (Collin and Chandler) talking Greek to each other, ancient and modern respectively. It is, however, possible to be blinded by the relative glamour of these bright young things and to exaggerate their contemporary importance. They were simply learning how to be journalists, learning about the real world and having a good time; they neither saw themselves as engaged in a momentous activity nor imagined that the *FT* was at the start of something big. The indispensable core of the paper remained its mass of mundane facts and figures. However brilliant they were, these graduates had little effect on the outlook or policy of Newton, who would talk 'shop' with old pros like Roger or Kipling but hardly ever with them. And arguably, it was to be at least another ten years before the paper itself began to do full justice to the people who worked for it.

Nevertheless, within the confines of the newsprint rationing and his own highly cautious temperament, Newton did begin, relatively soon after he became editor, what was to be an almost ceaseless process of evolution. One of Parkinson's last actions had been to move 'Lex' on the front page to the top right-hand corner above 'Diarist' (having been alongside each other), and this arrangement Newton left alone for a while; but he never liked 'Diarist' on account of its tipping element, and by 1953 the unpronounceable S. F. J. Kraeusslach, always known as 'K.', had his column moved to an inside page. Indeed, as early as March 1950 Newton killed off the Saturday 'Autolycus' Stock Exchange column, which was of a blatantly speculative character. More positively on the City side, Newton encouraged Shillady to refine and develop his prices service, culminating in November 1952 which two major innovations. One was the start of daily publication of 'highs and lows', in other words the highest and lowest prices during the year for each of the 1,500 securities that were listed; and the other was the addition of 'cover' to the regular Monday service of prices, dividends and yields, that is, the number of times the latest dividend of a company was covered by its earnings. Meanwhile, on another specialist side, the paper had begun a month earlier the publication of a new index of world commodity prices, 'designed more as an indicator of general world trends than as a measure of the changes in values' and highly topical in the context of world commodity agreements and the reopening of commodity markets. For a wider appeal, non-advertising photographs started to appear with increasing frequency, including during the floods of 1953 a rather dramatic front-page shot 'of an aerial view of the inundated oil refinery at Coryton, in the Thames Estuary, owned by the Vacuum Oil Co.' There was also the first harbinger of subsequent sports coverage, when David Livingstone-Learmonth began in March 1953 a monthly series of 'Bloodstock Notes', concentrating primarily on the economic aspect.

These years also saw the faint beginnings of what would become the *FT*'s celebrated arts page. It was a development that owed at least as much to Moore as to the editor, though Newton always encouraged the venture and did not resent the space accorded it. The origins can be dated to 1951, when the art critic and historian Denys Sutton, who was suggested to Moore by Kenneth Clark, started to write a monthly piece on the London art market, a subject with obvious advertising potential. After about eighteen months Sutton temporarily dropped out and was succeeded by one of the young high-flyers from Cambridge, Victor Sandelson, who began writing regular, financially orientated features with titles like 'The Opening of the Art Season'. Early in 1953 he fell ill and in so doing joined the select band of those who received a letter from Newton:

> I am indeed sorry that you have been so ill. Life goes on here in the same old way despite the number we have sick. The Features Department, now reduced to two, is struggling, but we still come out each day.
>
> If you are well enough, there is one point on which I would like your advice. Your last article, which dealt inter alia with a sale in New York, in which you said a Renoir was sold for £550, appears to have stirred the art world to the core. Apart from two letters, one of which you have seen, and one from the Marlborough Galleries, there has been a concerted attack on me from two directions, one via Denys Sutton and one via Lord Moore. To quote one of these, you seem to have brought the whole market in London in French Impressionists to a standstill. All this is most interesting because it does show that the art article is read, but it is also rather embarrassing because without you I don't know what to say in reply . . . If you are strong enough to pick up a pen, would you let me know, first and foremost, how you are, and secondly what I should say or write to all these people.

Soon afterwards, on Moore's continuing prompting, aesthetic was added to the purely economic, in the form of dramatic criticism. This time it was Laurence Olivier whom Moore approached for a suitable candidate:

> He instantly told me that by far the best person we could engage was one Derek Granger, the theatre and film critic of the *Sussex Daily News*. West End theatre

managers, he said, often gave their plays an advance run in Brighton in order to get the benefit of Granger's critical notices, which he said were highly perceptive and never unfair. As Sidney Henschel used frequently to visit Brighton I asked him whether he could help. With his usual resourcefulness he had arranged within a few days for Derek to come and see Gordon Newton and myself.[8]

The triumvirate duly landed their man. Granger's first notice, reviewing Graham Greene's *The Living Room* and written at speed in the reading room at Simpson's, appeared in the *FT* on 17 April 1953.

However, the truly important editorial thrust of Newton's early years was the one that took place on the industrial front. Hargreaves Parkinson had paved the way, but it was under Newton that from about the autumn of 1952 it gathered real momentum, typified by a series of eight articles that October on 'Training for Management', later reprinted as a pamphlet, that would have been unthinkable in the pre-war *FN* or *FT*. One of Newton's favoured vehicles, in what by the third year of editorship was a conscious campaign, was the feature article, of which almost throughout the 1950s there were usually two on the leader page. He was attracted by them partly because they were one of the few variables in papers of restricted size, partly because they were a forcing-house for his graduates, but above all because they offered a chance to tackle a range of subjects and variety of industries, often quite small, that would otherwise not have been covered. The features of this time were far shorter and less thoroughly researched than their modern counterparts, but in the course of a full year they seemed to cover almost every highway and by way of the British economy. Taken almost at random, features during 1952–3 included 'Making Cars at Luton', 'Ten Million Bottles a Day' (about the glass container industry), 'The Home of Nets' (about industry in Bridport, Dorset), 'My Daily Problem' (by 'An East Lancashire Mill Manager'), 'Making Chocolate' and 'Soap from Port Sunlight'. Newton liked a feature to get to grips with the industrial process itself, though not too technically, and often there were rather pleasing line drawings by Peter Dunbar to illustrate that process. It is easy now to mock them, but these features were almost all readable and informative, and they played an important part in broadening the content of the paper.

It was the day-to-day coverage of industry, though, that really counted. Crucial to this coverage was the labour side, the responsibility in the early 1950s of 'Bill' Parkinson. He has recalled illuminatingly his two years on the paper, before he was seduced (to his subsequent regret) to the *Daily Herald*:

Both in the labour movement and in Fleet Street there was considerable interest in the *FT*'s new concern about labour affairs. I was often asked why a high Tory financial paper gave so much space to labour. Here the labour leaders were far behind the awareness of Gordon Newton and Andrew Shonfield that it was high time that industrialists and the City should know what the unions were about. Labour affairs were considered in board rooms only at the confrontation stage and personnel officers rarely reached any level in the industrial hierarchy. In the City, trade unionism and nationalisation were just dirty words. Yet it was obvious to thinking people that wage demands, long-running disputes and Labour Party policies for public ownership could threaten the stability and success of companies, if not Britain's future as a trading nation. A better understanding on both sides was needed and the far-sighted men in control of the *FT* realised it.

On a personal level I too was being educated. At the outset I feared I would not be able to write what I thought ought to be written, and I was totally wrong. Of all the newspapers I served (and there were several) I never had so much freedom as I enjoyed on the *FT*. My reports appeared as I wrote them except when space dictated otherwise.

In terms of industry itself, the handful of provincial correspondents put into place in the late 1940s now came into their own. The man in the Midlands, for instance, was Peter Cartwright, who during the early 1950s made it his job to introduce the *FT* to as many industrialists as possible, persuading them that the paper was deeply serious in its intentions about industry and getting them into the habit of ringing him up to ask him to come and see things. It was a relationship that depended on trust and, inevitably, on an assumption on the part of industrialists that the *FT*'s attitude towards them was friendly and, if critical, always constructively critical. In practice, it meant that the paper at this stage tended to write about particular industries as a whole rather than about individual companies, though often that was a perfectly valid approach. And if there was an implicit price to pay, it was well worth it, for the *FT* during these years established a unique and also permanent industrial foothold. 'We can in truth claim that we publish more industrial news than any daily newspaper in the British Commonwealth,' Bracken truthfully told his shareholders in June 1953, less than four years after Newton had become editor.[9]

There was one other major innovation, but in the field of views rather than news. Soon after he became editor, Newton asked Harold Wincott if he would start writing a weekly column, under his own name and on any subject he liked to choose. Wincott agreed, rather reluctantly, and the first column, entitled 'Rediscovering Capitalism', appeared on

Tuesday 11 July 1950. He took a while to adjust to writing under his own name (having always been 'Candidus' in the *Investors Chronicle*), but after about six months he suddenly clicked, to such enduring effect that he continued to write a Tuesday column almost up to his death in 1969, moving to a monthly basis only near the end. His column acquired a devoted following – especially amongst small investors, whose steadfast champion he was – and was soon being syndicated on a world-wide basis. Although Wincott was never on the staff of the *FT*, his contribution to the developing reputation of the paper was inestimable, giving it a human face and making it liked as well as merely respected. How did he do it? Lionel Robbins was near the mark in the foreword he wrote to a collection of Wincott's writings in the 1960s:

> If I were asked to name the salient quality in these papers, I think I should sum it up in two words, humanity and candour. Expository skill and technical competence one takes for granted in anything that Mr Wincott writes. But the special characteristics of his approach are the width of his sympathies and the frankness of his argument. He discusses his problems in terms of their implications to the welfare of ordinary men and women and at each stage he discloses with attractive forthrightness the grounds for his judgements. He argues hard but he argues fairly.[10]

Many of Wincott's columns took the conventional form of 'think-pieces', but the device which caught his readers' imagination, and made his name, was that of imaginary dialogues between himself and his son. The first of these appeared in October 1951, and, though to some tastes they were cloying, they were a means for him to get across his arguments in the simplest, least jargonized English possible. But it is probably fair to say that the pieces more likely to stand the test of time – not of course that that was the point – are the more straightforward ones.

Over the years Wincott covered a considerable range of subjects, but his speciality as an expositor lay in relating the financial markets to the real economy, for some reason traditionally a slum area of journalism. This exposition was knowledgeable and lucid and was underpinned by a deep-seated faith in the virtues, moral as well as economic, of what a post-Wincottian age knows as 'popular capitalism'. He began a column in July 1951: 'As you will probably have guessed by this time, I carry several pet bees around in my bonnet. One of these bees is a passionate belief that the more widely spread ownership of British industry becomes, the more we can give ordinary folk a stake in real wealth, the better it will be for all of us.' There was in Wincott's outlook a strong element of 'good housekeeping', which manifested itself particularly when he laid into the

Labour Party or, as in December 1950, the more paternalist Tories: 'If a British electorate wants the Santa Claus State, it will vote Socialist, anyway, because it knows instinctively the Socialists will always beat the Tories at that game. The Conservatives' forte, trite enough though the observation is, is conserving. The Great British Public could do with some conserving – of the purchasing power of its money – right now.' Sometimes his anti-socialist rhetoric could go over the top, as in a column in August 1951 about Labour's Chancellor of the Exchequer (Gaitskell) that was headed 'Herr Finanzminister'. But there is no doubt that over the years, whatever the contrary fashions of economic thinking, Wincott carried an absolutely consistent banner for the cause of economic liberalism. The upwardly mobile direct intake might snigger slightly and consign him to the ranks of the unreconstructed right, but he knew that his true constituency lay far beyond the confines of Coleman Street or indeed Great George Street.

Meanwhile, from the definitely unreconstructed right, Bracken continued to sound off each Monday, demanding cuts, it sometimes seemed, in everything except his own column. 'To ask horny trades unionists to accept a wage freeze from Mr Gaitskell, who is a precious Wykehamist and an obvious child of privilege, is to ask the impossible', was his considered view of the government's wages policy in October 1950. Or at the time of ministerial resignations the following April: 'Of Mr Wilson it may be said that he was over-promoted and has now been over-demoted. His performances in the House of Commons and on public platforms at home and in North America show that power too easily went to his head.' His friend Beaverbrook thought it all good knock-about stuff, writing to him in June 1951 that 'the column is so vigorous that I would like to employ you for the *Daily Express*, and I offer you £20,000 a year'. Bracken was suitably encouraged and, despite his growing mood of world weariness, continued to write it for another four years, leaving Hodge to try gamely to imitate his style during his increasingly long absences from London. The range of targets expanded, taking in the Assembly of the Council of Europe at Strasburg, UNESCO and the British Council, but his real ire and dismay were reserved for the failure of Butler at the Exchequer to refute the precepts of Keynes (the man who, according to Bracken, 'made inflation respectable') and to cut back severely on public expenditure. The tone was still mild enough in May 1952: 'In open-handed times a Chancellor must have an infinite capacity for saying No. Mr Butler has not yet developed this quality.' But by the following February despair had set in: 'What he does not seem to grasp is that we have little time left if we are to avoid a crash, from the effects of which this country might never recover.' Two months later the spurned prophet summed up his economic message: 'Leading men on both front benches know perfectly well that we are living on what is left of the savings of our thrifty Victorian ancestors and on the savings of industry, which ought to be applied to replacing well-worn plant and equipment.' In the eyes of this particular 'Observer', the new Elizabethan age was dawning bleak and chilly.

FT leaders during these years tended to veer uneasily between Bracken-style fundamentalism on the one hand and the gradually emerging post-war 'Butskellite' consensus on the other. This in a sense was to be the pattern throughout Newton's editorship, and indeed beyond, resulting from the essentially tolerant method (although almost always eschewing controversy) by which editorial policy evolved. The experience of the mildly leftish labour correspondent of the early 1950s was probably typical:

> Nobody leaned on me or suggested my views were outrageous. When I took my leaders to Gordon Newton he never attempted to rewrite them. Sometimes he would say: 'No, that's not quite it. Have another go.' Then after the second or third attempt he would be satisfied. But he never indicated where the faults lay or what I ought to be saying, and in the end, after toil and tears, I usually believed that my leader was much improved.

The constantly shifting emphasis of the leaders at large that emerged was exemplified by the markedly different general election leaders in Newton's first two years. In February 1950 the question was posed, 'Which Way To-Day?' and the answer was clear: 'One road leads towards increasing State control, increasing rigidity and a lower standard of living . . . The other road leads to change, expansion, freedom and independence. Which way shall we go?' One 'wrong' way and twenty months later, however, the *FT* gave the Conservative opposition only the most grudging of endorsements. Although accepting that 'the strength of the Conservative case is the comparative realism on which it is based', especially concerning the need to attack inflation at its roots, the leader went on:

> The Tory case has, however, lacked something of completeness. The methods which a Conservative government would use have been left much vaguer than even the desire to be free in office would demand. And the party has included one proposal – that for an Excess Profits Tax – which is in direct contradiction to the spirit of its other economic policies. All that can be said is that EPT would be less damaging than the combination of dividend limitation and a capital gains tax which the Socialists have promised.[11]

There were no ringing tones, no grandiose pronouncements, to herald what would be thirteen years of Tory rule.

The cardinal event of the last two years of Labour in power, with profound long-term economic consequences, was the Korean War. The *FT* made its position plain at the outset, with a leader on 'The Korean Incident' in June 1950 two days after North Korean forces invaded South Korea: 'The unscrupulous determination to exploit any situation to the advantage of Communism, even to the point of endangering world peace, is the brute fact that is common between this incident and the Berlin blockade.' The government immediately promised to support United Nations action and a month later announced formal measures, earning for its pains the criticism from the *FT* that 'the additional £100 million now spent on defence is unimpressive compared with the American effort'. Soon afterwards the government increased its rearmament programme drastically, to a total expenditure on defence of £3,400 million over three years. The leader on the new programme at no point questioned its economic wisdom. Finally, in January 1951, the defence budget for the coming three years was upped yet again, coming to a grand total of £4,700 million. 'Not without Tears' was the title of the *FT*'s leader, which began: 'The Prime Minister's defence statement yesterday displayed a greater sense of realism and urgency than the government's critics had expected. It reflects a determination, at last, to match the vigour of the United States in defending Western security.' The rest of the leader dwelt on the inevitable adverse effects on the country's investment and consumption, but never once considered the possibility that, to put it crudely, the size of the Korean game was not worth the British candle.

Subsequently, historians of the post-war British economy were less diffident. In the words of one: 'Britain's uncalculated act of sacrifice during the crisis at the start of the Korean War, in embarking on a defence programme which used up all the resources in sight and more, continued to exercise an unfavourable influence on economic development long after the event.' The rearmament programme was, in fact, 'thoroughly badly conceived'.[12] The writer of these words (in 1958) was Andrew Shonfield, doubling as the *FT*'s foreign and features editor in 1950–1. Perhaps his voice had not carried sufficient weight, perhaps he changed his mind in the interim, perhaps indeed there was never any debate. Whatever the case, it is clear that the *FT* of the early 1950s was not prepared to quarrel with the underlying national assumption that Britain's place remained on the top table, irrespective of the damage caused to the domestic economy.

Yet the warning signs were there, as Western Europe in particular started its impressive, increasingly unified economic recovery. During the summer of 1950 the Schuman Plan began to take the shape that was to lead to the establishment the following year of the European Coal and Steel Community. The *FT* accorded the scheme a couple of fairly inconclusive leaders that were generally sceptical in tone. It was, the paper asserted, 'fatally hampered by the vagueness of its central idea and by the failure of anyone to look with any degree of realism at the kind of decisions that would have to be taken by a Common Authority'. Neither leader specifically addressed the question of whether or not Britain should participate, and certainly neither criticized the government's reluctance to do so; though, to be fair, one did make a rather interesting reference to how 'the practical question of the extent to which sacrifice of coal pits and steel mills might be involved is still obscured by the theoretical and perhaps illusory question of the sacrifice of national sovereignty'.[13] In general, the *FT*'s attitude towards much of the rest of the world was still distinctly insular. The ANZUS pact of 1951, for example, received barely a mention, let alone a comment; while on 7 March 1953 the main leader of the day was devoted to a 'Pause in Markets', with the death of Stalin nowhere. The paper may have been broadening its horizons, but the direction was still north of Watford rather than east of Dover, and with the square mile firmly in view.

Butler's early policies generally received the paper's approbation, including his arguably over-severe first Budget in March 1952: 'To cut the food subsidies is an act of considerable political courage . . . In spite of capital losses, there are few in the City who will not agree that a rise in interest rates is appropriate.' The following month a leader on 'Monetary Policy' viewed sanguinely enough Butler's reliance on changes in the Bank Rate rather than physical controls for regulating the economy: 'The object of the new disciplines is not to create unemployment for its own sake but to ensure that some of the men, materials and machines now engaged in non-essential activities are diverted to other forms of employment where they can contribute to the urgently needed expansion of defence and export production.' Bracken, incidentally, was less enamoured, grumbling in May that 'the Treasury now increasingly inclines to believe that monetary disciplines are all that are required to restore solvency to Britain' and that 'foolish indeed is this belief and altogether worthy of the costive ostriches of the Treasury'. In April 1953 the *FT* greeted the tax remissions in the next Budget with a palpable 'Sense of Freedom': 'Mr Butler's determination to relieve the taxpayer at all costs and to trust to natural forces (aided by the interest rate) to ensure that savings in the private sector are sufficient provides a noticeable lightening of the general gloom left over from the worship of austerity.' As for the Labour Party's attack that it was 'a rich man's Budget' in which the income-tax payer gained most, this, according to the leader, was 'one of the Budget's main virtues': 'For to be an income-tax payer, you also have to be, with very few exceptions, one of the country's skilled workers, either by hand or by brain. And it is precisely these men who need the greatest incentive, and who are likely to react to the greatest national advantage. They have been "equalised" too long.' With these sentiments at least Bracken would have concurred, though he would of course have liked the process to have gone far further, with Butler's monetary mumbo-jumbo abandoned altogether.

The authentic voice of the *FT* – pragmatic, balanced and sane – was heard a few weeks later in two leaders occasioned by the Coronation. On 30 May, with the ceremony about to be televised, the paper considered the inexorable spread of the small screen and concluded: 'Is this a good thing or a bad thing? Something to be encouraged or resisted? "There is nothing good or bad, but thinking makes it so." At any rate it is what is happening.' On 3 June there were front-page photographs of the Coronation, together with a detailed descriptive account; on the leader page a lengthy feature on the queens Matilda, Elizabeth I, Anne and Victoria; and a leader on the new reign that ended:

> In spite of the dangers and the difficulties in which the new reign opens, there are good reasons for hope. As the United Kingdom has declined as a world power the new Commonwealth, in the midst of its changes, has grown and strengthened. If the world is divided into two camps at least communication is being kept open while the frontiers, both moral and physical, have been maintained. In the United Kingdom itself, though some old industries have declined and others are backward by the standards of the modern world, the manufacture of what is up-to-date has always gone forward, and the new industries of aircraft and electronics have taken and keep the lead; there is no sign that inventiveness is lacking. If there are many difficulties there are also opportunities. The task of the new reign is to use what we have to better advantage.

The vision was not a glorious one but it was at least fairly realistic, though without as yet any glimpse of the emerging European dimension. It was just starting to sink in, rather earlier in Coleman Street than in some places, that the beginning of national wisdom lay in accepting that the 'glory days' would never return. But even in Coleman Street it was to prove a hard lesson to accept.

★

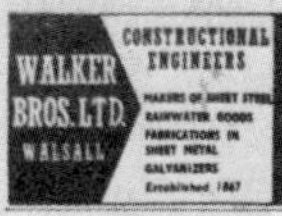

CITY EDITION

THE FINANCIAL TIMES

INCORPORATING THE FINANCIAL NEWS

INDUSTRY · COMMERCE · PUBLIC AFFAIRS

No. 20,000 · LONDON WEDNESDAY JULY 8 1953 · THREEPENCE

KNIGHT FRANK & RUTLEY
MAYFAIR 3771

FRESH FALL IN UNEMPLOYMENT

TOTAL LOWEST SINCE NOVEMBER, 1951

DROP IN SHORT-TIME WORKING

ENGINEERING INDUSTRY LOSES LABOUR

By Our Industrial Correspondent

Latest manpower figures issued by the Ministry of Labour show that the fall in unemployment which has persisted since the beginning of the year is continuing.

At June 15 the total number of unemployed was 297,700—a decrease of 42,500 during the month. This was the lowest level since November, 1951, and represented only 1.4 per cent. of the estimated total number of employees.

Only 22,000 of those unemployed were temporarily stopped, compared with 23,500 in the previous month, while 133,500 had been unemployed for more than eight weeks.

A year ago, on June 16, 1952, there were 440,100 out of work, representing 2.1 per cent. of the working population, with 143,900 temporarily stopped.

The increased activity in industry generally is brought out in the following table, which shows that unemployment has now fallen by 154,800 since the high level reached at the turn of the year:—

112,000 were affected and losing the same average time.

At the same time 1,306,000 were working an average of eight hours' overtime—a slight increase on the February figure.

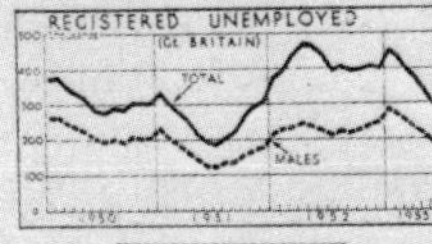

MINERS' EXECUTIVE TO HANDLE PAY CLAIM

From Our Labour Correspondent

PRICES TRUST ORDINARY

OFFER BY UTD. DRAPERY

The Board of United Drapery Stores announces that it has agreed to purchase from Sir Henry Price all the Ordinary shares in Prices Trust Company controlled by him (amounting to approximately one-third of the total Ordinary share capital) at a price of 30s per share.

DEMAND FOR ALUMINIUM

SPECIAL SURVEY

THE £ ABROAD

DUTCH GOLD STOCKS UP AGAIN

CONVERSION OF WAR BONDS

OFFER TO HOLDERS OF 2½% 1952-54 ISSUE

Financial Times Reporter

Holders of the £810m. 2½ per cent. National War Bonds, 1952-54, maturing next March, are offered conversion by the Government into 2½ per cent. National War Bonds, 1954-56, at the rate of £100 nominal for each £100 nominal of bonds tendered for conversion.

If all holdings are converted, the 1954-56 issue will amount to £1,236m., which will be the second largest Government issue, ranking next in size to the £1,910m. of 3½ per cent. War Loan.

The conversion date is September 1. Acceptances may be made at once and will be effective only if they have been received at the Bank of England, London (or, in respect of bonds on the Belfast register, at the Bank of Ireland, Donegall Place, Belfast), not later than July 17.

Only last month there was a Government operation — namely, the issue of £100m. 3 per cent. Exchequer "A" stock, 1960.

"ASSENTED" STOCK

Reference by "Lex" Col. 7; Editorial comment Page 6 Col. 2

GOVT. AND PURCHASE TAX "UPLIFT"

By Our Parliamentary Correspondent

Mr. R. A. Butler, Chancellor of the Exchequer, last night rejected pleas that he should abolish the "uplift" element in purchase tax, but his words held out hope that some concessions will be made before next year.

The Chancellor maintained that he had not yet received a sufficiently wide measure of opinion from the trade on its views on the reports of the Grant Committee on the problems of "uplift" to enable him conscientiously to take a decision.

"I am not satisfied we should be right to-day to come to a conclusion to give up £15m. of public money and accept the views put forward essentially from the big stores and multiple stores. ...

... ported the clause to abolish "uplift" moved by Mrs. Barbara Castle, Labour, and held that the additional purchase tax charged through "uplift" was a tax on efficiency.

The change-over from the buyers' to the sellers' market since "uplift" was first imposed and the new freedoms from controls, justified a "new look" at the problem, he said.

The new clause was defeated by 251 votes to 224, Government majority 27.

A. B. PICTURE CORPN.

SPONSORED TV DANGER

The hope is expressed by Sir Philip Warter, chairman of the Associated British Picture Corporation, that it may still be possible to persuade the Government to abandon its plan to allow commercial television in this country.

HOUSE OF FRASER

MAY SEEK "FRESH CONQUESTS"

TIN PRICE NEAR £600 A TON

NOTES FOR INVESTORS

INDUSTRIAL MARKET AGAIN GOOD

THE NATIONAL WAR BOND CONVERSION OFFER

By LEX

NEWS SUMMARY AND INDEX TO FEATURES

8 July 1953: the 20,000th issue and new masthead

On 8 July 1953 the *FT* reached its 20,000th issue. It marked the event in a twofold way: firstly by publishing (on Monday the 6th) an eighty-page survey of the British economy, which included articles by worthies like the chairmen of the Stock Exchange, BOAC and Rolls-Royce, Professor Lionel Robbins on 'Britain in the World Economy', Professor Simon on 'The Future of our Power Supplies' and an anonymous two-page historical piece about the *FT* and the City of London, illustrated by Lynton Lamb; and secondly, by starting, on Bracken's suggestion, to include the words 'Industry, Commerce, Public Affairs' under the title block on page one. An explanatory leader referred to the paper's broadening readership, how it now served 'directors of public companies, business men, investment managers, and Government servants' as well as 'the remaining private investors', and considered the implications of this, though not without a reassuring nod in the direction of its traditional readership:

> If a man is not to be taken unawares in Birmingham or in Manchester, in Whitehall or in Brighton, he must know (for example) what are the prospects of the United States economy, whether a South American republic is intent on nationalisation, what the wool cheque has been in Australia, whether the OECC countries will continue to support EPU – indeed, what these cabalistic signs denote . . . Finance has always been, in the last analysis, the reflection of changes in industry, commerce and world affairs. The *Financial Times*' new sub-titles are no more than a recognition of the logic of reality.

The new wording did not add to the beauty of the masthead, but it did serve over the next thirteen years as a useful summary of aspiration as well as achievement. In the context of the somewhat stagnant City, business and general economic coverage of both *The Times* and the *Daily Telegraph* during the mid-1950s, it made absolutely clear to the outside world the expanding patch that the *FT* was now seeking to occupy.

The issue of the last Wednesday of October 1953 gives some idea of how far the paper had come over five years. It was twelve pages long and had a distinctly 'industrial' layer to it on top of the staple financial fare of Stock Exchange closing prices and dealings, market reports from London, the provinces, North America, South Africa and the Continent, company news, comments and reports, and columns by 'Lex', 'Diarist' and 'Lombard'. Thus the front-page 'splash' was sent from Liverpool by 'Our Northern Representative' (Daniel Duxbury) and dealt with the likely reopening of the cotton market there; while elsewhere on the page, Einzig reported on the government's policy towards horticultural products, and Bromwich on the Gas Council's decision to spend a million pounds over the next five years on large-scale explorations for deposits of natural gas. Inside the paper, apart from particular industrial stories, regular columns like 'Trade Notes', 'Science and Industry' and 'Appointments' all featured and would have been of interest to a general business-cum-industrial readership. In addition, there were leaders on the economics of the film industry, the Gas Council's fourth annual report and the prospects for cotton trading, as well as features on the impact of dollars from United States troops stationed in Britain and the search for natural gas. As for the foreign coverage this day, it was not especially prominent, as was still usual at this stage; nevertheless, besides the regular 'U S Business Points', there were several quite substantial articles from abroad, including a front-page dispatch from Tehran on the latest report of the Persian Government Oil-Study Committee, a feature opposite the leader page on the economic situation in the Soviet Union's satellite countries, and from Kuala Lumpur a story on how 'high rubber and tin prices would not, on their own, solve Malaya's problems, Mr Richard Nixon, U S Vice-President, declared here today'. The paper continued to rely on a world-wide network of 'stringers', paid per contribution and numbering about fifty at this time; they produced an adequate, if not inspired, flow of foreign news and, to a lesser extent, analysis. Finally, this 28 October 1953, there were the entertainment listings on the penultimate page, started recently on Moore's initiative, although they never produced much revenue. Starring that evening at Drury Lane (tel. Tem. 8108) were Valerie Hobson and Herbert Lom in Rodgers and Hammerstein's *The King and I*.

As it happened, it was the field of popular entertainment that provoked an indicative contrast a few weeks later between the attitudes of the *FT* and *The Times*. On 13 November the government published a White Paper supporting the idea of commercial television. The *FT* the next day was sanguine enough: 'The scheme as it has been outlined will introduce competition into television, while safeguarding standards and keeping public expenditure to a minimum.' Some days later, in the context of fierce debate in Parliament, *The Times* argued strongly against the idea, declaring that those in favour 'want the educational purpose of broadcasting debased, and vulgarity – or, at best, triviality – enthroned'. It was almost certainly with this outburst at least partly in mind that the *FT* on the 27th, following the House of Lords vote in favour of a second channel, devoted a further leader to the subject, in which it referred disapprovingly to 'the use of moral superiority as a weapon in debate'. It went on: 'The new policy is designed to improve the standard of television by bringing in new men, new ideas and new money. It is odd that this should be thought revolutionary. It is even odder that it should be thought wicked.'

Yet the *FT* was like any paper prepared to use a moral tone if it suited its book. This particularly applied to trade unions that threatened or took industrial action, as with the railwaymen in December 1953: 'Men in public service, be they porters or heads of nationalised industries, have a great responsibility, which they generally recognise. Civil servants and the police are dissatisfied about their pay, but it is unthinkable that they would strike.' Similarly, the following month there appeared a hostile leader about the Electrical Trades Union and its increasing 'guerrilla strike action', under the heading 'Ruthless Men'. But in general, though with these and other exceptions, the *FT* under Newton moderated its tone towards labour and, as Parkinson's testimony suggests, tried much harder than it had done before to understand the causes of disaffection and strife rather than immediately condemning them out of hand. This also applied to the paper's attitude towards the Labour Party, where the almost puerile abuse of the 1940s virtually disappeared, apart from the columns of Bracken and, on occasion, Wincott. Of course, when it came to it, as on general election day in 1955, the political judgement of the *FT* remained unwavering: 'The Labour Party has become the party of economic protectionism, with all its economic policies coloured by the fear of crisis or slump. The Conservative Party has become the expansionist party.' Faced by a choice between 'the hand of restriction and the opportunities of growth', there was no doubt what that choice should be.

The overall quality of economic analysis in the leader columns was still variable. In 1954 an attempt was made to explain why West Germany was doing so much better economically than Britain, particularly in its exporting. This was a phenomenon that the *FT*'s representative in Bonn since 1949, Julius Hollos, had been a pioneer in explaining to a British readership, but all that a leader on the subject could adduce were such 'special', short-term factors as the rearmament programme sucking in labour, the steel shortage until recently and scarce materials in general.[14] The following year, when discussing the wage increase for miners coming hard on the heels of one for railwaymen, a leader expressed the pious but perhaps fatuous hope 'that higher wages and the better industrial relations they imply will not only help to increase productivity, but will persuade those who co-operate so eagerly in good times to co-operate in bad'.[15] Yet at other times there was a sharp analytical edge to the paper's economic comment. In January 1954, in a leader on Britain's failure to develop high-speed aircraft, the government was strongly criticized for its 'cautious and hesitant approach' towards helping to provide the necessary capital. Again, six months later, some pertinent questions were asked about the government's capital investment policy: 'Within the rising total, is enough going for example to transport, whether on the railways or the roads? Is the rate of investment in manufacturing industry high enough? Are not some sectors of the economy, especially housing and the electrical industry, absorbing too great a proportion of the available resources?'

The usual economic leader of the period, however, was somewhere between the bland and the astringent, typified by one in May 1955 on what was becoming a much-debated subject, 'Finance for Industry'. The overriding context was explained with admirable lucidity:

> The prospect is that the UK will need a much higher rate of capital formation than it achieved either in the decade before the war or the past decade if it is to take full advantage of technological advances and the industrial uses of atomic energy and electronics, since by their nature these developments are likely to have their chief impact on those industries which already have a high capital–labour ratio.

But as to what to do about it, the concluding sentences adopted a disappointingly (if quite possibly justified) negative tone:

> In the long run, if long-term investment on the basis of credit creation – that is, through inflation – is ruled out, the problem is not one of what type of institution should actually channel funds to industry. It is one of increasing the total of real savings, which is a problem about which the banks can do relatively little.

Other papers might over the years go in for 'whiz-bang' solutions to the problem of the faltering British economy, but whether in the 1950s or the 1980s the *FT*'s leader columns very rarely did or do.

It was in 1955 that Butler's chancellorship, hitherto highly successful, reached an unfortunate climax, and the British economy entered its fateful 'stop-go' cycle. On New Year's Day it all seemed very hopeful, with the economy apparently booming as never before. The paper looked ahead to the Budget in the spring and declared that 'with the monetary weapon available to check inflation, the Chancellor should be able to concentrate his attention on finding those reductions in taxation which are likely, in the long run, to produce the best incentives to higher production and increased productivity'. By 23 March, as the Budget approached and it had become clear that the economy was in a seriously overheated state, notwithstanding a rise in Bank Rate in February, the *FT* was more cautious about what Butler should do with his likely position of surplus:

> It would be possible for the Chancellor to make concessions equivalent to a 2*s.* 6*d.* cut in the standard rate of income tax and still retain an orthodox balance in the Budget.

Such concessions would be possible, but it is only too clear that they are most unlikely. The inflationary pressure in the economy is already sufficiently strong and a Budget which gave everything away would add greatly to it.

The leader argued, however, that there was *some* room for fiscal concessions – such as the abolition of purchase tax on cotton textiles, the raising of allowances and the removal of anomalies – and stressed not only that Bank Rate existed as a means to check inflation, but also that whatever 'the short-term pressure of the present inflation', quite as serious was 'the long-term problem of over-taxation'. That, as it turned out, was more or less the paper's final advisory word on the subject, for three days later a strike by electricians and engineers brought the national newspaper industry to a complete standstill for almost a month, causing the *FT*'s first-ever break in publication and what it called on its resumption a time 'of anxiety, suspense and frustration'.

The world at large, however, did not pause. On 6 April Eden succeeded Churchill as Prime Minister. Soon afterwards it was announced that the general election would be held on 25 May. On 19 April, Butler presented his Budget, in which he cut the standard rate of income tax by *6d.* and emancipated 2.4 million people from paying the tax altogether. Two days later the *FT* reappeared and delivered its verdict: 'There can be criticisms of the Budget's details, but there can be little doubt that it was well fitted to the economic situation in which it was produced.' After accepting Butler's statement that recent adjustments to the credit mechanism had brought the balance of payments situation under control: 'The Chancellor was right to take his risks on the side of expansion.' The next day the paper returned to the subject, responding to Gaitskell's charge that it had been an inflationary Budget. This the *FT* did not deny, but it argued that 'as Mr Butler has been prepared to use the Bank Rate, there was no need for him to rely on the Budget as the sole disinflationary influence he can exert'. It continued: 'The condition of the economy still needs to be watched with great care, and until recovery can be officially recorded, dear money policies are likely to continue.' The patient, however, did not seem unduly fragile to the tax-paying electorate, and a month later the Conservatives were returned with an increased majority. Butler's fourth Budget, it is not unfair to say, had achieved its main political task.

The economic reckoning followed swiftly. Sustained pressure on sterling led to a further round of credit measures in July, followed in October by an autumn Budget that flashed the red lights of 'stop' with a vengeance and took a particularly severe toll of public capital expenditure and private investment. Two months later Butler was replaced at the Treasury by Macmillan, at the end of a year in which, as the *FT* tactfully put it, 'things have been more difficult, and his monetary policies have had only a gradual and partial efficacy'. Yet arguably the *FT* itself bore some degree of responsibility for Butler's sad decline, in particular through failing to put his budgetary options under a sufficiently candid and rigorous scrutiny during the crucial first few months of the year. The leader columns of these months neither picked up on the impending sterling crisis – though the economic signs were unmistakably there, additionally so in the context of continuing confusion over Britain's convertibility plans – nor sought to get across the vital theme that, faced by an economic and/or sterling crisis, the fundamental choice would have to be made between economic expansion at home and world-ranking stature abroad. Not surprisingly, it was a choice that both ministers and electorate preferred not to make. Of course, the newspaper strike did not help, as Andrew Shonfield recalled a few years later of the circumstances in which Butler had shaped his economically disastrous Budget:

> It is perhaps not sufficiently realised how much cabinet ministers rely on the printed word in newspapers to turn their ideas over. Most of the time, they are so busy acting that they have no opportunity to think much beyond the next decision. Newspapers, and conversation with those who write them, often provide stimulus for self-examination in the context of a somewhat longer perspective . . . What they want above all is a mirror. Where else are they to find one?[16]

For a few weeks that mirror was absent, but most of the time it was present and too clouded, or at least in public. It was not as if those in Coleman Street did not know the score, for as early as February that year Bracken wrote to Beaverbrook:

> Butler is now very worried both about sterling and our export trade. When he was lunching at the *Financial Times* he held forth to us about his problems and the only comment my colleagues made after he had gone was that it was incredible that a man who had had the Treasury for three years should be so naïve in his approach to financial affairs.[17]

It was not, as the ghosts of Labour Chancellors past might have noted wryly, an attitude that ever surfaced in print.

In the less rarefied world of production rather than policy, the newsprint restrictions continued gradually to ease during the mid-1950s – though as late as December 1954 Bracken was complaining to the shareholders that 'our reasonable request for a little more newsprint for a paper which does credit to British industry at home and abroad and earns a useful amount of foreign exchange has been steadily refused'.[18] As the size of the paper gradually increased, so Newton pressed on with his policy of recruitment, from both within and without the ancient universities. The direct intake of 1955 proved a particularly distinguished crop, including as it did Robert Heller, subsequent editor of *Management Today*, and Samuel Brittan, one of only two members of the 1950s Oxbridge intake still on the paper thirty years later. Brittan recalls that Moore was mildly reluctant to take him on ('he seems so nervous'), but as usual in these matters bowed to Newton's judgement. Also joining the editorial staff that year, and in his way an equally important recruit, was Arthur Bennett, who had been editor of *Technical Journal* and came specifically as a qualified technical-cum-industrial journalist. He took over a recently started weekly column called 'New Products' and then the following January began, on Newton's suggestion, a weekly column on the advertising business. Able, conscientious and uncomplaining, he showed himself over the years to be the ideal workhorse, of whom Newton took the fullest possible advantage as the paper continued to expand its coverage.

Even by 1954 the innovations were starting to come quite quickly. In June there was published for the first time *The Financial Times Annual Review of British Industry*, which was 100 pages long, sold separately at a shilling and contained a mixture of articles by *FT* staff and 'men recognised as authorities in their special fields'. The following month the first of 'Know Your Competitors' appeared, being an occasional and, as it turned out, very successful series on foreign firms and business men. Subject number one was 'Nordhoff of Volkswagen', the beetle's general manager. In December, on the suggestion of Rees-Mogg, who in turn had borrowed the idea from Anne Temple of the *Daily Mail*, the Saturday paper began what was to be the hardiest of features, 'Finance and the Family'; this went beyond the problems of ordinary investment and offered the services of a financial 'agony aunt' on matters like taxation, insurance and banking. There was, however, one weekly column which no longer appeared by the autumn of 1955. Perhaps because of illness, perhaps because he could no longer muster the enthusiasm, Bracken ceased after July to contribute his observations, and 'Men and Matters' went into a period of temporary abeyance. It was in a way a sad departure, but Hodge and Newton, to name but two, probably heaved sighs of relief.

The arts side of the paper had taken a further step forwards with the employment from late 1953 of a music critic, again on Moore's initiative and this time nominated by Granger. He was Andrew Porter, who had fairly recently left Oxford and combined the qualities of high enthusiasm with immense erudition. His notices could also be devastatingly critical, sometimes of productions at Covent Garden, such as the 'insultingly primitive' *Tannhäuser* in November 1955. That particular notice, after describing 'a poky Venusberg', went on: 'No wonder Tannhäuser longed to escape! So he did, but not to the spring valley which Wagner describes. Oh no, twenty-two bare posts, midway between telegraph-poles and thorn-twigs, formed the pastoral setting.' It was the type of review that could lead to a certain coolness between music critic and managing director, though Porter was not the sort of person to be bullied, whether by Moore or anyone else. It was, as Porter subsequently described it, a case of pity a poor sub who took liberties: 'When I am asked, "How did you get established?" I answer, "By intransigence", and recall the night when I tipped a tray of loose type – a review of mine that, in early *FT* days, *had* been cut – onto the floor rather than let it appear in mutilated form.'[19]

As for Granger, he now began a weekly column of film reviews as well as continuing with his theatre criticism, which in August 1955 included a review of the first London production of *Waiting for Godot*, at the Arts Theatre: 'It is, in a manner of speaking, a cast-iron, copper-bottomed, rubber-lined, waterproof, high-brow's delight with knobs on – not a bit the thing for the wilting business man, but doubtless an ideally gruelling evening for the members of an experimental theatre club in need of a little corrective discipline.' Much of the rest of the review continued in this faintly Bertie-Woosterish way, culminating in the assertion that 'even its "great thoughts" seem just the kind that we ourselves might have fathered given moody enough circumstances and a dull day'. It was no thanks to the man from the *FT* that Beckett's play struck lucky.

All this editorial expansion depended, as Newton was the first to concede, on a healthy bottom line. Profits by the mid-1950s were running at about £550,000 a year and in 1955 would have attained a considerably higher figure than that but for the newspaper and railway strikes, together with increasing labour and newsprint costs that at the start of 1956 resulted in the price of the paper going up to fourpence. Trade or 'industrial' advertising continued to rise by leaps and bounds; from 3,157 in 1953, its columnage (including surveys) jumped to 4,000 in 1954, 4,612 in 1955 and 5,732 in 1956. Revenue from the more traditional financial advertising was steady rather than spectacular, though it was at this time that 'Bertie' Bradberry began what became virtually his crusade to try to persuade almost all companies to pay for having their share prices quoted in the paper. He encountered a certain amount of resistance from the editorial side on the way, but within a few years the principle was well enough established that the quality of the paper's share information service was such that it merited some payment to be included in it.

The most dramatic sign of growth came on the circulation side. Here at last, partly in the context of newsprint alleviation, there was 'take-off', going from just under 60,000 in the first half of 1953 to almost 72,000 by the second half of 1954, and then continuing to climb to an average daily net sale in 1955 of 80,360, before dropping by a few hundred in 1956 following the price increase. This rapid increase was profoundly exciting at the time, especially for Newton and his editorial staff, giving them a sense that all the hard and apparently unavailing work of the early 1950s was eventually paying off. 'We are particularly gratified', the chairman told shareholders in December 1954, 'by the remarkable growth of our sales in the principal industrial centres of the country'; while the following April, Bracken received a typical communication from Beaverbrook: 'I saw the newspapers for Monte-Carlo this day in transit. There were more *Financial Times* than any other paper except the *Telegraph* and *Daily Express*. And that's a good sign.'[20] It was indeed, especially as during these same years the circulation of *The Times*, which the *FT* was now supplanting in its City and business coverage, failed to attain any lift-off at all. Bracken's child had, in fact, just about arrived as a national quality in its own right.

As such, it required more commodious premises than the exceedingly cramped (though thoroughly cheerful) Coleman Street, where space was becoming so tight that in 1955 most of the advertising department had to move to the sixth floor of the adjoining Lloyds Bank building. Bracken elaborated the theme that December at the annual meeting of the FN Group:

> Our editorial department is separated by more than a mile from the printing plant. Our staff is working uncomfortably and uneconomically in six scattered buildings. Most of our leases are running out. The war and building restrictions have too long prevented us from building premises adequate to our ever-expanding needs.
>
> Last year I asked for your authority to obtain a site which would enable us to rehouse our newspapers and the St Clements Press and to provide room for future expansion. We have now got one. We shall soon sign a lease granted by the Corporation of the City of London for a site lying between Cannon Street and Queen Victoria Street, a little east of St Paul's Cathedral.
>
> I don't like spending much money on bricks and steel at a time when builders' costs are very big and indeed often incalculable. But there is no alternative unless

someone is brave enough to assert that in this age of creeping inflation building costs are likely to fall. We hope to take possession of the new building before the end of three years.[21]

A considerable history lay behind the project. As early as 1950, when it was clear that the merger of the two papers had been a commercial success and that there was potential for expansion, the board agreed that a bomb site to the south-east of St Paul's, conveniently midway between the City and Fleet Street, would be appropriate 'to erect a building to house St Clements Press, *Financial Times* and associated companies'. Bracken soon afterwards unilaterally found his architect in the person of Professor Albert Richardson, who was in his seventies, devoted to all aspects of the eighteenth century and was to be fairly described in his *Times* obituary in 1964 as 'a fighter on the side of the angels, if perhaps more trenchantly and constructively in the field of preservation than in the newer one of an architecture serving contemporary social needs'.[22] It is doubtful if he was the right man for what was to prove an extremely long haul. Progress for several years was virtually nil, but by the beginning of 1955 a building licence had finally been obtained from the Ministry of Works; the City Corporation had fixed the rental at £20,000 a year for a 99-year lease ('without any nonsense about periodic rent reviews', as Moore later put it); and the board had considered its building committee's suggestion that provision be made in the new building for a Grade 'A' nuclear shelter and rejected it, 'having regard to the improbability of its being possible to continue to print in London in the event of an atomic war and as there was no direct Government grant towards the cost of a shelter'. Richardson that March gave an expansive interview to the *Evening Standard* in which he showed off his detail drawings:

> See here. This cornice is supported by pillars of crystal glass. They'll be floodlit at night, giving the effect of an immense tiara. And look at this magnificent bronze clock over the entrance. I want sculptures round the dial in the grand manner, bronzes in the style of Cellini or Goujon. That's the way to be modern! There's no such thing as originality. Only variation. This building must express Administrative Power. It must be a City Palace – not a factory for clerks!

The interviewer was convinced by the Professor's eloquence: 'I went away telling myself how opulent and majestic it was going to be.'[23]

At this stage, with the likely cost going above £1½ million, Bracken began to get cold feet and in April 1955 persuaded his board to 'explore the possibilities' of developing the site 'as an office block of which a substantial proportion would be let, and to provide a separate printing works for St Clements Press on another site'. Moore was absent from the meeting, but on his return from the USA wrote to Crosthwaite-Eyre to say that he was 'quite frankly appalled' at the prospect of scrapping the planned development at such a late stage. This opposition was too much for Bracken, and he backed down, deciding henceforth to wage a rear-guard campaign against what he termed to Moore his 'beloved colleagues' passion for costly and stately buildings'. It began in September, when the board agreed that Richardson should be authorized to advise the builders that a contract would be signed with them 'on the understanding that luxury embellishments of which the cost had been estimated by the chairman at £115,000 should be deleted from the plans'. Nevertheless, as *Trade News* described it the following month in a series on 'New Homes for the Press', it remained an impressive conception:

> The building will be of unusual design, its interesting layout comprising basically two tall office blocks divided by an octagonal structure housing the 'factory' where the physical production of the paper [and the magazines, prospectuses, etc. also printed by SCP] will be carried out.
>
> The new building will be no skyscraper – its height is limited by the City of London development plan. There will be six floors above ground level for the offices, while the factory octagon, which is to start from the second floor, will rise to five floors. The structure will be steel framed and dressed with brick and stone.
>
> The sub-basement will house the wells for the presses, while the basement will take in the main press hall, the main foundry, canteen, ventilating plant and storage space . . .
>
> Apart from its unusual design, the building will certainly be as distinctive to those in the trade as is the newspaper to be published there. The reason? The main facing of the building will be in Hollington Stone, which, we hasten to explain, is a type of sandstone – of a delicate shade of pink.[24]

It was a distinctive and dignified design, but Bracken continued to be a spanner in the works, wrecking negotiations to have the *Observer* printed in the new building, vetoing Richardson's wish to have a top storey sheathed in copper (which would have turned green with time and thus complemented the Hollington stone) and knocking out another £77,500 worth of 'embellishments', including the proposed heating and ventilation system. Moreover, as late as February 1956, a month after the company announced that it was to raise through a debenture issue £1.3 million out of the estimated cost of £1.6 million, he was still backtracking on the whole thing, inspiring a reproachful letter from Moore:

I am unable to suggest how the new building project could be abandoned at this stage without loss of dignity by the directors or damage to the reputation and credit of the Company. It appears to me that we are irrevocably committed to putting up a building on the Cannon Street site.

Whether or no printing is an attractive or profitable business to be engaged in, the fact remains that the publishing of the *Finanacial Times* depends heavily on printing. Thinking back over my years with the *FN* and the constant disagreements with the Argus Press, I feel that a newspaper which has ideas of expansion and classifies itself among the national dailies should have control over the plant on which it is printed.

In one of our many conversations with you regarding the new building, I was expressing doubts as to the wisdom of so large an expenditure and you told me that one must have confidence in the future. It is not unreasonable to expect that, in a properly planned works, St Clements could not only operate more profitably but could handle a larger turnover, and the *FT* would have control of its printing works.

The penultimate sentence was a particularly shrewd thrust, as one would expect from someone who during the previous few years had become a master at handling his increasingly unpredictable chairman. Moore's soft impeachment had its effect, and the building, more or less as planned, went ahead.

For both paper and country, 1956 turned out to be quite a year, and in many ways was the culmination of Newton's first phase as editor. The regular contents continued to expand. Thus Wragge-Morley's 'Scientists' Notebook' became a frequent and widely read column; Denys Sutton started to write every Tuesday on 'The Arts'; and the labour coverage became so comprehensive that the Minister of Labour, Ian Macleod, half-seriously complained that the paper was making his life a misery, because Eden kept reading in it of minor strikes and then ringing him up to ask what he was doing about them. Many of the features continued as usual – a classic of the genre, 'Cut-Throat Competition', about the razor market, appeared in March – but it seems that by now Newton was also looking for harder-hitting features, with a more topical news angle. The surveys flourished, including a notable 64-page one in April on atomic energy, published when Calder Hall, the first full-scale atomic power-station in the world, was about to start operating under trial conditions. Leader comment, both this day and on other occasions later in the year, was wholly enthusiastic and at no point mentioned the safety aspect. The year 1956 was indeed one with something for everyone, including at the Royal Court in May the epochal *Look Back in Anger*, which Granger reviewed: 'Mr Osborne communicates no sense to us that he has taken even three paces back from the work that has so hotly and tormentedly engaged him. But for all this it is a play of extraordinary importance.' It was just a pity that there was as yet no cricket correspondent to get his teeth into Laker's nineteen wickets at Old Trafford.

There was also during the first half of this year a perceptible moving up of gear in the leaders written about the related themes of British economic policy and Britain's place in the world. Rees-Mogg and Shonfield, by now the chief leader writers, made between them a powerful and highly readable team. 'All the Burdens', responding to Macmillan's February austerity measures, set the tone, especially the closing sentences:

> Judged by manpower, industrial capacity or economic potential we are not a world Power in the same sense as the United States or the Soviet Union. It is to that fact, and to the ultimate dependence of our whole position in the world on productive investment, that we must adjust our thinking. The attempt to carry too great a defence burden, setting a military standard of parity of equipment with the United States, combined with an extraordinarily high level of social expenditure, has made it impossible to absorb a comparatively small and long overdue increase in industrial investment. In such a situation to cut investment rather than the other excessive burdens may be immediately necessary. Yet it is an expedient rather than a remedy. It is also a defeat.[25]

Similarly trenchant – and implicitly moving away from economic liberalism towards a more 'managed' economy – were two leaders in May on the wages question. In 'A Waste of Breath' the paper argued that government exhortation, such as Eden's recent speech at Perth, was useless in terms of achieving wage restraint. Whereas: 'A balanced labour market, consumer resistance, falling profits, these are the conditions which moderate wage increases.' The second leader reiterated that talk alone could not control wages, ruled out 'a controlled wages policy', on the grounds that the unions would not accept it, and stated that 'the other and right way of dealing with the problem' lay in accepting the premise that 'if the demand inflation is brought to an end then the wage inflation is bound to be checked'.[26] It was a conundrum to which *FT* leader writers would return again and again.

Also during 1956 significant events were talking place in both halves of Europe. In November 1955 Britain had withdrawn (apparently without comment from the *FT*) from the Spaak Committee that eventually led to the Treaty of Rome in 1957 and to the creation of the EEC. Instead, the government sought during 1956 to achieve within the already existing OECC a form of economic co-operation that was less institutional and did not remotely threaten national sovereignty. The *FT* gave this initiative its enthusiastic support, declaring in July that 'a common market which excludes Britain' would 'represent the absolute failure of British policy and would be a severe blow to the British economy'. Three months later it returned to the theme:

> British industry needs a new and vitalising competitive force already. A Free Trade Area would double the opportunities for success as well as the penalties of failure. It would stimulate the whole of British industry and give a new urgency to the improvement of production. It also offers a market of Continental size. If the European economy continues to be divided up by the frontier of a historic pact, it cannot compete with the Continental economies of America or Russia. All the European powers need a European market: this is the chance to create one.[27]

In fact, Britain had already missed the European economic bus that mattered. Nevertheless, this leader's tone and arguments offered interesting pointers to future attitudes, at a time when there was still considerable scepticism about any sort of European venture.

Absolutely unequivocal was the *FT*'s attitude towards the Soviet intervention in Hungary that began in late October. 'However events may go,' it wrote on 30 October as the forcible suppression was still going on, 'the people of Hungary have written an inspiring and indelible chapter in European history.' A week later a leader wrestled with the question of the Soviet Union itself, contending that 'there must be almost as great pressure for freedom as there is in the satellites' and that 'the whole tyranny of Russia must now be balanced on a knife's edge', before concluding: 'As yet we can have little idea how these pressures are developing. In the long run it is unlikely however that they can be prevented from showing themselves.' On 20 November even the *FT* board stood up to be counted:

> Lord Moore asked whether the Company should make a contribution to Hungarian Relief. Lord Bracken expressed the view that a contribution to a relief fund was rather impersonal and thought it would be better to make a contribution towards the education of a refugee child. He undertook to make some enquiries as to the possibility of assisting in the education of a refugee child at a school such as Ampleforth.

Relatively few causes could now move Bracken to action, let alone action that cost money, but this was one of them.

The dominating event of the year was of course the Suez crisis. During July the *FT* had little to say about the question of financing the Aswan Dam, which in a sense precipitated the crisis, but on the 28th of the month reacted as strongly as any paper to Nasser's nationalization of the Suez Canal Company:

> He has now shown that his word will not be kept even for two months at a time. In the history of dictators there often comes a point when it is apparent that there is no purpose in negotiating because no treaty will be respected, and no purpose in making concessions because no concessions will be deemed sufficient. That point Colonel Nasser has reached and passed . . .
>
> It is for the United States, Britain and France to concert a joint policy towards the Suez Canal problem. The Prime Minister has defined his policy as one of firmness. It will need to be so.

Over the succeeding weeks and months, various negotiations proceeded (of which the *FT* was generally sceptical) and schemes were hatched, but the crucial underlying question was always whether the West would use force against Nasser. On 13 September the paper was doubtful about this option, 'which at any rate in the short run might do more to jeopardise our Middle East oil supplies than to safeguard them'. Instead, it argued that the best approach lay in exerting 'the pressure of world opinion', even though this was a method that 'takes time and requires patience'.

By the last day of October all had changed. Israel had attacked Egypt, apparently spontaneously, and an Anglo-French ultimatum had been issued to the belligerents. The *FT* was fully supportive of Eden's action:

> Everyone must be anxious about the outcome of a difficult and dangerous act of pacification, but if there is a settlement it could provide at least a new start. The tension in the Middle East had reached a point at which no power could feel safe. The Government has taken on a grave responsibility. It was right to do so.

That day Anglo-French military action began, including the bombing of military targets in Egypt. The leader on 1 November was headed 'No Time for Delay' and concluded:

> There cannot be the least doubt that world opinion is generally opposed to the Anglo-French action. We are as unpopular now for intervening in a dispute as we were before the war for failing to do so. How world opinion will move in the coming weeks may well be determined by the duration and success of the campaign itself. If there is an early end to it, and if that can be followed by a rapid pacification, then the general climate of opinion may change. We shall have gone to restore peace and we shall have restored it.

If, on the other hand, the campaign is delayed and long drawn out, then we shall only have aggravated the problem of the Middle East. It is a swift settlement that is needed. If it is not achieved then our whole policy will be in ruins. Even those who have not approved the Government's policy must see that its failure now would be a mortal blow at the position of Britain in the world, and, indeed, at the prospect of a settlement in the Middle East.

It was in no sense a 'gung-ho' leader, but it did unashamedly call for a spirit of national unity behind the military intervention.

Alas for such sentiments, there no longer existed, within as well as without Coleman Street, an overriding mood of 'my country right or wrong'. National opinion was deeply divided. Faced by this, there seems to have come over the leading figures in the paper an awareness that the *FT* should abandon a moral stance – either way – and instead concentrate in its comment on the practicalities of the evolving situation. Thus on the 2nd a leader considered 'Economic Consequences', on the 3rd 'Gold Reserves' and in neither case referred to the merits or otherwise of intervention. On the 6th, 'After Seven Days', the leader reiterated that 'pacification in the Middle East has to be swift if it is to be successful' but was basically a progress report couched in politically neutral tones. On the 7th, following the end of intervention as a result of intense financial as well as political pressure on Britain from the United States, the leader frankly began: 'The cease fire in the Middle East comes as a most welcome conclusion to the brief but very anxious days of hostility.'

The *FT*'s coverage of the protracted crisis, with its complex interaction of the economic, the political and the military, was a major challenge to a paper that was still finding its fully adult feet. On the whole the *FT* responded pretty well, partly through the device of hiring a hardened news man from the *Daily Mail*, who was looked upon with some awe by the resident staff as 'a real journalist'. Peter Tumiati was sent from Rome to Cairo after the nationalization of the Suez Canal and stayed there for several months, game but hopelessly outnumbered by the bigger dailies such as the *Express*, which sent no fewer than eight specials to Egypt. In London, Ian Trafford performed with great zeal and intelligence in his new capacity as oil as well as industrial correspondent. In particular, the paper did its best during these months to offer a consistently detailed and critical scrutiny of received governmental wisdom about the specific consequences of the crisis, such as the oft-made assertion, which the *FT* effectively disproved, that the Egyptians could not navigate ships through the canal. Moreover, out of the crisis there emerged a feature that was almost certainly pioneering in Britain, possibly in the world. This was the news summary on the left-hand column of the front page, which began on 2 November as 'Suez Briefs' (though that title was then dropped) and on the first day comprised eleven condensed news items about the crisis. Over the next two months this summary continued to appear each day, concentrating almost wholly on the Middle East, though quite often with an item or two about Hungary at its foot. It was soon taken over by a sub called Alan Chalkley and in due course he brought to it a neatly humorous touch, but at this stage, when all was doom and gloom, it was still played completely straight.

Suez also marked, with brutal clarity, the end of Britain as a world power. During the rest of the year there appeared in the *FT* a series of leaders – lucid, provocative and at times brilliant – that examined Britain's post-Suez future and further developed some of the arguments the paper had been putting forward a few months earlier. The tone of 'Mending the Future' (1 December) was fairly typical:

> We cannot return to prosperity if we pursue the same path as has already helped to destroy that wealth. If we pay 10 per cent of our national income on arms – which we are then unable to use either in time or effectively – we shall not also be able to use that money for investment. If we go on building over 300,000 houses in a year of acute inflation, because no one has the will or the sense to stop it, then we shall deserve to be poor. If we impose penal taxation on business profits then we shall continue to destroy the foundations on which a return to wealth could be built.

Four days later, with an early withdrawal from Port Said announced and Macmillan about to go as supplicant to the IMF, it was time for 'Facing the Truth':

> International influence depends upon economic strength. Economic strength can only be obtained by investing a high proportion of the national wealth in new factories and equipment, and by giving big rewards to people who create wealth. To do that we must stop pretending that we can afford £1,500 million on defence forces which we cannot then use. We must also be sure that we do not try to maintain luxury standards of Government expenditure on an inadequate income. We must put the economic strength of the country first – whatever consequences may follow from that. If we do that we shall not have to see our Chancellors, Conservative or Socialist, tinkering like unskilled mechanics on an engine that is rusting through.

'What Must Be Done' the next day took up the by now familiar theme: 'Only if Britain's economic resources are devoted to economic growth, above all else, shall we be able to make progress during the next

20 years, or take advantage of the nuclear age when it comes.' So did 'Dollar Borrowing' on the 13th:

What is now needed is a clear sign that the failure of the last decade has been appreciated. A high cost, low investment, high tax and low incentive economy is capable of absorbing money as dry desert sand will absorb water, with little lasting benefit to itself. What it needs is not an occasional thunderstorm but a comprehensive irrigation scheme.

Finally, on the 15th, two crucial long-term questions were asked about sterling: 'The first is whether the extent of Britain's banking commitments through sterling is not excessive in comparison to the country's real economic power and resources. The second is whether British economic policy is not now too much influenced by attempts to calculate the reactions of foreign exchange dealers to British policy.'

It was all heady stuff, but somehow mundane life in Coleman Street staggered on. The summer and autumn's direct intake was well up to scratch and starred Nigel Lawson and 'Jock' Bruce-Gardyne. Also interviewed at this time, but not starting until the New Year, was John Murray, who was to become a notable 'Lex'. His session with Newton was interrupted by Einzig rushing in to say that Crosthwaite-Eyre had collapsed, though in the event he recovered. Einzig himself was by this stage not much longer for the paper. He had made the mistake of complaining to Newton about the chopping of his stories, and in the end it came down to Newton saying that either he or Einzig would have to go. Einzig went at the end of November, ostensibly (and to an extent justifiably) on the grounds of ill health. The post-war years of his tenure had been generally disappointing to all concerned, but he had had a long and distinguished run. In the true words of a reviewer of his memoirs a few years later: 'To Einzig journalism was not so much a profession as a crusade. He was always seeking not simply to record events, nor even simply to comment on them, but to shape and influence them.'[28] Meanwhile, to distract, console and encourage during traumatic times, there was always the flickering screen. On 17 December, Granger reviewed *High Society*: 'The characters are for the most part so smart that they sting like after-shaving lotion, and though the prevailing *bon ton* is not exactly "U" it is staggeringly rich in its manifestations.' In the same column he also cast a mildly jaundiced eye over *Love Me Tender* and 'the Presley technique in action – or how to make a very odd noise accompanied by an even odder shimmy from the hips'. One way and another, it was at the end of 1956 out with the old and in with the new.

[NINE]

BRACKEN'S MEMORIAL: 1957–61

During the early weeks of 1957 the country acquired a new Prime Minister and the *FT* a new owner. For several years the relationship between Bracken and Crosthwaite-Eyre had been deteriorating, partly because of Bracken's condescending manner, but also increasingly because of what was becoming his almost pathological reluctance to sanction the expenditure of money, whether as chairman of the *FT* or as an Eyre trustee. There were several specific bones of contention between the two men; these included Crosthwaite-Eyre's natural wishes to make improvements to his New Forest farm and to buy a sailing-boat, but the one over which feelings ran the highest concerned his desire to buy a beautiful but expensive Scottish estate called Knoydart, which Bracken felt he could not permit without betraying his duty to Crosthwaite-Eyre's children. In the publishing sphere there were also disagreements over the printing of the *Observer* at the *FT*'s new building and the merger of the book publishers Methuen with Eyre & Spottiswoode, both of which plans Crosthwaite-Eyre advocated strongly and Bracken vetoed. The situation became so strained and indeed impossible that finally, probably in November 1956, Bracken was asked to cease being an Eyre trustee. The letter was delivered in person by Crosthwaite-Eyre's father, who was temporarily back from South Africa and who, more than thirty years earlier, had been the crucial sponsor of Bracken's newspaper career.

Bracken was devastated. Even though the letter had made no reference to the *FT*, he decided in a state of deep despair to sever all connections with the Eyre family, including resigning his chairmanship of the paper and the FN Group. The devoted Moore at once implored him not to do so:

> I am filled with gloom by what you said after lunch today. I know how trying your trusteeship has been to you, but that should surely cease now that you have ceased to be a trustee.
>
> The effect upon everyone here not to mention our shareholders of your ceasing to be chairman would be deplorable. I do beg you not to resign, and also

not to announce your intention of resigning at the Annual Meeting. I need you, we all need you very much, your leadership was perhaps never more needed than now, and if you go I shall follow for my heart will no longer be in it.[1]

Bracken agreed to delay making an announcement, but his mind was made up. True to his word, Moore informed Oliver Crosthwaite-Eyre and his father that if Bracken went he would be going too. This came as an unpleasant shock to them; in dismissing Bracken as a trustee they had not anticipated losing him as chairman of the *FT*, let alone as a result also losing the paper's managing director. In some alarm, Oliver Crosthwaite-Eyre consulted his friend and financial adviser, Luke Meinertzhagen of the stockbrokers Cazenove & Co., who told him in fairly forcible terms not only that the paper would suffer from the simultaneous loss of both chairman and managing director and that the City would take a dim view of it, but also that in any case he had too much of his capital locked up in the paper and that he would do better to spread it across a range of other investments. Faced by an intractable set of circumstances, and not without a heaviness of heart, Crosthwaite-Eyre agreed to take Meinertzhagen's advice.

Thus the *FT* was up for sale, though only in the narrowest, least publicized of market-places. This was so largely because Meinertzhagan knew, and was able to tell Crosthwaite-Eyre, of the existence of a probable satisfactory buyer. The knowledge came through his brother Daniel, who was a managing director of the merchant-banking firm of Lazards, which in turn was part of the Pearson empire under the third Lord Cowdray. Daniel intimated to Luke that Pearsons would be willing to pay a fair price to acquire the *FT* and the rest of the group, and with great swiftness and secrecy this was what happened, a deal being concluded by late January or early February 1957. The price paid to the Eyre family was £720,000 for just over 50 per cent of the FN Ltd, which itself controlled 51 per cent of the *FT*. It was not an exorbitant price, granted that the paper (including St Clements Press) was already making a pre-tax profit of some £550,000, but Bracken informed Beaverbrook on 4 February that 'the Eyre family will make a vast profit' and added: 'A good business is the ownership of the *FT*. Ellerman made a big profit by selling to Camrose. He made a much bigger one by selling to the Eyres. They make twice as big a profit by selling to Cowdray.' Beaverbrook was unconvinced and growled back five days later: 'I am sorry that Cowdray has bought the *Financial Times*. It would have been much better in the hands of the Eyre family.'[2]

In a sense the Beaver missed the point, or at least the underlying logic.

Relations between owner and management had become unsustainable; the Eyre family did not have the resources to develop the paper properly; the continuing presence of Bracken (and thus Moore) was indispensable to any deal with a would-be new owner; and the Cowdray interest was one of the very few that Bracken, still much upset by the turn of events, would have been willing to countenance as possible purchasers. Indeed, as it happened, Bracken as early as 1951 had paid a significant tribute in 'Men and Matters':

> The Cowdray family is a remarkable one. The present peer's grandfather founded the firm of S. Pearson and Sons, which was one of the most enterprising of its generation. It built bridges all over the world, it developed Mexican oil and it pioneered the production in electric light and power in South America . . .
>
> The present Lord Cowdray is a comparatively young man, and not at all handicapped by his loss of an arm in the service of his country. He is still a crack polo player.[3]

Two years later, in a letter to a friend, he described Cowdray as having 'a wonderful war record' and being 'a very sound steward of his manifold business affairs'.[4]

By the 1950s these affairs comprised five main spheres: oil and gas production (mainly in North America); banking and finance through Lazards; investment through the Whitehall Trust; industry through various specific holdings; and, the fifth pillar of the empire, publishing in the form of the Westminster Press, which since the 1920s had acquired a considerable body of local newspapers, including in recent years in the London area. Under John Cowdray's chairmanship the general approach of S. Pearson & Sons was by this time becoming one of concentrating on certain well-defined sectors and within them looking for specialist, preferably quality products that filled a certain niche in the market and could be gradually developed over a period of time. The company was still wholly private and it was able to adopt a long, relatively relaxed view towards its holdings. All of which meant that in 1957 the *FT* fitted the Pearson bill perfectly – not at all as a future gold-mine or indispensable provider of cash flow, but instead as a sound, conservative investment that it would be pleasant and rather fun to own, especially as it gave the City and the economy at large a unique service that deserved to be supported. Times would change and become less relaxed, but to the *FT*'s immeasurable benefit something of that philosophy was to persist.

In the course of 1957 two Pearson appointees joined the *FT* board. The first was R. P. T. ('Pat') Gibson, who had come to the Westminster Press as a trainee and risen fast to become editorial director. His impact was immediate and positive, as Moore was justly to record: 'His arrival on the scene was for me most welcome. He had a wide-ranging knowledge of the newspaper business, and a wise, robust and balanced approach to problems which was most refreshing.'[5] Gibson was also devoted to opera, which made for a further bond. The other appointee, from 24 September, was Oliver Poole. He was joint managing director of Pearson, had come up on the Lazards side, was in the House of Lords and was now deputy chairman of the Conservative Party, having been a highly effective chairman. During the 1950s he had become, and was to remain for a long time, Lord Cowdray's chief lieutenant and financial supremo. Some years later he was described by Anthony Sampson as 'very much a City figure in his own right, with a tall, aloof presence and a single intimidating eye', who 'speaks in epigrams and gives clipped decisive opinions punctuated by "y'know what I mean?", without much fear of contradiction'.[6] Poole was altogether a formidable person and on the *FT* board was soon elected deputy chairman to Bracken.

The change of ownership was announced baldly and without explanation on the front page of the *FT* of 5 February 1957. After noting that S. Pearson Industries Ltd had acquired a controlling interest in the Financial News Ltd and the Financial Times Ltd, the statement concluded: 'Lord Bracken will remain as chairman of these two companies, and their management and policy continue exactly as at present.' It was a necessary and scrupulously upheld rider, as Moore some twenty years later testified:

> There was a clear risk that if a group controlling a leading merchant bank also controlled the only exclusively business-orientated newspaper, criticism would arise. It was therefore important that Pearsons should go out of their way not to interfere at all in the policy of the paper. They had given Bracken a categorical assurance to this effect, and I can say with absolute conviction that they never did so. Indeed, from a staff relations point of view it might be argued that they went too far in this respect, for John Cowdray himself was conspicuously absent. His determination not to interfere almost seemed to us in the office an attitude of aloofness. He seldom came near us, and this we regretted. It may have been his noted shyness, but I think it was more his desire not to be accused of interference.[7]

Poole and Gibson were both powerful figures at board level, but both fully subscribed to the guiding Pearson principle, established by the first Lord Cowdray, that each holding should be allowed a high degree of autonomy in its management, while maintaining access, in principle, to the capital resources of the whole. From a specifically editorial point of view, a certain regret about the more impersonal character of the new ownership was more than outweighed by satisfaction at the continuing absence of editorial interference, together with a gradually dawning realization that Pearson offered the paper a potential that had not been available before. Describing the 1960s, Newton later put it well: 'The advent of the Pearson interests had in some indefinable way brought a new dimension to the *FT*. It was an attitude of mind rather than any definite act which caused this but it was there and could be felt none the less.'[8] The process of broadening and expanding was already well under way before Bracken and Crosthwaite-Eyre fell out, but the new attitude of mind underwrote a continuing, even accelerating momentum and ensured that there was no turning back.

Ten months after Pearson acquired the controlling interest, Bracken in December 1957 delivered what was to be his swan-song address. Appropriately, he summed up in it the *FT*'s post-war achievements:

Profit for the year at £724,410 is about £172,000 more than it was in the previous year. This is a pleasing but hardly surprising result.

It would indeed be surprising if in good times we did not gain something from the expansionist or 'transformation' policy we formed in 1946, and have followed ever since. This policy has required large plough-backs from heavily taxed profits and what might be described as a good deal of brain bruising by an able and energetic editorial and managerial staff.

There were, of course, some risks inherent in this policy. It is not easy and it is generally unwise to try to change the character of newspapers, more especially if the change requires the introduction of much apparently forbidding statistical material and much serious writing on applied science, currency, engineering, and other obviously unalluring matters. A decade ago we thought that there was a place for a first-rate daily industrial newspaper in Britain which would report or explain technical developments in simple, lively English. Dullness is not a hallmark of seriousness: knowledge and liveliness go well together.

Time has shown that the paper we planned in 1946 attracts readers in ever-increasing numbers at home and abroad. Industrial and commercial businesses, who in number must now run into thousands, rate the *Financial Times* as a first-rate advertisement medium.[9]

Indisputably the *FT* was becoming a force to be reckoned with in the quality market. At the time that Bracken spoke, the paper's circulation of 84,000 was more than 40 per cent higher than what it had been in 1949; whereas over the same period, the circulation of the *Daily Telegraph* had risen by 12½ per cent and that of *The Times* had fallen. It was a situation that a few months earlier had prompted the editor of *The Times*, Sir William Haley, to write the following internal memorandum:

The main impression is that *The Times* is predominantly a political paper. Politics are undoubtedly important. The world has probably never been on the boil in so many places at once . . . At the same time the world is struggling to move away from any exclusive pre-occupation with politics. This is particularly true of the new generation. There is a growing interest everywhere in science, in technology, in economics, in artistic movements and so on . . .

The first serious newspaper which wakes up to this trend and deliberately sets out developing it, will lead the way. *The Times* should be that paper.[10]

Such was Haley's vision, approximately ten years after Hargreaves Parkinson had started to put a similar one into practice in the *FT*. It was a decade that made all the difference: by the late 1950s the *FT* had arrived to stay as a quality national paper and could not be shifted.

Thus things continued to go well during the second year under Pearson and the final phase of Bracken's chairmanship. Profits for the eighteen months ending 31 December 1958 were £1,052,618; circulation for the second half of 1958 was above 86,000; advertisement columnage for the year was a record 12,569, compared with 11,154 in 1956, which in itself had been a record. More than half of the advertisement revenue in 1958 took the form of industrial and other types of display advertising. There was, however, a small portent that year of a later revolution, in the shape of one or two Eurodollar market 'tombstone' advertisements appearing for the first time in the paper, to record foreign government issues such as the $17,500,000 bond issue for the Kingdom of Norway. This market, still tiny, was to grow significantly following the establishment of sterling convertibility at the end of 1958 and later the imposition in the United States of Federal Reserve restrictions, especially the notorious Regulation Q; but it was not until 1970 that the advertisements of record which the market generated (called 'tombstones' because of their appearance) became a major enough form of income to justify a separate category in the accounts of the *FT*'s advertising department. In other words, from the point of view of revenue and thus inevitably editorial direction, the 'industrial' design attributed by Bracken to 1946 still remained dominant through the 1960s, at least until the 'foreign' take-off later that decade.

Meanwhile, back in 1957–8, there were more immediate matters in hand. In 1957 Leslie Dearlove retired as general manager and was succeeded by Jim Hunter, who, reconciled now to not becoming editor, proved a great success in his new position, did much to promote staff welfare and acted as an important and hitherto absent link between the editorial and the business sides of the paper. People came to him with their problems in ever greater numbers; he thoroughly knew the ropes of the newspaper business and altogether was the ideal right-hand man of the more mercurial managing director, acting almost as a nanny figure. Moore himself succeeded as Earl of Drogheda in November 1957 and soon afterwards came near to leaving the paper. He was offered a position with great potential by the merchant banker Siegmund Warburg and wrote to Bracken in South Africa to tell him of the offer. Part of Bracken's lengthy reply was as follows:

> Remembering all I owe to you and the happiness I've derived from our long partnership I must stifle very selfish feelings and advise you to seize this rare opportunity.
>
> Working for shareholders in a large public company will never enable you to create capital. The only way (it's hardly ever to be found) is to come across a rich, international enterpriser many of whose doings are outside Britain and the lawful jurisdiction of Somerset House.
>
> Your going from the *FT* must be a very sharp loss. No one can swiftly take your place and you will long be missed and will yourself miss things for which you care. But you have to think of the advantage to Joan and Derry of your getting that rare thing called capital – some of it, I hope, not in sterling.
>
> Dear G. newspaper life will never be what it was before. I shall always miss you.

Whether consciously or not, it was a masterly letter that tugged at Drogheda's heart-strings and, as he later put it, 'of course had the effect of confirming me in my deeply felt instinct that I could not move elsewhere'.[11]

On the editorial side, Hunter's move 'upstairs' led to the creation of a tier of deputy editors in the persons of Roger, York and Rees-Mogg, of whom Roger was the most senior, while York remained in charge of news and Rees-Mogg was responsible in departmental terms for both leaders and features, though without being features editor as such. Staff turnover during 1957–8 was quite high. Trafford left in order to run a new *FT* subsidiary called Industrial & Trade Fairs Ltd, which achieved its greatest fame through arranging the British Exhibition at Moscow in 1961; Shonfield became economics editor at the *Observer*; Granger decided to try his hand at television with Granada and bowed out with a typically sparkling notice of *My Fair Lady* ('delicious, perfectly delicious'); and Dick Wilson after three years on the paper, latterly as labour correspondent after Shanks had succeeded Trafford as industrial editor, left to edit the *Far Eastern Economic Review* and start his career as a notable expert on that part of the world.

During this period five recruits stand out, all educated at Oxford, but not all direct intake. Two were future editors: M. H. ('Fredy') Fisher had been a diplomatic historian and soon became an important figure on the foreign side of the paper; while Geoffrey Owen, joining some eighteen months later in September 1958, was recruited to the features department almost in spite of his strikingly handsome appearance, although Newton was probably favourably impressed by his sporting prowess as well as his academic record. The other three were Patrick Hutber, who came at the suggestion of Nigel Lawson, wielded a trenchant if not always statistically precise pen and like Lawson subsequently became City editor of the *Sunday Telegraph*; Robert Oakeshott, who was soon complementing Fisher on the foreign side; and thirdly, John Higgins, who on the *FT* and then *The Times* was to become a justly renowned arts page editor. To these and other recruits of the time Newton was still a somewhat intimidating figure. Once when Oakeshott got in a muddle over the weekly coal figures, in the course of spending a year as a labour reporter, he received a severe rap on the knuckles. Yet at the same time Newton could bend over backwards to help; every day for his first three or four months Fisher took his putative copy to Newton, who painstakingly taught him how to construct and write a news story. Above all, he visibly *cared*, about the quality of the paper and the accuracy of the stories it carried. There was no more valuable lesson he could pass on to his young or youngish hopefuls.

The *FT* continued to evolve steadily, very much at Newton's own pace and in his own style. When Anthony Vice as features editor suggested that a feature on jam be called 'The Public Preserve', Newton shot down the title on the grounds that he did not understand it and instead suggested 'The Declining Consumption of Jam and Marmalade'; so it was. In general, industrial coverage remained the predominant forward thrust of the paper – including in the spring of 1958 a series of features on leaders of British industry, followed in July by the inclusion of the 'Annual Review of British Industry' in the main body of the paper – but there were other growth areas as well. 'Architecture To-Day' under Trystan Edwards, now abetted by Kenneth Swan on the commercial side, had found a new source of strength in Britain's power-stations, nuclear and otherwise. 'The Arts' had become a daily heading by the spring of 1958 and found a home in the top right-hand corner of the penultimate page, above a sea of prices. New critics included T. C. Worsley on theatre, David Robinson on cinema and Clement Crisp on ballet. Arthur Bennett in September 1958 began a weekly column called 'News from the Retail Shops', anticipating the paper's future consumer coverage. On the political side, Ronald Butt had succeeded Einzig and was starting greatly to expand and

THE FINANCIAL TIMES

INCORPORATING THE FINANCIAL NEWS

INDUSTRY • COMMERCE • PUBLIC AFFAIRS

No. 21,086 LONDON TUESDAY FEBRUARY 12 1957 FOURPENCE

NEWS SUMMARY

PREMIER FOR BERMUDA

BRIGGS TALKS FAIL

SHOP STEWARD NOT TO BE REINSTATED

RISK OF OFFICIAL STRIKE BY 21 UNIONS

By Our Labour Correspondent

Ford Motor Company yesterday flatly refused to withdraw its dismissal of Mr. J. McLoughlin, the Briggs Motor Bodies shop steward who called an unofficial strike.

This means that the company now faces the risk of an official strike by the 21 trade unions with members at Ford's. These include the three biggest unions in the country—the Transport and General Workers, Amalgamated Engineering Union and the General and Municipal Workers.

Yesterday's decision was made in reply to what is described as a "very strong plea" by leaders of the main unions concerned. It represents the end of the negotiating procedure.

Who Pays the Rates?

How Rates Have Risen	
1956	22s 2d
1955	22s 1d
1950	17s 3d
1945	12s 11d
1939	12s 3d

	New List*	Old List
Houses, flats	54	60
Shops	11	11
Offices	23	21
Industry	7	4
Other	5	4

*Since April 1, 1956.

Rates produced £476m. in 1955.

U.K.'s TRADE GAP RISES TO £104M. IN JANUARY

HIGHEST EVER LEVEL OF IMPORTS

By Our Industrial Correspondent

The full impact of the Suez crisis on shipping schedules was revealed last night in the publication of the U.K.'s foreign trade figures for January.

Imports, which had fallen back in November and December, while the arrival of ships re-routed round the Cape was awaited, rose to £376.2m. in January—the highest figure ever recorded.

TRADE FIGURES COMPARED

	1957 January†	1956 December	1956 January
	£m.	£m.	£m.
Exports (f.o.b.)*	272.7	264.9	272.1
Imports (c.i.f.)	376.2	307.8	346.3
Adverse balance	103.6	42.9	74.2

* Including re-exports. † Provisional.

BIG FUNDING ISSUE

£300M. OF 3½% STOCK AT 80

RE-RATING OF INDUSTRY

TO-DAY'S COMMONS STATEMENT

NOTES FOR INVESTORS

IRREGULAR TREND IN MARKETS

THE SEARS' BID FOR SHAW & KILBURN

By LEX

PETROL STOCKS LITTLE BELOW YEAR AGO

By Our Parliamentary Correspondent

As a result of rationing and by the co-operation of all classes of consumer, stocks of petrol in the U.K. are now only a little below the level of a year ago, Mr. Reginald Maudling, Paymaster-General, stated in the Commons yesterday.

NEW YORK DOCK STRIKE TO-DAY

OTHER PORTS MAY ALSO BE HIT

O.E.E.C. TALKS TO-DAY ON FREE TRADE AREA

From Our Own Correspondent

PARIS, Feb. 11.

The meeting of the O.E.E.C. Council of Ministers which opens here to-morrow will be invited to agree in principle to the plan for setting up a European free trade area.

U.S. REFINERIES OUTPUT CUT

GERMAN CEMENT PRICE RAISED

MARKET NOTES AND INDEX

INDEX TO FEATURES

CHIEF PRICE CHANGES YESTERDAY

12 February 1957: the first 'News Summary' with a globe

deepen the coverage, including becoming one of the earliest political correspondents to attend Labour Party conferences, hitherto usually the monopoly of labour correspondents.

The *FT*'s political antennae, however, still needed some fine tuning. A fairly detailed report of Macmillan's speech at Bedford in July 1957 completely failed to mention his assertion that 'you've never had it so good'. One might have expected the phrase to have turned up in the page-one 'News Summary', which that February had become a formal column on the left-hand side of the page, complete with a drawing of a globe on top. It was a globe that proved an irresistible temptation when the Soviet Union launched Sputnik on 4 October that same year. On the 5th a dot appeared by the globe, succeeded from the 11th by a small, satellite-looking shape that was in a slightly different place each day. From 3 November there were two such shapes, following the launch of Sputnik II, but on the 15th they disappeared, even though the satellites themselves were still orbiting. Bracken had at last noticed these extra-terrestrials and called an end to the fun.

It was during these years that the paper for the first time appointed full-time staff correspondents to Paris and Washington, in the persons of 'Jock' Bruce-Gardyne and Robert Heller respectively. Heller during his three years in the United States capital received precisely two communications from Newton: early on a request to relax the 'cablese'; and after the Presidential election of 1960 a telegram stating, 'Your election coverage excellent.' In terms of day-to-day foreign coverage, there was, under George Bull as foreign news editor, half a page of 'Commonwealth and Foreign' news each day under the Wall Street prices, expanding by the end of 1958 to a full page on most days. Arthur Bennett, meanwhile, had begun in April 1958 yet another column, 'On Sale in the U S', culled from material sent by a correspondent called Larry Stuntz. In October that year Nigel Lawson, who had succeeded Vice as features editor, initiated what was to be a valuable annual feature on 'The Cost of Living round the World', based on information sent from correspondents abroad and revealing Caracas to be the priciest capital city. There was still a long way to go, but occasionally the foreign coverage achieved genuine distinction, as on the Soviet Union's scientific and technological achievement during the Soviet *annus mirabilis* of 1957 – coverage that embraced aviation successes as well as Sputniks and included an article on 'I. V. Kurchatov, the leading Russian atomic scientist', which was full of praise for that country's organization of scientific research work. Newton, however, remained characteristically cautious; when Wilson, shortly before deciding to leave, suggested himself as Commonwealth correspondent, to cover the world outside Europe and the United States, he was told that the time was not yet ripe for such a position, but might eventually become so. The editor would not, in a word, try running until the paper was walking properly. Arguably, this particularly applied to the foreign side, where Newton's hunches and instincts were less developed.

In the wider policy-making domain, this was a period dominated by the legacy of Suez and its stern lessons – lessons that bore equally on Britain's domestic economy and the country's place in the world, with the two often inextricably bound. Thus on New Year's Day 1957 the *FT* declared that, in the context of the 'unremitting challenge' of 'permanent technological revolution' (an ironic nod to Trotsky), the basic decision was going to have to be made 'whether the United Kingdom's resources are to be devoted primarily to our own industrial investment or to those of the sterling area'. The leader made clear what its choice would be, arguing that 'high investment is the only policy which will enable Britain to overcome the problems which now confront her'. Three months later there was a predictable welcome for the reforming White Paper on defence: 'The attempt to carry a huge defence commitment with little regard to changing needs was both economically damaging and provided too little value in terms of national security, or the ability to conduct a campaign. The Suez episode was a demonstration of that.' Unlike *The Times* a year earlier, however, the leader failed to raise a questioning voice about the cost and efficacy of the independent deterrent, nor indeed even mentioned it in an otherwise thorough review of the defence programme. A similar silence pervaded the paper about a year later during and after the CND's famous Aldermaston march of Easter 1958. Partly due to Professor Simon's influence, the *FT* had been since the late 1940s a stong advocate of the civil use of nuclear energy; but when it came to the military aspect, it still apparently lacked the confidence to express an opinion.

Altogether more tangible and nearer to the paper's traditional concerns, if at times highly confusing, was the question of Europe, which the *FT* continued for the most part to perceive in essentially economic terms. For many months the conventional British wisdom remained that political obstacles (including United States and Commonwealth) to membership of the EEC were insuperable and that a plausible alternative strategy lay in the more narrowly economic European Free Trade Association, which would embrace those inside as well as outside the Common Market and in which Britain would take the lead. It was a wisdom to which the *FT* subscribed. Thus in July 1957, four months after the Treaty of Rome and in the immediate wake of the Commonwealth Prime Ministers' Conference, a leader on 'The Link' looked ahead still hopefully to a future in which EFTA had taken its rightful place:

There can surely be no doubt that British policy must not be focused either on the Commonwealth or on Europe to the exclusion of the other. Now that the whole idea of Commonwealth economic expansion has been given fresh life, while the new system in Europe is being created, British economic statesmanship is offered the greatest opportunities. The penalty for failure would be high, but if Britain can link Europe and the Commonwealth, helping to expand the trade of both and between both, then the rewards of success will be almost immeasurably great.

The rather cosy dream lasted until late in 1958, when France rejected the struggling-to-be-born EFTA and in effect divided Europe into two economic camps, of which the EEC was by far the stronger. The *FT* reacted to the threatened 'trade war' with a mixture of old-fashioned bluster and implicit sympathy for the wider European idea:

On the Continent it is still widely believed, almost as an article of faith, that the root cause [of the division] is British hostility to the Common Market. Such a belief has no foundation in fact. Successive British Governments have – for whatever reasons – fought shy of joining in moves towards European integration, but that does not mean that they have not welcomed them . . .

Palmerston once said: 'We have no eternal allies; our interests are eternal, and those interests it is our duty to follow.' Chancellor Adenauer and General de Gaulle would do well to ponder these words. If they pursue a policy which excludes Britain from Europe, they may not find it easy to persuade this country to reverse course when it is in their interest that it should.[12]

It was about this time, or soon afterwards, that Newton made a European tour in which he met Robert Schuman and others. Between them they converted him, on largely political grounds, from being a Little Englander into a supporter of European unity, above all as a means of preventing future warfare on the Continent. Backed at home by the enthusiasm of Fredy Fisher (who was of a German Jewish background), it became one of the *FT*'s few 'causes'.

To a greater extent than ever before, however, national attention by the late 1950s focused on the occupant of No. 11 Downing Street. The country's economic problems and progress were becoming front-page news in all papers and being widely discussed on radio and television, in the process inevitably raising the prestige (and pay) of economic journalists and their craft. In April 1957 Peter Thorneycroft prepared to deliver his first Budget and was told by the *FT* that 'the Chancellor can put expansion first or he can put sterling first, but he cannot put them both first'. The leader continued:

Of course in the end one has to come down on the side of economic expansion. It must not be heedless expansion, it must not be expansion through reckless inflation. But it must depend on the view that, whatever the economic difficulties, a steady rise in production is the only humane and realistic aim in an industrial society. The Chancellor may have been warned by the Treasury that such a policy involves risks. There are risks whichever way he turns. He should take his chosen and calculated risks on the side of growth.[13]

Thorneycroft did not heed this advice. 'The overall balance of his Budget is disinflationary', the *FT* noted a few days later, 'and its main purpose must be taken as the short-term support of sterling rather than the expansion of the economy. This may be a matter for regret.' Characteristically, however, the leader added that the Chancellor was not to be damned: 'Concessions which encourage inflation are in the end no concessions at all.' Five months later Thorneycroft raised Bank Rate to 7 per cent and imposed various credit squeeze measures, cuts and so on, all in order to defend sterling, but this time did not receive the semi-benefit of the doubt. Not only was it possible that foreign opinion might see the dramatic hike in Bank Rate (the highest rate since the early 1920s) 'not as a favourable indication of British determination, but as an unfavourable indication of the seriousness of the British difficulties', but also 'as an economic policy for the future his measures do not take us very far', in that 'apart from exchange speculation the weakness of the British economy rises largely from the constant pressure of trade union demands'.

In January 1958, preferring to be hung for a lamb rather than a sheep, Thorneycroft (and two other Treasury ministers) resigned over a question of public expenditure. The *FT*'s leader the next day was unsympathetic, arguing that the Cabinet had 'gone a long way towards meeting the Chancellor's point of view' and that 'the sum of £50 million seems small to set beside the shock to the sterling system which the resignations could involve'. The new Chancellor was already announced as Heathcoat Amory, under whom the paper looked forward to an economic policy 'somewhat more expansionist, but inside the limits set by confidence in the pound'. There of course lay the rub, but two days later the *FT* categorically disavowed one possible way out: 'Any devaluation of sterling with its world-wide repercussions on the under-developed areas would be a major economic victory for Communism.'

The *FT*'s sanguine attitude towards Thorneycroft's resignation contrasted notably with that of *The Times*. That paper's leader (written by Maurice Green) was called 'Flinching', blamed Macmillan for not having supported his 'courageous' Chancellor and asserted that 'if ever there was a point at which the Treasury team had to stand on a matter of principle, this was it'.[14] The following Tuesday in the *FT*, Harold Wincott took a similar line:

Mr Thorneycroft last October said very publicly in America that one aspect of the Keynesian doctrine had gone overboard. No longer, he said, would internal policies take precedence over the external value of the currency. 'What this episode [i.e. Thorneycroft finding himself in a minority in the Cabinet] has made plain', said Lord Hailsham last week, 'is that we are none the less determined to adhere to our social policies.' There you have it. Mr Thorneycroft's policy, if you like, makes him a hard-faced, hard money man. That makes two of us (at least).

Wincott then elucidated the context of 'the realities of our position in 1958', before concluding in characteristically vernacular-cum-portentous tones:

In the ultimate resort, if Mr Amory is not to be as expendable as Mr Thorneycroft was, it is the attitude of mind in the Conservative Party which has got to change. For over six years now, that attitude has been the 'Dear-Mother-I-am-going-to-save-7*s*. 6*d*.-but-not-this-week' attitude. It still is. But the supply of weeks is running out.[15]

Events in the spring of 1958 confirmed that the paper itself could go some but not all of the way with its Tuesday columnist. On 12 April a leader argued in 'hard' enough fashion that 'the decision reached in the railway wages issue will either mean that as a country Britain is condemned to an indefinite period of wage inflation or that it has the strength to resist it' and that 'if the Government gives way it will open up the road to all the rest of the unions'. Attention then turned to Amory's first Budget, which the *FT* hoped would offer 'a few measures in the direction of increasing demand', but which disappointingly turned out to be 'as self-effacing as the temperament of the Chancellor himself'. However, the paper's criticism was only mild: 'Moderation was itself the right policy, even if the Chancellor's moderation may have been a little overdone.'[16] Economic historians have subsequently argued that this was when Amory should have gone for full-blown expansion, rather than a year later; but at the time the gnomes of Zurich (as they were starting to be called) still loomed large, including to the financial press. Yet a month later, when the railwaymen received a fairly generous pay award, there were no tears shed:

A speech a few days ago by Lord Chandos made what are in fact the essential points. He said that labour would in fact get 'dearer and dearer', and, whether we like it or not, that will happen. He said that labour had the 'right to demand' less effort for a given output and better working conditions. He said that this was not a matter for regret or despondency but that it could only be met by increased productivity and increased mechanisation. It is still right to urge restraint; it is still right to maintain a cautious economic policy, but from now on to sacrifice increased productivity to the delusive and unattainable objective of a wages freeze would show a complete inability to learn from repeated experience.[17]

Practical acceptance of practical circumstances, within a larger social and political reality, was gradually becoming the norm, as the affluent, Butskellite road to 1959 and beyond beckoned.

One particular episode of this high policy-making came directly into contact with the *FT* and caused the paper's ailing chairman much anxiety. This was the famous Bank Rate 'leak' when, in the aftermath of Thorneycroft's announcement in September 1957, the Labour opposition accused various merchant banks – including Lazards – of having made illicit gains through advance knowledge of the steep rise. The charges led to the establishment of a tribunal of inquiry, which reported in January 1958 and entirely cleared the names of the bankers under suspicion, including Oliver Poole. The tribunal also considered whether there had been any unauthorized leaks to the press. It transpired that on 18 September, the day before the announcement, Thorneycroft had seen various newspaper representatives, including Moore, and told them that restrictive financial measures were in the offing, but without giving details. Moore then told Newton of the interview, but no hint of impending measures appeared in the earlier editions of the next day's paper. However, Newton late on the evening of the 18th read the first edition of the *Daily Telegraph*, where there was an intimation of an announcement, and wrote a brief article along similar lines (referring to 'an early whisper'), though not allowing it to appear in the later editions until his political correspondent had got the go-ahead for it from a Treasury official. Two aspects of the whole affair rankled from the *FT*'s point of view and in particular Bracken's. Firstly, as he wrote to Moore, 'Thorneycroft's performance in trying to by-pass Newton is inexplicable and a just cause of strong resentment by the *FT*.'[18] Secondly, and more importantly, Bracken was greatly perturbed that the paper's independence was now compromised by the fact of being owned by the same company that owned Lazards. In the event, neither the tribunal nor the Labour Party dwelt on the link as they might have done – and of course the conduct of Lazards was vindicated – but there is no doubt that the episode considerably affected Bracken.

He also continued to worry himself about the new building, which in the course of 1957 began to rise from the mud and mess of 'our hole', as the *FT* staff were wont to call it as they wandered over from Coleman Street at lunchtime to view progress. By November 1957 the contractors were roughly six months behind schedule, and, the story goes, this was attributed by some to a militant foreman on the site who was the brother of Brendan Behan. By 1958 the basic structure was up, but there was still plenty to do and decide. Thus Bracken in July received from Richardson an estimate for furnishing part of the sixth floor and on the 11th sent his response to the company secretary Arthur Knock:

> The Professor wanted me to say that this estimate should be accepted at sight. I say 'no'. We should get some competition in estimating. £3,000 is a lot of money to spend on the furnishing of two rooms.
>
> I hope, therefore, you will see that all largish projects at the *FT* building are put out to competition among a limited number of firms of acknowledged craftsmanship.

The letter was written from the Westminster Hospital and was one of Bracken's last. He had been suffering greatly for at least a year or two; the sight of him at Coleman Street lunches eating a boiled egg tipped into a cup and clutching his throat after each spoonful had been a painful one. In January 1958 his doctors had formally diagnosed cancer of the throat. By June he was in hospital, but soon after his letter to Knock he moved to the flat of a friend of his – Patrick Hennessy, chairman of Fords – that overlooked Hyde Park. And there, on 8 August 1958, he died at the age of fifty-seven.

Bracken had borne his last illness bravely, but in many ways it had been, as Newton later wrote, a pitiful death – 'pitiful not only for the nature of the disease but for the loneliness, apart from a few faithful friends, with which he had surrounded himself'.[19] The tributes flowed in. Perhaps the most apposite in an *FT* context was the one printed in *The Times* from Sir Geoffrey Crowther, for many years editor of the *Economist*:

> He mastered the very difficult act of being a newspaper proprietor. His editors, once appointed and trusted, knew that they had in him the perfect shield against all pressures and influences. He would advise (rarely) but never insist, and would remember to send the word of support when it was chiefly needed; the only prohibitions he imposed were against anything in the nature of personal publicity

for himself. Not that working with Brendan was pure joy – no one could be more infuriating about small things. But on all important matters he could be utterly relied upon, and if any of his colleagues found himself in a real difficulty, personal or professional, he could be sure of getting from Brendan not only generous help but unquestioning support.[20]

The board of the *FT* paid its own tribute by deciding to name the new building Bracken House, which he certainly would not have allowed in his own lifetime. He himself had suggested calling the building the Octagon on account of the distinctive shape of the central printing area, but as Drogheda has rightly observed, 'it would have conveyed little to the outside world, and our choice after his death was surely very much better'.[21]

For those in Coleman Street, there is no doubt that the passing of Bracken, untimely though it was in one sense, came as a considerable relief. It had, in Drogheda's words, 'the effect of lifting a heavy dark cloud from our heads, while in no way affecting the love and sense of gratitude which we felt towards him'.[22] The relief was understandable. Over recent years he had become increasingly morose and withdrawn; it had become hard to discuss matters rationally and objectively with him; in short, he had represented a significant obstacle to further growth and expansion. By contrast, the new owners were somewhat alarmed, having bought the paper less than two years previously on the strength at least as much of the name and stature of the chairman as of the *FT* itself. It took a year or two for Pearson fully to reconcile themselves to their Bracken-less acquisition, though shortly after Bracken's death Poole (who now became chairman) did come round to Coleman Street to indicate to senior editorial staff the willingness of Pearson to carry on. Much hinged at this time on the generally harmonious relations established between Poole and Gibson on the one hand and Drogheda on the other. Subsequently a certain underlying tension developed – caused by Drogheda's resentment at not having the ultimate power – but in the late 1950s and through most of the 1960s the relationship worked extremely well, as Poole and Gibson appreciated the qualities of their managing director, gave him a more or less free hand and sat back and watched the generally satisfactory results.

It was in fact the 'benchmark' issue of Wednesday 29 October 1958 that announced that Poole had been elected chairman. This particular issue of the *FT* was eighteen pages long and showed some signs of unassimilated growth, with two or three distinctly messy-looking pages. Page seven was the worst: two company-meeting reports, a dozen miscellaneous home and foreign news items and a handful of display advertisements – all thrown together in seemingly unplanned, higgledy-piggledy fashion. On other pages, however, the use of shoulder-heads helped to give the paper an appreciably sharper feel than it had had five years earlier. This issue also had a rather pleasing leader page: on the left, two columns of leaders (still alongside rather than on top of each other); in the centre, four 'Company Topics' at the foot, with above features on the second-hand car market and Canada's oil policy; and on the right, letters to the editor and an advertisement for Leyland Motors. Dominating the second half of the page, apart from Stock Exchange dealings and prices, was a three-page inset on metals that were starting to become important industrially, with most of the articles written by members of the ICI metals division. Also catching the eye were Wragge-Morley's 'Scientists' Notebook'; 'On Sale in the US'; and 'Your Business Problems', a high-powered version of Saturday's 'Finance and the Family' and almost equally popular. In the 'Arts and Entertainment' (as it was now called) quarter-page, Andrew Porter contributed a lengthy review of a new book about Bartók. Altogether, it was a solid and informative fourpennies' worth. What it missed, perhaps, was the human touch. When about a fortnight later Tyrone Power died on the set of *Queen of Sheba*, the *FT* covered it with a small piece by its insurance correspondent that was headed: 'Film Star's Death: Re-Filming Cost to Insurers $1m'. Subsequently there appeared in *Queen* an article about how the different papers had reacted to the news. Newton was shown the article and was mildly horrified, saying, 'Are we really so inhuman?'

Still, his mind was perhaps elsewhere, for during the last weeks of 1958 and first few days of 1959 there took place the epic 'Aluminium War', which was arguably the single great set-piece episode in the City's post-war history and certainly the first of the major contested take-over bids. The war fell into three distinct phases. The first began, at least in public, on 27 November, when British Aluminium issued a statement announcing that 'discussions are taking place with other parties in the industry, the outcome of which is as yet uncertain'. The following morning, 'Lex' in the person of Arthur Winspear analysed the statement. He described it as 'masterly only in its vagueness', hazarded a guess (ahead of anyone else in the press) that BA was the subject of a bid by Tube Investments and concluded: 'One thing is certain – the sooner the British Aluminium Board makes its further announcement the better.' The next day Winspear considered another statement issued by BA. Obviously anxious to avoid the embrace of TI, it now proposed that the Aluminium Company of America should subscribe for the company's £4.5 million unissued ordinary capital. 'Lex' was unimpressed: 'The issue of authorised but unissued capital other than to existing shareholders is rarely defensible, and certainly does not appear defensible in this case.' Over the next few days TI made public the nature and timing of the offer it had made to BA a month earlier, and Winspear in his column made much of the fact that in the week beginning 10 November the BA board had entered into an agreement with Alcoa without consulting its shareholders and despite an offer from TI having been received. On 6 December the *FT*'s leader columns endorsed Winspear's criticisms of the BA board, arguing that, although 'no precise definitions can be laid down' and 'these decisions are all a matter of degree', nevertheless 'the whole instinct of the City of London is that there are some matters so substantial in their bearing on the life of the company that full disclosure in advance to the shareholders is essential'. In sum: 'That is an instinct which it is right to defend.'

The next phase began a week later when TI posted its offer direct to BA stockholders. Winspear naturally devoted his column to it, which he considered to be a good one in the short term, while as for the long term: 'It is the handicap of the BA Board, as it must presumably recognize, that it has so far been able to put forward only vague statements to support its argument that holders will eventually be better off by sticking with the company.' Four days later, on 19 December, the BA board announced that, if the Alcoa deal went through, it would increase the 1958 dividend from 12 to 17½ per cent. Winspear, however, still thought the TI position the stronger, though he added: 'With both sides so desperate to win, shareholders should certainly take no action yet.' Two days later he was still looking for more information from the BA board, demanding that 'it should come forward with its appreciation of how profits are likely to develop [i.e. after the proposed Alcoa deal], even if it has to hedge any estimate round with assumptions about costs, etc.' In the same issue of the *FT* there appeared for the second time in a week a half-page advertisement by BA recommending rejection of the TI offer, due to close on 9 January. It was the start of defensive advertising, which was to become an art form.

After a brief Yuletide break, the final and most dramatic phase of the war began on New Year's Eve when fourteen of the City's senior financial institutions, including Lazards and the Whitehall Trust, informed BA shareholders by letter not only that they themselves held two million shares in BA but also that they were prepared to buy shares at four shillings above the TI offer. The consortium added that the TI bid (backed as it was by the US firm Reynolds Metals) should be opposed in the 'national interest', rather ignoring the equally American Alcoa aspect

Hargreaves Parkinson, editor of the *FN* and *FT*

Lord Drogheda, late 1950s

Gordon Newton soon after becoming editor, 1950

The bombed-out site of Bracken House soon after the war

A later version of the 'Games man'
(reproduced by permission of Abram Games)

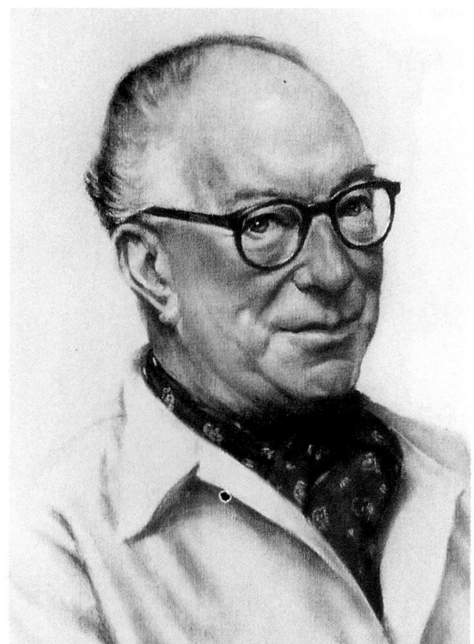

Sidney Henschel, advertisement director

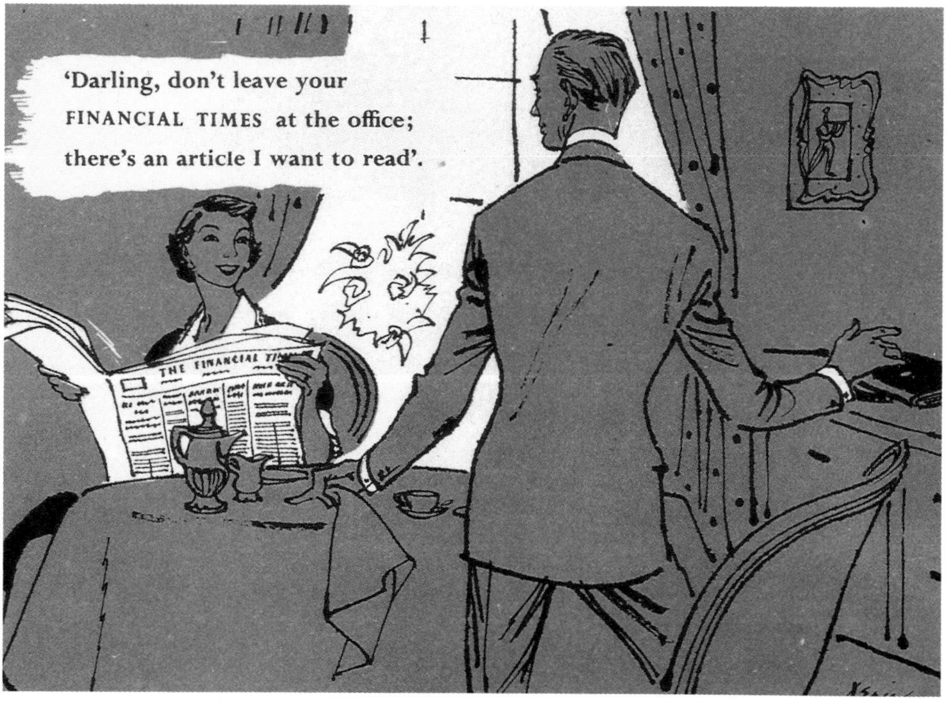
'Darling, don't leave your
FINANCIAL TIMES at the office;
there's an article I want to read'.
THE FINANCIAL TIMES

Illustration from publicity brochure, 1953

Newton in the early 1960s

Newton and his news team: Ben Kipling, Doug York, Cyril Ubsdell

Harold Wincott

Drogheda shortly before his retirement

of the BA alternative. 'Gloves Off in the BA Fight' was the headline to the first 'Lex' column of 1959. In it Winspear remained non-commital: 'Quite clearly, holders should do nothing until all the hands have been revealed.' The next day, the 2nd, the *FT* devoted its main leader – 'This Has Gone Far Enough' – to the war. It began: 'The British Aluminium dispute has now reached a stage at which it could do serious damage to the interests of the City of London. The two sides now seem to be in a mood of considerable material bitterness and recrimination.' It went on: 'This mood of ill-feeling . . . is building up grudges which should not exist between the leading institutions of the City.' Two days later TI, master-minded by the distinctly non-establishment, non-consortium Siegmund Warburg and Lionel Fraser, increased its offer. In the light of this, Winspear on the 5th at last offered his advice to BA stockholders on their best course of action: 'Few may now see the advantage of accepting the offer put forward last week by a syndicate of brokers and others, although some will remain shareholders of BA in principle.' Winspear's advice alone did not sway the issue, but it certainly had a significant effect. Three days later the *FT*'s main headline signalled the end of meaningful hostilities, although considerable acrimony lingered: 'TI – Reynolds gains control. Over 50 per cent held in British Aluminium.'

It had been a notable episode in the *FT*'s as well as the City's history. Winspear as 'Lex' had performed a *tour de force*, unearthing evidence, demanding information, offering stringent and unbiased analysis and throughout seeking to do his best on behalf of the shareholders of the company that was being bid for. It was the culmination of his several years on the column, and not long afterwards he left to become a merchant banker, appropriately with Warburgs. Still more important for the paper, however, was the proof that the episode gave that, following the change of ownership, the *FT*'s editorial independence remained sovereign. Granted the participation of both Lazards and the Whitehall Trust in the consortium there could hardly have been a more critical test of that independence, but at no point did Poole or Gibson seek to influence the paper's attitude towards the merits or otherwise of the TI bid. Nor after the rather ignominious failure of the consortium did either comment on the role that the *FT* had played in the outcome. As a result, Newton and Drogheda knew that in future they need have no fear of any editorial interference from Pearson – a rare privilege in the warped history of Fleet Street and its proprietors. The only pity was that Bracken was not alive to take reassurance.

Over the Easter weekend of 1959 the *FT* moved from Coleman Street to

Cannon Street. It was followed at Whitsun by St Clements Press, which found 100,000 square feet at its disposal in the new buildings, compared with 75,000 at Portugal Street. Early public reaction to Bracken House was at best mixed. A group of architectural students known as the 'anti-uglies' demonstrated outside the building in front of television cameras. Professor Richardson remained unrepentent:

This is one of the finest examples of modern brickwork in the world. It is based on the Palazzo Carignano in Turin. The red stone was chosen by Lord Bracken. But I agreed with it. Oh, yes, I agreed.

All this glass and concrete will be out of date in 100 years . . . My building is designed to last at least three or four hundred. Glass is much quicker and more expedient – but it has no drama.

I chose my materials to suit the atmospheric conditions of London. Bracken House will mellow in three or four years; London is kind to brick. But modern buildings don't mellow; they get dirty. These white concrete structures have already become crazed. Soon they'll be black.[23]

An outsider's view was that of Arthur Christiansen, a former long-standing editor of the *Daily Express*. Writing later in 1959, he admitted that he 'did not in the least like Bracken House on first sight', but went on:

Suddenly I found its point of beauty. As I passed St Paul's in my car the other night, I realised that for me the building needs to be seen from an angle. I got out of the car and walked back.

Head-on Bracken House was still a box – and not a very attractive box at that. But angled, it acquired depth and character, and unexpected simple beauty.

Just the same, Bracken House seems to be incongruous in the City of London. It ought to have been built in the middle of a park, where its pink bricks would tone with every season.

Against the mass of St Paul's it is a midget. Against the antiseptic sparkle of the Wiggins Teape building it looks rusty.

Christiansen concluded: 'For me, Bracken House is the right building in the wrong place.'[24]

Over the years, as more new buildings have gone up, opinion has warmed to Bracken House, and it has come to seem a rather splendid anachronism, surrounded by what Richardson called 'the monotonous repetition of cellular façades cloaked with vitreous indifference'. Quite apart from its general effect, it has been a building with much to admire about it: on the outside, for example, the marvellous astronomical clock, with its face of Churchill at the centre and its capacity to tell one almost everything except the time; while inside, one should mention the cinema downstairs and the well-proportioned entrance hall going up the height of two floors, both of which features Drogheda successfully insisted upon. Aesthetically the major disappointment was the colour of the building, which came out and remained much darker than Coventry Cathedral, the original inspiration for Bracken's choice of brickwork. In functional terms, there were two major drawbacks. One was the lack of proper air-conditioning, caused by Bracken's veto. It was a lack quickly felt, for 1959 turned out to be a sweltering summer. Drogheda recalls the unfortunate chain of events that resulted from Bracken's hasty decision:

Instead we installed a horrible thing called plenum ventilation, which warmed the air in winter, filling the offices with smuts in the process of its circulation, but failing to cool it in summer, and not cleaning it at all. Later we were obliged to install air conditioning into certain sections of the building, but it was piece-meal and costly; and resulted in some hideous metal excretions on the outside of the building, which Richardson would have loathed.[25]

The other mistake was the basic decision to have general printing, including monthly as well as weekly magazines, in such a prime site, when it could have been done equally easily, and much more cheaply, elsewhere. This general printing did not in the event last long in Bracken House, but it crucially determined the awkward design of the building and used up a great deal of space to unprofitable effect. But at the time it seemed the natural thing to do.

The *FT* staff generally welcomed the move. It made life much easier, in terms of sending copy and reading proofs, not to have to rely on motor-cyclists threading across London. It gave ever-expanding numbers room to breathe. It confirmed the success of the paper and helped to give it a sense of professionalism that had been missing before. It encouraged the growth of a more organized and structured approach, including the setting-up, still on a very small scale, of permanent committees, one of which dealt with the relentlessly burgeoning surveys. Not all of this, of course, was wholly welcome to everyone, while inevitably there lingered a certain nostalgia for the clubbiness of Coleman Street, where the very smallness and intimacy had encouraged a sense of common endeavour and intellectual ferment. One particular regret lay in management's decision not to reproduce in Bracken House the taking of afternoon tea in the canteen, which had been one of the great Coleman Street ceremonies. Instead, it was to be brought round on trolleys by tea-ladies, conveniently perhaps but at a certain loss to Socratic discussion. Nevertheless, it would be hard to quibble with the *FT*'s own sober verdict, delivered on the Easter Tuesday: 'The move is a symbol both of the much greater strength of the paper and of the expansion of its services.'

The year 1959 was fortunate for a financial paper committing itself so palpably to further growth. 'Forward in Confidence' was the title of the year's first leader, which, after noting with satisfaction the recent end of credit controls and the convertibility of sterling (with the latter's pleasing effects on the City's invisible earnings), declared that 'now, for the first time, it is possible to claim that the post-war period, with all its artificial pressures and constraints, is over and done with'. The stock market agreed, and the *FT* Index, which had been rising since the start of 1958, continued upwards almost without interruption. The *FT* responded by starting in March a new Saturday feature, 'What Readers Are Asking', in which investment queries were answered by the paper's Investment Bureau, which already provided a commercial service of replies not for publication. Meanwhile, the paper had also been looking ahead to Amory's Budget in April and warning him against a repeat of excessive caution: 'The right relationship between Chancellor and Treasury officials is perhaps that of a vigorous swashbuckler whom the officials contrive to restrain.'[26] The call was renewed on Budget day on 7 April, just over a week after the move to Bracken House: 'It is now necessary to raise consumption not only to expand the use of available resources and to raise the level of employment, but also to encourage confidence and investment.' Amory this time produced the goods, including £366 million of tax reliefs:

This Budget rests upon a number of assumptions. There is the need to encourage expansion, and the need to revive productive investment; there is the British contribution to restoring [after the U S recession of 1958] an expansion of world trade; there is the belief that the rising level of savings will permit the Government to meet even so large an overall deficit [estimated at £721 million for 1959–60] out of borrowing. The Chancellor must accept some risks in his policy. He himself forecasts that the gold reserves will fall somewhat this year on account of our repayments to the International Monetary Fund; he recognizes that in a period of expansion imports will start rising before exports; he does not expect our balance of payments surplus this year to be more than respectable. Yet on the whole the Chancellor's courage is justified. He will need to watch the external position very closely, and he will need to make sure that the various stimulants do not all produce a simultaneous effect. The early months of 1960 may be a period of some difficulty if all the measures have the effect one would suppose. Yet neither the British economy nor the world economy can grow as they should unless countries are prepared to take some of their risks on the side of expansion. That precisely is what Mr Heathcoat Amory had done.[27]

Economic historians have continued to debate the justification or otherwise of Amory's 'give-away' Budget, but as a leader it was, in its way, a superb exercise in legerdemain.

The general election followed in the autumn as surely as stop follows go. On 1 October, a week before polling day, the paper noted that the index of production was up by 6 or 7 per cent since the start of the year: 'The Prime Minister is fully entitled to point to this achievement and to take some credit for it. By any standards, the behaviour of the British economy this summer has been remarkable. Britain has become without question a dynamic and expanding economy.' Five days later a leader on 'Labour's Blind Spot' attacked the opposition's isolationist approach towards the British economy: 'The parochially protectionist nature of the Labour Party's manifesto and the subsequent long-term pledges with no regard to their possible effect on the balance of payments indicate that the Party's old economic devils have not been exorcised.' On the 8th itself the main headline was 'Stock Markets Strong and Active', while the leader on 'The Day of Decision' concluded in dignified tones:

> The thoughtful voter will probably have greater confidence in the Party which is more restrained in its pledges, has a more statesmanlike attitude towards the outside world, and is more firmly wedded to a policy of ensuring that the pace of economic growth is fully compatible with a sound currency, strong reserves, and stable prices. We believe that a majority of the electorate will share this view and return the Conservative Party to power today.

A majority did share that view. The Tories were returned, once more with an increased majority.

The *FT* on Saturday the 10th sought to wrap it all up. On the front page there was a photograph of the crowd outside Bracken House watching the election result boards. There was also a piece by the financial editor on the election and the redoubling of the bull market: 'The most remarkable week in the history of the Stock Exchange ended yesterday in an atmosphere of extraordinary excitement. Conditions, particularly in the Steel market, were the most hectic in living memory.' Inside, an *FT* correspondent contributed a psephological feature on 'The Pattern of the Polls', including a photograph of the National-Elliott 405 data-processing computer system that was used to provide the analysis for the article. On the same page, a leader attempted to elucidate 'The Lessons':

> The 1959 election may well come to be regarded by historians as a turning-point in modern British history. Two main lessons stand out. The electorate showed that it accepted the Conservative claim to be a party, not of one class only but of

the country as a whole; and, by registering a significant swing from Labour to Liberal, it showed conclusively its distrust of Socialism.

Such was the mood of the time: an unblushing acceptance of the consumer society and a belief in the imminent end of ideology. The *FT*'s post-election leader caught the mood well, above all in its stern message to the Labour Party: 'It cannot go on depending on the old loyalties and fighting again the old battles of the 1930s. It cannot hope to win many votes by cries of "soak the rich", by attacking a capitalist system which is patently giving its potential supporters a better life than they have ever known before.'

The good life continued. By 1961 industrial production and gross domestic product were each some 30 per cent higher in real terms than they had been a decade earlier; over the same period the proportion of income that was being saved had risen from 2 to 10 per cent; and in May 1961 the *FT* Index of Industrial Ordinary Shares, which had stood at 154 early in 1958, reached a then record height of 366. On the back of these highly favourable circumstances, the FT Ltd's pre-tax profits rose accordingly: from £650,000 in 1959 (a year affected by a dispute in the general printing industry) to £873,000 in 1960 and £1,006,000 in 1961. These profits would have been higher but for the loss-making general printing side of SCP; in 1959 the newspaper itself made an operating profit of £786,717, rising in 1960 to £994,817, on a turnover of some £3 million. During these same years the *FT*'s circulation rise was nothing short of phenomenal. Having been some 86,000 towards the end of 1958, it rose to 95,163 for the first half of 1959, to 109,374 for the second half, to 122,164 for the first half of 1960, flattened during the second half and climbed again to 131,631 for the first half of 1961. It was the steepest rise in the paper's history and, in that circulation spurts always cost money until the advertising rates catch up, conveniently came after the heavy expense of erecting Bracken House.

Advertisement columnage (excluding, as usual, paid-for quotations) told the same story: from 14,349 in 1959 to 17,244 by 1961, with revenue increasing by more than 20 per cent each year. Industrial display advertising remained the crucial growth area; during 1960, for instance, it brought in some 58 per cent of the year's advertisement revenue, compared with 17 per cent in the last full year for the *FT* before the war. By now Henschel's commission arrangement had been altered, so that he was receiving 1½ per cent on revenue of this type when it went above £260,000 in a year (which it always did), but with a ceiling of £800,000. The new arrangement was, in effect, the price that Henschel paid to stay in a job he loved. All the time surveys and insets packed with advertising continued to appear frequently, with a 112-page survey on Australia in 1959 as a particularly notable effort, marred only by the photograph of sheep on the front cover, which was not what the locals would have chosen.

If the main thrust was elsewhere, interesting things were also happening on the financial advertising side. From 1959 the government no longer placed restrictions on capital issues, which was good news for the future of prospectuses, that former staple of the financial press. Also during the late 1950s there was a rapid growth of unit trusts, leading to many full-page 'block offer' advertisements in the press; though in this particular field, where the small investor predominated, the *FT* always ran second to the *Telegraph* stable as an advertising medium. In the sphere of persuading companies to pay for their quotations, Bradberry's devoted campaign was flourishing. By 1960 the revenue from this source, some £29,000 a year when he began, was up to a rate of almost £130,000 a year. The most interesting development, however, lay in the consequences of the post-war tendency for the publication of company-meeting reports to be replaced by publication of the chairman's statement, usually some weeks before the meeting. To quote Newman, the historian of financial advertising:

> Beginning in the mid-1950s the old-fashioned small-type editorial format gave way to blocked-off squares and rectangles – quarter-, half-, and occasionally full-page advertisements, characterised by larger type, differential type, bold headlines, illustrations, creative borders and areas of white space around a full speech or statement [usually the latter] or an abridged version, often embellished with a portrait of the chairman . . . What had been for many years an advertisement disguised as editorial became an advertisement obviously looking like an advertisement . . . The change in presentation obviously affected the canvasser's argument. Before the introduction of semi-display he could ask chairmen to publish their speeches and statement rather than advertise. To publish the speech in the old format was almost seen as a duty but to advertise introduced choice.[28]

As a development it made the *FT* more attractive visually, but undoubtedly increased the problems of the people in the advertising department. Still, they had in their corner the supreme canvasser of them all; few chairmen could resist the argument, if it was being put to them by Drogheda, that they had an obligation to publish their statements in the paper that devoted itself to the cause of keeping British industry informed.

Expanding with the paper was the *FT* board. Poole, Drogheda and

Gibson were joined in 1959 by Jim Hunter, John Smith and Lionel Robbins. Smith was a friend of Gibson's, a director of Coutts and Rolls-Royce and came from a long-established City family. He was an *FT* director for nine years and, in Drogheda's words, 'brought to our board meetings a very original quality'.[29] As for Robbins, he had been the subject of a couple of laudatory paragraphs by Bracken eight years previously. After pointing out that 'it is a common mistake to think of the London School of Economics as a nursery of Socialism' and that 'that acute commentator on our economic affairs, Professor Lionel Robbins, has held the Chair of Economics in the University of London since 1929', Bracken had gone on: 'This country owes much to Professor Robbins. During the war he was a most successful Director of the Economic Section of the War Cabinet Offices. Since then his wisdom in counsel has been at Britain's disposal on many important national and international occasions.'[30] It was Poole's idea to bring in Robbins, and he probably could have started as chairman but preferred first to see how the *FT* suited him, while he also had to formalize his position with the university. The latter took time, but Robbins found the world of the *FT* highly congenial from the start; and in December 1960 he was elected chairman, to take effect from the New Year. Poole had always made it clear that he was only a stop-gap chairman, in the wake of Bracken's death, but more than willingly remained on the board.

Robbins, in his early sixties when he became chairman, was a man of immense charm, integrity and decency, a formidable conversationalist and a marvellous host. He was also, in the words of John Carswell, 'a bland silver lion', with a gentle manner but 'a giant paw from which a claw or two would sometimes make a carefully modulated appearance'.[31] In addition, he was someone who was always sure he was right, who (this time in the words of Lord Annan) 'tolerated disagreement, but it made no impression on him'.[32] It is likely that Poole had hand-picked him in order to 'referee' the sometimes temperamental Drogheda, and this might have led to an awkward relationship between chairman and managing director. In practice, partly because the two already knew each other through the board at Covent Garden and got on well, partly also because Robbins was new to the newspaper industry (though he had been very friendly with Oscar Hobson in the inter-war years) and did not wish to impose from a position of ignorance, that did not prove to be the case. Each in his memoirs paid a handsome tribute to the other:

> Drogheda had entered the business early in his career, and in his time he had served in most of its departments. This had made him one of the most truly

professional businessmen I have ever known, resourceful, indefatigable and knowledgeable – there were few departmental heads with whom he could not argue on at least equal terms – and his knowledge of the relevant parts of the world of business outside was wellnigh exhaustive.[33]

It would be hard for me to exaggerate his helpfulness in giving me balanced and constructive advice. At the *FT* he felt very much in his element. As a leading economist who had spent many years of his life instructing the ablest students, he took a tremendous interest in the younger members of the staff. He arranged a series of regular lunches to which he invited a cross-section of those working on both the editorial and the business sides of the paper: and he took great delight in the talk, always saying that he found it as good as and more stimulating than that of most senior common rooms.

Elsewhere, Drogheda added that Robbins 'was always most assiduous in his attendance at the office, and was constantly ready with advice, although he left to me the basic responsibility for the day-to-day running of the paper'.[34] It was in almost every sense a fortunate appointment. Perhaps most importantly, it helped, through Robbins's academic distinction, to give the paper a certain added intellectual authority – at a time when that was precisely the quality the *FT* was looking for in order to build on the foundations so painstakingly laid by Newton in the 1950s. Robbins himself never sought to influence editorial policy, but the connection was there, both formal and informal, to the paper's immense benefit.

Further down the ranks, several of the Coleman Street stars did not stay long in Bracken House: among those leaving in 1960 were William Rees-Mogg, who went to the *Sunday Times* as business editor, and Nigel Lawson, who became the *Sunday Telegraph*'s first City editor. Lawson, with his yellow waistcoat, green bow-tie and confident manner, had not been everyone's favourite person; but he had been an excellent features editor, with a keen, open mind, before for about a year succeeding Winspear as 'Lex'. From Newton's point of view, however, the tendency of the bigger national papers to poach the people whom he had trained up became such that he was almost afraid to go away on holiday because of the resignations that would be on his desk when he returned. The advent of the Pearson regime had in fact already led to a mildly more liberal approach towards salaries, but in June 1961 a special board meeting was called to consider Newton's problem, and in return for signing service agreements for two or three years his leading twenty-five or so people received significant salary increases. The problem did not go away

– as the rest of Fleet Street discovered the lucrative nature of City advertising and looked for qualified financial and economic writers – but it was alleviated.

The fact of people leaving had the healthy effect of creating early opportunities for Newton's recruits. Two such who arrived in 1960 were Christopher Johnson and Christopher Tugendhat. Johnson was the son-in-law of Robbins, had been in Paris for *The Times*, and his first job for the *FT* was to succeed Bruce-Gardyne there. Tugendhat, new to journalism, took the traditional plunge into features and was nursed through his early months with great kindness and sensitivity by John Higgins, who had succeeded Lawson as features editor. There was by now a deputy features editor in the person of Anthony Harris, who had come from the *Oxford Mail*, where he had caught Gibson's eye. Arguably the most significant recruit of these years, however, was already *in situ*. This was Sheila Black, who, married to a journalist and having done a certain amount of journalism herself, wrote to Newton out of the blue in 1958 a rather critical letter, saying that it was time the paper started to expand its consumer coverage, about the products that companies made that were part of everyday life. Newton interviewed her, said that he knew he would have to have a woman writing for the paper some time and took her on. She joined soon after the move, becoming the *FT*'s first woman's editor. She was probably the single most important influence in relaxing the style of the paper during the 1960s, as well as becoming, in Drogheda's words, 'a sort of sister-confessor' to the rest of the editorial staff, being 'both kind and infinitely resourceful'.[35]

The paper itself continued inexorably, though never in a consciously planned way, to grow and evolve. Nor did it ever do so at a breakneck speed, for Newton hated the thought of losing a reader, however many he gained; but in the late 1950s and early 1960s it was probably changing at a faster pace than ever before. There were many manifestations of this, one of which was pagination alone; in 1959 the average issue size was 16.8 pages, in 1960 it was 18.35. In January 1960 the leader columns were given a more modern look, with three leaders giving way to two, and those two being placed one on top of the other (as now) rather than in vertical columns running on. Another visual innovation occurred in the Budget issue of April 1961, when for the first time full-page half-tone advertisements were included.

Three editorial areas on the go were the share information service, arts and foreign coverage. From August 1959 the back pages gave not only the daily closing price and price change on the day for some 1,700 Stock Exchange securities, but also the highest and lowest of the year, the current rate of interest or dividend, the latest earnings cover and the current gross yield. An accompanying leader described 'A Unique Service':

The magnitude of this task can be best appreciated when it is realised that it involves in the course of a year the calculating, checking and printing of over 3.5 million groups of figures, and that the great bulk of this work is concentrated into the hours between the closing of the Stock Exchange at 3.30 p.m. and the catching of the first transport for the distribution of the paper at 9.35 p.m.[36]

As for 'Arts and Entertainment', by June 1960 it had consolidated itself as a regular half-page, which in February 1961 moved across to the pre-penultimate page. The foreign coverage, still predominantly stringer-based, continued to grow steadily in both size and scope, especially from 1960 when Newton showed the imagination to give Robert Oakeshott his head in responding to the momentous events that were happening in Africa. Oakeshott's running mate in charge of foreign affairs was the rather more traditional Fredy Fisher, whose main focus was Europe. It was a sign of how far the *FT* had come that in 1959 he flew out to Moscow to cover Macmillan's visit there; but it was also a sign of how far it still had to go that there was a proud front-page announcement of the fact that, as diplomatic correspondent, he *was* flying out.

In terms of new columns and columnists, the most 'business' one (apart perhaps from 'Industry in the Common Market', which had started by 1959) was that provided by the inevitable Bennett. This was the Monday 'Building Contract News', which from March 1960 was called 'Building and Civil Engineering News'. Building and contracting were at this time one of the busiest sectors of the economy, and the column was well received. As for the related 'Architecture To-Day' page, this from about late 1960 became appreciably *less* commercial; H. A. N. Brockman succeeded A. Trystan Edwards, and the writing went up-market, as in number 515 in the series, published in June 1961: 'Progress at Imperial College: Striking a Balance between Varied Styles'. The days of the power-stations, rich though they were in advertising fodder, were over. One other mainstream column that should be mentioned was that on 'Industrial Films', which had begun in 1958 and was by now well established.

Increasingly, however, Newton was turning his attention to specialist columnists, often outsiders, who would be able to write on a particular 'leisure' activity at a high enough level not to let down the rest of the paper. In practice, he often decided on the activity first and then had the patience to wait for up to a year or two until the appropriate writer came along, often by chance. Two such columnists were A. G. L. Hellyer, editor of *Amateur Gardening*, and Dudley Noble, the well-known motoring writer and a long-standing friend of Sidney Henschel. Both by 1959 were writing on their respective specialities in the Saturday paper, with 'Solving the Weed Problem' being the alluring title of Hellyer's first column. The *FT* also acquired its first sports writer, when towards the end of 1959 Dare Wigan, racing correspondent of *Country Life*, took over Livingstone-Learmonth's 'Bloodstock Notes'. At first Wigan stuck to retrospective commentary on race meetings, but by the end of 1960 he was making predictions, though by no means on a daily basis. Newton's logic was simple and could not be faulted. City men are as keen as anyone on the horses and are not averse to a gamble, so why not provide them with a tip or two in their own paper?

Also in 1960 a familiar column returned from the dead. This was 'Men and Matters', which reappeared on 12 April and was still by 'Observer', but henceforth to be on a Monday-to-Friday basis. As a result, 'Company Topics' moved from the leader page to the company news page, where it was to be 'amalgamated with Diarist's Notebook to form an extended column of comment on company news'. Kraeusslach himself had died the previous year, and Newton was keen not to encourage another such Pepys. The idea for reviving 'Men and Matters' was probably Rees-Mogg's, though Drogheda was certainly instrumental in persuading Newton to accept it. On 12 April 'Observer' rather archly described himself: 'We are not among those who call the Prime Minister "Harold" and we do not think he would like it if we did. We do not expect to refer to the Chelsea set more than once a year, and we are not often to be seen in the Markham Arms.' He added of the revived column: 'It will write about people because the character of men determines the fortune of business and public affairs. It will not write about people merely as gossip; in any case good gossip is usually either libellous or improper.' The writer was Rees-Mogg, who during his final months on the *FT* edited the column before being succeeded by Bruce-Gardyne and, in 1961, Heller. Under them it returned to its original pre-Bracken, pre-didactic function, although, with both Newton and Drogheda taking a keen interest, it could still be something of a minefield to edit. Drogheda in particular was capable of 'spiking' stories about friends, such as one that Bruce-Gardyne had come up with about Lord Chandos. 'Am I to have no friends left?' he pleaded. But for the most part it was fairly harmless semi-pap, like an interview in July 1960 with 'the "Golden Boy of Show Business", 27-year-old Mr Lionel Bart': 'He is not excited by making money. "I just like having it. Any money I have, I spend," he said.'

On the features side of the paper, Professor Roy Harrod, for many years resident outside expert on the state and prospects of the British economy, was now joined by Professor Paul Samuelson, the famous textbook writer, as the *FT*'s pundit on the United States economy. Together they made a powerful and authoritative double act, especially at the time of the ritual New Year forecasts. But in general, features during these years chugged along much as usual. Titles taken almost at random from the pages of 1959 included 'Battle for the Soap Market', 'Battle of the Breakfast Table' (about the cereals market), 'The Soap War Warms Up', 'Bright Picture for TV Sets' and, best of all, 'Sticky Times for Sweets'. Seemingly little was different by July 1961; there was 'Hot Competition in Cookers', 'Disharmony from Records' and questionably 'Carpets on a Firm Footing?'.

Two significant tendencies were starting to make an impact. One was towards the longer single feature, more cerebral and wider-ranging than the norm. An example of this more 'modern' feature was 'Paying One's Way – Britain's Hopes and Fears', a lengthy analysis in March 1960 by an *FT* correspondent on the state of Britain's balance of payments. Or again, when credit was tightened in June 1960, the heart of the *FT*'s response was a lengthy feature by Patrick Hutber on 'The New Restrictions – What They Mean to You', assessing in detail their effect on individual lenders and borrowers. The master of the genre on the paper's staff was probably Michael Shanks, who with the publication in 1961 of *The Stagnant Society* was becoming a considerable name. In his preface, incidentally, he mentioned that the *FT* had given him two months' paid leave to write a book 'in the full knowledge that much of what I had to say might conflict with the paper's editorial policy'. The other tendency, towards a greater frankness and more 'consumerist' approach, was embodied in the person of Sheila Black and epitomized by her famous feature of March 1960 on contraception, following the announcement by British Drug Houses of a new oral contraceptive. The subject-matter was entirely unprecedented for the *FT*, and agonized discussion took place over what to call it. Finally, 'Limiting the World's Population' was hit upon. A reader wrote to Newton to say that the only thing wrong with the article was that it should have been called 'How to Be a Prostitute and Get Away with It'. On Black's suggestion, Newton replied: 'The headline would not have fitted.'

Meanwhile, across the page, the leader columns were tending to revert to their more staid norm after the relative pyrotechnics of the 1955–7 period. This was especially so once Bob Collin – a fine expositor, but not a man who wore his socialist heart on his *FT* sleeve – succeeded Rees-

Mogg as chief leader writer. Even Collin, though, was sometimes frustrated by Newton's preference for eschewing the grand utterance in favour of the specific and tangible. 'I've got to do a leader on pigs,' he once remarked bitterly after the editorial conference. In November 1960, for example, the paper had no opinion to offer either on the *Lady Chatterley* case (although Sir Allen Lane was interviewed in 'Men and Matters' after the verdict) or on the respective desirability of Nixon or Kennedy winning the U S Presidential election. Nevertheless, it did take lines over certain foreign issues, including supporting in February that year Macmillan's historic 'Wind of Change' speech at Cape Town: 'It is right that the South African people should know fully that their best friends in Britain believe that the racial policies of their present Government can only lead to disaster.' However, like Macmillan, the *FT* did not approve of a policy of boycott. At home, a week earlier it cautiously but in the end clearly supported the government's plan to abolish resale price maintenance: 'On the whole the balance comes down in favour of a change.' Or in March 1961, when British Railways acquired a new chairman: 'Dr Beeching's appointment is to be welcomed. There is clearly a lot to be said for bringing in an able private industrialist to run the railways.' Furthermore: 'The important thing now is to give Dr Beeching enough rope.'

Looking at 1959–61 as a whole, three areas stand out as litmus tests of *FT* editorial policy: the management of the economy by successive Chancellors; the rising cult of economic 'planning'; and the question of Europe. All three came to a head in the closing days of July 1961.

On the economic front, the 'stop' duly took place within months of the 1959 election. Bank Rate rose to 5 per cent in January 1960, while in April a range of credit restrictions were imposed. The *FT* supported both moves and argued that, since the government's aim was 'to moderate the pace of expansion and not to check it', therefore 'analogies with 1957 are out of place'. But in June, Bank Rate was increased by a further point, and the *FT* lost patience. Asserting that the inflationary pressure leading to the rise was mostly the fault of the government, which had 'made little effort to balance the claims of industrial investment against those of its own social investment', it went on:

> Broadly speaking it has been the lack of a consistent expansion which has been the most serious weakness of the British economy since the war; each time expansion has started it has been chopped off in its prime. As a result the British economy, measured in terms of production, investment or exports, has done considerably less well than those of our competitors.

The *FT* concluded that even in the very short term the move was misguided, since the boom it was designed to check 'may be running out in its natural course'.[37]

A month later Amory was replaced by Selwyn Lloyd. The paper described him as a figure 'in the past often and most unfairly maligned' and argued more in hope than confidence: 'Somehow the pace of expansion has to be restored.' To an extent it was, but by 1961 Lloyd was faced with continuing inflation, balance of payments problems and pressure on sterling. A counter-inflationary Budget in April failed to do the trick (the *FT* was sceptical at the time that it would), and on 25 July he announced what the paper on its front page called 'the toughest economic restraints since the austerity period of Sir Stafford Cripps'. These included various personal credit and government expenditure restrictions, a rise in Bank Rate from 5 to 7 per cent and a call for a 'pay pause'. Rightly, granted that demand had not in fact been bursting its seams in recent months, the *FT* gave the package a jaundiced response: 'This is not the first time that a sterling crisis had induced Governments to restrict demand without achieving useful long-term results.' Of the 'pay pause' aspect the paper commented that 'if the Government is now convinced that it must depress home demand further below the level of capacity for the sake of holding back the rise in incomes and prices', then 'it will have to show greater political courage than it has shown in the past'.

There was, however, one hopeful part of Lloyd's speech: 'He showed a welcome awareness of the long-term measures which must be taken if the economy is to break out of the vicious cycle of short-lived boom and payments crisis into a more rapid rate of growth.' In particular the leader noted his reference to 'the need to co-ordinate the work of the various bodies in which the Government already works with both sides of industry'. On 26 July the Chancellor duly proposed to set up a body that would represent government and both sides of industry and would examine the country's economic prospects for several years ahead and plan accordingly. Thus was born the National Economic Development Council, or 'Neddy'. It was the fruition of a growing feeling that there was much to learn from the French emphasis on economic planning.

Harold Wincott as early as May 1960 had characterized the debate in terms of 'the two economic archetypes of this day and age':

> On my right, the type which used to be known as 'liberal'. Believes that even in the twentieth century we can still learn something from Adam Smith. Believes that the market place can decide most things better than the gent in Whitehall. Prefers bank rate to special deposits. Prefers, in fact, freedom to direction. On the

whole, pretty inarticulate and not very good at stating his case. Probably the present day equivalent of the type Keynes had in mind when he talked in the *New Statesman* of the 'elder parrots'.

On my left, 'the moderns'. Dashing, dogmatic: or alternatively, with larger than life chips on their shoulders: the economic John Osbornes. Impatient and intolerant of orthodoxy, The Establishment, and of course, mumbo jumbo. *Dirigistes* to a man. Believe inflation to be not only inevitable but rather delightful. Very fluent, very vocal. Very good on the telly, where they reduce the Elder Parrots to speechless rage.

During the rest of 1960–1 the men of fluent tongue clearly won the debate, though the *FT* itself (Wincott apart) did not significantly participate. When Lloyd made his proposal, the paper's first response was tepid ('Planning will always suffer from one great disadvantage in a democracy: there is no means of enforcing the plan'), but by 10 August the attitude was more positive:

The important thing – and here is where the French have been successful – is not to enforce a point of view, but to encourage those actually in charge of industrial operations to take an active part in the exchange of ideas, plans and forecasts, and not leave everything to a few men at FBI [Federation of British Industry] and TUC headquarters. This is still very much a distant hope, but it must not be lost sight of, if the Chancellor's brave new thoughts are to result in worthwhile action.

In characteristic *FT* leader style, they were sentiments that were probably equally acceptable to the 'elder parrots' and the 'telly whiz-kids'.

The French example was highly topical in every sense, for during the course of 1960–1 it had become all too clear that EFTA (finally established in January 1960) was a damp squib and that if Britain was truly to become part of Europe it would have to join the EEC. The *FT* had already seen this as desirable by 1959 (ahead of most papers) but politically impossible. By April 1960, following de Gaulle's visit to Britain, the impossibility was beginning to seem less:

Since the war, British policy has been based on the concept of the three groupings to which Britain belongs: the Commonwealth, Europe and the North Atlantic Community. It is time for this concept to be re-examined. Throughout the last few years it has been said repeatedly that if Britain were made to choose between Europe and the Commonwealth she would have to choose the latter. These statements really begged the question. More recently, especially, a number of Commonwealth countries have made no secret of their concerns at the widening rift between the rest of Europe and the Six. Overriding all other considerations, the Commonwealth must wish to see Britain as strong as possible. This she cannot be while Europe is divided.

It was a view that over the following year gained considerable acceptance, with the *Economist* (probably more influential than the *FT* in government circles) in particular propagating the belief that Britain's destiny lay in Europe, which in turn could mean only the EEC.

On 31 July 1961 Macmillan announced that Britain would be making formal application to join, a decision described by the *FT* the next day as 'undoubtedly right' despite natural fears that 'exposure to stiff competition would not invigorate but cripple British industry':

We prefer to believe that the economy is fundamentally sound and that industry, after a short period of uncomfortable adjustment, would be able not merely to withstand competition in its home market but to take full advantage of the greater opportunities opened to it abroad . . . Britain as a small, sober power, withdrawn from international responsibilities, is an idea ruled out not only by our history, but by the necessity of providing rising living standards for a large population. And the Commonwealth? The Commonwealth in its present form is no alternative to Europe, and there is little reason to suppose that the other members are ready for the measures needed to convert it into an alternative.

Three days later, in the context of 'the great debate' in Parliament on Britain and the Common Market, the leader columns returned to the theme:

There is no reason to suppose that adhering to the Treaty of Rome will impose on us a surrender of sovereignty which is not more than outweighed by the benefits which we shall derive from membership. If the result of such a decision were to be an increase in Britain's wealth and influence, the links which bind the countries of the Commonwealth together would be considerably strengthened.

But perhaps the final word should go to Wincott, who in his first Tuesday column after Macmillan's announcement looked forward to the economic implications of joining the Community as not only the country's best but also its last hope:

If by any other means we could get the necessary competition here in our own market, with compensating benefits and advantages for our exporters, we could afford to remain outside. But we can't. Demonstrably, on the record of the nearly 40 peace-time years which have passed since 1919 we cannot produce a single-party Government strong enough to stand up for more than a month or two against the pressure groups and the ignorant men who have steadily dragged us down. Demonstrably, the embittered history of those 40 years rules out a coalition. Only the judgement and the cathartic properties of a market of 260 million people remain. But what a promise also resides in this new chapter of our economic history which we must pray is opening up.

[TEN]

'BELOW STAIRS'

The 'stop-go' cycle, economic planning and the Common Market were all preoccupying matters in the early 1960s, but they were probably not the cause of sleepless nights to Fleet Street managements. In his chairman's statement of May 1961, issued not long after the demise in quick succession of the *News Chronicle*, *Star*, *Empire News* and *Sunday Graphic*, Robbins touched on a theme that was becoming of acute concern to the national newspaper industry and would dominate its affairs for at least the next quarter of a century:

> Newspaper costs, as the public has learnt from some tragic examples during the past year, have mounted relentlessly since the end of the war. We have had to face increases in successive years of the order of 20 per cent and more, and the rise still continues. Had the paper remained in the pattern of pre-war days, and dependent solely on its former sources of revenue, it would have had a hard struggle to survive. It is the success of this policy of expansion under the inspiring editorship of Mr Gordon Newton that has enabled it to reach out to new sources of advertisement revenue and thus surmount these rising costs, and, at the same time, to find money for the post-war expansion and development. A Royal Commission is at present enquiring into the whole question of costs and other matters affecting the well-being of our industry and we await with interest such enlightenment as in due course its members can throw upon our problem.[1]

Robbins was able to look at the 'problem' from the relatively comfortable point of view of an excellent product, an expanding market and a quasi-monopoly position. Nevertheless, even by the early 1960s the *FT* management was starting to feel anxious about its cost structure, and over ensuing decades it was an anxiety that at times turned to near desperation. Or put another way, once the *FT* joined the big league of national papers, as it did during the 1960s, then it was no longer immune to big-league problems, however much it might have wished (and sometimes pretended) otherwise.

The immediate roots of the Fleet Street *malaise*, for such it undoubtedly was, lay in the events of the late 1950s. It is true that in 1955 there had been a national newspaper strike, lasting almost a month, but this had been caused by electricians and engineers rather than the mainstream print unions and had been related to a general wave of union militancy at that time (also involving busmen, miners, dockers and railwaymen) rather than signalling any particular long-term militancy in Fleet Street itself. Of much more lasting significance were the consequences of the ending of newsprint restrictions. These took different forms in different sectors of the industry, but may be briefly summarized in terms of larger papers, ferocious circulation wars, rapidly climbing payments and above all manpower on the production side, and increasingly effective control of the labour market by the print unions. Frank Rogers of the *Daily Mirror* later recalled this crucial phase:

> With the lifting of paper-rationing, the *Mirror* was only concerned to capture advertising; this meant increasing the size of the paper and this, in turn, meant negotiating with the unions. For whatever reason – perhaps the unions wanted greater membership at the TUC – the chapel negotiators wanted more men, mainly casuals, rather than more pay. At one stage we had negotiated for 800 people each in the machine and publishing rooms. If they had all turned up on one night they would have suffocated. It had become so bad that the larger the pagination, the higher the manning and the greater the loss.[2]

In the words of Ted Blackmore, the *Mirror*'s labour relations director at the time: 'It was gradual attrition. Each time we wanted to change the number of pages, it would be two bob for this and three bob for that, but, by God, they mounted.'[3] Gross overmanning and a mass of apparently minor concessions in terms of payments – together they made a formidable recipe for commercial disaster.

Why did management, individually and collectively, fail to resist these fateful trends? The short answer is that Fleet Street management, protected from foreign competition, blinded by some of the temporary fat profits of the late 1950s and oppressed by the fact that if an issue failed to appear then that day's revenue would be lost for good, simply lacked the spunk and the foresight to do so. Their tradition was amateurish, deriving from the owners themselves; their own 'trade union' (the Newspaper Proprietors' Association, from 1968 the Newspaper Publishers' Association) was the bluntest, least unified of tools; and, it has to be said, some of the papers that were doing especially well in the immediate wake of the freeing of newsprint were not averse to negotiating agreements that, when applied as they inevitably were to their struggling rivals, added a further nail to various coffins. In 1959 the NPA did make an attempt to break the cycle. It dissolved its Labour Committee, which at an ever-increasing rate had allowed a multiplicity of disadvantageous piecemeal additions to the basic 1947 industry agreements, and replaced it with a body known as the Labour Executive, whose brief was to wrest the initiative away from the unions and chart a new course in Fleet Street industrial relations. The Executive, comprising various managing directors and general managers, tried quite hard but almost from the start was fatally undermined not only by the tendency of individual houses to make separate agreements off their own bat, but also by the failure of the proprietors as a whole to lend their efforts adequate support and authority. In the closing months of 1960 four newspapers folded. Early the following year the government announced the setting up of a Royal Commission, under the chairmanship of Lord Shawcross, to examine what was wrong with the industry.

Many thousands of words of both written and oral evidence were submitted to the commission.[4] Three well-known witnesses were particularly trenchant, starting with the first witness of all, Sir Geoffrey Crowther:

> There is an appalling state of affairs in deliberate cutting down of the amount of work that can be done; in demarcation disputes between unions; in restriction of entry to the trade and in general quarrelsomeness . . . You will not find it easy to get the evidence because for obvious reasons very little about it appears in print . . . In the early days the cost of printing was a relatively small part of the total cost of producing a newspaper or journal and it always seemed better than having a stoppage to concede what was asked for . . . You can go to a newspaper printing house in the middle of the night in London and find a staggering amount of people standing about doing nothing . . . I should say, generally speaking, the further you get away from Ludgate Circus the less intense does the restrictionism [in the printing industry as a whole] become. This is chiefly because the Press is the great consumer of printing that cannot afford a stoppage of half-an-hour . . . Papers are born, they die. At present they die; but they are not born.

Crowther with his *Economist* background spoke as a semi-outsider in terms of the newspaper industry, but the same was not true of Cecil King, nephew of the legendary Lord Northcliffe and chairman of the *Daily Mirror*. King during his evidence castigated the NPA: 'Newspaper proprietorship tends to inflate the ego, and it is very difficult to get a number of proprietors to agree to anything at all.' He went on: 'Of course, the whole of the relationship between NPA members and the unions has been based on the fact that at the last moment at least one of the members will usually run away.' Which in practice meant that no one took a stand, granted that, in King's words, 'a newspaper cannot afford to cease publication while all its competitors are running'. As to the future of the industry: 'If we go on as we are we will end up with three morning newspapers in London.' King's pessimism was echoed in the evidence of the commission's most distinguished witness:

Do you think the arrangements in the newspaper industry for negotiating with the trade unions are satisfactory? – We have always thought that the trade union people have been very clever and very able negotiators. From my experience we find them much abler than our people.

You do not think very highly of the Newspaper Proprietors' Association then? – I think it is a pretty ineffective organization. It is difficult to get agreement, and then somebody always tries to railroad something through.

Thus spoke the aged Lord Beaverbrook. He was the last witness to appear before the commission, and to him fell the final, unambiguous words: 'The trade unions are more powerful than the NPA.'

In September 1962, on the basis of the evidence it had collected (including a detailed examination by a firm of management consultants of the workings of the *Daily Express*, the *Daily Mail*, the *Daily Mirror* and *The Times*), the commission submitted its report. In some detail, and in a wholly objective tone, it portrayed Fleet Street in a state of early but unmistakable *malaise*. Overmanning ('at its least in the composing rooms and at its worst in the publishing rooms') was of the order of 34 per cent. Demarcation was often excessive, even 'grotesque', and particularly damaging because, 'apart from its capacity to irritate, it impedes the development of new processes'. Casual non-craft labour was rife, 'paid at premium rates', and in the extent to which it was used could 'be justified only on the hypothesis that a man cannot be expected to undertake from time to time any work significantly in excess of his normal standard'. But as the report mildly observed: 'There would be more in this justification if the normal standard of work involved men being employed to their reasonable capacity. This is often not so in the newspaper industry.'

There was also the whole question of 'house extras negotiated to meet special conditions', a 'substantial' number of which were 'based on reasons sometimes anachronistic and often fictitious'. According to the commission, a particularly insidious example of the latter was 'the extra which is paid for "ghost" workers':

Thus when the number of pages to be produced on a particular night exceeds the normal, more men (or in some offices more machines and men to run them) are accepted as necessary by agreements made between managements and machine room chapels. Sometimes the necessary number of casual workers cannot be mustered (and in some houses the extra machines do not exist). The extra pages are therefore produced by the existing crews on the existing machines without falling behind schedule. The wages which would have been earned by additional men or the notional crews of the 'ghost' machines have nonetheless to be paid and are shared out amongst the crews actually at work.

'Agreements of this kind,' the report added, 'are symptomatic of a relationship between management and labour which cannot possibly conduce to efficient production and is well calculated to daunt even the most optimistic from attempting to launch a new newspaper.'

The very method of conducting industrial relations did not help: 'The multiplicity of unions and more particularly of house chapels in itself conduces to great difficulty in negotiating efficient standards. In one comparatively small house we were told that there were thirty chapels.' But the report, in the last analysis, was not prepared to blame one side more than the other for 'the present unsatisfactory state of affairs':

If individual managements pay heed exclusively to their own competitive position and none to the common good of the newspaper industry, the industry as a whole is bound to suffer. The trades unions for their part – some more than others – have taken continuing prosperity for granted in pressing for high earnings and high manning standards regardless of the level of productivity. Both management and labour have lacked the incentive to improving efficiency which in many industries is provided by foreign competition. Some are now beginning to realize that inefficiency may help to kill at least some of the geese which lay the reputedly golden eggs.

The commission had three main remedies to offer: 'better and more authoritative negotiating and consultative machinery'; 'unity on the part of employers'; and 'a more constructive spirit on both sides together with a genuine will to work the machinery', in that 'good industrial machinery is no substitute for good relations'. They were noble sentiments, but it was to prove a long and stony road to the fellowship and good cheer of Wapping.

The *FT* welcomed the report, but discounted its chances of achieving more than minor reforms for the better. The leader commented wryly: 'The Commission is scathing about the "feather-bedding" and restrictive practices to be found in many newspaper offices. These criticisms may come as a surprise to the general public, but hardly to those who have worked in newspapers.'[5] It is impossible to make confident generalizations, because of the almost total absence of surviving records from before the 1960s, but as far as one can tell most of the commission's strictures would have fully applied to the newspaper side of St Clements Press, above all in relation to overmanning in the warehouse and the machine room. The *FT* was one of the many newspapers that submitted evidence, both written and oral. The written submissions mostly summarized the paper's history but did touch on the ubiquitous theme of new technology:

> When the *Financial Times* was first published it was entirely hand-set. Some six years later, it was the first London [morning] daily paper to be set by Linotype composing machines. No further comparable advance in techniques seems to have been achieved since, although it is difficult to believe that printing should not share in the revolutionary advances that are being made in other productive processes; and there can be little doubt that both existing piece-work scales and current practices as regards manning have created difficulties in this industry. The *Financial Times* has not hitherto seriously had to consider printing in the North. If that point came, it would clearly be interested in the conditions under which systems of facsimile transmission could be employed, as it is doubtful whether traditional means of production would be economically possible for a paper of this type. On a smaller scale [to do with the prices service], it has found the introduction of teletypesetting solely for the purpose of saving time, and with no intention of economising in costs or manpower, has been fraught with difficulties. The machinery was operated [in 1959] for a short time without success largely because a satisfactory basis of payment could not be agreed. Discussions have recently been re-opened and a three-months trial is in contemplation but no clear conclusion has yet been reached on payment.

This particular piece of new technology proved of illusory benefit (teletypesetting was tried again later in 1961 and, turning out to be slower than ordinary setting, was quickly abandoned), but the obstructive attitude of the unions was entirely symptomatic.

As for the *FT*'s oral evidence, a seven-man team of Robbins, Drogheda, Hunter, Henschel, Shapland (by now the doyen of circulation managers), A. J. Rampling of St Clements Press and the company secretary Arthur Knock (shortly to die) assembled before Shawcross and his colleagues on 10 July 1961. An undue proportion of the exchanges focused on the fact, amazing to the questioners but almost a self-evident proposition to the witnesses, that the general printing side of SCP operated as a separate sphere to the side that printed the newspaper and that therefore, when the newspaper 'needed' additional men on a particular night, it looked to outside casuals rather than men employed on the general side. However, there were some characteristic and quite revealing moments. One came when Shawcross asked whether the *FT* was 'completely safe from any possibility of a takeover', and Drogheda replied: 'Until Lord Cowdray gets bored with us.' Another came with Henschel's magisterial response to the suggestion that he should charge more for company-meeting advertisements and thus earn higher profits for the company's shareholders:

I would reply that profits have nothing to do with me. I do not really look at profits. I fix a rate, which I have confirmed by the board, of what I think is right and just: what I think advertisers would like to have, and what I would like to have, quite independent of any question of circulation. It is entirely dependent on value.

The heart of the evidence was reached when first Drogheda and then Rampling answered questions about the *FT*'s labour costs, above all in the composing room, which Drogheda conceded was probably where the best rates were paid in Fleet Street:

Why is that? – For a variety of reasons. First of all, these are piece rates, and they have got to work to earn the money. But undoubtedly, in what is called the London piece scale there are all sorts of extra payments and bonuses, which are not necessarily for extra output, but are for different styles of setting. The *Financial Times* is not only narrative; there is also a great mass of statistical material, and statistical material is paid at a very much higher rate.

This is under a house or London agreement, is it? – That is under the London agreement. It is laid down in this elaborate scale that you get so much extra for a setting of figures and tabulated material. Also, we have a great deal of material which is set in very small sized type, in particular, the Stock Exchange dealings, and also, I think, a number of the classified advertisements. There, again, there is a very substantial extra payment.

Again under the London agreement? – Correct. Then there is the fact that a great deal of our work has got to be compressed into a very short time. We go to press now two hours earlier than we did before the war.

At what time? – We go to press at 9 o'clock instead of 11 o'clock. That is chiefly because now so many of the papers print in Manchester, and we have to get our copies up there to share in the distribution arrangements from Manchester. That has also involved extra payments. I think there is no doubt that the London piece scale is out of date. In the old days this tabulated matter probably was difficult to set up, and it was reasonable to pay these higher sums of money. Today we do not think it is reasonable but, on the other hand, we cannot alter that piece scale in isolation.

You do say there are many extra payments which are not covered by the London agreement, but which you make in the Financial Times. What sort of things are they, and why? Mr Rampling: The specialised type of setting in this paper calls for a house agreement in one or two cases. For instance, we have what we call the tapes. This is Stock Exchange dealings. Normally, you get two lines for one.

Under the London agreement? – But with ours, owing to the class of setting and the copy that we receive, they are paid four lines for one.

If the London agreement gives very high earnings to a man, and you say it is out of date, why do you have a house agreement to give double the London rate? – Because we cannot get them to alter the piece rates.

But the house agreement is your own agreement? – Yes, but we are constantly getting at the trade union concerned to revise this, because of the mechanisation that is going on in the industry, and they will not have it.

The answer, I suppose, is that you are forced to pay it, because you will have a strike? – Exactly.

The commission could hardly have been told the score more plainly.

The men enjoying these rates were the Linotype operators and piece case hands, Fleet Street's true aristocrats of labour. Unlike the traditional aristocrat of labour, however, the mid-twentieth-century 'lino' no longer had a genuine craft to justify his superior remuneration. Indeed, quite the reverse had been the case since the modern 'London scale of prices' had been introduced in 1905 concurrently with the arrival of the Model 1 Linotype Machine: not only had the prices in the 'scale' been adjusted upwards with each wage award over the years, but there had been no downwards alteration to reflect the considerable developments in speed of operation and mechanical refinements in typesetting equipment. In other words, the Linotype operator was by the 1950s (if not earlier) enjoying the best of both worlds, receiving ever-increasing payments for manual operations that he was no longer performing. This applied throughout Fleet Street, but, as Drogheda and Rampling explained, particularly on the *FT* because of the densely factual nature of the paper. They might also have mentioned that in the late 1950s and early 1960s the father of the composing-room chapel was a charismatic figure in the person of David Minchin, under whom the pace of financial advance further accelerated.

From management's point of view, it was, by the time of the Royal Commission, probably already too late. For one thing, the decision had been taken in the late 1950s to print the paper a hundred yards away from St Paul's Cathedral, thereby missing the opportunity to take the paper's printing out of London and thus away from the Fleet Street unions. No one at the time even considered the possibility – the 'Fleet Street problem' had yet to be properly recognized – but undoubtedly it was a unique opportunity missed, almost at the same time that the *Wall Street Journal* was, to its immeasurable benefit, getting its production out of New York City. In addition, another crucial might-have-been was subsequently described by Drogheda in his memoirs (published in 1978):

> There was a time, nearly twenty years ago now, when the average weekly earnings of the compositors at the *FT* were some £45 a week. I was sorely tempted to propose an annual salary basis of £3,000 a year and the total elimination of the piecework scale, but the arguments against were too strong. There was no doubt that the piecework scale gave a real incentive to high output. Aside from that there was the problem of the repercussions on other sections of an annual salary to compositors of over £3,000 a year, when the average pay of journalists was perhaps under £2,000 a year. So nothing was done, and the compositors' earnings continued steadily upwards.[6]

It was a keenly felt regret, tinged with guilt on Drogheda's part. At about the time that he left the *FT* in 1975 he privately justified his stewardship to a colleague:

> I realise that I have a substantial share of blame for the high earnings of the composing room, but it is quite certain that we could not have got away from them without a prolonged stoppage, and a stoppage in isolation, with incalculable cost to the *FT*, for the other NPA members would never have shut down in sympathy with us.

So the paper whose founding father had been a printer entered the last quarter of its first century ever more vulnerable to the muscle of the print unions and their chapels, outside as well as inside the composing room. Again and again during the 1960s, whenever management sought to enhance the *FT*'s revenue, whether through an increase in pagination or the introduction of pre-set advertisements or colour pages or plant or technical development, it faced a choice: between an immediate and disproportionately large loss of revenue, if threatened strike action went ahead, or the less costly expedient of conceding some increase in payment or manning or some adjustment in working hours. The advent of pre-set advertisements, coming from the agencies from the mid-1960s, was particularly aggravating. The *FT* paid not only the agencies for the work they did but also the compositors (in the form of what were known as 'fat' payments) for the work that they no longer did. Yet faced by the choice of standing up and fighting or submitting, the *FT* management, like the rest of Fleet Street, always took the easier option. The unions had Drogheda and his subordinates over a barrel. They knew they were in an ideal bargaining position, able to apply eleventh-hour pressure at will; they knew that the company was making reasonable if not stunning profits and would not want to jeopardize them; and, perhaps most crucial of all, they knew that there would never be a shortage of potential buyers of the *FT* if Pearson became 'bored' of the industrial relations tangle. It was a formula for a defeatist management culture, partly disguised by a genuine element of paternalism, but primarily concerned that the paper should appear every day, at whatever long-run cost. It was a culture consolidated by the key events of the late 1950s and their aftermath, but its roots went back at least to the war and probably earlier. Documentation is thin on the ground, but there is a choice memorandum from Hargreaves Parkinson to Moore, dated 25 September 1946 and marked 'urgent', that in a sense foreshadowed all that lay ahead:

> Mathew [Francis Mathew, manager of SCP] rang up after you had gone tonight. One of the points we both regard as important for expediting the printing of the paper is that the men should take their half hour for supper from 6.30 to 7 p.m. instead of 7 to 7.30 p.m. as now. This, in fact, would save almost a full half hour's slating, as the setting of the lists is now completed by 6.30, but the mass of edition copy does not usually reach the Works until about 7 p.m.
>
> The men have now been consulted and have intimated their willingness to make the cut at 6.30 on every night except Sunday (when it doesn't matter anyway). They will do it for an extra payment each night of 8*d*., which Mathew says would mean a total of £2 a night, i.e. £10 a week. They can do it starting Friday night, if it is authorised Thursday.
>
> I recommend it strongly. It would be well worth the money and it may be indispensable if we are to get our eight-page issue out tomorrow (Friday) night.

Moore returned the memo the next day with a pencilled note: 'I have said OK to Mathew.' Could he, then or ever, have said anything else?

[ELEVEN]

CONSOLIDATION: 1961–6

In the early 1960s future Bracken House traumas still lay well ahead. The British economy was broadly prospering (unemployment below 2 per cent, disposable incomes rising), the stock market was bullish almost continuously from the spring of 1962 until the autumn of 1964, and over three successive years the *FT* made an operating profit in the range of £1 to £1¼ million. It was true, as Robbins emphasized in his annual statements, that inexorably rising production costs prevented any major growth in profits. Also, the decision taken in the autumn of 1961 to continue with general printing at SCP for another five years proved an expensive one; though it was understandable in the context of not wanting both to antagonize the unions and to write off a great deal of expensive plant. These were problems, but as yet serious rather than grave. Both advertising revenue and circulation (up to about 144,000 by the end of 1963) showed a fairly steady increase. This was despite limited promotion and a certain lack of enterprise in opening new offices abroad, above all in New York, where it was not until the 1970s that the *FT* attained a corporate presence. In short, there seemed no cause for alarm. The 'triumvirate' was more firmly in control than ever, with Henschel staying on despite being well past retirement age and Drogheda starting to achieve legendary status as the ultimate public relations man, though never losing his memo-sending grip on the day-to-day business. The white heat of technology could wait.

The existence of a long, gradually burning fuse on the production side was further masked by the enhanced status of the paper during the first half of the 1960s, of which perhaps the happiest sign was the private visit paid by the Queen to Bracken House in November 1962. She lunched with the board, together with Newton and Wincott, and leaving the building was shown the astronomical clock. The following year a couple of readership surveys showed how far the paper had come. One was commissioned by the *FT* itself and ascertained from almost 3,000 chief executives which daily papers they read in order to keep in touch with business news and developments. Eighty-five per cent read the *FT*, 50 per cent the *Daily Telegraph* and 48 per cent *The Times*. The other, less favourable survey was initiated by *The Times* and was based on questionnaires sent to people in *Who's Who*, revealing that of 'top business men' 79 per cent read *The Times*, 55 per cent the *FT* and 52 per cent the *Telegraph*. But whatever the precise figures, 'top' people were beginning to take note of the paper to a far greater extent than ever before, impossible though it is to quantify the trend. Thus in June 1964, reviewing Fleet Street in the course of his annual speech as chairman of IPC, Cecil King observed, perhaps to the surprise of his listeners: 'A paper that has come up in the world is the *Financial Times*. Instead of being a trade paper for stockbrokers, it is becoming a serious paper in its own right. It is necessarily Conservative in a general way, but it represents Conservatism at its more enlightened.' [1]

Later that year Labour won the election. The Cabinet diaries of Richard Crossman are increasingly full of references to the paper, as in June 1965 when, as Minister of Housing, he prepared to announce some local boundary decisions: 'I had special interviews with the *Guardian*, *The Times* and the *Financial Times* so as to make sure that in commenting on my decisions they would understand the general philosophy behind them.' [2] The culmination of this phase of public recognition for the paper came in June 1966 when Gordon Newton, sixteen years after becoming editor, received a knighthood. His fellow knights on the list included the composer Michael Tippett, the football administrator Joe Richards and the merchant banker Siegmund Warburg, appropriately enough in the context of the paper's arts page, increasing sports coverage and its rôle in the 'Aluminium War'. Newton himself was genuinely surprised, and accepted with misgivings, but at the same time was keenly conscious of the honour that had been bestowed on the paper as well as himself.

Why did the *FT* start to achieve such renown during the 1960s? It was not on account of its traditional core of financial coverage, which, apart from 'Lex' (in every sense a boxed-off compartment), was rarely more than competent. This was epitomized by the company pages under the direction of Wallace Whelan; highly reliable and a major constituent of the paper's reputation for accuracy, their main purpose was to provide a factual *record*, covering as many British companies as possible, rather than seeking to dig beneath the surface in a more analytical or investigative way. The companies side tended to be staffed by sound, non-graduate 'professionals'. They were usually older than the Oxbridge intake, who were often gone before they were thirty, and they received little encouragement from Newton to increase the penetration of the companies coverage. Nor was it through its general news coverage, under the sound but ultra-cautious York, that the *FT* in the 1960s acquired its particular lustre. Although Newton towards the end of the decade did try (not unsuccessfully) to get the front page competing with the rest of Fleet Street, it would be fair to say that the news room for much of the decade was a somewhat 'depressed' area. The problem resided in what was accurately known as the two-class system, operating functionally as well as culturally and to pernicious effect. Thus gilded feature writers wrote features, newsmen of ancient vintage or recruited from the provinces wrote news, and rarely the twain met, especially as newsmen stayed on in the evening to get the paper out long after the 'amateurs' had left. The situation was not in fact as clear-cut as this, but undoubtedly there was a strong element of 'gentlemen' and 'players', abolished on the cricket field about a decade before it was in Bracken House.

Nor was it on the high ground of editorial comment that the paper sought to establish an ascendancy over its rivals. The retrospective interest of *FT* leaders of the 1960s is considerable, but at the time they were written quickly, without much conscious premeditation or debate and certainly with no expectation of being quoted in Parliament or elsewhere. This is not to deny that they were often works of considerable craftsmanship and skill, rather that they were not central to the paper's thrust but in a sense were there because, by convention, they had to be there. In adopting this rather low-key approach, aiming at detached exposition rather than potentially controversial opinion-mongering, the *FT* was reverting to type, after those few years in the 1950s when Shonfield and Rees-Mogg had, probably to Newton's discomfort, transformed the leader columns into a forum of genuinely high-powered debate. The key figure in this process was undoubtedly Robert Collin, who between 1960 and his death in 1976 wrote almost a leader a day, mainly on domestic subjects. In many ways his was a poignant career: after various disappointments in the early 1960s (failing to land prestigious jobs outside the *FT* that instead went to Rees-Mogg, Lawson and Brittan) he seems to have retreated into himself, become a highly self-contained though much-liked figure within the paper and concentrated on fulfilling the important but rather unambitious brief as chief leader writer implicitly given him by his editor. For someone of such considerable intellect it was sad that he had to rely on a pseudonymous column in the *New Statesman* to express himself fully. Nevertheless, one should not underestimate Collin's achievement. He may have been ground down by the process of writing some 4,000 leaders, resulting at times (by no means always) in a somewhat formulaic approach and lack of sparkle. But his virtues of clarity and balance justly earned him considerable admiration, both inside and outside the paper, and were precisely those of the *FT* at its best.

Essentially, however, the tide on which the *FT* rode to glory in the 1960s was the larger tide of the new orthodoxy, which saw economics as lying right in the centre of public and political life and did not question the necessity of detailed economic planning on the part of the state. In an era of big Neddy and little Neddies, of prices and incomes boards and National Plans, of a Department of Economic Affairs designed to supplant the Treasury, the primacy within the media of economic expertise and, above all, articulacy was absolute. Having painstakingly established over the previous decade an enviable reputation for objectivity, fair-mindedness and accuracy, the *FT* was now able to capitalize to the full – or almost to the full – on the prevailing spirit of the age. It did so through the high quality of certain well-defined parts of the paper, of which the most important were the 'Lex' column, the industrial and labour coverage, the economic analysis in general, the much-improved main feature and, not least, Tether's still trenchant, well-informed 'Lombard' column. Underpinning it all as a package – a package so accomplished that the *FT* was almost becoming a daily *Economist*, but without any of the tendentiousness or unctiousness – was Newton's almost infallible nose for what his readers wanted. He never forgot that most of them were *not* permanent secretaries to the Treasury racking their brains over the fine tuning of economic management. Thus in July 1961, when Selwyn Lloyd announced his credit squeeze, what distinguished the *FT*'s coverage the next day was not so much the intellectual quality of its response as the range of authoritative features about the practical implications of the move. It was, in other words, a supremely pragmatic value that the *FT* possessed, imparting precisely the knowledge and analysis that was most at a premium. Newton could not have communicated with his readers as he did without a team of talented and highly productive writers: writers who earned their Newtonian credit-rating partly through their fluency and reliability, but also through their ability to generate ideas for articles and features. Altogether it was a superb formula. In a leftish climate an essentially right-wing readership was kept on the inside track by a largely leftish team of young, highly motivated journalists, whose editor combined the roles of ringmaster, midwife and ruthless chucker-out of superfluous ideological baggage. Unlike the economy that was the focus of the paper's attentions, it worked a treat.

Newton himself remained a somewhat intimidating figure, though he no longer seized copy from a typewriter in order to tear it up in front of the journalist and only occasionally bawled at people in front of their subordinates. He was still strangely short of small talk, and the silences could be long and glacial; but he now smiled rather more than he had done in his first decade as editor and generally, in the warm glow of public acclaim for himself and his paper, was a mellower, more relaxed presence, perhaps particularly on his visits to correspondents abroad. In addition to his instinctive affinity with the temper and desires of his readers (though never yielding to their wish, as shown by market research, to have share tipping reinstated), he retained all his formidable qualities as an editor. Success did not reduce his appetite for work or attention to detail. He could still make life miserable for his night staff by telephone after the first edition had been delivered to his home. The atmosphere perceptibly slackened when he was on holiday. He ran the show as if he was a prep school headmaster, at times deliberately creating what he once called 'a seething cauldron of unfulfilled ambition'; yet he permitted and indeed encouraged enormous freedom of expression and subject-matter. He knew when something was not right, but still could not articulate his reasons. He protected his journalists from any pressure from management or advertisers, which meant that they never felt they were hacks. He continued to rely utterly on personal judgement rather than paper qualifications in his recruitment policy, capricious though it might seem to outsiders. Perhaps above all, he retained the marvellous quality of taking genuine satisfaction in the achievements of his journalists and never attempting to outdo them or show that he was a greater or cleverer man than they were. None of this was inevitable; there have been many editors whom worldly success has coarsened and corrupted. It did not happen with Newton. Nor was it inevitable that the person who in the 1950s had laid the austere foundations of the modern *FT* would be the right person in the 1960s to inspire and oversee the more ornate upper storeys. With his strange mixture of obstinacy and modesty, brutality and shyness, he rose – supremely – to what was arguably the greater challenge.

As Newton entered in the early 1960s into his prime as editor, and the size of the paper gradually increased, so the numbers of editorial staff under him grew, though probably (and deliberately) at a lesser rate. In the last year at Coleman Street in 1959 there had been 129 on the editorial side, while by 1963 there were 173. The *FT* remained, in most editorial departments, an under-resourced, high-morale outfit. Newton continued with his policy of direct intake from Oxbridge, a policy that by this time was attracting not only the high-flyers of the 1950s mould, who had seen the *FT* as a stepping-stone to greater, more worldly things. Now it was also drawing people like Paul Lewis, Antony Thorncroft, Ian Davidson, William Keegan and Reginald Dale, all of whom would become high-level career journalists. Another of the Oxbridge recruits, and taken on despite wearing a bow-tie at his interview with Newton, was James Joll, a future finance director of Pearson. With John Gardiner (who had been an economist at the Prudential before joining the *FT* on the companies side) he was trained up by John Murray to succeed him as 'Lex', which they did to great effect when Murray left in 1965, having in his own words used up all his jokes. As a trio they fully maintained the high standard of insight and criticism that Winspear had set in the 1950s. Also from Oxford was Patrick Coldstream, who had completed two years of social work before coming to the *FT* in 1960, and in the course of his six years on the paper wrote an enormous number of features.

Probably the most influential newcomer during the first half of the 1960s was George Cyriax. He had read economics at Cambridge, worked on the *Economist* for three years and joined the *FT* in 1960 as a reporter, becoming economics correspondent the following year when Brittan went to the *Observer*. He was an exciting, exuberant figure, a highly fluent and professional writer and mildly left-wing in outlook. In conjunction with Michael Shanks, who remained industrial editor until 1964, it was probably Cyriax who did most during these years to set the paper's intellectual tone and agenda. His fluency was never more severely tested than on the evening of Friday 22 November 1963, as a sequence of conflicting news and rumours came through from Dallas. In the course of five or six editions, Cyriax had to transform a routine leader on the state of the markets in Wall Street into an appropriate tribute to the late President Kennedy, something he achieved with remarkable adroitness in the most trying of circumstances.

It is clear that whatever the lack of a master-plan, Newton was seeking to turn the *FT* into a complete paper for the business man in the 1960s. Increasingly he placed a high value upon, and gave considerable space to, specialist writers who would not have been given that space in an old-style financial paper. Half a dozen stand out from the early 1960s. One was C. L. Boltz, who had been the BBC's first science correspondent, was the author of a number of technical best-sellers (including *Wireless for Beginners*) and in 1961 succeeded Wragge-Morley, covering the field from technology through to science and medicine. Another was Ronald Butt, who, after several years of hard work raising the paper's political news coverage, now came into his own as a commentator in May 1963 with the beginning of a Friday column on 'Politics To-Day'. Then there was John Cherrington, who in the course of 1963, following a chance meeting with Newton while fishing on the Test, succeeded Tristram Beresford as agricultural correspondent. Cherrington had written briefly for the paper soon after the war, having been recruited by Shonfield, but had been dissatisfied with the poor pay and not being allowed to write under his own name. Now he became a permanent fixture and, on the basis of his considerable farming experience, wrote a thoroughly informative, hard-nosed column. Also to be a long-term contributor was John Chittock, who from the early 1960s was writing an authoritative, well-respected column on industrial films. Fifth, there was Professor H. C. Dent, a veteran educationalist and former editor of *The Times Educational Supplement*, who in September 1963 became the *FT*'s education correspondent. The momentous Robbins Report on higher education was about to be published, and it behoved the chairman's paper to have a qualified commentator on the subject. Finally, one must mention the pseudonymous 'Justinian', whose weekly article on 'Businessmen and the Law' began to appear under that name from February 1962. This was the *nom de plume* for the increasingly well-known barrister, Louis Blom-Cooper, who over the next quarter of a century provided the *FT* with a legal commentary, not only on matters of commercial law, of the very highest calibre.

Sport was a category of its own. Newton himself was a considerable sports enthusiast and, starting with Dare Wigan on racing, saw no reason why such a popular subject should not receive a certain coverage, though for financial reasons always of an occasional and analytical nature rather than daily and statistical. Thus in June 1963 John Barrett, the former British Davis Cup captain, considered that year's Wimbledon prospects; while three months later Newton's erstwhile *FN* colleague, the Labour politician J. P. W. Mallalieu, penned a piece entitled 'The Football Season Opens'. The main sports initiative came on the cricketing front. During the winter of 1962–3 England's tour of Australia was covered in fair detail by the former Australian captain Ian Johnson. For the 1963 season Newton recruited the services of the former England all-rounder Trevor Bailey, whose county career was drawing to a close. It was a highly appropriate choice for the *FT*, granted that 'the Boil' had been perhaps the ultimate percentage player. 'I cannot see the West Indian pace pair, Hall and Griffith, breaking through our batting twice,' he confidently asserted in his First Test preview, which was headed 'The Odds Are on England'. He was wrong by ten wickets. In fact, Bailey proved to be the most perceptive of cricket writers, if perhaps of a rather dogged style somewhat lacking in the poetry of the game. Within a few years he was also writing for the paper about soccer, and in both fields he fulfilled Newton's criterion that the 'non-business' writers should be as capable as the 'business' ones.

It was also at this time that the arts page became a fully fledged entity, being awarded a whole page from the end of 1962. It deserved no less, for its contributors were almost uniformly distinguished, its range of interests was considerable, and it had a genuinely international dimension, typified perhaps by the regular 'New York Theatre Letter' from Marya Mannes. During the early 1960s its five 'core' correspondents were Denys Sutton, Andrew Porter, David Robinson, Clement Crisp and Cuthbert Worsley. 'Francis Bacon – Too Shrill a Cry?' was the title of a typical Sutton piece, while from the autumn of 1963, in addition to his film reviews, Robinson was also writing a television column. One began: 'In much less sophisticated times, Dickens's readers wrote to beg him not to kill off Little Nell; but it is beyond doubt that Granada would be equally pressed by its viewers if it ever threatened serious harm to Ena Sharples.'[3]

The pivotal figure of the five arts writers was Porter, who subsequently described how he built up the musical side of the page:

> I decided that, since critics write most interestingly about events that interest them, I would try to assemble for the *FT* a team of colleagues whose particular interests were complementary to mine; no one would be directed to go to an event he or she didn't positively want to attend, since, sooner or later, such direction produces bored, routine reporting. So sometimes it happened that when other papers told of, say, Rubinstein's playing the Brahms Second Concerto for the umpteenth time, the *FT* told of an amateur performance of Alessandro Scarlatti's *Rosauro* in a suburban church hall. And sometimes the editor was cross. But as the team grew, it usually included someone who would leap at the chance of hearing Rubinstein.[4]

The entrepreneurial Porter could not have achieved what he did without the overall guidance provided by John Higgins, who by 1963 had become responsible for the page as a whole. Higgins was a superb arts editor. He had an instinct for the unlikely event that would turn out to be important, preferred to give plenty of space to one 'big' event rather than cover two or three routine ones, responded quickly and helpfully to the writings of his contributors and held the ring between Porter and Drogheda if relations between the two threatened to break down. Drogheda himself, of course, continued to be the page's patron saint, ensuring that, whatever pressure on space there might be for the paper as a whole, the arts page would remain inviolable, as indeed it has continued to be. Quite apart from his personal interest in what it was writing about, he appreciated that it was the arts page *par excellence* that conferred the inestimable quality of respectability upon the paper – a quality that both Drogheda and Newton, in their different ways, valued exceedingly.

Finally on the 'non-business' side, the Saturday paper continued into the 1960s on its high-circulation-but-thin-contents course. There were the reviews of the week's markets, the agony columns 'Finance and the Family' and 'What Readers Are Asking', and one particular page that never seemed to change, comprising in its top half 'A Correspondent' on 'Travel and Holidays', Hellyer on 'Gardening' and Noble with his 'Motoring Notes' and devoting its bottom half to a collection of advertisements under the heading 'Hotel and Tourist Guide'. It was all sound stuff, but it still represented only a partial stab at the whole small-investor-cum-leisure-and-consumer weekend market. There was, however, one significant Saturday innovation. In December 1961, two Saturdays before Christmas, 'Our Woman's Editor' (Sheila Black) contributed a feature on 'Mink, Masks and Money', which began: 'Before he settles down to a relaxing Christmas holiday, a man has other problems to add to his working day – presents for the women in his life.' She then made a series of specific suggestions, some illustrated, before sadly concluding that 'most men will settle, as usual, for frilly nylon nightdresses, négligés and lingerie because they are easy to buy'. The article aroused enormous reader interest (stimulated by Newton's old ploy of not giving brand names) and the following March there began a regular Saturday column by Black called 'Shopping Guide'. Its flavour was fairly up-market, while brand and retailers' names were not given until the column was almost a year old. On one occasion Lady Cowdray inquired where she could obtain a particular type of hunting gloves that had been featured, which according to Newton was the first sign he had ever had that anyone in that family read the paper. The column was accurate and discriminating, enjoyed considerable drawing power and was in its way a pioneer in daily journalism.

Operating on rather more familiar terrain was another major innovation of 1962, the *FT*–Actuaries All-Share Index. Since 1929 the Institute of Actuaries in London and the Faculty of Actuaries in Edinburgh had been compiling a broadly based Actuaries Investment Index, covering more than 200 shares, but its calculation, necessarily by manual methods, was so slow that it was produced only monthly. With the coming of the computer, massive and fallible though the machine still was, it became possible for the first time to calculate an even more broadly based index on a daily basis. The actuaries approached the *FT*, and it was agreed that they would be responsible for the design and management of the index, including its many component parts, while the paper supplied the data, provided for the calculation and published the results. The index, covering 594 equities, appeared for the first time on 26 November, and a lengthy article by Shillady explained that whereas the *FT* Thirty-Share Index 'is presented purely as a price index', designed to measure the often rapidly fluctuating mood of the equity market, the new indices 'are designed also to measure portfolio performance'. It then gave some background detail:

> The new equity indices are virtually all-embracing. The All-Share Index, for instance, covers shares which had a market valuation at April 10, 1962, the base date, of £18.170 million, or about 60 per cent of all those quoted on the London Stock Exchange in the markets concerned . . . The new indices are being calculated each day by the Financial Computing Centre of the National Cash Register Co. on National-Elliott 803 computers. While the *FT* index is geometrical – that is, it is calculated by logarithmic process – the new *FT*–Actuaries' indices are arithmetical . . . The purpose of the new indices is to reflect the performance of the whole Ordinary share market of the London Stock Exchange, that is, the combined experience of all investors . . . All-in-all, the investment world should find valuable employment for the new indices.

They were indeed found valuable, especially to professionals, coming as they did at a time when the institutional investor was starting to supplant the private investor in overall ownership of equities. It was hardly surprising. The different component indices allowed investors to track the performance of particular sectors; and the All-Share Index itself increasingly accurately reflected the whole market. In addition, being a weighted arithmetic index designed to behave as an actual portfolio would behave, it served as a reliable yardstick against which to assess portfolio performance. These have been abiding virtues and, though the general investing public took some time to appreciate that the new index performed an essentially different function to that of the traditional Thirty-Share Index, by the 1970s, once a ten-year continuous record was available, it became fully accepted in 'the investment world' at large.

Also pointing to the future was the emergence, almost as a daily rule, of the single big feature on the leader page. A sample of a dozen, from one week in March 1962 and another in April 1963, gives a fair idea of the subject-matter. Three were by Cyriax, on methods of controlling government expenditure, on 'Capital Gains Tax: How It Works Abroad' and on the extent of railway redundancies following the Beeching Report; three were by 'A *Financial Times* Correspondent' (presumably direct-intake trainees), dealing with the antiques market, 'The Overdue Renaissance of the British Hotel' and how 'The New Cars Ride High on the Maudling Boom'; two were articles by Wincott; two were by 'Our Commercial Editor' (Hutber and Coldstream successively), on the market in meat and 'Caution Above All from the HP Companies'; one was by Tugendhat as oil correspondent on 'Discounts and Experiments among the Petrol Pumps'; and the last was by Boltz, on 'Hovercrafts: A New

Dimension in Transport?' Taken as a whole, they tended to deal with 'the world of affairs', often from the consumer's point of view, and represented a significant though not revolutionary advance on their 1950s counterparts. Only one of the dozen (and that for comparative purposes) tackled a foreign subject.

A missing name from the sample, as it happens, was Shanks, who was possibly the best of the feature writers and specialized in the lightning tour of industry followed by the 'big sweep' article. One such appeared in May 1963 when, five days after Macmillan had declared that 'Britain is on the move', he delivered a sector-by-sector report offering a qualified endorsement of the truth of the claim. Shanks also started to popularize a theme that within a few years would come to be seen almost as a complete panacea for Britain's economic ills. 'Not Enough Technocrats at the Top', 'What Kind of Education for Management?' and 'Britain's "Harvard" Begins to Take Shape' were the titles of three of his features during 1963.[5] It was an enthusiasm for management education – and the end of the cult of the amateur – soon shared by others on the paper, including Coldstream and Owen, and the dim beginnings could be seen of the *FT*'s eventual management page.

In fact, the main resting-place of the old-style feature was no longer the leader page but the page opposite, in the top right-hand corner, and sometimes on an earlier page. The titles of some subsidiary features of 1963, all by a youthful '*Financial Times* Reporter', reveal their salient quality: 'Soap: On the Scent of International Sales', 'A Steady Appetite for Sausages', 'More of a Crush for Squashes', 'Overseas Tonic for Gin Sales', 'The Heat's On for Electric Blankets' – the list is potentially endless. The *FT* of the 1960s had a pleasing element of quirkiness, of not taking itself too seriously. Thus one Thursday in November 1961 the main photograph on the front page was of Rembrandt's *Aristotle Contemplating the Bust of Homer*, which 'was being auctioned in New York late last night'; there would not have been such a photograph, at least on the front page, twenty years later. Or when Marilyn Monroe died in August 1962, the laconic response of the column-one 'News Summary' was to quote two comments: '*Izvestia*: "Hollywood made her . . . and murdered her." Vatican Radio: "A person can be poisoned by environment."' Four months later, when Lady Tweedsmuir became Parliamentary Under-Secretary for Scotland, the treatment by 'News Summary' was par for the course. It showed a photograph of her and underneath described the new minister as 'Scottish, 47, and photogenic'.

In terms of 'human interest', probably the prize item of these years occurred on Friday 18 October 1963. Coming into work one day,

Newton had heard the Beatles on the radio recently installed in his red Jaguar, thought they were rather good and now sent Coldstream off to interview them at the BBC Playhouse Theatre. The intrepid commercial editor encountered the full force of Beatlemania ('I myself was forced to leave the Playhouse by a side exit, for the glass doors of the foyer, chained, padlocked and protected by a row of policemen who linked arms, were being battered by a crowd of some hundred girls'), but the result was a main feature on the fab four entitled 'The Drive behind the Beatles'. Coldstream analysed the economic aspect: 'The Beatles are a well-integrated business operation. Operating costs are kept low because two of them, Lennon and McCartney, write and compose the songs they sing (though neither can read music).' He then discussed the Mersey pop phonomenon as a whole, before wondering in his final paragraph when the Beatles' commercial star would begin to wane:

> Whether that will be sooner or later is anybody's guess. Next year at least is scheduled to include a film contract and a world tour. But beyond that the Beatles themselves have few illusions. Few pop singers have stayed on the crest of the wave for longer than two or three years and already, one Beatle told me, physical and nervous strain is beginning to tell. Making hay while the sun shines is an exhausting, seven-day week, business.

Within hours the Bracken House switchboard was jammed, as the serried ranks of stockbrokers' clerks at last caught out the *FT*. The next day Coldstream meekly apologized: 'Our Teenage readers have properly been quick to point out my aberration yesterday in attributing the current hit "You'll never walk alone" to Billy J. Kramer. It is of course sung and played by Gerry and the Pacemakers.'

If such features were the jam, the many surveys were undoubtedly the bread and butter. By the early 1960s only the really major ones – about five or six a year, such as the prestigious annual surveys of British industry and of banking – were still being produced in the labour-intensive, magazine-style tabloid form. The great majority were included in the main body of the paper and consisted of such subjects, to take a small alphabetical sample from 1962, of sixteen pages each on advertising and aerospace, four pages on agricultural engineering, eight pages on aluminium and light alloys, two pages on anti-corrosion, sixteen pages on brewing, eight pages on ceramics, four pages on chemical and petroleum engineering . . . It was an impressive and profitable array, though two major thrusts, towards the regional and international, were on the whole yet to come. Few of the articles were written by editorial staff (with the limited exception of the prestige surveys), and Newton once remarked that it was a hard job keeping the advertisements apart.

Perhaps the most impressive survey of these years was the one that appeared on Monday 11 February 1963, to mark the imminent seventy-fifth anniversary of the paper. It was called 'The Forces That Shape our Lives' and, apart from a brief introduction by Newton and a résumé of the *FT*'s history by Bill Roger, consisted entirely of articles by distinguished outsiders. To name but five, Noel Annan wrote on 'Mankind's Major Problem' (man himself), the Archbishop of Canterbury on 'Religious Faith', Denis Brogan on 'Democracy', Richard Crossman on 'Sound Radio' and Mark Abrams on 'The Influence of Advertising'. The accompanying leader in the paper on 'Forces That Shape our Lives' was suitably think-piece in style, concluding portentously but optimistically:

> The ever-present threat of a nuclear war, the spread of education, the diffusion of greater wealth and security among the bulk of the population, the rapid pace of scientific advance and technological change have all greatly weakened the influence of established institutions and accepted ideas. New generations are coming forward, unhampered by strong preconceptions, who regard much of the conventional wisdom as obsolete and irrelevant to our present position. Iconoclasm has become a national pastime.
>
> The enthusiasm for tearing down the old must first be welcomed and then put to work on producing a new set of working assumptions about the way we live and wish to live. A different sort of society is already beginning to evolve, and some of its distinctive qualities are becoming apparent. It will be diverse, tolerant, sceptical and curious. It will place a high value on education and the arts. And it will be essentially undogmatic, aware of the fact that human behaviour is often irrational but concerned to understand and control the many other forces which shape our feelings and our actions. We, on our 75th anniversary, look forward to it.

Eight months later, the 'benchmark' issue of Wednesday 30 October 1963, just another day in the life of the *FT*, offered twenty-four pages for fivepence. It embodied various changes that had been introduced the previous December, including not only a whole page for 'Arts and Entertainment' but also fuller treatment of 'Food and Raw Materials', as the commodities page was now called. There also began then the modern system (though for a long time only on a Tuesday-to-Friday basis) of having home and foreign news in the front half of the paper and company news, stock-market reports and so on in the back half. The front page of this particular issue was almost wholly British in focus and was dominated by labour news, concerning Ford and Vauxhall car workers and also the dockers. There was also a main industrial story about 'Steel Production Running Close to All-Time Peak'. Inside the paper, as usual there was foreign news on pages 3, 5 and 7, neatly arranged into 'North America' (including the headline 'Nixon May Face Kennedy in 1964 Poll'), 'Europe' (including a piece by the paper's 'Common Market Correspondent' in Brussels, an innovation of the early 1960s) and 'The Rest of the World' (including one of the familiar 'Scene' articles, this time 'The Indian Scene' by the paper's stringer in Calcutta, dealing with the state of the capital market). The foreign coverage was still limited, but it did hang together quite well – unlike the home news, which was still scattered about much of the paper in semi-random fashion. Its emphasis was heavily industrial, though there was a report on the proposed schedule for the BBC's imminent second television channel ('Each Evening with Own Character'). In an obscure corner 'To-Day's Events' still lingered, announcing that Mr John Bloom, managing director of Rolls Razor, would be addressing the Society of Investment Analysts at 5.30 p.m., within the august portals of the Institute of Bankers. The two leaders of the day concerned the pay settlement at Ford and the state of tin, 'the *enfant terrible* of the commodity markets'. The leader-page feature was 'By Geoffrey Owen, our US Correspondent', the only person to get a by-line that day outside the arts page, and concerned the chequered progress of the United States space programme. Owen doubted whether it would fulfil Kennedy's target of landing an American on the Moon by 1969. In retrospect, perhaps the most interesting piece of writing that day was Tether's 'Lombard' column. It was headed 'Finding a Solution for Latin America's Debt Problem' and dealt sympathetically and imaginatively with the issue, from the point of view of the debtor as well as the creditor countries. But perhaps what strikes one most forcibly is the visual aspect. On no fewer than ten pages there was a photograph of some sort of industrial or technical process in everyday action, ranging from 'lengths of steel gas pipe being welded together in a field near Norwich' to 'a convoy of six tractors being driven on to the Transport Ferry Service's "Dorric Ferry" at Tilbury before being shipped to Antwerp'. The photographs may have been there primarily as space-fillers, but cumulatively they gave an excellent, nuts-and-bolts sense of things *happening*. They symbolized an ultra-empirical dimension to the paper, in many ways a legacy from the 1950s, that subsequently rather went missing as the *FT* raised its intellectual sights.

In the world at large, the big question during the early part of the second half of Newton's editorship was whether Britain's application to join the EEC would succeed. At the end of 1961 the *FT* was quietly confident, asserting that 'despite differences among the Six on agriculture, the chances are still greater than evens that by January 1, 1963, Britain will have joined'. The year 1962 proved to be one of tortuous, fluctuating negotiations, and then on 14 January 1963 de Gaulle pronounced his momentous 'Non'. The *FT* the next day rather bitterly interpreted the decision in terms of 'anti-Americanism' and French power-lust:

> Logical, inward-looking, often brilliant, the French bureaucrats who have dominated policy-making under the Treaty of Rome have prepared their blueprints for the future of Europe; its elements are French leadership, a Franco-German *entente* and planned economic growth that would make Europe undeniably into one of the world's great powers. In these blueprints, there is not as yet any place for Britain. The French insistence that Britain should accept the Treaty of Rome without reservations is the logical, but absurd, outcome of thinking that sees the Common Market not as a balance of members' interests – in which case the entry of a new member with new interests would of necessity mean changing the rules – but as a vehicle for a French view of the world.

The paper had been strongly pro-Europe for several years, so the tone of manifest disappointment was natural. Negotiations continued for a while at Brussels, but by the end of January the French veto had become definitive. The paper was defiant in defeat, arguing that 'there is no alternative to British membership of the European Community', in that 'the Commonwealth does not offer such an alternative, and there is no other grouping of comparable importance in the world to which we can readily attach ourselves'. It admitted, however, that the immediate prospect was 'a fairly prolonged stalemate', before concluding: 'Nothing will ever be quite the same again for any of the participants. Ironically, one of the facts of the new situation is that Britain – in or out of the Community – is and will remain more inescapably a part of Europe than she was before the Gaullist *démarche*.'

Three months earlier Bracken House, like the rest of the world, had held its breath during the Cuban missile crisis. A grateful leader on 29 October signalled its end: 'A challenge has been thrown down, firmly resisted, and withdrawn. The West, thanks to President Kennedy, has shown that there is a point beyond which it will not be pressed, whatever the consequences.' But there was a kind word for Khrushchev too: 'At least he has shrunk from persisting in a provocation that could have destroyed us all.' The conduct of the crisis was yet another sign that Washington was the centre of decision-making power within the Western alliance, and when at Nassau in December 1962 Kennedy's offer to sell Polaris to Britain led to some Conservative MPs voicing dismay that Britain would not have its own independent deterrent, the *FT* gave these critics short shrift. It argued forcibly that although 'Britain probably possesses the resources to produce her own Polaris as well as her own nuclear submarines', the attempt to do so 'would be a gamble', would 'impose strains on an economy which is already by no means buoyant', would alienate the United States and would 'probably postpone only for a few years, even if successful, the time when nuclear independence becomes too expensive'. The US President, however, was not above reproach. 'President Kennedy in Trouble' was the title of an editorial in June 1963 highly critical of his failure to take a strong economic and social lead, especially over the question of discrimination against blacks. It concluded: 'Events may yet thrust upon him the greatness he seems reluctant to achieve.' One event was enough, and the leader mark five or six by Cyriax, entitled 'What Will Happen Now?', began: 'The shooting of President Kennedy, while on a political tour of Texas, must be counted as a major international disaster.' The leader paid tribute to Kennedy as a man 'of great personal stature' who had 'stood behind many of the most hopeful developments in world politics in the past few years – the Atlantic alliance, the slow and painful easing of relationships with the Soviet Union, the liberal trends in the internal policies of the United States'. Furthermore:

> Perhaps the most important thing, at such a grievous moment, is to keep a sense of proportion. The US, and the West, has received a blow, but it is one which, if taken calmly, can be surmounted. In the United States, there will be complicated and potentially dangerous emotions to deal with. It is imperative that they should be dealt with in the calm by which, in the last resort, great nations are known.[6]

On an evening of despair, it was, in the best *FT* tradition, a level-headed message, to the markets and elsewhere.

On the broad domestic front, a handful of issues stand out from the early 1960s. One was the ICI take-over bid for Courtaulds in 1961–2, at that time the biggest such bid in British financial history. 'Growing Too Big?' was the title of the *FT*'s initial leader, which argued that 'mergers in general are subject to too little scrutiny in this country' and in particular wondered 'whether such a merger does not create a group too large to be in the national interest'.[7] For a long time the attempt looked likely to succeed, but by the beginning of March 1962 a significant voice against it was that of 'Lex':

THE FINANCIAL TIMES
INCORPORATING THE FINANCIAL NEWS
INDUSTRY · COMMERCE · PUBLIC AFFAIRS
SATURDAY NOVEMBER 23 1963 No. 23,168 FIVEPENCE

PRESIDENT KENNEDY IS ASSASSINATED

SHOT DURING VISIT TO TEXAS

President Kennedy, 46 years old, one of America's youngest Presidents, was assassinated yesterday when riding in an open car with Governor John Connally, of Texas. He was on a visit to the Southern States to win support and close the divided ranks of the Texas Democrats over his Civil Rights Bill.

Early reports indicated he was shot in the head, and Mrs. Kennedy, who was with him in the car, was trying to hold up her husband's head. He was rushed to a nearby hospital, where he was to have made a speech, and given a blood transfusion.

Almost at once his condition was stated to be critical, and at 7.30 p.m. G.M.T. last night it was announced that he had died

One reporter covering the President's visit said he heard three shots fired as the President's car entered a highway underpass.

THREE SHOTS

Vice-President Lyndon Johnson assumed the full constitutional responsibilities of the Presidency immediately on the death of Mr. Kennedy and before taking an oath of office.

Mr. Johnson will remain President until the end of the present presidential term late next year. The election will be in the first week of November, 1964.

Pandemonium broke out after the shooting, but Secret Service agents waved the cars on to a road which led to the Parkland Hospital, and within five minutes the President's car was there. Reporters saw the President lying flat on his face in the car. Mr. Kennedy lived for 25 minutes after the assassin shot him.

NORTH AMERICAN MARKETS CLOSED

The first news of the shooting resulted in a selling wave in securities and commodities. Then the Governors of the New York Stock Exchange announced that trading would be suspended for the rest of the day.

The Mid-West and Pacific Coast Stock Exchanges and commodity markets were also closed. Prior to the closure, grain prices had tumbled, and sugar, cocoa and other commodities had declined.

On Wall Street the ticker was delayed by thirty-four minutes as prices tumbled sharply. Until yesterday, Thursday's market decline had been the widest of 1963. Yesterday's plunge produced losses ranging for the most part to two points or more. Only the quick cessation of trading prevented wider declines.

SENATE SUSPENDED

The U.S. Senate suspended its sittings even before news of President Kennedy's death. On the first reports that the President had been gravely wounded work came practically to a standstill in all Government offices.

Montreal and Toronto Stock Exchanges also suspended trading until further notice.

CANADA BUYING U.S. JETS INSTEAD OF ONE-ELEVENS

By Our Air Correspondent

Trans Canada Air Lines' decision to buy six U.S. Douglas DC-9 short-range jet airliners, worth £8.6m., announced in Ottawa yesterday, is a setback to the progress of its British rival, the B.A.C. One-Eleven short-haul jet, in the North American market.

Another blow to the U.K. aircraft industry yesterday was a decision announced by Sir Patrick Hobson, chairman of British West India Airways (in which B.O.A.C. has a small shareholding) to buy three Boeing 727 medium-range jets, costing nearly £7m., including spares. The alternative aircraft was the U.K. Hawker Siddeley de Havilland Trident.

Hawker Share

LONDON BUS OVERTIME BAN TO CONTINUE

By Our Labour Correspondent

AUSTRALIA ORDERS 900 LAND ROVERS

£60M. SUBSCRIBED FOR TOY OFFER

FORTE'S INVESTMENTS

MORGAN GRENFELL PLANNING BIGGEST TENDER OFFER

R.T.B. ISSUES £50.2M. EQUITY TO I.S.H.R.A.

Intended Aim

ALL-PARTY SUPPORT FOR PRIVATE BILL ON TRADING STAMPS

By Our Political Correspondent

Meetings Next Week

A NEW MAJOR UNCERTAINTY

CONTINENTAL INSURANCE BUYS INTO PHOENIX

By LEX

It is now impossible even to guess at the immediate future of the market since it has to react to the appalling fact of President Kennedy's death—a major disaster for both America and the whole of the West. President Kennedy's singular success in international relations and his ability to deal with Mr. Khrushchev was a tremendous asset which we have all now lost.

Impact on Earnings

Phoenix Assurance

Pyrotenax

REYROLLE IN INDIA

NEWS SUMMARY

More Judges—and their Pay Will be Raised

Retired on Pension

Tito Urges Atom Free Balkans

More Aid to Kenya

Disarmament Talks

KASHMIR AIR CRASH TOLL

Malaysia Snag

Congo Expulsions

Convoys Wrangle

Soviet Shortages

QUICK LOOK ROUND

WORLD WEATHER

MARKET SUMMARY

U.K. DAILY STOCK INDICES

CHIEF PRICE CHANGES YESTERDAY

THE £ ABROAD

FEATURES IN TO-DAY'S ISSUE

23 November 1963: assassination of Kennedy

In my view those who can take even a medium-term view would be well-advised to reject the offer and stay with Courtaulds.

First because the case is established that the offer undervalues Courtaulds in terms of earnings, and earnings should be the basis of such a bid. Second because while it is hard to assess the *immediate* price of Courtaulds in the absence of a bid, 50 shillings seems well towards the lower end of the scale of possible prices in any but the shortest run.

Within a fortnight the bid had failed. The *FT* also supported competition by continuing to back, unlike many interest groups, the proposed abolition of resale price maintenance. Thus in May 1962 it described the existing system as one which 'tends to raise costs, hold up new methods of retailing and thus denies the consumer the opportunity – which he need not take – of buying cheap'.

In general, the *FT* leaders of this time strongly advocated the virtues of modernization, rationalization and technological advance. In November 1963 the government was criticized on account of 'the slow pace of the Beeching closures', while three months later a leader argued 'The Case for the Concord', at the time a highly controversial issue. Interestingly, however, there was a surprisingly sceptical response in October 1963 to Wilson's famous 'white heat of technology' speech at the Labour Party Conference:

Mr Wilson, in the heat of oratory, seemed at times to be inclining towards the magical view of life. He suggested that we needed many more scientists and technologists (no figures, no reasons) and that we needed (no reasons, no figures) to spend much more on science: honour the mysticism with adequate offerings, he implied, and all will be well.

Instead, the leader argued, what mattered as much was that research was properly directed, and that, in terms of that direction, 'What to investigate, what to manufacture, and how to sell are questions of practical importance which neither the scientist nor the non-scientist is necessarily better qualified to answer.'

A similar faith in the liberal virtues underpinned the paper's response a few days later to the Robbins Report on higher education, which advocated a much faster rate of expansion than most people had expected. Whereas *The Times* in three leaders on consecutive days attacked the report, arguing that it was a fatal mistake to put so many additional resources into new universities rather than improving the country's technological and technical education, the *FT*, in a fairly bland editorial ('Investing in Higher Education'), followed the conventional wisdom of the time that expanding higher education as a whole had the potential to be a prime motor of arresting national economic decline. Seen strictly as 'an investment', it was 'almost certainly a profitable one'.

Inevitably, though, it was the government's management of the economic cycle, and the political implications of that management, that dominated the purview. During his final year as Chancellor, the deflationary Selwyn Lloyd received only moderate support. In particular, though not questioning the need for some sort of incomes policy, the *FT* doubted the government's ability to sell it to the unions, especially once the Electricity Council had broken the 'pay pause' in November 1961 and made a mockery of the Chancellor's rhetoric: 'A sense of national purpose and co-operation for the common good are very desirable things. But in practice, in wages as on exports, it is up to Governments to set the conditions in which these things flourish.' Also, though pleased that the creation of the National Economic Development Council ('Neddy') reflected a 'general realisation that economic policy ought to be something more purposeful and stable than an intermittent dose of short-term restrictions', the paper criticized the rather dour Chancellor for his failure to get that commitment across. 'The Lessons of Orpington', following the sensational Liberal by-election victory in March 1962, analysed the Tory unpopularity as much in terms of medium as message: 'It is plainly boredom rather than active discontent that has swung so many people into the rather ill-defined Liberal camp . . . A reasonable policy of restraint has no chance of winning public support unless it shows at the same time the possible fruits of its own success.'

The following month, on Budget day, the *FT* argued that public opinion was 'becoming increasingly suspicious of anything which appears to smack of *immobilisme*' and needed 'to be reassured that stagnation is not an endemic feature of the British economy, that growth is both possible and attainable'. Yet characteristically, when Lloyd declined to reflate, the paper the next day expressed no particular disappointment and accepted Treasury forecasts about rising personal consumption. Lloyd's days, however, were numbered. On 13 July, Macmillan wielded the long knives, and the Chancellor got one of them. The next day's leader paid tribute to his 'integrity and courage' but welcomed his replacement by a better communicator in the person of Reginald Maudling. Wincott, however, was aghast. In his first column after the bloodbath, 'The Betrayal of Selwyn Lloyd', he berated the Prime Minister: 'The truth is that Mr Macmillan is and always has been an inflationist . . . The truth is that Mr Macmillan still lives and thinks in the atmosphere of Stockton-on-Tees in the early thirties.' As for the new Chancellor: 'If Mr Maudling thinks we can go back to indiscriminate expansion, to flooding the economy with credit, and without tackling the fundamental maladjustments which still obtain in many of our basic industries, he will find he has created the same sort of mess that Selwyn Lloyd inherited.'

It was soon clear that Wincott was swimming against the tide. As early as 20 July, Cyriax in his first post-Lloyd feature discussed 'The Great Debate: Does the Economy Need a Boost?' After a careful analysis of what exactly had been happening in the economy in recent months, he concluded that the margin of spare capacity was now too great and that 'a small stimulus at home' would be justified. Four months later, by such steps as cutting the purchase tax on cars and increasing investment allowances for industry, Maudling gave that stimulus. 'Just What Was Needed', the *FT* declared in a leader of lavish praise: 'He has been much concerned, as he stressed yesterday, to avoid slipping back into old habits of short-term stimulus and restriction and to introduce only such measures as would remain useful when the economy was again working close to full capacity.' Faith in the possibilities of planned expansion was starting to run higher than ever, as shown most graphically in an editorial of January 1963 in the context of the Common Market trauma:

> If the Brussels negotiations fail, the best thing the Government could do for the country's future as well as for its own would be to go all out for a faster rate of economic growth. This means assuming responsibility for it, instead of handing it over to bodies like Neddy and Nicky [the National Incomes Commission]. It means knowing precisely what one wants and dealing ruthlessly (as ruthlessly as the French planners, perhaps) with all the mental and physical obstacles which stand in the way. It means hurting established ideas and vested interests. It means governing, in short, even at the risk of unpopularity. If the Government is able and ready to do this, to provide the country with the leadership and sense of direction which at present it often seems to lack, there is little doubt that people will respond quickly and at last produce a British economic miracle to match the rest.[8]

In the here and now, however, 'Neddy' and 'Nicky' would have to do. The *FT* was always sceptical of the latter's chances of delivering the voluntary goods ('Nicky's problem seems to be to discourage the most anti-social features of free negotiation without attempting the impossible task of reducing the free market in which wage claims have traditionally been hammered out'); but in February 1963 it welcomed as suitably ambitious 'Neddy's' setting of 4 per cent as an annual growth target. It also expressed general warmth towards the body itself: 'Neddy has several qualities which the Treasury badly lacks; it has close contacts with industry which, over the years, are bound to get closer and a sense of propaganda about proper economic policies which the official machinery has never managed.'[9] The mood was clearly ripening for an alternative ministry, irrespective of which party was in power.

For several weeks during the summer of 1963 the question of the state of the British economy lost its grip on the public imagination. 'It *is* a moral issue,' thundered *The Times* about the Profumo affair, but the *FT* declined to deliver a moral judgement either way, concentrating instead on its political consequences and generally rather playing the episode down. 'Foreigners Judge Less Harshly' was the title of the principal editorial comment, published a week after Profumo's resignation and mostly taken up with quoting the opinion of the world press, before pointing out that, although one should not 'minimise the seriousness of what has happened', nevertheless 'it is worth while remembering that what we are faced with is a domestic crisis, not an international one'.[10] Still, there was a widespread feeling, implicitly shared by the *FT*, that the episode at one level represented yet another sign of the decay and incapacity of the traditional British ruling class. Suddenly the Edwardian Supermac seemed more Edwardian than super.

A leader written in July, in the context of National Productivity Year, caught something of the desire for change at all levels:

> The current interest in improving facilities for business training is a product of the managerial revolution which has been taking place in industry. It is part of a renewed national interest in education, in the provision of skills, which is fully reflected in the Neddy report on 'Conditions for Growth'; the national mood is moving away from the traditional belief in amateurism, towards a greater degree of professionalism. This new trend needs to go much further – in Government and in the unions at least as much as in industry – if Britain is to get the extra productivity of which she is capable. But the trend is clearly in the right direction. The next few years may well be ones of exciting achievement for Britain.[11]

At which point enter the fourteenth earl with his matchsticks. The *FT* paid the retiring Macmillan judicious tribute: 'In the long retrospect of history, perhaps, to have set Britain on the path which leads to Europe will appear his most lasting claim to greatness.' The next day, 12 October, little enthusiasm was expressed for either of his likely successors. 'His administrative ability falls short of his eloquence', was the verdict on Hailsham; while of Butler, it was reckoned that he 'lacks panache' and that 'his choice would rouse little enthusiasm in the constituencies'. In the same issue, almost a week before a new Prime Minister finally 'emerged', the front-page headline hit the jackpot: 'Lord Home May Be

Compromise Choice'. It was a tribute to Butt's perception as political correspondent. And when Home did form a government, the response of the *FT* to this surprising development was not only generous but also acute: 'His reputation for selflessness, integrity and amateurism may even be an advantage at a time when many people are a little disillusioned with the performance of more run-of-the-mill politicians, and Mr Wilson will have to be careful in his choice of stones to throw at this particular Aunt Sally.'

During Home's year as Prime Minister, with an election due within the year, there was the famous or infamous 'dash for growth'. Maudling's Budget of April 1964 fired the starting-gun. It was, according to the *FT* the next day, 'A Calculated Gamble':

He has deliberately decided to gamble on the chance that things will go well in the months ahead. There are arguments which can be brought forward in favour of such a gamble. First, there is the fact that there are self-regulating factors in each boom and the danger that official intervention may check instead of merely moderating the growth of the economy. Second, there is the possibility of using the regulator . . . Third, there is some reason for hoping that personal savings will continue to increase and that voluntary abstention from consumption will make a small increase in taxation adequate.

Mr Maudling has given these arguments more weight than many economists – including those most anxious to achieve a faster rate of long-term growth – would have recommended. His judgement may well prove to be correct. But, in choosing to take a risk, he has incurred an even greater obligation to watch the progress of the economy closely in the months ahead and to take further restrictive action if ever it becomes clear that he has miscalculated.

There was a curious reluctance to draw parallels with the similar strategy of Butler in 1955 and Amory four years later.

In September 1964 an election was called for the following month. Cyriax weighed up the question: 'How Much Better Off Are We Than In 1959?' His feature began: 'Should people go with Labour? Or should they be content with what they have, and keep it with the Conservatives? It depends very much on what has happened to living standards in the last five years.' Cyriax reckoned that money incomes were up by about a third since 1959 and that the spread of prosperity was fairly broadly based, before concluding:

How secure is this prosperity? In terms of the labour market in the short term, the position today is stronger than 1959; unemployment in July 1959 was 1.8 per cent of the labour force while this July it was 1.4 per cent. But in July 1959, the current balance of trade showed a surplus of £153 million, while in 1964 it will show a deficit of around £320 million. For any Government concerned with security, this is the greatest challenge.

It was an underestimate of the poorness of the balance of payments position. But, as both parties knew, trade gaps alone do not determine the outcome of elections.

The 1964 general election was the first to which the *FT* gave the coverage of a quality daily. Specialist writers like Tugendhat (recently called 'energy editor' in an inspired moment by Newton, ahead of anyone else in Fleet Street) and John Horam the transport correspondent were particularly adept at turning their hands to features on 'key marginals'. Nevertheless, the election was not allowed complete sway. Only a week before polling day Cyriax contributed a major two-part feature entitled 'Engineering: The Industrial Problem' and offered a close, wholly non-political scrutiny. During polling week itself, a series of leaders focused on the respective claims of the parties. 'Britain's Place in the World' was the theme on Monday, when Labour was criticized for having 'so far given no indication that it has appreciated the fundamental problem which the new Government will have to resolve', namely, 'to elaborate a foreign policy which we can afford in terms of the military effort required'. On Tuesday the problem of how to attain more rapid economic growth than had yet been achieved was nominated as 'The Great Election Issue', while on Wednesday the question was asked of the parties, 'Which is The Radical One?' in terms of making the 'clean break with the post-war tradition of easy-going regulation' that was needed to solve Britain's economic problems.

Finally, 'To-Day's Choice' pulled the strands together. After an unenthusiastic assessment of the Conservatives' economic record ('the very state of the economy at present shows that they have only just begun to grasp the size of their task'), the main focus switched to the pretensions of the opposition:

Its dependence on trade union support and the Socialist prejudices which still colour its economic thinking may well prevent it from carrying its vision successfully into practice. State ownership may be out for the moment, except in the case of steel, but state direction and control is very much in. Even this might be tolerable in an emergency such as we are facing if there were any certainty that it would produce the desired results. But Labour is not attuned to the need for competition. It is protectionist by instinct. It refuses to admit the importance of the profit motive in a mixed economy. It tends to assume that the main problem is to produce larger quantities of heavy machinery, when the real problem nowadays is to produce more of anything which people at home and abroad are anxious to buy. Above all, it appears to believe that it can carry through its programme without reference to what is happening elsewhere in the world.

There then followed a double hit at Labour's foreign policy, for its apparent determination to abandon the nuclear deterrent and its lack of interest in joining the EEC should the opportunity arise, before the leader reached its overall conclusion: 'The *Financial Times* has always attached such importance to the European issue that we would have been tempted to come down on the Conservative side even if the balance of economic argument were more favourable to Labour. As it is, we have little doubt that a Conservative Government is the more likely to meet the country's needs.' So – perhaps against the odds, granted the prevailing mood of the early 1960s – the *FT* remained true to form. Planning was one thing, but 'socialism' on polling day was another.

The day after Labour had scraped home by four seats, the paper warned the new government, almost exactly in 1945 style, that it would deserve general support 'on one condition – that it is clearly out to serve the interests of the country as a whole and not that of any particular minority'. On the 19th a mildly sanguine leader greeted the news that the left-wing union leader Frank Cousins was to be Minister of Technology, arguing that 'his readiness to accept a post and the responsibility to the Cabinet which goes with it is an admission that some doctrine will have to be watered down if it is to be acceptable to the British electorate'. At the end of October the *FT* accepted as necessary the first round of measures aimed at remedying the trade deficit; but in the second half of November a major sterling crisis followed that threw into doubt the government's whole economic management to date, in particular its apparent commitment, as expressed in Callaghan's first Budget, to the primacy of its social policies. 'Something Will Have to Be Done', the *FT* declared on 23 November, after almost a fortnight of heavy selling of sterling. That something did not include what would become over the next two years the great unmentionable:

Confidence has been shaken and there is sporadic talk of devaluation again. This is silly stuff in itself. Britain's deficit has not suddenly become larger than it was; it is generally agreed in fact that it will be considerably smaller in 1965 . . . There can be no question of a forced devaluation . . .

Yet a voluntary devaluation of sterling is still less credible. Internally, it would do nothing to improve the economic position. It would make permanent the undesirable protection from foreign competition already provided by the import surcharge [introduced a few weeks earlier]. It would also – unless accompanied by those restrictions on demand which would make it unnecessary – lead to a rise in prices sufficient to cancel out quickly a large part of its effect on exports.

Externally, it would inflict serious loss on all foreign holders of sterling and impose great strain on the working not only of the sterling area but of the international monetary system as a whole. No Labour Government is likely to contemplate incurring for a second time the odium of such a step. Yet the devaluation gossip, however silly, cannot be safely disregarded. The Government must demonstrate convincingly that it is determined to maintain the existing parity – and such a demonstration will probably have to include a rise in Bank Rate.

Bank Rate duly went up that day by 2 per cent ('an expensive lesson in the value of imagination and tact'), but the crisis did not go away. Indeed, the sales of sterling became such that by the 25th the Bank of England felt itself compelled to raise an overseas credit of $3,000 million to save the pound. The expedient worked, but to the *FT* on the 27th the outcome of the crisis marked the bankruptcy of economic policy since July 1961:

In the past forty-eight hours, three years of illusion have been swept away. Gone is the illusion in the Labour and Tory manifestos that more benefits for all could be squeezed from static production. Gone is the illusion that growth can come from talk. Gone is the illusion that planning can ignore finance; with the UK's massive credit the Bank of England and the Treasury [as opposed to the recently created Department of Economic Affairs] must now gain prestige. Gone, too, is the idea that the UK can continue to take on world commitments and defence expenditures without selling more abroad. Power, independence and benefits hinge on solvency. Solvency is what, over the years, this country has lost.

The tone was understandably bleak, yet tinged perhaps with a certain *Schadenfreude*, together with an implicit satisfaction that within the making of policy a more familiar order of things would be returning.

This early phase of the Labour government had an unfortunate sequel. On 15 December, several weeks after Callaghan had outlined in his Budget the nature of the government's proposed capital gains tax and corporation tax, Wincott devoted his Tuesday column to an 'Open Letter to the Chancellor'. In it he not only attacked the proposed measures as such, but asserted that they represented a 'fiscal putsch' on the part of the government's economic adviser, Nicholas Kaldor, and that 'there really hasn't been anything like it since Hitler wrote "Mein Kampf"'. Indeed, the 'letter' as a whole was headed (presumably not at Wincott's choice) 'Nothing Like It since "Mein Kampf"'. It ended: 'Send him back to

Cambridge, Mr Callaghan, and rely on your own good, common sense.' Callaghan at once wrote to the paper: 'I must protest most strongly at the personal attack which Mr Wincott levelled at Mr Nicholas Kaldor. Mr Kaldor is a highly distinguished economist who has served the country well and, like others before him, is now a civil servant. As Mr Wincott must know, civil servants are precluded from defending themselves against personal attacks.'

There then followed a considerable correspondence in the letters column, in which the great majority of *FT* readers supported Wincott. Thus M. G. de St V. Atkins, of Merton Park, SW19, argued:

> With due respect, the Chancellor of the Exchequer is wrong: Mr Wincott's article is not an attack levelled at Mr Kaldor; it is an attack levelled at his appointment . . . At a time when the Conservative Party in opposition is being as limp as it was in office (please, please, read Bolingbroke), Mr Wincott chose the only way possible to question the wisdom and propriety of the appointment.

The principal complaint about the piece came from Noel Annan, Provost of King's College, Cambridge, of which Kaldor was a fellow. He described Wincott's attack as 'gross' and went on: 'Mr Kaldor is of Jewish descent, and to compare him as Mr Wincott did with such delicacy to Hitler was peculiarly offensive.' Wincott himself in his next column hotly denied that he had based his attack in any way on racial grounds and added: 'I am proud to number among my friends many Jews. Odd though it may seem to Mr Annan, it never occurs to me that they are Jews.' Altogether, it was not a happy episode, and at least one member of staff rang Kaldor to apologize on the paper's behalf for what had been, whatever the fiscal and political arguments, an uncharacteristic lapse of taste.

In less parochial spheres, several momentous international questions were coming to the fore during the first Wilson government. One was Vietnam. 'The policies for ending the Vietnam war being advocated by Senators Fulbright and Robert Kennedy represent a dangerous challenge for President Johnson', a leader of February 1966 on 'Johnson's Dilemma' asserted. The paper offered no opinion as to whether the United States should recognize the Viet Cong and negotiate with it. But it tacitly accepted the 'domino' theory that the existing regime in Saigon must be upheld, since if it fell 'all the other non-communist governments in South East Asia would be threatened by attacks from so-called liberation fronts'. An even longer-term thorn in the side of the USA would be Iran, where in January 1965 the Prime Minister was almost assassinated. The *FT* pointed out that 'religious fanatics combine with extreme nationalists to oppose the Shah's policy of co-operation with the industrial powers', but concluded that 'if the Shah and his team of technocrats can show real progress in the living standards of the people, this will be a basis for further progress towards democratic institutions'.

At this stage, however, neither Vietnam nor Iran captured the headlines in the same way as the dramatically developing situation in Southern Rhodesia. Robert Oakeshott in the early 1960s, during the break-up of the Central African Federation, had written a series of agonized leaders over what seemed an insoluble problem, at one point suggesting that the white settlers be bought out – a suggestion that had earned him a mild reprimand from Drogheda. By June 1963 a leader headed 'What Now for Rhodesia?' admitted that 'we have no practical means of preventing the territory from becoming independent if it chooses to claim independence for itself' and that 'British troops, whatever the advice of African spokesmen at the United Nations, will never be used to force Southern Rhodesia into line.' However, it went on: 'We committed ourselves to the idea of a multi-racial Commonwealth, even at the cost of losing old friends, over the question of South African membership. We cannot shift course now because Sir Roy Welensky is a more familiar and sympathetic character than Dr Verwoerd.' Again, in February 1965, the paper avowed that 'the UK can do nothing to stop Mr Smith seizing independence' and that 'people in this country would not stand for the use of force against the white settlers'. It also made the point that 'whoever may be responsible for the existing situation, African rule if it came overnight would not be the rule of law and order.' That autumn Smith declared UDI. The *FT* declined to support the Archbishop of Canterbury's suggestion that immediate use of force was the answer and instead stood behind Wilson's policy of sanctions: 'The UK is publicly committed to them and international opinion is on the same side.' Few if any doubts were expressed about the speed with which the weapon of sanctions would do its job.[12]

Meanwhile, during 1965 and into 1966, the Labour government semi-recovered from its early economic traumas. The *FT*'s attitude towards its handling of the economy was generally sceptical, but not ill-naturedly so. Thus in March 1965 when Aubrey Jones was appointed chairman of the Prices and Incomes Board: 'Will the Government be prepared to back the Board in its attack on inflationary wage and price movements even at the cost of alienating its own supporters? It should, but it will not be easy.' The next month, following the introduction of the corporation and capital gains taxes, the paper rather doubtfully hoped 'that Mr Callaghan has not cancelled out the moderate effect of his Budget with the more extreme nature of his ideas about tax reform'. In July a round of government cuts was welcomed as 'Putting the Pound before Politics', while two months later the paper christened the Department of Economic Affairs' much-vaunted National Plan 'a small but not unpromising baby', though not to be taken too literally or to be used as a substitute for economic management. The government's interventionist approach was further fleshed out in January 1966 with the publication of a White Paper proposing the establishment of an Industrial Reorganization Corporation. The *FT*'s leader on this was less than enthusiastic, concluding: 'If ministers are really anxious to work with the City and with industry, their aim should be to supplement the working of the market, not to subvert it.' Finally, the next month, the government produced its Prices and Incomes Bill, giving itself certain statutory reserve powers, but still essentially relying on a voluntary approach. Again, it was viewed as potentially helpful, but as 'no substitute for economic policy'. Or put another way: 'A safety valve fulfils a very useful function. One thing, however, one cannot do is to sit on it.' The paper was under no illusions that it was by National Plans or Prices and Incomes Bills that the battle to save the pound would be won or lost.

In March 1966 there was another general election, as Wilson sought to enlarge his threadbare majority. He had a new opponent by this time. In July 1965, following Home's resignation as Conservative leader, the *FT* had described Maudling as 'not only intelligent but tolerant, easy-going and well-liked', whereas his rival Heath 'is regarded by many Tory members as pushful and unreliable, and their opinion may be shared by a sizeable part of the electorate'. Nevertheless, the paper argued, Heath 'has a force which would command respect and enthusiasm enough to outweigh the superficial unpopularity of his policies'. It concluded: 'We, things being what they are, would just prefer to take a risk on Heath than to play safe with Maudling.' Heath was duly elected, thereby showing to the electorate 'that the party is fully aware of the over-riding importance of industrial and economic problems at this stage in the country's history'.

Nevertheless, when it came to it eight months later, the new leader failed to command the support of the *FT*. The set-piece election pronouncement noted Heath's far greater enthusiasm for the Common Market than that of Wilson, but rather discounted it on the grounds that 'it is not certain that the opportunity of joining will arise quickly'; while in terms of cutting down defence commitments in the East to match resources, the clear potential edge went to Labour. The leader then considered Labour's economic record in office and argued that 'once the new Government had recovered from its initial blunders, realized the full implications of its undertaking to defend sterling, and shown a willingness to learn from experience, it did succeed in getting a large number of things done'. The concluding passage then made a small piece of *FT* history:

Mr Wilson is probably the more skilful politician, moving forwards slowly and empirically, while Mr Heath is more straightforward and impetuous. But impetuosity, and a readiness to admit the need for drastic changes of policy both at home and abroad, is perhaps what our present situation calls for. If, as the polls suggest, a large majority of the public prefers the Wilson it knows to the Heath it doesn't, the public is probably wrong. It is certainly wrong if, as the polls again suggest, it is ready to return Labour with a sweeping majority. A Government with a large majority usually in the end becomes a bad one.

This is not to say that the public is necessarily wrong in believing that the Labour Government should be given the chance to go on for some time longer. It has many faults, but so had the Government before it. If it can keep old prejudices under control it may be able to attract the support of many businessmen while retaining that of organised labour – a double support which it will need if it is to carry through the job it has scarcely yet begun. The Opposition has not yet recovered from its defeat of 1964 which itself stemmed from the events of the two previous years; it is still divided on some issues, and Mr Heath, who has developed a lot during the campaign, has not yet had time to convince all Conservatives (as he will do) that his own approach is the right one.

On the Presidential basis we would, then, vote for Mr Heath. But we do not regard the return of a Labour Government, with a reasonable majority, with any misgiving. A very large majority could be dangerous both for good Government and perhaps for the Labour Party itself.[13]

It was not the most ringing of endorsements (and hardly influential, granted the inevitability of the result), but nevertheless it was the first time that the paper of MacRae and Barrett, of H.P. and B.B. had commended to its readers the case for Labour. Newton wondered at the time whether he might get some come-back from Pearson, but he never did.

Within four months the Labour government was being faced by its worst sterling crisis yet, partly as a result of the seamen's strike earlier in the summer. In a series of stern leaders during the middle of July 1966 the *FT* made its view clear to the government that if the sterling parity was to be saved, in the immediate future and thereafter, it was going to have to dispense a highly unpalatable dose of medicine. That of 15 July – 'This is *the* last chance' – set the tone:

Whatever measures the Government decides on will have to be harsh if the pressure on sterling is not to recur at an intolerable strength. Either it takes steps itself to avoid devaluation, or the rest of the world will make up its mind for it. It seems inevitable now, therefore, unless exports suddenly become more buoyant, that industrial investment will fall off sharply, that unemployment will rise considerably, and that production will at best stagnate for the next 12–18 months. This is the bill for nearly two years of pretending that things were better than they really were.

On 20 July, Wilson announced his massive £500 million deflationary package, including a wage freeze. Many of his supporters were dismayed by the statement, but the *FT* believed that it would achieve its declared objective of restoring confidence, above all foreign confidence, in the government's determination and ability to maintain the existing exchange parity: 'If it does not succeed in doing this, it is hard to think of anything that will: Mr Wilson threw in everything within reach. It was, as he had promised, a statement to end statements.' Indeed it was, ending as it did any chance that the National Plan of the previous year, purportedly ushering in a golden age of planned and sustained economic growth, would be more than mere words.

Neither the Prime Minister nor the *FT* actually uttered the deathless phrase 'there is no alternative', but in July 1966 they never hinted, let alone stated, what that alternative was: in a word, devaluation. The only glimmer in the *FT* came from Tether. 'There are signs', he wrote in his 'Lombard' column on 20 July, 'that in some parts of the world a devaluation of the £ is no longer seen as the unmitigated disaster it was earlier on.' He went on:

The idea appears to have been gaining ground that, while the disruption of trade and financial patterns produced by a sterling devaluation would be considerable, even that would be better than to allow the sterling nightmare to go on casting a deep shadow over the whole world economic scene in the way that it has done during the past two years.

But as Tether correctly added, inside the sterling area itself there remained as much concern as ever that the pound should be upheld. It was in many ways an extraordinary situation. For at least a year, if not longer, several members of the Cabinet, together with a majority of economic commentators (including those at the *FT*), had been convinced that, if it came to the implacable choice, devaluation was preferable to deflation, that indeed it was perhaps essential if Britain was to solve its balance of payments difficulties. Yet no sense of this debate, this alternative policy, surfaced in the press, least of all during July 1966, apart from what Samuel Brittan later rightly called 'a brave leading article' in the *Observer* on 10 July, putting the case for devaluation and thereby doubtless incurring the Wilsonian wrath.[14]

The cause of this silence was the so-called 'self-denying ordinance', by which the press agreed not to discuss the possibility of devaluation, for fear, so the reasoning ran, that such a mention would be self-fulfilling and cause a perhaps fateful run on the pound in the foreign exchange markets. It was of course an argument that applied with particular force to a specialist financial newspaper, and Newton accepted it, perhaps reluctantly but never questioning its validity. It was not so surprising: there was a strong streak of old-fashioned patriotism in his character; he had lived through the financial crises of 1931 and 1949, at the sharp end both times, first as a small business man and then as a newspaperman; and with his innately cautious temperament, on behalf of his paper as well as himself, the possibility of being accused of having 'rocked the boat' was not one that he would have relished. His journalists, ultimately deferential to him and likewise fearful of recriminations if they 'pulled the plug' (the other much-used metaphor), fell into line and obeyed the ordinance. Most of them have subsequently regretted the fact and even confessed to feeling a certain element of intellectual guilt. Perhaps not wrongly: the *FT* did fail in its wider duty, as an organ seeking to promote disinterested opinion, by agreeing to take part in what was in effect a conspiracy of silence. Its reasons were understandable, but surely inadequate – particularly as it probably overrated its own power to influence the markets. In the month that England won the World Cup, the *FT* played the square pass, though it was not alone in so doing.

The paper's economics editor by 1966 was Samuel Brittan, who, after three years at the *Observer* and then a little over a year at the Department of Economic Affairs, had returned in January to the Bracken House fold, replacing the departing Cyriax. By this time Brittan already had a considerable reputation as an economic analyst, commentator and historian, especially following the publication in 1964 of *The Treasury under the Tories*, which revealed much of the inner process of economic policy-making over the previous thirteen years. Now, with the *FT* as his power base, Brittan was to establish himself over the next two decades as the pre-eminent economic journalist of his generation, distinguished not only by the quality of his thought, but even more by the purity of his search for the right approach towards economic management. Many have disputed his conclusions, but never his motives, which, in an often self-seeking profession, have stood out as a shining light. To quote Sir Keith Joseph, introducing a Brittan pamphlet of the 1970s: 'All who know Sam Brittan must relish the contrast between his gentle, modest character and the vitality of his written analysis and argument. Lucid and humane, penetrating and civilised in his judgements, his comments have been and are a continuing guide to better prospects.'[15] It was a deserved tribute to a shy, awkward man, who had left the DEA partly on account of Britain's involvement in the Vietnam War and who in the 1980s would stand out as a lonely dissenting voice against the Falklands War.

The paper to which Brittan returned in 1966 had bolder page headings than the one he had left five years earlier and was getting steadily fatter. For the week beginning 21 March 1966, for instance, the average length was just over twenty-four pages. The character of features remained fairly constant. Thus on the Wednesday that week the main one was by Coldstream on 'Domestic Appliances: Can the Growth Market Return?'; while on the opposite page, 'Financial Times Reporter' was 'Waiting for Panda Chi-Chi'. The classic such feature of the mid-1960s was that which appeared on 23 September 1964 and was called 'Cut and Thrust in Razor Blades'. One innovation occurred during 1965, when each Wednesday that top right-hand corner opposite the leader page was filled by 'our independent contributor' Nigel Lawson, who had left the *Sunday Telegraph* and for about a year wrote pungently about the political as well as the economic situation. Newton apparently wanted him back full-time, but Lawson had other fish to fry.

The regular weekly features continued, including 'Building and Civil Engineering' on Monday, 'Products and Processes' on Tuesday, 'Scientists' Notebook' on Wednesday, 'Advertising News' (becoming 'Advertising and Marketing' by 1966) on Thursday, and on Friday 'What's New in the World', likewise changing name by 1966 to 'The World of Industry'. In addition, a regular column on management was begun. During 1964 Shanks and Coldstream had continued to write various features on the subject, including one by Coldstream in October on 'Business Schools – Finding the Money and the Men' that had aroused considerable response in the letters column. In December the *FT* sponsored a conference at the London Hilton on 'New Techniques in Management'. It mostly comprised lectures by American business men, but in his welcoming address Robbins asked, 'What actually is the nature of this mysterious subject which is called management?' *FT* readers were soon able to find out, for on 7 January 1965 Coldstream began a fortnightly column called 'World of Management', which aimed, in the words of the front-page 'blurb' that day, to 'examine aspects of management and especially new methods which are being used to reduce as far as possible the area of uncertainty involved in making business decisions'. The 'blurb' also explained the context: 'Over the past year the idea that industrial management should acquire a new "professional" outlook has gained ground. Business education is at last fashionable; management consultants and computer experts have had something of a boom.' The new column was the *FT*'s response, even if 800 words each fortnight was hardly likely to 'Harvardize' the British economy overnight.

Also beginning at this time, from January 1965, was half a page of 'Export News', the precursor of the subsequent 'World Trade News' page. It ran on a Tuesday-to-Friday basis, devoted itself to the subject of British export orders won and lost, and was very much inspired by the 'export or die' mood of those days. In terms of general industrial coverage, Shanks was succeeded as industrial editor in 1964 by Owen, who tended to adopt a more 'micro' approach and contributed leader-page features in 1965 with titles like 'Machine Tools: An End to Living in the Past?' and 'New Strategies in the Brick Industry'. Complementing Owen's features was the excellent day-to-day industrial news coverage, with much of the leg-work being done by the industrial correspondent Dennis Topping, who had joined the *FT* in 1960, having been industrial correspondent of the *Yorkshire Post*.

Yet, perhaps inevitably, it was in response to a Budget that the coverage provided by the paper was seen in its very best light. The Budget issue of 7 April 1965 was fairly typical. On the front page the 'splash' was by the political and parliamentary correspondents, the industrial staff reported 'How Industry Sees the Chancellor's Proposals', and 'Lex' declared, 'Not a Budget for the Investor'. Inside, three pages were given to the full text of the Chancellor's speech, together with a photograph of Callaghan walking down Whitehall to the House, and another page gave details of the proposed fiscal changes. On the leader page, the main editorial obviously considered the Budget, while the leader-page features were by Murray on 'The Corporation Tax in Operation' and Coldstream on 'How Capital Gains Tax Will Work'. On the opposite page, Owen wrote on 'Now the TSR-2 Has Gone', Horam on 'Drink and Tobacco – the Traditional Revenue Raisers', and 'Our Taxation Correspondent' on 'Covenants Lose Some Appeal'. On another page, Tether had his say, reckoning that 'Budget Should Pave the Way for Real Recovery in the £'.

Following the introduction of the highly contentious Selective Employment Tax a year later, Newton's editorial instincts were well shown by a quintet of features that appeared two days after the Budget and considered how specific parts of the economy were likely to be affected. Owen wrote on 'Doubts on Definitions in the Building Industry', Black on 'The Stores Prepare for a Protest', Tugendhat on the hotel trade 'Passing on the Cost to the Clients', Jonathan Radice on 'A Spur to Mechanisation in Banking', and Joe Rogaly on how 'Show Business Looks to the Part-Timers'. They were not erudite features, but they were objective, reasonably well informed and (looked at twenty years later) surprisingly readable. Above all, following the announcement of the new tax, they exactly hit the mark in terms of what the *FT*'s readers needed and wanted to know about.[16]

The foreign coverage in the mid-1960s, with Christopher Johnson succeeding Fisher as foreign editor, remained fairly rough-and-ready, with a small foreign news desk in London, a handful of full-time foreign correspondents and an array of stringers, including in Dublin the future Irish Prime Minister Garret FitzGerald. The story goes that some years later FitzGerald was rung up late one night and asked for a quick 300 words on peat exports, only for the foreign desk to be told that their one-time humble stringer had by now moved on and become deputy leader of the opposition. Offices were opened in the mid-1960s in Tokyo (only temporarily at this stage) and Brussels, where Ian Davidson went as Common Market correspondent. In terms of London-based people on the foreign side, three figures with particular 'beats' stand out. Hugh O'Shaughnessy was beginning his distinguished career (interrupted briefly later in the decade) as the paper's Latin America correspondent. Michael Connock, though an able journalist, had become the paper's first East European correspondent largely on the basis of the fact that he spoke Russian – a typically haphazard Newtonian style of appointment. And J. D. F. Jones, who had come to the *FT* in 1964 via Oxford and two or three years in Africa, became diplomatic correspondent in 1965, specializing in African affairs and spending much of his time on the Rhodesia story.

At this stage perhaps the pick of the foreign correspondents was the *FT*'s man in Washington from 1964 to 1967, David Watt. Newton in the early 1960s had noticed the high calibre of his work as the *Daily Herald*'s Common Market correspondent and subsequently recruited him when Owen returned to England. Watt – intellectual, slightly reserved, possessing a very good sixth sense – did much to politicize the paper's United States coverage, became a much respected figure in Washington and was particularly good at securing interviews for a still semi-unknown London paper. Such was the excellence of his sources that the IMF once complained that it turned to the *FT* to read its own minutes. He also had an effective style of writing, typified by a couple of sentences on Lyndon Johnson in a piece in April 1966 about the making of US foreign policy: 'He detests fixed machinery, he is distrustful of empire-building assistants, he adores secrecy and inscrutability. He distributes responsibility freely, but retains every scrap of power for himself.' These were charged times in the USA, and it was important for the paper that it had someone of Watt's quality in the field, even if it meant a shifting from the economic to the political in the emphasis of the coverage.

Meanwhile, the Saturday paper continued to stagnate, though in a small gesture to modernity 'What Readers Are Asking' was renamed 'Your Savings and Investments'. At one point Newton and Drogheda toyed with killing off the Saturday edition altogether, but decided that the *FT* had a duty to appear six days a week. Sheila Black continued to write her 'Shopping Guide' and, in general, to extend the range of the paper's consumer coverage. Typical features by her in the mid-sixties were on Green Shield stamps, on 'Fashion Raises the Gold Standard' and, in a four-page inset on home central heating, on 'The Choice and the Cost' involved. She also introduced in January 1965 a new grocery prices index, published monthly and based on 100 items bought in eleven different areas throughout the country. Newton also pushed on with modestly expanding his leisure and sporting coverage: new recruits at this time including Edmund Penning-Rowsell on wine, E.P.C. ('Pat') Cotter on bridge, Peter Robbins on rugby and Ben Wright on golf. In July 1966 the World Cup was covered not by Bailey but by Walley Barnes, who correctly predicted that England would win the final by 'sheer determination', even if they 'at times lack skill and control'. Reflecting the boom in the sport at this time, the *FT* also acquired a yachting correspondent in the person of David Palmer, who had come to the paper in 1964 after Oxford and two years of travelling round the world – a combination that appealed to Newton. Unusually for a graduate, Palmer began in the news room, where he underwent the ordeal of being put through his paces by John Hay. He decided to do reports for yachting magazines on dinghy open meetings in which he was participating and, as was necessary with outside work, asked the editor's permission. A day or two later Newton came into the news room: 'You're Palmer, aren't you? I gather you sail. I need an ocean-racing correspondent. You're it.' As with Michael Donne and aviation some twelve years earlier, Newton was prepared to back his intuition and give a young journalist the break he needed.

The *FT*'s arts coverage flourished. Of a notably high standard (as indeed had been the case since the 1950s) were the book reviews. Of Evelyn

Waugh's autobiography *A Little Learning*, published in 1964, David Pryce-Jones memorably wrote: 'The claws no longer scratch at the surface, they rip the flesh.' That same year another characteristic tone was well caught in a review by Peter Quennell that began: 'A recent and rather regrettable film based on the life and loves of Tom Jones, and an even more regrettable dispute concerning the sexual influence of Fanny Hill, have no doubt left the ordinary newspaper-reader with a strangely erroneous impression of the English 18th century.' Elsewhere, Sutton continued to write his weekly art column, Worsley became the television critic ('Goodness, how I am enjoying the World Cup!'), and Clement Freud emerged as a fairly regular and witty contributor to the arts page, typified by a missive from Vittel in September 1965 on the thermal season there. About the same time David Robinson gave John Schlesinger's film *Darling* a typically perceptive review, describing it as 'a very serious and conscientious attempt to isolate a wholly contemporary character, born of post-war Britain and moulded by some of its pressures'. In the end, however, the character was unconvincing and uninvolving, at least compared with Thackeray's Becky Sharp. In November 1965, at the Institute of Directors' Conference, Peter Ustinov gave a speech advocating encouragement of the arts by industry, in the course of which he praised the *FT* for the quantity and quality of its coverage, describing its arts page as 'one of the best in the country'. The following month Newton offered one of his relatively rare comments on the page. B.A. ('Freddie') Young had recently become drama critic, after a long time as assistant editor of *Punch*. Though normally the mildest, most gentle of critics, he now panned the new musical *Charlie Girl*, describing it as 'a show that would have seemed old-fashioned in the thirties' and adding that 'almost everything about the production seemed to be obstinately second-class'. Newton, who had been to see it and had enjoyed it hugely, was livid, calling it a filthy, disgusting review. Whatever the truth of the charge, the old Newtonian instincts were again spot-on, for *Charlie Girl* proved to be one of the great commercial successes of the post-war London theatre.

Against a troubled general economic background, the mid-1960s were years of watchful consolidation rather than carefree expansion. Circulation went over 150,000 in 1964 in the context of that year's bull market, but then flattened to an average daily net sale of 149,166 and 149,804 for 1965 and 1966 respectively. Advertising revenue continued to increase (including from colour advertising, which first appeared in January 1965); but so too, even more inexorably, did production and distribution costs, with the *FT* now firmly part of the wider Fleet Street syndrome. The situation was not helped by the continuing drain on resources of the general printing of St Clements, though in January 1966 the board took the decision that all printing other than that of the *FT* would be taken out of Bracken House within the next two years. The *FT* itself made a trading profit in 1965 of £1,369,410, which was only marginally an improvement on the £1,360,856 for 1964. By February 1966 the mood in the board room was one of gloom, as the minutes show:

> Lord Robbins said the position at the moment was causing some concern and with the present conditions going on it would seem that this year would not be a very good one. Lord Drogheda said that so far there had been a 20% drop in advertisement revenue. In view of this and the economic situation he wondered whether steps ought to be taken to try and cut down expenses. Lord Poole said that while the situation gave cause for concern he did not think that policies should be altered over what might be a temporary period of depression. If such a trend went on for a year or more then would be the time to think of cutting back.
>
> Lord Drogheda asked if Lord Poole had heard any comments from his people in Lazards as to the content of the paper. He thought it would be extremely helpful if opinions could be obtained. Lord Poole said he had heard no averse comments on the *FT*. As regards competition he said he was in the habit of reading the *Sunday Times* Business Section [which had begun in 1964] but he did not think this was very well done. He was impressed by the quality of *The Times* City pages which he felt had improved considerably.

A month later Hunter, the general manager, told the board that, according to his estimates, the paper's profits for 1966 were likely to be about half those for 1965, a fall attributable equally to increased costs and reduced revenue. Within days of this ominous forecast Labour was returned to power at the general election with a handsome majority.

It was in this context that the *FT* now embarked on one of the great might-have-beens (arguably, the greatest might-have-been) of its history. By 1965 everyone who was anyone at the quality end of the newspaper industry knew that *The Times* was more or less actively looking for a suitor. Over the previous five years its ratio of profit to turnover had fallen from 10.7 to 3.4 per cent, its home sales had gradually declined from 239,600 to 228,300, and its circulation share of the market was down from 14.7 to 12.7 per cent. In the subsequent words of its owner Gavin Astor:

> There is no standing still in newspapers. They either progress or they die. *The Times* was not only standing still but others were overtaking it. It was becoming

imperative to restore the health of the paper; and the best way to do this was to ensure that it was better than any of its competitors so that it would attract readers as well as advertisers.[17]

In the course of 1965 it became clear that the cost of such a development programme over the next five years would be some £2½ to £3 million – funds that the paper simply did not have available at a time when it owed almost £2½ million to the bank. It was a burden compounded by Astor's thorough awareness that, if he died, the appalling liability of estate duties could lead to a forced sale of the paper to the highest bidder, who might or might not be the suitable owner of a 'national institution'. For these reasons *The Times* during 1965 entered into talks with both the *Observer* and the *Guardian* about some form of union, but neither set of talks achieved significant progress. From March 1966, following a chance meeting between Drogheda and Astor's financial adviser, Kenneth Keith, it was the *FT* that for six months took up the principal running.

Over these six months the initiative from the *FT* side very much came from Drogheda. Why was he so keen? Partly of course because of the immediate rather depressing outlook for the paper, but partly also for reasons he subsequently touched on in one of the most interesting passages of his memoirs:

> I realised that the *FT* had had a good run, having built itself a position that was basically extremely strong, and having enjoyed a degree of success which far exceeded my expectations. However self-satisfaction was a mood which I constantly resisted, for I was always fearful that something might happen to disturb our happy state . . . I was very much aware that because of our specialised nature we were inescapably bound to remain a second newspaper. The *FT* certainly carried much general news, and the volume of foreign news which we published was in terms of columnage higher than any other [probably not true until later in the 1960s]; but when it came to sport, the law courts, social news and so on we did not attempt to compete. To have done so on top of providing all our specialised business news coverage would have crippled us financially. We should have needed a limitless purse to draw readers away from *The Times* and the *Daily Telegraph*, with no certainty of success after years of striving. It was our job to try to provide the best possible business newspaper, interpreting the word 'business' as widely as possible, but we could never hope to give a complete service. However, there was the constant possibility that following a change of control *The Times* might greatly enlarge its business news coverage, and this in times of difficulty could strike a hard blow at the *FT*. (A similar risk did not exist in relation to the *Daily Telegraph*, because of its circulation of over one and a

quarter million, and the consequent cost to it in terms of paper and distribution of adding several more business pages.)[18]

Drogheda was a curious, perhaps healthy mixture of pessimist and expansionist. Both elements now came strongly into play. That July, in the midst of negotiations, he summarized in a memorandum to his colleagues the eight main reasons why he was seeking to achieve a merger between the *FT* and *The Times*:

1. First of all I believe that the profit of the new paper would be materially greater than the profit we can anticipate from the *FT* on its own. The reason for this is that the higher advertisement rate which we could charge, coupled with the substantially greater revenue from classified advertisements and circulation, would comfortably exceed the increase in costs.
2. I think that the business climate is going to be difficult for some time to come. This would affect the combined paper just as much as it will the *FT* on its own, but one must remember that dependence on display advertisement revenue would be lessened and a larger proportion of revenue would be derived from classified advertisements and circulation.
3. Bringing the two papers together would give a tremendous incentive to the business staffs at a time when such incentive is lacking. There would be a splendid sales story to tell.
4. We should be able to move production into a building which is far better designed for daily newspaper production and a fair amount of accommodation would be freed which could be profitably rented.
5. *The Times* situation cannot remain static. If we do nothing, somebody else will go in and whoever it is is bound to make a dead set at our sources of revenue. Our Editor has no doubt that *The Times* and ourselves would then be on a collision course. It would not be difficult to build up the business side of *The Times* and if times are going to be hard I can well see readers opting for a general newspaper which has a first-class business section and I can see the sale of the *FT* suffering.
6. A merger would enable us to get rid of a number of the costly practices which have over the years been allowed to creep in on the production side. The move to a new centre of production would enable a fresh start to be made in certain important respects which it is unrealistic to suppose would be possible if we stayed where we are.

   There is likely to be important changes in production techniques during the course of the next few years, computerised setting and colour printing, for instance, and these will be far easier to face up to if we have a broader based group.
7. There appears to be some doubt about the title of the merged paper. It would

in my view have to be *The Times* and *FT*, not simply *The Times* followed in very small type by 'incorporating the *FT*' which would not do at all.

8. There must to my mind be a great attraction in producing what would undoubtedly be the leading newspaper in the land and one which would have great influence throughout the world. We have an exceptionally able staff and I believe that to give them a wider scope would be in the general public interest.

Drogheda added his belief that 'there is no reason at all why the paper should not make a profit from the word go' and estimated £1,465,000 as a minimum profit projection, rising considerably higher in better economic times. He was now increasingly coming to see what had begun as essentially a pre-emptive strike as the most natural of marriages.

Editorially no insuperable problems emerged during the negotiations. It was agreed from the outset that Newton would be editor of the merged paper. Newton himself was almost as keen as Drogheda on the whole idea. He saw it as a hybrid, combining the best of the two papers, and was especially attracted to the prospect of increased sports coverage. During these months he was constantly pulling dummy copies out of his pocket to show people. In short, the project appealed to him greatly as a journalist, quite apart from his apparent acceptance of the Drogheda argument that *The Times* under other ownership could prove a serious threat to the *FT*. There is conflicting evidence about what precisely the nature of the combined paper would have been, but it seems that the original notion was of a fairly conventional *Times* at the front, with the *FT*, still on pink paper, attached at the back to provide the business coverage. Increasingly, however, it seemed absurd, to Newton in particular, that a paper that was making a huge loss should dominate the combined paper in this way; and what appears to have evolved over the summer months was a more unified paper, printed throughout on white paper, in which the *FT* writers and approach permeated almost all the pages and not just the specialist business coverage. 'It's a take-over,' remarked Sir William Haley, editor of *The Times*, at one point to Newton.[19] In a sense that was true, editorially as well as financially, but at the same time it was never intended to discard such traditionally excellent features of *The Times* as its law reports and obituaries, together with its full complement of foreign correspondents and its increasingly good sports coverage.

The Times side was also worried about whether ownership by Pearson would guarantee the new paper the editorial independence to which *The Times* was more or less accustomed. The solution devised to this problem

– a somewhat artificial one, granted Pearson's track record – was that Haley would become both chairman of the new paper and, in the American sense of the word, publisher. This would enable him, to quote the historian of *The Times*, 'to put a broad pair of shoulders between the editor and anyone, from anywhere, who was out to apply pressure on that editor', while at the same time leaving the editor to get on with the day-to-day business of editing.[20] Drogheda would be managing director of the new paper. By the beginning of August it all seemed to be coming together.

Yet within the *FT* camp there were significant doubts. The 'triumvirate' was solid enough, but Hunter's attitude towards the proposed merger was one of what Drogheda later called 'somewhat irrational hostility'; while Robbins was, again in Drogheda's words, 'sceptical because of his fear that we might be submerged by the losses of *The Times*'.[21] The crucial doubts, however, were those felt by Pearson. At the decisive board meeting Gibson did not oppose the project as such, but expressed concern that the independent identity of the *FT* would be lost at the hands of a paper with historically far greater prestige and range of subject-matter. Poole was distinctly unkeen; the project ran diametrically counter to his whole 'niche' approach towards business, and he could see no advantage in paying money to take on an enterprise that was losing considerable sums at a time when the problems of the national newspaper industry as a whole were compounding rapidly. Cowdray himself did not express a view either way, but in practice found it easiest to authorize Poole on behalf of Lazards to make a low bid for *The Times* that would almost certainly be rejected.

The rest of the story is told by Drogheda:

> An indication had been conveyed to us that if Gavin Astor were to be offered a 12½ per cent or one-eighth interest in the combined group [to include the Westminster Press, the *Banker* and so on as well as the *FT* itself and *The Times*] he would be willing to accept. However, the financial experts advising Pearsons suggested that his proportion should be no more than 8¼ per cent. I pleaded that this figure should be increased, because I was certain that it would not prove acceptable (in terms of assets as opposed to profits, figures suggested that one third of the assets of the new company would derive from *The Times*) and I felt that far more was at stake than a small percentage either way; but to no avail . . . To the profound dismay of Gordon Newton, Sidney Henschel and myself the offer was duly and predictably declined. No increased figure was proposed and within a few weeks it was announced with a great flourish of trumpets that control of *The Times* has passed to Roy Thomson.[22]

Irrespective of the rights and wrongs of the larger judgement, Pearson had not conducted themselves particularly creditably. Making an offer that was almost certain not to be accepted was in practice a way of aborting the project without having to go to Drogheda and say outright that the idea had been turned down. Not surprisingly, Drogheda's account of the episode is tinged with a certain bitterness.

The question remains: would the merger of the two papers have taken place even if Pearson had favoured the idea and come up with an appropriate offer? Newton for one came to believe not: partly because, in his own words, 'there would have been an uproar from the unions'; and partly also because of likely opposition on the part of the Monopolies Commission, especially granted the presence of an alternative suitor in the wings, Roy Thomson, who did not own a national daily and would not be turning two papers into one. These are plausible grounds for doubt, but of course one cannot know what would have happened in practice. The successful arrival of Thomson on the scene – so soon after Drogheda and Newton had been led (or felt they had been led) to understand that union with the *FT* was a way for *The Times* to be saved from Thomson – rankled in Bracken House for a long time afterwards. The feeling undoubtedly existed that the *FT* had been little short of double-crossed. In fairness to *The Times*, however, there is at least some evidence that Thomson did not emerge as a significant negotiating force until the rejection of Pearson's nugatory offer.

More to the point is the question whether the failure of nuptials was ultimately a cause of regret. The *FT* journalists themselves, or at least those who knew something of what was going on, had mixed feelings. Tugendhat has put it rather well, saying that they felt the hope and excitement of an occupying army, together with a certain fear of being left behind in the rush of events. Perhaps in the end a sense of relief was uppermost. Twenty years on it is a feeling with which one is inclined to sympathize. It is hard not to believe that in the course of time, perhaps after Newton had retired, the smaller, younger, more specialized paper would not have been swallowed up by what was then, whatever its arthritic, non-commercial characteristics, a great and vastly respected national organ. As it happened, the *FT* on its own was able to go on to still better things, while *The Times* after 1966 had some more years ahead of it as a quality paper. For Drogheda and Newton it was the denial of the culminating master-stroke of their careers, but for the *FT* in the longer perspective it was, in the words of the famous exam question, the turning-point that fortunately failed to turn.

[TWELVE]

TOWARDS AN INTERNATIONAL PAPER: 1966–72

As the Drogheda–Newton 'axis' moved into its final phase the problems of the national newspaper industry, above all on the production side, cast an increasingly oppressive shadow. In 1964 had been established a Joint Board for the industry under the chairmanship of Lord Devlin, representing both management and unions and designed to usher in a new, more rational age. Chapel opposition effectively nullified its efforts, but for the historian it did sponsor a major investigation into the industry by the *Economist* Intelligence Unit, which was published in January 1967. The report, while predictably critical of overmanning, restrictive practices, union resistance to change and so on, also had harsh things to say of Fleet Street management, which it depicted as generally timid, of poor quality and amateurish in approach. Thus of the *FT* specifically:

> Because of the unique position of the paper and its numerically small organisation, it is possible to be financially successful without the use of more sophisticated management techniques . . . Although revenue and cost forecasts are prepared, the various departments do not appear to conform to a fixed budget and certainly there is no editorial budget in the true sense of the word. The forecasts themselves tend to be prepared on a rule of thumb basis by the General Manager . . . There is little interest in management training in the company, nor are attempts made to train representatives in the Circulation and Advertisement departments.[1]

Over the next few years, partly in response to these charges, a greater degree of budgetary control was introduced, together with an element of in-house training. Nevertheless, there was another side to the coin, as the report itself showed. Not only was it the case that 'among daily newspapers the *Financial Times* has the highest ratio of single column inches of advertising carried for each member of the advertisement department', but the same also applied in the editorial sphere. Taking the year 1965 as a whole, the number of single column inches of editorial space per member of editorial staff was as follows for various papers: *Daily Express*, 791: *Daily Telegraph*, 1,269; *Daily Mail*, 1,273; *The Times*, 2,115; *Guardian*,

2,281; and the *FT*, a staggering (to those who did not know the editor) 4,958. There was still the problem of 'below stairs', but nevertheless, in the slightly reluctant words of the report, 'it may be argued that there is no need to be particularly sophisticated, as the newspaper is sufficiently successful by use of personal judgement'.[2]

The *FT* in the late 1960s was, by any normal standards, a severely under-managed paper. Apart from Drogheda, whose time was increasingly taken up by other matters (including the chairmanship of the Newspaper Publishers' Association from 1968, a thankless task indeed), there were only four significant management figures. One was Alan Cox, general manager of St Clements Press. Another was A. L. ('Bert') Emerick, who after the retirement of Hunter in October 1966 became joint general manager of the paper. Emerick was the nicest of people and an efficient worker, who had started on the old *FT* in 1928 as a messenger boy, but he was not the sort of person who was going to guide the company into a new era of professional management. The other joint general manager was the Hon. Alan Hare, who had been at the Foreign Office during the 1950s and became manager of the *FT*'s foreign department in 1962. His elder brother was married to a sister of Lord Cowdray, and he was originally recruited by Drogheda, who later recalled how Hare 'was obviously very bright and produced the most fascinating convoluted sentences, to which I had to pay close attention in order not to get lost'.[3] He was a man of considerable qualities, including great integrity, but neither by background nor by outlook could be described as entrepreneurial. The fourth figure was Christoper Johnson, who in 1967 became the paper's first managing editor. There were various reasons for his appointment: the need to take some of the burgeoning work of editorial organization and recruitment off the shoulders of Newton; a desire on the part of Robbins and Drogheda to keep a certain check on Newton's expansionist instincts; and a feeling that it was a good position in which to 'run' him as a potential future editor. Again, Johnson was a thoroughly pleasant and intelligent man, but he lacked the personal weight, the streak of ruthlessness, to make a great impact in the job. He was also hindered rather than helped by being the son-in-law of the chairman. Finally, one should mention Newton himself. He was elected to the board in 1967 and in a sense became more formally accountable for his editorial actions. Nevertheless, during his last years as editor he had far greater freedom to pursue a policy of more or less untrammelled growth than a present-day Fleet Street editor could conceivably have. Nor was he the sort of editor who made the position of managing editor an enviable one.

As a management team they were no match for the print unions and their chapels, especially with the size of the paper rapidly increasing and thus yielding ever-greater bargaining opportunities. Old-fashioned paternalism remained, at least from on high, the order of the day, typified by the concluding part of an anxious discussion by the board in March 1968 about recent troubles:

Lord Robbins wondered whether we did everything possible to foster good relations on the productions side. Both Lord Drogheda and Sir Gordon Newton said that they thought this aspect was adequately covered and that from time to time notes of thanks were sent to various Chapels following difficult periods when the production side had been extremely co-operative. Lord Drogheda said he would not object to further cocktail parties being arranged but he did not think this sort of event should take place too often.

Cocktail parties or no, the whip hand lay ever more with the unions. Three months later a further board discussion practically said it all:

Lord Drogheda gave details of a dispute between St Clements Press and the staff of its composing room following a decision of SCP to discontinue certain special payments which were made in connection with the production of The Financial Times Annual Review when this had been produced as a separate publication. He said the payments originated some fifteen years ago when the Annual Review was treated as exported material because it had been available for sale separately from the paper. Although we had since stopped selling the Annual Review separately the payment had continued. However, now that the Annual Review would form part of the paper itself there was no longer a case for making special payment. The compositors had said, however, that unless the special payment was made they would not set any editorial copy or proof any advertisement material for the Annual Review. The cost of the original demand for this special payment amounted to about £5,000, but Mr Cox had negotiated a reduction of some £2,500 with the composing chapel. After discussing this matter further the Board expressed their sympathy with Mr Hare's view that the claim for the special payment was completely unjustified and should be resisted but felt that our case was not strong enough for a confrontation with the Union. It was agreed, therefore, that Lord Drogheda should arrange for Mr Cox to settle the dispute on the best possible terms which would not endanger publication of the Annual Review.

It was not the first time Cox had been issued such instructions, nor would it be the last. He had come from *The Times* in 1964, knew the printing industry inside out and in many ways was a superb negotiator, including having a well-developed line in brinkmanship. Inevitably, he was engaged for most of his years at St Clements in what was essentially a 'fire-fighting', damage-limitation exercise, and there were always a few particularly powerful groups of workers – above all the lino operators and those in the foundry – with whom he tried at all costs to avoid tangling. He worked incredibly hard at his job, never took a holiday, and for many years, certainly until the mid-1970s, played virtually a lone hand. It would not be an exaggeration to say that his fundamental brief from Drogheda was to make sure that the paper came out every day; precisely how he achieved that was, for the most part, left to him. It is all too easy, from the more favoured management perspective of the second half of the 1980s, to denigrate the key role that he played in keeping the show on the road for the best part of two decades.

Back in the first winter following the failure of *The Times* merger talks, the main preoccupation of both management and editorial lay elsewhere. It was clear from soon after the time that Thomson acquired ownership that he had ambitious plans to transform the business coverage of *The Times* – precisely the scenario that Drogheda had feared. In distinctly sober mood the *FT* board (joined by Newton and Henschel) met on 25 October 1966 to consider the paper's apparently threatened future:

> On the whole it was thought that most top businessmen read the paper. The aim now would be to reach more of the middle management strata . . . It was thought that the paper may have reached its ultimate circulation for its present format, although there could be about 5,000 investors who might come back in if stock markets became active again. Although new features aimed at helping circulation would increase costs, it was agreed that these should not be curtailed unless financial circumstances so dictated.
>
> Sir Gordon Newton said he thought in future the paper must be developed more for the industrialist than the investor. Competition would increase in all spheres of advertising and editorial. It would be foolish to ignore *The Times* venture. The City side of the paper and back page quotations might be vulnerable. Both Lord Robbins and Lord Drogheda thought the City aspect could be improved.
>
> Mr Smith and Mr Gibson both thought that enlargement of the page-one news synopsis might help circulation. Sir Gordon Newton said a previous experiment with this had failed, but he would reconsider it. A tentative new layout for the paper was now being prepared.
>
> Lord Poole said there were tremendous advantages on our side. We had an organisation ready to go. This was a wonderful chance to show its capabilities. It should start now with a great urgency.

Below board level there was, over the next five or six months, considerable nervousness in the ranks. The feeling grew that, faced by the

The Financial Times Tuesday January 10 1967 9

The Technical Page

Products

Computer specifies home heating needs

FULL domestic central heating systems of Dutch design are to be marketed on a greater scale soon in England. Calculations of the requirements for each individual house or flat are worked out with the aid of a computer.

In each of these systems a gas-fired stove acts as the heat source and this is connected in a ring circuit by means of a continuous ¾-inch square pipe. Water is circulated through the pipe by a noiseless pump which can be fitted out of sight at any point in the circuit.

Installation of the system can be made without doing any damage to the house, it is claimed. Only a few small holes need to be bored through walls, and because of its square section the pipe can be run externally along or on top of skirting boards. The stove itself looks like a large modern gas fire. It gives out radiant heat and is suitable for installation in place of an existing open fireplace.

Prefabrication of pipework is carried out in Holland and all the facts and figures for each installation are fed into a computer in that country. The computer output specifies radiator sizes for each room, but outputs required and costs and print-out is supplied to the potential purchaser.

It is claimed that by this "pre-piping" method full central heating can be installed in a three- or four-bedroomed flat in about 35 hours, the fitter only having to make about 20 connections. Cost of installation in an average-size semi-detached three-bedroom house is estimated at about £385, including stove radiators, pipework, pump and thermostat. The stoves have burners suitable for both town and natural gas.

The company marketing the system is **Ringheating**, of Northway House, High Road, Whetstone, London, N.20, which which is a subsidiary of Ringverwarming NV, one of the largest companies in the central heating field in The Netherlands.

In Holland the company operates a day and night servicing system with the aid of radio-equipped cars and it will do so in this country when operations are on a large enough scale.

Machine fills cans of many sizes fast

MANUFACTURERS faced with the problem of filling containers of various sizes—from ½-pint to 1-gallon cans—with liquids of many kinds are now being offered a machine which will do this with an accuracy of plus or minus ½ per cent.

Air-operated and flameproof, the machine will even handle semi-solids, claims the maker. Rate of filling varies with the viscosity of the material and size of container, but is generally about twelve 1-gallon or 50 half-pint containers per minute. Measures may be imperial, metric or U.S. The volume of each "shot" can be changed instantly to fill different-sized containers and the equipment is especially designed to cope with the problem of foaming.

The machine incorporates a reciprocating air motor driving a positive displacement pump and these are mounted horizontally on a portable steel frame. Only service required is an air supply above 80 lbs per square inch. Operation is by a hand or foot control to initiate a single fill, but the machine can be made fully or semi-automatic if required.

The manufacturer, **Neumo**, South Coast Road, Peacehaven, Sussex, says the machine will cost between £540 and £700, according to materials from which it is to be made and whether it is to be designed for filling from the top or bottom of the container. Similar machines with smaller pumps and designed to fill containers with capacities as low as 1 cc will cost about £350.

Cheap spreaders for garden lovers

DRIED BLOOD, bone meal and hoof and horn, though excellent for roses, are rather unpleasant to distribute by hand in a garden, while they can often be contaminated with various kinds of salmonella bacteria which cause food poisoning.

A simple powdering can made of polypropylene and ABS plastics has been designed and tested with powdered and granulated fertilisers as well as grass seeds and enables these to be distributed evenly over the surface of the ground with a movement of the wrist.

Sutton and Sons, of Reading, have tried out the design with some 40 different products, alone or in combination with dry soil or sand.

The can has been moulded with a very smooth surface, making it particularly easy to clean.

The Terry vented space heater seen on the left has improved working conditions at the Mitcham, Surrey, works of Microplas which produces about 300 cabin cruisers a year. Marketed in Britain by George Cohen Machinery, the heater is said to be particularly suitable for use where strict fire precautions have to be observed.

Large surfaces sprayed at speed

VERTICAL spraying machines designed to cover large surfaces at speeds of up to 300 feet a minute have been developed by **Automatic Equipment**, Daleside Road, Nottingham.

They will apply a variety of paints and lacquers to metals, plastics and timber in sheet form ships' plates, structural steelwork, acoustic panels and plasterboard. Self-contained, the machines can be used with existing plant and conveyors or incorporated into automated painting systems.

Scan lengths are variable from 2 to 8 feet and spray width adjustable accurately within the scan. The sprayer can be used with air atomisation automatic spray guns, airless equipment, electronic spray equipment or hot spray systems.

Facilities exist for incorporating pivoting mechanisms to arc the guns at the end of each stroke. This enables low and medium contour work to be adequately coated with only two guns.

Special-purpose oil pump

DESIGNED specially for use at London Airport is a vertical, suspended version of the 2½-inch RT.50 Rotan internal gear pump. Three are installed in the fuel storage area, where, suspended in tanks, they transfer lube oil to maintenance vehicles at rates of 70 gallons a minute.

The RT.50, available from **Jobson and Beckwith**, 62-66 Southwark Bridge Road, London, S.E.1, can pump against a total head of 260 feet, including a suction lift of 25 feet. It is available with built-in relief valve and steam jacket.

Control lowers grain-drying fuel bills

AT CHOSELEY Farm, near Odiham, Hants, in a specially constructed store, a **Matthews and Yates** on-floor grain drying installation with automatic humidity and conditioning control has dried 300 tons of grain this season at a cost of some £20 for electricity. Results are stated to closely resemble those produced by natural drying.

The store is a 75 by 40 feet "Arcform" building. M and Y equipment consists of a Cyclone PU 2.5 packaged drying unit, main on-floor ventilation ducting and slotted lateral ducting. The drying unit is fitted with the humidity and conditioning control (a major contributor to the lower fuel cost) which can be set to operate the fan only when atmospheric air is dry enough to remove moisture from the grain without use of additional heat.

The control has been perfected during field trials, it is stated, and is available from M and Y (Cyclone Works, Swinton, Manchester) for next season at £78. Total cost of the equipment at Cholsey, including installation, was £1,330.

Shatterproof containers

FIRST CUSTOMER in the U.K. for Cope Allman International's new Coplastic containers is Chesebrough-Pond. It is putting an eight-ounce pack of Vaseline in the lightweight, shatterproof material and finds that filling rates of 180-240 packs a minute are possible.

Coplastic is an injection moulded container for clear, opaque, rigid or pliable packs in various types of plastics material. With the machines at present being used the outside limits of size for the containers are six inches cube, but if economic runs were assured new machines could be installed for larger sizes. Liners are used to alter the basic sizes and shapes, giving a wide range of custom-built packs.

Two claims made by **Cope Allman** (27, Hill Street, London, W.1.) are savings of up to 30 per cent. on transport costs over heavier packs and that, depending on requirement and length of run, Coplastic is fully competitive with glass.

Promoting advanced machine tools

THESE are the three advanced machine-tools selected so far by the Ministry of Technology for support under a programme to help the machine-tool industry and improve productivity in engineering. All three represent a considerable improvement on anything available elsewhere.

The scheme provides money for pre-production models which are then placed with selected industries who use them for a specified period and then report on their performance. These reports will ultimately be used to tell industry what they can do.

At top left is a double action spring coiler which turns out two springs per cycle with an efficiency of 90 per cent. against one per cycle and 65 per cent. for existing units. It is made by **Bennett Tools** of the Tube Investments group. On the left is the **Ferranti** drawing measuring machine, which makes a paper tape when a user follows a blueprint with a stylus. The tape can go into the control unit of a machine-tool or into a computer for further processing.

Another Ferranti unit (above right) is a very high accuracy inspection machine which will quickly measure engineering components in three dimensions to tolerances of about one ten-thousandth of an inch. The Ministry is spending a total of £155,000 on the three contracts in the expectation that the time-lag between the development of up-to-the-minute equipment and its acceptance by industry will be appreciably shortened.

Science News

Spray hardens load-bearing soil beds

EXPERIMENTS are going on in the U.S. with a method of treatment that enables levelled ground to bear heavy loads after about an hour.

The basis is to spray a rapid-setting material on the earth and while many compounds have been tested, the best performance was put up by a mixture of a modified chlorinated polyester resin with fibreglass reinforcement and heat-resistant ingredients.

The surface it produces on the soil is strong enough after an hour to take the weight of a ten-ton aircraft and it is primarily for this purpose that the method has been developed—to provide quickly established landing and take-off pads for helicopters. It has obvious applications in many other areas of civil engineering.

The material can take blast pressures of 2,500 lbs per square foot and withstand heating to 3,000 F. It is now being tested in sub-zero and tropical conditions.

Leading the work on the method and the materials suitable for it is the **U.S. Air Force Research Laboratories**, Dayton, Ohio, U.S.A.

Coal chemicals by laser

EXPERIMENTS by scientists of the **U.S. Bureau of Mines**, Department of the Interior, have shown that it is possible to produce a whole range of valuable chemical building blocks directly from coal with laser light.

Using an intense beam to disintegrate the coal, they cooled the gases coming off to prevent further reaction and found they contained 25 per cent. acetylene, as well as ethane, ethylene, hydrogen cyanide.

There were no tars left after the heating process, which took a few fractions of a second, only a solid residue. Vaporisation of the coal was estimated to have been in the region of 50 per cent.

The whole process took a few thousandths of a second and the products obtained were different from those released during conventional carbonisation which requires minutes and even hours.

The research workers believe that laser heating could provide a method of extracting a whole range of industrial chemicals from coal at lower costs than with any method applied so far.

Thermal analysis solves problems

THE Inveresk Gate, Musselburgh, research laboratories of the **Arthur D. Little** organisation are making extensive use of the differential thermal analysis technique to carry out delicate analyses of milligramme samples of many complex substances.

DTA provides a fast and simple method of identifying very small amounts of plastics, rubbers, resins and metals since it can work at temperatures of up to 1,600 degrees C. This is done by comparing the heat absorption of a sample with that of a reference.

To spread information on the techniques and equipment involved, the Ministry of Technology's Edinburgh Liaison Centre recently sponsored a conference on the technique at which some of the work at the Inveresk laboratories was described.

This included crystallisation phenomena and irreversible chemical changes in food manufacturing processes. The technique has also been used to solve whether a non-iron finish has been applied to a cotton fabric and it is sensitive enough to differentiate between various types of non-iron finish.

Transatlantic microfilm service

EXCHANGES of technical drawings between manufacturing centres of the **Hoover** organisation in Britain and the U.S. are now taking the form of low-cost microfilm duplicates inset on data processing punched cards. Over 10,000 drawings of new and modified products travel between the centres each year and in addition there are frequent demands for copies from the Hoover library of 60,000 drawings. The system chosen is the 3M "Filmsort" and its use at Perivale has cut storage costs by 75 per cent.

Solvents cope with copper and zinc

COMPLEX ORES which defy ordinary smelting methods to extract their copper and zinc content may be treated by a solvent extraction process to be patented by the Metallurgy Research Laboratory of the **U.S. Bureau of Mines**, Salt Lake City, Utah.

Complex sulphides, for instance, would be roasted, leached with acid to remove the two metals in solution and the liquor fed to a mixer, where an organic chemical would be used to absorb one of the metals, leaving the other in the acid. The two liquids would be separated by gravity and their metal content recovered by electrolysis.

The laboratory says the equipment required is simple and can be established anywhere, eliminating the need for a long haul of concentrates from mine to smelter.

Materials

Porous metal cuts noise of engine

SINTERED, porous stainless steel sheeting called "Felt Metal," has been used to line the casings of jet engines and down the centre of the air passage as a splitter ring to provide worthwhile reductions in engine noise.

It is particularly effective in the range of 2,000 to 6,000 cycles per second, absorbing vibrational energy from the air which would otherwise emerge as noise.

Sintered aluminium is to be tried in place of the steel by the developers, **Huyck Metals** of PO Box 30, Milford, Connecticut and it is anticipated that the materials will find similar sound-deadening applications in other areas of engineering.

Better shielding from radiation

A NEW CLASS of shielding materials having excellent resistance to neutron and proton penetration has been developed by the **Chemtree Corporation**, of Central Valley, N.Y. 10917, U.S.A.

They are composed of lead and elements selected from the lanthanide series. One of them, for instance, contains 35 per cent. dysprosium and 40 per cent. lead and while slightly inferior to lithium hydride insofar as its neutron scattering potential is concerned, it is superior for thermal neutron capture and proton attenuation.

It is possible to get the best of both worlds by layering different materials so as to alternate the most efficient neutron capture product with the one which is best at scattering protons.

Coating resists water and wear

DEVELOPED for surfaces that have to stand up continuously to extreme conditions of humidity, pressure and water abrasion—encountered by submarines for instance—is a urethane-epoxy resin formulation containing ricinoleate polyol.

It cures in the temperature range 32 to 36 degrees F. and on surfaces in a continuous state of condensation, and while it was developed primarily for the maintenance painting of submarines it has many applications in chemical processing and electrical industries.

The developers, the **Baker Castor Oil Company** of Bayonne, New Jersey 07002, USA, claim at least six months' protection for their product.

Processes

Plastic powder spraying

CONFIDENT that there will be a growing demand for finishes produced from plastic powders **Aerostyle**, of Sunbeam Road, North Acton, London, N.W.10, is putting on the market new electrostatic equipment for applying them.

An important part of the equipment is the patented Powderstat hopper which meters the powder at controlled rates of flow from 1 to 100 lbs per hour. The spray gun is claimed to have a unique nozzle arrangement which enables infinitely variable adjustment between a straightforward spray and a wide cone shape.

It is further claimed that no blocking of the feed tubes between the hopper and the gun is possible because the trigger arrangement on the gun is such that the powder is cleared from the tubes completely before the air is cut off.

Plastic powder coatings, which have to be stowed after application, are said to be particularly suitable for producing smooth finishes on rough castings and for covering sharp edges and reaching into deep recesses.

Thinner layers of insulant

EXPERIENCE in operating a contractors' scheme has led the Oleochemical Division of **J. Bibby and Sons** to modify their one-shot polyurethane spray on thermal insulation for buildings and marine vessels.

The new formulation can be applied in a wider range of external temperatures, has a longer shelf life and provides a smoother and harder finish.

One advantage is that thinner layers can provide the same insulating effect. In a cold room designed by the C. Hemmings organisation a three-inch layer enables temperatures down to minus 5 degrees Fahrenheit to be maintained with a given power consumption against a range of 28 to 32 degrees Fahrenheit for a room with the same floor area and power using a 4-inch layer of material previously used.

The service operates from King Edward Street, Liverpool 3.

Covering pipes with plastics

HIGH VACUUM plant capable of applying a wide range of plastic coatings to pipes from one to sixteen inches in diameter has been installed at the Horseley works in Tipton, Staffs.

Using a new process to be known as "PRO-VAC," the plant is to be developed to tackle still larger pipe diameters and, at a later stage to apply liquid coatings.

The process was invented and successfully operated in Holland by Mr. J. J. Heilker who has been appointed technical director of a new company set up within the Horseley group under the name of **Horseley-Piggott (Coatings)** to sell the service to industry.

Apart from pipes, valves, fan and pump impellers and objects of difficult shapes are simple to protect with the process which gives even surfaces with high adhesion.

10 January 1967: the first 'Technical page'

seemingly bottomless Thomson millions that were being poured into *The Times*, the *FT* was going to be hard pressed to compete. If a certain complacency had crept into the paper by the mid-1960s, there was none by the spring of 1967. Newton's response was admirable. He refused to panic and took the view that the *FT* was a quality paper which, with a generation of experience behind it, would not only meet the challenge but even thrive on it. It was a characteristic level-headedness at a time when that quality was at a premium.

During the early months of 1967 Newton made three main changes to the paper, each of which has endured. In January he began 'The Technical Page', which appeared four times a week and on its first day received the following billing:

> Besides incorporating the material formerly included in weekly columns – Products and Processes, Scientists' Notebook and New Materials – it will extend its coverage to all fields of industrial, scientific and technological research and innovation. News will be given of the latest developments in fields as diverse as automation, agriculture, and new gadgets and equipment for the home. The aim is to present to industrialists a broad but detailed picture of what is new in every branch of industry.

The page's co-editors were Arthur Bennett and Ted Schoeters, who had been a press officer with the Atomic Energy Authority. As a page it was invented, in Newton's own words, 'out of the wastepaper basket', being largely composed of press-release material that the *FT* had found itself receiving in increasingly large volumes. It was the first Fleet Street page devoted to technical matters and it obviously chimed in with 'white heat' and the existence of a Ministry of Technology, but to begin with it was terribly bitty, comprising on any one day up to twenty items divided into sections like 'Products', 'Materials', 'Science News' and 'Processes'. Gradually, though, it started to do a little more than merely regurgitate press releases and began to acquire a certain standing and authority, eventually leading to the infinitely more sophisticated technology page of the 1980s.

The second development had a more auspicious start. This took place in February when, after two years of fortnightly articles headed 'World of Management', 'The Executive's World' page began, forerunner of the modern 'Management' page:

> It will appear two or three times a week and will deal with topics which concern business executives at all levels – problems of finance, marketing, labour relations, training and education, planning, and all the other management problems which

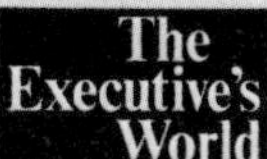

HOW TO STAY ON TOP

The virtues of specialisation

By GEOFFREY OWEN

A. L. TRUMP

P. T. STEPHENS

P. C. E. ROSE

Courting the new graduates

DESPITE British industry's alleged indifference to business school graduates, a strong demand is building up for the first products of the London and Manchester Business Schools.

At Manchester the recruiting process for the first year's students, who will complete their course in the summer, has already begun. About half the class has been "sponsored" by their previous employers and will be returning to them.

The students at London are on a two-year course, and arrangements are now being made to provide them with summer jobs, on the American pattern, before they begin their second year's training. There is no shortage of firms offering jobs; they are clearly eager to find out what business school students are like, with a view to

IF THERE IS ANY management principle which has some claim to universal validity, it is this—stick to what you are good at, and don't diversify into fields where you have nothing special to contribute. Too many British companies are active in many industries, but leaders in none. The most successful firms are often the ones which have deliberately confined their efforts to a narrow area where they have a proprietary position, a technological or marketing edge over everyone else. An outstanding example of such a policy is Saunders Valve, based at Cwmbran in Monmouthshire, which is the world's leading producer of diaphragm valves. It exports 60 per cent. of its output, and no one, either on the Continent or in the U.S., has come near to challenging its hold on world markets.

It was a help, of course, to be first in the field; the diaphragm valve was invented and patented in South Africa 35 years ago by Mr. P. K. Saunders. But it is one thing to invent a new product and establish a patent monopoly in that field; it is quite another to retain a dominant position in world markets long after the patents have expired. Saunders' success has been based, first, on its specialisation, and, second, on its consistent policy of treating the world as its market; because of the wide spread of sales

Line managers

Lack of warmth

Desert island

The big push

A different style

A language class for scientists

BY W. VAN DER EYKEN

Boosting sales in a stagnant market

BY ANTONY THORNCROFT

Profit margin

Impulse buying

OR man at Warwick

The Lombard Column

Central borrowing for local authorities?

BY C. GORDON TETHER

Change of plan

Where advantage lies

Treasury interest

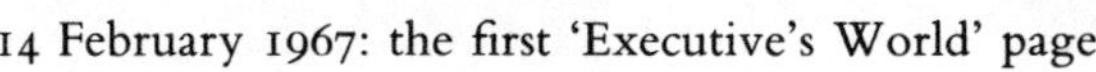

14 February 1967: the first 'Executive's World' page

face businessmen today. It will describe how companies are tackling these problems, and what modern techniques can be used to solve them.

The preparatory work for the page had been done by Owen, who edited it for the first few weeks. He also wrote its main article on the first day, which was headed 'How to stay on top: The virtues of specialisation' and began: 'If there is any management principle which has some claim to universal validity, it is this – stick to what you are good at, and don't diversify into fields where you have nothing special to contribute. Too many British companies are active in many industries, but leaders in none.' Any one 'Executive's World' page usually had two or three fairly substantial articles, and some early pieces included Willem van der Eyken on 'Management Simulation: Decision-Making without Tears', James Ensor on 'Automation in Steel: Controlling the Flow' and Antony Thorncroft on 'Market Research: How to Launch a Newspaper'. There was a long way to go, but it was still a fair start in an almost wholly undeveloped field, certainly in daily or even weekly journalism. Owen himself left after a few weeks to join the Industrial Reorganization Corporation and was succeeded by Anthony Harris, who over the next eighteen months or so developed the page as a mildly satirical organ, showing up the 'guff' of charlatan management analysts, of whom then as later there were not a few. The solemnization and professionalization of the page lay in the future.

The third main change early in 1967 was more gradual and took the form of an increasing number of articles being accorded by-lines. Thus on 16 March there were signed front-page stories by Mark Gapper (labour correspondent), Dennis Topping (industrial correspondent), Christopher Tugendhat (energy editor, hitherto named only in features) and Ian Dunning (commodities editor). The spread of by-lines was not an innovation that altogether met with the approval of Drogheda, as he later wrote: 'I could not help feeling that this was being allowed to be overdone, even quite trivial news items being signed, but Gordon Newton assured me that it was necessary in order to retain his staff, and certainly there was a similar trend at *The Times* and elsewhere.'[4] Newton has argued that, with the growth of the specialist correspondent, such as Tugendhat on oil and related matters, *other* specialists in the same field needed to know who that correspondent was, and that, if they had not, then the authority of the anonymous correspondent would have suffered. At the time, however, it was probably the loyalty-retention consideration that was decisive. During the early part of 1967 the Thomson chequebook was luring journalists to *The Times* virtually by the dozen; but in the event only one now went there from the *FT*, namely the industrial and commercial reporter Maurice Corina, followed a year later by Topping. It is impossible to know how much by-lines helped, but they presumably played a part.

As it turned out, not one but two potential rivals now took the field, for early in April, a week before *The Times* launched its initiative, the *Daily Telegraph* started a new investment and business section, under the editorship of Kenneth Fleet. In the eyes of the *FT*, however, the real danger resided in Printing House Square. It was formally announced in February that *The Times* would soon be starting a daily business news section, which was to be in separate pull-out form, the thinking being that the husband would take it to the office while his wife read the main part of the paper during the day. Launch date was set for 11 April, Budget day, and considerable publicity attended the venture: 'This new section will be entirely devoted to industry and finance. It will provide a complete service for business executives and investors . . . Thirty additional full-time business journalists, backed by specialist contributors, have been recruited for the Business News.'[5] The *TBN*'s editor was Anthony Vice, the former *FT* journalist who had subsequently been on the *Sunday Times*, and its economics editor was Peter Jay. It proved a fatally flawed project. Launched before it was properly ready, it was plagued by inaccuracy and continued to be so for almost another two years; and it was often hard-pressed to decide whether stories should go in the business news section or the main paper. Bracken House breathed a collective sigh of relief, and some of the journalists were soon referring to the *TBN* as 'Comic Cuts'. Typically, this was not the response of Drogheda. On about the second day after the launch someone mentioned to him, during a sixth-floor lunch, how bad it was, and he replied, 'Never underestimate your competition.' Fortified by that certain streak of neurosis in him about the *FT*'s ultimate prospects, it continued to be his mission to keep people forever on their toes.

That autumn a further significant change took place. During its overview discussion of October 1966 the board had considered the future of the Saturday paper and bowed to Drogheda's view that for the time being it would be better to concentrate on developing the weekday paper, which would be less expensive and likelier to generate more immediate revenue. Robbins, however, had added his opinion 'that the Saturday issue should not be overlooked in future planning even although the weekday issues would have priority'. Just under a year later, on 7 October 1967, a revamped Saturday paper made its bow. The announcement of the previous day detailed the principal attractions:

How to spend it

Making it hot for yourself

BY SHEILA BLACK

TWO YEARS AGO a big commercial group asked directors of two divisions to review what had become a costly and haphazard system for allocating company cars to representatives and executives. One evolved a points system, based on rank, which put all but top-flight management into small, cheap cars.

The other, with an almost identical division, had a different approach. He gave bigger, more powerful cars to those who had to cover the greatest mileage in their jobs, regardless of rank. Which meant that a lot of executives had to settle for rather smaller runabouts than before.

The first director's bill rose by nearly £1,500 in the first year for a fleet of about 50 cars, with an increase of about £3,200 in the second year. The other director saved £1,800 and £2,900 respectively. Both gain and loss were made largely in maintenance.

This preamble is more relevant to central heating than might appear, since high running costs provoke more complaints than anything else, with expensive installation running close.

Like a car, heating installations must be geared to individual requirements—rather more so since they cannot be traded in. The basic steps will crystallise what you really want, and make it easier for your dealer to offer alternatives and estimates. Draw a house plan, upstairs and downstairs, however rudimentary. Decide how much time is spent in each room, by whom, when and what temperature you want—an hour or so with a thermometer in various rooms may surprise you by showing you that your comfort is in higher or lower ranges than the recommended temperatures.

Is the home heating to be on the same system as the hot water, regardless of whether the latter is already satisfactory? Often, it is cheaper in the long run to convert old water-heating systems when whole-house heating is installed.

If home heating and water are to run off the same source, be sure to consider a programmer rather than a time switch. The latter will cost anything from £5 to £10. These will switch on and off twice a day but will control only one circulation system. A programmer will cost between 12 guineas and 18 guineas but it will operate water and room heat separately, switching both on and off twice daily or keeping the water on all day and switching the room heat on and off.

The problem of choice

Now comes the first stage in the difficult problem of choice. The main headings for the system would be: (a) by circulating hot water into radiators of some kind, fed from a boiler burning any fuel. (b) Warmed air, ducted around the house from a central unit run on any fuel. (c) Floor warming, by electrical elements embedded under the floor on insulated beds to obviate downward loss of heat. (d) Individual, portable units such as fires, convectors, electrical oil-filled or other radiators, and suchlike. (e) Electric storage radiators using cheaper, off-peak electricity (anything from 30 to 40 per cent cheaper according to the area).

All but (d) and (e) can make the entire house comfortable without additional heat. The last two categories are usually only background or periodic heating methods—or else wildly expensive ones if whole home heating is the aim.

Olde phones from modern Denmark. All shapes, sizes, prices. Anne Storm, 119 Portobello Road, London, W.11.

Warm-air systems are rarely practical in old houses. Much the same applies to floor warming, although one might be having a floor re-laid. In such cases, the method is not too expensive—say about £150 in a room measuring 12 feet square, but that heats only the one room. Arguments rage about the running costs, generally found to be high. However, the secret is in the laying of the element rows at the right widths apart.

Since the majority will, therefore, be faced with a final choice of either (a) radiators fed by a central unit or (e) off-peak electric storage heaters, this might seem to be the time to end all this personal domestic research.

But wait. What about the psychological factor? If you want a glowing fire to sit by, you will be faced with turning off individual radiators in the living room, and the consequences of having to come down to a cold room because you forgot to turn them on again before bedtime. One simple answer might be to have either a smaller radiator or only one instead of two in the lounge. This does mean that the supplementary glowing fire is indispensable most of the time but, if you like it that way, well and good. By reversing this idea and having extra-large radiators or two in rooms where one would serve, one can cater for invalids or extra-chilly mortals without either subjecting the rest of the family to an inferno or investing in a programme sophisticated enough to be a mini-computer. 3.

There are still minor problems to work out. Where will you put those radiators? As far as possible, they should be under the source of greatest cold, usually the windows. If there are several windows, consider several small radiators. If furniture clutters the room, and there is only one window in a large room, consider a double radiator of narrow and short dimensions. They look unattractive, but learn to live with them. Skirting heaters are unobtrusive and highly efficient since they look like no more than wide skirtings with grilles atop. But they do mark walls very faintly, so don't go for them unless you have washable walls or annual redecoration agreements.

Having added up the radiators, the hot towel rails and any other thing, note this down and measure each room. The radiators cost anything from £8 to £16 each for roughly 5 feet long by 2 feet high (double types £3 to £5 more). 4. Now think about what fuel you want. Oil costs rather more to instal—a pressure-jet boiler costs about £140 (give or take £25 according to make) but it burns a heavy, cheaper oil than other types and gives more heat.

Oil is trouble-free except with cheaper boilers which occasionally give trouble or are noisy. It needs storage tanks, which can be small enough to fit into tiny London courtyards. Bills are worked out so as to spread the load if wanted. There is no standing charge (£10 with gas and £2 with off-peak electricity per year at *present* averages). Little attention needed.

Gas boilers are probably going to cost the average household anything between £105 and £135. Installation will be cheaper than oil, running costs higher and remember the standing charge. Radiator prices as for oil. Little attention needed.

Solid fuel boilers will be around £60 if you are prepared to play stoker or £100 to £135 for the gravity-feed type which "draws" its supplies from a big hopper built behind the boiler. The hopper does have to be filled and there is some work involved in clearing ash or the occasional clinker, though very little these days. If you don't mind the work, these are good value.

Electric storage radiators for off-peak current can cost as little as £25 or less each, but must be considered as background heating only except early in the morning, when they will supply enough heat to sit in comfortably. Controlled output models are about £35 to £40 each, but give comfortable heat for ten to fourteen hours a day according to whether they have an afternoon boost or not. Installation might be a little higher than gas in large houses, and similar in smaller ones requiring fewer radiators. Allow about £350 for our pre-mentioned average house and complete comfort but this varies enormously according to the number of units each buyer thinks necessary. No work and, unlike gas or oil, you can take the things with you. But they are big, bulky, and probably no cheaper to run than gas.

Electric radiators, usually oil-filled, have a lot of advantages, although they are expensive to run. They are cheaper to instal since all they require is a normal power socket and no fixing. They are portable so that you can change the furniture around or even store them away in summer if you must. They need no space for the central boiler or other unit—flats and small houses often lack this vital space, and the smaller the dwelling, the less heat it needs which helps to control the running cost. They can give all the heat you need or just background heating to your fire, as long as you ensure you get only those fitted with thermostats. They can be bought in "instalments," one at a time. They are portable and do not attract higher rates on valuation increases as most fixed systems do. And you can take them with you. They are also efficient. Probably well worth considering by those whose life at home is rather part-time, or for small flats and houses, or for those who still want to be spartan in some rooms but cosy in others. Our average house might be warmly furnished with these for about £200 though the annual cost is likely to be at least double any other system.

An extra-large radiator

Another system that needs no boiler—gas this time—is the Servowarm, where the heat supply unit is an extra-large radiator—probably in the living room. Servowarm (and one or two others remotely like it coming along) is sufficient for whole comfort. About £200 to instal with four radiators including the parent, but nearer £300 if you want extra radiators, programming, and so forth. There is a limit to the amount of heat available so watch that you buy the size you want if you need more than, say, five or six radiators.

Having told you how to make it hot, next week we shall tell you how to keep it hot, how to pay for it, how to find your dealers, and how to insure yourself against those non-deliberate mistakes.

Fashion and function blend in this electric coffee maker as harmoniously and tastefully as the coffee is blended. Probably the first of its kind in the world—this is a fine, bone china coffee pot by Wedgwood to their most popular designs with the practical plus of automated electrical control by Russell Hobbs. Perfect coffee makes itself in 10 minutes, then switches off and keeps itself hot to the last drop. I find the china-made coffee tastes best and like the idea of being able to match electricals to cups and things. In "Barbican" with the light brown glaze at £9; in "Gold Marguerite" bordering white china at 14 guineas; and in the well-known Napoleon Ivy at £10. Matching cups, bowls and saucers at their usual prices. In the shops early November.

YOUR COOKING ADVISER

Trompetto of the Savoy on pheasant

CHOOSE CAREFULLY. Hens are always best but cocks are good early in the season. Feel up under the feathers to the top of the leg beside the body for full, soft flesh. The same softness should be at the top of the wings, underneath.

Hanging time is a matter of taste. The favourite flavour nowadays is less "gamey" than in the '30s and birds are hung no more than two or three full days (Saturday's bird can be cooked on Tuesday or Wednesday). Hang, fully feathered, in a medium-temperature, dry, airy room, never in a cold or airless place. Pluck and dress (or get the butcher to do it) on the day of cooking or, at most, one day ahead. Do not refrigerate.

INGREDIENTS

One pheasant (preferably a hen)

One celery heart cut into matchsticks

¼ lb unsalted butter

¼ pint double cream (very fresh or it will curdle)

One sherry-glass Madeira or Sherry or ½ sherry-glass of brandy

Salt and pepper to taste

Pieces of larding fat (from butcher)

Season the bird by rubbing salt and pepper all over, then tie larding fat to cover breast. Lay the bird in a thick, heavy saucepan and simmer slowly for 20 minutes with lid very slightly back off the pan to expose about an inch-wide slit to keep succulence. Baste three or four times, then turn the bird over on to its other side and repeat for the next 20 minutes. Now lay the bird on its back and surround with cut celery. To check it cooked at the end of the hour (since heats vary, time may vary a little), lift it carefully to see if the fat drips white. When cooked, remove it to gentle warmth. Pour off excess butter, leaving a thin layer at bottom of pan. Add Madeira and bring to boil, stirring slowly. Then add cream, and bring that slowly to boil, stirring all the while. Serve sauce separately with the carved pheasant. This recipe can be followed for a jointed bird in a shallow, thick pan to take all the joints. Halve the cooking time and serve the joints and sauce separately.

Clement Freud

Sad we lost India

IF THE TOWER over the entrance had been 30 feet higher, the place could only have been a castle . . . but the battlements stop just above the fourth floor which tells those of us who know about 1920's architecture that it is an hotel.

Actually it is THE hotel Gleneagles. The pride of the British Railways fleet: 300 rooms; 300 staff, and a 2,000 square foot lounge in which occur such wild afternoon scenes as eight people and I sitting on unmatching, uncomfortable, uncut moquette chairs contemplating three-tiered cakestands lightly filled with standard goodies.

The history of railway hotels is not without interest. There was a time when train journeys were the highpoint in the nation's entertainment programme; soon after this the wise old railroaders, realising that station waiting-rooms were not the money spinners they might be, built hotels. As a result you could not only travel from London to Perth; once arrived there you could sleep in a bed hard by the the station before having the pleasurable journey home.

Over the years railway hotels fared as badly as other bad hotels; some were sold, some pulled down, some turned into institutions and a few survived. Gleneagles remained imperiously unaffected by the wind of change and flourished quietly, annually from March to October.

The prevailing atmosphere of the place makes you weep for the loss of India, and the spirit of Harold Macmillan walks slowly, approvingly, down the wide corridors.

The visitor is received with all the ceremony of an arrival at a country house. You go in to the immense hall and no one takes any notice. As you adjust your eyesight, you observe a considerable number of people all around, people perfectly prepared to help with the mechanics of signing the register, handing out keys, taking luggage—on their own terms.

By the time you get to your room and are confronted by a single red rose standing a leisurely guard over a bowl of fruit, Gleneagles time has become your time. There is no conflict of interest.

You pick up the telephone, ask for room service and request a menu—and, when it comes 15 minutes later, you feel that they have taken considerable trouble to send you the right menu in the hands of the only possible waiter who could competently take your order. On reflection, you feel that it is surprising they have achieved this with such despatch.

The waiter recommends smoked salmon—as one man to another. He comes back with the best smoked salmon I have eaten this year and it occurs to me that if I met the man in the hall downstairs I would not remember his face — though I would remember the smoked salmon.

The hotel, the service, the over-riding air of utter decency with which they go about their business, is bigger than the individuals concerned in the play.

On closer inspection the salmon is served on a silver tray decorated with half a lemon. There is also a plate containing six slices of brown bread generously spread with unsalted butter; salt, pepper, Cayenne and a peppermill; a bottle of olive oil and another of wine vinegar; two each serving spoons and forks; a fish knife and fork; a bread knife; and a dish of crisps. A coffee pot sits on a hotplate and there is a bowl of white sugar, another of Demerara, a napkin.

And I am not sure I mentioned that behind the waiter who pushed the trolley there stands another waiter; the reasoning is clearly that, if the first man collapsed, the second would brush him gently out of the way and ease the salmon from dish to plate.

Look where you will, there is the feeling of irrevocable rightness in all they do. At 8.15 pm all the lights fused. I waited in the room because I knew that candles would come. Two of them appeared. The lights went on again. A man came to collect the candles. I went down in the lift. It is marked "LIFT" in simple, unostentatious golden letters, and contains an easy chair lest you should tire on the journey down.

Actually, I did not go for the food; the paté seemed to be a strange mixture of gall bladders and seaweed but it was properly called "Maison" and served with serious authority.

My sole was lemon which is not really sole, and the saddle of lamb was carved across into chops instead of lengthwise in slices. One would no more have complained than have written a rude letter to the Queen Mother. Throughout, the the head waiter watched, the manager hovered, the waitress smiled. Which is what matters.

In the bar, in spite of the BTH ashtrays and multitudinous pieces of paper pointing out a service charge of "about 12½ per cent" plus a token 5 per cent. to help with Selective Employment Tax, the atmosphere was relaxed and civilised; the barman, urbane and knowledgeable about the Battle of Bannockburn and, outside the bar over yet another faultlessly polished oak panelled door, was the legend "Bank of Scotland"; I tried the handle, the door was locked—the first visible sign that they trusted me less than I trusted them.

Come the end of the month, Gleneagles will be cocooned until the spring. About a third of the staff will be assimilated by other British Transport hotels; a similar number do not wish for employment because they devote the winter to recouping the income-tax they reluctantly paid in the summer months.

Of the rest, the majority are foreigners working on short-term permits. They will return to their native lands with a certificate that they have worked for BTH and the feeling that they have learnt something of the British way of life.

They have little idea of how unrepresentative is their knowledge.

7 October 1967: the first 'How to spend it' page

The Saturday edition from tomorrow will be enlarged to give a greatly improved service to readers on investment, personal finance, and home and leisure activities.

Exisiting features which will be given more space are The Week in the City, Finance and the Family, Your Savings and Investments, and Unit Trust Review.

New Saturday features to be introduced will cover residential property in all its aspects; personal insurance problems and how to obtain the best value for money; careers and education, indicating where the best opportunities lie; and a column for collectors of all kinds, whether for pleasure, profit or both.

Sheila Black's Saturday column will have a wider scope as a guide to good living, and with guest writers on house furnishing and decoration, food and cooking, beauty treatment and other topics.

In addition to our regular features on travel and holidays, motoring, and gardening, there will be articles on golf, racing and bridge.

It was from this point that Sheila Black's Saturday page (as it now was) was called 'How to spend it' – a title that was not intended to be provocative but has perhaps become so with the passing of time. In general, it was an inviting enough prospectus, and in the overall context of fairly bullish markets and offices not yet cutting out Saturday copies, the Saturday circulation rose steadily to some 215,000 by 1970, almost 50,000 above the average weekday circulation. It remained, however, the obstinately 'non-advertising' Saturday paper, an essentially different animal to the Monday-to-Friday version and unable to compete in terms of *mass* circulation with the quality Sunday papers. Nevertheless, in purely editorial terms it was a vast improvement on its almost embarrassingly thin predecessor.

Meanwhile, the weekday paper continued to develop during 1967–8. The technical page was soon appearing five times a week, the management page four times, and by early in 1968 the building and civil engineering column on Mondays was transformed into a weekly full page. Also at this time Newton recruited a specialist writer of particular importance, who, though operating largely outside the technical page, was able to give the paper both authority and readability in the critical area of science. This was David Fishlock, who in the summer of 1967 succeeded Boltz as the paper's science editor. He had previously been technology editor of the *New Scientist*, had written various books (for example on man–machine relationships) and had been 'spotted' by Bob Collin, who gave his name to Newton. It proved an excellent choice. During the late 1960s Fishlock wrote an enormous amount for the paper, making a particular speciality of elucidating and exploring the implications of specific areas of scientific research that subsequently became important industries or large-scale activities: subjects that would come into this category included uranium enrichment, the reprocessing of nuclear fuel (practically unheard of in the late 1960s), safer cigarettes, carbon fibres and composite material, and the automatic factory. On all these (and many more) arcane matters Fishlock was providing a journalistic early-warning system that no other paper could match. Whereas Boltz had dissatisfied Newton by failing to initiate enough ideas, Fishlock provided an almost ceaseless flow for news and above all features, which for the most part Newton was happy to publish. Occasionally he took a real interest in what Fishlock was writing about, as with the subject of heart transplant surgery, one of enormous popular appeal at the time and pushed by Newton in the *FT* for all it was worth. Despite a knighthood, despite worldly fame, he remained to the last the perfect Fleet Street market researcher.

Certain significant changes also occurred in the core economic and financial spheres of the paper. In 1966 there was instituted a detailed and valuable monthly review of the state of British industry, while by 1968 there was a small section devoted to international company news and a Monday survey of Eurobonds. This last market was one that the *FT* had been slow to pick up on (apart from the occasional mention in Tether's column) and would continue to receive less than adequate treatment for several years yet, but at least this was a start. Much of the day-to-day economic coverage was by now in the capable and energetic hands of William Keegan, aided often by Kelsey van Musschenbroek. A typical feature by them in November 1968, on prospects for the motor industry, confidently began: 'Another dose of hire purchase and consumer credit controls has been in the offing for some weeks, as readers of the *Financial Times* know.' The dose was duly applied the same day. There was also an increasing emphasis on regional reports, such as by Andrew Hargrove from Scotland, while in 1968 Roy Hodson was recruited from *The Times* as the *FT*'s first regions editor. 'Lex' continued to enjoy its golden age for a year or two more, still under Joll and Gardiner and exercising particular influence during GEC's successful bid for AEI in the autumn of 1967.

These two were largely responsible for recruiting to the *FT* in 1966 someone who was on the paper for only three years but during that time fulfilled a role that, until very recently, was unique. Christopher Gwinner, who had been trained by Patrick Sergeant on the *Daily Mail*, was a man of formidable intelligence and considerable personal charm, and on behalf of the *FT* deployed these qualities to great effect as an authentic financial reporter. Gwinner moved freely in the City and uncovered (often anticipated) the implications as well as the details of the many take-over bids, mergers and suchlike of this period. In short, he made a very fair stab at trying to discover what at any one time the City was up to. Newton, his instincts entirely against upsetting the square mile, was never comfortable with his work, but he gave it a reasonable amount of front-page exposure. In 1969 Gwinner left to go into industry and, to the paper's enormous loss, was not effectively replaced – at the very time when events in the City were becoming ever more 'interesting'.

The late 1960s also saw a stepping-up of the *FT*'s political coverage, including the start of daily reports of parliamentary proceedings. Lobby correspondent was John Bourne, who established himself as one of the coveted inner lobby whom Wilson would agree to talk to. Returning from Washington in 1967 to succeed Ronald Butt as political correspondent, and holding the post for the next ten years, was David Watt. The Friday 'Politics To-day' column initiated by Butt was Watt's particular forum, and together with Bourne he did much to further enhance the *FT*'s political 'clout', as odd entries in the Crossman diaries testify. In November 1967 Crossman referred to Watt and James Margach of the *Sunday Times* as 'two key journalists', while the following October he quoted at some length from Watt's description of Wilson's speech at the Labour Party Conference and then commented: 'Harold won't like that kind of discriminating praise but it's worth a great deal more than the uproarious backslapping which the popular press have given him.' Again, in February 1969:

> The story of the Kindersley award finally came to an end yesterday afternoon, when the evening papers published banner headlines 'Big Awards for the Doctors'. We were lucky this morning, though, as there were a lot of other sensational stories and only one paper, the *Financial Times*, fully understood the significance of the conflict between Aubrey Jones on the university teachers' award and Kindersley on the doctors' award, and the contradiction in the Government's accepting both.

Finally, on 24 November 1969, a Monday, the Secretary of State for the Social Services took lunch in Bracken House: 'They have a magnificent dining room, facing the finest view of St Paul's. I sat next to Robbins, with Drogheda opposite, and a nice gang of young men round me, but before we could really settle down to a proper argument I had to be back in the House for Question Time.'[6]

Replacing Watt in Washington was Joe Rogaly, a South African who had come to the *FT* in 1965 after six years on the *Economist*. He was an ambitious foreign correspondent, a fluent writer and in the course of 1968, that traumatic year in United States history, received considerable licence from Newton to get his stories across in the fullest, most colourful way possible. 'America is stumbling in the dark today', was the opening sentence of his front-page 'splash' dispatch from Washington on 3 April, in the context of the Vietnam War and President Johnson saying he would not stand again – an opening sentence inconceivable in an equivalent situation in the *FT* two decades on. Later in the year Rogaly's reporting of the infamous Chicago Democratic Convention was particularly striking, while in November he described in vivid terms the outcome of the Presidential election:

> Today, as he appeared on television to announce his victory and to muse upon it, Mr Nixon seemed somehow softer and more conciliatory than I have ever before found him to be. It was as if a great and ancient weight had been lifted from his shoulders and a relaxed man had emerged from beneath the burden of non-success he had been bearing so long.

If this was a more 'green eye-shade' approach than the *FT* was accustomed to, it was not the only change now taking place in the foreign coverage. The issue of 7 November 1967 exemplified the trends. On the one hand there was a modern-style 'profile' of Governor Reagan of California, describing him as 'a skilled politician, a relaxed, persuasive public speaker, with some good speech writers, a warm personality, sincere in his views, and, so it is said, a "decent sort"'; while on the other hand there was a detailed account of the ongoing Nigerian civil war 'by a correspondent recently in the battle zones'. The foreign editor by this time was J. D. F. Jones, who over the next few years would steer the coverage into uncharted and also controversial waters.

That lay mostly in the future. Before then, in the immediate face of the challenge from *The Times*, the paper underwent some major physical surgery. In 1967, at Newton's request, the group's deputy chief promotions manager and chief designer, Victor Clark, moved to editorial design and, directly answerable to Newton, was charged in effect with bringing the appearance of the *FT* into the second half of the twentieth century. This he did over the course of about eighteen months: partly by joining the rest of the world in having both upper- and lower-case headings; partly by much improving the look of the leader page (especially helped by the removal of letters to the editor); but above all by the role he played in taking Stock Exchange prices off the back page, moving 'Lex' from front to back page and filling the rest of the back page with news.

For up to a year Newton sat on this proposed change, deeply apprehensive of how the City would react, but at last in October 1968 he let it happen. He need not have worried. There was only a handful of complaints from brokers and investors about their prices being moved to the penultimate and ante-penultimate pages. Other changes took place at the same time: letters went to page two, joined by television and radio listings (making their *FT* bow); arts moved to page three; Wall Street prices made a belated move to the back half of the paper; and Tether's 'Lombard' column, following an uneasy spell on the 'Executive's World' page, went to the back. Perhaps most importantly, the front page from now carried on its left-hand side not only a general news summary but also a business summary – in order, in Johnson's words at the time, 'both to supply a news feature that is readable in its own right, and to act as a trailer by means of cross-references to fuller stories carried all over the paper'.[7] Since the size of the paper was by now anything up to forty pages, it was a sensible idea. The changes were generally welcomed, though Drogheda was annoyed at the 'typographically displeasing way' in which 'Lex' on the back page ran horizontally across it, as well as believing that the historically appropriate slot for 'Lombard' was on an inside rather than the outside page.[8] Taken as a whole, however, they represented the paper's sense of confidence and maturity, a formal, irrevocable recognition that the *FT* was no longer just a City paper. The long revolution inaugurated by Hargreaves Parkinson was complete.

The question would continue to be asked, in time with increasing force: if by general consent more than a City paper, how far precisely should the *FT* go beyond its central historical function of recording the doings of the Stock Exchange and other main markets? In a rare moment of conscious articulation about the *FT*'s long-term destiny, the editor tried to answer this question at a board meeting in January 1968:

> It was mentioned that a number of people still appeared not to appreciate the scope of reading within the paper. Sir Gordon Newton pointed out the dangers as well as the advantages in over-diversification from financial reporting bearing in mind that half the paper's revenue came from the City. Looking into the future he felt that concentration on specialist markets would offer better prospects of growth and profitability than would be offered by becoming a more general newspaper.

This opinion of where the paper's best future lay is particularly interesting because after Newton's retirement his editorship tended to be depicted as one that *throughout* its duration was seeking to push the boundaries of the *FT* ever outwards. The views he expresses here suggest quite otherwise, that the time had come for a process of consolidation, refining and deepening the product no doubt, but no longer seeking to enlarge its fundamental terms of reference. One might ask: was Newton perhaps seeking to pull the wool over the eyes of the board? No, he was not that sort of man. The probability is that he genuinely believed that a halt should be called to what was perhaps becoming, even if not by design, an attempt to turn the *FT* into a complete general as well as specialist paper for the business man.

The 'benchmark' issue nine months later, on 30 October 1968, enables one to see how far the *FT* had come down the 'generalist' path by this time. On that side of the ledger (that is, items that need not have been in the *FT*, granted that the business reader would also have access to an explicitly general quality paper) one would put, in a 34-page issue: the arts page, together with the 'Entertainment Guide' and (just introduced) television and radio listings; a handful of both home and foreign stories that had no apparent business relevance; the day's racing tips; the crossword; and really not much else. In other words, the true nature of Newton's achievement, one is tempted to conclude, had not been to make the *FT* into the business man's sole paper (foreign coverage was still inadequate, sports even more so, and there was little of what one might call broad social texture), but rather to turn it into a paper which the business man, and not just the City stockbroker or investor, would be ill advised not to read. A closer look at this particular issue shows most of the things Newton had introduced on the business man's behalf: a full commodities page (still in the front half of the paper); half a page of 'Export News'; the 'Technical' and 'Executive's World' pages; a mass of industrial and labour news; a specialist main feature, by Fishlock on the Ministry of Technology's research laboratories; a six-page regional survey, on Yorkshire and Humberside; and a highly detailed share information service. Two other impressions linger from this particular issue. One is of the end of the old-style industry-in-action photographs and an attempt, not yet taken very far, to replace them with more 'newsy' photographs, such as one on the front page of Rupert Murdoch, in the midst of his bid battle with Robert Maxwell for the *News of the World*, leaving the Savoy Hotel the previous night for London Airport. The other is of how certain names kept cropping up. One was Reginald Dale, the Common Market correspondent, who contributed three stories, including one with an already familiar refrain, 'EEC Ministers face soaring butter stocks poser'. Even more prolific was Harold Bolter, who had recently come from the *Birmingham Post* and was to be an extremely able industrial correspondent for several years. On this particular day he had no fewer than five stories:

'Government hinders road haulage – Sir D. Stokes', 'Increases must lead to BOAC redundancies', 'Teething troubles ahead as the builders "go metric"', 'BOAC and pilots continue talks to avert stoppage' and '"Too many amateurs in too many industries"'. For a keen young reporter the sky was the limit on Newton's *FT*.

There were two other major strands to the paper's response to the challenge apparently posed by *The Times*, which continued to run a separate business news section for three or four years until abandoning the struggle. Sidney Henschel outlined to the board in October 1966 one of the initiatives: 'He hoped that display advertising could be maintained particularly through the use of insets and he said that his department could produce every inset which the editor was able to cover.' This was the cue for a rapid expansion of the *FT*'s programme of surveys, which after 1967, with the demise of the expensive tabloid 'magazine' format, were all produced (until 1984) as insets integral to the main body of the paper. The figures, though not complete, are adequate to tell the story: advertisement columnage in surveys increased from 2,959 in 1966 to 3,278 in 1967, 4,537 in 1968 and 5,328 in 1969; pagination, 768 in 1967, was up to 1,114 for 1968 and 1,377 for 1969; and the number of subjects covered in surveys expanded from 140 in 1967 to 176 in 1968 and 205 in 1969. Newton greeted this development with only modified enthusiasm, but was determined that if there was going to be a survey virtually every weekday then they should be of a higher standard than before and, in particular, that a much higher proportion of them should be written by members of staff. In the new circumstances he was more than ever conscious of the possible charge of log-rolling in connection with surveys.

Two people who played an important part in the editorial direction and quality control of the expanded programme were Christopher Johnson the managing editor and David Watt, the latter doubling up for some time with his political duties. They certainly showed great ingenuity in finding new subjects for surveys, with a particular bias towards the regional. Sixteen pages on the North West, four on Norway, four on offset litho, six pages on pipes and pipelines, three on premium promotions, four on quarrying, three on retirement and security, one on the Royal Mint, two on Swindon town centre – such were some of the surveys of 1968. Perhaps the ultimate was the modest page devoted to Reading Car Park. Drogheda observed to the board that February that 'there were indications that our enlarged programme of insets might be trying the patience of some of our readers', but he himself was unrepentant, as he later explained in his memoirs: 'Many of the suggestions for surveys stemmed from the industry or country concerned, even though we made perfectly clear to them that they would have no say over the editorial content. I had no compunction about developing the programme ruthlessly and planning it for anything up to a year ahead.'[9] And, as the world and Newton knew, a compunctionless Drogheda on the hunt for new frontiers of advertising revenue was not to be gainsaid.

The other main post-*TBN* thrust was acknowledged by the board in January 1969, when Robbins referred to how 'there had been significant change in the last three years in the methods adopted for selling advertising space', and 'Mr Hare added that we were now near the top in producing sophisticated arguments for selling space.' In this respect science came late to the *FT*. Prior to the mid-1960s the selling of advertising space, or decisions about promotional campaigns, had little more to go on than circulation figures and an impressionistic idea of who read the paper, though the occasional readership survey was undertaken or sponsored. The key figure in changing this was Michael Ryan, who came to the paper in February 1967 as market research manager, in charge of an as yet non-existent department. At the time there was no equivalent to Ryan's position on the *Daily Telegraph*, but at *The Times* by now there was the considerable muscle and finesse of Thomson Group Marketing. It was Ryan's task, one in which he succeeded to a great degree, to lend statistical credibility to the efforts of the advertising and foreign departments, with whom he worked closely.

A small brochure issued some two years after Ryan began his job, entitled 'It's not just being pink that makes the *Financial Times* different', gives some idea of how he went about his work. In it he produced a series of figures and commentary, comparing throughout the *FT* to *The Times* and the *Guardian* and demonstrating, on the basis of various disinterested readership surveys, that the *FT* was read by more readers (four) per copy; that it had a smaller proportion of women readers (185,000 out of 630,000); that it was read by 44 per cent of the 450,000 'A' class business men in the United Kingdom (those earning over £2,000 a year), which was a higher percentage than the other two papers combined; and finally, that of the 108,000 business men with a corporate purchasing power of more than £50,000, some 56 per cent read the *FT*, compared with 31 per cent *The Times* and 17 per cent the *Guardian*. The point was not that these were figures which would have particularly surprised advertisers. Rather, they were figures that the *FT* needed to make sure that advertisers never forgot the importance of. In so reminding advertisers, Ryan's role represented a certain step towards the paper attaining a greater awareness of itself as a product and of the nature of its market.

How did it all work out on the bottom line? The economic climate was generally inauspicious until the autumn of 1967, but then improved. Indeed, in 1968 the Stock Exchange enjoyed a bull market that saw the *FT* Ordinary Share Index going for the first time above the 500 mark. As usual, the paper's vital statistics reflected these larger trends: advertising volume was down in 1966 to 24,863 columns (compared with 26,571 the previous year), but then increased to 25,033 in 1967 and 29,306 in 1968 (the year of the great surveys expansion); while the circulation, after staying static from 1965 to 1967 at just over 149,000, rose in 1968, despite a price increase the previous summer from 6*d* to 8*d*, to a record average daily net sale of 159,536. The best that could be said about profits was that they did not bear out Drogheda's worst fears as expressed while he had been pushing for *The Times* merger. Operating profits for the paper during these years came out at approximately £997,379 for 1966, £790,792 for 1967 and £1,085,439 for 1968. Of course, one should add the rider that by comparison with most of the rest of the national newspaper industry these figures were positively glittering. In its report on the industry published in October 1967, the Prices and Incomes Board described the *FT* as 'an extremely successful newspaper' which showed that 'the secret of success need not necessarily be size in the sense of circulation' but rather 'is the formulation of an appeal which marries readership with advertising'.[10]

Nevertheless, there was sombre truth in the words of Gibson in June 1969: 'If the *Financial Times* had had to meet the total outgoings of 1968 with the revenue of 1967 there would have been no operating profits for the year. Hence our anxiety to secure some more rational basis for our costs of production in the interests of all concerned.'[11] Gibson was speaking in his capacity as chairman of S. Pearson Publishers, which in 1968 had replaced the Financial & Provincial Publishing Company, itself created only in 1967, as the name of the group combining the interests of the FT Ltd, the FN Ltd (which finally ceased autonomous life), the Westminster Press and (from 1968) Longmans the book publishers. The parent company, with the controlling interest, remained S. Pearson & Son. The idea behind the grouping was not to undermine the individual management of either the *FT* or the Westminster Press, but rather rested on the belief, in Gibson's words, that 'a pooling of resources will enable us to take advantage of the opportunities ahead', including new technology, it was fondly believed, in modes of production.[12] Robbins remained chairman of the *FT* itself, but clearly it was a move towards the paper becoming part of a bigger, more powerful player in the publishing industry.

Inevitably, Newton in his last five or six years as editor was becoming a larger-than-life figure, the stuff of Fleet Street legends. In March 1967, the year after his knighthood, he received the Hannen Swaffer Award as 'Journalist of the Year', for having 'selected, trained and given scope to a team of journalists who, under his direction, have vastly widened the field formerly associated with a specialist journal'. Philip Howard the next day went to interview him on behalf of *The Times*: 'The Journalist of the Year sat in his office gazing out at St Paul's, behind a massive modern semi-circular desk, looking acutely embarrassed by the whole business . . . For his prize he receives £500 and a golden quill, which will look slightly bizarre in those practical, professional hands.' The piece went on: 'He is a reticent, grey man, aged 59, with the inquisitive beady eyes and the restlessness of Water Rat in *The Wind in the Willows*. He taps his teeth with a pencil in a characteristic gesture.'[13]

Nor did the other salient qualities and quirks desert Newton during these last, celebrated years. He retained his essential modesty and lack of pomp. He maintained, even developed, his remarkable ability to hold the paper in his head, quite often at six or seven in the evening suddenly deciding to change the mix and, if he felt it was too heavy, telling his features editor to replace a feature on industry with one on, say, the football pools. He continued to insist on the absolute primacy of factual accuracy, coming down as hard as he had once done on Einzig when his motoring industry correspondent referred to a Jaguar engine size as 2.8 litres instead of 3.5. His briefings, especially for foreign correspondents, remained minimal. 'I want you to cover the stories', was the full extent of his instructions to Rogaly before he went to replace Watt in Washington. Yet at the appropriate moment he could say the appropriate thing, however simple and mundane it might be. Thus at the end of the Presidential election in 1968, with the three-man US team having been up some thirty hours filing extensive double copy (because of the uncertain result) and finally sitting round spent and exhausted, there came over the telex a painfully typed message: 'Well done ed.' It so rarely happened, and when it did it meant such a lot.

To anyone coming new to the paper, there was no doubt who bossed the show. David Fishlock (arriving in 1967) has recorded some of his memories of the Newton of this final phase:

> Bob Collin told me I would never know the real G.N. He had already been mellowed by success. I was just getting to know him well enough to be slightly scared – in a way I cannot recall of anyone else I have ever worked for, or with. Later, another old hand told me G.N. knew he had this capacity to inspire fear, did not like it, but nevertheless made it work for him.

G.N. as editor held all the strings. Everyone deferred to him in what was a dictatorship, albeit a benign one.

I rarely felt comfortable in his presence, except perhaps in the bar, where he mixed freely with his journalists. He also walked round a lot during the day – something his two successors did not do. I was told he had had the portholes put in the offices. You never knew when G.N.'s face would loom in your porthole. I never felt any urge to put my feet on my desk in his day.

He offered journalists enormous encouragement, often giving very young writers the chance to write major pieces. But I remember an old hand telling me that if G.N. felt someone was getting too cocky, he would spike a couple of his features – to bring him back to earth.

G.N. loved news. He kept his office door open and encouraged people to drop in and tell him what was going on. He bawled out the Malta correspondent – a chum of his when he holidayed there – for getting into a row with Dom Mintoff, the Malta Prime Minister, and letting G.N. learn about it through agency reports.

G.N. could also be very vindictive if he felt the victim deserved it. One colleague told me how he'd gone to G.N.'s office to find him giving another colleague a bad time. He called the new arrival in and sat him down, to listen to a highly humiliating dressing down. I heard other similar stories and once got caught up briefly myself in overhearing G.N.'s displeasure. G.N. was absolutely ruthless in protecting the good name of his paper and dumped heavily on anything that smacked of dishonesty or professional misconduct such as share-pushing.

G.N. was not given to smiling. I cannot ever recall a hearty laugh. Some said the only humorist he found amusing was Jak's cartoon in the *Standard*. He once threw out a Men and Matters story I had persuaded the column to take, with the comment that 'there's too much lavatory humour creeping into my paper'. How could he have known that I had copied it from a lavatory wall?

Fishlock was in his thirties and an experienced journalist when he came to the *FT*, but clearly he found Newton a unique, formidable and, despite everything, sometimes endearing figure.

Accounts vary as to how completely in control he was in his last years of all aspects of the paper, as irresistibly it increased in size. He had a certain innate reluctance to delegate, but according to Sheila Black, who knew him well, in practice he proved surprisingly adept at learning that difficult art. During these years his main focus, perhaps increasingly, was on the front, back and two middle pages. Indeed, to this day the two centre pages are known to the printers as 'the editor's pages', thereby requiring special attention and care. Although accepting that there were certain limits to how much of a 'general' paper the *FT* could become, towards the end of his career Newton was anxious that, at least on the outside pages, the paper should be competing hard with the rest of Fleet Street, in terms of getting the big stories, hitting the news hard (while not losing accuracy) and making a certain visual impact. In trying to achieve this, an important part was played by his own instinct for what those stories were. During the *Torrey Canyon* saga of 1967, for example, Rogaly was told to go to it, had Newton on the phone every night and was given plenty of space, reflecting Newton's belief, to which he was now starting to give expression, that City people liked the odd dose of melodrama. Rogaly was in the bomber with the RAF, but Newton blue-pencilled all the rude words (even 'bloody') from the interview, making the immortal remark: 'You can only say fuck on the arts page.' Or again, less obviously, when in May 1969 a feature by Tugendhat on the Alaskan oil rush mentioned that in the autumn there would be 'an auction of State-held lands situated near the recent fields', he made a note and four months later sent Palmer from New York to Anchorage to cover the sale. Over the course of a week his young correspondent, fired by the challenge, wrote a series of highly atmospheric splashes and features on the cloak-and-dagger drama taking place, culminating in a main feature on 'Alaska's $900 million gusher' that began:

> It is six o'clock in the evening of the great Alaskan lease sale. The last bid was opened half an hour ago. Up on the 15th floor of the Anchorage Westward Hotel, leaning against the bar of the exclusive Petroleum Club, is a senior officer of one of America's largest petroleum companies. Drinks are on the house tonight, and as the bar quickly fills up to sardine proportions, the drinks are flowing fast.
>
> For months this oilman has been living with top-secret information of the progress of his company's wildcat wells. For three days he has not slept but has lain awake at night, worrying over bids which have already been sealed. Now he can talk. And as fast as I ask him questions, the answers come flowing out . . .

An oil lease sale in Alaska was far removed from the strait-jacket of City reportage, and this was just the sort of stuff that Newton relished – getting a major economic story across in a vivid and accessible (albeit detailed) way. But it could not have happened without his spotting the original lead and guessing it could produce something big.

Another important development added to the way in which the *FT* was becoming more mainstream in feel, if not altogether in subject-matter. This was the increasingly effective pressure being applied by the National Union of Journalists, throughout Fleet Street but of a particular significance for the *FT*, that henceforth journalists on national papers were to be recruited from the ranks of those who had received the traditional but not always obligatory provincial apprenticeship. The pressure did not effect an overnight change in terms of ending the system of direct intake from the universities, but as early as 1966, following a word from management, Newton felt unable to recruit Guy de Jonquieres direct from Oxford, as he would have wished. De Jonquieres in the event spent eighteen months with Reuters and then came to the *FT*. The last year of classic direct intake proved to be 1968 and included in its crop Nicholas Colchester, who survived an interview well up to Newtonian standards of terror. Finally, in 1970, the NPA and the NUJ signed a memorandum formally stating that henceforth journalists would be expected to undertake three years of provincial training before coming to Fleet Steet, with graduates allowed half a year less. Specialist writers could be engaged if there was consultation with the NUJ, but the union would not recognize literary excellence alone as a specialist qualification. It was the final nail in the coffin of the old system.

Newton did not particularly pine, having come to feel during the 1960s that the absence of two years of National Service adversely affected the quality of the direct intake, while also recognizing that the greater size of the paper and its staff made it harder for him to take the personal interest in them that he once had. Increasingly, the people who were to be weighty names on the paper in the 1970s and 1980s were now coming from the provincial press or had had a provincial training: recruits from Newton's last few years like Michael Cassell, Ray Dafter, Roger Matthews, Barry Riley, Michael Hand, David Walker, Christian Tyler and John Wyles. As the paper grew in size this trend would have occurred anyway, irrespective of the NUJ, but undoubtedly it was accelerated. Nevertheless, there was still the odd loophole and a little room left for the editor's famed intuition. In 1970 he received a bold letter asking to be taken on from Peter Riddell, then completing his last year at Cambridge, and despite the new dispensation agreed to do so after interviewing him. It was an amply rewarded impulse buy, with Riddell becoming in due course a notable economics and then political correspondent, for all his lack of experience in reporting village fêtes and motorway pile-ups.

There were of course exits as well as entrances, none more publicized than that resulting from the 'Connock affair' which took place early in 1969. Michael Connock had come to the paper in 1957 direct from Oxford and had done the usual stint in the features department, before being sent to commodities. This move disenchanted him, and he went to the *Daily Express*, but returned to the *FT* in 1961 to help run 'Men and

Matters'. Later that year he was appointed East European correspondent, based in London but four or five times a year making trips behind the Iron Curtain. In February 1969, in the course of doing research in Poland for a coming survey on Polish engineering, he found himself the object of an attempt by the secret service to blackmail him into working for them. Their particular lever was his close friendship with a married Polish woman. Connock returned to London and told his story to Newton. It transpired that in Poland he had signed a document by which he 'voluntarily' agreed to 'co-operate with the intelligence of the Polish People's Republic in political, economic, intelligence and counter-intelligence matters', in return for 'the non-production of certain compromising documents'. To Connock's surprise, Newton, after consulting with Robbins and Drogheda, decided that his correspondent would have to leave the paper. There ensued a considerable storm, fuelled by a lengthy justificatory article by Connock in the *Observer*, but Newton sat tight and declined either to elaborate or to reverse his decision. It ran directly counter to the paper's long non-sacking tradition, but in this particular situation Newton was not prepared to jeopardize (as he saw it) the integrity and independence of the *FT*, so painstakingly built up over the years.[14]

It was a doubly traumatic time, for on 5 March, four days before Connock's *Observer* article, Harold Wincott suddenly died at the age of sixty-two. He had recently begun easing down – his *FT* article had become monthly rather than weekly – but it was still a terrible shock. His last article, 'How deficit finance wrecked the gilt-edged market', was published on the day of his death. Newton was moved to write a fine obituary, the last paragraph of which began with a classic Newtonism that enhanced rather than lessened the effect of the whole:

> What made Harold such a great journalist, to many people a peer without equal in his own field? There can never be any one answer to this. He was a kind man. He was a completely honest man. He felt things deeply. He never wrote a word in which he did not believe. And given these qualities, his writing came as it were from the heart, so that even those who disagreed fundamentally with his views found him compulsive reading and respected him. His career is an illustration of how sincerity exerts its own influence. Missed so much by his family, colleagues and friends, he cannot be replaced.[15]

He was indeed irreplaceable, both as a moral force and as a commentator relating the financial markets to the real economy. After his death more than £100,000 was raised, much of it from ordinary readers, to form a charitable trust called the Wincott Foundation, which sought to continue to propagate his ideas and also, through annual awards, to encourage high standards in economic and financial journalism. But perhaps the most telling tribute was paid some years earlier, while he was still alive. Visiting Malawi on business, John Waring of the advertising department had found that all doors were open to him once the Minister of Finance had learnt that he was from the *FT*. 'Do you *know* Wincott?' the Minister kept asking in some awe. Not many British journalists have earned that sort of reputation in Blantyre.

Wincott lived long enough to witness Britain's second devaluation since the war and to argue that if it was to succeed in its aim of shifting resources from public and private consumption into exports, and thus right the balance of payments deficit, then the best way was not through more taxation but by way of a new campaign to boost personal savings, including wider share ownership. It was a theme to which most ears were still deaf. The paper itself, as it became clear that the measures of July 1966 had not worked, at last began publicly to take on board the possibility that a devaluation might be a lesser evil than another huge foreign loan. On Friday 17 November 1967 the main leader argued that 'we would do better to take whatever steps are necessary to put the balance of payments straight by ourselves', since 'previous loans have allowed the Government to put off the moment of truth when the need to get out of deficit at last becomes clear'. Over the weekend the value of sterling was reduced from $2.80 to $2.40 to the pound, and Wilson made his 'pound in your pocket' television broadcast. The *FT*'s Monday-morning leader opened portentously:

> The ball is over. The Government has finally been forced to devalue the pound. The Prime Minister may claim that nobody forced it to act in this way, that it was blown off course by a gale that nobody could have foreseen and that it then freely chose devaluation as the best means of getting back on. Nobody will pay the least attention to such a claim. Maintenance of the sterling exchange rate has been the overriding aim of the Labour Government's economic policy since it took office in 1964. Devaluation is an open and humiliating admission that the policy has failed.

The leader then went on to express gratitude to Britain's international creditors for deciding at last not to bail the nation out: 'Another loan would merely have postponed the day of reckoning. Given the size and persistency of Britain's balance of payments deficit, moreover, there is a good theoretical case for lowering the exchange rate: the *Financial Times*,

HILLIER PARKER MAY AND ROWDEN
London and Edinburgh

THE FINANCIAL TIMES

INCORPORATING THE FINANCIAL NEWS

No. 24,393 — Monday November 20 1967 — EIGHTPENCE

HALE OF TIPTON — for Modern Malleable CASTINGS — HALE & HALE (TIPTON) LTD., DUDLEY PORT, STAFFS.

What $2.40 is meant to achieve

An improvement in payments balance of £500m. expected

BY M. H. FISHER

The Government expects that the devaluation of the pound, coupled with the measures to restrict home demand, will lead to:—

1—An improvement in the balance of payments of at least £500m. within a comparatively short time.

2—A rise in output which in twelve months should be running at a level 4 to 5 per cent. higher than it is now.

3—A fall in unemployment within the next twelve months to a seasonally adjusted figure of 1.7 to 1.8 per cent. (as against the October figure of 2.3 per cent.).

4—A gradual increase in the cost of living which, once the rise in import prices is fully reflected, should not exceed 3 per cent. This would be the pure devaluation effect.

The output and unemployment forecasts are not greatly different from the latest figures the Treasury was working on before devaluation and which helped to persuade the Chancellor that the decision was inevitable. But the "mix" of the economy and the timing now look different.

Because home consumption will be hit immediately whereas exports will respond more slowly, output will rise and unemployment will fall more gradually in the next few months than would otherwise have been the case.

The various Government restrictions are designed to produce a marked shift in resources to exports and private manufacturing investment at the expense of Government expenditure and private consumption.

Maximum benefit hoped for

Whether the forecasts will be met must depend on events both abroad and in this country. The Government so far appears to have good cause for its view that the exchange rate adjustment has been such as to give this country the maximum competitive advantage.

Watch on prices—and rents: Wilson

On other pages

	Page
Editorial comment	12
Foreign reactions	10
Home reactions	9
Impact of higher Corporation tax	11
Travel industry fears bleak period	11
Basic defence policy not disrupted	11
How invisible exports should go ahead	11
Why more domestic measures may be needed	12
Prices that will go up	12
The impact on industry	13
Men and Matters	13
Lombard	5

Control of prices and incomes

Industry's cash flow should improve

The impact on other countries' currencies

Most of the world's major currencies, including the U.S. dollar and Common Market currencies, were unaffected yesterday by Britain's decision to devalue. But some smaller countries announced they would follow Britain and some Commonwealth countries were finding difficulty in deciding how to act.

There were fears in Whitehall that an Australian devaluation might provoke similar action by Japan and undermine much of the advantage gained for British exports by devaluation.

But it will be some months before the full impact of the British move is felt by other countries. In the meantime, close attention will be focused on the behaviour of the dollar and movements in the gold price.

Main reactions to the British move yesterday are listed below.

Countries which have or will probably devalue

New Zealand: Devaluation in line with pound a virtual certainty. Decision to-day.
Kenya, Uganda, Tanzania: Expected to devalue when their central bankers meet in Nairobi to-day.
Hong Kong: Devaluation in line with pound.
Malta: Devaluation in line with pound.
Fiji: Is devaluing.
Israel: Devaluation at least in line with pound, possibly more.
Denmark: To devalue by 8 per cent.
Ireland: Devaluation in line with pound.
Spain: Devaluation in line with pound.
Nigeria: Expected to devalue to-day.

Countries not devaluing

United States
Canada: Finance Minister said U.K. action would not substantially affect Canada.
Common Market Countries
Malaysia, Singapore, Brunei: No change in new national currencies introduced last June.
Middle East Oil Producing Countries: No devaluations expected.
Norway, Sweden, Finland: No devaluations. Finland devalued recently.
South Africa and **Rhodesia:** Decided late last night not to devalue.
Portugal: No immediate devaluation expected.
Greece: No immediate devaluation.
Japan: Not devaluing but disturbed by U.K. move.
India: Devaluation unlikely after last year's 36.5 per cent. cut in value of Rupee.

Countries which are uncertain

Australia: Decision expected to-day. Devaluation thought unlikely on balance.
Ceylon: No decision yet. Business circles "cautiously forecasting" some devaluation.
Pakistan: Decision to-day.
Cyprus: No decision yet.

U.S. raises re-discount rate to 4½%

BY JOE ROGALY, U.S. EDITOR

WASHINGTON, Nov. 19.

In a mood designed more for its psychological than its physical impact, the Federal Reserve Board raised the rediscount rate (the equivalent of Britain's Bank Rate) by ½ per cent. to 4½ per cent. to-day. The increase takes effect to-morrow morning.

It is hoped that this will keep the inevitable flow of funds back across the Atlantic (in view of the British devaluation and accompanying 8 per cent. Bank Rate) under some sort of control and that it will calm the markets, while keeping the dollar out of trouble.

In fact, the Administration was keeping its fingers crossed for the dollar this weekend. The hope was that the effect of the devaluation of sterling on the main reserve currency would not be too drastic.

Contingency planning for what one official said this morning would be the "rough ride ahead" has been in existence for some months and it was sharpened up in the second half of last week as the Treasury and the Federal Reserve Board came to know what lay in store.

Heavy support

SE & banks closed to-day

THE LONDON and regional Stock Exchanges are closed to-day because of devaluation and, in addition, dealings of any sort by members are forbidden to-day.

By Royal Proclamation all banks will be closed to the public to-day, while the cocoa, coffee, fishmeal, soyabean oil, sugar and wool markets will also remain closed.

Brazil buys 2 British One-elevens

Credits are designed to discourage speculation

Where does the market go from here?

By LEX

The Government's Saturday night package contains plenty for the market to think about. Luckily, with no dealing to-day, official or unofficial, it will have time to reach some rational conclusions. On the economic front, the most important point to bear in mind is that the combined effect of devaluation plus the various restrictive measures should leave the economy roughly where it is now.

Corporation tax

Thus in terms of overall corporate profitability, this is not a return to July, 1966. Output is forecast to rise 4-5 per cent. in 1968 with consumption static in real terms. However this is no recipe for companies operating in the retail sector, who are likely to see their margins squeezed to boot as higher import prices work their way through. Secondly a 2½ point rise in corporation tax to 42½ per cent. will cream off a portion of the extra profits accruing

[...]

market. Clearly the ideal situation is a company which keeps its hard currency prices largely unchanged and has very narrow margins to begin with. Stone-Platt and Holman look to fill the bill with pre-tax margins of 4.6 and 2½ per cent. respectively.

Other, more profitable, exporters who look bound to prosper include the whisky trade in general, and DCL, Teacher's and IDV in particular, BSA, English China, Lesney, Mettoy, Pergamon and London Rubber. Rolls-Royce, already a strong contender for the Lockheed airbus engine, could well find this a clincher. And Swan Hunter should now find competition from Japan for super-tankers less onerous.

It is less easy to identify the beneficiaries on the import side. Since Sweden is not following us down then the U.K. papermakers will breathe a small sigh of relief—in Reed's case matched by the gloom higher pulp costs from Canada must induce. And the price-cutting in man-made fibres should ease off considerably, to the

Good for Gilts

Export rewards

Features Today

20 November 1967: devaluation

though heartily condemning the way in which affairs have been allowed to develop, is not opposed to devaluation in itself.' The paper insisted, however, that devaluation alone was not enough, that 'consumption and investment at home have to be curbed to make room for the additional exports that devaluation should make it possible to sell'. Over the next week, with the Conservative opposition out for the Chancellor's head, it argued that Callaghan should stay at No. 11 precisely in order to push through the necessarily unpopular accompanying measures. In the event he resigned and was succeeded by Roy Jenkins, greeted by the *FT* as 'a highly intelligent politician' and one who, 'with luck, firmness and patience' in the post-devaluation situation, 'might even find himself presiding over the long-delayed British economic miracle'. But (the time-honoured warning) 'he will do well to remember that the best path to political success in his present post is to behave as unpolitically as possible and to leave the next election to look after itself'.[16]

As Jenkins prepared for his first Budget, during the early months of 1968 there were two particularly piquant economic developments. One occurred at the Colt Heating factory in Surbiton, where five young women started the 'I'm Backing Britain' campaign, involving half a day's extra work without pay, which for a time promised to sweep the country. 'It is easy to be cynical – but they *mean* it', was the title of a main feature by Arthur Sandles. The next day an approbatory leader appeared full of moralistic fervour:

> The 'Back Britain' campaign is a beacon of light in an otherwise dismal economic and industrial prospect. It shows that there are at least some people who are willing to look beyond their immediate comfort and convenience, and do something for nothing . . . It is the spirit of the people that matters most. Aside from the mistakes made by successive Governments – and these have been considerable – the main reason why the country is in a mess is that there has been a general unwillingness, at all levels of society, to do a good day's work . . . It is absenteeism, restrictive practices and the rest that is dragging the country down. Too many people expect to be paid for work they do not do. The 'Back Britain' campaign should be devoted to changing this attitude, and encouraging individuals to identify their efforts with the success or failure of the country as a whole.[17]

Two months later, far away from Surbiton and following a dramatic flight out of paper money (above all the dollar) into gold, the international monetary system came close to collapse. On 15 March, in response to urgent United States requests, the London gold market was closed, for a fortnight as it turned out. It was the end of the Gold Pool and signified, as the *FT* called its leader of the 16th, 'The end of an era'. That same leader considered in some detail various possible solutions to the crisis, but rather discounted the two-tier system that was in the event adopted, on the grounds partly that 'the separation between official and private transactions could hardly be maintained', but above all that it 'would do nothing to reduce the American deficit', described as 'the root cause of the gold rush'. Three days later Jenkins presented his austerity Budget and received from the *FT* a warmer commendation than any Labour Chancellor before or since, producing as he had a package 'which is designed to hold back consumer expenditure hard without weakening the incentive to earn more profit and income through greater efficiency'. In short, clearly marking out the new Chancellor as a coming man: 'It is a Budget of opportunity, which fits the special needs of the moment remarkably well.'

Also at about this time, though not reflected for several years yet in the leader columns, a seismic shift was taking place in the thinking of the paper's principal economics commentator, Samuel Brittan. He subsequently (in 1975) described why it had taken him so long to abandon the Keynesian orthodoxies of his youth, with their 'conventional "full employment" policies pursued through monetary expansion and deficit finance':

> My slowness in seeing the light was explained, though not excused, by the fact that the case for 'sound money' was usually stated in terms of misconceived objectives, such as the maintenance of the sterling exchange rate or the sterling area. Moreover the distinction between a steady inflation and an acceleratory inflation, and the likelihood of 'full employment' policies producing the latter, were rarely stressed by sound money men, who were too shocked by the very idea of inflation to go much further into the matter . . .
>
> It was Professor Milton Friedman who removed the scales from my eyes – not by his more technical views on money, but by his analysis of the effects of demand management on unemployment. He did so in one single paper: his 1968 Presidential address to the American Economic Association.[18]

Articles influenced by Friedman started appearing soon afterwards in Brittan's 'Economic Viewpoint' column. But as he later stated, their main thrust was not so much an adoption of Friedman's specific views on correct monetary policy as a 'conversion' to Friedman's tenet that (in Brittan's paraphrasing words of April 1969) 'the authorities have no more than a temporary power to influence output and employment' and 'that the difference between high demand and low demand policies affects in the long term the price level alone' – a tenet that Brittan found particularly congenial in the context of his passionate belief (derived from David

Hume rather than Adam Smith) in the primacy of the individual over the collective. Moreover, in terms of the price level, Brittan was accepting by April 1969 the Friedmanite line that 'a very large amount of inflation is required to purchase quite a small lasting improvement in employment'.[19] A passage from a May 1970 article shows the way in which instead he was increasingly looking:

The way to reduce the natural rate of unemployment in any country is by the boring and humdrum process of better training of the labour force to match the skills required, more even regional distribution of demand, better employment exchanges, and so on. A more controversial suggestion might be to treat the unions' employment-reducing behaviour (because that is what it really is) no more favourably than that of other monopolists who raise prices at the expense of turnover.

Brittan was also strongly propounding the virtues of flexible exchange rates, arguing that they would greatly reduce the 'problem' of the balance of payments, so dominant and so harmful, he plausibly maintained, throughout the 1960s. One way and another, his column was doing much to set the intellectual agenda for the next decade and more.

Nor was the economic arena the only one in which some of the key themes of the future began to show themselves in the late 1960s. In April 1968, following Powell's 'rivers of blood' speech, the *FT* ruled out of court repatriation as a solution to Britain's 'racial problem' and declared that 'the only practicable course' was, 'while maintaining strict control over any further immigration', that 'of seeking to ensure by a whole range of policies the speeding up of the process of assimilation of those immigrants now in the country'. The paper thus accepted the need for the new Race Relations Bill, while warning that 'in racial questions, the law can never be more than a deterrent' and that, like the nuclear bomb, 'if the threat ever has to be implemented, the policy has failed'. A little over a year later, in June 1969, the government announced that it was no longer going to attempt to impose its *In Place of Strife* industrial relations legislation against the will of the unions, in return for the TUC General Council's 'solemn and binding undertaking' that the unions themselves would comply with the TUC's own guidelines concerning unofficial strikes. The *FT* the next day, sceptical anyway of the worth of Barbara Castle's proposed Bill, was strangely sanguine about the sticking qualities of Mr Solomon Binding:

The threat of legislation has undoubtedly caused the TUC General Council to move much further and faster than most people expected earlier in the year. It has now assumed fresh responsibilities for mediating in industrial disputes and acquired new powers over member unions. If it is willing and able to use these powers and discharge these responsibilities, real progress can be made towards removing the 'tinge of anarchy' that the Bank for International Settlements has detected in our industrial affairs . . . If they fail the test, the call for legislation will become more insistent than ever. That, perhaps, is the best reason for hoping that the General Council will now take advantage of the opportunity it has won for setting its own house in order.[20]

Two months later Ulster exploded, and the troops went in. In a grave leader entitled 'Heading for the precipice', the paper on Friday 15 August 1969 even-handedly lambasted (in uncharacteristically strong language) the Northern Ireland government's 'incredible act of folly in allowing the march of the Apprentice Boys of Derry' and 'the ineffable irresponsibility of Mr Jack Lynch, the Prime Minister of the Irish Republic, whose speech on Wednesday night and subsequent playing at soldiers on the Border might have been expressly calculated to create the maximum tension'. Would the use of troops be only 'a very temporary expedient adopted for one grave emergency', as Callaghan the Home Secretary believed? The closing sentences of the leader read presciently almost twenty years later: 'If the British Government is to be involved it will immediately find the burden of responsibility placed upon it. And it is a sound principle that those who hold the responsibility should also hold firm control.'

The state of the economy remained, however, the central preoccupation of public life. Cecil King, recently deposed at IPC, had some stern words in his diary entry for 13 December 1968:

The papers are all very optimistic this morning because of the trade figures, which are better. The *Financial Times* takes off into the realms of pure fantasy. It is a strange aspect of our affairs that newspapers like the *Financial Times*, essentially hostile to a Labour Government, go out of their way to emphasise the cheerful points of Government propaganda.[21]

By this time King saw doom and decay all around him and was bound to be disappointed by the *FT*'s tendency to eschew the apocalyptic.

A similar caution imbued the paper's attitude during the general election of June 1970, turning as the contest did on conflicting analyses of the economy. It was not an election that appealed much to David Watt in his polling-day retrospective: 'Everyone seems agreed that this has been a thoroughly depressing election campaign – dull, parochial, mercenary and, occasionally, downright nasty. The British, one might say, have got their feet in the trough and the only argument is about who gets most of the swill.' In the end, with little enthusiasm, Watt accepted Labour's 'unfinished business' argument, involving 'the paradox that it is the Labour Government's own failures and omissions which entitle them to another term'. On the same day John Bourne the lobby editor asserted (like most of Fleet Street) that 'taken as a whole, the polls indicate that the national pattern will be sufficient – barring any last-minute switches of opinion – to return Labour to power with an adequate working majority'.

The election leader concentrated entirely on the economic aspect, questioning in various respects Labour's apparent confidence that all was well, but declining in the final paragraph to commit itself either way:

> The immediate task of the new Government must be to curb the rise in costs. It must do this to maintain the external surplus, to prevent a further erosion in profit margins leading inevitably to a fall in investment and to ensure that social justice is done. It should have no illusions about the difficulty of that task. Once inflationary habits are firmly entrenched they are not easily broken as the American administration has found to its cost. Whether in the end Mr Wilson's confidence in the economic strength of the country or Mr Heath's forebodings about the future prove justified will hinge on how quickly the new Government can persuade the nation as a whole that the present rate of inflation [about 6 per cent] must do serious damage to this country.[22]

It was arguably the paper's weakest post-war election leader, indicative perhaps of divided counsels at Bracken House. And it was doubly weak granted that the eventual victor was committed to 'rolling back the frontiers of government', reviving market forces, letting lame ducks die and other controversial, Selsdonian principles, all of which marked a clear break with Labour and demanded (but did not get from the *FT*) considered debate and response.

Wilson was still Prime Minister when he attended, as one of the guests of honour, the splendid dinner given by the paper at the London Hilton on 11 November 1969 to celebrate the publication (on the 12th) of the 25,000th issue of the *FT*. The idea was Drogheda's and it was planned and executed with typical flair and attention to detail. Thus the banqueting room was decorated in pink as far as possible; the guests on arrival were given pale pink carnations for their buttonholes and before leaving they received copies of the 25,000th issue. It was an immensely impressive guest list, coming to some 600 people and including half the Cabinet, the pillars of the City, the chairmen of 25 out of the 30 companies in the *FT* Index, most of the press barons and in general the great and the good in almost all walks of life. In addition to the Prime Minister and the Governor of the Bank of England, the guests of honour were Robert McNamara, President of the World Bank, and Jean Monnet, both men much admired by the paper. The only regret, perhaps, is that some names from the history of the *FT* itself were missing, including Archie Chisholm and Paul Einzig. The room was divided into seventy-six tables, with at least one member of the paper's staff at each table to act as host. The table plan reveals some intriguing groupings, perhaps none more than Table A8, where the young education correspondent, Michael Dixon, found himself playing host to Margaret Thatcher (opposition spokesman on education), Sir Siegmund Warburg, Peter Wilson of Sotheby's and the Belgian Ambassador, amongst others. By contrast, David Watt had a relative snip with Frank Cousins and Michael Heseltine, or even Doug York with Sir Lew Grade and John Cuckney. One of the journalists was so apprehensive of his task that he arrived at the Hilton somewhat the worse for wear and was sent straight home by Drogheda. The next day he went to see Newton, half expecting to be sacked, but Newton told him to forget about it. Newton himself had taken on Hugh Cudlipp, the Soviet Ambassador and Arnold Weinstock, so perhaps he sympathized. The evening as a whole was a great success, the speeches by the guests of honour were fully if rather blandly appreciative of the achievements of the paper, and the occasion aroused considerable media attention. It was yet one more recognition of how far the *FT* had come over the previous two decades.

The old order was now starting to break up. The last day of the halfpenny, 31 July 1969, was Sidney Henschel's seventy-sixth birthday and his farewell as advertisement director. Bracken and Drogheda had always referred to him as 'the founder of our fortunes' and they spoke no less than the truth. His had been an exemplary career, and he enjoyed a happy retirement until his death in 1983. He was briefly succeeded as advertisement director by Wilfrid Gabriel, until 1971 when Peter Yeo took over and fully implemented the 'scientific' as opposed to 'ambassadorial' approach towards the selling of advertising space.

The year 1971 also saw the retirement of Robbins as chairman, shortly after his seventy-second birthday, after eleven fruitful years in the position. Drogheda became the new chairman, with Hare succeeding him as managing director. Drogheda later described their relationship:

> I requested [Pearson Longman] that I should be regarded as chief executive in order that in the unlikely event of a disagreement between us I should have the final say. But during the time that I was managing director and he was general

manager we had each developed our own particular spheres of activity so that things fell naturally into place, and no difference arose, at any rate none of any significance that I can recall. On all important issues we usually saw matters in the same light . . . I did everything in my power to leave the day-to-day running of things to him, although, having had the responsibility for running the business as it grew from its relatively small beginnings in 1945, and being rather bossy by nature, it was inevitable that on occasion I had an irresistible urge to engage in matters of detail.[23]

Most observers would feel that it was a rather more charged relationship than that, especially towards the end of Drogheda's time in Bracken House, but it is still probably true that on the fundamentals they were in broad agreement. There was one other significant management appointment in 1971. This was the coming of Justin Dukes as the company's first industrial relations adviser, very much in the context of the Heath government's Industrial Relations Act of that year. He had previously been a ship's architect, a lecturer in management and group manpower adviser to McCorquodale & Company. He was still young and full of ideas, and soon emerged as an influential figure in what remained a distinctly under-managed organization.

Dukes was to be intimately involved in what had become from the late 1960s, and would remain until at least the 1980s, the single major direction of the newspaper: internationalization. It was a direction outlined in the course of a BBC World Service radio programme about the *FT* broadcast in November 1969 (a further 25,000th-issue spin-off) and featuring various leading Bracken House voices. The linkman knew to whom to turn to bring the programme to a suitably worldly end: 'Let's leave the last word to Lord Drogheda, the managing director. High up in his elegant suite, with its views of St Paul's and the City of London, placed as it were between God and Mammon, he gave me this thoughtful summary':

We try our level best to be impartial and to be accurate and to be comprehensive. We don't have any passionate political addictions, we believe in free enterprise, provided that it is enlightened free enterprise. And we try to develop the paper abroad, we want to see the paper read widely by the leading businesses throughout the world. We see the frontiers of the world are shrinking and we think particularly in the case of the United Kingdom which is so desperately dependent upon foreign trade, that, the more we can get the *Financial Times* known, the more we can get the point of view of the United Kingdom accepted abroad, so that we are rendering some service to this country.

It was an international vision based on Britain's traditional role in the pattern of world trade rather than on any awareness of the country's place in the incipient globalization of the world's financial markets – nevertheless, it was an international vision. During the next three years, with de Gaulle no longer ruling France and Britain at last able to sign the treaty of accession to the Common Market, taking up membership from the start of 1973, it was a vision that began to appear the appropriate one.

On the commercial side, another key figure in defining and implementing that vision was Adrian Secker, manager of the foreign department from 1966 and justly described by Drogheda in his memoirs as having 'an agreeably vague manner which concealed a very shrewd judgement'.[24] His was another of the radio voices:

At the old rate we used to do about twelve supplements a year, that's one a month, on various countries, perhaps just a little bit further from England, a little bit outside Europe. Then about two years ago, the editorial people and the foreign side got together and we drew up a programme of some forty foreign supplements, individual countries. And we carried that programme out and produced forty supplements in 1968 and in 1969 we shall have produced by the end very nearly sixty . . .

Supplements on countries are a joint operation in the very early planning stages, between the advertisement staff and the editorial staff. Somebody suggests a thing at a meeting, and I think, well, that I might be able to get the revenue and then we're off and we prepare a synopsis . . .

The curious thing was that neither Drogheda nor Secker by temperament and affinity particularly liked foreigners. Yet between them, together with Henschel and his colleagues in the advertising department, they did an enormous amount to set the *FT* on its future and, as it now seems, indispensable road.

Overseas revenue rose dramatically as an immediate result of this initiative, increasing by some 65 per cent between 1968 and 1971 and reaching an annual total of more than £1½ million, a figure no other Fleet Street paper came anywhere near to matching. The majority of the increase was attributable to display advertising in foreign surveys. Inevitably, it was an increase that involved considerable promotion. Towards the end of 1970, for example, under the auspices of the promotion director Tony Martin, four-page pink paper insets were put into *Le Figaro* in France, *Die Welt* in Germany and *24 Ore* in Italy. The insets reproduced a typical front page of the *FT*, gave circulation details and advertising rate, and invited readers to apply for a fortnight's free copies. It was an ambitious effort and involved shipping 7,500 tons of pink newsprint across the Channel. At about the same time, in December 1970, an *FT* symposium was held in New York on the 'Challenge of Europe', at which 600 representatives of United States finance and industry gathered in the grand ballroom of the Waldorf-Astoria Hotel to hear the thoughts of five European experts, including Baron Guy de Rothschild, Giovanni Agnelli (President of Fiat) and Roy Jenkins. There was also a new and highly effective slogan, in which the *Financial Times* was billed as 'Europe's business newspaper'. The slogan was almost entirely confined to Continental use, but from 1972 passengers travelling through Heathrow Airport were confronted by a jumbo-sized poster (40 feet by 10 feet) bearing the message. Readership abroad also rose during these years, though much more slowly than advertising revenue, going up from just over 10,000 in 1966 to a little more than 18,000 by 1972. Around three-quarters of this overseas readership was European. The numbers were not particularly impressive – hampered by perennial problems of cost, distribution and language – but the profile was. In 1968 the British Market Research Bureau examined the reading habits of 352 chairmen and managing directors of major European (non-UK) companies and discovered that the most-read English language publication, on 39 per cent, was the *FT*, followed by the *Economist* on 35 per cent and *Fortune* on 29 per cent. Of other daily papers, *The Times* scored 14 per cent, the *International Herald Tribune* 13 per cent and the *Wall Street Journal* 10 per cent. It was in the light of these and similar figures, with their obvious advertising implications, that the *FT* pressed on in the early 1970s with circulation campaigns in Europe, problematic and loss-making though the selling of the paper abroad still was. The prospect of printing in Europe was as yet only a distant gleam in one or two people's eyes.

It was for its export achievement that the *FT* in 1971 deservedly became the first newspaper to receive the Queen's Award to Industry, but on the foreign front equally significant developments were also taking place in the editorial sphere. Indisputably the key figure was J. D. F. Jones, who in 1967, while still in his late twenties, became foreign editor. In addition to a host of articles, mainly on African subjects, he had won his spurs during the Indo-Pakistan war of 1965, when he was the *FT*'s first real war correspondent. His appointment as a foreign editor was a fine example of Newton trusting his hunch, though for six months he watched over Jones closely and gave him a pretty hard time, before more or less allowing him his head. It was an appointment that produced dramatic results which Newton could not possibly have foreseen. In the course of his eight years as foreign editor, Jones not only developed the existing stringer network to a point where there were more than 100 round the world, but above all he increased the number of full-time foreign correspondents abroad from a mere handful to almost thirty, more than any other paper in the world had except the *New York Times*. Some of this development took place after Newton's retirement, but most was under Newton, if for the most part permitted by him rather than positively sponsored. It was an achievement that revealed a strong entrepreneurial streak, but in addition he was the most inspirational of foreign editors, absolutely on top of his job, full of editorial flair and instilling his correspondents with a marvellous sense of *élan*, trust and confidence.

It was Jones, moreover, who gave a further dimension to the paper's foreign coverage by developing the concept of the regional specialist, of whom by the late 1960s there were about ten, based in London but travelling abroad frequently. Their job was to provide an analysis not only deeper and more specialized than that previously offered by the *general* international specialists (the diplomatic and Commonwealth correspondents), but also more quickly and certainly available than that coming from the correspondents in the field, who might be uncontactable when a major story broke, or might have cable problems, and so on. It was a role that, as Jones explained to the BBC in 1969, was becoming central to the paper:

> What we are more and more concerned with these days is the feature coverage, the analytical explanation of the meaning of the news. After all, there are plenty of agencies to supply the news, and then there's radio and TV. Most of our readers probably see television or something every night. They don't necessarily, we think, want to read next morning just the actual news, just what happened. What they want to know is what that means and thus the function of the journalist in a British serious newspaper today is surely to analyse, not to report.

It is a view that has stood the test of time.

Subsequently, Jones's foreign editorship came under a certain amount of criticism – for empire-building, for recruiting correspondents inadequately numerate for a specialist financial and industrial paper, for concentrating too heavily on Africa and the Middle East, on guerrillas and 'small wars', to the detriment of the European, North American and Far Eastern mainstream economic coverage that the *FT*'s business readership primarily wanted. There was some truth in all three charges, but equally undeniable was the transforming nature of what he did on behalf of the paper. At a time when most papers were cutting down on their foreign staff, the *FT* was doing quite the reverse and getting the people in place to provide full coverage and analysis of what became during the 1970s and early 1980s economically and financially an ever more interlocking world. Subsequent foreign editors could tailor that legacy to the particular needs of the *FT*, but the legacy itself was, to a remarkable extent, the work of one man.

Among the people making names for themselves during this foreign expansion of the late 1960s and early 1970s was Richard Johns in the Middle East. In 1967 he had been sent to cover the Arab–Israeli war without ever having been in the area before, but over the coming years he emerged as one of the world's great experts on OPEC and its momentous doings. Tehran correspondent for six years from 1969 was David Housego, making a considerable cultural shift from his previous job of deputy letters editor of *The Times*. Serving as the paper's Africa specialist was Bridget Bloom, who had come from the magazine *West Africa*, was aggressive and broke stories, and whose coverage of the Nigerian civil war made the front page of the *Washington Post* in 1970. In Europe, particularly capable correspondents included Malcolm Rutherford in Bonn (succeeding Wolf Luetkens after an eleven-year stint), Paul Lewis (whose particular forte was the Bank of International Settlements in Basle) and Robert Mauthner in Paris (having been with Reuters and come to Newton's attention with a series of reports on the Prague spring); while as EEC correspondent in Brussels, Reginald Dale produced a regular flow of perceptive and detailed stories about an institution beginning to loom large in British eyes. In the United States there was Jurek Martin, whose first assignment was to write a feature on a hobby of his – baseball – a characteristic Newton touch. Yet not all the big foreign stories appeared under an individual by-line. Perhaps because the *FT* lacked a plumbing specialist, the first mention of Watergate was as a semi-humorous item in the 'Men and Matters' column on 19 June 1972: 'The US political scene was enlivened by a cloak-and-dagger mystery at the weekend. Five men carrying cameras and bugging devices were arrested inside the Democratic national headquarters in Washington early on Saturday morning.' The piece ended: 'Why they broke into the offices, and whether they were working for any other organisation, remains an enigma.'

There were other developments, less dramatic but in the long run equally significant for the internationalization of the paper. One was the increasing though still inadequate attention to the financial Euromarkets. In the late 1960s Ian Davidson wrote a certain amount about the Eurodollar market, but the main journalistic practitioner, and very close to the dealers themselves, was William Low, who in the autumn of 1970 began the weekly *FT Euro-Market Letter*, available on subscription. The following March the paper carried a sixteen-page survey of Euromarkets, including an introductory article by Low that began: 'Like Topsy, the Euromarkets have just growed and growed. In the space of one decade, the Eurodollar sector has expanded from around $1,000 million in 1960 to over $45,000 million by the end of last year. The growth of the Eurobond market is only slightly less impressive.' In the regular main body of the *FT*, by 1970 Low was writing an article each Monday on the Eurobond market in addition to editing the daily quarter-page of 'International Company News'. Then from April 1971 'International Company News + Euro Markets' became a daily page heading, at first occupying half a page but within a few weeks a full page. Among its regular contents was 'Selected Eurodollar Bond Prices: Mid-Day Indications'. And there, with Low receiving only moderate encouragement from Newton or indeed almost anyone else, the coverage of both international companies and the Euromarkets remained until after Newton's editorship. The Euromarkets in particular were somehow regarded as cultish and beyond the pale, a freak that was not the proper business of the *FT* – the paper of record for the Stock Exchange – to engage in overmuch. Low himself, disenchanted, left in 1972. The *FT* had not entirely failed to respond to what was taking place almost literally on its doorstep, but it would be fair to say that if it had had a real competitor it would have been seriously embarrassed by the tepid quality of that response.

On more familiar terrain, the paper ably met the European challenge on the eve of Britain's membership of the Common Market. From 11 April 1972 not only was the 'Export News' page broadened into a 'World Trade News' page, including a high proportion of news of European trade, but from Tuesdays to Fridays a second page of European news was also added to the foreign pages. The 'generalist' correspondents were mostly in place, the political context was appropriate, and it was the sensible, logical thing to do. The paper, however, could not genuinely claim to be 'European' until similar expansion also took place in the back, specialist half of the paper, which in practice did mean the international companies coverage. Newton himself wrestled with the problem, and revealed something of his thinking, in an interview he gave to the paper's house journal, *Bracken House News*, in October 1971:

> I don't believe there is such a thing as a 'European' paper. All experience shows that the language barriers are too great and the people too nationally minded. Anyone who tries that is going to come unstuck in a big way.
>
> That does not mean, however, that in a specialised field such as the one in which the *Financial Times* operates – and business is the only common language in the Common Market – we should not look at Europe in a rather broader sense than we do at the moment.
>
> We have got to carry a greater amount of European business news, which

means increasing our European representation. Anyone can look round Europe now and see the areas that we will need to reinforce, and it follows from that, that in the end we will inevitably put more men on the ground, and have to find more space in the paper for the news that they cover.

One only hopes that the cost of that will be covered by greater European advertising. It is a gamble.

It was one on which Newton, with his innate caution, was prepared to have only a modest flutter, certainly in terms of space if not representation.

The sense of growth and potential on the foreign side was not, however, shared at this stage by the traditional core of the paper's business, financial advertising. This now lay principally under the direction of the ebullient Robert Piper, who found himself fighting against certain adverse long-term secular trends, especially in the field of company-meeting reports and statements. The continuing tendency to go for the display-style advertisement (unlikely to appear if the results were unfavourable), the wave of take-overs and mergers reducing the number of companies, the inclination to spend more money on glossy reports to shareholders than on reports and statements in newspapers: all these factors contributed, so that the volume appearing in the *FT* steadily declined from its peak of 1965.

Nevertheless, in the context of the 'Barber boom' of 1972, it was by no means all tears, both within and without Piper's specific sphere. Euromarket 'tombstones' started to make a perceptible impact; prospectuses flourished, with often as many as eight pages appearing on a Monday; there was considerable trade advertising from merchant banks and secondary banking areas; and as a consequence of the accompanying property boom, there was much advertising by the construction industry, the profitable advent of the property investment bond in the unit trust market, and a phenomenal quantity of commercial property advertising, sometimes up to seven pages on a Friday. As a result, in conjunction with the surveys programme, the total advertisement columnage for 1972 came to a record 32,299 (excluding quotations), compared to 26,773 in 1971, which had itself been a record.

The *FT* would not have been able to take advantage of this particular boom if it had not had extra capacity installed by 1971, resulting for the first time in integrated issues of more than forty pages, with a maximum of forty-eight pages, which was to remain the ceiling for a long time. The other great technical gain of this period, in terms of advertising revenue, was the ability to offer fully registered colour of high and certain quality, as opposed to the less satisfactory 'wallpaper' method with a repeating pattern that had been used for the first tentative colour pages in the mid-1960s. The result was a big jump in these highly lucrative pages, going up from only 5 in 1968 to 37 in 1969 and 67 by 1972. During the 'wallpaper' days there had been some talk of printing the *FT* on white paper in order to accommodate the technical problems of colour advertising, but by the early 1970s these revolutionary thoughts had been long banished, and the slogan 'When five colours are better than four' was making confident play of the native salmon pink.

Circulation in this period went up to more than 170,000 in 1969, then flattened for two years largely in consequence of three price rises (including going up to a shilling in April 1970 amidst much anxiety) and finally in 1972 saw Newton out in grand style by jumping to an average daily net sale of 188,485, comprehensively a record. The feverish 'Barber boom' contributed greatly to that dramatic leap, while in the words at the time of the circulation manager Leslie Bentley, 'interest in the state of the economy, the Common Market, VAT and the labour situation can only help us'. These were years of flourishing publicity and marketing, with John Geddes coming in 1969 as public relations adviser to join forces with Tony Martin and Michael Ryan. The 'Games man' was finally and regretfully pensioned off as unhelpful to the image the paper was trying to project of itself as the *complete* business paper; and at last, after years of oral usage, the abbreviation '*FT*' began to be used in written form as well. There was a particularly interesting campaign in the spring of 1971, when full-page advertisements were placed in the *Daily Telegraph*, the *Guardian*, the *Daily Mail* and the *Daily Express* tailor-made for each paper and presenting the *FT* not as an alternative but as a complementary purchase, fulfilling the role of 'the business partner'. It was an explicit acceptance of the paper's essentially specialist function.

At about the same time Ryan wrote a piece in *Bracken House News* about the nature of the paper's British readership. He revealed predictable domination by men (75 per cent), an average age of thirty-seven (lower than that for any paper except *The Times*) and a high readership per copy of almost five people (probably attributable to being read mostly in offices). Geographical breakdown showed 55 per cent of readers in London and the South-East, though Ryan pointed out that 'our regional distribution of readership matches fairly closely the regional distribution of men in the professional and managerial classes, with only a slight bulge in the London area'. Within that 'AB' grouping, among *FT* readers there were 100,000 directors and managers in industry and commerce, 43,000 accountants and company secretaries, 35,000 engineers and technologists, 34,000 proprietors and managers in retailing and 23,000 sales and marketing executives. Stockbrokers and insurance brokers came sixth on 20,000, while senior civil servants and local government officials contributed a disappointing 12,000. Still, that was four times the number of officers in the armed forces who read the paper; perhaps they had become jaundiced over the years with the *FT*'s persistent calls for cuts in the defence budget.

The operating profits of the paper held fairly steady at around £1 million pounds for three successive years, but then jumped to more than £2 million for 1972. In March that year a survey of the newspaper industry by the brokers Hoare Govett considered some of the *FT*'s salient commercial characteristics:

> The readership is obviously very heavily weighted to businessmen and the AB or higher social income groups and this enables it to charge the highest relative rates for advertising space. Despite this, the paper is a very attractive advertising medium for commercial and industrial as opposed to consumer goods advertisers and this provides the paper with a relatively stable high volume of advertising. The paper's share of display advertising in the quality daily papers increased from 30% to nearly 31% in 1971 and compares with the 19% of *The Times*.
>
> The paper's cost structure is very different from the other nationals, with newsprint only accounting for some 15% of the total because of the low circulation and production about 35% because of the high composing costs. Overhead costs are also higher than average, but the most striking difference is the paper's profitability, with a return on sales of over 15% in 1970 compared with the average of about 1% for all national newspapers. Also, because of the high price of advertising space, a marginal increase in its volume is extremely beneficial to profitability. The most variable part of revenue, and hence the main determinant of profit fluctuations, is that derived from financial advertising, which is closely related to the state of the stock market.

In January 1972 the *FT* Index crossed the 500 mark for the first time in nearly three years (after a long slide from September 1968 until March 1971), thus setting up the paper for the bumper profits of that year.

From January 1971 an organization under Christopher Johnson's direction known as FT Business Enterprises was established, which grouped together the existing syndication department, Investment Inquiry Bureau and library external services, as well as developing an ambitious programme of conferences and list of business books and publications, including the *FT Diary*. Generally, a rather sharper commercial edge was now being developed. In 1969 Pearson had gone public (as much as anything to mitigate death-duty problems), while still remaining family-controlled; in 1970 Frank Taylor, finance director of Pearson Longman (as S. Pearson Publishers were now called), joined the *FT* board; and at the end of that year Pearson Longman moved its head office to Bracken House. The logical culmination came in 1972 when, at the request of Pearson Longman, the paper drew up a corporate plan for the first time, covering the next three years. In presenting the plan in draft form to the rest of the board, Hare 'in particular mentioned the problems which arose from the company being a high fixed costs type of business where a relatively small variation in revenue had a disproportionately large effect on profits'. Gibson in response 'said that a study of the plan showed that the main benefit of the exercise was that it highlighted problem areas', but added that 'it could not however produce solutions to these problems'.

No problem was more acute than that of production costs. 'Unless ways can be found to bring about a closer connection between productivity and the rise of money incomes, no newspaper publishing enterprise, however profitable at present, will be able to sustain its position': Gibson's words of April 1970 in his annual statement remained as true two years later, despite the introduction between times of a series of so-called 'comprehensive' agreements, part of a general wave of such agreements in Fleet Street.[25] Their introduction was a complex, time-consuming business, but the basic *FT* management thinking behind them was that, in the context of ever-larger papers, it would be easier to contain and plan production costs if, for each chapel, all the mass of individual payments for work done and time spent were lumped together into one 'comprehensive' rate to cover the job as a whole, irrespective of how long or short a time it took to do. The belief was that such a change, by ending increasingly expensive overtime, extra page payments and so on, would lead to drastic and permanent savings. Certainly something needed to be done to counter years of wage drift: between 1963 and 1969 the page content of the paper had increased by 38 per cent, whereas over the same period the total labour cost had gone up by 105 per cent in the case area, 94 per cent in the linotype area and 99 per cent in the stab area. A letter from Drogheda to Cox in December 1969 about the overriding need to achieve comprehensive agreements was indicative of the management mood of the time: 'So far as we are concerned, the prospects for growth of the *FT* look pretty good, but it is pointless trying to assist that growth if all the fruits thereof have to go to the men under your command. I feel that at the moment we are desperately handicapped.'

Yet once completed, the benefits of these agreements proved somewhat illusory. It is true that they allowed greater budgetary control, as well as reducing the potential number of 'flashpoints' over individual payments;

but against that, they necessarily had all the various abuses and 'Spanish customs' built into them that had evolved over the years, were highly inflationary in what was to be the decade of hyper-inflation, and were all too liable to have extra individual payments tacked on to them. Nor did these agreements lead to the end of the London Scale of Prices in the composing room; it remained firmly in place and ever more costly in its consequences. Moreover, the coming of these agreements also had a damaging psychological effect, providing for a set number of people to do a job and thus impairing production flexibility, encouraging the chapels to gain control from the overseers over determining who did the work, and inevitably leading to a general attitude of trying to get through the work as quickly as possible, whatever the corner-cutting and loss of pride involved. Perhaps management had no alternative but to go comprehensive, but the results were at best mixed.

The other major production development of this period was the move towards computer-assisted methods of calculating and photosetting the tabular matter in the paper, above all the share information service. It was clear from the late 1960s that the existing manual methods were not only very labour intensive but also increasingly unable to cope on days when more than about a third of the securities quoted showed price changes. On some evenings up to half the labour force was being employed on tabular matter, at a time when the size of the paper as a whole was steadily increasing, yet for understandable reasons the management was seeking to hire as few new people as possible until the comprehensive agreements were reached. Finally, in 1972, with the paper frequently going to press late despite copy deadlines being pushed earlier, Cox was authorized to go ahead and purchase the Linotron system developed by Linotype-Paul. The new equipment, which came into operation in 1973, meant no saving on labour costs (the compositors continued to be paid as if they were still engaged in hand composing in movable type according to the London Scale of Prices, even though their function was now changed to keyboard operation) but otherwise had the anticipated beneficial effects, soon leading to the question of whether the computer might also have a role to play in other parts of the paper.

These were also years in which the *FT*, like the rest of Fleet Street, was increasingly being affected by industrial action. Between 1970 and 1972 a total of sixteen issues failed to appear, usually because of general as opposed to house disputes and sometimes for 'political' reasons, such as four days lost in July 1972 in support of dockers gaoled under the Industrial Relations Act. In June 1970 four days were lost shortly before the general election, as a result of SOGAT terminating a wage agreement three months prior to its date of expiry. The *FT*, after the resolution of the dispute, optimistically argued that out of it there might come good for Fleet Street:

> The newspaper industry, which notoriously has great scope for increasing its efficiency, has now taken at least a step in the right direction. First, management has been able to negotiate and reach a settlement with all the printing unions [i.e. chapels] simultaneously rather than with each individually. If this practice is kept up in the future, there will be an end to the leap-frogging of wage claims that has in the past made it impossible to keep labour costs under control.
>
> Second, and of even more potential importance for the future, management and unions have agreed to set up a joint working party that will review the whole wage structure of the printing side of the industry and make recommendations based on the most efficient use of manpower and equipment. If this review is thorough and if its recommendations are accepted, the economics of the national newspaper industry could be transformed.[26]

Neither hope was fulfilled. There was a speedy return to the leap-frogging approach; while as for the joint working party, as usual it was no match for firmly entrenched (especially after the comprehensive agreements) chapel power. Moreover, within days of the editorial being written, a new government was elected, and industrial relations began to enter their harshest phase yet in post-war British history.

Predictably, the *FT* had little patience with the strong, sometimes violent opposition displayed by the unions towards the Heath government. In August 1971, for example, when the Industrial Relations Bill became law, it called upon them 'to realise and admit, now that the legislation is an inescapable fact, that they have much to gain from it'. The following winter the paper was particularly unsympathetic towards the miners when they went on strike after rejecting the National Coal Board's offer. 'A bitter and fruitless stoppage', was the paper's view on the eve of the strike. Some six weeks later, after mass picketing of power-stations and an inquiry chaired by Lord Wilberforce treating the miners as an 'exceptional' case and awarding them three times the NCB's offer, a major leader weighed up 'The cost and the lessons'. The conclusions reached were thoroughly gloomy: that 'the authority of government has been damaged'; that there was 'the renewed threat of wage inflation'; that 'the law on picketing was anything but clear' and 'must be clearly defined'; and that the miners had won because the government had lost the propaganda war, having 'failed to drive home the lesson that inflationary pay awards for one sector of workers which then spread through the economy must mean higher unemployment'.[27]

The tone of the leader was strong, but as nothing compared with the one on 'What is now at stake' on 28 July 1972, in the context of dockers being gaoled under the Industrial Relations Act and the resulting massive industrial turmoil, including the start that day of a national dock strike:

> The Government must persuade the public that what is at stake now is the way in which this country will run its affairs. Will the country accept that the wishes of the majority and the law must be respected, that the interests of all those who cannot protect themselves against inflation are nonetheless legitimate and a matter of concern to all? Are we to go back to feudal times and the over-mighty subject who pursues his ends and his alone no matter what the cost to anyone else or are the normal political processes to be allowed to work?

The final paragraph turned to an aspect especially close to the heart:

> Fleet Street was one of the very first to be hit by the political strikes against the Industrial Relations Act. The public must recognise the danger that the Press will become nothing more than a political football, to be stopped at any time for political reasons. We are only one step away from a situation when a newspaper may be stopped from publication because of the views which it might express, where the free expression of opinion becomes impossible . . . It does not require much imagination to see what sort of a political system – whether it be dominated by extreme right or extreme left – lies at the end of that road.

The 1970s were to be a crisis-ridden decade, economically as well as politically, and at times the bunker mentality was one that the *FT*, like the governments of the day, found it difficult to avoid.

As for the specific economic policies of the Heath government, going as they did from *laissez-faire* to interventionist in less than three years, the paper offered more or less consistent support through the successive phases. In 1971 the phenomenon known as 'stagflation' manifested itself, being a uniquely puzzling combination of rising wages and prices, falling production and increasing unemployment. And in January 1972 there was that deeply embarrassing moment for the City when the *FT* Index went above 500 on the same day that the jobless total reached seven figures. The paper's leader on the conjunction could not deny that it made 'an easy anti-capitalist debating point', but maintained that historically 'the behaviour of the Share Index is, if anything, an encouraging sign', in that 'every major downturn in the Index has heralded a rise in unemployment' and usually vice versa. It also went on to argue, in language that would become deeply familiar, that granted 'a large part of economic progress consists of finding ways of saving labour', unfortunately 'improvements in labour productivity are not spread equally over different industries', while in addition 'there have been major shifts in both home and overseas demand away from certain industries and regions'. Therefore, 'full employment cannot be restored simply by boosting overall demand, but must actually involve a change in the distribution of workers between occupations'. In which context, it was a pity that 'union behaviour aimed at preserving existing wage differentials instead of encouraging the required movement of labour'.[28]

Yet two months later, when Barber presented his famous (or infamous) arch-reflationary Budget, which *did* seek to provide a massive and general stimulus to the economy, the *FT* greeted it with some warmth and in the final paragraph of the next day's leader (called, as in April 1964, 'A Calculated Gamble') played down its obvious inflationary dangers:

> But the Government is now talking with the TUC and the CBI. It is expanding the economy along the lines for which the TUC has been pressing; it is adopting the argument, the level of unemployment being what it is, that a rapid rate of industrial growth is the best way of preventing higher costs from spilling over into higher prices. There is a reasonable chance that everyone concerned will now co-operate in the attempt to get inflation in check. The Chancellor is taking a calculated gamble.[29]

Inflation continued to rise; tripartite talks about its voluntary control broke down in November, and the government introduced a wage–price standstill, the fourth 'freeze' since the war. The *FT*'s response to the move noted that 'it represents a reverse for the Government, which has been forced into doing what it said originally would never work', but characteristically concentrated on the practical implications, above all on the sequel to the immediate freeze. It concluded: 'It is to be hoped that both the CBI and the TUC, once over their initial disappointment, will feel able to play their part in devising workable machinery.'

A further major strand occupying the *FT*'s leader-writing attention in the early 1970s was monetary. In August 1971 President Nixon, faced by a continuing trade deficit, suspended gold convertibility of the dollar, introduced an import tax of 10 per cent and announced that he was asking the IMF to recast the international monetary system established more than a quarter of a century earlier at Bretton Woods. The United States move took the rest of the world by surprise, but the *FT* reacted with admirable calm and percipience, pointing out that 'facile phrases, like "the toppling of the dollar", should not be allowed to obscure the fact that the basic power relationship between the US and her allies has not changed merely because of an alteration of exchange parities'. Four months later, in the Smithsonian Agreement reached by the Group of

Ten at Washington, the import surcharge was abandoned in return for a new pattern of exchange rates, multilaterally agreed, by which the dollar was devalued by some 12 per cent. The *FT* viewed it as 'a considerable achievement' that ended a lengthy period of uncertainty, though rather shied at Nixon's own estimate of it as 'the most significant monetary agreement in the history of the world'.

The rapid pace of monetary change continued when in June 1972, in the context of a sudden sterling crisis caused partly by the threatening labour situation, the British government decided to leave the exchange rate free to float, as an alternative to outright devaluation. At what was potentially a critical juncture, it received decisive support from both the *FT* and the *Economist*. Six months later, in the final editorial of 1972 ('Ringing out the old year'), the principal cause of optimism was viewed as Britain's imminent membership of the Common Market, which 'will have a far-reaching influence in almost every sphere of national life'. The concluding paragraph, however, supplemented this vision with the emerging monetary dimension:

> At the same time, the decision to float the exchange rate and keep it floating until inflation is under better control demonstrates that the Government means to be inhibited neither by traditional prejudices nor by excessive subservience to conventions which may damage the national interest. Once in the Community, we shall be able to play a full part in working out a course of development which will benefit not only its members individually and collectively but the world as a whole. It is not only the old year but a fusty collection of old ideas that we shall be ringing out.[30]

It was an appropriately forward-looking tone for the last leader to be written under Newton's editorship.

As ever, his paper in these final years continued to evolve, not only on the foreign side. Thus in 1972 the 'Farming and Raw Materials' page (as 'Commodities' was now called) made a logical move to the back half of the paper; while already in existence by this time was the *FT*'s monthly survey of business opinion. Or again, one day in 1970 the creative advertiser Michael Manton was lunching with Drogheda, suggested that there should be more marketing in the paper, Drogheda put it to Newton, and Newton made Antony Thorncroft marketing editor virtually on the spot. The upshot was 'Advertising and . . . the Marketing Scene', occupying a page to a page and a half each Thursday and capitalizing on what was becoming one of the great growth industries. Meanwhile, 'The Executive's World' page was starting to move towards its modern form, becoming distinctly more analytical in approach and also international in scope. A full books page each Thursday also began by 1970, edited by Anthony Curtis and with C. P. Snow as its chief reviewer. It was a brilliant move to recruit Snow, who had recently finished his *Strangers and Brothers* sequence, was looking for a new direction and proved the most wide-ranging, perceptive and also industrious of book reviewers. It was, however, an old feature, that well-established favourite 'Finance and the Family', which provoked a public reaction, when Bernard Levin wrote in *The Times* in May 1971 that the questions asked in it 'paint a picture of life in Britain so horrifying that I think the Government would be fully justified in seeking from Parliament power to prohibit, on pain of massive penalties, the export in any form of any Saturday issue of the paper, Queen's Award or no Queen's Award'. Levin then gave such a detailed account of the impression given therein of British life – 'people going to almost insane lengths to avoid the payment of income tax or death duties, cheating those to whom they have loyal obligations, defaulting on payments of every kind, divorcing one another in the most appalling circumstances, and sitting about waiting eagerly for the deaths of those from whom they have expectations' – that perhaps he was only half joking.[31]

Of the individual journalists now making the day-to-day running outside the foreign pages, one of the most prominent was John Elliott, an energetic, highly combative labour editor, who sharpened up the paper's news coverage of what was becoming an ever more central area of concern. Two others who should be mentioned are John Graham, a resolute and capable correspondent in Belfast, and Arthur Sandles, who not only became the paper's first expert on the leisure and travel industry, but also in increasingly inflationary times made something of a speciality of the workings of the family budget. His pieces often featured a mythical couple, Sally and Jim Jones, who usually seemed to live in Richmond and drive a Ford Cortina. Also in the 'leisure' area, the paper had a second gardening writer in the person of the young Oxford historian Robin Lane Fox, who contributed a much appreciated column each Wednesday. There were also frequent pieces by the always readable Clement Freud, who in December 1970 reported on a Muhammad Ali fight at Madison Square Gardens 'feeling a shade awkward as the only man in my section not dressed in full-length fur coat and matching hat'. In the arts page proper, Andrew Porter continued to add lustre, in December 1971 hailing Kiri Te Kanawa as 'the new star' and describing her in *Le nozze di Figaro* at Covent Garden as 'such a Countess Almaviva as I have never heard before, not at Covent Garden, nor in Salzburg, or Vienna, at once young, full-throated, a singer of great accomplishment and a vivid character'.

If one had to name the two writers who most caught the eye in the early 1970s they would probably be C. Gordon Tether and Joe Rogaly. Tether by this time was starting to use his back-page 'Lombard' column not only to provide a monetary commentary but also to offer his personal perspective on a whole range of issues, of which the one that recurred most often was the Common Market and the method as well as the implications of Britain joining it. 'Free vote would be another charade' was the title of one such column (in August 1971), arguing that 'even a referendum could hardly do democratic justice with the scales weighted as heavily in the pro-Marketeers' favour as they must be with the media so much on their side'. It was a judgement, as well as at times a style, that sat increasingly uneasily in the *FT*'s pages as a whole.

An altogether happier column, in terms of the development of the paper, was that on 'Society To-Day', started by Rogaly in 1969. It aimed to be a free-ranging look at society both home and abroad, was soon complementing the other weekly columns by Watt and Brittan, and was always stimulating if sometimes tendentious. 'It would be easier for the present Government', Rogaly wrote typically in June 1972, 'to find and converse with creatures on Mars than it would be for it to get any kind of meeting of minds with British workers.' His general approach to the problems of society was liberal, to the vexation of Cecil King on 14 December 1971: 'Rogaly in the *Financial Times* has what is to me a disgraceful piece saying that governments are not concerned with morals, and no one should be concerned with what adults do in private.'[32] One might or might not agree with Rogaly's opinions, but undoubtedly the column as a whole provided the paper with a valuable social dimension – a dimension that after he stopped writing it in the late 1970s rather went missing.

Newton had always hated the idea of staying on as editor with people secretly thinking he was no longer the man he had been. By 1970 at the latest he decided that he would retire on or soon after his sixty-fifth birthday, which fell in September 1972. In the event, he retired at the end of that year. The choice of successor, decided in 1970, was virtually a one-horse race, once it had become clear by about 1969 that Christopher Johnson was not a realistic candidate. There was some possibility of Nigel Lawson returning to the fold, but when approached he expressed unwillingness to serve an initial probationary period as editor of the *Investors Chronicle*. Moreover, it was strongly felt by Newton for one that, after the paper's great achievements of recent years, it would be a source of considerable resentment to the editorial staff if the new editor did not come from the existing ranks. In practice, this almost certainly meant that the new editor would come from the first generation of direct intake, of whom by 1970 there were only three still in Bracken House: Robert Collin, already an ill man; Samuel Brittan, temperamentally unsuited; and Fredy Fisher. This is not to say that Fisher did not have many positive qualities to offer as potential editor, merely to make the point that there was no plausible alternative. So in January 1971, after several years as assistant editor, he became deputy editor, with Bill Roger moving to managing editor for his last few years on the paper and Johnson to business enterprises; and in November 1972 it was formally announced that on Newton's retirement Fisher would succeed him as editor.

The making of the original decision in 1970 is not documented, but probably the three key people in choosing Fisher were Drogheda, Newton and Robbins, perhaps in that order. They were well aware of the internal politics of the situation; they knew that Fisher was likely to leave the paper if he did not become editor; and Newton in particular would have been less than human if he had not wanted to confer the succession upon someone whom he had trained as a journalist and who could fairly be trusted to uphold the character of the paper that he was now bequeathing. There was one other significant appointment at this time. Geoffrey Owen, after working for the Industrial Reorganization Corporation and then British Leyland, returned to the *FT* in September 1972, with a brief to write about European industry, but within four months became deputy editor to Fisher. Lines of succession were starting to take shape.

Meanwhile, the old guard took its leave. 'Shill' had already gone in 1971; and shortly before Newton himself left, both Doug York and Ben Kipling retired after many years of service. Also, Sheila Black decided to move on, feeling perhaps it was the end of an era. But of course, the departure that overshadowed everyone's was that of Newton. There had been no more influential figure in the history of the paper, and the prospect of the *FT* without him seemed almost inconceivable.

What in the end does one make of Newton's long editorship? Some have argued that although manifestly a winning formula, fuelled by his own industry and intuition as well as the conducive climate of the time, it was in the end an intellectual evasion, a failure to attempt to make the paper into an organ that tried to shape opinion and not merely reflect it. It is also argued (not always by the same people) that the Newtonian *FT* was crucially flawed by its subservience towards the City, which it recorded in a two-dimensional way, but on the whole neither criticized nor even properly understood. Both arguments can be exaggerated. What they ignore is the intangible legacy that he left, quite apart from the quadrupled circulation and hugely expanded coverage, remarkable

FINANCIAL TIMES

No. 25,946 Monday January 1 1973 6p

EEC—exciting time ahead: PM

Britain has joined the Common Market—entering a new and challenging political and economic era with the New Year.

A movement begun in 1946 by Sir Winston Churchill's visionary call for "a kind of United States of Europe" has thus been completed and the major objective of Mr. Edward Heath's Government finally realised.

At the historic moment of Britain's admission—diplomatically recognised at a minute after midnight in both Brussels and London despite the one hour time difference—the Prime Minister was returning from Ottawa. "A very exciting time is now beginning," he said.

Mr. Heath called on the people to forget their fears and seize the opportunities open to them. "This is only the first stage, the work is not completed."

A united Europe would now begin to work towards new objectives, including the creation of a fresh balance with the U.S. in trade and monetary affairs, he added.

The enlargement of the Community—Denmark and the Irish Republic became members at the same time—was welcomed in all the capitals of Europe.

The flags of the nine nation members were raised at dawn in Brussels and were flown in London but generally there was a notable lack of ceremony to mark the successful conclusion of more than a decade's debate about the terms of British membership.

A day of prayer for the new Europe will be held in Westminster Abbey to-day, and Fanfare for Europe, an 11-day festival of the Arts, begins on Wednesday.

Amid the celebrations yesterday, however, Mr. Harold Wilson, the Opposition leader, said that the terms of entry would be "crippling" for the country. He reaffirmed that a future Labour Government would renegotiate with the Community and let the people, still divided on the issue, have the last word.

See Page 9, Back Page
Editorial comment, Page 12
Britain and the New Europe Pages 13-22

FINANCIAL TIMES EDITOR RETIRES

Sir Gordon Newton

On Saturday, November 19, 1949, the following announcement appeared on the front page.

THE FINANCIAL TIMES

Mr. Hargreaves Parkinson has been elected into a directorship of The Financial Times. Mr. Parkinson was, for many years, a member of the editorial staff of The Economist and was associate editor of that newspaper until his appointment to the editorship of The Financial News in 1938. After the amalgamation of The Financial Times in 1945 he became editor of the combined newspaper.

Mr. Gordon Newton will succeed him as editor of The Financial Times as from January 1, 1950, and Mr. T. S. G. Hunter has been appointed deputy editor.

Thus, without any biographical detail, without any sounding of trumpets, was announced the appointment of Gordon Newton as Editor of the paper which he was so signally to transform, and which from a modest eight pages selling 50,000 copies a day was to grow to an average size approaching 40 pages and a circulation approaching 200,000.

For nearly a quarter of a century he has been at the editorial helm of a newspaper which has increasingly earned the respect of the business community not only in this country but throughout the world. His colleagues would all have liked him to complete the full 25 years, but he had always been insistent that he would not continue as Editor beyond his 65th birthday. He was in fact 65 on September 19 last, and he only carried on as Editor until the end of the year because of various staff changes with which he was actively concerned.

It is perhaps not unreasonable at such a moment to claim that the growth and development of the Financial Times during recent years has been a story of success. Gordon Newton would be the first to agree that many factors have contributed to this story, not least the vision of Brendan Bracken, and the immensely strong advertisement staff built up by Sidney Henschel, who was Advertisement Director from 1946 until he retired at the age of 76 in 1969, but who still comes weekly to the office.

Gordon would, I think, also say that he had been considerably assisted by the constant support and encouragement of the controlling shareholders of the Financial Times, who at no time have interfered with or sought to bring any pressure to bear upon him in his task of editing the paper. It is nevertheless essentially to him that credit for its success is due.

What are the qualities which he has above all brought to bear? Each of his colleagues would place the emphasis differently, yet each of us would agree that modesty ranked high, and therefore he will be embarrassed by the opportunity we now have to pay our tribute.

Working alongside of him day by day, his tremendous singleness of purpose has never ceased to impress itself upon us all. From the moment of his appointment his greatest desire has been to make the Financial Times the world's most authoritative and comprehensive journal for the man of business. He has judiciously broadened the scope of the paper. He has paid endless attention to detail, and he has insisted upon the facts being as accurate as they can be. He would rather not carry a story than get it wrong, for he has realised the hurt and the harm which inaccuracy can do. He has shown unerring wisdom in his choice of staff, and he has earned the deep affection and respect of those working under him, to whom he has contrived both to give a lead and yet to allow very considerable freedom.

At all times he has made himself readily available as a point of reference for guidance and advice. His open-mindedness and his objectivity have been a delight to experience. Upon countless occasions he has been required to make judgments upon fundamental questions of policy (and how right he has usually been), in the knowledge that views expressed by the Financial Times will be regarded as an authoritative guide; but the responsibility he has borne has in no way aged him, and to most of us he appears as young to-day as he did when he was first appointed.

It was a happy day for all his colleagues when in 1966 the Honour of Knighthood was conferred upon him, closely followed by the bestowal of the IPC Hannen Swaffer Journalist of the Year Award in March 1967. The Knighthood was, I hope, essentially in recognition of his great services as Editor of the Financial Times. It should however be recalled that he has rendered considerable public service. At the request of the Prime Minister from December 1970

until March 1971 he carried out a personal review of the aims and functions of the Central Office of Information. He also served as a member of the Committee on Privacy from April 1970 until July 1972. There have been many other occasions when his advice has been sought informally on major issues; and it is certain that he has never betrayed a confidence.

He has been good enough to refer elsewhere to his and my collaboration together. We have been close colleagues, not only during his period as Editor, but also extending back to pre-war days, when we both worked on the old Financial News, he as one of the bright young editorial men, I as a humble canvasser for financial advertising. While our tastes and hobbies may not in all respects be identical, on fundamentals we have always seen very much eye to eye, and we have constantly worked together in complete harmony. I am profoundly grateful for all the support he has given me over the years; and I am most thankful that we are to continue as colleagues on the Board of our parent company.

DROGHEDA

NEWS SUMMARY

ULSTER

Hunted man seized

Martin McGuinness, No. 1 on the British Army's wanted list in Londonderry, has been arrested by Irish police, 14 miles from the Ulster border.

He was seized with another man, named as Joseph McCallion, after a car containing 5,000 rounds of ammunition, and 250 lbs of gelignite was discovered near Ballybofey, Co. Donegal.

McGuinness, 22, and McCallion are being held under the Republic's Offences against the State Act, which allows police to hold suspects for 48 hours without making a charge.

Peace talks to resume

Peace talks are expected to resume in Paris next week following the decision by President Nixon to call off the bombing of Hanoi and Haiphong.

Aircraft are still hitting targets in the North below the 20th parallel. The latest raids have set the country back two years, according to one semi-official assessment. **Pages 6 and Back**

More pig fever

Two new outbreaks of swine vesicular fever, the first for 10 days, have been reported. The outbreaks hit farms 30 miles apart, in Staffordshire and Warwickshire. After the slaughter of 3,611 pigs, it was thought the disease had been beaten.

Air crash puzzle

Early investigation reports into the crash of a Lockheed TriStar at Miami, which killed 97 people, indicate there was no technical failure of the aircraft or its Rolls-Royce engines. **Page 9**

Fog menace

Heavy week-end fog throughout Britain cut visibility on some roads to 10 yards and delayed dozens of flights at London Airport, Heathrow. As temperatures plunged, motorists also had to contend with black ice.

£25,000 premium bond first prizewinner — number 2WS 870556—lives in Hertfordshire.

BUSINESS

Industry outlook improves

● **THE FT** Monthly Survey of Business Opinion shows that the freeze has helped to moderate industry's fears of inflation. The effect, however, has been blunted by continuing uncertainty over what is likely to happen when the freeze ends. Prospects for the economy are seen as having improved, with expansion continuing unabated and both orders and deliveries at their highest level yet.
Page 38 and Back Page

● **CHANGES** in Bank of England rules governing takeovers of members of the Accepting Houses Committee, the 17 elite merchant banks, come into effect to-day.
Page 40

New Year honours

Mr. William Batty, once an apprentice and now chairman and managing director of Ford of Britain, gets a knighthood in the New Year Honours list.

With Sir Robert Maclean, who receives a KBE, he heads a list of 36 awards for export services—12 fewer than in the Birthday Honours.

The list of 34 knights include Mr. William Ryland, chairman of the Post Office Corporation, Mr. K. C. P. Barrington, a director of Morgan Grenfell, and Mr. G. N. Butterworth, chairman of English Calico.

● **LAY-OFFS** for 1,500 men at British Steel Corporation plants at Scunthorpe, Lincs., begin to-day.
Page 9

● **PRUDENTIAL ASSURANCE** led the way for 1972 in new life business with net new sums assured leaping by £241m. to £2,276m. New annual premium income was £52.3m. (£43.7m.).
Page 34

● **ASSOCIATED ENGINEERING** chairman Mr. H. R. Moore forecasts a further increase in profit in his annual statement.
Page 34

● **MR. L. J. MATCHAN**, chairman of Cape Allman International, expects new records in turnover and profitability in the New Year.
Page 34

We wish our readers a happy and prosperous New Year

ON OTHER PAGES

A New Year message from the Chancellor of the Exchequer

A CHALLENGING YEAR—BARBER

TO-DAY WE become full members of the European Economic Community. This is the climax of negotiations which have extended over 11 years.

In these years the Community has gone far towards achieving its primary aim of freedom of trade and movement between its members. And now the scene is set for further advance. The Summit Conference in Paris in October took a number of major decisions, including the development of common industrial, social and regional policies, and a common approach to international monetary reform and tariff negotiations. These are all matters of great importance to the United Kingdom. We are now in a position to exert our full influence on the way in which these policies develop, and my personal experience over the past year leaves me in no doubt that we shall be expected to do just that.

Joining the Community involves no change in our own economic objectives. The goals of greater price stability, full employment and economic expansion are shared by our fellow members. The difference is that we now have a better chance of achieving them. We now have a home market of nearly 300 million people. It is therefore only commonsense that Government and industry alike should be thinking and planning on a European scale, in order to take full advantage of the new opportunities. There is nothing more encouraging than the confidence in our ability to compete which is shown by those of our firms which already have experience in the Common Market—except perhaps the concern of some Continental enterprises that they are now to be exposed to British Competition!

On the economic and financial front, the Government's primary purpose has been to create the conditions which will help our industry and commerce to compete effectively. We have done this by massive reductions of taxation, by liberalising the system of credit control, and by introducing free depreciation on plant and machinery to encourage investment.

Next April, the three main structural reforms of our taxation system will all come into operation—the unification of income tax and surtax, the new system of corporation tax, and the reform of indirect taxation, including the abolition of purchase tax and SET and the introduction of VAT. Change and transition are never easy, but over the years these reforms will provide new incentives for enterprise and efficiency.

We enter the Common Market with an expanding economy and a reserve of unused resources. To sustain this expansion, however, we need a higher rate of capital investment and a lower rate of inflation. On the first of these, it is not unfair to comment that the ball is now unquestionably in industry's court. Almost all the major actions which I have taken have been designed to set the economy on a 5 per cent. growth path—twice as fast as during the previous decade. Furthermore, the forecasts for world trade suggest a faster growth rate this year which should help our exports.

On inflation the present standstill has the overwhelming support of the British people. And the policy which is to follow it will recognise that our most immediate task is to ensure that inflation is checked. The action we have taken to contain the growth of the money supply is designed to match the action we have taken to slow down the rise in prices but not to put a brake on our rising prosperity.

Expansion has inevitably meant, and will mean a change from the very high balance of payments surplus which was associated with excessive unused capacity and high unemployment. We are at the moment in the lower part of the familiar J curve which follows the change in the rate of exchange. In other words, import values are swollen by the higher prices, but the increased competitiveness of our exports which the change has made, has not yet had time to work through into actual sales. This is a temporary phenomenon. And two further facts should not be forgotten. First, we have repaid all our outstanding short and medium-term official debts. Second, our reserves are now twice as large as they were when we took office.

1973 will be a year of challenge—the year in which we will be competing on more equal terms with our European neighbours. I believe that it will also be the year in which we finally show that we can break away from the slow economic growth which for too long caused our standard of living to lag behind. It is one of the economic facts of life that real prosperity can be achieved only as a result of higher output. This is why I am determined to sustain a faster rate of economic growth.

ANTHONY BARBER

● **G. D. N. Worswick, Director of the National Institute of Economic and Social Research, discusses the prospects for the U.K. economy on page 12. Professor Paul Samuelson examines the U.S. economic outlook and Ian Davidson writes on European trends on page 33. And on page 8 leading U.K. businessmen discuss the prospects for their industries in the coming year.**

FT Survey: Britain and the new Europe

To-day the Financial Times is publishing the first part of a three-part survey on "Britain and the New Europe" to mark the start of British membership of the European Community. Part II will appear to-morrow, and Part III on Wednesday.

The survey is introduced by a major article by the Prime Minister, the Right Honourable Edward Heath, and the list of distinguished outside contributors includes Sir Christopher Soames, one of the two British members of the Commission, who analyses the tasks ahead, Professor Walter Hallstein, the former President of the Commission, who assesses the achievements to date, Mr. Vic Feather, General Secretary of the Trades Union Congress, and Mr. W. O. Campbell Adamson, Director-General of the Confederation of British Industry.

In all, the survey runs to 60 pages and over 80 articles, and examines in depth the implications for all aspects of political, industrial, commercial, social and cultural life in Britain.

1 January 1973: Newton retires, Britain joins the EEC

achievements though those were. It was a legacy that was essentially an ethos – an ethos of accuracy, of caution, of disinterestedness, above all of placing the cause of the paper above the demands of personal ego and opportunism. The ethos derived from the man, and it seems right to end this chapter with Newton's voice, explaining on the radio in 1969 how the *FT* had achieved what, by universal consent, it had:

We didn't have a plan. We've never really had a plan. We've just produced, or tried to produce, a paper which we thought was a good paper. And we got fun out of doing it. And the staff as a whole has thought it fun. They've seen the paper grow and they've been happy and proud, I think, to be with the paper. But the whole idea really has been that of gradual growth, adding a bit to this, seeing whether it was right and if it was right going ahead more boldly and that sort of thing. But I would emphasize that at the beginning of each year we've never sat down and said, 'We're going to do this.' Someone has had an idea. It looked good. Try it out. If it's good in practice, push ahead . . .

[THIRTEEN]

NEW HORIZONS, OLD TECHNOLOGY: 1973–9

'He still retains something of a Teutonic accent, but this is matched by a fierce enthusiasm for all forms of British sport.'[1] Thus *The Times* described the man who on 1 January 1973 took on the almost impossible job of succeeding Newton as editor, the journalistic equivalent perhaps of going in to bat after Bradman. Appropriately, it was the same day that Britain at last entered the Common Market, for by both background and outlook the new editor was wholly European. M. H. 'Fredy' Fisher was born in 1922 in Berlin, the son of a distinguished lawyer, and was brought up bilingually in German and French. In 1936 his family was forced to leave Germany and went to Switzerland, while he was sent to boarding-school in England. Soon after the outbreak of war he was shipped as an 'enemy alien' to an internment camp in Australia, but by 1942 he had persuaded the authorities where his sympathies lay and returned to Britain to join the army, taking part two years later in the Normandy invasion. After the war he read Modern History at Oxford; then for seven years worked in the Foreign Office library, editing the German Foreign Ministry documents relating to the war; and in 1957, looking for a new career, landed up almost by chance in Coleman Street. Until the mid-1960s his main work was on the foreign side, but in 1965 he became economics editor and took as his brief the paper's overall economic and industrial coverage, writing a wide range of leaders and feature articles. The editorship was always Fisher's goal, and by 1971, if not earlier, it was clear that he was going to achieve it.

As an editor he was not the easiest of people to work for. He did not always listen, could be authoritarian in manner and had a tendency to 'bark'; he could be tactless, though not deliberately, and like Newton did not often congratulate; he could also be snobbish, culturally and intellectually rather than personally. Perhaps most importantly in the context of a daily paper, his mode of discourse tended to be an argumentative one, which could make life tiring and sometimes dispiriting for his subordinates, especially when they approached him with new ideas. Nevertheless, even at his most frustrating as an editor, Fisher never forfeited the loyalty, indeed affection, of those who worked most closely with him. They recognized the many positive qualities – including considerable personal charm and kindness – that more than outweighed certain flaws. There was, as his life history had shown, the sheer 'bounce' of the man, full of force and vitality, always restless, always looking for new challenges. They also respected him for the element of steel in his make-up, the capacity to take the necessary but unpopular decision – something that Newton, for all his day-to-day semi-despotic rule, had at times shied away from, perhaps especially towards the end of his editorship. Above all, Fisher won the minds if not invariably the hearts of his staff because they knew that, at the particular stage the *FT* had reached in its evolution, he was the right person for the job. Not only was he a highly intelligent and cultured man, with a wide range of interests and the inclination as well as capacity to encourage those around him to debate the issues of the day in a far more thoroughgoing way than had been the case under Newton. But even more crucially, he was by both background and temperament a genuinely internationally minded person, at the very time when internationalism was ever more where the destiny of the paper lay. Believing implicitly in the best Newtonian traditions of objectivity, non-partisanship and accuracy, and upholding them to his utmost, Fredy Fisher was also supremely well qualified, in a way that his predecessor could not have been, to take the paper into a new, more worldly era of broadening horizons and deepening sophistication.

As one would expect, the 44-page 'benchmark' issue of Wednesday 31 October 1973 shows the state of the paper still as essentially that bequeathed by Newton at the start of the year, with plenty to do for a reforming editor. Home news remained all over the place, in the back as well as the front half of the paper, including an incongruous mix on one page of the money market, the *FT*–Actuaries share indices and a story about how 'owners of more than 13,000 Ford Cortinas are being contacted for a check on a possible fault in the fuel system'. The technology page was still very bitty, comprising on this particular day thirteen small items. The back half was generally messy, including Lane Fox's weekly gardening column appearing on one page amidst a sea of classified advertisements for 'Business Opportunities'.

Yet in this random issue there was as ever plenty that impressed. One full page was devoted to setting out in authoritative detail 'stage three' of the government's counter-inflation policy. Another whole page tackled the Middle East crisis and accompanying oil shortage from a genuinely international perspective, showing to the best advantage the paper's newly enhanced human resources abroad. And on the centre pages there were substantial feature articles not only on the hopeful third stage, but also on 'The urge to merge in Sheffield steel', the latter by Ken Gofton, a notable industry specialist since the late 1960s. Various other names catch the eye: on the arts page Chris Dunkley was now in residence as television critic and writing about the Thames series *The World at War* with characteristic incisiveness; a few pages on, the paper's splendid legal correspondent, A. H. Hermann, reported at some length on the first day of the *FT*'s conference on company law; on the 'Executive's World' page the much-liked house doctor, David Carrick, submitted his regular prognosis on 'Executive Health'; and towards the back, Mary Campbell examined in detail the relationship between the Euromarkets and British public sector borrowing overseas. On the front page, one small but indicative change was the complete lack of jokiness in the news summary, with not even a single 'human interest' item. While on the back page, Tether's 'Lombard' column was far removed from the traditional preoccupations of the street of that name and considered the larger implications of the recently publicized Ethiopian famine, emphasizing that similar tragedies 'are being enacted day in and day out on an enormous scale throughout the less-developed world' and arguing that 'the real culprits are those who, being in a position to see that the affluent peoples are made aware of their duty to tackle the world poverty problem in appropriately serious fashion, fail to do so'. It was strong stuff – but was it, some were beginning to wonder, what the *FT*'s readers needed to read about? Still, it was at least as relevant as the list across the page of temperatures at holiday resorts, which passed on the vital information that on a Tuesday at the end of October it was 52 degrees in Blackpool.

During the early years of Fisher's editorship the foreign side continued to expand, including the opening of an office in Tokyo in 1973 by Charles Smith, who for the rest of the decade produced sound economic coverage at a time when Japan was starting to make its global presence felt. In the autumn of 1973 events in the Middle East enabled Richard Johns to establish his reputation as supreme interpreter of the actions of Sheikh Yamani and his colleagues, while at home Adrian Hamilton earned wide praise as energy editor. A less happy area was Watergate, of which the paper was slow to discern the significance, only towards the end achieving proper coverage. An early sign of coming times occurred in 1973 when Christopher Lorenz, after two years spent establishing the Frankfurt office, became the first of the J. D. F. Jones school of foreign correspondents to transform himself into an industrial correspondent. Over the next four years, tracing the development of Silicon Valley, he put the *FT* on the map as the definitive paper on the business aspects of international electronics and telecommunications, hitherto adequately covered only by *Business Week*. Significantly, a frustration he had found in Germany was being bound by geographical constraints at a time when industries in general were becoming increasingly trans-frontier. At the consumer end of the economic process, the task of telling people how to spend their pounds was now in the hands of Lucia Van der Post, who in September 1973 visited the new Biba store in Kensington High Street with Sandy McLachlan and declared of the household section that 'there is something over-blown about it', that 'the joke has been taken too far: one bright pink nylon broom is fun, but a barrowful is a little worrying'. Meanwhile, the daily racing tips now passed from Dare Wigan to his son Dominic.

As for the City's equivalent of the racecourse, the Stock Exchange, the prestigious 'Lex' column of market analysis, which had had a bad patch in the last part of Newton's editorship, was put by Fisher into the capable hands of Richard Lambert and Barry Riley; the former was one of the late direct-intake recruits (1966 in his case) who were trained on the companies side of the paper in lieu of the more or less dissolved traditional features department. Generally, however, the financial coverage in the mid-1970s was still weak. Mary Campbell, lacking resources and under-supported, struggled to convey the importance of the Euromarkets; there was surprisingly little on the secondary banking crisis; the paper was well behind the pack on stories like Slater Walker; and on the whole, no less than Newton before him, Fisher viewed with some distaste the *Sunday Times*-style 'Insight' investigative approach, arguing that it was bound to go factually wrong at some point, tended to confer a stamp of importance upon unworthy subjects and altogether was to be eschewed in favour of the cardinal *FT* goals of seeking to be accurate, analytical and non-controversial. It was a case that could well be argued, but in practice it meant that the 'unacceptable face of capitalism', as the famous phrase now went, was not much seen in the City's own paper.

Fisher's underlying approach to his editorship was to consolidate the Newtonian achievement, but this did not mean that the product stopped evolving. From August 1973 the share information service and unit trust prices were set by computer, though contrary to expectation the computer proved unable to deal with the whole of the paper's tabular matter, so the Wall Street prices, currencies and other statistics continued to be manually set. Soon afterwards an office page began on Mondays, which made the mistake of concentrating on office products rather than life in the office and lasted only a few years.

On January 1974 an announcement that might have been expected to shake the foundations of Bracken House appeared on the front page: 'In view of the present general situation and in particular the need to conserve newsprint stocks, it has been decided to discontinue the publication of Stock Exchange dealings in the *Financial Times* issues of Tuesday to Friday. The week's Stock Exchange dealings will continue to be published on Saturdays.' Everyone then sat back and awaited the barrage of protests. There were many more protests than in October 1968, when the prices moved off the back page, but not enough to tempt Fisher to reverse his decision. It was perhaps at last generally recognized that the dealings (based on voluntary marking by members) were an unreliable guide to Stock Exchange actuality; while from an editorial point of view their demise on a daily basis released up to a page and a half of the paper. A week later, under David Palmer as news editor, 'Home News' became a page heading for the first time. After years of dispersion the British news was at last systematically gathered together, creating a far more satisfying effect for the paper as a whole. Palmer also developed what was called for some time a 'News Analysis' piece, being a news feature deriving from the news room and thereby giving the home pages more shape and authority, comparable to the old 'Scene' articles on the foreign pages.

Finally, in January 1975, to a considerable extent at Drogheda's urging, significant overall layout changes took place. 'Letters to the Editor' were moved from page two to opposite the leader page in an attempt to enhance their pulling power; labour news, much of which had for years been on that page, now received a page of its own in the front half of the paper; Tether's 'Lombard' column was moved from the back page to page two; and on the back page this change enabled not only the 'Lex' column to go down rather than across the page (as Drogheda had wanted in 1968) but also the page as a whole to become much more of a news page, second only in importance to the front page itself. The paper was coming close to taking a shape familiar to readers of the 1980s.

A close statistical reading of the editorial contents of the national press, including the *FT*, was provided by the third post-war Royal Commission, which was set up in 1974 by the Labour government and three years later published various detailed reports relating to a sizeable sample of issues taken in 1975. Not surprisingly, more than 69 per cent of the *FT*'s total news space in the sample issues was taken up by financial and market news, over twice as much as any other paper. Otherwise, 20 per cent was devoted to home news and 11 per cent to external news, in both cases a much lower percentage than the other quality papers. In terms of feature space, the *FT* was the leader in its financial and business allotment, but significantly its 18 per cent devoted to British political, social and economic subjects, and its 13 per cent for similar foreign subjects, was comfortably ahead of *The Times* and the *Daily Telegraph* and lagging only slightly behind the *Guardian*. Where the *FT* trailed in its features was in spheres such as 'personalities' (2 per cent), 'sport' (1 per cent), 'women's features' (2 per cent) and 'picture features' (0 per cent). The reports also analysed various subject areas in considerable depth. In the field of foreign coverage (excluding specifically financial, business and 'travel' content), the geographical breakdown was particularly interesting, showing that (contrary to subsequent conventional Bracken House wisdom about the mid-1970s) there was no marked bias towards either Africa or the Middle East. Indeed, Africanists fared better in *The Times*, the so-called 'camel corps' in both the *Guardian* and the *Telegraph*. In industrial relations, the *FT* led the way with 300 items in twenty-four sample issues, followed by the *Morning Star* with 248 items. Interestingly, those were also the two papers more likely than any other to have cited redundancy as the cause of a strike. By contrast, the *FT* came easily bottom of the qualities in terms of the percentage of editorial space devoted to the area of 'social welfare', with *none* of its 63 sampled items (again from twenty-four issues) originating in court cases, pressure or action groups or the National Union of Students. Analysis of letters-to-the-editor columns showed that, although the *FT* received only 240 letters a week (of which sixty were printed), this resulted in a figure of 6.7 for annual letters received as percentage of circulation, second only to *The Times*, which scored a commanding 24.6 per cent. In terms of supplements, the *FT* was predictably dominant, with an average of 4½ pages added by them to each issue, compared with 1¾ pages to *The Times* and 1¼ to the *Guardian* – a fact that also meant that by the 1970s the *FT* had replaced the *Daily Telegraph* as the daily paper with the largest average size. Finally, there was 'picture content' as a proportion of editorial space, which revealed the *Daily Mirror* and the *Sun* leading with 17 per cent each, with the *Guardian* and the *Telegraph* both on 9 per cent, *The Times* on 6 per cent and the *FT* on 3 per cent.[2] However, one might add that compared with the *Wall Street Journal* (not to mention *Le Monde*) the *FT* was and is a visual feast.

This scrupulous fieldwork, however, gives little or no inkling of what was taking place behind the scenes on the editorial floors. Certainly, on the *FT* there were some particularly charged developments during these early years of Fisher's editorship. Two stand out. One was the way in which, partly through the conscious efforts of Palmer in the news room to upgrade the status of the news function, the old 'two-class' system amongst the journalists at last disappeared, though it had been on the wane since the late 1960s with the phasing out of direct intake. Increasingly, 'industry specialists' came to the fore, who were expected to take responsibility for all aspects of that industry's coverage, whether in the form of news or features. Undoubtedly this made for a more harmonious working atmosphere, while also giving proper writing opportunities to certain journalists hitherto denied them. On the other hand, there were some specialists, highly knowledgeable though they were, who lacked the literary ability to write the extended feature of authentic quality, to the inevitable detriment of the reader.

The other development, about which it is even harder to be dogmatic concerning its consequences, was the pattern of recruitment. During the 1950s and 1960s Newton relied essentially on his flair. Of course on occasion he erred, though usually it did not matter because the newcomer who turned out to be unsuitable was often a young graduate who was not intending to make journalism his ultimate career and could easily move on to another pursuit. During the 1980s the process of recruitment to the *FT* became highly systematic and even sophisticated, placing the highest possible value upon a potential recruit's intellectual cutting-edge. Between times, however, the paper almost completely failed to put in place a satisfactory vetting machine, at the very time when the Newtonian instincts were now absent from the procedure and the size of the paper was demanding a much larger staff than had customarily been the case. As a result, abetted by lax budgetary procedures, there was a tendency during part of the 1970s for some departmental heads to hire an unregulated number of people with little cross-vetting – people who, unlike many of the recruits of previous generations, *were* intending to make journalism their career and over the next decade would often feel little inducement to leave what was by now a well-paid job. One should not overstate the problem: many of the very best journalists of the *FT* of the 1980s were recruited during this period. Moreover, even those recruits who, in a broad-based sense, lacked long-term potential as writers were still able to fulfil useful, even important roles within the paper. Nevertheless, it was a problem and, although one by no means unique to the *FT*, it was arguably of particular importance to the *FT*, granted the increasingly ambitious editorial aspirations of the paper.

Much of this lay in the future. During the first winter of Fisher's editorship the more immediate and striking drama of the oil crisis, the miners, the three-day week and the fall of the Heath government was played out. 'History has always shown that it is unwise to try to exploit a monopoly position ruthlessly,' the *FT* warned the Arab oil-producing countries at the end of October 1973, but two months later the paper was rather belatedly accepting that things would never again be the same for the West and that the age of automatic economic growth was finished:

The interlude of cheap oil – which lasted only a couple of decades – is now over, as the Shah has rather too bluntly explained. We face now a demanding decade or two of adjustment, of payments imbalance (like the old dollar famine) and of heavy investment – a prospect rather like that of 1945. Given the same common will, the problem is no more insoluble than it was then.[3]

The real ire of the *FT* was reserved not for the sheikhs but for the National Union of Miners, as in a fairly typical leader on 29 November, following a ban on overtime and weekend working in the context of sharply reduced oil supplies:

The plain fact stands out that the miners are seeking to obtain even more than the relatively generous pay increase offered them and that yielding to their demands would, by destroying a policy approved by Parliament, make the economic situation of the country dangerous and could put its political stability in question. The Government has no choice but to uphold the terms of Stage Three. Public opinion will prevail in the long run, and public opinion will probably swing increasingly against the miners as the results of their action become clearer.

The first such result was the announcement a fortnight later of the three-day week, earning the government praise for having 'acted firmly and sensibly', even if rather late in the day, and accepting that 'there is no longer to be any pretence that the $3\frac{1}{2}$ per cent growth target on which Stage Three was based is relevant'. Over Christmas and into the New Year the crisis dragged on, baths were shared in order to save power, and by the end of January the executive of the NUM had decided to go for a ballot for full-scale strike action. The *FT* on 25 January declared that 'if the miners choose to come out on strike in these most difficult of circumstances for Britain the case for calling a General Election will be overwhelming'.

So it happened. The miners voted to strike, and an election was called for the last day of February. The *FT* fully supported Heath's decision – arguing that it was the only way of avoiding either the misery of a long strike or the larger consequences of agreeing to the miners' demands. But what was particularly interesting was its discussion of *why* it believed the miners had to be resisted:

Do the miners realise the implications of this appeal for the uncushioned operation of supply and demand? Do they recognise that what they take for themselves will be at the expense of others and that their manner of taking it is likely to lead, one way or another, to the growth of unemployment for their fellow-workers? Does the TUC not see that it is the weaker members of the community, whether or not organised into unions, who are likely to suffer most from inflation and have the greatest interest in preventing supply and demand from operating without restraint? No doubt the moves towards an incomes policy which have so far been made can be criticised as ineffective, partly at least because they have been inadequately supported by fiscal and monetary policy. But surely the attempt to work out an acceptable policy in co-operation is well worth continuing? The heart of the present matter, ironical as it may seem, is that the Conservative Government is rightly unwilling to let the miners bring back unfettered 'free enterprise' into the running of the economy.[4]

It was, as they might have observed in points north, a piquant viewpoint from EC4.

Three weeks later the country went to the polls, and the paper's election-day leader began by expressing irritation that 'several analysts of the British Press, ranging from the *Economist* to Moscow University, have recently suggested that the *Financial Times* could always be counted on to support the Conservatives'. The last three election leaders, all at best lukewarm towards the Tories, were cited in defence of 'a newspaper which does and can claim political impartiality'. On this particular occasion, however, 'we see no alternative but to hope for an adequate overall Conservative majority'. This was so less because of the merits of the Heath government ('If the Conservatives have had bad luck, they have also displayed bad judgement'), but rather because of the perils of the Labour alternative, which 'could increase the polarization of society, exacerbate the problems of inflationary stagnation, and create bitterness which before long might lead to another election and the return of a Government pledged to policies much more extreme and divisive than those pursued in the early days of the Heath Administration'. It was, as the title of the leader proclaimed, 'A difficult choice', for 'just as Labour failure might lead to an extremism of the right, so Conservative failure might lead to an extremism of the left'. But in the end (in a characteristic final sentence), 'We support the Conservatives because the risk of failure seems smaller in their case – provided they interpret a victory primarily as an authorization to deal with an economic crisis for which they are themselves in part responsible.'[5]

Heath lost his electoral gamble, and by 4 March the *FT* was calling on Wilson to 'find the resources within himself' to transcend party considerations and 'promote a national effort to solve the economic crisis'. Over the succeeding weeks the paper's attitude towards the new government was not one of thoroughgoing hostility. 'Provisionally correct' was the verdict on Healey's first Budget; while at about the same time Geoffrey Owen profiled as 'Man of the Week' the new Secretary of State for Industry, Anthony Wedgwood Benn, and concluded that it would be foolish to dismiss his ideas as irrelevant, in that 'they are designed to meet the aspirations of people who are dissatisfied with the present economic system' and that 'such dissatisfaction is widespread, and those who wish to preserve the system need to develop policies which will make it work better than in the past'.[6]

Increasingly, though, as the Labour government outlined its plans, the *FT*'s editorial attitude became unashamedly antagonistic. The proposed industrial relations legislation was viewed as giving the unions unwarrantable privileges, while as for Benn's intended National Enterprise Board, 'as a recipe for economic recovery it can only be described as nonsense'.[7] One sentence in August 1974 about plans to nationalize the shipbuilding industry could have come straight out of the late 1940s: 'The fact is that the Government's proposals have nothing whatever to do with efficiency, but stem from out-dated doctrines which are quite irrelevant to the problems of shipbuilding.' Two months later Wilson sought an increased majority, and the *FT* came out much more strongly for the Tories – or, at least, against the alternative – than it had done in February:

> We are quite clear where we stand. We do not believe that the Labour Party has an effective policy to deal with inflation. We do believe that the division in the Labour Party on Europe is potentially a major threat to this country. Just where Mr Wilson himself stands is a legitimate question to which there is no answer. And we also believe that the greatest danger to the economy would arise if a Labour Government with a large majority in the House of Commons but a minority popular vote were to try, either under pressure from its extremists or that of events, to shift the political and economic balance sharply to the left.[8]

Again Heath lost, but again the electorate declined to give Labour a convincing mandate.

Meanwhile, as the election leader suggested, the issue of Britain and the Common Market continued to rumble high on the political agenda. As one would expect, the *FT* under Fisher's editorship never wavered in its formal commitment to British membership. The leader on his first day in the editorial chair celebrated Britain's simultaneous entry and looked ahead optimistically to the time when there would be 'a more closely integrated Community', not only in the trading and monetary senses, but also 'institutionally equipped to take on one day much greater responsibility also in the area of ultimate sovereignty, that of defence'.[9] This latter theme was picked up again in the leader of June 1974 about the nuclear deterrent, following a British nuclear test undertaken in Nevada. After noting that the arguments of the 1950s were long dead and that 'few people now think unilateral renunciation would have the slightest effect on anyone', the leader went on: 'The new Goverments in London and Paris have both shown they wish to remain in the nuclear league; they could do it better together, even though it would require a degree of political co-operation not yet contemplated.' Two months later, during Nixon's Watergate death throes, the paper drew one positive lesson from the sight of Europe's 'natural ally' hamstrung by domestic political scandal: 'It is that the case for European unity, especially in the political field, is stronger than ever.'

The EEC referendum of June 1975 prompted the paper's major set-piece on the whole subject:

> For about 15 years now the *Financial Times* has held the view that for the sake of Europe and for the sake of this country British membership was the right choice. Initially – and in those days tariffs were very much higher than they are today – we attached considerable importance to the short-term economic advantages of forming part of the fastest growing market in the world. But then we swung to our present position, that the economic advantages are there, but will have to be worked for over a number of years, and that political considerations are paramount.

The next paragraph outlined the *FT*'s belief that 'greater European unity must be the objective for which the Community must strive', even though there were no short cuts to such unity, before moving to what was clearly intended to be a resonant conclusion on a historic day:

> Among all the pros, only Mr Edward Heath and Mr Roy Jenkins have held out a positive vision of the future. They, as little as any of us, can foretell what form future European integration will take. But they reject totally, as we reject, the prospect of Britain as a tight little island, seeking refuge in a siege economy, opting out of the main stream of world politics. We do not believe that a 'Yes' vote will solve a single one of Britain's pressing current problems, but we are certain that coming out would make their solution immeasurably more difficult.
>
> We do believe that in a world dominated by the superpowers, at a time when the US is more uncertain than at any time since the end of the war on how it should use its power, Europe has a vital role to play. It can only hope to make its voice heard, whether it be in relations with the third world or in the dialogue

with the oil and raw materials producers, it can only hope to temper the rivalry between the US and Russia if it can defend common interests in common.

Can anyone really deny that Europe will be weaker if we withdraw from the EEC and that Britain as a result will be weaker too? 'No man is an island, entire of itself', John Donne wrote. Nor can Britain be today. It is because getting out would be a gratuitous act of irresponsible folly, because we have a contribution to make to the building of a more closely knit Europe and a better and safer world that the vote must be 'Yes'.[10]

The vote was 'yes' overwhelmingly – and two days later the *FT* enjoined its readers now to 'Behave like Europeans'.

By this time there was a new Conservative leadership embodying, as it now seems, a new political and economic philosophy. On 4 February 1975, when Heath came under challenge from Margaret Thatcher and Hugh Fraser, the paper saw the contest in rather less grandiose terms, asserting that 'it is plain that the main reason for today's election is a negative wish to be rid of Mr Heath rather than a general desire to appoint any particular alternative'. No doubt at the time that was an accurate assessment. And according to the *FT* it was an unworthy wish, for it concluded that Heath's 'undoubted gifts are enough to justify allowing him another period of grace in which to show that he can carry out the necessary task of reconciliation'. The college of voters judged otherwise, Heath stood down, and six days later Thatcher, William Whitelaw and four others were the candidates in the second and, as it turned out, final ballot. 'The choice is Thatchlaw', the *FT* declared on the day, arguing that each candidate was handicapped – Thatcher by her 'reputation for unfeeling dogmatism', Whitelaw by his 'paternalistic and very untechnocratic character' – and that consequently 'whoever Conservative MPs pick, the new leader will need the virtues of his or her chief rival in the coming months, as well as his or her own'. In short, 'the choice is very finely balanced', and the paper declined to express its preference.

The next day an intellectually rather more purposeful editorial welcomed a 'New start for the Tories':

Nowhere is the need for a fresh approach more urgent than in the field of economics. Largely because of Mr Heath's reversal of the policies embodied in the 1970 Election manifesto and the subsequent failure of his new policies, the Conservative Party is deeply divided on economic issues and, above all, on the central problem of how to tackle inflation. The role of prices and incomes policy, the importance of fiscal and monetary policy, the power of the trade unions – there is no consensus within the party on all this. There is a philosophical conflict between the concept of a 'fair' society, implying some logical relationship between the incomes of different groups, and the consciously non-egalitarian approach associated with Sir Keith Joseph.

On the basis of her past statements and associations it is fair to assume that Mrs Thatcher will wish to move the party, however gradually, more in the direction of what Sir Keith Joseph has described as the social market economy. This is to be welcomed. The experience of both Labour and Tory Governments in the past ten years suggests that the expansion of State influence over the economy and industry, and the replacement of market forces by bureaucratic decision, almost always has harmful consequences. This is widely recognised, even on the Left. If Mrs Thatcher can develop a practical and non-doctrinaire programme for reducing State control and enlarging the area of individual choice, she will win considerable support.

On a more personal note, the paper added: 'To the public at large Mrs Thatcher is still something of an unknown quality and this should be a source of strength. In the present mood of disillusionment with party politicians, she has the opportunity to develop a new style of leadership.'[11] The words almost echoed those some twelve years earlier about the rather different fourteenth earl.

By the summer of 1975, as the government in the wake of the EEC referendum sought finally to bring inflation under control, the *FT*'s editorials were moving towards accepting the economic precepts of what would become known as 'the counter-revolution'. On 2 July, after Healey had announced that if an effective voluntary agreement was not concluded quickly with the unions then the government would introduce a statutory incomes policy, the top leader ('Some action at last . . .') expressed satisfaction, but the one below ('. . . and what remains to be done') stressed that serious dangers remained of 'unforeseen increases in the borrowing requirement and increasingly lax monetary conditions', that indeed 'without a financial context, the policies are empty: arithmetic without economics has been tried before, and failed'. The next day Samuel Brittan's column was headed 'Still under the delusion of incomes policy', and soon afterwards the government announced that wage rises were to be limited to £6 a week. The *FT* on the 14th offered its considered opinion on the pay package, accepting straight away that it was perhaps for the best: 'Given the situation in which the country found itself – notably a high and rising rate of wage settlements at a time of falling output combined with a special relationship between the Labour Government and the TUC – there was much to be said for the introduction of a temporary but drastic incomes policy.' The rest of the leader, however, was distinctly unenthusiastic about its potential long-term implications, arguing that 'the

Government's policy is bound to cause serious inequities between one group of workers and another' (particularly, the *FT* noted, for those unfortunate business executives earning above £8,500 a year, who did not even get the £6) and that 'such a state of affairs cannot persist for long without either immobilising the labour market and inhibiting initiative or encouraging widespread evasion of official policy'. The concluding passage sternly asked the government what its intentions were beyond the immediate crisis:

> If members of it are flirting with the idea which has long been popular with some officials in charge of economic policy, that control of incomes should be a permanent tool of economic management, they should come out into the open. We ourselves believe that incomes policy can be no more than a temporary expedient, inevitably accompanied by many disadvantages, and that the proper tools for regulating the economy in all but abnormal times are fiscal and monetary policy. Only the proper use of fiscal and monetary policy can make the present policy effective. The debate which should begin at once should be about how to get back to the use of these tools alone as rapidly as possible.

The leader was called 'Getting back to normal'. In 1975 it was many years since this 'norm' had held sway for any length of time, but in due course it would indeed return, its passage in some measure eased by influential leaders such as these.

Four floors up from where these thoughts were emanating, the management of the *FT* during the mid-1970s was enduring some fraught times. From the autumn of 1973, within months of Fisher assuming the editorship, not only was there the general economic *malaise* of the oil crisis, the three-day week and continuing stagflation, but there also existed a specific financial dimension, with the secondary banking crisis lasting until 1975 and prices on the Stock Exchange on a rapid downwards spiral, culminating in January 1975 with the *FT* Index hitting a low of 146. In this context, circulation held up well enough, with a record average daily net sale of 194,289 for 1973 even rising to 194,592 for 1974; though the British component of that circulation was two thousand down and was now beginning a long, difficult period of relative stagnation, not helped by the frequency of major cover-price increases throughout the rest of the 1970s. A further aspect was the declining increased sale on Saturdays: in 1965 the difference between the Saturday and the weekday circulation had been some 60,000, but by 1972 it was down to 39,000 and by 1974 to 31,000, with the difference continuing to narrow for the rest of the decade.

In the mid-1970s, however, the immediate pressing problem was that of advertising. In 1973 the total columnage was a record 45,490, but in 1974 it fell sharply to 39,901. This was partly because of a collapse in financial advertising (especially in terms of new issues) but also because secondary banking, commercial property and Development Area advertising were all severely affected by the adverse climate, as was old-fashioned industrial advertising as a whole. Nor was this all. Between the start of 1973 and the end of 1974 the price of newsprint almost doubled, a factor that was less ruinous to the *FT* than to the mass circulation papers, but even so added an extra £½ million to the paper's costs for 1974, even allowing for slightly reduced paging. Inevitably, the figures told their story on the bottom line: in 1973 the paper made a trading profit of £2,148,000 (which would have been about a million more if the Price and Pay Code had not prevented a rise in the advertisement rate until the end of the year), working out at 15.6 as a percentage to revenue, which was 3 per cent down on the previous year; but in 1974, despite high inflation, the profit was down to £1,075,000, or 7.6 per cent to turnover. The equation, in short, was no longer working, for whereas revenue between 1970 and 1974 increased by 80 per cent, over the same period costs went up by almost 94 per cent. Panic and emptiness did not actually stalk the corridors of Bracken House, let alone fear and loathing, but Alan Hare in December 1974 caught the prevailing management mood when his front-page article in the house journal was headed 'A Grave Period Ahead'.

Fleet Street as a whole was by now in a state of crisis, and for a few months during the winter of 1974–5 there seemed a chance that the four quality daily papers would come together to take drastic collective action in an attempt to retrieve their fortunes. The prime mover was *The Times*, on whose behalf Marmaduke Hussey proposed to the *FT*, the *Guardian* and the *Daily Telegraph* (in that order) that they should form a consortium by which they would undertake their production on one site and take the opportunity to introduce labour-saving new technology already long common in the United States. From a management point of view, the potential advantages of such a joint production arrangement were profound: enormous economies of scale; the chance to attain far lower manning levels and an altogether more rational wage structure; the forming of a common front by traditionally divided employers; and, by reducing alternative working opportunities, limiting the power of the unions to resist change. Hare responded to Hussey's proposals with considerable enthusiasm and anticipated using the real-estate value of Bracken House to help to capitalize the venture, which was to be based in 'a hole in the ground' (in his own later phrase) in Gray's Inn Road. The *Guardian* too was willing to join the consortium, but the crux was the *Telegraph*, with its greater volume and thus muscle-power in terms of making the scheme a success. Various approaches were made to Lord Hartwell (the former Michael Berry, one-time managing director of the *FT*), the conclusive one from the *FT*'s point of view occurring on 28 January 1975 when he lunched with Gibson. At this meeting Hartwell, though not formally declining to join the consortium, in practice killed the project by saying that he was not prepared to enter without the *Daily Mail*. And as Gibson the next day reported to Drogheda: 'Obviously the *Daily Mail* is not an appropriate partner and would not move without the *Daily Express* . . . What is certainly quite clear is that he is in no hurry. I do not think we ourselves can contemplate a move without the *Telegraph*, though I greatly appreciate the consequences of doing nothing.'

There the matter rested, with both the *FT* towards the *Telegraph* and the *Telegraph* towards the *Mail* subscribing to the conventional wisdom of the time (subsequently rather disproved by events) that a paper *permanently* lost market share to a rival if it was off the streets for any length of time – which was a contingent possibility if such a bold, highly controversial move as the consortium was to be executed. The question remains: if Hartwell had come in, could it have worked? Both Hare and Drogheda certainly thought so and subsequently regretted its failure. On the other hand, granted the prevailing culture of the time, it is hard to feel that the four managements concerned would have had the professionalism and the ruthlessness required to carry through a scheme against what would have been massive union opposition. Indeed, the real interest of the episode arguably lies less in what might have been and more in the way it shows the feeling of desperation of the managements of three at least of the quality papers at this time. It was a desperation that would take a long time to banish.

In April 1975, on his sixty-fifth birthday, Drogheda retired – somewhat reluctantly – and was succeeded as chairman by the recently ennobled Gibson. Enough has been said to suggest the inestimable contribution that Drogheda made to the post-war transformation of the *FT*, not to mention the merger that preceded it, so perhaps the last word should go to his old sparring partner, Gordon Newton, who paid a warm tribute in the paper to 'this essentially nice and kind man' who 'has played a great part in building something which lives, something which is there'.[12] Newton least of all would have denied Drogheda's contribution.

With Drogheda's going, and thus the final break-up of the old triumvirate, day-to-day control passed ever more into the hands of the managing director and now chief executive, Alan Hare, who in November 1976 became vice-chairman and at the start of 1978 succeeded Gibson as chairman. Hare is not an easy person to whom to do historical justice. Undeniably he possessed to the full the qualities of integrity, loyalty and conscientiousness – qualities that have rarely been synonymous with Fleet Street management and were indispensable if the best traditions of the *FT* were to be maintained. Yet there were some crucial flaws in his make-up when it came to running a national paper in the harsh climate of the 1970s. For all his attractive traits, there was a certain shyness about him that tended to distance people and meant that he lacked the charisma (however maddening at times) of a Drogheda. For much of his period in charge he failed to impose adequate unity and cohesion upon the management team beneath him. He seemed to expect people in general, including the print unions, to be as civil and reasonable as he was. And, what might have made up for these deficiencies, he was without either money-making verve or a thorough knowledge of newspaper production, having come to it late from a quite different world. Paternalism, unfortunately, was no longer enough in the Fleet Street of the 1970s – as most other houses also found to their cost. In Alan Hare the *FT* had a chief executive in the very best paternalist tradition, in many ways to the paper's benefit as well as to its loss.

He was not helped by the fact that the two men now under him as joint general managers were temperamentally incompatible. Alan Cox was a superb production manager and bargainer of the old school, but was not really qualified for wider management responsibilities; while Justin Dukes, after three years as industrial relations adviser, suddenly found himself promoted to a very senior position at a time when, for all his vision and flow of ideas, he had not yet properly developed the necessary management skills. A further element in this team was J. D. F. Jones, who in 1975 became managing editor and soon was not only at odds with Fisher but also found himself swamped by the sheer burden of coping single-handed, from union negotiations to a shortage of paper-clips, with an expanding journalistic staff of some 250 people. One way and another, in the post-Drogheda world of Bracken House, it was not a management formula designed for either success or harmony.

The downturn in the *FT*'s prosperity continued through 1975. The overseas circulation held steady at a little over 23,000, but the British sale was almost 14,000 down on 1974, to an average daily figure of 157,178. The advertisement columnage similarly tumbled, from 39,882 to 35,725, while pagination naturally did likewise, from an average of thirty-five pages in 1974 (itself three less than in 1973) to thirty-two pages in 1975.

One might have expected production costs to have fallen accordingly, but as Hare explained to the board in October 1974, this was unfortunately not the case: 'Production wages showed a favourable variance against budget in line with the reduction in pagination, but a continuation of this trend would not be matched by a proportionate reduction in wage costs [which had rocketed during the fat papers of the early 1970s] due to the existence of a guaranteed minimum level of payments under the comprehensive wage agreements.' It was a crippling burden, as the figures for total earnings in 1975 on the printing production side amply show: in the course of that year, the seventy lino operators in St Clements Press earned an average of £25,800 each; they were followed by the foundry (30 people) averaging £18,600, the case piece-workers (26 of them) averaging £17,900, and the timehands (57) and readers (33) each averaging £15,500. For all the 470 regular workers on the printing production side, the average for the year was £14,500. To get these figures in some sort of perspective, one has only to mention that the national average income at this time was barely £3,000. Not surprisingly, the paper's pre-tax profits continued to fall, down to £745,000 for 1975, representing a nugatory (for the *FT*) 4.8 per cent to turnover.

For a paper that, in its own terms at least, had always prospered for almost as long as anyone could remember, it was psychologically a hard situation to adjust to. Hare, in a memorandum written in the spring of that year, attempted to set down the salient, unpalatable facts as he saw them:

1. We have the highest manpower costs in Fleet Street (46% of total costs).
2. We pay the highest rates to individuals. Under the national settlements, increases are on a percentage basis, which thereby widens the gap between the higher and lower paid under each annual settlement.
3. We have the highest dependence on advertising revenue in Fleet Street (82% compared with 71% Times Newspapers and 61% *Daily Telegraph*), at a time when our advertisement rates cannot be safely increased unless our competitors, who can get infinitely more revenue than us for a cover price increase, do so also.
4. We are entering a period when advertisement revenue in our sector of the market may well be on the decline, not only cyclically but absolutely, with the decline of London as a business centre and the ability and willingness of business and commerce to spend sufficient money on financial and institutional advertising to meet our needs.

It was a reversal of fortune not lost on that former Coleman Street leader writer and now editor of *The Times*, William Rees-Mogg, when he had addressed a group of chartered accountants a couple of months earlier on 'The Finances of Fleet Street':

We are aiming this year at a new record – that every daily newspaper published in London should operate at a loss. That is a record which owing to the unsportsmanlike conduct of the *Financial Times* we have never been able to attain before. But in January, I am told that even the *Financial Times* has not made a profit and that they have therefore joined the rest of us in the league of the righteous.[13]

Thus anointed, the *FT* management decided by the spring of 1975 that it must go it alone. On 11 July – following approval from a rather anxious parent company and amidst considerable presentational fanfare – Hare and his colleagues announced the broad outline of what was known from the outset as the Development Plan. Suitably grave emphasis was laid upon the *FT*'s recent poor performance and parlous outlook unless something fundamental was done, but in practical terms the plan at the outset divided into two main areas, the technological and the social, which were primarily the responsibility of Cox and Dukes respectively.

The technological aspect could not be faulted for lack of ambition. What was proposed, to take effect by the end of 1976, was a totally integrated computer system embracing not only the typesetting requirements of the paper but also the commercial functions of the company as a whole. The existing photocomposing system, which was now producing the share and unit trust prices, was to be integrated into the new system. Provision was also to be made for direct input by journalists into the computerized photocomposing system that was planned to 'originate' the whole of the paper, with cold composition thus replacing the traditional hot metal. The actual printing and distribution systems were to remain basically unchanged, but otherwise, in the words of Cox on 11 July, the impact of the technology 'is almost total in that it will produce changes in virtually every area of the business'. As for the human consequences of making redundant up to a third of the company's work-force of some 1,400, which was what the plan envisaged, Dukes at the presentation stressed to the union representatives that 'we share a common concern for the hardship which the actions we are forced to take will cause', adding that 'it is a fact that the ultimate hardship which would result from taking no action is in the long term greater, more far-reaching, and less capable of alleviation'. He looked forward to 'continuing discussion'.[14] Other papers, notably the *Mirror*, were also in the process of preparing to cross the frontiers of the new technology, but none at this stage matched the enormous leap to which the *FT* was now publicly committed. It was a leap to be explained only by the perceived wisdom that drastic troubles demanded drastic remedies. Or in the words of the *Sunday Times* two days after the presentation: 'Time, even for capitalism's own paper, is running out.'[15]

Could management sell the plan? At the end of July, Dukes told the board that in his opinion 'success would be primarily dependent on the company's ability to develop an acceptable social package and secondly the extent to which the demarcation issues could be overcome'. Over the next three or four months, considerable theoretical progress was made in both respects. In terms of a 'social package', the company by November was offering not only to underwrite the retraining of those made redundant and help them find alternative jobs, but also, during the retraining and as long as an earnings difference existed, to bridge the gap between an employee's net salary in his new job and his net earnings as of July 1975. This last part of the package did not command the approval of Drogheda (still on the Pearson Longman board), who wrote to Gibson at the end of October:

> We seem to be in a real cleft stick. It is obvious that the scheme must go forward, but it is depressing that already the anticipated benefits have had to be so much written down. I think that the guarantee of maintained earnings, especially *net* earnings, is fraught with dangers, and offers great scope for argument stretching out for years ahead. Personally I should have been happier to pay each man affected a lump sum, and say: 'that is that'.

Times, however, were changing, and the Dukes approach carried the day. As for the demarcation aspect, the initiative taken by management was even more radical, involving the proposed establishment of what would be known as a Joint Technology Section. This was to be formed of employees operating the new technology and would seek to ensure that traditional 'territorial concepts' no longer applied when jobs were allocated at the time of the implementation of the Development Plan itself. As a placebo, each union was to be paid the subscriptions covering the total membership of the JTS, irrespective of its true membership.

As a final part of the whole deal, the *FT* management by the autumn of 1975 was also proposing the establishment of a Joint Supervisory Board, which would be responsible for the overall supervision of the execution of the plan. Its membership would comprise three senior management directors and a senior official from each of the seven printing unions, and would be under the chairmanship of the chairman of the TUC's Printing Industries Committee, who was Bill Keys, general secretary of SOGAT. Even more than the net income provisions and the

Joint Technology Section, the proposed JSB was a child of its times – the world of Bullock writ large and, as it seemed, inescapable.

The role of Keys was a sign of how the fate of the *FT*'s plan was becoming increasingly entwined in the wider Fleet Street movement for reform by late 1975, at least within the industry's higher echelons. There was a genuine feeling that the newspaper industry was in a state of crisis; management and union leaderships shared a desire to bring chapel power to heel; and of course the union leaders were concerned to ensure that, if change was inevitable, it would be brought about as much as possible on their own terms. On 10 October the TUC Printing Industries Committee specifically commended the social aspects of the Development Plan being mooted by Dukes:

In further discussion, the point was made that an industry-wide approach should not be used to delay initiatives taken at house level. The management of the *Financial Times* had put forward imaginative and extensive proposals for accommodating technological change and had fully consulted the unions. These could form the basis of an agreed strategy to the problem of the industry. Other managements had been far less positive and had shown very little concern for proper negotiation and consultation. The less progressive should not be permitted to hold back the more advanced.

This sort of praise was highly encouraging to the *FT*'s management, as reflected a fortnight later in Hare's memo to the rest of the board when he asked them to give their approval to the social package being proposed:

The approach we are now proposing, although it could cost us more to achieve the savings we are seeking and will involve even longer and more complicated negotiations than we had first envisaged, is a very real step forward in dealing with the major difficulties in a development plan of this kind. It may or may not be saleable by union leaders to their members, but it represents a position which we can defend and advocate in public and in private and we at least have allies on the union side.

It is clearly worth our while to pay some price to achieve the joint co-operation of the union leaders, since this will greatly reduce the chances of major disruption arising either from demarcation disputes or from resistance to re-dundancies. A new and imaginative approach of this kind should also arouse the interest and support of the Government, the Royal Commission and the public, and however difficult these advantages are to evaluate, they must be a plus factor, if only from the effect they will have on our employees.

It was an understandable belief, but essentially misguided. Real power in the newspaper industry by now resided firmly in the chapels, as much in Bracken House as anywhere else. If new technology and/or more rational working arrangements were going to be successfully sold, the selling was going to have to be direct to them and not via the union leaders, who were in any case the objects of considerable mistrust within the workplace. Instead, what happened was that at industry level there gradually lumbered into action between December 1975 and July 1976 what became known as the Joint Standing Committee, comprising a mixture of employers and union leaders and using many of the *FT*'s ideas in its attempt to put forward proposals for industry-wide change. The *FT* management, like those of other papers, came increasingly to pin its hopes on the JSC coming up with an overall package that it would be able to sell to the union membership.

Inevitably this meant that within Bracken House the internal momentum for change was lost. This particularly applied to the social aspect of the plan, where, in the words of Roderick Martin's authoritative study of Fleet Street and the new technology in the 1970s: 'After two years no formal or informal discussions had taken place with chapels in-house on the social proposals . . . Full reliance was placed upon the achievement of agreement at national level, successive failures to meet anticipated deadlines resulting in little more than exasperation and frustration at house level.'[16] By contrast, some apparent in-house progress was made on the technological front. During the winter of 1975–6 a team from the computer manufacturers ICL arrived to conduct a detailed study of the requirements of the editorial and business departments; seven working parties examined specific applications of the new technology; and a group of senior journalists visited the United States and was favourably impressed by seeing the new technology in action, reporting back that a system of photosetting accompanied by direct inputting by journalists 'gives the editorial department much more complete control over what actually appears in the paper' and 'can be regarded as a powerful tool to help the editorial department produce a better product'. It remained inconceivable that the NGA leadership would agree to try to sell a package involving journalistic direct input and thus abandonment of the union's traditional monopoly of keyboarding, but nevertheless by the spring of 1976 the Development Plan was still broadly intact, if already a considerable way behind schedule.

In the course of the summer, however, the *FT* management came to the conclusion that it was desirable to make a certain tactical retreat from what was becoming the increasingly exposed July 1975 position. At the end of June, Hare outlined to the board his proposals 'whereby the

Development Plan should be tackled in self-contained packages each of which would be capable of being separately costed and evaluated'. Gibson in the chair 'welcomed this more gradual approach, especially in view of the misgivings expressed by the Pearson Longman board at the shape of the original proposals'. In August the ICL team was told to stop work; and at the beginning of September the company formally announced that 'in the current situation of the industry we shall make progress faster by introducing a plan on a phased basis rather than attempting to introduce the whole system overnight', so that 'we reach the position that all those processes have been computerised which can produce useful savings'. In the words of Cox at the time, quoted by the *Sunday Times*: 'Our intention is still to go ahead, but to use a more piecemeal approach to the same final objective.'[17]

Four principal considerations lay behind this new note of caution. One was the improved economic climate, affecting the whole of Fleet Street but particularly the *FT*, which in the first half of 1976 made a pre-tax profit of £1,108,000, being a healthy 12 per cent to turnover. There was therefore less urgency to achieve instant, cost-reducing results, with the attendant risk of outright confrontation and its likely consequences. Secondly, there was a natural reluctance to go it virtually alone at a time when all the other papers (with the partial exception of the *Mirror*) were adopting an increasingly piecemeal approach towards radical technological change. Related to this was a wish to see what happened when the Joint Standing Committee produced its long-awaited proposals – proposals that were likely to take much of their inspiration from the *FT*'s various initiatives of a year earlier. Finally, there was some sense in which doubts were starting to spread about the viability of the technology itself, certainly in terms of introducing it in the dramatic across-the-board form originally envisaged.

Some commitment to the new technology survived. The specifications worked out by ICL were submitted to tender to various companies, and the seven working parties were disbanded in favour of a pilot scheme on the computerized production of the survey pages. In a memorandum written towards the end of the year, Hare accurately summed up the overall situation:

> The relatively good results in monetary terms for 1976 should not blind us to the fact that we have not yet succeeded in overcoming the basic obstacle to growth, namely an unstable cost base. We have not succeeded in stabilising our wage structure on the newspaper by introducing the Development Plan, which remains the key to our future. We must still persevere in our efforts to introduce the Plan

as part of a national plan agreed between unions and employers for the industry, but if this fails, which should become clear within the next few months, we shall be faced with some hard decisions. In any case the introduction of the Plan is proving slower and more difficult than we had hoped, but we are making progress with mastering the technical problems involved and educating all concerned into the implications of what is to be done.

How much progress is debatable, but by this time the fate of the plan no longer depended primarily on decisions taken in Bracken House.

On 2 December 1976 the JSC published its *Programme for Action*, with a foreword signed by the general secretaries of the NGA, SOGAT, NATSOPA and the NUJ, together with a representative of the EETPU, commending its proposals to the union memberships and stating that the consequences of rejecting them would be 'extremely grave and have a serious effect on the continued viability of some titles in the industry, the maintenance of employment, and the continuation of a strong and effective trade union organisation'. What did the proposals amount to? To quote again from Martin's study of Fleet Street and the new technology:

If it was felt that the industry was facing severe difficulties, it is difficult to see what union members could have wanted that was not provided in *Programme for Action*. There was a guarantee against compulsory redundancy, very generous terms of voluntary redundancy, and considerable scope for bargaining over the basic issues of manning levels and demarcation lines. The agreement did not open the flood-gates to employers' proposals for new technology.[18]

However, when it came to voting on the proposals in the early months of 1977, the chapels did *not* feel that the industry was facing such a crisis (as indeed seemingly it was not by this time) that titles would disappear if the proposals were rejected. The NUJ did accept them, but was the only union to do so. The NGA voted against by 3,778 to 889 and NATSOPA by 4,598 to 4,296, with in both cases a greater majority against in London than in Manchester. The union leaders had proved poor salesmen. Not long afterwards, on 13 June, Hare issued a briefish statement that 'after a very careful examination of current union attitudes and negotiations with other companies, and despite the economic considerations, we have regretfully come to the conclusion that we can make no progress with the Development Plan until all the unions are ready to respond to the principles contained in our original proposals'.[19] A tortuous episode, lasting almost two years, was finally played out.

There have been many retrospective opinions on why the plan failed and what the consequences were of that failure. Martin has argued that management had no alternative but to attempt to negotiate it on an industry basis, granted the fundamental nature of the changes proposed and the sense in which (pre-Wapping) Fleet Street 'is a distinct world, whose separation from the conventional routines of industrial life reinforces unity within it', at least on the union side; though he adds that 'the speedy creation of joint institutions at house level' by *FT* management might have done something to alleviate, if not remove, local fears and confusion.[20] Others have argued that the expectations invested in the mid-1970s in computerized technology were ridiculously high and that it was a blessing in disguise that it was not put to the test. Others still have pointed to the appalling experience of *The Times* in 1978–9 as evidence of the *FT*'s wisdom in deciding in 1977 to abandon the plan. At the time, however, there is no doubt that a considerable loss of face was involved, undermining the credibility of management and making it much harder in future to wave the 'accept-change-or-we-go-bust' stick, since manifestly the *FT* was still alive and, to most intents and purposes, well.

One particularly interesting perspective belongs to Rex Winsbury, who had joined the paper as a trainee in 1959, left in 1961 and then returned in 1970, becoming features editor a few years later. By the time of the Development Plan he had joined management as, in effect, project planner and co-ordinator in relation to the new technology. Of those most committed to the introduction of the plan, he was probably the person most closely involved in propagating its potential editorial as well as economic advantages. Like that of all participants, his viewpoint is necessarily a partial one; but a decade on, with *FT* management again in the throes of trying to introduce fundamental changes in production methods, his analysis of why the plan failed makes interesting reading:

1. It was mainly seen as an anti-trade union device (however dressed up) and not much interest was shown in what the technology could do, positively. We were in the absurd position of not being able to tell the *FT* chapels what we were doing – let alone ask their advice. Coming after years of management connivance in union malpractices, this meant that the *FT* (and other) managements were up against a highly paid, highly motivated workforce that had usually got its way in the past; knew that something was going on; and rejected it on principle. We had no chance to educate them/warn them/train them/consult them – it *might* have made a difference.
2. There was little real understanding of the *actual* state-of-the-art of technology as it stood at that time. Senior managers had excessive expectations of what could

be done, and were impatient with suggestions that the *FT* was different from (say) the *Baltimore Sun* – the trend-setter of that time.

3. The *FT* was (in most years) a great cash-generator for Pearsons – I suspect that senior management was frightened of a lengthy strike over technology, which would have hit group profits hard.
4. Thus the general idea was: '*All* Fleet Street must move together, and go for a *big bang* approach to new technology – or nothing happens.' So after the negative union vote, everything collapsed.
5. Management itself at the *FT* (such as it was) was divided, on tactics and technology: working 'down the line' was very difficult because one was never clear who would decide (or when).
6. It was generally ignored that the USA had been evolving its 'new technology' over a period of 20 years, and that Fleet Street was *primitive* even by *USA 1955* standards. The 'big bang' theory could not work. Nevertheless, something could have been salvaged from the débâcle, if there had been a clear management strategy – by gradualist but determined methods, ignoring what any other Fleet Street papers were doing, but over time building up the 'electronic infrastructure' of the *FT*.
7. This was the first time that the *FT* had 'looked at itself' – introspectively – to see how it could produce itself better. It was an unsettling prospect for *many* (not just NGA) and they were only too happy to see the Development Plan dropped, so that they could relapse happily into bad old ways. The *FT* is (or was) a very introverted organisation, very tribalistic, and therefore profoundly conservative. This is often a *great strength* – but sudden change is anathema to it.

Did it matter? Yes, profoundly, according to Winsbury, writing in June 1986 (a month before the company publicly announced once more its intentions of thoroughly embracing the new technology):

I believe the abandonment of the 1975 Development Plan may turn out to have been the crucial failure in the eventual decline of the *FT*. It may or may not matter what technology the *Daily Mail* uses, as long as it is roughly comparable to, say, the *Daily Express*. But the *FT* is a world-class newspaper up against world competition (the *Wall Street Journal*, *International Herald Tribune*, *Business Week*, etc.). It is *ridiculous* that a paper of the *FT*'s quality and scope should sell only circa 250,000 copies world-wide. It should be selling 500,000 and rising. But it cannot promote itself to these levels because its technology is primitive, its 'base costs' are high and its competitors are running away with the game. The *FT* European edition is far too expensive to produce (because of crude technology): editions in the USA, Far East, etc. have been too late, too expensive, too small scale, or non-existent – all because the *FT* had *not* got the technology to expand easily, and diverts into the pockets of the NGA (still) money that should go into product expansion world-wide. Technology is the *FT* Achilles heel.

Time alone will deliver the verdict on the 'lost' decade and its fatefulness or otherwise for the long-run history of the *FT*.

Back in the mid- to late-1970s, and masked to an extent by Fleet Street's technological impasse, editorial developments of high importance were taking place on the paper. One of them evolved under unhappy circumstances. Even under Newton's editorship, C. Gordon Tether had been increasingly using his 'Lombard' column as a platform for his views on extra-monetary subjects. With the coming of Fisher as editor, Tether pushed this tendency still further and in particular devoted a large proportion of his columns to the iniquities of British membership of the EEC. Inevitably, his campaign rose to a crescendo during the referendum of 1975, with its tone typified by a couple of sentences on 2 June: 'The sacrifices made by the dead of the two World Wars have been featured in pro-Market publicity. One wonders what these heroes of yesteryear would think of a Britain which rated patriotism so low that it was prepared to sink its identity and individual freedom in a European super-State for such unworthy reasons.' In general, it would be fair to say that while many of his wide-ranging columns in the 1970s were trenchant and provocative, others were windy, overblown and repetitive affairs. But whatever their merits, the cardinal fact was that by 1975 at the latest the relationship between editor and columnist had – for a variety of personal, journalistic and political reasons – completely broken down.

A distressing chain of events ensued. In July 1976 Tether's column was terminated; he then went to an industrial tribunal court accusing the *FT* of unfair dismissal; and the result was a record 45-day hearing ending with the rejection of Tether's claim. In the course of his evidence, Fisher said that 'he knew of no Fleet Street journalist who had the right for his articles to be published against the wishes of his editor', and that 'it would be impossible to edit if this was the case'. He added: 'He had certainly felt that Mr Tether's writing was becoming strident to the degree which could prejudice the reputation of the *Financial Times*, which said the things it had to say in a manner which was not strident or ill-tempered although, on occasion, it could be forceful.'[21] The NUJ chapel at Bracken House declined to support Tether, aware that he was claiming rights for himself that no other journalist had, but at the same time there was a widespread feeling that the whole problem had been badly handled.

The episode also took a heavy toll on Fisher himself. During the 1950s and 1960s Tether's column had been one of the strongest parts of the paper, and this was a sad end to a distinguished career.

One good thing, however, that emerged was the transformation of the 'Lombard' column after Tether into a vehicle for staff writers – not just one man – to express their opinions in a rather more personal, intellectually open-ended way than had previously been possible. Thus in the random week beginning 13 September 1976 there were five 'Lombard' columns, comprising a critical piece by Colin Jones on a recent decision by the Monopolies Commission, Joe Rogaly on how 'Mr Vorster is a poor risk', Eric Short on 'Playing fair on pensions', Geoffrey Owen on how 'Industry must fight back' and Peter Riddell on 'Waiting for the boom'. By definition, not all columns could or can be equally good and sparkling, but over the years it has proved an excellent means of raising the level of debate within both the pages and the corridors of the paper.

It was at about this time that the nature of the paper's foreign coverage came under close and, as it turned out, decisive scrutiny. A feeling grew not only that this coverage was increasingly haphazardly related to the prime concerns of the paper's particular readership, but also that the foreign side had become an élite empire within an empire and needed to be reintegrated within the main body. It was a feeling shared, to a greater or lesser extent, by Hare, Fisher, Owen and Palmer, four leading players of the 1970s. The debate was not one that was committed to paper, but seems to have surfaced early in 1976. On 17 February, for example, half a page was devoted to 'The Conflict in Western Sahara' between Morocco and Algeria. Two days later, considerable space was given to Eirene Furness, who, 'with the Polisario guerrilla forces in Western Sahara, reports on Warfare by Land Rover'. Or again, on 4 March the story of Mozambique closing its border with Rhodesia took up half a page, consisting of four articles, together with a photograph of patrolling Rhodesian security forces. The question began to be asked: how relevant was such detailed treatment of these and similar stories (granted that space was not limitless) to a paper whose principal readership comprised business men in Britain, Northern Europe and North America?

From this question there emerged over the next few years, not without considerable heartache, a certain orthodoxy: that the *FT* was a paper aimed squarely at 'decision-makers' and that a foreign story had therefore to pass the 'so what?' test; that 'small wars' in relatively remote or non-developed places were not a central priority; and that even within highly developed countries like the United States and France the main thrust of the coverage was to be at least as much on the economic, industrial and financial aspects as on the political, diplomatic and social. The change of emphasis did not happen overnight, nor was it total. In March 1978 Dan Connell reported 'on the state of the war in Ethiopia's northern province of Eritrea after spending six months in the region with the rebel forces' – a James-Cameron-type story that would be unlikely to appear a few years later. Nevertheless, gradually and ineluctably, the emphasis *did* change, also reflecting crucial changes in the larger world. The breakdown of the Bretton Woods system meant that international affairs were becoming more market-dominated than government-dominated. The paramount importance of OPEC was putting economic news into the top rank of world affairs. And with the expansion of international capital markets and the continuing growth of multinational companies, the City of London was becoming ever less parochial. For all the heat that the debate over foreign coverage engendered, it is hard in retrospect to deny that the paper's response, granted the market it was serving, was the appropriate one.

There were additional pressures by the late 1970s pushing the *FT* towards an editorial character simultaneously more international in ambition and more specialist in function. In his keynote memorandum of late 1976, anticipating 'some hard decisions' over the future of the Development Plan, Hare argued that the paper required, as a fall-back in the event of the plan's failure, a greater diversification of its revenue base:

> Although the present economic situation inevitably affects us, since we are a British newspaper and our home market is less attractive to overseas customers and our own reputation to some extent suffers with that of the country, we must invest in improving circulation of the newspaper on the Continent and in building up our market in one way or another in the United States.

In March that year Hare had already examined the latter problem in some detail, pointing out that 'unlike the position in the Common Market and most other developed parts of the world, the *FT* is little known and therefore little respected in the United States'. Hare had then suggested, on the basis of proposals from Archer Trench, chairman of the *FT*-owned *Oil Daily*, that 'a weekly American edition of the *Financial Times* is probably the best and most economical way of combining the objectives – at a stroke – of getting a sizeable new profit centre and getting the paper better known in the area'. It was a suggestion fully supported by Fisher, but it took another two and a half years, until the autumn of 1978, to come to fruition, under the editorship of Joe Rogaly. Unfortunately, *World Business Weekly*, sixty-four magazine pages on pink paper culled from the daily *FT*, did not work and after three loss-making years ceased publication. It was good enough editorially, but the history of foreign magazine publishing in the United States was against it, as were the restricted terms of promotion and circulation under which it operated, together with the inauspicious economic climate, coinciding with the second oil shock. Perhaps most importantly, it was also, in a bets-hedging way, launched at a time when the *FT* was about to hit North America with another, more frequent product, thereby saturating an already difficult market. Sooner or later one of the products would have to go, and it was *World Business Weekly* that departed.

This other product had as its genesis the realization by the middle of the decade that, with the British economy in possibly terminal decline, the *FT* urgently needed to tackle the European market on a more ambitious and systematic basis, building on the already considerable progress since the late 1960s in terms of both revenue and (to a lesser extent) circulation. In July 1977, under the auspices of Justin Dukes, the 'European Project Group' was set up, presenting its findings to the board two months later. Much of the presentation naturally concentrated on the revenue and distribution aspects of the *FT* in Europe. It was argued that if the paper's European circulation was to rise from the existing 13,785 to, say, 20,000 copies a day, this would greatly enhance the *FT*'s appeal to non-UK advertisers, particularly those in media-conscious countries such as the United States, Japan and Switzerland – countries which were providing an increasingly significant portion of the paper's advertising revenue. Much stress was laid on the fact that the *FT*'s expanding European market was already under threat, not only from the *International Herald Tribune*, but also in prospect from the *Wall Street Journal*, which had already launched an Asian edition and would logically make its next play in Europe. How was the desired circulation rise to be attained? Apart from improved marketing, the proposed answer was twofold: by launching a five-day-a-week international edition tailored to suit a non-UK readership; and by printing that edition in Frankfurt, which would not only greatly improve European distribution (especially in the context of likely further bans on night flights from London) but also offer the potential, through a 4 a.m. flight from Frankfurt, of reaching New York before breakfast as opposed to the middle of the afternoon. The proposals were readily accepted by first the board and then Pearson Longman; and over the following winter, with Dukes as the major driving-force on the management side, 'Frankfurt' began to take shape. The date set for the launch of the international edition was 2 January 1979 and, unlike many such dates, it was one that was kept.

The decision to introduce an international edition had profound edi-

J. D. F. Jones (managing editor), Fredy Fisher (editor), Geoffrey Owen (deputy editor), late 1970s

Alan Hare

Samuel Brittan

First night of the Frankfurt edition, 1979

The astronomical clock over the main entrance

Bracken House

'No comment' poster, 1983

The management in 1985: Michael Gorman (finance director), Joe Rogaly (FT business information), Richard McClean (deputy chief executive), Frank Barlow (chief executive), Geoffrey Owen (editor), David Palmer (general manger and chairman of SCP), Alan Cox (director)

The news room in 1987

The printing presses in 1987

torial consequences, furthering as it did an awareness, specifically articulated in the September 1977 presentation, that the paper badly needed to improve the quality of its international financial coverage. Since the core of the international edition was going to come from the London edition, and the cost of improving that coverage was going to be considerable, it was obvious from the outset that any such change for the better would affect both editions. Even before an international edition was seriously mooted, there had been a certain realization that this was an area requiring attention; but it was the September 1977 decision that proved the crucial spur. Two people's contributions stand out. One was that of Palmer, who temporarily left the news desk in order to be the editorial representative on the Frankfurt project. During the summer and autumn of 1977 he was commissioned by Fisher to examine the whole question and sent him a series of detailed reports about what was needed to improve the coverage. The other key person was Nicholas Colchester, who at about this time returned to Bracken House from foreign tours and harnessed a formidable, highly analytical intelligence to the experience he had acquired first in New York and then in Bonn. In theory his new brief was to write about the British financial system, working with the 'Lex' team of Lambert and Riley, but in practice he made it his business to get a grip on the world of international capital markets, also spending time on the international companies side and on foreign exchanges. At a critical juncture for the paper – as critical in its way as the need after the war to attain an authoritative industrial presence – it would be only a slight exaggeration to say that Colchester 'saved' the *FT*.

The capital markets side was perhaps particularly important. There had been some editorial progress on Euromarkets during the first half of the 1970s, and then in 1976 the paper had started publishing a monthly list of Eurobond quotations and yields as compiled by the Association of International Bond Dealers. Yet there remained much to be done:

> While the Euromarkets have grown into the world's second largest capital market, providing us with well over £1 million a year of tombstone advertising, our coverage of these markets has been irregular. One result of this is that the *International Herald Tribune*'s financial editor, Karl Gewirtz, is universally regarded as the number one commentator in the market. Another is that we have allowed the vacuum that we have left to be filled by three weekly newsletters (one of them our own) and two monthly magazines (*Euromoney* and the *Institutional Investor*) and we are beginning to see the English language weeklies responding to this challenge. Luckily, none of our major UK daily competitors, nor the posh Sundays, have chosen to develop this area of coverage.

The message of Palmer's 1977 report was clear. Unless the paper radically improved the quality and scope of its coverage, the substantial revenues that it was garnering from 'tombstones' would be vulnerable. In particular, what was imperative was that the daily price list should become both large enough to satisfy the professionals and comprehensive enough (including redemption yields) to satisfy the market's users. The self-scrutiny worked, for over the following year the *FT* at last did attain the high standard of coverage expected of it, improving the Eurobonds daily prices service so that the prices quoted were closing prices, together with an increased amount of data per bond. The Monday financial page was now introduced, consisting of the existing Eurobond column, a new New York bond market report and reviews of national capital markets. There was also, under Colchester's auspices, a perceptible improvement in the quality of analysis. All of which not only improved the *FT* as an international product but also meant that the paper was reasonably well positioned for the 1980s, which were to be *the* decade (to date) of Euromarket expansion.

Similarly, international company news coverage was an improving feature of the paper before 1977, more so indeed than Euromarkets coverage. In September 1976 a second ICN page was added, very much at Fisher's instigation. This gave the *FT* a range of coverage in this sphere unique to any daily paper available in Europe and elicited such a favourable response that within a few months some advertisers, particularly US advertisers, were prepared to wait up to two weeks to secure an ICN slot. What was needed by 1977, in the looming context of Frankfurt, was both more space and a more systematic approach, deciding which were the world's important companies and, in terms of covering their results, seeking to turn ICN into a section of record in the way that the paper's home companies news pages already were. The following March this was achieved, with a third page of ICN added and a list compiled of some 800 United States companies and 600 companies from the rest of the world that henceforth would be covered on a regular basis. Attention was also given at this time to the paper's quotation of stock exchange prices from the USA, Europe and Japan, resulting in the summer of 1978 in expanded lists, together with the grouping of overseas bourse reports on to a page devoted to 'World Stock Markets'.

In 1977 Palmer put one further financial area under the spotlight:

> Foreign Exchange and Money Market reports are an almost classic example of one of our European readers' major complaints – that we are too UK oriented, and that we write about things from a UK point of view. Our Money Market

report is almost exclusively a UK affair, reflecting the official view of what is going on in the UK Money Markets. In the Foreign Exchange sector, three of the seven tables are related to Sterling which, though still an important world currency, is no longer what it used to be.

With the increasing growth of video terminals and the modern network of communications, the *relative* importance of statistical tables to the copy that surrounds them is on the decline. This does not mean that the tables have no value – quite the reverse. But increasingly the role of a newspaper is to provide for its readers an authoritative and well-researched commentary on how the markets are moving and why the dealers and/or the central banks think this is happening.

The international Money, Gold and Foreign Exchange markets are increasingly linked to one another. At present, they are reported on different pages, and in different sections of the paper. They should be merged.

Change did not happen overnight, but within about a year 'Currency, Money and Gold Markets' had become a page heading, embracing an enhanced standard of commentary and statistical material expanded to take in more cross-rates, more Eurocurrency rates, a dollar and a forward-dollar table and some basic New York money-market statistics. It was all nuts and bolts stuff, deeply uninteresting to many readers, but indispensable if the *Financial Times* were to live up to its name in a truly international sense.

This was not all. In manifold, seemingly unconnected ways, the paper in the mid- to late 1970s was refining itself as a product and becoming more sophisticated. By the end of 1978 it was, in terms of content and appearance (including page title designs), not very different to the *FT* of seven or eight years later. On the whole this was a conscious process. In June 1976, for example, Hare at a board meeting pointed out that 'no research had clearly established why an *FT* reader bought a second newspaper'; Roger Brooke on behalf of Pearson Longman 'asked whether the absence of adequate sports coverage might not be one of the main reasons'. To which Hare responded by saying that he 'considered that the costs involved in providing adequate sports coverage would be substantial', and the matter was dropped, probably conclusively. It was a view with which Fisher entirely concurred, arguing then and subsequently that fully fledged sports coverage would have been liable to knock out two pages of advertising (with the continuing 48-page capacity), would have required a staff of at least twenty people, would have been at the cost of better foreign coverage and, perhaps most important, would have crucially diluted from an advertiser's point of view the 'profile' of the readership.

Other examples of the refining process are almost arbitrary, but each in its own way is of significance. The arts page at about this time became appreciably more 'high' art in character. The Saturday paper was reorganized so that it had a more logical flow, with the excellent books page now becoming a permanent fixture that day. The classified advertising, having been all over the place, was sorted out so that there was a particular type of advertising on particular days of the week: business opportunities on Tuesday, jobs on Thursday, commercial property on Friday and residential property on Saturday. As for the new 'sophistication', inevitably gradual though its advent was, a good example was the role of Malcolm Rutherford, between 1975 and 1977 covering diplomatic and defence matters. Hitherto defence had been treated by the paper almost purely in hardware terms, but Rutherford in his approach now added a much-needed strategic dimension. It was, in a sense, a new *worldliness* that was increasingly the *FT*'s hallmark – a worldliness of omission as well as of commission. When the Thorpe case started at Minehead in November 1978, Fisher took a particular pride in the fact that the *FT*'s coverage of it was confined to the front-page news summary, which might not have been the case some years earlier. It was the sort of story that would continue to be a problem area, whether it was a bomb in Belfast or a royal wedding, but increasingly the paper knew, or felt it knew, what its purpose was and how it was seeking to fulfil that purpose.

The 44-page issue of Wednesday 25 October 1978 incorporated most of the developments of the previous two or three years, including the layout changes introduced at the start of 1978 by which the 'Lombard' page and the arts page moved to the spread immediately before the leader page. This allowed European news to move to pages two and three, in the light of market research which suggested that new readers expected a run of news pages in the early part of their paper. The front and back pages were overwhelmingly economic in character, with the five stories on the front comprising Michael Donne on France's decision to allow Britain to rejoin the Airbus project, Philip Bassett and Nick Garnett on 'Luton men reject strike as Ford prepares offer', 'Our Own Correspondent' in Canberra on 'Australia tightens mineral rules', David Freud on 'Big new fall in jobless' and Jurek Martin from Washington on 'Carter aims for 7% pay rises'. Inside, eight of the thirteen European stories were primarily economic or financial, seven of the American nine, and six of the 'Overseas' nine. Nevertheless, on the overseas pages, always *the* battle-ground of the foreign debate, the three non-economic stories included Connell from Eritrea ('This dispatch was written on October 11 and delayed by communications difficulties') and a major piece by Patrick Cockburn on Syrian–Iraqi attempts to forge an alliance against the Camp David agreement. As for 'World Trade News', the headline 'Italy bids for more deals from Peking' evoked the page's perennial flavour. The home news pages were, as usual, economically oriented, including Antony Thorncroft's 'Saleroom' column, but there was also a substantial piece by Rhys David to mark the Queen's opening that day of Liverpool Cathedral. 'The Technical Page' remained unchanged in its 'hundreds and thousands' character; but 'The Executive's World' was now (and had been since 1976) called the 'Management' page, under the editorship from 1977 of Christopher Lorenz, who in alliance with Nicholas Leslie was seeking to give the page a more consistent, better-thought-out identity. In particular, they aimed to illuminate applicable themes rather than merely giving corporate profiles almost for their own descriptive sake, as had tended to be the case in the past. It was yet another part of the refining, deepening process. In general, what strikes one about the issue is how its whole *feel*, with the notable exception of the still very messy 'Lombard' page, was appreciably more professional, more coherent, altogether better assembled than a few years earlier – reflecting enhanced production standards, the rising status of the sub-editors and to some extent the balance of control moving towards their desks and away from the writers. In short, a certain paradox was at work: while in a fundamental editorial sense starting to return to specialist roots and also to strengthen those roots, the *FT* was simultaneously becoming more of a 'real' newspaper, staffed by trained, professional journalists and about to compete with the world's as well as the country's best.

Commercially, 1976 to 1978 were years in which the paper no longer looked at the abyss; but, as with the rest of Fleet Street, nor were they particularly prosperous for the *FT*. In December 1976 the editor struck a gloomy note to the board: 'With regard to management's plans for building up circulation, Mr Fisher explained that unless the national economy was to pick up and making money became respectable again with a corresponding relaxation in managerial salaries, the circulation base of the newspaper would continue to be eroded.' In the event, the economy did start picking up soon afterwards, though the recovery was essentially consumer-led and thus filtered through rather late to the *FT*. With recovery, the decline in the paper's UK circulation was checked: having dipped to 153,000 in 1976 (21,000 down on 1974), it modestly ascended to 158,000 in 1978. Meanwhile, overseas circulation grew by about a thousand each year. The advertising recovery was similarly undramatic – a total columnage in 1978 some four thousand up on the nadir year of 1975. Signs of the times were not only that the surveys department was looking increasingly to the Middle East for its subjects, but also that, as the advertisement director Richard McClean explained to the board in June 1977 about recent improvement, 'the principal contributory factor had been the strength of the "tombstone" market'. Profits similarly were only reasonable, with the best of the three years being the £2,311,000 for 1977, or 10.4 per cent to turnover. These were still years of high inflation (by January 1978 the cover price was 15p, more than twice what it had been less than four years earlier), so profit to turnover becomes an increasingly telling guide. There was one other significant 'business' element to these years, which was the decision in 1977 to start a joint venture with Extel, not unnaturally called Fintel and intended to be the *FT*'s entry ticket to the highly lucrative world of disseminating information by electronic means. By 1979 Fintel was the largest provider of information to the Post Office Prestel service. From the start it was a venture that had its teething troubles, including industrial relations, but in the late 1970s there still seemed rich electronic pickings to be had from it.

The unique world of Fleet Street production was now entering into what was to be its Indian summer, in terms of riches if not of tranquillity. By 1979 the average total earnings of SCP printing production workers were almost £16,000 a year, for an average working week of little over twenty hours, with the lino operators averaging £31,300 a year. In fourth place, on £14,900, were the sixty-one time-hands, whose job was to assemble the type into pages for casting into plates for the presses and who in 1977 had been involved in the *FT*'s most serious industrial dispute prior to that of 1983. The origins of the time-hands' dispute lay in an entirely unofficial agreement reached in the summer of 1975 between them and the head printer, by which they were allowed to take regular time off from their normal working hours while still being paid, amounting in practice to some thirty-one ghosted man-days a week, known in this particular rota arrangement as 'blue' days. The head printer had been given the job because, as a popular figure, it was felt that he was most suited to get the best out of the chapels, but this was ridiculous.

Two years later, with the size of the paper returning to 1972 levels and serious production difficulties being encountered at the time of issues in March, the matter blew up. The deputy printer, who had always been against the agreement, gave eloquent testimony to the problems it had led to:

The arrangement was meant to remove the continuous aggravation over cuts [i.e. men leaving shifts early when the paper was thin]. Cuts would cease, but they did not. It was meant to cover sickness, but 'blue' days are taken regardless of sickness. And the arrangement provided that if more men were needed on the nights the Chapel would get them in. This has not worked. There are always arguments when extra men are needed and Chapel excuses that they cannot get the men in on time, or that they cannot contact them. On Budget night and particularly the night after. When I saw the list on Monday [i.e. of that week's 'blue' days] I said I needed another two men on each shift. After a lot of arguing they gave me one man. They say that they have covered the job and got the paper out. They don't worry about how it goes out nor that Staff Hands have to work like the clappers to cover the 'blue' days to get the paper out. The aggravation over cuts goes on.

Soon afterwards, in July 1977, management decided that it could not sanction the arrangement and started to deduct money from the wages of time-hands who continued to take unauthorized days off. The dispute escalated, and in August a stoppage took place that lasted for sixteen issues. Management, backed by Pearson Longman and knowing that August was an inexpensive month to be off the streets, held firm and, at some financial cost, emerged from the end of the dispute with the 'blue days' arrangement ended. In the wake of the Development Plan back-down earlier in the summer, it was for the sixth floor a rare and sweet moment of victory, however minor.

Industrial relations in Fleet Street were an extreme example of the British economic *malaise*, to which the *FT* naturally continued to devote a high proportion of its leader comment. During the second half of the 1970s, its analysis was of an increasingly 'dry' nature, reflected in November 1975 in Barbara Castle's diary reference to 'the new philosophy which is now spreading, not only in the *Financial Times* but among right-wing members of the Cabinet, to the effect that cuts in public expenditure are positively socially desirable'.[22] In December 1975, for example, the government's decision to rescue Chrysler prompted a major attack on its industrial policy, for all the pious words of ministers: 'It is no good talking about the evils of overmanning if the Government continues to prop up badly managed, loss-making enterprises in the private sector and continues to prevent, or at least to discourage, public sector enterprises from tackling their manning problems.' Two months later the paper strongly criticized the Treasury, arguing that its recent reply to the report of the Parliamentary Expenditure Committee showed that it remained wedded to 'the conventional progressive wisdom of 30 years ago', namely demand management, and had failed to take on board the monetarist lesson 'that money spending is one of the few things that overall economic policy can determine', whereas 'output and employment cannot be so determined'. Also in February 1976, with the publication of the public expenditure White Paper, the *FT* in similar vein welcomed its 'fairly blunt discussion of the tax consequences of failing to rein back expenditure' and offered the homely wisdom that 'the more the Chancellor can rub his colleagues' noses in the fact that, in the current American phrase, there is no such thing as a free lunch, the likelier he is to restrain their spending enthusiasm'.

Thus it may be gathered that the overall approach of the Labour government continued to go down poorly in Cannon Street. When, in March 1976, Wilson surprised everyone by deciding to step down, there was little in the way of a warm tribute paid to him, with instead a tart reference to how 'we remarked many years ago that the Prime Minister's characteristic weakness is to mistake activity for action', a weakness that left his party with 'the legacy of hurried commitments made to heal this or that party rift, or to exploit some past Tory embarrassment'. He deserved 'much credit' for having over the past year developed 'a workable arrangement with the trade unions in support of sane economic policies', but there the praise stopped. It seemed a long, long time since those joint battles in defence of the pound.

Who should succeed Wilson? James Callaghan – 'an avuncular figure with considerable appeal to the electorate, a man without too much doctrinal baggage, yet with enough "bottom" to restrain his more impulsive and committed colleagues' – made a certain appeal to the *FT*, but at the age of sixty-four 'would have an insuperable problem in persuading the party to regard him as more than a temporary leader'. He would, moreover, 'be quite unable to give the party the new sense of direction it now urgently needs', lacking as he did 'a vision which stretches beyond the needs of the moment and the tactical objective of winning the next election'. Instead, granted that the Labour Party was going to 'try to become in good earnest what Mr Wilson always intended it to be – a party of government', the *FT*'s preference was for Roy Jenkins, who of the likely candidates 'has shown the most consistent philosophy, and a political courage which has at times neared recklessness'. In addition, 'his political appeal to the centre, which Labour must win back if it is to retain office, is powerful'. In short, 'the sight of Mr Jenkins at No. 10 Downing Street, with Mr Healey remaining at No. 11, would be one to inspire new confidence'.

That dream ticket was not to be. A fortnight later, coming to the second ballot, the paper considered the merits of the first-round leader:

Mr Foot is a national institution, a fine rhetorician and a civilised man. But he simply will not do. Naturally the *Financial Times* is not anxious to see Tribunite men and still less Tribunite measures in Downing Street. But even Mr Foot's own supporters must see that his age, his lack of administrative background and above all the unacceptability of his radical image in the country must make him, in the end, a gigantic electoral liability.[23]

The drawbacks of Callaghan were again rehearsed, so this time the paper plumped for the third remaining candidate, Denis Healey, who, albeit 'a heavy-footed politician and an indifferent handler of men', nevertheless 'has in greater measure than his rivals the necessary personal assets of determination, experience and intelligence, as well as the political qualifications of a central position within the Labour Party, and a good standing in the country'. The *FT*'s choice again proved the kiss of death, and Healey was knocked out, leaving Callaghan to defeat Foot in the final round. On 6 April the paper summed up the new Prime Minister's main task in the immediate future: 'To persuade his supporters that the sacrifices now demanded will bring their rewards, and that it is only by meeting the challenge, rather than by retreating into still deeper debt behind protective barriers, that we can achieve sound growth and full employment.'

Over the next three years other world statesmen came and went. No departure was as epochal as that of Chairman Mao, but his death in September 1976 inspired a leader that concentrated more on the future than the past. It was safely forecast that his passing 'may well exacerbate the power struggle between radicals and moderates', but no bets were laid. Four months later, in January 1977, the paper greeted 'A new era in Washington' with the characteristic concluding remark that 'the real challenge to the new President is not only whether he can bring charity into government, but whether he can restore prosperity to America'. That May, Carter made his major Indiana speech on foreign policy, committing his administration to a moral approach and referring to 'that inordinate fear of Communism which once led us to embrace any dictator who joined us in our fear'. The *FT* responded warmly to the speech – 'The rest of the world is to be treated as adult' – though it added with some prescience:

It would be foolish to deny that there are grey areas where it will be difficult for President Carter to put his principles into practice. Saudi Arabia, Iran and South Korea all come to mind as countries where the American interest in stability is too great to insist on conformity with anything like American standards of democracy. One may wonder too how the principle of majority rule for southern Africa (which means South Africa as well as Rhodesia) is to be put into effect.

The honeymoon with Carter did not last long. By April 1978 his change of mind over the question of the neutron bomb earned him a leader headed 'An erratic President'; while, in the same month, 'Carter fails to convince' was the verdict on his latest economic policy statement, viewing appeals to 'the decency and good sense of the American people' as no substitute, in the eyes of 'international opinion', for 'the convincing lead by the President that is needed if confidence is to be restored'. That September his Camp David agreement on the Middle East received cautious praise ('Still a long way to go'), but within months the USA and the West were anxiously weighing the consequences of the most dramatic exit of all: 'All the Shah's efforts – his hand-picked army, the secret police, the handouts, the massive support from the West – clearly failed to amount to much more than a house of straw.' This was in February 1979, barely three months after the paper had at last made the point that 'it is not sensible to link Western interests with the success or failure of a particular form of regime', two months after the description of Ayatollah Khomeini as someone 'whose ideas are out of tune with those of most of his countrymen'. Still, in this particular situation it was not only the watch-towers of Bracken House that had been found wanting.

On the home front, the *FT* had by the autumn of 1976 a new chief leader writer. The death that summer of Robert Collin removed from the paper a voice wholly sane, lucid and dispassionate, whose leaders for the course of some sixteen years had been a consistent source of enlightenment, perhaps especially to those in key places like the Bank of England. His successor had a more populist touch, a knack for the telling phrase, and an intellect equally penetrating but more mercurial in character. This was Anthony Harris, who had been economics editor of the *Guardian* from 1968 to 1973 before returning to the *FT*. He had gone to the same Cambridge college as Samuel Brittan, and like Brittan he was originally a historian who took to economics late. Yet between the two men there has been over the years a fundamental philosophical difference: whereas Brittan tends to perceive the world in terms of problems and solutions, for Harris there exist only dilemmas involving choices. It is an intellectual tension that has done much to enrich the paper's columns.

Another voice that now departed was that of David Watt, who in 1977 left to become director of the Royal Insitute of International Affairs at Chatham House, a position earlier held by Shonfield. He had been doing the 'Politics Today' column for ten years, and his final piece deserves quoting, if only from a few paragraphs that, in isolation, do not do it full justice:

Turning over the pages of my cuttings book, it seems to me that the most significant thing I have been reporting, though I have not always realised it, is the decay of a political culture and the demoralisation of a political class. The British political world and its occupants have not yet discovered a convincing reaction to the very rapid movement of British society in the last ten years along the path towards a mass culture already travelled by the Americans – a world of high expectations and high demands which brushes aside slogans like 'More Means Worse' with the answer: 'Well, we'll have more anyway.'

The fact is that the assumptions of the whole of the Conservative and Liberal Parties and at least half the Labour members of Parliament are in a contrary sense. They instinctively subscribe to the fears of unbridled democracy of the Victorian middle class . . .

By background and temperament I share all the values and fears of [John Stuart] Mill. But journalism imposes other values of its own – a belief in public discussion, a distrust of closed societies and a belief that ordinary people can be persuaded (contrary to Mill's expectations) to act rationally and far-sightedly if things are adequately explained. That is why the political event which has given me most pleasure in ten years was the referendum on the EEC. We shall not solve the problems of modern society by government diktat. The distribution of power and wealth and amenity is too complex and too sensitive to be encompassed either by paternalism or by a return to *laissez-faire*. The only alternatives are education, persuasion, debate, trust.[24]

It was, in its way, a classic statement of the *FT*'s rationale. The new political editor and writer of the Friday column was Malcolm Rutherford, who had a hard act to follow.

Meanwhile, the landmarks of a crisis-ridden decade continued to be strewn across the paper's pages. The major sterling crisis of September 1976, leading to the calling in of the IMF, induced editorial wrath:

The Government may argue that it has conceded a great deal less to Labour's left wing than it has been asked for. But it has conceded a number of measures over the past couple of years, many as part of the 'social contract', which the country cannot afford at present even if there were no doubts about their desirability. It has created the effect of a Nero, fiddling away with great political artistry while the town burns, and an increasing number of people are beginning to wonder whether it is not spending an utterly disproportionate amount of time and effort in accepting or staving off the demands of those who represent only a small proportion of the electorate. There is coming to be seen a clearer opposition between what is economically necessary and what is conventionally regarded as politically practicable.

What was economically necessary? There were, according to the same leader, only two possible courses of action. One was 'to tighten the money supply more effectively – a process which, as the experience of Germany has recently shown, may well reduce unemployment by bringing down inflationary expectations'. The other was 'to cut public expenditure still further, especially in those areas which absorb large amounts of relatively unproductive manpower'. As for the strong union opposition this would involve, 'conventional ideas of what is politically feasible will now have to be revised'.[25]

Over the next few months (and to an extent over the rest of its life) the government followed both courses, culminating in Healey's package of public expenditure cuts in December 1976, grudgingly accepted by the *FT* as 'the very least that the IMF would accept as a condition for allowing the Government the first instalment of the loan for which it has asked'. During 1977 and into 1978 the economic situation improved, though not to a point where the paper could disagree in December 1978 with Callaghan's decision that the time was not yet ripe to join the incipient European Monetary System: 'The fact is that the outlook for the UK economy, and especially for the rate of inflation, remains a mystery wrapped in an enigma; and in such circumstances, membership of an obligatory currency intervention club is definitely not an unmixed advantage.' All the time, a strong monetary vein ran through the *FT*'s economic analysis, summed up in a leader of February 1979: 'Monetary restraint is not a magic formula, which solves problems on its own; but it is a realistic one, which makes the nature of problems clear. That is why we need it.' The language was moderate and the conversion was intellectual rather than emotional, but as an economic standpoint it still came nearer to Friedman than to Keynes.

No economic theme during these years consumed more tons of newsprint (and amply justified the paper's recent decision to have a labour page) than the annual rounds of pay 'norms' and unfree collective bargaining. For most of the late 1970s the *FT* accepted the need for this process, though emphasizing its preference for as much flexibility as possible. By July 1978, after a detailed examination of the current police pay claim, the tone was becoming ominous:

> The wider point is the question of devising a flexible approach to pay policy which can accommodate the necessary adaptations to reality without a renewal of general wage-inflation. The Prime Minister has been talking of wage increases

of around 5 per cent over the next year. If the Government is led into trying to apply this or any other figure in a manner which further compresses differentials and prevents adaptation to market pressures, the policy will contain the seeds of its own undoing.

So it proved, as Samuel Brittan by October was not ungleefully observing: 'If there is a hero of the hour it is Mr Moss Evans, the new General Secretary of the Transport and General Workers' Union, who has made it clear that he will have no truck with pay norms of any kind.' And this long-time opponent of incomes policies added: 'After ten years of counter-productive effort in this field we could do with a decade of *laissez-faire*.' Three months later, deep into the 'winter of discontent', the paper was viewing quite sanguinely 'the undignified tussle over wages which is now disrupting various sectors of our economic life': 'They are not so much an outbreak of anarchy as a return to normality, with all its faults.' The leader was headed 'Back to the pig trough', but the prospect did not dismay. If the government stuck to a policy of 'monetary control and a relatively strong exchange rate, and educating the public in its consequences', namely that 'higher settlements mean lower growth and fewer jobs', the trough would soon sort itself out.[26]

These were also the years that saw the power and ambitions of trade unions at their zenith. It was not a trend that the *FT* welcomed, as was shown by its combative response in January 1977 to the Bullock Report on industrial democracy, asserting that, if the government tried to legislate on it, 'industrial management, already tried exceedingly hard, is now ready to fight back'. Another emotive subject was the long-running dispute with the Grunwick Processing Laboratories and the issues it raised. The *FT*'s own mind, as expressed in June 1977, was clear enough: 'the state of the law about picketing is unsatisfactory and the attempt to improve it must be renewed'; 'workers who do not wish to belong to a trade union should be free not to do so'.

The tone of the paper towards the unions was usually measured enough, but in September 1978 the economic resolution adopted by the TUC provoked a set-piece passage of lofty rebuke:

It would be hard to contrive a recipe more likely to provoke inflation and inhibit growth than the blend of job protection, higher public spending, tighter price controls and confiscatory attacks on wealth applauded by the delegates. Unfortunately it is only too easy to persuade some men in the street that price controls stop inflation, that giving unproductive work to the jobless solves the problem of unemployment, and that any damage done by compressing profits and destroying incentives can be put right by an indiscriminate application of

North Sea funds. Most people have now learned that they cannot get the moon by being paid in confetti; some may still be persuaded that they could after all have the moon if only the Government would adopt the illogical 'alternative strategy' sponsored by the TUC and supported by some Labour MPs.

The leader then went on to argue that though there was no chance of Messrs Callaghan and Healey ('men who have learned realism in a hard school') falling for 'this nonsense', nevertheless it was nonsense that mattered:

A Labour Government opposing the basic ideas of the trade union movement has to pay a price in what it considers less essential matters – exchange controls, the structure of tax concessions, expensive rescue operations, an attempt to enforce wage norms through back-door pressure on employers, unrealistic proposals for workers' participation, and burdensome employment legislation. In total this is a high price to pay for the apparent harmony between Government and the trade union movement.[27]

If the *FT* felt this to be a price no longer worth paying, it was a feeling reinforced by the paper's progressive disenchantment with incomes policies. In fine, the corporatist dream, born *circa* 1961, was over.

That same TUC was addressed by the Prime Minister, giving an opportunity to examine 'the Callaghan philosophy' in the context of a probable election in the near future. Unsurprisingly, it was found wanting: 'The kind of Britain outlined by Mr Callaghan yesterday leaves little room for individual skills and even less for individual rewards. It is firmly based on the assumption that British industry cannot stand on its own feet and does not wish to try.' The leader also took the line that, if a philosophy, it was one that had 'been made up higgledy-piggledy as the Government has gone along'. Thus for example, 'the NEB may be presented as an attractive half-way house between private ownership and nationalisation, but in practice it is a bit of a hotch-potch whose role is uncertain'.[28] The following spring, with the election at last fixed for 3 May, it was this theme of unacceptable and often unsystematic interventionism to which *FT* editorials returned several times. The leader on 19 April was fairly typical: 'Unlike some of his colleagues, Mr Callaghan does not want to change the capitalist system in any radical way. He merely wants to be able to intervene at any point in the system where he feels that the interests of some group which he wishes to protect are threatened.' Consequently, 'more and more industrial problems become the subject of Cabinet-level debate, with the result that decisions take longer to reach and the outcome depends more on the strength of the various lobbies than on economic realities'. In short: 'Arbitrariness is the hallmark of the Labour Government's approach to industry.' The *FT* was more than happy to pay tribute to the 'sense of realism' that had informed the Callaghan administration since the autumn of 1976, as it did in its election-day leader, but towards the underlying tenets of that administration the paper remained unsympathetic.

There was an alternative. 'Similar but different' was the title of the rather low-key leader in October 1977 on the Conservative Party's policy document *The Right Approach to the Economy*. After noting the existence of 'a remarkable degree of consensus between the two major parties on the need for strict control of the money supply, firm cash limits on public expenditure and "responsible" wage bargaining', it then pointed up the central difference between the two: 'The Tories believe in the market economy: Labour's attitude to it is, at best, ambivalent.' However, 'in the light of the record of the last Conservative administration some of the comments about non-intervention may be regarded with scepticism.' It was a scepticism that persisted. The same April 1979 leader condemning Labour interventionism was headed 'Would life be any different under the Tories?' and gave a cautious answer: 'Mrs Thatcher seems determined to dismantle much of the apparatus of intervention which has been built up since 1972, but there are influential voices in the Party which argue that the Government cannot sit on the sidelines while British industry sinks without trace.'

On polling day, however, the *FT*'s leader did not doubt the choice facing the electorate was a clear-cut and potentially historic one. After outlining in familiar terms Labour's deep-rooted interventionist instincts, the final paragraphs argued the case for, in the leader's title, 'A change of direction':

> The Tories, in total contrast, believe that it is the role of the individual rather than that of the state which is crucial. It is against this general background that their promises to reduce direct taxation, to deal with such issues as the closed shop, their determination to cut government spending have to be seen.
>
> They believe that not only the economy but our everyday lives are over-regulated, but that the vision of the future held out by Labour is grey and drab and stifling of individualism. Judging by what has happened to this country it is an argument which cannot be rejected easily. It applies not only to domestic affairs but to Britain's place in the world and in the EEC. Labour's manifesto introduces the section on foreign policy with the statement: 'The Labour Party's priority is to build a democratic social society in Britain.' The Tories have a broader vision.

FINANCIAL TIMES

PUBLISHED IN LONDON AND FRANKFURT
No. 27,856 Friday May 4 1979 15p

CONTINENTAL SELLING PRICES: AUSTRIA Sch 16; BELGIUM Fr 25; DENMARK Kr. 3.5; FRANCE Fr 3.5; GERMANY DM 2.0; ITALY L 600; NETHERLANDS Fl 2.0; NORWAY Kr 3.5; PORTUGAL Esc 35; SPAIN Pts 50; SWEDEN Kr 3.25; SWITZERLAND Fr 2.0; EIRE 20p

North-South split clear, but overall Conservative majority looks certain

Thatcher set for Number 10

BY RICHARD EVANS, LOBBY EDITOR

AT 3 am this morning Mrs. Margaret Thatcher was set to oust Mr Callaghan from 10 Downing Street and become Britain's first woman Prime Minister.

The Conservative Party scored substantial general election gains to ensure that Mrs. Thatcher leads a majority administration in the next Parliament.

But the variation in voting patterns was considerable throughout the country and the Tories owed their victory to their supremacy in the Midlands and the South of England.

Labour's support held up well in Scotland and the North, and one of the most important implications of the election was the Tories' failure to break out of their southern strongholds.

The marked North-South divisions could cause considerable political problems for an incoming Conservative administration which tries to implement its economic and industrial policies, particularly if these involve a loss of jobs, as predicted by Labour.

Nevertheless, all the signs early today were that the Conservatives would get a sufficiently large majority to retain power for the full five years of a Parliament.

Mrs. Thatcher's intention is to await the remainder of the results later today before considering the composition of her Cabinet, which is expected to be announced over the weekend.

There were inevitably some eminent casualties during the night, including Mr. Teddy Taylor, one of Mrs. Thatcher's closest lieutenants and almost certainly destined to be Secretary of State for Scotland.

Shortly before 3 am Lord Thorneycroft, Conservative Party chairman, said the party was on course to get the majority it needed to govern the country for five years. "If we go on at this pace we are plainly going to have a very adequate majority," he said.

Mrs. Thatcher had a highly successful result at Finchley, where she nearly doubled her previous majority of 3,911 and Mr. David Steel, Liberal leader, also greatly increased his majority at Roxburgh, Selkirk and Peebles.

Overall the Liberals had mixed fortunes but seemed likely to keep most of their 14 seats, including their by-election triumph at Liverpool Edge Hill. Both Mr. Clement Freud at Ely and Mr. Geraint Howells at Cardigan held their seats for the Liberals.

The most spectacular Conservative swings came in East London and the Essex suburbs in both Labour and Tory-held seats. Walthamstow stayed Labour but the swing to the Tories was 9.1 per cent, and there were several swings of more than 7 per cent in seats such as Romford and Upminster.

The first Labour loss in Greater London was at Putney, where Mr. Hugh Jenkins, the former Arts Minister, was defeated by nearly 3,000 votes.

Labour was holding its own much more in the North with swings to the Tories confined in many cases to under 3 per cent. But with many marginals in the North West vulnerable to the Conservatives, there were early losses there as well.

At Nelson and Colne, a Labour Left-wing member of the National Executive Committee, Mr Doug Hoyle, was defeated by 436 votes, with a swing to the Tories of 1.4 per cent, and at nearby Rossendale Labour MP Mr. Michael Noble also lost his seat.

The only good news for Labour in the early results came from Scotland, where the party held safe seats with increased majorities and cut savagely into the Scottish National Party vote.

The Labour Party's General Secretary, Mr. Ron Hayward, admitted that the tide was going towards the Tory Party. Mr. Hayward, like other organisers gathered in Transport House, took some small comfort from the much smaller swings in the North of England.

But he said he was particularly disappointed at the defeat of Mr. Doug Hoyle.

Tory leaders were confident of an overall victory for two reasons—the desire they found for change before and during the campaign, and the signs of a drop in the total Liberal vote even though some individual Liberals did well.

Crucial to a Conservative win must have been the troubles on the industrial front since Ford workers won their 16 per cent pay award in December and smashed the 5 per cent pay barrier. The Tories have benefited substantially from the discontent that followed.

It is not clear what Mr. Callaghan will do after the defeat, but close aides believed before the election that his inclination would be to retire quickly to leave the succession clear for Mr. Denis Healey, Chancellor of the Exchequer.

Any successor to the Labour leadership would find a difficult inheritance, with a Labour Party in disarray and Mr. Callaghan's ultra-moderate economic and industrial policies discredited. There is certain to be considerable pressure from the party in defeat to swing sharply to the Left.

Mr. Callaghan is the first Premier for more than 50 years to be forced into a general election by the Commons and he has paid the price. He wanted to hold on until June or October to distance himself from the winter's strikes but was defeated by the Conservatives and a combination of minority parties over the result of the Scottish referendum on devolution.

The Labour leader will inevitably face criticism of his personal decision not to go to the country last October when many Labour tacticians were convinced he had a much better chance either of a narrow victory or of containing the Tories.

But having made his decision, Mr. Callaghan fought a dedicated paternalistic campaign based on the Government's concordat with the trade unions and the need to avoid confrontation.

● Early results confirmed the predictions of the opinion polls, showing variations in the voting pattern, but generally in line with the 6 per cent to 7 per cent Conservative lead suggested by the polls.

The swing to the Conservatives was 6.8 per cent in London and 5.9 per cent in the South-east. In the North-west, the shift to the Conservatives was less marked, around 3.7 per cent.

STATE OF THE PARTIES - 3.30 A.M.

	Seats	Gains	Losses
LABOUR	152	5	16
CONSERVATIVE	125	18	3
LIBERAL	2	—	—
SCOTTISH NAT	2	—	5
OTHERS	1	—	—

SWING—4.25% TO CONSERVATIVE

SEATS GAINED

Conservative
Nelson and Colne (Lab)
Rossendale (Lab)
Putney (Lab)
Fulham (Lab)
Hornchurch (Lab)
Ilford South (Lab)
Anglesey (Lab)
Angus South (SNP)
Ealing North (Lab)
Banff (SNP)
Newark (Lab)
Northampton North (Lab)
Peterborough (Lab)
Dartford (Lab)
Enfield North (Lab)
Rochester and Chatham (Lab)
Liverpool Garston (Lab)
Coventry South West (Lab)

Labour
Paisley (SNP)
Stirlingshire East (SNP)
Glasgow Cathcart (Con)
Dunbartonshire East (SNP)
Workington (Con)

NEWS SUMMARY

GENERAL

Terrorists kill officer

Extreme Left-wing terrorists raided the Rome headquarters of the Christian Democrat Party, killing one policeman, seriously injuring two others, and causing extensive damage by throwing bombs in the building.

The raid, on the eve of Italy's general election campaign, marked the climax of a fresh outburst of political violence, including the kneecapping by Red Brigade terrorists of a Genoa state company manager and 27 bomb attacks in the northern region of Veneto earlier this week.
Back Page

Autonomy plan

Egypt rejected an Israeli autonomy plan for the Palestinians on the Jordan West Bank and Gaza Strip, and said it would obstruct peace efforts in the Middle East. Page 4

N-reactors shut

Both nuclear reactors at the Dungeness A nuclear station in Kent, one of the UK's earliest nuclear plants have been shut because of delays in repairing cracks found in the No. 2 reactor last winter. Back Page: Nuclear accident costs, Page 29; EEC safety committee, Page 2; U.S. closure Page 4

New U.S. weapon

The U.S. Senate authorised money for the development of a new type of nuclear intercontinental weapon, the MX missile, without which senators said they will not vote for the SALT II treaty.

Butter surplus

The EEC will end this year with a record surplus of butter of between 500,000 and 600,000 tonnes, Fin Olav Gundelach, the EEC Agriculture Commissioner, said in London. Back Page

Briefly...

At least eight people were killed and 40 injured in northern India when a lorry carrying a marriage party overturned.

Nearly 9 lbs of heroin worth £2m at street prices was seized when customs officers swooped on a Mercedes car being driven ashore at Harwich.

BUSINESS

Gilts up; Copper falls back

● **EQUITY opened sharply higher and the FT ordinary index closed off its best but still at a new high of 553.5.**

● **GILTS** achieved rises of up to ¼ with the Government Securities index rising 0.26 to 75.58.

● **STERLING** rose 90 points to $2.0770 and its trade-weighted index rose to 67.5 (67.2). The dollar showed little movement but its index rose to 86.7 (86.6).

● **GOLD** fell $¼ to $246¼ in London, and in New York the Comex May settlement price was $247.30 ($246.40).

● **COPPER** prices fell with cash wirebars off £8.5 to £980 a tonne on selling by speculators. Page 39

● **WALL STREET** closed 2.08 up at 857.59.

● **WORLD NICKEL** price has risen again, the French-based producer, Le Nickel has announced. The UK price will rise £374 to £3,049.5 a tonne. Back Page

● **AN OIL FUTURES** market in London is to be considered by a special study group drawn from London commodity market traders. Back Page

● **JAPAN'S** Prime Minister Mr. Ohira has said that his government will seek to cut Japan's tariffs earlier than agreed in the GATT trade negotiations.

● **EEC COMMISSION** has launched a cash grants scheme for European steelmakers and has begun work on a directive to cut overtime working throughout the Community in an attempt to ease the EEC's growing unemployment problem. Page 2

● **BUILDING** and civil engineering industry unions seem likely to reject current pay proposals for 700,000 construction workers. Page 10

● **LONRHO** has been unsuccessful in its first attempt to take over Scottish and Universal Investments. The first closing date has passed with acceptances of only 17 per cent of the shares. Back Page and Lex

● **CHRYSLER CORPORATION** of the U.S. has turned in a $53.8m loss for the first three months of 1979. Back Page

CHIEF PRICE CHANGES YESTERDAY

(Prices in pence unless otherwise indicated)

RISES					
Treasry. 9¼% 1983	£97¼	+ ¼	Laporte	137	+ 9
Exchqr. 12¼% 1999	£105¼	+ ¼	Lex Service	118½	+ 6½
Aberdeen Const.	88	+ 7	Lonrho	85	+ 5
Anchor Chemical	80	+ 7	Lucas Inds.	309	+ 17
Avana	93	+ 5	MEPC	208	+ 10
Averys	258	+ 8	More O'Ferrall	140	+ 7
Bambers	280	+ 18	Mothercare	188	+ 8
Beecher McConnell	357	+ 12	Porter Chadburn	103	+ 7
Boot (H.)	98	+ 8	Rowntree Mackntsh.	454	+ 15
British Land	81	+ 4½	Sainsbury (J.)	383	+ 16
Brocks Group	162	+ 9	Sound Diffusion	119	+ 8
Clarke (Clement)	148	+ 17	Tricoville	94	+ 4
Edwards (L. C.)	84	+ 8	Ward White	143	+ 8
European Ferries	175	+ 8	Whitbread	141	+ 5
Furness Withy	288	+ 22	Wimpy (G.)	100	+ 4
Hambro Life	685	+ 25	East Driefontein	689	+ 20
Hambros	294	+ 20	Marievale	94	+ 5
Hanger Invs.	76	+ 8	RTZ	354	+ 8
Hill Samuel	120	+ 13	Selection Trust	568	+ 22
			FALLS:		
Imry	748	+ 38	Ultramar	292	− 16

Scottish Nationalists almost eliminated from the scene

BY PHILIP RAWSTORNE

THE Scottish Nationalists were virtually eliminated from the political scene as their vote crumbled to both Labour and Conservatives.

Labour, in contrast with the rest of the country, gained strength throughout Scotland.

Its greatest single triumph was scored against the Conservatives in Glasgow Cathcart where Mr. Teddy Taylor, the Right-winger who would have been Tory Secretary for Scotland, was defeated.

Mr. Taylor, who had held the seat for 15 years, fell to a swing of 4.4 per cent to Mr. John Maxton, a college lecturer.

Labour had fought a vigorous campaign to oust Mr. Taylor, one of the leading Tory anti-devolutionists, and appear to have been helped by some tactical voting by former Nationalist supporters.

He said: "It is a miracle that we held the seat for so long. I am disappointed but we have the consolation of a probable Tory Government tomorrow."

It was ironical that Mr. Taylor should have been defeated as the Nationalist cause which he opposed so fiercely collapsed throughout Scotland.

The first sign that they were to take a drubbing came in Hamilton, scene of the party's emergence on to the national political scene with Mrs. Winnie Ewing's by-election victory in 1967.

The SNP candidate in Hamilton was pushed into third place behind Labour and the Conservatives. Mrs Ewing subsequently lost her seat at Moray and Nairn.

Campaigner

Mr. George Reid, the party's devolution spokesman, lost his Stirling East seat shortly afterwards to Labour.

Then Mrs. Margaret Bain, one of the party's most colourful campaigners, lost Dunbarton East. A member of the party's national executive, she had gained the seat from the Tories by 22 votes in 1974. This time Labour took it.

The Conservatives, however, also made advances at the Nationalists' expense.

A Tory lawyer, Mr. Peter Fraser, recaptured Angus South from Mr. Andrew Welsh, the SNP housing spokesman.

Throughout Scotland, the SNP challenge to the two main parties, which fuelled the devolution debate of the past few years, declined.

In nearly all the Labour seats where the Nationalists had run close in 1974, the SNP candidates fell to the foot of the poll, behind the Conservatives.

The Nationalist vote generally fell by 6-8 per cent; and the number of lost deposits mounted steadily.

It clearly signalled the end of devolution—for the next Parliament at least—as a major political issue.

Proposals

Both major parties can gain some satisfaction from the outcome.

Labour's devolution policy has clearly contributed to its renewed political force in Scotland. In spite of the referendum rejection of the proposals, Labour would have been much more vulnerable to a Nationalist assault if it had rigidly opposed the movement for self-government over the past five years.

The Tory anti-devolution approach has also been justified by events.

Mrs. Thatcher, who had said a Tory Government would hold further talks on the issue, will now be under little pressure to do so.

Tories gain in South

FINANCIAL TIMES REPORTER

THE CONSERVATIVES made their most dramatic gains in London and the Home Counties, where in addition to defeating the former Labour Arts Minister, Mr. Hugh Jenkins, in Putney, they gained Ilford South with a swing of 6 per cent.

The Tories also gained Fulham, a seat once held by Mr. Michael Stewart, the former Foreign Secretary, with an 8.1 per cent swing.

Mr. David Howell was the first Tory Shadow Minister to be returned when he won Guildford with 31,595 votes, and increased his majority to 19,906, a swing of 4.8 per cent. He polled 25,584 in 1974.

The biggest swing to the Conservatives was at Barking, where they cut the Labour majority from 16,290 to 7,008, a 13.9 per cent swing.

At Sidcup Mr Edward Heath retained his seat with a 13,458 majority, a 6.9 per cent swing. The Tories also held Bexleyheath with a swing of 8 per cent.

Sir Nigel Fisher held Surbiton with a 10,802 majority, a 6.3 per cent swing. Mr. Patrick Jenkin held Wanstead and Woodford with a 7.4 per cent swing, and Mr. Norman Tebbit retained Chingford with a 11,983 majority, an 8.2 per cent swing.

Labour held Hackney South and Shoreditch with a 6,704 majority but the swing to the Tories was 11.6 per cent. Mr. John Tyndall, the National Front chairman, lost his deposit.

At Bermondsey, where Mr. Robert Mellish, former Labour Chief Whip, held his seat with an 11,756 majority, the swing to the Tories was 10.4 per cent.

The City of London was held by Mr. Peter Brooke, the Tory candidate, with a 9,784 majority (7.2 per cent swing).

The smallest swing to the Tories was in Southall, where Labour held the seat with a 11,278 majority (0.3 per cent to the Tories).

The Conservatives also increased their majorities at Sutton and Cheam, Romford, St. Marylebone, Orpington, Acton, Upminster and Harrow Central. The swings ranged from 3.6 to 7.8 per cent.

Labour retained Islington Central with a majority of 4,139, reduced from 6,818, a swing to the Tories of 10.7 per cent. At Edmonton and Brent South, the Labour candidates held their seats with reduced majorities.

Boost for shares and pound

BY PETER RIDDELL, ECONOMICS CORRESPONDENT

SHARE PRICES and sterling both rose sharply yesterday on hopes of a Conservative election victory.

The FT 30-share Industrial Ordinary index jumped by 12.7 at the start of business following the publication of final opinion polls favouring the Tories. This was followed by some profit-taking and the index ended 8.7 up at a new all-time closing peak of 553.5.

Money Markets, Page 31
Stock Exchange Report, Page 40

Longer-dated gilt-edged issues showed gains of ¾ of a point. But business on the stock market was generally thin as both jobbers and brokers and investors awaited the election outcome.

Sterling gained ground quickly, rising by nearly 1½ cents at one stage to $2.08. Dealers believed that the Bank of England might have intervened on a small scale to prevent too large an appreciation.

The pound then slipped back slightly before closing 90 points up on the day at $2.0770.

The trade-weighted index, measuring the value of sterling against a basket of other currencies, rose by 0.3 points to 67.5. This represents an appreciation of 2.1 per cent since the middle of last week.

The other main development on the foreign exchange markets involved the currencies in the European Monetary System. The Danish krone, which has recently been stronger, weakened sharply and dragged down the Belgian franc. The result was that the franc moved beyond its permitted divergence limit in terms of the European Currency Unit, a basket of all EEC currencies.

The Belgian franc is permitted to diverge by 1.53 per cent from the European Currency Unit. But after adjusting for the special position of sterling and the Italian lira its adjusted divergence was 1.56 per cent.

Under the rules of the European Monetary System a movement beyond the divergence point is a warning signal. The government concerned should choose between intervening directly in the markets, changing its monetary policy, altering its central exchange rate, or revising its overall economic policies, or some combination of these actions.

Belgium can claim to have followed the rules since the Belgian National Bank raised its Bank Rate by one point to 7 per cent on Wednesday.

STERLING

£ in New York

—	May 3	Previous
Spot	$2.0755-0765	$2.0675-0685
1 month	0.19-0.14 dis	0.40-0.35 dis
3 months	0.55-0.50 dis	0.74-0.69 dis
12 months	1.65-1.80 dis	1.90-1.80 dis

CONTENTS

For latest Share Index phone 01-246 8026

4 May 1979: general election

Whether that vision can be realised in the Britain of the eighties is what this election is really about. If the Tories were to make the attempt and fail, the chances are that the Labour government which succeeded them would lurch further to the left, towards more interventionism, greater isolationism, further curtailment of personal freedom and choice. Yet in our view that risk is one that has to be taken. The time to arrest the trends of decades of post-war history is now. The task will have to be approached with great care and patience. No one can be certain that the Tories will succeed. But they must be given the chance to try.[29]

Austria	Sch 15	Luxembourg	Fr 24
Belgium	Fr 25	Netherlands	Fl 2
Finland	Fm 2.75	Spain	Pta 50
France	Fr 3	Switzerland	Fr 2
Germany	DM 2	Portugal	Esc 25
Greece	Dr 22	Turkey	L 16
Italy	L 500	U.S.A.	$1.50

FINANCIAL TIMES

PUBLISHED IN FRANKFURT AND LONDON

● Helmut Schmidt on the future of EMS, Page 10

No. 27,753 Tuesday January 2 1979 D 8523 B

NEWS SUMMARY

AN ICY START TO THE NEW YEAR

Winter freeze hits Europe

SEVERE winter weather gave northern Europe a freezing start to the New Year, causing chaos on roads and railways and creating dangers for shipping.

Roads remained blocked by snow in northern areas of Britain, France and East and West Germany, with further blizzards sweeping southwards to Bavaria and the Alps.

West Germany's northern border with Denmark was impassable. In West Germany's worst-hit state of Schleswig-Holstein, three people were reported missing and private cars were banned from the roads.

At Swiss Alpine resorts, holiday-makers were warned against straying from established ski runs following the avalanche deaths of two West German skiers.

Many roads in the north of France were closed by drifting snow. French police advised extreme caution to the thousands of motorists heading for home after the New Year holidays.

In the Atlantic off north-western Spain, 29 crew members of the stricken tanker Andros Patria were feared drowned after their lifeboats capsized in rough seas.

Swedish and Danish Air Force helicopters rescued 57 seamen and women from two stranded Soviet fishing vessels, blown ashore from the Baltic Sea on to the Swedish coast.

Moscow's coldest spell for a century relented in what, by local standards, was a slight thaw. Temperatures in the Soviet capital rose to −23C from the previous day's low of −35C, while in London, temperatures rose slightly to −3C.

GENERAL

Peking celebrates U.S. link

China's Vice-Premier Deng Xiaoping (Teng Hsiao-ping), the diplomatic architect of the normalisation of relations with the United States, last night took his first step into American territory – the U.S. liaison office in Peking.

He led a number of high-ranking Chinese foreign affairs officials who were guests at a reception hosted by Mr Leonard Woodcock, head of the U.S. mission.

The reception was the only ceremonial observance of the normalisation of relations which became effective yesterday. No practical results of the new diplomacy are expected until March, when the two Governments exchange ambassadors. Page 12, feature, Page 2.

Sadat seeks aid

President Sadat of Egypt said the issue of a peace treaty with Israel had dropped to second or third place in Egypt's list of priorities. First place was now occupied by the "Carter plan" for increased U.S. aid to Egypt. Page 2

Smith warning

Mr Ian Smith, Rhodesian Prime Minister, said that the Anglo-American plan for an all-party conference on Rhodesia had failed. He added that only the internal settlement could save the country from tyranny and totalitarianism. Page 2

Callaghan plea

Mr James Callaghan, Britain's Prime Minister appealed to the trade unions not to abuse their power in what could be "a year of decision and advance". A general election is due to be held this year. Page 12

Refugees move

Health chiefs in the Philippines were considering transferring 2,300 Vietnamese refugees from a freighter in Manila Bay to smaller vessels in a bid to ease health hazards. The Government has refused to allow the refugees to land there.

Briefly . . .

Festive Neapolitans who drank and danced their way into 1979 awoke to count the cost–131 injured and 50 fires.

Two men died and six were injured in an accident on an offshore oil rig in Bass Strait, south of Melbourne.

Sri Lankan lawyer has broken the world twist dance record in Colombo by dancing for more than 102 hours without stopping.

BUSINESS

Scottish hauliers to strike

Scottish lorry drivers are to strike from today after rejecting a 15 per cent pay offer.

Although it appears that nothing can stop the strike, further talks are taking place in many English regions of the UK's Road Haulage Association. Page 12

● **PROSPECTS** for a solution to West Germany's five-week-old steel strike improved after talks between Herr Friedhelm Farthmann, the north Rhine Westphalia Minister of Labour, and the two sides involved in the dispute. Page 2

● **KRAFTWERK UNION**, the power plant manufacturing subsidiary of Siemens, of West Germany, is going ahead this year with plans to build a $120m turbine-generator factory in the U.S. state of Florida. The move comes as the General Electric Company, Siemens' UK counterpart, is also planning major U.S. investment. Page 4

● **SHARES** on Wall Street ended 1978 with the Dow Jones index at 805.01, 26 points lower than the 1977 closing figure. It was a year of sharp peaks and falls, with the Dow ranging from 750 to over 900.

● **ITALY** is within reach of achieving a trade surplus for the whole of 1978 for the first time since 1942. The recovery follows the restrictive measures adopted in the country's currency crises two years ago and the steadying of the domestic market. Page 4

● **MR ERIK HUSS**, Swedish Industry Minister, has appointed a two-man team to negotiate State support for Swedish pulp and paper concerns in financial difficulties. Page 4

● **SUN ALLIANCE** and London Assurance Company of Britain, the life company of the Sun Alliance and London Insurance Group, has improved its reversionary bonus rates for 1978. Page 14

● **PRUDENTIAL** Corporation, the largest life company in Britain, increased overall annual premium income by 23 per cent in 1978. Single premium business declined by 4.3 per cent during the year. Page 14

Franc and lira in currency link despite EMS row

BY PETER RIDDELL, ECONOMICS CORRESPONDENT IN LONDON

THE FRENCH franc and the Italian lira are unofficially to be linked closely with other Common Market (EEC) currencies from today as if the European Monetary System (EMS) was in full operation. This has been agreed although the formal start of the EMS has been delayed.

The original intention, agreed by EEC leaders in Brussels early last month, was that the EMS would start from the beginning of January. But this was blocked last week by France's decision to refuse to allow the EMS to take effect until outstanding problems on agricultural trade and prices had been settled.

The central banks of the eight EEC countries participating in EMS without Britain have agreed to intervene to keep their currencies within specified narrow margins of each other.

For seven of the countries this means that their exchange rates must be within 2.25 per cent of each other. The eighth, Italy, has been allowed a 6 per cent margin.

Five of the currencies are already linked in the present European joint float known as the snake. So effectively there will be a change only for France, Italy and Ireland.

During recent weeks their exchange rates have been within the agreed range.

The hope is presumably that the arrangement will be enough until the French worries about farm subsidies have been solved. For the time being, countries will only be able to call on the present credit facilities rather than the increased amounts available when the full EMS comes into effect.

None of this should make any difference to Britain, which is outside the formal currency arrangements, because the Government is anyway committed to keeping sterling stable. This should also ease the position of the Irish pound in view of the Irish central bank's intention to maintain a one-for-one parity with sterling.

The decision to link EEC currencies informally follows talks during the weekend between officials. They have not removed the confusion about when, and in what form, EMS will start.

The delay may simply be the result of a simple dispute between France and West Germany about the level of farm subsidies, as the French statement said on Friday.

If this is the case, there have been a surprising series of misunderstandings in view of the strong political commitment to EMS by President Giscard d'Estaing. Although the issue should be capable of resolution by political compromise, officials were not underrating the difficulty of sorting out the agricultural argument in view of the strength of French views.

But the delay may reflect a deeper French concern about the future of

Editorial comment, Chancellor Schmidt: Page 10

Continued on Page 12

Slick from holed tanker threatens Spanish coast

BY DAVID GARDNER IN BARCELONA

A GREEK supertanker carrying 208,000 tonnes of crude oil was last night drifting helplessly off the north-west coast of Spain trailing a slick several miles long and threatening serious pollution.

All but three of the crew of the Andros Patria are believed to have drowned after the captain gave the order to abandon ship in severe weather. The dead are thought to include 29 crew members and the captain's wife and his two-year-old son.

The tanker is carrying only 12,000 tonnes of oil less than the Amoco Cadiz which last year hit rocks off the north-west coast of France and devastated a huge stretch of Brittany shoreline.

The tanker, owned by Seas Transportation Corporation of Piraeus, was holed above the waterline by an explosion when it was about 30 miles of the north-west of the Spanish port of Coruna on its way to Rotterdam from the major Iranian oil terminal of Kharj Island.

The salvage operation yesterday was being co-ordinated by Seas Transportation Corporation's New York agents, who had signed a Lloyd's open-form salvage agreement and brought in a salvage tug from Holland.

The tug was yesterday afternoon standing by, trying to get men on board and take it in tow when weather permits.

The tanker is insured in London primarily with the London Steamship Owners' Mutual Insurance Association.

THE SHETLAND Island's Council is to enquire into the weekend oil spill at Britain's Sullom Voe North Sea oil trans-shipment terminal. The spill of several hundred tonnes of fuel oil came after the 190,000 tonne Esso Bernicia was holed while mooring. And is the second since the port opened in November.

It's oil, which the Lloyd's agent in Coruna said was owned by British Petroleum, has already been leaking extensively. The naval authorities in Coruna said the slick was more than three miles long.

The ship's bosun who was rescued along with the chief engineer and pump man said that the tanker was holed just above the waterline and therefore relatively high up on the storage tanks. This, as well as that only three tanks, holding about 50,000 tonnes of crude, were holed, has limited the spillage so far.

High winds were driving the tanker towards the north-western corner of Galicia. A change in wind direction, however, could direct the oil slick further south towards the port of Vigo and Portugal.

The accident happened at 9.35pm on Sunday. The three surviving crew-members said there was a crack on the vessel's port side, followed quickly by two explosions, and then a fire which extinguished itself.

The ship was left holed in a force nine gale and the captain gave the order to abandon ship in the vessel's two life-boats.

The survivors said that all those who abandoned ship were swept away in the storm when the lifeboats capsized. They are presumed drowned. A Norwegian ship in the vicinity had by yesterday afternoon recovered seven bodies.

The three survivors had stayed on board the ship and yesterday were lifted off by navy helicopters in two trips.

IMF takes hard line in Zaire

BY MICHAEL HOLMAN IN KINSHASA

ZAIRE'S Central Bank has issued a list of 50 customers to whom further credit will be refused. They have also been ordered to repay outstanding debts and repatriate hundreds of millions of dollars held in overseas accounts.

The list has been sent by the Banque du Zaire to the country's commercial banks as part of a campaign against widespread and damaging corruption. The list of businessmen includes at least two Commissaires Politiques (Members of Parliament) and other political figures, many of whom have been dealing in commodity exports, particularly coffee.

A further 55 companies have been warned that their affairs are under investigation by the five-man team from the International Monetary Fund (IMF) now working at the Central Bank in Kinshasa. The team is led by Herr Erwin Blumenthal, of West Germany, who signed the list which was sent out last month.

As another part of the Government's attempt to stop irregularities, which are ruining the economy, French and Belgian officials are expected to arrive early this year to supervise a new section of the customs department.

Western economists here estimate that although the 1977 coffee crop was worth more than $400m only $120m returned to Zaire. The discrepancy is accounted for by smuggling, under-invoicing, and the export of best grade coffee beans declared as low grade.

Considerable significance is attached to the list blocking credit which is the talk of the business and diplomatic community. If it is effective Zaire will not only save millions of dollars but, as one Western economist said: "The first stroke of the axe will have been successful."

It is assumed that the move has President Mobutu's backing, since one of the country's most powerful figures is involved. Herr Blumenthal's willingness to confront him and others like him has earned the 60-year-old German the title "Bula Matadi" – the Stone Crusher.

The development is regarded as a key feature of efforts to reform and revive the ailing Zaire economy. The effectiveness of the rescue depends on the extent to which expatriates can control this rich, sprawling nation. All key sections of the economy are now, or are about to be, under the control of foreigners in what amounts to a surrender of economic sovereignty.

At the Banque du Zaire the IMF team functions in terms of an unequivocal pledge by the Government contained in its recovery plan presented to a meeting of the 12-nation "Zaire club" in Brussels last October.

Continued on Page 12

Financial Times prints in Germany

Financial Times Reporter

COPIES OF the Financial Times for sale in large parts of Europe and the United States were last night printed for the first time in Frankfurt, West Germany.

By printing in Frankfurt, distribution of the Financial Times will be much improved. In all but extreme weather conditions the FT will in future be on sale in major European capital cities before breakfast. On Wall Street, it will be available at 9.30 a.m.

The European FT is being printed on the traditional salmonpink newsprint. The printer is Frankfurter Societäts-Druckerei, an old-established contract printing house in the centre of Frankfurt.

The bulk of the Frankfurt paper will consist of pages sent from London using full page facsimile transmissions–essentially sending photographs of full pages across a high-quality telecommunications circuit.

But parts of the paper will be specially written and edited for the FT's overseas readers.

Frankfurt was chosen as the FT's second printing centre because of its prime position at the centre of the European road network.

The FT will be delivered to major European capitals by specially designed Citroën vans with a top cruising speed of 100 miles per hour.

Last night's print run in Frankfurt was 20,000. This will be raised over the next three months to 30,000. Approximately 20,000 copies are being dropped from the London production run.

The Financial Times at present has a circulation of around 181,000, and a world-wide readership of about 825,000. About 14 per cent of that sale is overseas.

Over the coming months, the FT is mounting a major marketing drive aimed at increasing its penetration of the European and American markets.

The Frankfurt-printed paper is being distributed from today to major business centres in Germany, Austria, Belgium, Italy, the Netherlands, Switzerland and Turkey, as well as to the United States.

Over the next few months seven other countries will be included. They are France and Luxembourg (in February), Finland, Greece and Portugal (in March); and Canada and Spain (in May).

Details, Page 11

VIOLENCE PERSISTS IN IRAN

Chaos grows as Shah stays silent

BY SIMON HENDERSON IN TEHRAN

THE SHAH of Iran yesterday failed to clarify persistent reports that he is about to leave the country temporarily amid signs that the growing chaos in the country is hampering the mass exodus of foreigners.

The Shah of Iran, failed to clarify reports

Appearing in public for the first time since the reports that he was to leave "for medical reasons and relaxation," the Shah merely said he would like to go away for his annual winter holiday when things had settled down.

He appeared before TV cameramen with his wife and three younger children as violence persisted in the provinces and efforts to form a Government in the capital seemed to be running into difficulty. Mr Ardeshir Zahedi, his close adviser and ambassador to Washington told cameramen, however, that the Shah would remain.

The new Prime Minister designate, Dr. Shahpour Bakhtiar, who claims he took the job on the basis that the Shah would step down has said his Cabinet list is two-thirds complete by Thursday. Separately on Tehran radio, Dr. Bakhtiar said he would move his Government in the direction of social democracy. He said he would gradually lift martial law and he would allow compensation for the formalies of those hurt in the recent troubles.

Yesterday General Azhari, the present Prime Minister and head of the armed forces, submitted his resignation in what is seen as a formal move preparing the way for Dr. Bakhtiar. The Shah accepted it on the understanding that the General would stay in office until Dr Bakhtiar was ready.

A new Government would have to be presented to Parliament, now in recess, but no special session has yet been called. Officials say that one of General Azhari's deputies will be in charge of affairs, as the general suffered a heart-attack last month and has still no yet fully recovered. A deputy has not been named.

The rapid succession of political moves over the weekend has so far failed to calm anxiety over Iran's future. Violence has continued in many towns and cities with several hundred anti-Shah protestors reported to be shot dead by the army in Mashad. Western embassies advised nationals on Sunday to leave, unless they had an important reason to remain.

The official reason for being asked to leave is concern over the economy: petrol is now largely unavailable because of disruption by oil workers, as is heating oil, fuel for cooking stoves, and some foodstuffs. There are also nightly power cuts.

By yesterday afternoon most of the employees and dependants of the Western oil consortium who were no longer needed had left from Abadan. During the previous two days, 1,200 have taken charter flights out of the country.

Westerners who try to leave Tehran, however, were prevented by a strike of air traffic controllers, who were only allowing food and medical cargo to arrive. A Swiss Air flight managed to land and depart, as did an Israel El-Al Airliner, which landed without using the control-tower.

Hopes have been raised that oil production can be resumed to the level of domestic demand. The army has conceded some of its control of the oil fields, and an opposition politician has been pleading with striking oil workers to convince them of the need not to alienate the general population.

Shah and the army lose control, Page 2

CONTENTS

2 January 1979: the first Frankfurt edition

[FOURTEEN]

INTERNATIONALISM 1979–85

The second of January 1979 was probably the most important date in the *FT*'s history since 1 October 1945. For the first time, the paper was printed abroad as well as in London, thereby bringing to the first stage of fruition an internationalizing vision that, as it matured over the years, not only transformed the outlook of the *FT* but in retrospect may come to be seen as having redefined its very terms of reference. The presses that now rolled in Frankfurt were those of the well-established contract printers Frankfurter Societaets Druckerei (FSD). On that first day David Palmer described in the paper the gist of what was involved in production terms:

The process by which we shall be transmitting most of the paper to Frankfurt, though expensive, is well tried, and is already being used by newspapers all over the world. It is called 'full page facsimile'. The page of this paper that you are now reading was composed and made up by the traditional hot metal process in London. A very high quality image of this page was then taken, using a machine called a 'proofing press'.

The 'proof' – in effect an image of this page up to art photography standards – was then wrapped around the drum of a Muirhead facsimile machine. At the press of a button, the drum started to revolve at 3,000 revolutions a minute. As the page revolved, a beam of light 'read' it, and translated the image into signals which were sent down a 48 kHz line to Frankfurt. In Frankfurt, these signals were translated back into an undeveloped film. The whole process described in this paragraph took less than three minutes.

The film was then developed; made into a hard plastic plate; and fastened on to the rotary presses of our German printer. The London page now had an identical twin in Frankfurt, 400 miles away.[1]

It was an impressive script, but the 'clerk of the weather' fluffed his lines on opening night, swathing the whole of northern Europe in snowstorms and sub-zero temperatures. The first European print run was successfully completed shortly after midnight on the night of the 1st, but distribution was badly affected, especially to points north. Present in Frankfurt was Justin Dukes, who rightly paid tribute to the people who – under-staffed in some areas and against a stern deadline – had achieved the launch on time. It was, on a corporate level, a considerable morale-booster after the failure of the Development Plan. As for the initial teething problems, Dukes put them in perspective: 'It would be unwise and inappropriate to judge the success of the project after the first night, or even the first hundred nights. We take a long-term view of this because we view it as a major development over a long time.'[2]

The initial difference between the international edition and the London one was of style rather than of substance, reflected in particular by the physical sectionalization of the paper, in accordance with European and North American convention. Roughly speaking, the front and back halves of the London edition were each accorded a section, with a section also being given to surveys of four or more pages. To begin with, the only pages different from London were the two main news pages in the first section and the international company news pages fronting section two – a minimalism caused to a large degree by the fact that the only production choices were taking a page intact from London or setting and composing it in Frankfurt, the latter an especially expensive process because of the terms exacted by the NGA as recompense for the work 'lost' to its members. By the mid-1980s, however, from twelve to twenty pages in the Frankfurt edition were, as a matter of course, different in whole or in part from the London edition. This evolution would not have been possible without the development and refinement of what became known as the strip-in technique, by which London-produced pages were sent by facsimile (or 'faxed') to Frankfurt, where, following the layouts drawn by the Frankfurt desk in London, elements could be removed or deployed as necessary, allowing locally set copy to fill parts of a page. The Frankfurt edition also acquired major new components of its own: from February 1982 two extra European pages on Mondays; and a year later, a third section from Tuesdays to Fridays devoted to international markets, with the second section concentrating on international companies.

Under the editorship at the London end of first David Bell and then Dominick Coyle, the difference between the international edition and its London progenitor remained fundamentally cosmetic until at least the mid-1980s. The fact of sectionalization, the physical juggling of stories, the shorter sentences, the dollarizing of all money figures, the labelling of Mrs Thatcher as 'the British Prime Minister' – all these devices did not alter the basic truth that both editions came out of largely the same set of stories and facts, even though they succeeded to a considerable extent in persuading the market that the international edition *was* significantly different. Of course, there was less British and more international news in the international edition. But in 1983 a telling episode occurred when, after only a few months, the UK companies element was reinstated in the second section as a direct result of reader demand. The opening shots were starting to be fired in an as yet unfinished editorial war between the globalists and the regionalists.

The Frankfurt edition was unlucky enough to be launched just before the second oil shock and a further bout of Western recession. For about two years it was a somewhat unpopular animal amongst the Bracken House journalists, where the feeling existed, fuelled by wildly exaggerated surmises, that the costs involved in producing it were bleeding the paper dry. There was also a certain resentment at the way in which their copy was being rewritten for it into what some regarded as a rather flavourless Europeanese. Management did not disguise the fact that there would be an initial shortfall. As Hare told the staff in June 1979: 'We reckon that the costs of the Frankfurt development over the next three years will exceed the revenues attributable to it by some £4 million, but after that we hope to be reaping the rewards of a much broader international readership base.' To his considerable credit and also that of Pearson Longman, Hare stuck to his guns two years later, in the context of the paper's overall loss for 1980:

> We need Frankfurt for the future. Besides producing extra jobs and payments in some departments of the newspaper already, Frankfurt provides the best hope for the newspaper expanding its revenue. We must invest in this sort of development, if we are to move forward in the market, for if we do not move forward, we will move backwards. There is no other development with half Frankfurt's potential for us.

Over the next year or so the case for Frankfurt was generally accepted, with circulation growth during 1981 being entirely attributable to the international edition, which increased its sales from 25,500 in December 1980 to 33,000 a year later. Even from Frankfurt, distribution remained the major European problem; but increasingly this was solved, for city centres at least, by improved subscription services and in particular a system of hand delivery. Most of the attention focused on Europe, which by March 1982 was responsible for 28,970 copies out of Frankfurt's daily circulation of 35,314, with the rest going to the USA (4,469) and Asia (1,875). Other parts of the world were still served by the London edition. Over the next year the international edition continued to increase its circulation and by March 1983 was running at a satisfying 43,200, virtually double the sales in those areas previously covered out of London. What could not be precisely established over the years, however, was what effect this growth had on the paper's advertising revenue, for the simple reason that (with only partial exceptions) advertisers did not yet have the option to buy space in the Frankfurt edition only, which was still a long way from attaining the 'critical mass' necessary to command profitable rates off its own bat. Nevertheless, as a very rough guide, overseas advertising columnage continued to rise during these years; while it was generally accepted, outside as well as inside the paper and reflected by advertising rates successfully going up more steeply than in other quality papers, that the growth of the Frankfurt edition had done nothing to impair the quality, and much to improve the quantity, of the overall readership profile.

By 1983 there was a direct competitor in the European field. Although almost certainly not intended as a pre-emptive strike as such, Frankfurt had in practice played some part in deterring the *Wall Street Journal* from embarking on a much-anticipated European venture of its own. By the early 1980s, however, the *Journal* was ready to move, though not without first engaging in some high-level dialogue with the *FT*. At a series of three meetings, held in the spring of 1982, Dow Jones floated to Hare and his colleagues the idea of a joint *Wall Street Journal/Financial Times* daily paper for the European market, with both names on the masthead and having the avowed intent of thereby avoiding head-on competition in Europe. The talks progressed only a limited way and foundered decisively on the question of editorial control, which the *FT* was not prepared to cede in any such joint venture. Not unnaturally, the London organization felt that it had invested considerable sums in Europe and, from a position of reasonably well-established strength, was prepared to take the risk of the competition. That it was a risk was graphically shown a few weeks later by Richard Lambert's article in the *FT*, following the announcement that the *Journal* would start in the Netherlands to print an edition for European consumption early the next year:

There are powerful resources behind the new paper. If Dow Jones decides that the European market is worth exploiting in a big way, it will not be held back by financial constraints.

The reason is that the *Wall Street Journal* is an extraordinarily profitable newspaper. Stockbrokers Kidder Peabody estimate the paper contributed some 73 per cent of the group's $149 million (£83.2 million) operating income during 1981. Mr Joseph Fuchs, of Kidder Peabody, says there are two reasons for this commercial success. One is that the paper is very tightly edited for a specific demographic sector which has great appeal to advertisers. The other is that the paper is 'superbly managed' on an operating basis, and has used modern technology to create new opportunities.

By the mid-1970s, all the *Journal*'s printing plants had been converted to photocomposition. After establishing its first satellite printing plant, the paper will have a network of 17 printing plants across the US.

This development means that the paper can be delivered more quickly to a much wider readership at a lower cost than was ever possible in the past. A typical printing plant employs a total of perhaps 25 people and can turn out 100,000 copies a night – a phenomenal level of productivity by Fleet Street standards. While the *Journal*'s circulation has risen from 1.2 million to over 2 million since 1970, the number of production workers has fallen significantly.

The *Journal*'s higher circulation has brought an increased volume of advertising and generated more profits to invest in new plant which can boost the circulation yet further: a sort of virtuous circle.[3]

It was a circle so virtuous, so utterly different from the British national newspaper industry, that henceforth the *Wall Street Journal*, already printing in the Far East as well as in the USA, would loom large in the *FT* collective consciousness.

The early 1980s were not in general a good commercial time for the paper. After the freak year of 1979 (showing a profit of £3.38 million, caused largely by the non-appearance for most of the time of *The Times* and also the lengthy ITV dispute), the next three years settled into a stagnant, rather depressing pattern: rising international circulation offset in the main by declining British circulation, a decline caused partly by the cover price increasing from 15p at the start of 1979 to 30p by August 1981; advertising volumes steady at some 40,000 columns for the year (5,000 less than in 1973), though disguising an increasing market share by 1981; and, on the bottom line, a small loss in 1980 (the first in recent history) picking up to trading profits of about £1.8 million in 1981 and £2.1 million in 1982, better than nothing but each time representing only about 4 per cent to turnover. Not only was the cost of the Frankfurt development a continuing if necessary drain, but the general economic climate, both national and international, was unfavourable for most of this period, being characterized by rising oil prices, sky-high interest rates and widespread industrial recession. By the summer of 1982, however, this crucial, perennial backcloth to the *FT*'s performance began to brighten, with inflation falling fast in Britain and the economy seemingly bottoming out. In the USA the domestic equity market, after years of somnolence, suddenly came to life. In October 1982 the *FT* Thirty-Share Index reached 600 for the first time (fourteen years after it had first crossed the 500 barrier) and the following May it reached 700. Inevitably the *FT* benefited. During the first four months of 1983 the paper was selling a record 214,800 copies per day (almost 15,000 more than a year earlier), and by May a small amount of advertising was even having to be turned away because of capacity problems.

A particularly gratifying aspect was that the British circulation was at last starting to enter a period of growth. This was a reflection not only of changing circumstances but also of the impact of the major corporate promotional campaign launched in the autumn of 1981, the first sustained one (in Britain at least) in the paper's history. At the heart of the campaign, which was mainly concentrated on London and the South-East, lay the 'No *FT*, no comment' theme. This had been devised by the advertising agency Ogilvy & Mather, was very nearly rejected by the *FT* as a slogan on account of its double negative, and in the event became one of the great catchphrases of the 1980s, doing more to establish the paper in the minds of people than any previous advertising. The format of the television arm of the campaign stayed constant for the first five years. It showed two business men with the *FT* and one without, mentioning a mix of recent issues (usually one international, one national and one light-hearted); and it asked the guilt-inducing question to the odd man out: 'In the week when the *FT* considered all these questions, what was *your* point of view?' For the first two years the campaign's posters similarly twisted the knife, but from 1983 a more relaxed, humorous dimension was added, beginning with the appealing photograph of a spaniel and a dalmation (the odd dog out not carrying the *FT*) and perhaps culminating with the beautifully executed 'Partridge in an *FT*' Christmas campaign of 1986. Witty, stylish and highly effective, it was an award-winning campaign that owed much to a sympathetic as well as discerning attitude on the part of the agency towards the product it was seeking to promote.

Before then, however, the generally disappointing results since the mid-1970s began to raise the question by about 1980 of what sort of animal the *FT* was and whether its best commercial future lay in seeking to broaden out from being primarily a daily newspaper. The main proponent of this approach (an attitude as much as a strategy) was Justin Dukes. He argued that the *FT* should be transformed into a single editorial resource seeking to attain a world stature in the burgeoning financial information market, whether by means of traditional newspaper publication, electronic publishing or syndication. Dukes had seen the in many ways fortuitous growth since 1973 of the Reuter Monitor Service – a service epitomized by flickering green screens in the trading rooms of the world, underpinned by the technology of the microchip and fed by (as well as feeding) highly volatile currency markets. He now wanted the *FT* to be a leading player in the wider information-technology revolution, even if it meant downgrading the traditional primacy of the paper itself and those who worked full-time for it. Dukes was quite open about the high-risk nature of his proposed approach, as well as the constraints it would impose on short-term profits, but believed that in the long run it was a route that the *FT* could not afford not to take. However, he failed to convince either Hare or Pearson Longman, who believed, partly because of the problems encountered by Fintel, not only that the benefits were too uncertain, but also that the new emphasis was likely to damage the paper.

Dukes himself left in 1981 to apply his talents to the world of Channel Four, with Richard McClean and Alan Cox becoming joint managing directors. The newspaper remained the centrepiece, and the various forms of attendant business information continued for the most part to expand; but electronic publishing persisted as a sphere of activity in which the *FT* did not excel, at the very time when Reuters were enjoying soaring profits as a result of key improvements in the Monitor Service by which subscribers were able to talk to each other 'direct' and thus fix deals almost instantly. Was the negative decision of *circa* 1980 therefore a mistake? The short answer is that it is too early to say; Dukes was suggesting an initial game-plan of at least five to ten years. But in 1980 – after a bruising decade, with Frankfurt still in its early stages and with severe production problems remaining on the newspaper side – there were neither capital nor management resources to spare for such a major change of long-term direction with such an uncertain yield. Even a newspaper publishing organization like Dow Jones, which *had* got its production sorted out, was to find electronic publishing an almost bottomless hole for several years. Moreover, at some level it is hard not to feel that cobblers should stick to their lasts and that the traditional, highly refined main purpose of the *FT* (unlike that of Reuters) was to provide a value-added service in hard copy, relatively worthless without its interpretative and analytical dimension. If such an activity failed to bring in sufficient noughts, the remedy was probably a case of changing the internal economics of the product rather than its fundamental nature.

Back among the day-to-day realities of the editorial work-face, these were also the years in which the *FT* appointed only its third editor since Hargreaves Parkinson and the merger. Fredy Fisher's last eighteen months or so were not a happy time, as he became a somewhat isolated figure and came close to appearing to retreat into his intellectual shell. In particular, industrial action taken by the journalists in July 1980, causing the loss of one day's issue and leading on the part of Dukes to a higher-than-expected settlement, reflected larger discontents than the ostensible issue of pay. It was still, however, a complete surprise when it was announced in the autumn of 1980 that Fisher would be leaving the paper at the end of the year and starting a new career as a banker, on the international side as a director of Warburgs. He had done much for the *FT* during his eight years as editor: supporting the Frankfurt project; never losing sight of the commercial aspect, especially through the development of the international company pages; demanding in tone and outlook a greater professionalism and internationalism; playing a key part in the crucial redefining process of the mid- to late 1970s; and in general helping the paper to start to become a presence on the world stage, as an opinion-forming as well as a news organ. Perhaps most importantly, during an editorship conducted for most of the time in a highly discouraging economic climate, he neither lost his faith in the paper and its future nor allowed his subordinates to lose theirs. It is relatively easy to be editor of the *FT* when markets are bullish and the mood is upbeat, but quite the reverse during a period of gloom and pessimism such as characterized much of the 1970s. A lesser man would have allowed a corrosive sense of doubt to spread, but it was a tribute to Fisher's strength of character, as well as to the intrinsic merits of the *FT* itself, that at no stage did this happen among the editorial ranks. At the end of a difficult, sometimes unrewarding editorship, he left the paper in excellent shape to take advantage of the generally more propitious circumstances of the 1980s.

The choice of Fisher's deputy, Geoffrey Owen, to succeed him at the start of 1981 was almost automatic. There was no serious internal rival nor indeed external, though the name of David Watt was bruited. David Palmer was chosen as deputy editor. A potentially significant footnote occurred almost two years later, when the NUJ chapel expressed to management its view that in future the selection of the editor should be a participative process and that this was essential if the editor was to enjoy a status beyond that of an ordinary employee, to some extent independent of management. In reply, Hare made the point that the final approval of the editor by the parent company could fairly be seen as the *quid pro quo* for its 'hands-off' approach to *FT* editorial policy; but he added that he himself was in favour of widespread informal consultation with senior journalists. At which point the bust of Bracken in the entrance hall probably began to twitch.

What sort of person was the new editor? Towards the end of his editorship, Newton is said to have remarked that relatively speaking it did not matter who succeeded him, because the momentum already established would keep the paper going, but what really mattered was who the editor after that was. There was perhaps some truth in the observation. The *FT* by 1981 had had its period of protracted post-war expansion, had also had its difficult period of redefinition in the wake of that expansion and now needed someone to pull together and further redefine the diffuse threads of the previous thirty years, to renew journalistic loyalty to the collective enterprise and, like his two predecessors, to uphold the best standards of the paper at a time when those of the quality press in general were in danger of being eroded.

In many ways it found the ideal man. Geoffrey Owen was in his mid-forties when he became editor and still had the striking physical presence befitting someone who had been a notable tennis and hockey player, winning blues for both sports at Oxford. There he had read Greats at Balliol, an appropriate culmination to an education during which, at both prep school and Rugby School, he had been a 'hero' figure to a generation of schoolboys. After doing National Service in the RAF, he had learnt his journalistic craft under Newton and imbibed to the full the Newtonian ethos. In the 1960s, in the United States and as industrial editor, he had developed a keen interest and knowledge across the range of the industrial spectrum. He had also, from 1967 to 1972, experienced the outside world, first with the Industrial Reorganization Corporation and then at British Leyland. Under Fisher he had been a very quiet, understated, utterly loyal deputy editor. Now in 1981 he came into his own, imposing his authority through the quiet strength of his personality, healing internal wounds and reaffirming in the minds of his journalists the high seriousness of the task to which they were committed. It was all done with sweet reason and a sense of humour, quite different from the Newtonian approach and involving an implicit acceptance that an abrasive style of leadership was no longer acceptable, or even feasible, in a paper like the *FT*. Yet Owen also shared many of Newton's qualities: the dedication; the integrity; the open-mindedness; the absence of any hint of the prima donna; the dislike of publicity; the ability to motivate; perhaps above all the genuine self-effacing pleasure taken in the achievements of others and his role in orchestrating those achievements. To a remarkable extent, Bracken House has remained in the 1980s a place where egos are not inflated, pockets are not lined and rows do not fester. Much of the credit for this is due to Owen, who has commanded more than any of the post-war editors the respect *and* affection of his staff. These things alone do not make a great editor, but they go a long way towards satisfying the fundamental prerequisite of a successful paper, which is to have a united crew sailing in roughly the same direction.

What was that direction? Owen on taking over described the job ahead in terms of 'finding ways of extending the appeal of the paper to new readers – perhaps making it more readable in certain ways – but at the same time maintaining our basic position of accurate, comprehensive reporting of everything relevant to our readers'. In practice, however, if it came to a choice between these two tasks, the latter imperative almost always won. Owen, like Fisher before him, believed that the function of the *FT* was to address itself ever more thoroughly and systematically to a certain fairly well-defined market and that it would be folly to risk losing (or even diluting) this market by attempting to be a paper that, historically and by collective temperament, the *FT* was not designed to be. Granted that Owen himself had played a major part in the redefining process of the 1970s – on the one hand more specialist but still capable of the broad political or social brush, on the other hand more international in tone, perspective and range – it was hardly surprising that he should have sought to consolidate this achievement.

The new professionalism of the paper was well testified to by Dennis Topping, who after some twelve years on *The Times* returned in about 1980 to the Bracken House news room and found it revolutionized, not only physically but also in the way it approached its daily task. Its procedures were far more sophisticated; it demanded a high degree of accuracy and would take back a page for just one literal; and by the mid-1980s it was changing more pages between editions, up to thirty-five a night, than even the *Telegraph*. The news editor since the late 1970s was the very reliable David Walker, who possessed a complete grip on detail and valued clear, lucid, unjargonized reporting. Yet it is arguable that in the 1980s the *FT* has not always hit the news quite as hard as it might have, going for the big story, imposing its stamp on it and bringing it to life. Possibly this is no longer what it seeks to do, by virtue of its 'redefined' view of its own function, but even so in some sense that still leaves a missing journalistic dimension. This has not always been the case – the Chernobyl disaster of 1986 and its consequences would be a classic example to the contrary – but in as much as it has been, it would to some degree reflect the character of Owen, who has lacked the 'kneejerk' reaction to news that, say, typified Newton. The Falklands war is in this respect the most often cited episode, when Owen spent roughly a tenth of the time that Newton would have spent on supervising the paper's news coverage and front-page presentation of the story, but ten times as much on helping to shape the paper's editorial policy.

On the foreign side between 1979 and 1983, under the editorship of Palmer and then Colchester and amid one or two last whiffs of grapeshot, the 'battle' was conclusively won by the specialists and laid to rest.

Henceforth it was a rule of thumb that a foreign correspondent would be appointed only if he or she possessed a reasonable amount of financial and/or industrial experience. 'Are you as happy to write about Renault as Mitterand?' would become the test question. It was a sign of the times that when Roger Matthews went off to cover the early stages of the Iran–Iraq war he was told not to put himself in a position of danger; *that* was no longer the purpose of an *FT* correspondent. Inevitably the overriding specialist brief could lead to a certain schizophrenia in the coverage of a certain type of foreign story. In 1982, for example, there was major coverage of the Israeli invasion of Lebanon for about three months, but it then went abruptly to the back of the field, not to take up the running again. The specializing process also led at times to a certain loss of colour, a diluting of the individual correspondents, perhaps particularly in the European field because of the needs of the international edition. John Wyles in Brussels, for instance, encountered some resistance when he tried to get across in more human terms the notoriously inaccessible EEC story. On the other hand, Europe was now much more thoroughly covered than it ever had been before, with the advent of the Frankfurt edition prompting much greater consistency and continuity, as opposed to what Colchester liked to call 'the swinging spotlight approach to foreign coverage'. And in general, there was much of distinction in these years. Ian Davidson began a wide-ranging weekly column on foreign affairs that was new to the paper. Andrew Whitley was named 1980 Foreign Correspondent of the Year for his reports from Iran. Richard Johns continued to scoop the world about the intentions of the Arab oil cartel. In the well-remembered words of Sheikh Yamani at an OPEC press conference: 'Where is Richard Johns? We cannot begin without him.' Alain Cass was in Kabul at the end of 1979 to cover the Soviet Union's invasion of Afghanistan. And in succeeding years, under Cass as Asia editor, there was a belated recognition by the paper of the vast economic potential of what was becoming known as the Pacific rim, resulting in offices being opened in New Delhi, Singapore, Sydney and Hong Kong. Yet it would be misleading to suggest that the daily foreign coverage was becoming solely economic in its purpose and character, for that was not the case. Thus when Jurek Martin went to Tokyo in 1982, his brief (superbly fulfilled) was to write about Japan as a whole, to convey the totality, social and political as well as economic, of this immensely powerful player on the world stage, seen through the eyes of a quizzical outsider. And realistically, it was and is not an either/or choice. The deliberations of international bankers may be the subject of arcane analysis, but there also needs to be objective evaluation of the likely social consequences of these deliberations in, say, Mexico. One without the other would not give the complete, interwoven picture. It is a tribute to the *FT* that to a remarkable extent it has succeeded in the last ten years in performing this demanding double task.

There were also significant improvements during these years in the mainstream industrial and business coverage, partly as a result of the fact of Owen's own journalistic roots and strongest sympathies lying in this area. In the autumn of 1980 the paper ran a notable series of features on fifteen British companies, one a day over three weeks and given the collective title 'Wrestling with the Recession'. At a time when the British economy seemed close to two submissions and a knock-out, it was a major contribution to furthering understanding of the depth of the problem. The following March, in pre-Budget week and in the context of the worst recession since the 1930s, a series of five articles on the industrial heartland towns of Halifax, Ellesmere Port, Stevenage, Sunderland and Coventry appeared, dealing with the human as well as the economic impact. The changing pattern of the British and indeed the international economy also affected the coverage offered by the two war-horses of 1967, the management page and the technical page. The former underwent relatively minor modifications: the Thursday 'Marketing and Advertising' page was brought under its remit, and an attempt was made to broaden it out from consumer products; while at about the same time, in November 1981, it followed the example of the *Guardian* and began a small business section on Tuesdays, the first article being 'a look at why a senior company executive set up his own engineering business'. More fundamental were the changes to the management page's historical twin. In 1981 Alan Cane took over the editorship of the technical page, renamed it the technology page and completely refocused it. He swept away almost all the short little pieces, turned it into a features page and concentrated heavily on computer-based stories and on electronics, an accurate reflection of where the industrial sun was rising. Indeed, if one had to name a 'quintessential' *FT* journalist of the first half of the 1980s, reflecting the mood and priorities of the paper and the world at large, it would be tempting in this respect to choose Guy de Jonquieres. After successive stints in Paris, Washington, New York and Brussels, he returned to Bracken House in 1980 wanting to do something different and also something that was on the up. Electronics fell into his lap, and – much encouraged by Owen, even though his own natural affinity was with old-style, 'visible' industry – he was soon providing high-quality coverage in a crucial area. It was also coverage that, as with other industries, was of an increasingly international nature. This global dimension was one now more and more demanded of the industry specialists, and by the mid-1980s they would sink or swim by their ability to provide it.

Also improving in the early 1980s, in the wake of the changes to the back half of the paper following the Frankfurt decision, was the overall financial coverage. Even the rather stolid UK companies pages enjoyed something of a renaissance, with the appointment in 1979 of Richard Lambert as the first specifically designated financial editor since the 1960s, and with the conscious decision that youthful talent should not solely go to the 'Lex' part of the financial operation. The companies coverage retained its essential paper-of-record function, but the infusion of new blood now gave its comments on the results of individual companies an altogether sharper edge, as well as generally leading to a broader, more satisfactory range of financial feature writing. Moreover, almost in spite of this policy, the 'Lex' column itself now enjoyed for a short time one of its very best practitioners, in the person of Martin Taylor, who brought to it all the finest qualities of youthful attack and coruscating prose. Extracts from 28 July 1982 suggest something of the incisiveness:

> Sir Denis Rooke must be the sort of chap who would complain, were he the owner of an ice-cream van, that the August sun threatened to melt his strawberry sundaes. British Gas, he writes, has 'withstood the worst effects of the winter weather', and the Corporation's annual report contains pictures of disconsolate gasmen standing in snowdrifts . . .
>
> The profit and loss account, not for the first time, gives off a peculiar smell; customers are advised not to strike a match and reach for the hundreds of millions of pounds that they are leaking away . . .
>
> British Gas is also deep into the policy of double write-offs. As well as charging full replacement-cost depreciation of its assets, it sets against trading profit the cost of actually replacing them as it does so. It really is time that all capital-intensive businesses adopted this convention, even if that means that the entire published earnings of British industry will be wiped out. All this capitalizing of capital expenditure has simply got to stop.

Even so, the question remains: did the *FT* in the early 1980s at last start to do its stuff in terms of financial investigative reporting, as opposed to retrospective comment? The answer must continue to be a qualified negative, even though John Moore's coverage of the developing scandals at Lloyd's in 1982 won him a British Press Award as 'Specialist Writer of the Year'. It was certainly excellent reportage on his part – accurate, sometimes breaking new ground and far superior to, say, the paper's treatment of Slater Walker – but taking the Lloyd's saga as a whole it is probably fair to say that the *FT* has been a follower rather than a leader, at least in comparison with the *Economist*.

Meanwhile, the paper's general, increasingly international rediscovery of its financial roots continued apace. In October 1982 the annual *FT* 500 made its debut, being 'the first survey of the top 500 publicly quoted European companies, ranked in order of market capitalization'. Easily top was Shell, followed by British Petroleum, with S. Pearson coming in at number 218. The eight-page survey – a much belated riposte to *The Times* 1,000 – also contained listings of the top European companies by turnover and of Europe's biggest banks, together with analyses of trends in the main industrial sectors.

At this time much of the financial action was happening in the United States, where, during an eighteen-month spell in Wall Street, Richard Lambert began to alert both the paper and its readers to the rapidly progressing globalization of financial markets. Also in the USA the *FT* in July 1982 enjoyed a certain coup when it was approximately three weeks and twenty-five articles ahead of the *Wall Street Journal* in picking up on the importance of Penn Square, a smallish bank in Oklahoma whose collapse sent earth tremors through much of the rest of the US banking system. David Lascelles saw the possibilities, quarried the story for all it was worth and in doing so did much to win respect for the *FT* among the Wall Street professionals.

Another of the key figures in the first half of the decade was Peter Montagnon, who was recruited from Reuters in 1980 with a double brief: to take overall charge of the *FT*'s Euromarkets operation; and in particular to cover the hitherto neglected Eurocredits market, which was now bigger than the Eurobond market and, involving as it did lending to developing countries, had considerable macroeconomic implications. By 1981 the syndicated loans in the Eurocredits market were starting to go wrong. Montagnon swiftly built up an authoritative line on the whole debt story, with its rescheduling and its impact on the world banking system, and became recognized as one of the leading experts on the subject. In what was commercially as well as editorially a crucial area – with 'tombstone' advertising by 1982 running at thirteen times the level of 1971 – the *FT* had found the right person to build on the pioneering spadework of Colchester in the late 1970s.

There were various other changes that occurred at this time, unconnected but all pointing in the same direction. In September 1981 the visually displeasing 'Lombard' page was disbanded, with the column itself moving to its present place, thereby allowing the paper's major comment columns and features to be located on a double-page spread in the middle, together with letters and 'Men and Matters'. Soon afterwards the daily racing tips and regular sports reports both faded out, so that sport became a Saturday-only phenomenon. On the centre pages, features editor for most of the first half of the decade was David Bell, who reshaped the pages, improved the variety of subjects, gave more attention to the illustrative element and was prepared to put the articles and their writers through the mill to ensure that the *FT*'s features were as well written and constructed as those of the *Wall Street Journal.* He did not always succeed, but the improvement was palpable.

Two areas that now began to be covered more systematically were defence, with Bridget Bloom becoming the paper's first full-time defence correspondent, and local government under the auspices of Robin Pauley. Both were areas involving enormous sums of money and thus indispensable to any proper treatment of the British economy, let alone their respective political implications. But in a way the really interesting marker for the future was put down in November 1981, when the commercial law reports of the 1960s were revived on a much more ambitious scale (thrice a week during the legal terms) by the barrister Dr Rachel Davies, thereby complementing the long-established 'Justinian' column each Monday by Louis Blom-Cooper and the Thursday column on business law written since 1974 by A. H. Hermann. The decision to revive them was very much taken in the context of the new ownership of *The Times*, reflecting a certain feeling that in the long run, perhaps the very long run, there would be room for the *FT* to expand its status as an indispensable paper of record.

Who was reading it all? The National Readership Survey for the second half of 1980 showed that 71 per cent of the *FT*'s 714,000 UK readers were male, that 54 per cent came from the social grades A and B, that 51 per cent lived in London and the South-East and that 42 per cent were aged thirty-four or under. A year later MORI polled MPs and discovered that of the four qualities the *FT* was the daily paper read the least regularly, but also that by a considerable margin it was adjudged by the same parliamentarians to be the 'most useful'. The most telling survey, however, was the biennial National Businessman Readership Survey, which in 1982 showed that, of an estimated 806,000 business men and women in Britain, only 19.7 per cent read the *FT* compared with 30.4 per cent the *Daily Telegraph* and 19.8 per cent the *Daily Mail.* Interestingly, the *Guardian* on 12.3 per cent was just above those stablemates the *Sun* and *The Times.* More encouraging for the *FT* was its 27.6 per cent readership among the country's 121,000 directors, but even here it was more than six percentage points below the *Telegraph.* There was still a long way to go before becoming the indispensable second paper of the business communtiy. As for Europe as a whole, the European Businessman

Readership Survey for the same year, seeking to cover an estimated 232,000 senior business men and women (including Britain and Ireland) in companies with more than 250 employees, showed that 19 per cent read the *FT*, compared with 10 per cent *Business Week*, 9 per cent *Time* and *International Management* and only 3 per cent the *International Herald Tribune*. The *FT* had clearly secured a useful continental foothold, but the major challenge of the *Wall Street Journal* still awaited.

Whether *FT* readers or no, British business men were by 1982 starting to emerge from two years of deep and destructive recession, during which the underlying editorial message coming from Bracken House was, by and large, to brace up and trust the new Conservative government to see them right in the long run. 'Six weeks ago the country voted for a radical change of direction and yesterday it got it', the *FT* greeted Sir Geoffrey Howe's first Budget in June 1979. It involved major cuts in direct taxation, a large increase in indirect taxation and 'an unprecedented assault on public spending in the current year'; altogether it 'will result in a short sharp shock to the economy', although 'as much from the pressures in the labour market and the depressed external outlook as from any plan of a Chancellor who has forsworn demand management'. The leader's concluding sentiment was sanguine enough: 'Overall, we are witnessing a change of direction which offers hope for the future to help us get through what looks like a very rough year.' Four months later there were no qualms at all about the abolition of exchange controls. Apart from removing a market distortion and encouraging thrift, 'it also, and perhaps most important in the long run, makes it possible for Britain to resume her traditional role as a capital exporter, as is vital if the windfall of North Sea oil is to provide any lasting benefit to the economy'.

By the spring of 1980 and Howe's second Budget the famous medium-term financial strategy had emerged as the centrepiece of macroeconomic policy, the principal components of which were specific targets for monetary growth, substantial cuts in public expenditure over a period and an avowed intent to squeeze inflation out of the economic system. The *FT* offered almost unqualified approval:

> Taken as a whole, this seems to us a sane and credible strategy, which should in due course convince the financial markets that so far as Government policy can make it possible, we are now set on the road to recovery. However, the strategy also has a message for both sides in industry which may not be so readily apparent. It is that under a Government prepared to give such total priority to reducing monetary inflation, the threat implied by uncompetitive costs is not going to go away. On the contrary, it will intensify.

> This was apparent not only in the Chancellor's warning that the Government could not manage the exchange rate, but in his decision to take only the most limited steps to relieve the cash flow of the corporate sector, which is under such heavy pressure. He preferred, he said, to take steps which would relieve the pressure on interest rates.
>
> This decision may disappoint some employers, but seems to us a right one. A tax reduction, as much as a relaxation of monetary control, would risk conveying the old message – or the deadly illusion, as the Chancellor called it – that in the last resort a Government will always come to the rescue of those who have run into difficulty through their own folly. A reduction in interest rates, achieved by a tough Budget and cuts in spending, is another matter.

In short: 'If the Government can stick to the strategy outlined, this was an historic occasion.'[4] Unfortunately, partly because of events across the Atlantic, interest rates (like the exchange rate) did not come down, unemployment mounted rapidly during the rest of 1980, and by the autumn there was considerable dissatisfaction within as well as without the Tory Party. The Prime Ministerial tone at the party conference remained unyielding, however, as did that of her Treasury team. The *FT* supported them, demanding more stringent efforts to control public spending and borrowing and also arguing that 'to get the positive side of this economic message across to the public, the Government should perhaps try to spell out more clearly how it expects the long-awaited reduction in inflation to stimulate real economic activity and employment in the years ahead'. Increasingly, the theme of unsatisfactory 'presentation' was to become a central strand of the paper's critique of the Thatcher government.

During these early years of the new order, the weekly voice of Samuel Brittan enjoyed a particularly great weight and influence. He had done much to lay the intellectual groundwork for the market approach of Thatcherism. Now he was an influential proponent of the medium-term financial strategy, which itself owed much of its incorporation into official policy to the political muscle of his former Coleman Street colleague Nigel Lawson, the Financial Secretary to the Treasury. Brittan's reaction to Howe's first Budget had been one of disappointment – lamenting its lack of monetary planning and over-great emphasis on income-tax reduction – but in March 1980 he applauded 'a coherent Budget at last', marking as it did something of a personal triumph over the Bank of England, which had been opposed to the MTFS. Another intellectual opponent whom Brittan sought to subdue was Wynne Godley and his Cambridge Group, of whose recommendations he wrote the following month:

Just as incomes policy was the fashion of the 1970s, import controls are going to be the vogue cry of the 1980s. The real danger is going to come not so much from the Left – where the Benn group can be taken for granted – as from the Government's natural supporters among industrialists and from self-seeking back-benchers looking for a U-turn with a difference.

He continued, in characteristic fashion: 'The popular appeal of the Cambridge Group is that it satisfies the popular craving for lurid horror predictions and also provides an intellectual veneer for the protectionist demands of special interest groups.'

Brittan also decried what he saw as cant in an 'Economic Viewpoint' piece in July 1980 headed 'De-industrialization is good for the UK'. In it he emphasized that 'although the recession is obviously adding to current pressures, the next recovery is unlikely to reverse the loss of manufacturing jobs', before concluding:

There seems no alternative but to abandon the spurious moralising which regards manufacturing as superior to other activities and to welcome the undeserved good luck [i.e. North Sea Oil] which has reduced the need for these arduous activities, as earlier we accepted the changes which made it possible for fewer people to go down the mines. If we are to have some de-industrialization anyway, we might as well enjoy it and concentrate on helping those who would otherwise lose out, rather than make everyone worse off in vain attempts to stop it happening.

The MTFS, however, remained the cause closest to Brittan's journalistic heart. In October 1980 he declared that, if the government allowed it 'to go by the board, it will become just another run-of-the-mill Conservative administration, remembered for its pre-occupation with guns, truncheons, and nuclear fall-out shelters'. The passage was a useful reminder that he was far from the blue-rinsed commentator he was sometimes mistaken for.

Meanwhile, it was political wintertime for the trade unions, a fact unmourned by the *FT*. When in September 1980 the TUC discussed its possible willingness to countenance an incomes policy, the paper was merciless in its demolition ('An offer we must refuse') of what it saw as an attempt to return to the centre of the political stage: 'When a Conservative Government is bent, like the present one, on reducing the privileges which enable some unions to enforce economically short-sighted bargains on unwilling employers, the discussion of restraint policies is simply irrelevant. The Government is not appealing to the TUC for a compact; it is appealing to union members for common sense.' The final two sentences contained the kidney punch: 'The unions should stick to their last. When they are doing something effective about their own problems, they will earn the right to complain about the Government's faults.'

Within two months the *FT* was considering the not unrelated subject of 'Callaghan's legacy' to the Labour Party. It was not a happy one: 'Fudge is what we have had from the Wilson and Callaghan leadership in the past 15 years or so, and that is why the Party is in its present position.' Most of the rest of the editorial considered the movement in the party for constitutional change ('many of those who are pushing for the wider franchise are not remotely interested in an extension of democracy') and for new policies ('the Labour Party used to be in the mainstream of British political life'). For the second time Denis Healey received the *FT*'s theoretical vote as 'the only candidate tough enough to be capable of pulling the Party together'.[5] Again it served him poorly, and Foot won by ten votes. The new leader still did not do. Although 'a constitutional conservative' and possessing 'literary and oratorical abilities all too rare in British politics', he remained a liability to his party, feeling as he did the most strongly over divisive issues like nuclear disarmament and the Common Market and over the years having 'shown little interest in what has been the main issue in British politics almost since the war, namely the management of the economy'. His record as Secretary of State for Employment 'was a disaster, and there is no evidence of a learning process since'. In sum: 'The man elected to produce unity may in fact preside over a declining party. The Tories would have to make a remarkable mess of things for a Labour victory next time.'[6]

Europe too was feeling the cold, after a decade or more of thaw and *détente*. In December 1979 NATO's defence and foreign ministers were asked to approve a plan for the stationing of 572 new United States nuclear missiles (Pershing IIs and Cruise) in Western Europe. The *FT* argued that, in the light of new Soviet weaponry, there was no alternative but to go ahead: 'A gap has appeared in the Alliance's doctrine of flexible response or graduated escalation in the face of an attack by the Warsaw Pact.' In terms of possible arms control, 'past experience would suggest that such talks have a much better chance of success if the West negotiates from a position of strength'. Shortly afterwards the international temperature went to freezing point with the Soviet invasion of Afghanistan. 'Annexation in all but name' was the title of the *FT*'s New Year's Eve leader, which ended: 'President Carter is on the right track. If the Russians do not respond to reason, they can have the arms race which they will undoubtedly lose.'

Carter himself was to be a beleaguered man in 1980, but the paper was not unsympathetic towards his Entebbe-style attempt to free the Tehran hostages and emphasized that 'whatever criticisms European governments have of the American action, the first priority must be to maintain the alliance intact'.[7] In November he was one half of 'A poor choice for America', but the better half: 'What is needed is an American President who can give imaginative and mature leadership to his countrymen in coping with the uncertainties that lie ahead. On balance, Mr Carter may be better equipped by his intelligence and his four years' experience to offer that leadership, but it is not an enthralling choice.' Three days later the post-election editorial barely paused to congratulate the victor:

Now that the campaign is out of the way, Mr Reagan's top priority must be to study the real world more closely. It is one thing to seduce the American people with simple promises to take the country back to a golden age of greatness; it is quite another to imagine that there are simple solutions to complex problems. Above all, Mr Reagan should urgently acquaint himself with the views and predicaments of the European allies – not because Europe is right and America is wrong, but because in the difficult years ahead, whether in East–West relations, in the Third World, or in the management of the international economy, co-operation between Europe and America will be essential to the success of any American foreign policy.[8]

Coming from an international paper, it was suitably internationally minded advice.

Owen's succession to the editorship in January 1981 made a significant difference to the *FT*'s leader columns, though it was one that was felt only gradually. The difference was that of changing perceptions within Bracken House. Under Newton editorial policy had never been considered of great pith and moment, at least relative to most other parts of the paper; Fisher then initiated the practice of regular discussion at leader conferences about what lines of policy the paper should adopt; and under Owen the process has been taken considerably further, so that it has become a matter of collective pride that the intellectual quality of the leaders should be as high as, if not higher than, anything else in the paper. This would almost certainly have happened anyway in the 1980s, whoever was editor. The paper was gaining in international repute and therefore in self-confidence, and the feeling was growing that the time had come for the *FT* to try much harder to become an opinion-former in its leader columns, not merely reflector, and to seek to reach for the intellectual high ground that it had hitherto not often attempted. The value of lucid, objective exposition was not denied, but it was felt to be no longer enough.

One should not exaggerate the difference. There were plenty of trenchant views expressed before 1981, many 'on the one hand . . . on the other hand' leaders written afterwards. The change under Owen was not so much that the paper now began to spout 550 opinions a year, rather that when an editorial line was taken it was almost always a consensual view that had emerged as the result of sustained, wide-ranging discussion among the leading journalists. To his credit, Owen has not slavishly aimed at too great a consistency of view in the paper's leaders and has thus tried to avoid predictability. Nor has he been afraid to say that some issues are so refractory, so impossible to be certain about, that it would be absurd to lay down dogmatic lines. But above all, what he has done is seek to inculcate an attitude of mind that treats leaders as the intellectual underpinning of the paper, creating a certain set of values and having a permeating effect through the other pages. To the considerable extent that he has succeeded, it is in part a reflection of the quality of his own mind: open, absorptive and remarkably adept during a leader conference at gathering together the strands of a debate and imposing an accurate shape upon them. If he has aimed to create a collegiate structure and atmosphere within the paper, he himself has played the part of the best sort of don.

Economic questions almost immediately dominated Owen's leader conferences. 'The strategy under attack' was the title in March 1981 of a pre-Budget leader, in the context of reports hostile to the government's approach being published by both the House of Commons Treasury Committee and the CBI. The paper declared the existing strategy 'broadly preferable to the alternatives put forward by its opponents' and counselled the Chancellor to 'reaffirm his intention to stick to a strategy of monetary control and fiscal caution, suitably redefined to take into account the effects of recession and of some of the past year's policy errors'. When, despite a prevailing economic backcloth of rising unemployment and falling output, Howe duly stuck to the strategy amidst considerable political controversy, the *FT* did not stint: 'Praise is due for the courage to be "deflationary" at such a time, and by such unpopular means – that is, for imposing burdens on the personal sector and for relying mainly on reduced public borrowing to provide a balancing relief for the supply side of the economy.' Nevertheless, as the title of the leader conceded, it was 'The strategy's last chance'.[9]

So it proved. By July 1981 urban riots were vying with the royal wedding for front-page attention, unemployment was approaching three million, and Brittan was writing that 'it is too early for a requiem on the Thatcher experiment, but not too soon for an inquest'. His own inquest included an advance obituary of the MTFS: 'The difficulty about a medium-term strategy is that the numbers and forward projections which it must contain are anathema to Tory sceptics, while the admission that the Government can influence only monetary demand and cannot determine output and employment is anathema to more optimistic souls. So it has few friends.' Brittan also anticipated his next major thrust: 'The ultimate answer to unemployment lies neither in inflationary finance nor in palliatives, but in action to make wages more responsive to market forces, which means tackling union and other labour market monopolies in earnest.'

Over the next year and a half, the government gradually relaxed its economic policies, to the approval, indeed encouragement, of the *FT*. 'Agenda for the Tories' in October 1981 caught what would become the paper's prevailing tone:

What has been missing is the element of compassion. It has been the market economy that has been presented rather than the social market economy of Ludwig Erhard. The latter deliberately provides a safety net for the disadvantaged and the unemployed. It would be entirely compatible with this Government's approach and with the pursuit of growth without inflation.

There are areas, such as the power of the unions and the nationalised industries, which remain to be tackled. The decentralisation of wage bargaining, for example, could be taken much further . . . Equally, the Government should adopt a less restrictive attitude towards viable public sector projects which could be financed with long-term borrowing.

Such changes can be accommodated within the Government's present strategy. The crucial question, however, is whether the progress so far made in changing attitudes and expectations can be maintained. The Government has yet to convince the electorate, including many of its own supporters, that a permanent reduction in unemployment can only come from improvements in competitiveness, not from reflation.[10]

The Friedmanite strategy was dying, long live radical pragmatism.

It was a pragmatism on the *FT*'s part that defied glib meteorological labels, as had already been tellingly shown by two of the paper's leaders in February 1981. One was a strong attack on the British Nationality Bill, concluding that it not only would have harmful consequences but also was unnecessary: 'The real need is not for tighter controls on citizenship, but to create conditions in which relations between the different racial groups that are already established here can be improved.' A week later the government was again under the hammer ('With a view to surrender') for tamely giving in to the coal-miners over the question of pit closures. 'In Tory Britain, miners rule', the leader asserted, and the final paragraph in effect accused the Prime Minister of double standards: 'Mrs Thatcher might like to think of those industries which have accepted cuts and redundancies. She might also like to reflect on a private sector struggling to make itself more efficient and which now sees yet more public money going into uneconomic activities. She has offered them a poor reward for their pains.'

The following month the paper gave a warm welcome to the SDP: 'At its best, it could combine the virtues of the social market economy with the internationalism and humanitarianism that used to be found in the Labour Party and are lacking in Mrs Thatcher's brand of Conservatism.' The racked Labour Party itself continued to be the subject of many editorials over the next two years, including an outright attack in October 1982 on its non-nuclear defence policy ('not merely vapid and simple-minded' but 'positively dangerous'), as did the trade unions in the context of the Tebbit legislation on trade union immunities and the definition of a trade dispute. The *FT* praised its former employee for both the general thrust of his measures and their moderation: 'The Government seems to have accepted, rightly in our view, that the law can make only a modest contribution to the improvement of industrial relations; that task remains with management and unions at the level of individual companies and factories.'[11]

Perhaps the most characteristic tone was that of 3 January 1983, marking Britain's ten years in Europe. 'Time to join the EEC' was the title of the leader, dispensing even-handed justice in the best *FT* style. It was true that Britain had a long record of budgetary complaints, but by now Mrs Thatcher 'could and should be thinking of ways' to develop 'a broader, more constructive and more imaginative approach to the whole gamut of Britain's relations with Europe'. She herself 'is not naturally equipped for the role of international statesman', but 'has a reputation which commands respect and even admiration abroad'. In particular, it was 'time to reconsider the various arguments which have been deployed against full membership of the European Monetary System'. In the end, however, 'the most important question is this: can the Community play any constructive role in tackling the salient economic problems of today, low growth, high and rising unemployment, industrial maladjustment?' About *that* imponderable the *FT* made no forecast.

For a British paper in the early 1980s, there was no questioning what was the single stand-out news event. 'Jingoism is not the way', the *FT* declared on Monday 5 April 1982, three days after the Argentine seizure of the Falkland Islands and on the day that the British task force set sail. It was a leader that set the tone for the cool, considered approach that the

FINANCIAL TIMES

PUBLISHED IN LONDON AND FRANKFURT

No. 28,742 Monday April 5 1982 *30p

NEWS SUMMARY

GENERAL

Bonn invites Reagan to speak

BUSINESS

BP Oil reports £126m losses

Fraser pressured

Sicily N-protest

Diplomat killed

Gadaffi visit

Police probe

Women picket

Ballot aid banned

Cargo ship sinks

Swiss spy claim

Pot-holers found

Chay returns

Prisoners strike

Gut reaction

Briefly . . .

CONTENTS

Benjamin Menendez, Argentinian-appointed governor of the Falkland Islands, in Buenos Aires yesterday. Troop carriers outside the Falkland Island Company offices in Port Stanley show the strength of the invading forces

Tory whips seek to contain revolt as fleet prepares

BY PETER RIDDELL, POLITICAL EDITOR

FIRST elements of the largest British assault force assembled since Suez will set sail for the Falkland Islands this morning.

Mr John Nott, the Defence Minister, warned yesterday that Britain is prepared to attack the Argentine Navy now stationed off Britain's colony, 8,000 miles away in the south Atlantic.

Though stressing Britain's determination to achieve a diplomatic solution, he left open the option of an attack on Argentina itself.

Senior Ministers have become increasingly bellicose and explicit in their commitment to re-take the Falkland Islands from Argentina, if necessary, by armed force, in the face of continuing Conservative Party anger over Government handling of the issue.

The Government's freedom of manoeuvre is now severely limited as the Falklands invasion has become a major crisis of Tory Party confidence in the conduct of foreign and defence policy.

Tory whips were yesterday talking to all back-benchers in an attempt to cool tempers after Saturday's heated and enthralling Commons debate. Intense activity is likely in the next two days to avoid a significant back-bench rebellion after the full-scale debate scheduled for Wednesday.

The political futures of both Lord Carrington, the Foreign Secretary, and Mr John Nott, the Defence Secretary, remain precarious in face of widespread private criticism by Tory MPs and several public demands for their resignation.

However, the word in Whitehall is that no Ministers have offered to resign and no Cabinet changes are imminent.

Mr Nott said on ITV's Weekend World that he would "unhesitatingly" resign if he lost the confidence of Cabinet and parliamentary colleagues and the Prime Minister. "But for me to quit my post at this moment would be very damaging indeed for the Government."

It is clear, however, that if either the operation to re-take the Falklands fails or there is what is regarded by MPs as a "sell-out" to Argentina then the pressures for the departure of Mr Nott and Lord Carrington will become irresistible.

There was cross-party support for a tough line in Saturday's debate. But, as Mr Nott indicated in his interview, the Government expects public doubts and criticism over the coming weeks if there is armed conflict and Ministers will try to tie Labour down.

Tory MPs were drawing parallels with Suez in 1956, when Labour under Hugh Gaitskell initially took a very strong line but then attacked the Eden Government.

Mr John Silkin, the Labour Defence spokesman, said in the debate, however, that Labour would not offer a "blank cheque." The Shadow Cabinet, which is due to meet today, is likely to offer only qualified support.

There are differences between the strong line supported by Mr Peter Shore and the instinctively less bellicose attitude of Mr Michael Foot, who scored a much-needed personal success with a highly effective speech on Saturday.

Having failed to anticipate the invasion, the Government's internal party problem is that

Continued on Back Page

Invasion developments, Page 2; Falkland's sovereignty defined, Page 15; Feature and Editorial Comment, Page 18

Marines destroy helicopter and damage ship off South Georgia

Strict military rule imposed in Falklands

BY JIMMY BURNS IN BUENOS AIRES

THE ARGENTINE occupation forces yesterday imposed strict military rule on the mainly British-speaking 1,700 islanders against the background of persistant local hostility.

The newly-installed military governor, General Benjamin Menendez, issued a statement ordering the islanders to remain in their houses until further notice and threatening anyone breaking the ban with immediate imprisonment. Shops and banks were also closed until further notice, and a penalty of 60 days' jail threatened for "anyone showing disrespect for the armed forces."

Initial clashes between British marines and invading forces on the main island on Friday left one Argentine officer dead and several wounded. It emerged yesterday that on the island of South Georgia, several hundreds of miles away, a small detachment of British troops opened fire on two Argentine helicopters, destroying one and killing at least three Argentinians. An Argentine naval corvette is also believed to have been damaged by the British marines, who yesterday surrendered the island without further resistance.

The Argentines had been led to believe that the island was uninhabited, except for unarmed officials of the British Antarctic survey, and a group of Argentine scrap merchants, whose illegal landing on the island two weeks ago sparked off the crisis. There were also unconfirmed reports in Buenos Aires yesterday that six marines had managed to escape from the Falkland capital, Port Stanley, and were organising some resistance among islanders in the interior.

According to the Argentine national news agency, Noticias Argentinas, Gen Osvaldo Garcia, the chief of military operations in the Falklands, said yesterday that the captured marines in South Georgia would be treated "as intruders on national (Argentine) territory and not as prisoners of war." Evening papers in Buenos Aires yesterday were referring to the marines, in banner headlines, as "pirates."

Most Argentine airports and naval bases on the south Atlantic mainland yesterday continued to be the setting for constant troop and supply movements, although there was no official confirmation that the Argentine military presence in the Falklands had been increased from its original number of 4,500.

Diplomatic moves aim to avoid armed confrontation

BY DAVID TONGE IN LONDON

INTENSE diplomatic manoeuvrings continued yesterday, involving the two sides ... to have ruled out the imposition of immediate economic sanctions by Washington on ...

City shows concern over block on assets

BY WILLIAM HALL AND GARETH GRIFFITHS

The British Government's decision to block Argentine assets held in the UK and suspend official insurance cover on ex- ... terday that the move would damage the City's reputation as a neutral international financial centre. ... the Argentine Government or Argentine residents.

Bank of England will issue notices clarifying details later ... Argentina but it is clear that it will make the problems of both importers and exporters considerably more difficult.

Reagan refuses to defer tax cuts

BY REGINALD DALE, U.S. EDITOR IN WASHINGTON

FT business survey optimistic

BY MAX WILKINSON, ECONOMICS CORRESPONDENT

5 April 1982: the Falklands conflict

paper was to adopt over the next ten weeks. It did not deny that the seizure was 'an outrage' nor that 'military invasion is an illegal and immoral means to make good territorial claims', nor indeed that 'Britain must resort to every viable means to counter the *coup de main* which placed 1,800 unwilling Falkland Islanders under the Argentine flag.' But it strongly advised the British government to adopt a long-term and preferably objective view of the situation:

> A British naval force operating in the South Atlantic would be stretching its lines of supply to their limit and maybe beyond it. Even if a counterblow were to be struck and were to be successful, the problem of the Falkland Islands would not disappear. Argentine determination to gain possession would be reinforced. The anachronism of Britain seeking to retain control of an area thousands of miles away from its possible sphere of influence and remote from its present national interests would not be removed.

There was then a brief discussion of possible long-term solutions, each of which would, while 'recognising that the Falklanders have rights of self-determination', nevertheless 'also take account of the fact that geography makes the Falklands dependent to some degree on economic and communications links with Argentina and, in the long run, makes British protection for them a Herculean task'. The final paragraph summed up the paper's position:

> The results of negligence cannot be undone by something near panic. Ministerial statements in the first, humiliating hours of the crisis have suggested a determination to drive out the invaders and reoccupy the islands; but to what end? There is no point in a large expenditure of force to reassert a right which, as the Prime Minister herself pointed out [in the Commons on the 3rd], we have not the means to sustain in the long term. It is precisely because no substantial British interest was involved that the crisis was allowed to arise in such a careless way. The danger is that a process of escalation has begun which will be very difficult to control.

It was a leader of sufficient detachment that it perhaps already had the *FT* designated as an enemy within.

Thereafter – in an atmosphere feverish, muddled and sometimes unpleasant – the paper continued to keep its head while some at least were losing theirs. The line throughout was that it might come to war in the end, but that it must not do so until all possible means of negotiation were exhausted. There was also an insistence that Britain should not engage in hostilities until a coherent long-term plan for the future of the islands had been thought out. By 26 April, with South Georgia retaken and the fleet in place, the 'crunch' was approaching, but the *FT* sought to avert it:

> Britain cannot defend the Falklands indefinitely and has no wish to retain sovereignty. The case for what the Government is doing is based on the need to seek an international solution to a problem created by blatant national aggression. It is very important to show that now. The Government should offer to go to the International Court of Justice or to accept UN Trusteeship of the Islands. It should also formally call on the US to join the economic sanctions. Argentina is wrong, but there is no need yet for a military showdown.

Two days later 'Justinian' (Louis Blom-Cooper) contributed a main feature outlining in more detail the notion of trusteeship under the auspices of the UN. Britain would continue to administer the Falklands, but the trusteeship agreement would be written in terms recognizing the interests of Argentina, for 'implicit in trusteeship is the idea that at some stage the islands might, for strictly geographical reasons, become part of the Republic of Argentina'. It was a distinctive contribution to the debate. Over the next two or three weeks several prominent politicians, including Foot and Owen, took up the idea. Also adding to the debate was Samuel Brittan, who on 6 May, in the immediate wake of the *Belgrano* and *Sheffield* sinkings, wrote a 'Lombard' piece with the self-explanatory title: 'Stop the killing straight away'. On 21 May the *FT* accepted the parliamentary consensus of the previous day 'that the British Government has gone to very considerable lengths to secure a negotiated solution' and indeed took a certain satisfaction in the fact that 'concessions have been offered by Britain which must have seemed unthinkable to some sections of the Conservative Party – and perhaps of the Cabinet – at the outset of the crisis'. The leader finished by counselling that 'the strategy of limited military activity while keeping open all diplomatic channels should survive', but by now it was too late. Over the following week the military dimension took over completely, culminating at Goose Green on the 28th. There remained only the peace to be won.

During this crisis the BBC took most of the Tory flak and on 12 May received a stout defence from the *FT*, which praised its 'balanced coverage', noted 'the jingoistic bombast which masquerades as patriotism in some quarters' and declared that 'the Government should proclaim the freedom of the media rather than attacking it', especially as 'this is one of the values we are fighting for'. The approach of the *FT*, however, also earned less than universal approbation. The paper published several letters attacking its editorial policy, including one from the veteran Tory Julian

Amery, who accused it of 'still suffering from the withdrawal symptoms which have plagued so much of the British establishment since 1956'. Perhaps the strongest criticism appeared on 1 June from O. R. Durrant, City Recorder:

From your safe and snug financial fortress in Cannon Street, EC4, don't you think it would be more honourable and encouraging to the nation, the Government and the task force if your editorial comments and articles were less disparaging and negative regarding events in the south Atlantic?

The City of London is not a hiding place for the wets and weaklings and it is playing its part in our country's time of need.

To directly and indirectly continually convey otherwise to your readers is, in my opinion, quite deplorable.

Undeterred, within a week the paper was considering as dispassionately as usual the prospects for another, less snug fortress. It quoted Cecil Parkinson's recent remark that no deal with Argentina would be considered 'which diminished our sovereignty in any way' and described this as 'entirely the wrong approach', being one that would alienate international opinion and thereby increase the probability for Britain 'that what it gains by force it will have to keep by force'. On 16 June, following the fall of Port Stanley, the *FT* returned to the theme, arguing that to turn the Falklands into 'a powerfully armed fortress' was a 'grandiose imperial gesture' which Britain simply could not afford and that 'the 1,800 islanders are entitled to their share of British protection, but they are not entitled to jeopardise the security of the 55 million people who live in Britain'. Therefore, whatever 'the euphoria of victory', the twin objectives of British policy 'should be to explore any recipe which will enable the islanders to live in peace and security with their neighbours, and Britain to come to an accommodation, sooner or later, with this or a future Argentine government'. It was a suitably mature note on which to end a testing episode that, far removed from the world of equities and debentures, even monetary targets and fiscal strategies, had in a sense witnessed a coming of age on the part of the *FT*.

Within a year the country went to the polls. 'It is not the resolute approach', the paper remarked when 9 June 1983 was announced as election day, adding that 'we would have preferred Mrs Thatcher to have served more of her elected term'. During the rest of May the three manifestoes each received scrutiny. That of the SDP–Liberal Alliance was treated sympathetically, if slightly patronizingly: 'It invites nostalgia for the decent, orderly world of Butskellism; its appeal to a sense of partnership and common interest is addressed to anyone who has grown up with a well-developed common sense.' If the centre no longer held, even less did the left-wing policies of Labour, whose manifesto was dismissed as 'a muddled, backward-looking dream', in which 'instead of Mao's one hundred flowers we hear the buzzing of a hundred bees, let out of every party bonnet'. That left the incumbent Tories, who neatly 'avoided the danger of half-baked ideas by publishing a manifesto that contains hardly any new ideas at all'.

On polling day there was little doubt about either the result or whom the *FT* supported:

> By determined leadership and the strength of her personality, Mrs Thatcher has shown that it is possible to break with the past. She had forced people at many levels in British society to understand that their prosperity depends on their own efforts, and they cannot count on government to bail them out.
>
> Already there are some remarkable changes to record. Some industries have responded to danger with quite remarkable achievements in productivity. The atmosphere for bargaining over pay and work practices has changed almost out of recognition across a wide range of manufacturing. Cuts in higher tax rates and an imaginative programme of incentives have encouraged a large increase in the birth of new enterprises. This is the first election for nearly fifteen years not fought in the shadow of a major strike.

With Labour having 'succumbed to infiltration by the extreme left', the Alliance then received a brief pat on the head (with the exception of its 'unfortunate', retrogressive stress on an enforceable incomes policy), before the final paragraph touched on the subject of proportional representation:

> In a more representative voting system, the Alliance could emerge tomorrow as the main alternative to Mrs Thatcher, which we would count as a strong gain. This is highly unlikely under the present system; but it would do nothing but good if the underlying support which the centre party has always claimed were realised by the ballot box, if only as a marker for the future and a powerful argument for electoral reform.

Guardian readers at this point perhaps nodded their heads in sympathy, for it was there that the *FT*'s leader was published, the *FT* itself in June 1983 being off the streets. The reference to 'the shadow of a major strike' was not without intentional irony.

Against a background of unsatisfactory profits and national recession, the years since 1979 had seen a further attempt to introduce new technology into the production processes of the paper. This time it was consciously decided not to go for the 'grand slam' approach of 1975 and instead to try to introduce computerized photocomposition (in 'cold' as opposed to traditional 'hot' type) in a phased way over a five-year period, preferably with a minimum of press statements and publicized fixed deadlines. There was a specific reason for the new initiative: the existing cold-type system for setting part of the tabular matter was becoming obsolete and needed replacing. Beyond that there were powerful reasons why it was felt in 1979 that in the long term the *FT* as a whole, not just its statistical material, could no longer afford to continue being produced by traditional methods.

In the context of developments in the newspaper industry at large, at last even including the British newspaper industry, there were five main reasons why it was imperative to try again to move towards cold type: the high future cost of replacing increasingly anachronistic machinery; the fact that main sources of information like the Stock Exchange and Reuters were rapidly changing to modes of electronic transmission incompatible with traditional printing methods; a realization that, if production continued on hot metal, the quality of the printing would compare unfavourably with those papers that had changed to total phototypesetting; a belief that text setting through electronic 'qwerty' keyboards would be faster and lead to later deadlines; and finally, a fear that, with the rapid expansion of photocomposition leading to the supply of metal plates from advertisers being replaced by 'original artwork', some advertisers might no longer be willing or able to supply such plates. Altogether, in the words of the report to the board in June 1979, 'within the next five to ten years, if we continue to produce the newspaper on hot metal, we shall no longer be able to compete profitably in the international news medium market'. From the start it was accepted that the new technology would have to be introduced in a 'back-ending' way, with no possibility of direct input by the journalists, at least in the immediate future. That acceptance alone meant that the labour-saving potential of new technology mark two was relatively minor. Nevertheless, in the context of 1979, management felt that there was no choice but to go ahead, in the hope that one day half a loaf might turn into a full one.

Unfortunately, it became increasingly clear over the next three to four years that at best the new plan was going to produce crumbs. Although the basic decision was taken in September 1979, it was not until November 1980 that it was formally announced that the *FT* would be changing to a computerized typesetting system by 1984, at a cost of £1.8 million and with the new system to be designed and supplied by Linotype-Paul. The delay was mostly due to a policy of waiting for the general economic climate to deteriorate to a point that would strengthen management's notoriously weak bargaining hand. By 1981 complex negotiations with the various unions were well under way but were severely complicated by the decision taken in March that year that there were few benefits to be obtained from photocomposition unless an attempt was also made to buy out the London Scale of Prices. For at least twenty years the scale had been regarded as a millstone round the paper's neck, resulting in high costs of operation, reducing ability to introduce new editorial and advertising approaches and making increases in capacity disproportionately expensive. The director of newspaper production, Brian Lawrence, forcibly put the case to Hare in January 1981. After noting that, with current scale earnings of more than £500 a week, 'the pieceworkers appear since the early seventies to have protected their earnings remarkably well', he went on:

> The LSP earnings do not relate in any sensible way to the effort involved in securing them; with the change away from the technology and system that the scale has been adapted to and tolerated in, the need to relate effort and skill to earnings under a cold type system should not be only a management objective, but will certainly be one that not only will time-paid NGA and other composing area chapels push for, but also others, notably electricians. Equally, if among the objects of the move to cold type are to control costs and increase the efficiency of the business, the company's persistence in applying a system of payment such as scale is totally incompatible and at variance with them. Few managers understand its operation and scarcely any would be able to check precisely the docket claims and charges derived from it: to a very considerable extent the responsibility for managing the SCP typesetting operation in its widest sense is that of the Lino Chapel FOC [Father of the Chapel].

There probably was no alternative, certainly if management now wished to regain the long-lost 'right to manage'.

The negotiating price to be paid, however, was progress at a snail's pace, further retarded by technical problems. In September 1981 Cox told the board that 'meetings had taken place with the NGA, who have indicated that they will not agree to the piece scale buy-out until all hot metal production has ceased' and also that 'they had rejected the level of technology rates proposed'. The following February, Lawrence 'explained that there would be a delay in the introduction of the photocomposition equipment due to the problems being experienced with Linotype-Paul' and that 'it would be at least two years before setting of text on the new equipment was possible'. In June, Hare was admitting to the staff in his chairman's statement that 'progress on computerisation of the newspaper has been painfully slow', while at the same time Cox was telling the board that 'the NGA had, up to now, rejected any incentive-based scheme'. It was now decided to call in an outside firm of management consultants, who reported in December:

The company's proposals for the current negotiations on Linotype-Paul were ambitious by Fleet Street standards, well ahead of anything achieved in other national newspapers . . .

It is our view that, on the union side, there is little or no perceptible shift in attitude; no recognition that the world revolves around customers and competitors, not unions and management; therefore no willingness to change the rules to reflect this reality; no recognition of the need for lower costs to generate cash for investment; of the need to employ the number of staff actually needed; of the need to work contracted hours; of management's right to control the deployment of staff; or of the need for on-going change and improvement.

It was a gloomy but realistic view of a deeply embedded culture.

As the 1979 plan stalled and stuttered through the early 1980s, few felt the frustration, or indeed the sense of *déjà vu*, as keenly as Hare. In December 1982, at the same time as the report by the management consultancy, he gave vent to his frustration in a feature article in *The Times* about 'the unequal balance of power between trade unions operating in national newspapers and their managements':

A newspaper company loses irrevocable revenue in a dispute; most union members continue to be paid through stoppage or disruption. Since there is no apparent chance of change in the industrial relations legislation which helps create this situation, managements have tried persuasion towards reform. But management and unions do not even agree on which problems should be tackled, let alone on how. If some union leaders (at all levels) can agree about the problems, they show no willingness to lead their members to co-operate in solving them.

In a world in which other media are proliferating and attracting advertisers and readers away from newspapers, the Fleet Street workforce is overpaid, overlarge and protected by restrictive practices. Our outdated technology is the laughing stock of the rest of the world.

What could be done? According to Hare, almost everything hinged on the attitude of the union leaders:

Above all, they must recognise that under present circumstances they have an overriding responsibility to ensure that their members understand that they alone have the power to enable the changes to be made. The leaders should make a public declaration to commit themselves to work with, and not against, managements to restore companies to profitability.

In sum: 'Unless union leaders work together to achieve their members' acceptance of management initiatives and all that follows from them, Fleet Street's future is grim.' [12] For all its honourable intentions, it was in many ways a sad, intellectually bankrupt statement of belief, conditioned by the dispiriting experience of a decade and a half of almost continuous defeat. The message between the lines was there to be read: old-style paternalism, whether from management or union leadership, was a busted flush – if indeed it had ever been anything else in Fleet Street.

Even as Hare wrote, however, a quite different, altogether more aggressive approach to the whole problem was starting to be actively canvassed. Palmer and Lawrence were the two 'young Turks' most closely involved in this approach; and in December 1982 they were part of a five-man team (the others being Richard McClean, its chairman, Alan Miller, finance director of the newspaper, and John Hill, a management consultant) that presented a report entitled 'New Technology: The Way Forward'. The report argued strongly that the *FT*'s main competitor was now the *Wall Street Journal*, shortly to start printing in Europe, and that unless the paper took fundamental action it was engaged in a battle it was going to lose. The facts cited were eloquent enough. The *FT* in 1981 had shown an operating profit of £1 million on sales of £48 million, a margin of 2.2 per cent, whereas the *Journal* was regularly making 20 to 30 per cent; the *Journal* was printing eight or nine times more copies a day, with three-quarters the production labour force; the *Journal*'s production system allowed regionalization of editions, minimum distribution costs and late deadlines, none of which was possible for the *FT*; and the new European edition, to be printed by web-offset, would give advertisers a significantly higher quality of reproduction than that offered by the *FT*, an advantage compounded by the *Journal*'s ability to expand capacity without paying an exorbitant price. In the face of this formidable catalogue, the report stated that if the *FT* was to hope to compete it must plan to achieve five corporate production objectives:

1. Competitive production costs.
2. A flexible, high technology production system, including a front-end [i.e. direct input by journalists] editorial system and on-line wire and statistical services.
3. Web-offset printing.
4. Growth capacity.
5. Freedom continually to introduce new technology and improve efficiency.

Over the following years, however much immediate circumstances changed, these remained the central, abiding objectives.

The question was how to get there. Was it through the current negotiations, which were aimed at introducing into Bracken House a production system that was, at least in theory, not incompatible with eventually introducing direct input? The report argued that that would be a disastrous route to continue to take. Even in the unlikely event of the plan succeeding in every proposed detail, it would still 'leave us in Fleet Street, where labour relations agreements of this kind have a history of not sticking'; 'leave us with a relatively inflexible production system'; 'leave us with poor quality of print'; and 'take us no nearer front-end technology'. In short, it was a route that would gain little and lose much, in terms of both time (at least two years) and money (at least £10 million, including the buy-out of the piece scale).

The alternative was clear: to adjourn the current round of negotiations and instead to go for what the report called 'the remote production option', with the journalists remaining in Bracken House, the composition taking place at Bedford, Saffron Walden and Cheltenham, the paste-up at Saffron Walden and the printing at Pearson-owned Westminster Press plants at Uxbridge, Bradford and Oxford. The report accepted that a non-union distribution system in Britain was impossible and that therefore 'we are committed to working with and through the print unions'. It laid great stress, however, on the virtues of making a clean break with Fleet Street culture, as well as on the technological advantages and the dramatically reduced cost structure. Could it work? The report was sober enough: 'The history of industrial relations in Fleet Street gives no grounds for over-optimism that the *Financial Times* can succeed in breaking free from Fleet Street's culture where others have failed.' And: 'The *Financial Times* cannot get out of Fleet Street on its own. It needs the leverage of Pearson Newspapers as a group if it is to succeed.' There was still no guarantee of success, but the alternative was worse: 'The break with Fleet Street's culture has to be made. If we do not make it the *FT* has no long-term future and a pretty dismal short-term one.'

For a time remote printing seemed a runner. The management consultants thought that it might be achieved with 'a joint Westminster Press/*Financial Times*/Pearson bargaining position' and 'united and determined management'. Hare declared himself cautiously in favour. So too did James Lee, who in recent years had been a notably 'hands-on' chief executive of Pearson Longman, doing much to encourage *FT* management to plan more systematically and be more profit-oriented. He reminded Hare in January 1983 'that Frank Barlow [of Westminster

Press] has said on a number of occasions that the introduction of photo-composition [by the current Linotype-Paul route] will not provide the excuse to change basic management problems'. Discussions about remote printing took place in February between Lawrence and Barlow. By the spring, however, the option had receded, at least for the immediate future; the risks were presumably judged too great. Nevertheless, quite apart from possible subsequent revivification, the development of the option during 1982 and into 1983 had done much to clarify management's objectives concerning production and generally to raise the level of understanding, above all in the context of the United States challenge. But for the time being, it was back to the familiar negotiations, where at last some tangible progress was made with the installation in March of the replacement for the existing tabular-setting equipment. All concerned, however, realized that the heart of the plan was its second phase, namely the installation of 'cold' text-setting equipment, now due in January 1984. No agreements had yet been concluded on the new technology of this phase, nor on the buy-out of the London Scale of Prices and its replacement with a new rate, and by May 1983 it was still anyone's guess whether phase one would have a successor.

One specific by-product, which in time would be of great importance, did come out of the whole process. It was essentially the work of what was known as the Origination Committee, set up in 1981 to evaluate the Linotype-Paul system from an editorial point of view. One of its members was the night editor David Jones, who in the course of 1982 became increasingly involved in the burgeoning remote printing option. By March 1983 he was framing a project application very much in the light of the corporate objectives which that option had enunciated. In his own words: 'The target is the establishment of front-end journalist input for an international multi-centre printing operation making the most effective use of page make-up equipment and direct-to-plate techniques as they become available.' *That* was becoming the target – modern, international and ambitious – against which investment application decisions were being measured. The particular application for funds made by Jones was for the introduction in Frankfurt of a computerized editorial database. Frankfurt was chosen partly because it was a discreet but convenient venue for a pilot scheme involving editorial screens of a highly sophisticated nature, but primarily because the building up of a considerable body of copy (mainly foreign) there would give the Bracken House management greater room to manoeuvre in its industrial relations and production options. Jones emphasized that the Frankfurt database was as compatible with the existing photocomposition negotiations as it was with remote printing; but the real affinity was with the latter, since it ultimately envisaged a *Wall Street Journal*-type world of multi-printing and intercommunicating editorial screens. There was a long way to go, but a decisive first step was taken in April 1983 when Pearson agreed to the purchase of the equipment for such a database from System Integrators Inc. of Sacramento, California.

During the summer of 1983, however, all this was overshadowed by the protracted drama of the strike that took the *FT* out of circulation for ten weeks – a strike that, on the surface at least, had nothing to do with questions of new technology. Its origins lay in the machine room, where historically in Fleet Street a sharp demarcation existed between the minority, the machine minders, who belonged to the NGA (by tradition a craft union), and the majority, the machine assistants, who were less well paid and belonged to what was now SOGAT '82. The job of the machine minders was to ensure the quality of the print, in particular that newsprint was properly folded, that ink levels were correct and that the assistants ran the presses at the correct speed. By the 1980s, if not much earlier, many machine assistants felt, with some justification, that the job was little more skilled than that of a brake hand and therefore did not deserve to be paid at a higher rate.

What both sets of workers shared by this time was a common grievance that they had been left behind during the pay race of the 1970s, in Fleet Street as a whole but particularly at the *FT*. The machine room (or press room as it was also known) had been a neglected province of the Balkanized industrial-relations map, and in 1981, following a dispute between management and the machine minders, it was agreed at ACAS that the basis for future stability in the machine room lay in achieving, on the part of the company and the respective chapels, a 'joint press-room agreement'. Such an agreement was supposed to be negotiated within months, but by the autumn of 1982 it had still not been achieved. At this point management concluded a bilateral agreement with the assistants (SOGAT '82), who unlike the minders were willing to negotiate on a self-financing basis involving higher productivity and who were becoming increasingly exasperated by what they saw as the prevarication and shifting tactics of the minders. The minders regarded the agreement as a betrayal and after a winter of intensive negotiations, involving further charges and countercharges of bad faith, were still at odds with management, not to mention the assistants. By May 1983 they were demanding a weekly rate of £330, which the company was not prepared to concede. On the night of the 31st the presses stopped rolling.

The immediate expectation that it was a local dispute that would last only a few days was soon proved false. The process of escalation into a major set-piece strike took place with remarkable swiftness, triggered by three principal causes. One was the action of the NGA time-hands, who on 2 June took management by surprise by walking out in support of the machine minders. Here the long arm of new technology does seem to have played a part; with its introduction through the Linotype-Paul negotiations still possible, and indeed theoretically imminent, the time-hands wanted to ensure that they obtained a slice of that action. Their support for the minders may plausibly be interpreted as the *quid pro quo* of future negotiating support from the minders. The second 'trigger' was the decision of the NGA itself four days later, again to the surprise of *FT* management, to instruct all its members in St Clements Press (including the linotype operators) to withdraw their labour. Thirdly, there was the attitude of management and in particular Alan Hare, who almost from the outset seems to have been governed by two different levels of motivation. In house terms, he undoubtedly saw the behaviour of the twenty-four machine minders (only a third of whom were in regular employment at SCP) as outrageous, claiming an increase in one year of up to 24 per cent for working fewer hours. He was keenly conscious of the effects in the machine room on the much more numerous assistants, who would inevitably seek to restore the differential to the status quo ante, and he felt it was time that *FT* management took a stand against the whole upward spiral. Yet at another level he regarded the strike as one with far wider implications, not only for Fleet Street but for the nation at large, especially as it came in the middle of a general election campaign. On 3 June he wrote a letter to the party political leaders, the Secretary of State for Employment, the general secretary of the TUC and the chairman of the NPA, part of which read:

> The *Financial Times* is a non-political national newspaper. I think it must be common ground among all the main parties that it is undesirable that a national newspaper should be stopped by industrial action during a national election campaign. It is also highly regrettable that a British newspaper which has established a great influence on the Continent and in the rest of the world, and is facing a strong challenge to its position from the American *Wall Street Journal*, should be stopped at this time with all the overtones abroad that this conjures up about the malaise in British Industrial Relations.
>
> I think it should also be common ground that the enormous disproportion of damage which a union, such as the NGA, can inflict on a national newspaper at any time, by closing a newspaper by withdrawing a tiny proportion of its workforce, places an extra responsibility on the union or unions. Namely to

exercise their power moderately and sparingly by a strict adherence to freely negotiated agreements and a proper appreciation for the importance of the survival, efficiency and development of as many national newspapers with diversified views as possible.

Hare was due to retire the following April, and it is hard to resist the conclusion that he wished in his final year to win not just a local dispute but also that most dangerous of things, a principle.

With management for once not prepared to climb down, the NGA intransigent and highly disciplined (believing it held the aces) and the NPA its usual unhelpful self, the mould was soon set for a lengthy conflict. Over the ensuing two months, *FT* management tried or explored three main options in an attempt to emerge successfully from a dispute costing more than half a million pounds a week. The first was the well-trodden ACAS route, undercut from the start by the NGA's rejection of binding arbitration, which was against union policy. On 29 June the NGA agreed to an ACAS-appointed umpire making recommendations with a view to the securing of a press-room agreement between itself and the *FT* by 3 July. On the 3rd the umpire recommended that the comprehensive wage for the machine minders be £304 for a four-night week (as opposed to £270 for five nights during 1982). Four days later the NGA rejected the recommendation, to the dismay of the TUC's Len Murray, who on the 29th had expressed his confidence that the procedure would produce a settlement. Over the next few weeks Murray urged the NGA with increasing vehemence to accept the ACAS recommendation, but the union continued to insist that its pre-1983 pay differential of 19.5 per cent above the machine assistants' rate be restored. This was 7 per cent greater than the differential by now existing elsewhere in Fleet Street machine rooms. In the words of the general secretary of the NGA, Joe Wade, on 21 July: 'Our claim is justified and right. From the beginning of this dispute, the NGA has wished to negotiate a satisfactory settlement. This is still our aim. But we are not prepared to accept agreements made with other unions being unilaterally imposed on the NGA.'[13] The wheels of TUC indignation and wrath, however, ground slowly, so that it was not for another fortnight that the NGA faced the threat of expulsion, with Murray on 3 August due to travel to the union's headquarters in Bedford to make a last personal plea for acceptance of the ACAS formula. By then, however, events elsewhere in the dispute had moved decisively and made his initiative redundant.

The second main management thrust was the so-called 'SOGAT

option'. On 10 June, Hare wrote to the union's general secretary, Bill Keys, 'to ascertain from you what SOGAT '82 might be prepared to do to enable us to resume production of the *Financial Times* both in the UK and in Frankfurt'. Keys's immediate response is unclear, but on 20 June he received an anxious letter from the FOC of the 450-strong clerical chapel at the *FT*:

As far as it is possible to obtain a consensus view of our members, there is considerable resentment at the NGA action in stopping publication. In addition the NGA appear to be prepared to use the introduction of new technology to take over work presently done by our members and this attitude mitigates against inter-union co-operation.

We would welcome any assistance that you may be able to give in obtaining a resumption of publication and securing the jobs of all the SOGAT '82 members at the *Financial Times*.

Three days later Hare approached Keys again, this time with a major initiative designed to turn the *FT* into a high-tech, non-NGA house:

Our aim over the next few months would be a long-term new technology and production agreement which would secure the jobs of existing SOGAT '82 employees; and would offer considerable prospects for growth in employment as the *Financial Times* continued its expansion.

To do this, we would seek to conclude an equitable plant-wide wages and conditions agreement to cover all SOGAT '82 employees in our subsidiary company, SCP '83 (such agreement to embrace members of the EETPU and the AUEW).

SOGAT '82 possesses all the skills needed to produce the *Financial Times* somewhere in the UK, and my first interest is securing as many jobs as I can in this country. I have prepared a detailed plan phased over nine months, and I would like to discuss this with you. This plan in its interim phase would involve the distribution in this country of copies of the newspaper printed in Frankfurt.

The plan revealed that in its first phase, to start two days after union agreement, a sixteen-page paper (moving after about a month to twenty-four pages) would be written and edited in London as usual by NUJ staff; copy would be 'faxed' to Europe by a mixture of NUJ and SOGAT staff, cutting out the NGA; the setting and printing would be done entirely in Europe, probably in Frankfurt; and distribution in Britain of 150,000 air-freighted copies would be by the normal SOGAT-dominated channels. Phase two would start after about two months and last for some six to nine months, during which period the German-printed *FT* would be sent back to St Clements Press by full-page facsimile, and SCP would re-start using retrained SOGAT personnel. Finally, in phase three, the *FT* would be ready to bring back the typesetting of the London edition to SCP.

Did Hare think he had cracked it? Writing to James Lee at Pearson Longman on 7 July, he not unreasonably noted that, if the plan went into action, 'we must expect the NGA to attack us on every conceivable front with every conceivable weapon at their disposal'. What would be needed was 'a combination of TUC support and employer firmness'. He felt that most journalists would co-operate if SOGAT was seen to be committed to the plan. In sum: 'It is only feasible with SOGAT, the NUJ and the TUC all on board.' However, he went on:

The potential rewards are immense:
- Release from the grip of the NGA in months rather than decades.
- The advent of new technology within a year with all that means in terms of ability to develop our product and our markets.
- The achievement in 12 months of goals that Fleet Street has been seeking for 12 years.

Was it seriously believed that Keys would buy it? The NPA was highly sceptical (and indeed hostile) when the plan was outlined to it, with Hare vainly hoping for a degree of financial support to help meet the considerable early losses it would involve. Yet at least some of *FT* management seem to have had hopes, including the greatly experienced Cox. At the NPA on 28 June he said that 'when this situation started he was totally sceptical of SOGAT being able to do anything' and added: 'The fact was during the occasions they had met he was becoming more and more convinced that given the opportunity Keys would like to move down this path.' A week later, still hoping to get prospective support from his fellow publishers, Hare said 'he would hope to get some statement from Keys rather than a nod and a wink that this was a practical possibility SOGAT would go down this line'. On 11 June, four days after the NGA's repudiation of the ACAS solution, Hare formally put his detailed proposals to Keys, who replied two days later:

My worry about embracing the idea you are putting forward is that it would involve this Union in becoming the centre of a dispute that could escalate right through the national and provincial press.

I have to say that after careful consideration I do not believe that I could put at risk our members' livelihood right throughout the national and provincial press.

This point of view is shared by the senior officers of this Union.

A further point which disturbs me, and disturbs me greatly, if one was to embrace either phase one or phase two we could be held in defiance of the Bridlington Procedures of the TUC, and this could leave us open to exclusion from that body.

The plan was thus, in the words of the *The Times* reporting SOGAT's rejection, 'effectively squashed'.[14] Management thereafter did try to persuade Keys to allow SOGAT co-operation on producing a Frankfurt edition for European sale only, but on 29 July he ruled that out also, writing to Hare that 'your suggestion, in my view, will only lead to the dispute escalating'. As the *Economist* put it the next day, Keys was 'not a blackleg by nature and dreams one day of uniting with the NGA in a glorious federated association'.[15]

The final option was the most controversial in retrospect and for obvious reasons the least widely known about at the time. This was the entirely non-union approach, which began to take putative shape when talks, led by Lawrence and Miller, were held with T. Bailey Forman on 19 and 20 July. This was the Nottingham publishing firm that in the 1970s had made newspaper history in Britain by defeating the unions over the introduction of new technology. Managing director, *éminence grise* and notorious 'union basher' was the former naval officer Christopher Pole-Carew, subsequently to earn further fame as the inspiration for the erection of barbed wire outside the News International plant at Wapping. He now indicated his firm's willingness to take on the printing and (if necessary) the distribution of the *FT*, but stressed that he would win the ensuing conflict with the unions only if *FT* management was totally involved, committed and completely ruthless. He pointed out that over the years many companies had approached T. Bailey Forman for help in printing publications threatened by union action, but that almost without exception they had departed within a week or two.

Would the *FT* be the exception? Over the next ten days an intensive round of assessments, costings and projections took place. Almost all pointed in the same direction: the preparation was inadequate, the risks were too great, the benefits were too doubtful. The option would have involved the inevitable closure of Bracken House and the dispersal to other locations of journalists, advertising and support staff. It was highly unlikely that enough journalists would have stayed to produce a paper of the accustomed standard. Predicted circulation and advertising levels were both drastically reduced. A distribution system would probably have had to be started from scratch. Overall, a trading loss of between £10.5 million and £13 million was projected for the first full year of operation, falling in 1985 to between break-even and a loss of £5 million.

One way and another, it was not an enticing prospect. The final nail in the coffin of this third option probably arrived on about 1 August, when a group of *FT* executives went to see Pole-Carew. They were accompanied by Frank Barlow, who had emerged during the year and particularly the strike as a significant adviser to the paper. Pole-Carew was confident that he could perform the task, but Barlow was unconvinced. In the words of his report:

> Not one single doubt was uttered (by Pole-Carew) thoughout the entire meeting, perhaps suggesting insufficient appraisal of the technicalities of this project, lack of appreciation of the scale of the task and perhaps most important of all, complete naïvety of the 'trades union politics' of the proposal, thus preventing him from distinguishing between this and any other job he has undertaken.

The message was clear. The honour of the first great Fleet Street 'break out' was not to fall to the *FT*.

A day or two later, the paper's management went to the Millbank offices of Pearson and outlined the unpromising state of the various options, in particular the SOGAT and non-union ones. In the course of the subsequent discussion a common feeling emerged that there was little choice but to settle, in effect to sue for peace and live to fight another day. A dispirited Cox then, for once in his life, gave away more than was strictly necessary, so that the machine minders received £317 a week, £13 more than the ACAS recommendation. They were also to receive a further £6 a week when the joint press-room agreement was at last reached, which in theory was to be within a fortnight. The NGA accepted a differential with SOGAT of 12.5 per cent, having probably never expected to attain a higher one. What of the cost? At the time it was stated that the company had lost more than £10 million as a result of the strike, but a more accurate overall figure for the net loss would be £6 million, taking into account lost advertising revenue subsequently regained. Either way, it was a formidable amount.

The paper returned on 9 August, costing 5p more at 35p, and the main feature of the day was a notably objective account of the strike by the labour correspondent Philip Bassett. There was a shortfall of some 70,000 copies, and the next day the *FT* reprinted the article, in which Bassett argued that 'though essentially a traditional niggling row over differentials, the like of which Fleet Street has suffered for years, from the first day of the strike the *FT* management seemed tempted to invest it with a status it arguably did not warrant'. The *Daily Telegraph* on the 10th was still harsher, accusing the *FT* management of having 'acted with impetuosity': 'What might have been a little local difficulty, if handled differently, became an all-out confrontation with the National Graphical Association – the élite of the printing unions. To put it mildly, the NGA is nobody's pushover. But the *FT* decided to take the union on without any coherent idea of how success might be achieved.' It was true enough. There was no advance preparation, no fall-back position, no proto-Wapping down the road to use either as a stick or as an actual production centre. Instead, there was a naïve faith that ACAS, Murray and Keys would somehow deliver the goods, followed by a desperate and late approach to Pole-Carew. Lacking the size of operation to concentrate the minds of the unions, and the battle-hardened skills to play in the big league, the *FT* management was unequal to the situation it had done much to create. In a sense a member of the NPA Council said it all when, responding to Hare's request for help in pursuing the SOGAT option, he replied: 'We are willing to support when you get to the point where you are saying something to them that scares them. I don't think they are scared at present.'[16]

It was with a natural sense of relief that Bracken House returned to doing what it did best, producing a quality international newspaper. The 'benchmark' issue of Wednesday 26 October 1983 serves as a reminder of the sheer excellence, perhaps above all thoroughness, of a product that had been kept off the streets for the best part of a summer. It was, as it happened, a particularly interesting issue, because the dominant news of the day was the United States invasion of Grenada, thereby providing an unintentional test of the *FT*'s response to a major international, essentially non-economic story. By any standards it rose to the challenge. On the front page Reginald Dale reported from Washington and Peter Riddell from Westminster, while the paper's Barbados stringer, Tony Cozier, took up commentary from the Bridgetown end. Inside, in addition to parliamentary coverage and leader comment ('An ill-judged adventure'), most of a page was devoted to the story, with reports by Anthony Robinson on the Soviet reaction, Canute James in Kingston, Jamaica, on the participation of Caricom troops, and an informative piece by Andrew Whitley on the Grenadan background. Two other major non-economic stories were also prominent at this time, both of which the paper covered well: strategic missiles (with Cruise about to arrive); and the aftermath of the bombing of the US barracks in Beirut, with Patrick Cockburn on the spot. Otherwise, most of the coverage was economic, with the headline on one of the British pages, 'Lear Fan adds to aircraft manufacturing space', having a particular retrospective piquancy. The main feature was by one of an emerging group of young high-flyers, Anatole Kaletsky, who wrote from Rio about 'A battle of wills and wits' between Brazil and the IMF. On the opposite page David Churchill, consumer affairs correspondent, considered British consumer spending and 'The boom that refuses to die'; while next to him, and reflecting Owen's greater preference than that of Fisher for opening the pages to outside opinion, Roger Williams of Manchester University assessed the achievements of the UK Atomic Energy Authority (shortly to be thirty years old) and argued it was a case of 'Too high a price for too little return'. The back half of the paper was much the same as the 1978 version, though slightly more international in emphasis, with two less pages of British company news and one more of international companies and finance. In the interim there had also been some changes of nomenclature: 'Currency, Money and Gold Markets' was now 'Currencies, Money and Capital Markets', while 'Farming and Raw Materials' had become 'Commodities and Agriculture'. Still in the back half, but soon to move to the arts page and replace the theatre listings, were the TV and radio details, with a daily guide by Chris Dunkley. Main attraction of this day was coverage of the Booker Prize, and Dunkley committed himself to a prediction: 'Presenters of the programme are Simon Winchester and Selina Scott who cannot but make a better job of it than Russell Harty who was such an embarrassment last year.'

Despite its lengthy absence, the *FT* was named Newspaper of the Year for 1983 in the annual *What the Papers Say* awards. According to Granada Television's Gus MacDonald, it represented 'the entirely acceptable face of capitalism'.[17] Fortified by that vote of confidence, Owen early in 1984 gave an interview to the house magazine in which he sought to plot the future editorial direction of the paper and where his immediate priorities lay:

> We mustn't forget that people read us primarily for news. This means that our reputation as a comprehensive paper of record is very important. We mustn't miss things. But it also means that we have got to respond quickly and aggressively to important stories . . .
>
> A second point is the constant monitoring of quality control in all its various guises, ranging from the way a story is written, to the way it's sub-edited, to making sure unnecessary errors do not creep in. We must monitor that process as scrupulously and as rigorously as we can . . .
>
> Another continuing priority, where we've got a long way to go, is to improve our European perspective. Of course, we can't possibly neglect our UK readership, and our coverage of the UK is always going to be more detailed than any single country outside the UK. We still haven't mastered the task of looking

at subjects from a European point of view, whether it's financial, political, economic or social. So many issues are common to all the European countries that our various writers have got to be more prepared to make sure they've got access to European sources of information and look at things in that broader context . . .

I think the launch of the *Wall Street Journal* has certainly been good for us. In a number of areas it has provided a source of competition that previously didn't exist, particularly in European corporate and financial news. We're strong too in those areas, but we have to make sure that we stay ahead of them. And I think their news sense is good. They are ready to react to news rather well in one or two cases. We need to watch them carefully – not to be mesmerised by the *WSJ*.

Owen and his staff must have been doing something right. In July that year the former editor of *The Times*, Harold Evans, asked by the US media magazine *World Press Review* to name Britain's best paper, replied: 'The *Financial Times*. It is a paper of reason. It gives a more comprehensive view of the world than its American counterpart, the *Wall Street Journal*, does, and it is not so narrowly focused.'[18] And a year later the *World Press Review* itself named Owen as International Editor of the Year, an award given 'for his leadership in outstanding coverage and interpretation of international banking and debt problems, and other global concerns; for his newspaper's general excellence; and for his contribution to its international role'.[19]

Perhaps the most noticeable editorial progress during the two years after the strike was in the financial sphere. An important figure in this respect was Richard Lambert, who became deputy editor in the autumn of 1983 and whose experience on the financial side complemented Owen's natural thrust towards the industrial. Various new services emerged. In the area of money market funds, a daily table showing interest rates, annual equivalent rates, interest payment frequency and withdrawal notice required began in December 1983. Two months later, a new equities index was launched in the form of the *FT*–SE 100 Index, which was primarily the work of the Stock Exchange, but further gained in authority from having the *FT*'s name lent to it. The index was based on the minute-by-minute share price movements of 100 leading companies, and its primary purpose was to give to the futures and traded options markets a 'real-time' index on which to deal. The Thirty-Share Index was deemed unsuitable partly because it was unweighted and geometric, partly also because it was never intended to simulate a real portfolio of thirty shares; while the task of converting into real time the 747 share prices of the *FT*–Actuaries Indices was understandably deemed too daunting. The new index was generally reckoned a success on its introduction, though during its early years it has tended to underperform (by more than 6 per cent by December 1986) in comparison with the *FT*–Actuaries All-Share Index, a reflection partly of the better share-price performance of smaller companies. On the Euromarkets front, the monthly quotations and yields did not reappear after the strike, largely because the AIBD was by this time producing its own, much more up-to-date weekly list. From October 1984, however, the Monday coverage of the international capital markets was expanded by an extra page, with new features including an enlarged list of bond and warrant prices, supplied exclusively by the AIBD; more detailed coverage of the US money and credit markets; and, astonishingly for the first time, regular comment on the UK gilt-edged market. Finally, as a specific service, from May 1985 there was a notably expanded range of unit trust prices, reflecting the growth of offshore and money funds.

The mid-1980s were a time of profound financial change. The liberalization and internationalization of the markets, the rapid erosion of traditional barriers between different types of institutions, the growth of banking as an industry in its own right, the increasingly fierce battle for personal as well as institutional savings – these and many other developments meant that the *FT* had to ensure that the mechanism was in place to handle properly what was, taken as a whole, arguably *the* big story of the decade for the paper. By the end of 1984, under the auspices of Lambert, most of the right changes had been made. A particularly heavy responsibility fell to the financial editor Barry Riley, who over the next two years made a speciality of the intense, often dramatic run-up leading to the London Stock Exchange's 'Big Bang' of October 1986. There was also a conscious attempt at this time to give a harder focus to the UK companies pages, to give them a greater sense of overall direction. In Lambert's words: 'We would like to develop better co-ordination of our companies coverage, so that we can respond more rapidly and flexibly to new stories.' It was a hard task, especially granted that the pages retained their indispensable function as pages of record, but during the ensuing year or so some perceptible progress was made.

Also, for the first time since the days of Christopher Gwinner, a specific financial investigative brief was allotted, this time to Duncan Campbell-Smith, though he was to write features rather than news. In the course of 1984–5 he wrote some major pieces, including those on 'God's Banker' and the British Airways/Laker imbroglio, as well as the definitive article concerning Robert Maxwell and Lichtenstein. The *FT* remained, for a variety of long-standing reasons, a long way from being like the *Wall Street Journal* as an amply resourced paper of investigative journalism. The

British libel laws, costly of time as well as money, continued to discourage such an approach; it was never easy finding the right people to do this testing type of work; an innate distaste lingered for 'dignifying' financial wrongdoers by according their activities a lot of space; perhaps above all, the legacy of caution, founded by Bracken and passed down by Newton and Drogheda, still weighed heavily and was not to be easily cast aside. Increasingly, however, with the City changing fast in both working practices and ethical standards, the paper would find that it had no alternative but to reconcile itself to a type of journalism that it had rarely practised.

Moving out towards the larger British economic scene in these years, one prominent strand to the *FT*'s coverage was the June 1984 'Wrestling with recovery' series, a well-timed follow-up to 'Wrestling with recession' four years earlier and spotlighting several of the same companies. In a conscious effort to point up general lessons, the journalists writing the series posed the same questions to each senior company executive from the fourteen companies included. Owen himself wrote an upbeat introductory article, in which he argued that 'the shock administered by the recession has brought much-needed changes in attitudes and behaviour', thereby creating 'a good chance that Britain's new managers and entrepreneurs can maintain the momentum of industrial recovery'. Three months later, the paper ran a seven-part series of feature articles with the collective title 'The Selling of British Telecom', putting into a very full context – social and cultural as well as technical and financial – what may come to be seen as an epochal event.

The international coverage continued to develop under the foreign editorship of Colchester. By the end of 1984 there were (including stringers) 100 foreign reporters in the field, of whom the heart were the 30 staff correspondents abroad, second only to the *New York Times* (35 staffers) among English-language papers edited from one place. In some remarks at this time to the editorial department, Colchester set out his thoughts about the strategy, future as well as past, underpinning and justifying this formidable resource. He saw the principal aims as fourfold: to integrate the foreign coverage with the rest of the paper; to continue to provide consistent and continuous coverage of Europe and the United States; to increase coverage in the parts of the world developing fastest; and, last but not least, to consolidate 'the defence of the *FT*'s position as required reading for those investing or borrowing through the international capital market based upon London'. He went on:

The point about integration means that foreign coverage is not something that the

FT does rather nicely on the side but which isn't part of the editorial mainstream. The aim of the foreign department is to bring regional or country specialists to bear on every sectoral division of the home newspaper – economic, political, financial, industrial, management, etcetera. My ideal is a sort of matrix where almost any topic anywhere in the world could be attacked by at least two *FT* people – a homeside specialist who knows all about that sector or subject, and a regional or country expert who knows all about that place. In this respect we're actually ahead of the *Wall Street Journal* who, till recently, thought that coverage of the world motor industry was something that could be done by their Detroit correspondent.

Taken together with Owen's earlier remarks, it represented an internationalist strategy – as much an attitude of mind as a theoretical construct – well designed to take the *FT* into the last stretch of the twentieth century, comfortably ahead of the British competition and well up in the global field.

Moreover, by May 1985 a Saturday version of the paper fully worthy of the Monday-to-Friday staple at last existed. In 1983 an internal report recorded the generally sorry commercial history of the Saturday *FT* and examined, as part of an ongoing debate, the alternatives for the future. It was clear that something fundamental needed to be done: circulation was only marginally ahead of the weekday figures, with a readership that was lower and a social profile that was more 'C' and less 'B' than the weekday one, older, more female and in Britain more provincial; while in terms of advertising, Saturday revenue was some 30 per cent less than the weekday average, partly because of the greatly superior pull of the *Telegraph* in the financial sector and partly because consumer-directed advertising had never taken off, despite the quite marked consumer editorial emphasis from the time of the original 1967 revamp. Saturday obstinately remained a 'non-day' in the advertising industry, compared with lovely, leisurely Sunday. What was to be done? A Saturday colour magazine was seriously considered, but the feeling was that this was an overcrowded market and too high-risk an option. Instead, it was concluded that what was necessary was to make a *virtue* out of the special characteristics of the Saturday paper, as opposed to treating the whole thing as a mildly regrettable necessity.

There eventually emerged, on 4 May 1985, a Saturday paper in two separate sections: an orthodox 'news' section containing domestic and international news, leader pages and statistics; and a 'Weekend *FT*' under the editorship of J. D. F. Jones, designed to have a 'shelf life' of forty-eight hours and, in the words of its editor, aimed at the reader 'with his pullover on'. The basic admix of the weekend part was much the same as before – a blend of personal finance and leisure subjects – but it was assembled in a much more expansive and purposeful way, contained various new elements and generally had a more up-market feel. The first issue set the pattern for the future: on the front page, a substantial feature article (Colin Amery on London's Dockland) and below it Anthony Harris taking 'The Long View', an attempt in the Wincott tradition 'to treat the market as part of the economy, rather than a gambler's sideshows'; two pages on the week's markets; a run of four pages on personal finance, given the umbrella heading 'Finance and the Family', with *that* venerable column now called 'Brief Case'; and then, via property, moving into leisure for the last five pages, including two pages of 'Diversions', with 'How to Spend It' still prominent. A curious weakness was the absence of editorial matter to accompany the bare TV and radio listings: one would have thought that the reader with his pullover on would never have been far away from the insidious temptations of the remote control. In general, it was an impressive enough début package, handicapped only by restrictions by the unions on the Friday-night print run, resulting for several months in unsatisfied demand and no promotion.

There was, however, no more notable achievement in these years than the response to the year-long coal-miners' strike, which the *FT*'s labour team covered with such distinction that in a sense it was the culminating achievement of an area of excellence within the paper by now going back over thirty years. There was someone out on the coal-field almost throughout, thereby not only producing stories and contacts but also acting as a corrective to London-based thinking about the strike; the paper was first with some of the key developments, including the 'revolt' of the managers against the Coal Board; and John Lloyd, the industrial editor, was so acclaimed for his lucid, objective coverage that he was named both Journalist of the Year by *What the Papers Say* and Specialist Writer of the Year in the British Press Awards. Writing in the *New Statesman* on 8 March 1985, the former Labour MP Phillip Whitehead offered an interesting perspective:

> It is a minority view of the Left, but I believe the *FT* to be a first-class paper of its type. It gives more coverage to both sides of industry and their failings than any other paper, and can be unsparing with the faults of management. Since it is concerned with the health of capitalism this is not surprising. The kind of reader who buys the *FT* needs to know about lousy management. He also needs to know the real picture in industrial relations, not the kind of wild and unrealistic optimism which marks out the Rothermere and Murdoch papers. The sober

assessment of the end of the NUM strike in the *FT* on Monday was infinitely the best in Fleet Street.

The following year Lloyd became editor of the *New Statesman*, taking with him the accumulated authority of his nine years in Bracken House.

As for the *FT*'s editorial attitude during the strike, it was reasonably consistent, although not without some internal agonizing on the way. In March 1983 it had supported the appointment of Ian MacGregor to head the National Coal Board ('the new chairman will bring an understanding of the disciplines of the world market to the over-protected British coal industry') and thereafter it continued to back his policies, if not always his tactics or presentation. Some sympathy was shown towards the strikers as a whole. 'The fact is', a leader asserted in March 1984, 'that the mine-workers are battering themselves against a brick wall – not of National Coal Board and Government determination, but of the brute facts of the market and the effects of technical change, which together dictate a reduction in capacity and in the size of the workforce.' No sympathy, however, was extended to the miners' leader. An editorial the following month emphasized the political dimension to the dispute and that 'Mr Scargill has never pretended to be anything other than what he is – an old-fashioned left-wing militant, ambitious to deploy the power of the organised working class.'

Granted that and also the nature of the miners' pickets, there was, the *FT* concluded on 15 June, no alternative but that of 'Sitting out the strike', since 'for the Government and the Coal Board to give in now would be a total and unprincipled surrender to violence'. For Samuel Brittan, however, it was too soft a line, and in July he wrote an impassioned piece declaring that it was 'High time to fight back' against what he described as 'the use of violence and intimidation by a militant minority to terrorise fellow workers who do not wish to follow the lead of Arthur Scargill'. He also argued, in September, that 'if there is any industry which is crying out for decentralised workers' ownership it is coal mining', adding that 'Scargillism will not be made to go away by retaining the status quo.' As the strike dragged on through the winter, the *FT* increasingly took the line that 'what began as an industrial dispute is turning into a calamity for the left'; and at the end, in March 1985, it stated its belief that 'it is unlikely that there will be such a strike again in the foreseeable future, either by the miners or by any other large union'. MacGregor had won his opportunity 'to run the coal industry as a business', though typically the paper added that it had to be 'management by consent' if it was going to succeed in the long run. And that, the *FT* concluded, was 'as great a challenge as the defeat of Scargillism'.[20]

Towards the government's economic policy as a whole during the first two years of Mrs Thatcher's second term the prevailing attitude continued to be one of watchful and questioning support. There was certainly no enthusiasm for the economic alternative under Labour's new leader, Neil Kinnock. 'In a document entitled *A Future that Works*,' the paper asserted in September 1984, 'Britain's Socialists have served up a menu of policies that were not even considered credible by Labour politicians in the 1960s or 1970s and which certainly have no hope whatever of succeeding in the 1980s.' In March that year an enthusiastic welcome was accorded to Lawson's first Budget ('First stride of a tax reformer'), but by the spring of 1985 there was considerable disappointment that fiscal caution had become the order of the day, in the long as well as the short term.

Regarding privatization, by now moving centre stage in the government's programme, the *FT* consistently stressed that 'the introduction of competitive pressure to public sector enterprise is a far greater spur to efficiency than the act of privatisation' and that 'there is no merit in transforming a state-owned into a private monopoly'. Rather, the yardsticks for the worth or otherwise of privatization were 'the widening of consumer choice, removal of artificial barriers to entry, reduction of monopoly power (whether wielded by management or unions) and less politicisation of industrial decisions'.[21] There was as yet relatively little emphasis on the potential emergence through privatization of 'popular capitalism'.

Whatever the case for a privatized British Telecom, there was no escaping from the obstinate, unrelenting fact of mass unemployment, with all its profound social consequences. References to 'two nations' and 'the North–South divide' now became the stock-in-trade of leaders, as the paper developed various lines and approaches to treat the problem, though with diminishing conviction that it was in fact curable. Inevitably, it was hard to avoid a tendency to dart about from one would-be remedy to another. In March 1984 the emphasis was on tackling barriers of labour mobility, particularly in housing; in November there was a call for some infrastructural reflation; by February 1985 the prevailing needs were considered to be cutting non-wage labour costs, expanding schemes such as the Community Programme and improving work incentives for those receiving social security benefits; while by March, following Lawson's Budget, the new flavour of the month was the abolition of wages councils, which 'would send a powerful signal to all parts of the economy'. It was generally accepted, however, that the key lay in improving the workings of the labour market rather than in macroeconomic strategy, with little interest by this stage being evinced in the nostrums of monetarism, once so agenda-setting.

What else? Twice the *FT* quarrelled with the government over 'security' matters. 'A questionable proscription' was the title of the leader in January 1984 on the decision to ban the staff of GCHQ at Cheltenham from belonging to a union. Thirteen months later, when the jury in the Clive Ponting case 'accepted the defence that Mr Ponting's principal duty as a servant of the state was to the supremacy of Parliament rather than to an individual minister', the resulting acquittal was described as a 'welcome verdict'. The paper also argued in February 1985, reversing its line of five years earlier, that it was time to renege on Trident, there being 'no good case for stubbornly clinging to a commitment which is out of proportion to Britain's needs and financial reserves'. As for Ulster, the *FT* in April 1984 welcomed in advance the path-finding report of the New Ireland Forum, looked to 'a public commitment by Britain and Ireland to work together to resolve present problems' and called on Mrs Thatcher 'to make the Irish question a priority and to attach her personal authority to the search for a solution'. It ended with a surprising touch of rhetoric: 'She could do it. She could do it magnificently. It would be a tragedy if she were to walk away.'

Nearer to home base, there were certain causes of anxiety. The collapse of Johnson Matthey in the autumn of 1984 not only provoked 'a nagging worry about the whole process of bank auditing' but also raised the whole question of 'tighter control' on the supervisory part of the Bank of England; while the following January, the rash of take-over speculation on the London Stock Exchange was frankly described as 'not a healthy phenomenon' and all too liable to lead to 'bad corporate decisions'.[22] Towards the rapidly developing City 'revolution' as a whole, however, the *FT* was generally sanguine in its attitude, or at least aware that the pressures for change were too strong to be denied. The prevailing tone was set as early as November 1983, almost three years before 'Big Bang':

> The one thing that cannot be gainsaid is that mergers are happening and that these have important implications for the authorities. Conglomeration cannot take place in financial services without giving rise to new conflicts of interest, and as the boundaries break down further and foreigners take their place in an increasingly international market, the old formula of self-regulation becomes harder to operate since it depends heavily on a village concept in which the population is known to the Old Lady and other regulatory authorities.
>
> The Bank of England is aware of the dangers ... But in the long run a deregulated and more international environment in the securities markets can

only lead to some stiffening of the legal framework within which self-regulation takes place – as it already has in banking.

This is a price well worth paying if deregulation leads to a significant injection of outside capital and increased competition into the securities markets. There is at least a chance that financial institutions will become more sensitive to the needs of all participants, including the private investor.[23]

Freedom and responsibility: solving the conundrum would become more important than ever to the City of the 1980s.

On the wider stage, this was when years of budgetary wrangling between Britain and the rest of the EEC culminated in twelfth-hour *rapprochement* at Fontainebleau in June 1984. 'Time has come to settle it' was the title of the leader of the day of the meeting, with the paper accepting that 'there can be no denying that Mrs Thatcher's manner has caused profound antagonism, or that, despite Sir Geoffrey Howe's recent disclaimers to the contrary, the British Government has appeared to take a minimalist view of the Community'. Six months later, the *FT* had no doubt what should be the New Year's resolution for Europe's political leaders: 'that after a decade of stagnation and dissent, they will make a serious attempt to set the Community on a more dynamic course'. In particular, the hope was expressed that 'agreement can now coalesce on the proposition that the top priority for the future is the liberation of the internal market'. No one now questioned the sluggishness of Europe's recent economic performance, and in the summer of 1985 the paper ran a major series with the title 'Can Europe Catch Up?'

However, the *FT* through the 1980s was not greatly enamoured of apparently more virile Reaganomics. 'The President can be euphoric about the economic prospects so long as he declines to get to grips with the US $200 billion budget deficit', it noted sternly in January 1984 of the great communicator's State of the Union address. Or as it put it more idiomatically in November, the day before Reagan's re-election: 'In economic management, the administration has scored with what cricketers call a Chinese cut.' Nevertheless, whatever the future consequences of the budget deficit, the paper accepted, as in February 1985, that 'the prosperity and employment which the President's policies have generated are genuine'. Wholly sceptical was the attitude towards Reagan's strategic-cum-foreign policy, above all his 'Star Wars' project, enthusiastically though it was endorsed by the paper's science editor David Fishlock. According to a leader in January 1985, it was 'more likely to re-ignite the arms race, with all the attendant costs and dangers, than render it obsolete'. While as for supporting so-called 'freedom fighters' in Nicaragua, the *FT* tartly observed in April 1985, following the refusal of Congress to unblock funds, that 'it ill behoved the US Administration to be seen funding in public the overthrow of a government with which it has diplomatic relations'.

One issue of mounting concern on both sides of the Atlantic was what to do about the increasingly combustible situation in South Africa. While deeply opposed to apartheid, the paper continued to give Pretoria the semi-benefit of the doubt. 'Enlightened foreign investors must continue with their important contribution to reform', it asserted in February 1985; two months later, repeal of legislation banning mixed marriages suggested that the process of reform 'is under way'; and in June it was strongly argued that 'economic sanctions are not the best way to bring about change in South Africa', in that they would be 'perverse in their consequences', likely to damage the neighbouring black states and above all would 'fall upon a society in which change seems to be unfolding at a pace and in ways which are beyond that society's control'. The debate continued.

On Christmas Eve 1984 one of those big 'think-piece' leaders had appeared, seeking to transcend the local, perishable questions of the day and to elucidate some more lasting truths. Called 'Two prophets re-examined', it compared Orwell's *Nineteen Eighty-Four* and Huxley's *Brave New World* to the actuality of the 1980s and found that both prophets had misread the consequences of technology, having 'failed to see that as human existence becomes more complex, the ability of a central system to plan for its myriad desires becomes steadily more impractical': 'Above all, technology has recently created such a pace of economic change that governments find that they are less and less able to plan or control the impact that this change has upon their countries. There is a tide of economic liberalism running through Europe. Even in China the somewhat Orwellian system is cracking as free markets beckon.' Yet, as the final paragraphs made clear, there was a double-edged character to this technology-fuelled liberty:

> The electronic revolution has certainly made it easier to get in touch with each other. But curiously it has undermined proper human contact. It has allowed people to live more isolated lives, in which television provides them with a pale substitute for genuine community friendship.
>
> Huxley's book was about a romantic savage in revolt against the ordered perfection of the Brave New World. The savage was in search of the 'right to be unhappy, the right to have too little to eat, the right to live in constant apprehension of what may happen tomorrow'. We are still a long way from the luxury of such

a whim. There are many millions of Europeans for whom technology has delivered precisely these rights, along with unemployment, alienation and loneliness.

Europe's non-totalitarian governments are therefore forced to tread a dangerously narrow path between realism and lack of compassion. They are right neither to have, nor to foster, illusions that they can secure wealth and determine their people's employment under circumstances of such change. They equally have to be extremely careful to hold together that perception of common good which underpins the rule of law and prevents liberalism unravelling into anarchy.

Compassion, whose birth as a religious ideal is celebrated tomorrow, was absent from Orwell's and Huxley's future worlds, suppressed and replaced by fear in the one, and miraculously rendered obsolete in the other. In Europe, in the real 1984, compassion is not obsolete. It is a vital requirement of every section of society, including government, as our countries ride, rather than resist, waves of technological and economic change that are breaking up the established patterns of so many people's lives.

Toughness and tenderness: it was perhaps the nearest the *FT* could ever come to expressing its world view.

One section of European society notably reluctant to ride the waves of technological and economic change was the print unions in the basement of Bracken House. The 1983 strike had proved the Waterloo of the management old guard, and that autumn a new order was installed. In particular, Alan Hare effectively retired, followed soon afterwards from St Clements Press by Alan Cox. During an intensely difficult period of Fleet Street history, probably the most difficult ever, they had done much for the paper: maintaining better discipline and cohesion on the production side than in most houses; achieving, by the standards of the time, a high level of continuity of production; and keeping the *FT* roughly in the middle of the Fleet Street pay league, despite the nature of the paper requiring a sizeable number of phenomenally well-rewarded linotype operators. Indeed, in their swan-song year of 1983 the paper before the strike was heading for a record profit of more than £5 million. It was also to Hare's immense credit that he had not only backed the Frankfurt project but also strongly continued to do so during its early, much-criticized years. From a late-1980s perspective, the future of the *FT* would look very different and altogether less healthy if he had then precipitately abandoned Frankfurt. Yet it is probably true, as Owen wrote in his tribute, that Hare's most valuable contribution could not 'be measured in purely business terms'. Rather, it 'stemmed from his understanding of the newspaper's editorial objectives and his determination to maintain its quality and independence'.[24] With great integrity and dedication, Hare entirely fulfilled these abiding criteria.

The choice of his successor as chief executive marked a complete break with the patrician, paternalistic past. Frank Barlow, fifty-three years old when he came to the *FT*, was brought up in Barrow, Cumbria, and had spent most of his working life in newspapers. In the 1960s he had been with IPC, in West Africa, the West Indies, London and Ireland, where he had had overall responsibility for the set-up and operation of the Irish *Daily Mirror* and *Sunday Mirror*, the first national newspaper to use facsimile transmission and web-offset printing. In 1968 he had joined the Westminster Press, becoming general manager in 1976. His reputation in the defeatist newspaper management culture of the 1960s and 1970s was that of being almost a 'freak' – for being aggressive, for insisting that management should manage, for treating industrial relations as a power-play rather than as a mode of rational discourse. He was recognized as a tough operator who rarely fought a battle he could not win. He knew production intimately, and his early training as an accountant had given him an abiding appreciation of the importance of the bottom line, as well as a well-developed ability to control costs. In the particular context of 1983, with management credibility in tatters, it was an inspired choice (probably made by Gibson) to appoint him.

Deputy chief executive in the new regime was Richard McClean. He had come up on the advertising side of the paper during the 1970s, combining to a remarkably successful degree the old-style 'ambassadorial' and new-style 'facts-and-figures' approaches to the problem of selling space. The general manager, as well as chairman of SCP from the end of March 1984, was David Palmer, moving over (like Hunter in the 1950s) from the editorial side. Highly energetic and motivated, sometimes impetuous and with a rare ability to find himself in the middle of the action, he was well caught in one of the best phrases in Drogheda's memoirs: 'He can go as far as his defiant nature permits him.'[25] Also in the spring of 1984 Alan Hare was succeeded as chairman of the *FT* by Lord Blakenham, his son-in-law and chairman of Pearson since 1983. This chairmanship was a reversion to the earlier, 'hands-off' tradition of the position, and henceforth Blakenham chaired quarterly board meetings that concentrated on formal matters and major capital developments, while Barlow chaired the newspaper's monthly management board. The new chief executive's brief was to produce results. He was given a free hand and he now proceeded to make good use of it.

Above all this meant Barlow imposing his stamp on the production side. The obvious question in the autumn of 1983 was whether or not to press on in their entirety with the long-standing Linotype-Paul photocomposition plans. In an early interview with the Bracken House magazine, Barlow made it clear that he did not automatically view new technology as a panacea and that it all depended on matching the nature of the technology to the nature of the task:

> Photocomposition must be seen to yield a benefit to the company – a benefit in deadlines, or in profit, or something. But at present I can't see it; I can only see dis-benefits. I can see deadlines worsening; I can see the *FT* not getting out. I am very concerned because we publish such a complex newspaper. I can't think of any more complex setting job than the *Financial Times*, in the UK or US. No one involved in the discussions on photocomposition has been responsible for a change-over from hot metal to photocomposition. I have. The first time was 16 years ago, and I've experienced it four or five times since. There are innumerable problems . . . It's really the degree of the quality of the newspaper, and the *FT* is all about quality. That could suffer.

Not long afterwards, accordingly, the overall photocomposition negotiations, together with those concerning the buy-out of the piece scale, were put into abeyance.

However, all was not static in terms of new technology. Management embarked on a step-by-step process with the print unions, in which a number of concessions were achieved in a series of lengthy negotiations over the following two years, in return for a long-term commitment by the new management to bring the composing work being done in Frankfurt back to Bracken House. Also, following the purchase from System Integrators Inc. in 1983, the pilot project for an editorial word-processing international network, or 'Edwin' as it was popularly called, began to take shape in Frankfurt. By early 1984 there were fifteen screens, some of which were used by journalists in Frankfurt. The eventual idea remained a total communications system for the editorial department, enabling all *FT* journalists to write and communicate with each other on screen, thus attaining belated parity with their *Wall Street Journal* counterparts. Undoubtedly it was a form of preparation for the eventual era of direct input on the part of the journalists, but Barlow denied that the development should be regarded by the NGA as a kind of Trojan horse, arguing instead that Edwin had powerful and autonomous editorial advantages in its own right. This was true enough, but not unnaturally overlooked Edwin's other main role, developed from the initial 1982 concept, as a comprehensive editorial database. Options, in short, were being developed and thereafter kept open.

The perennial problems associated with the old technology did not go away. Barlow's initial strategy was consistent: to return the company to profit in the short term and therefore not to push conflict into all-out war, but at the same time to pursue a policy of allowing no *gains* to the unions through disruptive action and thus doing nothing to impair their already existing impression that he was a formidable opponent. In addition, there were to be no financial concessions without counter-concessions over working practices; there were to be no more secret deals; and management would honour written agreements in return for the unions observing dispute procedures. During his first two years as chief executive, there were lengthy disputes with various SCP groups. By far the most important was with the machine minders, who now engaged in a process of mutual testing with Barlow. The most acute phase occurred during the autumn of 1984, when in the course of six and a half weeks the *FT* lost some 2.3 million copies as the result of unofficial action; while taking 1984 as a whole, the company lost £3.2 million through the effect of shortfalls and industrial disruption. The production problems continued into 1985, so that by April management was publicly considering resorting to the courts against what Barlow called 'nihilistic and destructive industrial action', with a specific reference to repeated paper breaks and the breaking of printing plates.[26] All the time the joint press-room agreement, supposed to have been reached a fortnight after the end of the 1983 strike, remained the subject of attritional, unyielding negotiation. Moving into the second half of 1985 it was still uncertain, not only in Bracken House, whether the tide of Fleet Street history was to be reversed.

Barlow could afford to bide his time, in terms of both 'instant' new technology and his approach to the unions, because the general circumstances of the mid-1980s were highly propitious for a specialist financial and business paper. Not only were international capital markets flourishing, but so too were the stock markets of the world, with London well to the fore. In March 1984 the front page of the *FT* recorded the Thirty-Share Index at a record 901.4 'as Budget buying spree continues'; and the following January the index (in its fiftieth year) for the first time went through the 1,000 barrier, causing Bracken House electricians a hard day's work to install an extra digit on the window display. Circulation responded accordingly, reaching a record 229,423 copies per day for the first half of 1985. The bulk of the growth was in the UK, where sales by early 1985 were running at more than 176,000, at last going above the previous home peak of 1973. Overseas growth was steady rather than spectacular, and with the *Wall Street Journal*'s European circulation over half that of the *FT*'s European within a year of starting to print in Holland, it was already clear that a long-haul battle was in prospect. Despite the production problems, advertising also did extremely well. Indeed, in this area there was a notable production breakthrough in 1984, with the use for the first time of gravure colour, allowing 48-page papers with colour, four more than the previous maximum. The financial sector was especially strong, particularly from the spring of 1985. The bull market inspired not only a rash of flotations, and thus prospectuses, but also a phenomenal series of take-overs and mergers, resulting in many full-page 'defensive' as well as 'aggressive' advertisements, not all of a very pleasing character. As for profits, 1983 inevitably saw a loss (albeit small), but the 1984 figure of £7,389,000 was comfortably a record, as was the 1985 one of £12,036,000. Nevertheless, the profit-to-turnover figures for these two years, of 10 per cent and 14 per cent respectively, though much better than those of the early eighties, were still less than the post-1970 record of 18.6 per cent in 1972. Moreover, as Barlow himself pointed out in connection with the 1985 figures, the *FT* always had to remember that it was now competing, particularly abroad, with the *Wall Street Journal*, 'a newspaper whose profits are higher than our total revenue, and which is probably the most technologically advanced in the world'. It was a sobering thought, if by this time slightly less oppressive than it had been in the doom-laden days of 1982.

This mood of qualified optimism by the middle of the decade was accurately reflected by the development that took place on schedule at the beginning of July 1985. Six and a half years after the start of printing in Frankfurt, the *FT* now began to be printed on a third site, in New Jersey in the United States. It was a move that Barlow had anticipated in his in-house interview a year and a half earlier: 'I believe we need to print in America, just to improve our distribution system. We can hardly pretend that we can ever make any impact on the *Wall Street Journal* in America; their base market is so much bigger than ours. But we need to print in America to give a better service to our American readers and advertisers.' In a sense, there was little more to it than that: distribution by air freight from Frankfurt to New York had become increasingly unreliable, and also expensive, and the prospect of being able to expand internal distribution in North America by printing in the early evening and flying copies from Philadelphia airport had an obvious attraction. North American circulation had increased from 2,600 at the end of 1978 to 6,000 by the end of 1984, but it was reasonably felt that there was room for further improvement, which in turn would stimulate American advertising as the *FT*'s local profile rose. Although no other British paper had been transmitted overseas daily via satellite, the technology involved was well tried. It was, moreover, a relatively cheap project. The extra cost of printing and transmission was about £1 million a year, as was the capital cost, but against that some £400,000 a year was saved on air-freight charges. The pages transmitted to the Evergreen Printing and Publishing Company in Bellmawr were those of the Frankfurt edition, though omitting the two pages of Wall Street prices, which were regarded as coals to Newcastle. Indeed, the emphasis of the project throughout was on the distribution aspect – replacing an inefficient carrier with a more efficient one, namely facsimile transmission – and there was no thought at this stage of developing an American edition tailored to the US market. Nevertheless, there were the latent implications there. But also this coming of a second international printing site further confirmed that international cast of mind which, more than anything else, had emerged as the defining characteristic of the *FT* as a whole. Some 102 years after Harry Marks had returned from the United States to try out New World ideas in an English setting, the traffic was now two-way.

POSTSCRIPT: TOWARDS THE SECOND CENTURY

Exhaustive histories will come to be written about the 'newspaper revolution' of 1985–6 that, in the space of a few months, transformed the principles and practices of an entire industry. Here it is possible only to outline the key developments. It was a revolution that, from the point of view of Fleet Street as a whole, had at least fivefold origins. The profitable flotation of Reuters gave papers the cash to set in theoretical train by 1983 the removal of their production and distribution operations to 'greenfield' sites in the one-time Docklands area of East London. The trade union legislation of 1980 and 1982, as tested in 1983 by Eddy Shah's Warrington works, critically undermined the power of the NGA in particular to maintain its closed-shop control. The defeat of the coalminers had immense psychological repercussions. Three provincial papers or groups secured, during the winter of 1984–5, direct input on the part of their journalists. Fifthly, it was realized by the autumn of 1985 that the imminent launch of Shah's *Today* was more than a rumour and would involve, through the use of new technology, a drastic reduction of traditional labour costs.

It was against this background that Robert Maxwell, in the closing weeks of 1985, forced through at Mirror Newspapers a major redundancy programme that would have been unthinkable a year or two earlier. The truly seismic event, however, occurred in January 1986 when Rupert Murdoch, seemingly at a stroke and in defiance of the social consequences, transferred production of his national titles to 'Fortress Wapping'. Technology there was not only of the newest, but also put in the hands of the journalists and the electricians (the EETPU), with the traditional print unions firmly excluded. History is rarely so convenient, but the day that production began at Wapping was the day when, to all intents and purposes, old Fleet Street ended.

Over the following weeks and months, the pace of change did not let up. Most papers announced that they would shortly be moving their production to the Docklands, several (including the *Telegraph* and *Observer*) that their editorial offices would also be moving out of Fleet

Street. In October 1986, seven months after the start of *Today*, a new quality daily paper was launched, the first such since the First World War. This was the *Independent*, whose start-up costs of some £18 million were less than a third of those of the *Mail on Sunday* a few years earlier. The commercial potential of new technology, allied to the unaccustomed state of print unions weakened and forced on the defensive, appeared to be limitless.

By the autumn of 1986, however, some mildly sceptical voices were starting to be heard. One was that of the experienced Fleet Street watcher (and practitioner) Simon Jenkins, who argued in his book *The Market for Glory* not only that the basic structure of chapel power was still intact in most houses, but also that the prolonged and high-profile aftermath of Murdoch's Wapping *putsch* had given the print unions a vital 'breathing space' to, as he put it, 'win back negotiating leverage over new composing technology', even if they had to accept News International itself as a permanently lost cause.[1] There were some signs that they were succeeding. In July 1986 the managements of both the *Guardian* and the *Telegraph* dropped demands for legally binding collective agreements with the traditional print unions before transferring production to the Docklands. Two months later the *Telegraph* reached a comprehensive agreement with the unions which it described as a 'benchmark' for the rest of Fleet Street. It was undoubtedly far-reaching, including a no-disputes undertaking on the part of the unions, but some commentators detected lingering remnants of the 'bad' old days, including lack of management control and manning levels higher than strictly necessary.

However, no one by the end of 1986 would have denied that a revolution had taken place within the national newspaper industry, though the full extent of its long-term consequences was still unclear. The print unions might claw back some bargaining leverage, and much would depend on the political-cum-legal climate of the late 1980s and early 1990s, yet the balance of power had shifted. 'The gravy train has hit the buffers,' Maxwell informed the unions in a famous phrase.[2] It was a message they had often been told by Fleet Street managements, more in hope than expectation, but at last it seemed they had no alternative but to start to believe it.

Unlike in 1975, or even the early 1980s, the *FT* placed itself in the slipstream rather than the vanguard of developments elsewhere. This was largely a strategic decision on the part of the post-1983 management, but to some degree it was influenced by the fact that the *FT* had gained relatively little from the Reuters bonanza, having in 1968 downgraded its shareholding to that of a Sunday paper. Nevertheless, during 1985–6 momentous changes were under way at the *FT*, if in a rather less headline-catching way than in some other houses. Perhaps the key moment in redetermining Bracken House's balance of power occurred in October 1985 when, following a night in which half the paper's run was lost, the company secured an injunction against an NGA deputy FOC and took out writs for damages against eighteen of the twenty-six machine minders. At the same time, Barlow warned members of the NGA machine chapel that the company would use the law if they were not prepared to honour agreements. The threat worked, for production went smoothly for the rest of the year and then throughout 1986 as well.

Against this background of more stable industrial relations, a complicated, fourfold agreement, the outcome of more than two years of negotiations, was reached in March 1986. Composing work in Frankfurt was to be returned to London, meaning new work and more pay for the print unions; the setting of all regular statistics in the paper was to be, over a period of time, by direct entry – in many cases directly from computer to computer and thus markedly improving their accuracy; the prices operation was to be carried out by a newly created separate company, which would be housed outside Bracken House, manned by SOGAT staff and covered by a strike-free agreement featuring binding arbitration, thereby ensuring continuity of production and that, with the prices on line, non-newspaper markets could be properly exploited; and finally, a joint press-room agreement was at last arrived at, to run for two years and designed, for that period of time, to eliminate inter-union pay leapfrogging in the machine room. Altogether the package represented, in the words of Barlow at the time, 'a substantial step on the road to the electronic future that the newspaper has to embrace'.[3]

In an equally substantial step, agreement had already been reached, in February 1986, between management and the journalists, over the introduction into Bracken House of an extensive screen-based editorial system, alias 'Edwin'. There was still no explicit provision for the direct input of copy by journalists, but the strategy (different from that of other papers in Fleet Street) was to bring the new technology into play on the editorial floor without reference to the NGA, familiarize the journalists with it and thereby, because of the way the system had been customized, with typesetting procedures also, then go the whole hog when the time was deemed ripe.

Finally, there were significant capacity improvements. In the autumn of 1985 management had broken through the maximum number of sixth-unit working of the presses allowed in a year, with no effective riposte from the unions. A by-product of the press-room agreement was to allow up to 300,000 copies of the Saturday paper to be printed. And from the spring of 1986 the practice of having the larger surveys pre-printed began, thus enabling the pagination on any one day to go above the long-standing maximum of forty-eight. The markets were still strong, the financial world was buzzing, and at last the *FT* was in a position to take, by its own standards, full advantage.

In any normal time of newspaper history this would have been enough for most managements – but these were not normal times. On 9 July 1986, following several months of rumour, the paper announced a radical plan designed to take its production into the late twentieth century and beyond. Barlow, in his introductory speech to staff, spelled out 'Why we have to change':

> When Rupert Murdoch went to Wapping, he established a completely new and much lower competitive base to the one that he had been operating from in Fleet Street. His costs came down, I estimate, by £80 million per annum. His flexibility of operation magnified overnight. He now enjoys a huge cost advantage over the *FT*. Murdoch now has the ability – the financial ability – to reduce his advertisement rates, to reduce his cover price, to increase his promotional spend, or a combination of all three. The *FT* is extremely vulnerable.
>
> It is not Murdoch we have to worry about. The *Telegraph*, the *Guardian*, the *Independent* – all of them will soon be operating with far lower costs than we do at the moment. And don't forget the *Wall Street Journal*, one of the richest and one of the most technologically advanced newspapers in the world. Every day of every week of the year, we are engaged in a toe-to-toe slugging match with the *Wall Street Journal* in continental Europe. This is one of those heavyweight title fights run by the old rules. They don't stop after 15 rounds. You just go on fighting until somebody is knocked out.
>
> The truth is, both here in the UK and overseas, there is no future for us if we don't accept change. We need the same lower cost base as our competitors, we need the same potential for reduced advertising rates, for lower cover prices, for greater promotional spend and for developing the newspaper in the way that new technology is allowing our competitors. If we don't change, then we run the risk eventually of being overwhelmed by Murdoch; by the *Wall Street Journal*; and by new competitors who will come into the market if they see the *FT* floundering.

Would the *FT* have opted for fundamental change if Wapping had not happened? Almost certainly it would have – bearing in mind the long-term production objectives formulated in 1982 and the already changing balance of industrial power by 1985. But undoubtedly, as with other houses, the fact of Wapping accelerated the process. Not only was there the unwelcome existence, almost overnight, of Murdoch's new cost base, but also the print unions appeared weaker and more vulnerable than at any time in living memory: the pressures for change were wellnigh irresistible.

The plan outlined in July 1986 took three main forms. First, from 1 January 1988 the *FT* would become a fully front-end newspaper, with copy set directly by editorial and advertising staff on the 'Edwin' word-processing system, as opposed to being set by printers on hot-metal linotype machines. Second, in July 1988 the printing and publishing operation would move to a new £33 million plant sited in the Docklands and housing two lines of seven-unit web-offset presses, providing higher quality, greater use of colour and increased output of up to 25 to 30 per cent. Third, and perhaps most radical in terms of Fleet Street's negotiable plans and the history of chapel power, it was envisaged that in the new plant the existing twenty-five bargaining units would be reduced to only three (pre-press, press and publishing, and maintenance and services); the multiplicity of pay scales be cut to six; and traditional union and work-based demarcation lines would be replaced by the introduction of full work flexibility. Moreover, in the uncompromising words of the plan: 'There will be no casual employment of any kind at any time in any production operation at the *FT* after July 1988.'

What did it mean in terms of redundancies? According to the 1986 figures, no fewer than 386 redundancies would be required from the existing 639 workers employed on the production side and 18 from the *FT*'s editorial and administrative assistants' department. Most fell in the composing area, by virtue of technological change, but also the opportunity was being taken to end the traditional overmanning in the machine room and warehouse. In order to achieve these voluntary redundancies – billed from the start as central to the feasibility of the plan – the company offered a £22 million package of severance payments and pension increases as well as extensive provisions on redeployment and retraining for those made redundant. The last word at this stage went to Barlow: 'I do not intend to do a Wapping. I intend to do the very opposite of a Wapping. I intend to do an anti-Wapping.'

Would it stick? The *Daily Telegraph* the next day thought it would, offering the headline on its City page 'Change of scene should put the *FT* in the pink' and commenting that Pearson could now expect to 'unlock the goldmine of the *FT*', with the prospect of not only much reduced labour costs, but also '56-page papers, run-of-print colour if necessary, multi-spot colour to enliven the charts and graphs and even more frequent surveys'. In the *FT* itself the labour writers Philip Bassett and Helen

Hague explicitly accepted the validity of management's reasoning: 'It believes the unions will accept the inevitability of change – especially when cushioned with an attractive severance package – and is probably right to do so. The new leadership of the print unions *are* much more pragmatic than some of their predecessors. They know the Fleet Street tide cannot be stopped.' The compensation offered was attractive, especially the pensions aspect in comparison with what had been offered a decade earlier. Also, as several commentators noted, it was a sign of changing times that the paper itself appeared the day after management had proposed cutting the production work-force by some 63 per cent; a year or two earlier there would have been 'no *FT*'. It was also widely accepted that this time round, unlike in 1975 or 1983, *FT* management would have a fall-back position, an alternative production strategy ready and waiting to adopt, if negotiations failed.

If doubts lingered about the viability of the 1986 plan, despite the confident air and high professionalism with which it was presented, they took three main forms. One was the larger question, impossible to predict with certainty, of whether the prevailing political and legal climate might change, thus enabling chapel power in general to reassert itself. Secondly, there existed a certain feeling that *FT* management was possibly playing it too long for its own good, with an inherent danger that, as in the mid-1970s, the momentum for change would be reduced or even lost. However, it was a fair point that major and complicated matters needed to be negotiated, involving not only substantial redundancies but also fundamental changes to working practices. The third doubt raised the whole 'cultural' question: granted that management had been bemoaning the pernicious and ubiquitous effects of Fleet Street culture for at least four years, and the need to make a clean break with it, was it not a mistake to go with the rest of the pack to the Docklands, instead of sticking to the original decision to build a plant to the west of London near the M25? The reason given, perfectly logical in its own terms, was that a Docklands base allowed collective distribution, cheaper and more fail-safe, and also kept open the rail or road option. Moreover, when in December 1986 the exact location for the new plant was announced, it was clear that the *FT*'s production force would be physically well away from that of other houses, thus reducing the chances of being involved in any cultural transplant. The chosen site was in the East India Dock area, on the corner of the junction between the A13 and the eastern side of the Blackwall Tunnel northern approach road. The architectural feature of the new plant was to be a glass wall, through which travellers at night would see the 'heroic vista' of a line of double-width offset presses, about 100 metres long, printing the *FT*. It was an appropriate vision for a paper whose historical roots peculiarly lay in the printing industry.

Management's bullishness during 1986 was amply justified by the commercial success now being enjoyed by the paper. Circulation during the second half of the year was running at a record 254,236. This represented an 8.8 per cent increase on the figure for the same period the previous year, more than twice the increase of any other daily paper, most of which were losing sales. The component parts of that 254,236 also featured records: UK sales were 189,748, US sales 11,020 and sales out of Frankfurt 49,902 (almost twice the figure of the *Wall Street Journal* for the same area); the remaining 3,566 were overseas sales printed in London. Altogether, 25.4 per cent of the *FT*'s total sales were now overseas, compared with 14.2 per cent in 1978. A rising proportion out of a rising overall total: eight years later, it was eloquent testimony to the Frankfurt venture. The advertising figures were similarly flourishing. The total columnage for 1986 was 52,748, which was easily a record and for the first time included over a thousand columns of 'Frankfurt only' advertising. Further helped by continuous production (only £200,000 lost in disputes and shortfalls), the newspaper's profit for 1986 was handsome indeed: a record £22.5 million, itself representing a post-1970 record of 21 per cent to turnover. In a period of intense financial activity, with London at the centre of much of it, clearly the *FT* was in the happy position of being the right product at the right time. But if the circumstances were advantageous, in terms of both the City and the newspaper industry at large, it needed a clear-sighted, tough-minded management approach to maximize them to the paper's benefit. This the regime under Barlow had provided since 1983, and the remarkable results of 1986 were its vindication.

Meanwhile, what of the *FT* itself, as an editorial product, as it approached the close of its first century? The daily quota of fact, analysis and statistics continued much as usual – a formidable armoury all too easy to take for granted – but various themes or aspects stood out during the paper's ninety-eighth and ninety-ninth years. One was the continuing internationalization of approach, particularly in the spheres of industry and commerce, highlighted by the appointment in 1986 of Guy de Jonquieres as the paper's first international business editor. Two main features in December 1986 epitomized the approach, one by de Jonquieres on privatization in Europe, the other by Christopher Lorenz on transatlantic take-overs. Increasingly this was the terrain that the *FT* sought to make unquestionably its own.

On the foreign pages as such, there were many occasions when the range of correspondents and accompanying expertise at the paper's disposal resulted in exemplary coverage. A classic example was the United States raid on Libya in April 1986; stories were filed from Washington, Tripoli, Moscow, Paris, Abu Dhabi and New Delhi. Also on the news pages, Peter Riddell, Robert Mauthner and Bridget Bloom wrote about the British involvement in and reaction to the attack, Robert Graham and Quentin Peel narrated the build-up to the US response, A. H. Hermann considered the legal implications, and Leslie Colitt in East Europe elucidated the claimed Libyan involvement in a West Berlin night-club blast. On the centre pages, in addition to leader comment, Roger Matthews assessed the likely response of the Arab world, David Lennon provided a full historical profile of Gadaffi, and Reginald Dale described how 'Reagan bids goodbye to the Vietnam syndrome'. It is hard to believe that any other paper could have equalled either the depth or the breadth of the coverage. A less momentous example also showed the *FT* at its international best. This was in June 1986 when, following Mrs Thatcher's decision to appoint Richard Branson to head a campaign to clean up the environment, the paper devoted the best part of a page to a series of briefings from ten of its foreign correspondents about city cleanliness round the world, putting the British problem into due perspective. The most telling touch came from Lynne Richardson in Tel Aviv, which a favourably impressed Prime Minister had just been visiting. In her report she pointed out that municipal labourers 'had toiled for days to spruce up the city centre and a small fortune, by local standards, had been spent on flowers for the occasion'. In the words of the headline: 'Mrs Thatcher might have guessed'.

One of Owen's principal concerns by the mid-1980s was that, in the process of further developing its international character, the paper did not start to neglect its 'back yard'. On a day-to-day basis the domestic news pages were not always the most sparkling in the *FT*, but on the whole the fear was not realized. Indeed, early in 1986, in his annual progress report to the staff, Owen expressed his belief 'that the recent growth in circulation reflects in part the excellence of our domestic political, economic and business coverage'. He referred with justifiable pride to 'exclusive stories like Ford's negotiations to buy Austin Rover and our in-depth reporting on Rupert Murdoch's move to Wapping, the Westland Helicopter battle and its consequences, and the crisis in the tin market'.

By the middle of the decade particularly interesting developments were taking place in the paper's labour coverage. There continued to be a labour page, and the *FT* was almost alone in refraining from adopting a dismissive tone towards the unions, but in an increasingly strike-free, non-unionized context the nature of the coverage began to alter. Philip Bassett, in an article in the *New Statesman* in September 1986, described the change: 'Apart from the 1984–85 miners' strike, the *FT* labour page has, for the last few years, largely been about agreements, new industrial relations practices, new ways of working, not – as it was, say, five years ago – mostly about strikes over pay.' Bassett then outlined what he saw as the future of his craft:

> Partly in order to survive and thrive, partly in order to reflect properly the real pattern of the world of work, labour journalism, especially at the quality end of the business, will have to write about industrial relations much more widely: about unemployment; about employment as a whole – how it's changing, who the new workers are, where they are, what they do, how they do it; about redundancy patterns, about job content, about the impact of computer technology, about personnel thinking, about *management* as much as about *labour*.[4]

The keynote phrase was 'the world of work', for two months earlier the *FT* had put down a marker for this type of future coverage in the form of a superb 24-page special report entitled 'Work: The Way Ahead'. It was written mainly by John Lloyd and Charles Leadbeater, included contributions from Ralf Dahrendorf, Richard Layard and Martin Weitzman as well as Samuel Brittan, and on the basis of an analysis of the six biggest market economies tried to predict what the future of work was in the Western world. The report garnered only six pages of advertising, well down on the usual ratio for surveys, but as a *succès d'estime* it could hardly have been bettered.

In the year of 'Big Bang' the paper's financial coverage continued to expand. In January 1986 a fourth page was added to the 'International Company News' section, concentrating mainly on international capital markets. There was also improved coverage of financial futures and options markets, as well as in the burgeoning field of international equities. In September, reflecting the reality of global trading, the launch was announced for the following year of the *FT*–Actuaries World Share Index, covering the shares of about 2,000 companies from twenty-four countries and to be calculated daily after the close of the US stock markets. Its primary purpose would be to provide a benchmark against which the performance of international investment managers could be judged, but it was also intended to serve as an indicator of the health of the world's capitalist economies. 'Big Bang' itself occurred on Monday 27 October 1986, and the *FT* marked the event with a comprehensive, splendidly produced 48-page survey on 'The City Revolution', which, in conjunction with the main body of the paper, produced the biggest UK

FINANCIAL TIMES SURVEY

Monday October 27 1986

This survey is an integral part of the Financial Times and is not for sale separately.

THE CITY REVOLUTION

Today's Big Bang changes the London securities market irrevocably. The prize within the City's grasp is the leading position in the European time zone in a seamless market extending around the world.

NOBODY HAS ever come forward to claim the credit for coining the phrase "Big Bang," perhaps because it is an inelegant way of describing the process of deregulation. But it has stuck, because although there have been several intermediate "little bangs" since the Stock Exchange embarked upon the path of rapid reform some three years ago, it is the dramatic structural changes scheduled for October 27, 1986, which have always captured the imagination.

Yet since the historic Parkinson-Goodison deal in July 1983, and the realisation soon afterwards that the structure of the market would have to be transformed, the perception of Big Bang has subtly changed.

Originally the debate was about the need to bring competition into the Stock Exchange, with the focus on its scales of fixed minimum commissions. But more recently the emphasis has been on the scope for London to capture a leading role in the burgeoning global securities market.

That change of emphasis has had a tremendous impact. Only a few years ago the Stock Exchange was fiercely resisting the attempts by the Government to interfere in its rule-book. It regarded itself as a private club.

Now, however, the exchange has thrown its membership lists open to the world. Even more astonishingly, it has agreed to merge with Isro, a body representing the once distrusted Eurobond houses, because it sees that as being the only way to ensure that the exchange is plugged securely into the global securities market network.

The prize for London is the leading position in the European time zone in a seamless market that swings from Tokyo and other far eastern centres in the morning through Europe and on to New York. This market is well established in US Treasury bonds, and is becoming important for several hundred leading equities of international grade.

If London can capture the secondary market, then it will also be well-placed to attract the fees, commissions and trading profits that go with primary market financing.

London has already gained a leading time-zone position in the banking markets, of course. But these are hard times for international bankers, with few new creditworthy customers to be found, and many old ones on the sick list.

In pitching for the international securities business, London has the advantages of the native English language, a sophisticated cultural environment and good (and relatively cheap) international telecommunications. Such attributes keep the Americans, and a good many others, happy.

But in truth, there is really no contest. Apart from Amsterdam, which suffers from having too small a domestic base, continental centres have hardly been in the picture.

This is partly because they are often constrained by internal rigidities. More fundamentally, however, the idea of a free-wheeling financial centre is not to continental tastes.

Continental financial markets have been constrained to serve industry or finance governments, and tight regulation has been part of this framework. The idea that a financial centre could be a self-standing economic unit, creating jobs and earning foreign exchange, is not widely shared: rightly or wrongly, the dangers of conflict are seen to be great.

Nevertheless, the impact of London is causing significant changes in continental attitudes, as London securities firms attract substantial volumes of business in European equities, especially those of Germany and Scandinavia. Longer trading hours and new bourse structures are being introduced in several countries.

The City of London has still to face the possible political backlash from its current success. But already New York-style salaries, and the sucking of scarce talent from its ailing economic hinterland, have created respectively outrage and distress, not to mention envy.

A future Labour government would be unlikely to reimpose foreign exchange controls in a way that would seriously cramp the City's style, but it might well impose income taxes at 70 or 80 per cent. At a time when the top US domestic income tax rate is being cut to 28 per cent, that might be an effective way of curbing the City's ambitions by causing a brain drain.

Arguably, however, the City of London is giving the rest of the sluggish British economy some lessons in adaptability, innovation and sheer hard work and commitment. The lifestyle of securities market practitioners is much more like that of Americans than of traditional British professionals.

For example, citizens of the Surrey stockbroker belt town of Haslemere have just prevailed on British Rail to schedule a new train, the 6.44 to Waterloo, because the 7.18 already timetabled was not early enough. Previously, such trains were reserved for cleaners and security guards rather than City stockbrokers.

In this respect, the securities markets are following in the footsteps of the credit and foreign exchange markets, which have long been in the habit of opening at 8 am. This is because the continent of Europe, inconveniently, sets its clocks an hour ahead of the UK.

Readiness to embrace rapid change is also reflected in the huge quantities of the very latest technology that have been installed in the trading rooms of the Square Mile in the past few months. Brokers and traders, used to working with equipment no more complex than a telephone and a dealing book, have had to come to terms with banks of screens and a wide selection of databases and communications devices.

It has to be said that the flexibility shown by securities market practitioners has only been forthcoming by virtue of enormous financial incentives. In the process, the cost base of the securities markets has been raised sharply, to the extent that only large increases in the volume of trading can justify all the investment.

Nervous markets, in both gilt-edged and equities, ahead of Big Bang have prompted fears that the long bull market may be ending, and that a bear phase could put added pressure on the top-heavy structure. Certainly, a great deal will depend on the degree of flexibility that London's new securities firms have been able to build into their remuneration.

And there are bound to be major reshuffles of people over the next year or two, as the 1,000-or-so ex-partners, now locked in by "golden handcuff" arrangements, regain their freedom to seek more congenial positions with other firms—or perhaps to retire to the country.

At the same time, the continuing boom in the Euromarkets—which has nothing to do with Big Bang—is a reminder that international opportunities exist which could more than make up for any setbacks in London's domestic markets.

Yet there is real concern that the open-door policy, which has encouraged banks and securities groups from all around the world to seize opportunities rarely available elsewhere, has generated far too much capacity in London. Such over-capacity will be self-correcting, but the process could be extremely uncomfortable.

Meanwhile, in London, and around the world, securities market regulators are struggling to keep up with the pace of events. The next few years could bring severe problems for the supervisory agencies, not least in the UK where self-regulatory traditions now have to be made relevant to the problem of controlling the activities of global financial conglomerates.

It would scarcely be surprising if deregulation were to be followed by at least partial re-regulation. But the technology-driven advance towards an international market place is so strong that it is impossible to see the old barriers being reinstated.

Today's Big Bang is far from being an isolated phenomenon: it follows a series of other changes, and there will be further important developments in the future, including the merger with Isro and the progressive introduction of computerised auto-execution for small bargains.

But Big Bang is the event which guarantees that nothing in the London securities markets will ever be quite the same again.

Barry Riley
Financial Editor

IN THIS SURVEY

27 October 1986: the 'Big Bang' survey

daily newspaper edition ever, a record ninety-six pages. 'The prize for London', Barry Riley wrote in his introductory piece to the survey, 'is the leading position in the European time zone in a seamless market that swings from Tokyo and other far eastern centres in the morning through Europe and on to New York.'

Yet by the autumn of 1986 there remained gaps in the *FT*'s financial coverage. There was still a lack of market reporters for some of the major securities markets abroad, particularly Tokyo. The response to change was still insufficiently swift; one would, for example, probably not have realized from the paper's daily coverage that by this time the biggest area of growth in the debt market was the securization of debt, greater on an annual basis than US Treasury issues. An increasing technical problem was the difficulty of writing about continuous trading done mainly on screens far away from trading floors. The personal dimension remained unsatisfactory; it should have been the *FT*, not the *Daily Telegraph*, that provided a proper obituary in October of Julius Strauss, a prominent international financier for more than half a century and one of the founders of the Eurobond market, including the term itself. Perhaps most importantly, a certain weakness persisted in the sphere of *international* monetary affairs and policy, typified by rather disjointed IMF coverage. This is not to deny that in general much progress had been made since the 1970s. It had. But moving towards the late 1980s, with the pace of financial change declining to abate, nothing could be taken for granted.

Underpinning the daily staple fare – essentially that of a specialist paper with wide interests – was a broadly consistent editorial 'world view'. It was an outlook that embodied the belief, not always justified, that human beings are rational and guided by rational considerations. It eschewed ideology, whether of other people or self-made, and to almost every situation applied fundamentally pragmatic criteria. In more specifically economic terms, what this outlook usually entailed by the mid-1980s was a strong preference for allowing markets to work, with an accompanying dislike of price and exchange controls, a profound belief in the virtues of competition and a continuing scepticism about old-fashioned Keynesian notions of spending one's way back to full employment.

During 1986 there were several emotionally and politically charged episodes that showed this market-oriented side of the *FT* at its most 'dry'. Early in the year the board and shareholders of the Westland Helicopter Company, faced by rival US and European offers, were advised to make their decision strictly 'on a commercial basis', with the paper warning that 'if the politicians in the UK and Europe want to make Westland a protected species, barred from shareholding links with the US, they should do so openly and clearly'.[5] A few weeks later the question of the proposed sale to General Motors of the Land-Rover business arose. 'Patriotism is not the issue,' declared the *FT* in one leader, while arguing in another that 'the danger is that, in responding to strong political pressure to keep BL British, the Government may take the wrong industrial decisions'.[6] Political pressure duly carried the day, and in a stern leader on 25 March ('Irresolute approach') the paper stated its view that it was 'quite absurd' that 'the best guarantee of continuity, development and indeed local content' should be lost 'because of an outburst of jingoism on the part of a handful of backbenchers'. In August 'A bad decision in Cornwall' was the title of the editorial about the government's decision to rescue the Cornish tin-mining industry in the wake of the collapse of the international tin agreement: 'Britain may be engaging in yet another of those subsidy races, which are always futile in the end.' Finally, in a year of such decisions, there was the government's choice in December between the GEC and Boeing airborne early-warning systems. The *FT*'s advice was clear: 'Ministers have to weigh up for themselves the central issues of cost and technical performance; if those considerations point decisively in the favour of the US option, they should not be afraid to choose it.' This time the government overrode the political storm, and the *FT* sought to console the losing side: 'The company will simply have to work harder to win new orders and put the bad publicity behind it.'

As for economic policy as a whole, the paper consistently supported such supply-side measures on the part of the Thatcher government as employment legislation, tax reforms and privatization (provided that meant increased competition) – all of which, it was believed, would have a beneficial effect on the economy and therefore ultimately on the reduction of unemployment. Indeed, in an area like housing policy, especially concerning the rented sector, the *FT* would have preferred much greater 'radicalism' on the government's part. Supply-side measures were not, however, at least by the mid-1980s, regarded as the whole of the story. Thus in February 1986, looking ahead to the Budget, the paper argued that the priority was the reduction of long-term unemployment and that, in order to achieve something tangible in this respect, it was time for 'an unaccustomed touch of iconoclasm from the Government and the abandoning of some prejudices', including 'its distaste for direct employment subsidies for companies', its dislike of subsidized public works and its belief 'that public sector employment is invariably bad'. If the government changed tack to this extent, along the lines already recommended by the Commons Employment Select Committee and the Employment Institute, 'there is a sporting chance they would create nearly

750,000 jobs: enough to break the back of the long-term unemployment problem'. The cost of such schemes, over a three-year period, would be about £3.5 billion – 'well within the expected scope for tax cuts over this horizon'.[7] It was a significantly different approach to that of the *Wall Street Journal*, which three days later rebuked the *FT* for having 'editorialised in favour of more government subsidies for jobs programmes and public works projects, back to the Keynesian programme of spending one's way out of the problem'. According to the *Journal*, 'it has not yet dawned on Britain's leaders that those countries with the low rates of unemployment also, not so coincidentally, have lower tax rates'.[8] There was some unfairness in the criticism; the *FT* was not seeking to return through Keynesian methods to *full* employment. But the implicit broader charge was true: there was an intellectual incompatibility between the overall disciplines of the market and the particular expediencies of non-market palliatives.

Other domestic issues during 1985–6 provoked characteristic tones and responses. In November 1985 the Anglo-Irish Agreement was welcomed as 'a civilised acknowledgement that the two governments most affected by the Irish troubles should work together to resolve a common problem'. Four months later, in the context of legislative plans for a new criminal justice Bill, a leader on 'Alternatives to imprisonment' epitomized the social liberalism consistently espoused by the paper. It made much of the fact that nowhere in Western Europe outside Turkey was a higher proportion of the population imprisoned, and it castigated the government for failing to come to grips with 'so shaming a reflection on Britain's sentencing policy', in particular for 'dismissing an approach which in other countries has proved a civilised and effective solution for both default and many imprisonable offences – weekend and part-time prison which deprives an offender of valuable freedom without ruining his chances of remaining within work and society'.

As 1986 wore on, looming increasingly high on the domestic political agenda was the question of defence, culminating with the publication in December of the Labour Party's *Strategy for Defence*. The *FT* was not altogether hostile to Labour's proposals, quarrelling neither with the idea of scrapping Polaris and abandoning Trident nor with the anomalous nature of the fact that 'the world's 19th economic power should belong to the quintet of nuclear states'. What it could not accept, however, was Labour's case 'within the context of the alliance as a whole'. In particular, 'there is no evidence whatsoever that any of Britain's major allies want the country to embark on a course of unilateral disarmament'. It added: 'It is very difficult not to see the Labour Party's proposals as an attempt to write its own rules and to opt out of alliance responsibilities.' In short: 'An alliance is about sharing, about making some sacrifices in return for some protection. If it is to work at all, it has to be a collective enterprise.'

In these closing years of the *FT*'s first century, however, nothing consumed as much pink newsprint as events in the City of London. Two themes stood out as demanding editorial comment: the continuing wave of take-overs and mergers; and the vexed question of defending the City's reputation in the face of rapid change. 'A surfeit of takeovers' was the headline in December 1985 after Britain's biggest yet take-over bid, the £1.9 billion offer by Hanson Trust for Imperial Group. The leader argued: 'Takeovers are a useful part of the market system, but they can be overdone. As a cure for sick companies, they are often less effective than a change in top management, engineered by non-executive directors or outside shareholders.' The Hanson bid ultimately succeeded, against stiff competition from United Biscuits, and the following September the *FT* devoted a whole leader to the Trust's activities. 'Reshuffling of assets' was the title, and the tone was generally uneasy, especially about Hanson's image in the City:

> It seems that financial opportunism is more highly rated than the building of businesses and that the way to win the City's acclaim is to indulge in adventurous takeover bids which make large headlines – and earn large fees for City institutions. There is nothing wrong with financial opportunism or with takeover bids, but they are only part of what the financing of industry is about.

Towards the reputation of the City as a whole an equal sense of queasiness was the pervasive tone during this period. In December 1985, on the day of the introduction of a new financial services Bill designed to provide a greater degree of investor protection, the paper even declared that 'the City of London stands at a lower point in the public's esteem than it has for many years'. Scandals at Lloyd's, the excesses of Johnson Matthey Bankers, the revolution being undergone in Britain's securities industries – all were part of a pattern that necessitated a balance of statutory and self-regulatory controls, accompanied by 'self-restraint' on the part of the financial community. Ten months later, with the legislation still in the pipeline and continuing to receive broad support from the *FT* despite 'attracting a degree of weary hostility from market practitioners that borders on exasperation', *the* day arrived and the paper sought to put 'Big Bang in perspective' and also the new-style City as a whole. It welcomed the 'vast increase in competition' and with it 'the potential for more efficient capital raising' and the likelihood of 'more open pricing', and it did not object to the fact that 'the leisurely work style of City firms has been replaced by an American work ethic and American pay packages', but the final paragraph sounded a warning note:

Uncertainty and volatility in the international monetary system currently permit those who live off capital flows to earn above-average returns. But bankers cannot defy the laws of economic gravity by earning more than their customers for ever. Nor is there any correlation between a sophisticated financial system and a successful economy; if anything, hyper-active capital markets impose a short-term view on industry and inhibit real investment. In short, financial efficiency must not be allowed to become an end in itself.[9]

On the most important single day in the history of the City, let alone the Stock Exchange, it was a salutary reminder that the *FT* was also devoted to the causes of industry, commerce and public affairs.

The paper was also devoted to the more nebulous cause of international peace and goodwill. In this global area, an especially interesting event was the United States bombing of Libya in April 1986, using British air bases. If one had not been reading any earlier leaders during the build-up of the crisis, one would still have been able to guess with justifiable confidence the respective attitudes (pro, pro and anti) taken to the action by *The Times*, *Telegraph* and *Guardian*, even though the *Telegraph* was less strongly in favour than might have been expected. The same was not true of the *FT*, about whose response bets could easily have been laid either way – a mark of the value and genuinely disinterested quality of the paper's editorial comment. In the event, its reaction was unequivocal:

Yesterday's bombing was futile, deplorable and almost certainly counter-productive; not merely is it unlikely to halt Libyan-sponsored terrorism, it will leave in its wake significant political damage both to the US and to the UK. The British Government, by its unqualified public support for the US action, has compromised its position in ways which are logically and politically untenable.

During the next few months, the paper also seriously questioned government policy over South Africa and in particular its opposition to sanctions. A series of rather tortured leaders culminated in the position adopted by the end of June:

The time has now come for the UK to recognise that the policies of the Government of Pretoria have finally made sanctions unavoidable. There can, of course, be no certainty as to what sanctions would achieve, but this has ceased to be an adequate pretext for inactivity. There is now no alternative. As a leader of the Commonwealth and a pivotal member of the European Community, the

UK should take a positive lead, rather than reluctantly submit to the inexorable.

The purpose of external pressure cannot be to compel change, but to tilt the balance of argument within the white community, however slightly, over the feasibility of their present course of action. The chances of achieving that purpose must be recognised to be small. But the opponents of sanctions cannot prove that they would have no effect at all. If there is *any* chance of persuading the whites that they have no future on the present basis – and there is no evidence that they are indifferent to what the rest of the world does – it must be seized.[10]

Granted the sheer extent of Western capitalism's financial stake in white-controlled South Africa, it represented a remarkable shift of policy on the paper's part.

If those were the 'glamour', high-profile issues, there remained the problem to which a prestigious international business daily had continuously to address itself: how best to achieve satisfactory economic performance and growth in the sluggish, low-growth 1980s. The *FT* offered no magic solutions but plenty of helpful advice. In March 1986, in the context of 'nerve-racking times in a world of free capital movements', it called not for a return to the Bretton Woods system, which 'would mean swimming against the tide of new market technology, rapid communications and persistent innovation in financial instruments and techniques', but instead 'macro-economic policy co-ordination between the major currency powers and a greater readiness to listen to the International Monetary Fund in its almost forgotten role as monitor and arbiter of the exchange rate system'. As for individual components of the world economic engine, particular criticism was levelled at West Germany and Japan. In separate leaders in June 1986, Bonn was urged to 'give an international lead by adopting somewhat more expansionary macro-economic policies', while it was pointed out that 'a doubling of Japan's development assistance would solve the whole African resource problem at a stroke, yet cost Japan less than three weeks of its current account surplus'. In terms of world trade as a whole, with a new GATT round imminent, the paper declared in August 1986 that, in order to safeguard governments against domestic protectionist pressures, 'there is a very strong economic and political case for reasserting the Gatt principle of non-discrimination – that trade concessions agreed in a bilateral negotiation should be extended on a most-favoured-nation basis to all Gatt member countries'.

More than anything, perhaps, the *FT* by this time sought to fight against creeping complacency, epitomized in its eyes by the OECD's *Economic Outlook* of December 1986, which projected without evident concern a future of steady, non-inflationary growth of some 2½ to 3 per cent a year. While accepting that 'five years ago it was easy to dream up much worse scenarios for the world economy', the paper declined to share in the quietist optimism:

Unemployment in Europe at levels last seen in the Great Depression, unprecedented current account imbalances within the OECD, and the Third World's inability either to earn or borrow enough to sustain the momentum of development ought to be powerful antidotes to any tendency towards Panglossian complacency this Christmas.

The supply-side structural reforms introduced in recent years have been both necessary and beneficial. But they may not be sufficient to solve all of the world's economic problems on an adequate timescale. Unemployment, external imbalances and LDC problems could all be ameliorated by faster growth of real demand in the rich creditor countries. The OECD report demonstrates that, after five years of restraint and with inflation at a 20 year low, there is no fiscal constraint to expansion outside the US.[11]

Moving into a new year and the late 1980s, it was a suitably positive note struck by an increasingly distinguished international voice.

What then was the overall balance sheet by the ninety-ninth year? On the negative side, a feeling existed that, especially with the rapid growth of the informative but sometimes bland international company news pages, the paper was coming to mirror too closely and too uncritically what might be described as the corporate world. It was in a sense merely a refrain of the familiar critique that the *FT* at heart was still a local paper appealing to a particular constituency, and that like a local paper it was not in the business of upsetting its readers – except that in the *FT*'s case its constituency happened to be the rather important City of London. It was a critique not without historical validity, though one that grossly misrepresented the overall character of the paper. There was also the whole question of the *FT*'s tone, which was characterized by a certain lingering fastidiousness, even coyness, and was best epitomized in 1986 by its nervous, hesitant approach towards covering the Aids phenomenon. It was a tone that by the mid-1980s represented a strange misreading of the paper's audience; for it was undeniable that most of the *FT*'s readers were now rich, sophisticated and as intimate with the facts of life as with those of the world. Yet perhaps the really serious criticism of the FT by 1986 concerned its *feel*. It was hard to avoid a certain sense that, after almost a decade of deepening and strengthening the redefined product of the late 1970s, the paper had become, for all its enhanced professionalism, somewhat formulaic, a little tired and lacking in surprise. Somewhere along the line the human touch, arguably the entrepreneurial touch, had

gone missing. One former journalist, affectionate but critical, put it rather well, comparing the modern-day *FT* to a Japanese motor car. In both cases the machine was marvellous and all the bits worked, but somehow the overall effect was bland and uninspiring, lacking a certain identity, a certain personality. A paper in need of 'chutzpah': the charge was not altogether fair, but in the mid-1980s it had a certain germ of truth to it.

Nevertheless, if these were faults, they were faults that weighed but slightly in the scales compared with the *FT*'s overwhelming day-in and day-out virtues. Enough has been said to suggest what these virtues were, but any list must include the paper's general authority and weight; its factual accuracy; its objective reporting; its international dimension (no other British paper in 1986 covered in anything like the same depth, or with the same prominence, events like the Austrian general election or the change in the Vietnamese leadership); its reputation for fairness and integrity; its complete lack of proprietorial interference in editorial matters; its liberal attitude towards its writers, allowing on its pages a full spread of well-argued views; perhaps above all, its continuing commitment to the importance of the journalistic enterprise, in an era when the world had never more been in need of lucidly presented information and stringent, dispassionate analysis. The *FT* may have lacked a certain showmanship – for better or for worse – but its deeply imbued editorial qualities of sobriety, moderation and a general measuredness provided ample and abiding compensation. At times indeed the paper seemed one of the last bastions against an encroaching tide of shrillness, ideology and, for want of a better word, 'hype'. Writing early in 1986, Rees-Mogg gave full and just praise to his old paper:

> Both editorially and commercially the *Financial Times* is one of the great success stories of post-war British publishing. I think its influence has been wholly for the good. It sets a standard of seriousness in its coverage which everyone admires. It is an unegotistical paper, free of the personal follies of much contemporary journalism. It is trusted as much on the left as on the right, read by trade union leaders as carefully as by cabinet ministers.

'That is all a long way', he added, 'from the slim newspaper we produced in Coleman Street', and in an obvious sense that was true.[12] In a deeper sense, however, the papers of the 1950s and the 1980s were of the same breed. Both were honest, both tried to do their job properly and both added to the sum of human wisdom and knowledge, if not always to the gaiety of nations. The difference was that the *FT* of the 1980s had transcended its British rivals and joined the ranks of the select. It had become one of the world's great newspapers.

APPENDICES

PROPRIETORS

Financial News

1884–1916	Harry Marks
1919–26	John Jarvis
1926–8	Trireme Trust
1928–45	Eyre & Spottiswoode/Eyre Trust

Financial Times

1888	Jas Sheridan and brother
1888	MacRae, Curtice & Company
1888–1901	Douglas MacRae
c. 1905–19	Sir John Ellerman
1919–37	William and Gomer Berry
1937–45	Lord Camrose
1945–57	Eyre Trust
1957–	Pearson

CHIEF EXECUTIVES

Financial News

1884–1916	Harry Marks
1916–28	H. A. Woodcock
1928–41	Brendan Bracken
1941–5	Lord Moore

Financial Times

1888	Horatio Bottomley
1888–1901	Douglas MacRae
1901–15	F. M. Bridgewater
1915–19	Frank Bridgewater
1919–37	R. J. Barrett
1937–9	Michael Berry
1939–45	Lord Camrose
1945–75	Lord Moore (Lord Drogheda from 1957)
1975–83	Alan Hare
1983–	Frank Barlow

EDITORS

Financial News

1884–1909	Harry Marks
1909–20	Ellis Powell
1920–1	H. C. O'Neill
1921–4	W. A. Doman and William Lang
1924	Sir Laming Worthington-Evans
1925–9	Edward Hilton Young (knighted 1927)
1929–34	Oscar Hobson
1934–8	Maurice Green
1938–45	Hargreaves Parkinson

Financial Times

1888–9	Leopold Graham
1889–90	Douglas MacRae
1890–2	W. R. Lawson
1892–5	Sydney Murray
c. 1896–1909	A. E. Murray
1909–24	C. H. Palmer
1924–37	D. S. T. Hunter
1937–40	Archie Chisholm
1940–5	A. G. Cole
1945–9	Hargreaves Parkinson
1949–72	Gordon Newton (knighted 1966)
1973–80	Fredy Fisher
1981–	Geoffrey Owen

FINANCIAL TIMES CIRCULATION
1928–86

average daily net sale

Year	Sale	Year	Sale
1928	31,441	1957	83,305
1929	31,269	1958	84,858
1930	25,412	1959	102,269
1931	20,915	1960	122,334
1932	19,121	1961	132,279
1933	21,867	1962	137,048
1934	24,971	1963	142,358
1935	25,246	1964	152,212
1936	28,269	1965	149,166
1937	30,380	1966	149,804
1938	24,572	1967	149,311
1939	19,001	1968	159,536
1940	12,714	1969	171,789
1941	12,050	1970	169,900
1942	14,574	1971	170,466
1943	20,272	1972	188,485
1944	25,898	1973	194,289
1945	34,697	1974	194,592
1946	51,706	1975	180,506
1947	68,305	1976	175,155
1948	64,161	1977	177,545
1949	59,463	1978	181,678
1950	57,461	1979	204,599
1951	59,686	1980	197,096
1952	59,702	1981	198,487
1953	60,039	1982	203,283
1954	68,655	1983	213,302
1955	80,360	1984	217,430
1956	79,581	1985	231,514
		1986	252,895

EDITORIAL OFFICES

Financial News
1. 6 St Swithin's Lane (1884–6)
2. 11 Abchurch Lane (1886–1910)
3. 111 Queen Victoria Street (1910–29)
4. 20 Bishopsgate (1929–45)

Financial Times
5. 28 Budge Row (1888)
6. White House, Telegraph Street (1888–92)
7. 52 Coleman Street (1892–1900)
8. 72 Coleman Street (1900–59)
9. Bracken House, Cannon Street (1959–)

REFERENCES

Note: All unattributed references are to the *Financial Times*. The place of publication of books is London unless otherwise stated.

1. Beginnings: 1884–95

1. Francis W. Hirst, *The Stock Exchange* (1911), pp. 80–1.
2. *FN*, 23 January 1904.
3. *FN*, 27 December 1916.
4. *FN*, 23 January 1904.
5. *FN*, 9 May 1889.
6. *FN*, 23 January 1904.
7. *FN*, 25 January 1909.
8. *FN*, 12 October 1895.
9. *FN*, 22 October 1886.
10. David Owen, *The Government of Victorian London, 1855–1889* (1982), p. 175.
11. *The Times*, 22–3 January 1890.
12. *FN*, 26 November 1887.
13. *Statist*, 11 February 1888.
14. H. Osborne O'Hagan, *Leaves from My Life* (1929), Vol. 1, p. 106.
15. Frank Harris, *My Life and Loves* (1966 paperback edn), p. 463.
16. Ibid., pp. 464–6.
17. O'Hagan, op. cit., Vol. 1, p. 266.
18. A. J. P. Taylor, *English History 1914–1945* (Harmondsworth, 1970 paperback edn), p. 665.
19. Ibid., p. 243.
20. 4 April 1901.
21. O'Hagan, op. cit., Vol. 1, p. 265.
22. *Vanity Fair*, 8 June 1889.
23. H. G. Hibbert, *Fifty Years of a Londoner's Life* (1916), p. 169.
24. O'Hagan, op. cit., Vol. 1, pp. 106–7.
25. Ibid., Vol. 1, pp. 107–8.
26. 17 January 1922; *The Times*, 17 January 1922.
27. *FN*, 14 June 1897.
28. H. Simonis, *The Street of Ink* (1917), p. 118.
29. 8 January 1898.
30. 19 November 1889.
31. O'Hagan, op. cit., Vol. 1, p. 109.
32. 5 January 1892, 3 March 1894; O'Hagan, op. cit., Vol. 1, pp. 356–61.
33. *FN*, 22 January 1934.
34. *FN*, 23 January 1904.
35. *FN*, 3–6 November 1888.
36. 16–18 January 1890.
37. *FN*, 9–18 December 1890.
38. 14 June 1892.
39. *FN*, 30 September 1892, 1 November 1892.
40. O'Hagan, op. cit., Vol. 1, pp. 108–9.

2. The Rivals: 1895–1914

1. *FN*, 21 February 1899.
2. 6 April 1897.
3. *Linotype Notes*, May 1901.
4. 2 February 1899.
5. *Morning Post*, 28 May 1903.
6. *Rialto*, 10 April 1901.
7. *Surrey Comet*, 10 June 1899.
8. *The Times*, 4–6 August 1897.
9. 8 May 1897.
10. 2 July 1898.

11. *The Times*, 8–9 March 1900.
12. *The Times*, 19–21 July 1900.
13. *The Times*, 28 July 1898, 2 August 1898, 3 November 1898, 8–9 November 1898.
14. Francis W. Hirst, *The Stock Exchange* (1911), pp. 80–1.
15. *Rialto*, 30 January 1901; *Economist*, 8 February 1902, 21 February 1903; *FT*, 2 March 1904.
16. *FN*, 25 January 1909.
17. 4 April 1901.
18. *Daily News*, 26 September 1904.
19. Charles Duguid, *The Story of the Stock Exchange* (1901), p. 431.
20. 15 January 1902.
21. Records of the London Stock Exchange at the Guildhall Library, London.
22. 27 January 1904.
23. Charles Duguid, *How to Read the Money Article* (1901), p. 99.
24. H. Osborne O'Hagan, *Leaves from My Life* (1929), Vol. 1, p. 385.
25. 25 February 1908.
26. *Isle of Thanet Gazette*, 30 December 1916.
27. *FN*, 2 June 1922.
28. *FN*, 22 January 1934.
29. *Economist*, 18 February 1905; *FI*, 19 February 1907; *The Times*, 16 March 1909.
30. 26 February 1909; *The Times*, 16 March 1909.
31. 3 March 1911.
32. *FN*, 12 February 1913.
33. 3 March 1911.
34. 26 February 1909.
35. *FN*, 19 January 1911.
36. *FN*, 22 January 1934.
37. 28 April 1910.
38. 19 February 1907.
39. *FN*, 31 January 1908.
40. Parliamentary Papers 1913 (152) VII, QQ 8627, 8709.
41. *FN*, 9 February 1912.

3. *FT* in the Ascendant: 1914–28

1. 24 February 1915.
2. 23 March 1916.
3. 10 May 1918.
4. *The Times*, 31 July 1917.
5. *FN*, 27 December 1916.
6. *FN*, 5–8 December 1916.
7. Charles Duguid, *How to Read the Money Article* (1936, 7th edn), p. viii.
8. 21 June 1954.
9. *The Times*, 4 October 1950.
10. Donald Cobbett, *Before the Big Bang!* (1986), p. 56.
11. Paul Einzig, *In the Centre of Things* (1960), pp. 46–8.
12. Ibid., p. 67.
13. Einzig Papers, at Churchill College, Cambridge.
14. *Report of Annual General Meeting of Financial Times Ltd*, 23 May 1924.
15. *Financier*, 23 May 1924.
16. *Dictionary of National Biography, 1951–1960* (Oxford, 1971), p. 1090.
17. Anne Oliver Bell (ed.), *The Diary of Virginia Woolf, 1915–19* (1977), p. 130.
18. The personal journal of Collin Brooks is in the possession of his family.
19. Einzig, op. cit., p. 63.
20. Ibid., p. 63.
21. Kennet Papers at Cambridge University Library.
22. R. S. Sayers, *The Bank of England 1891–1944* (Cambridge, 1976), p. 377.
23. Einzig, op. cit., p. 166.
24. *FN*, 22 January 1934.
25. 31 August 1942.
26. Einzig Papers.
27. Einzig, op. cit., p. 51.
28. 8 May 1928.
29. Einzig, op. cit., pp. 102–3.

4. The Bracken Years: 1928–45

1. Charles Lysaght, *Brendan Bracken* (1979), p. 83.
2. *Brendan Bracken 1901–1958: Portraits and Appreciations* (1958), p. 51.
3. Paul Einzig, *In the Centre of Things* (1960), pp. 100–1.
4. Lysaght, op. cit., p. 88.
5. 10 June 1930.
6. *Report of Annual General Meeting of Financial Newspaper Proprietors Ltd*, 14 October 1929.
7. Anne Oliver Bell (ed.), *The Diary of Virginia Woolf, 1915–19* (1977), p. 170.
8. Compton Mackenzie, *Gallipoli Memories* (1965 paperback edn), p. 84; *FT*, 22 January 1952.
9. *Report of Annual General Meeting of Financial Newspaper Proprietors Ltd*, 14 October 1929.
10. Lysaght, op. cit., p. 102.
11. *FN*, 17 October 1930.
12. *FN*, 10 December 1931.
13. *FN*, 8 December 1932.
14. 9 June 1933.
15. 30 June 1932.
16. 30 June 1932.
17. Einzig, op. cit., p. 65.
18. Lysaght, op. cit., pp. 125–6.
19. Einzig, op. cit., p. 106.
20. *FN*, 25–6 April 1934.
21. House of Lords Record Office.
22. Supplement to *Advertiser's Weekly*, 4 December 1959.
23. Andrew Boyle, *Poor Dear Brendan: The Quest for Brendan Bracken* (1974), p. 224.
24. Lysaght, op. cit., p. 128.
25. *Brendan Bracken 1901–1958*, op. cit., p. 52.
26. *FN*, 10 October 1935.
27. Douglas Jay, *Change and Fortune* (1980), p. 67.
28. 1 July 1985.
29. *FN*, 8 October 1936.
30. *Lloyds Bank Limited Monthly Review*, January 1934; Boyle, op. cit., p. 224.
31. 19 June 1933.
32. Lord Drogheda, *Double Harness* (1978), p. 84.
33. Einzig Papers at Churchill College, Cambridge.
34. Lysaght, op. cit., p. 167.
35. *FN*, 24 November 1939.
36. 6 June 1940.
37. *FN*, 5 December 1939, 7 May 1940.
38. Einzig, op. cit., pp. 241–6.
39. *The Times*, 25 May 1950.
40. 2 December 1942.

5. Merger

1. Charles Lysaght, *Brendan Bracken* (1979), p. 256.
2. Ibid., p. 256.
3. Lord Drogheda, *Double Harness* (1978), p. 114.
4. 6 December 1946.
5. Einzig Papers at Churchill College, Cambridge.
6. Einzig Papers.
7. Paul Einzig, *In the Centre of Things* (1960), p. 253.

6. Towards a National Paper: 1945–9

1. Sonia Orwell and Ian Angus (eds.), *The Collected Essays, Journalism and Letters of George Orwell* (1970 paperback edn), Vol. 2, p. 99.
2. 9 April 1946.
3. 6 December 1946.
4. 12 November 1947.
5. *Guardian*, 25 March 1986.
6. Lord Drogheda, *Double Harness* (1978), p. 134.
7. 31 July 1969.
8. House of Lords Record Office.
9. *Newspaper World*, 31 August 1946.
10. Michael Cockerell, Peter Hennessy

and David Walker, *Sources Close to the Prime Minister* (1984), pp. 46–7.
11. Charles Lysaght, *Brendan Bracken* (1979), p. 259.
12. Ibid., p. 259.
13. House of Lords Record Office.
14. Cherwell Papers at Nuffield College, Oxford.
15. Simon Papers at the Royal Society, London.
16. Einzig Papers at Churchill College, Cambridge.
17. Hargreaves Parkinson, *Ordinary Shares* (1949, 3rd edn), p. 170.
18. 21 November 1945.
19. Einzig Papers.
20. Dalton Diaries at British Library of Political and Economic Science.
21. Paul Einzig, *In the Centre of Things* (1960), pp. 254–5.
22. 10 November 1948.
23. 22 June 1949.
24. Cockerell, op. cit., pp. 100–12.
25. Einzig Papers.
26. 14 June 1950.
27. Nicholas Davenport, *Memoirs of a City Radical* (1974), p. 111.

7. The Triumvirate

1. 31 July 1969.
2. Karin Newman, *Financial Marketing and Communications* (Eastbourne, 1984), p. 182.
3. 1 April 1975.
4. Lord Drogheda, *Double Harness* (1978), pp. 215–16.
5. *Director*, October 1972.
6. 1 April 1975.
7. *The Times Literary Supplement*, 24 November 1978.
8. *Punch*, 13 January 1965.
9. Einzig Papers at Churchill College, Cambridge.
10. Drogheda, op. cit., p. 131.
11. *Management Today*, September 1978.

8. 'Industry, Commerce and Public Affairs': 1950–6

1. 24 May 1951.
2. House of Lords Record Office.
3. *Newspaper World*, 18 January 1951.
4. House of Lords Record Office.
5. Einzig Papers at Churchill College, Cambridge.
6. 1 April 1975.
7. Einzig Papers.
8. Lord Drogheda, *Double Harness* (1978), p. 137.
9. 10 June 1953.
10. Harold Wincott, *The Business of Capitalism* (1968), p. xii.
11. 25 October 1951.
12. Andrew Shonfield, *British Economic Policy since the War* (1958), p. 92.
13. 11 May 1950, 28 June 1950.
14. 18 January 1954.
15. 16 March 1955.
16. Shonfield, op. cit., pp. 224–5.
17. House of Lords Record Office.
18. 8 December 1954.
19. Andrew Porter, *Music of Three Seasons* (1979), p. xiii.
20. House of Lords Record Office.
21. 14 December 1955.
22. *The Times*, 4 February 1964.
23. *Evening Standard*, 22 March 1955.
24. *Trade News*, 29 October 1955.
25. 18 February 1956.
26. 19 May 1956, 31 May 1956.
27. 2 October 1956.
28. *The Times Literary Supplement*, 30 September 1960.

9. Bracken's Memorial: 1957–61

1. Lord Drogheda, *Double Harness* (1978), p. 146.
2. House of Lords Record Office.

3. 30 July 1951.
4. Charles Lysaght, *Brendan Bracken* (1979), p. 320.
5. Drogheda, op. cit., p. 147.
6. Anthony Sampson, *The New Anatomy of Britain* (1971), p. 496.
7. Drogheda, op. cit., p. 149.
8. 1 April 1975.
9. 4 December 1957.
10. Iverach McDonald, *The History of 'The Times', Volume 5: Struggles in War and Peace, 1939–1966* (1984), p. 321.
11. Drogheda, op. cit., pp. 150–1.
12. 15 December 1958.
13. 6 April 1957.
14. *The Times*, 7 January 1958.
15. 14 January 1958.
16. 16 April 1958.
17. 17 May 1958.
18. Lysaght, op. cit., p. 321.
19. 8 September 1979.
20. *The Times*, 13 August 1958.
21. Drogheda, op. cit., p. 144.
22. Ibid., p. 161.
23. Supplement to *Advertiser's Weekly*, 4 December 1959.
24. Ibid.
25. Drogheda, op. cit., p. 143.
26. 28 February 1959.
27. 8 April 1959.
28. Karin Newman, *Financial Marketing and Communications* (Eastbourne, 1984), p. 21.
29. Drogheda, op. cit., p. 162.
30. 26 November 1951.
31. *The Times Literary Supplement*, 11 April 1986.
32. Ibid.
33. Lord Robbins, *Autobiography of an Economist* (1971), p. 291.
34. Drogheda, op. cit., pp. 163, 165.
35. Ibid., p. 170.
36. 4 August 1959.
37. 24 June 1960.

10. 'Below Stairs'

1. 23 May 1961.
2. David Goodhart and Patrick Wintour, *Eddie Shah and the Newspaper Revolution* (1986), pp. 36–7.
3. Ibid., p. 37.
4. Parliamentary Papers 1961–2 (1811–19) XXI, XXII.
5. 20 September 1962.
6. Lord Drogheda, *Double Harness* (1978), p. 200.

11. Consolidation: 1961–6

1. Anthony Sampson, *Anatomy of Britain Today* (1965), p. 144.
2. Richard Crossman, *The Diaries of a Cabinet Minister*, Vol. 1 (1975), p. 240.
3. 28 November 1963.
4. Andrew Porter, *Music of Three Seasons* (1979), p. xiii.
5. 9 May 1963, 17 May 1963, 17 June 1963.
6. 23 November 1963.
7. 19 December 1961.
8. 19 January 1963.
9. 6 March 1963, 28 February 1963.
10. 12 June 1963.
11. 8 July 1963.
12. 12 November 1965.
13. 30 March 1966.
14. Samuel Brittan, *Steering the Economy* (1969), p. 214.
15. Samuel Brittan, *Second Thoughts on Full Employment Policy* (1975), p. vii.
16. 5 May 1966.
17. Iverach McDonald, *The History of 'The Times', Volume 5: Struggles in War and Peace, 1939–1966* (1984), pp. 478–9.
18. Lord Drogheda, *Double Harness* (1978), pp. 189–90.
19. Ibid., p. 192.
20. McDonald, op. cit., p. 415.

21. Drogheda, op. cit., p. 190.
22. Ibid., p. 193.

12. Towards an International Paper: 1966–72

1. *Economist* Intelligence Unit, *The National Newspaper Industry* (1966), pp. 46–8.
2. Ibid., p. 48.
3. Lord Drogheda, *Double Harness* (1978), p. 174.
4. Ibid., p. 211.
5. *The Times*, 7 April 1967.
6. Richard Crossman, *The Diaries of a Cabinet Minister*, Vol. 2 (1976), p. 547, and Vol. 3 (1977), pp. 208, 359, 743.
7. 25 October 1968.
8. Drogheda, op. cit., pp. 211–12.
9. Ibid., p. 165.
10. Parliamentary Papers 1966–7 (3435) XLIII, pp. 8–9.
11. 4 June 1969.
12. 27 July 1967.
13. *The Times*, 2 March 1967.
14. *Observer*, 9 March 1969.
15. 7 March 1969.
16. 30 November 1967.
17. 5 January 1968.
18. Samuel Brittan, *Second Thoughts on Full Employment Policy* (1975), pp. 11–12.
19. 10 April 1969.
20. 19 June 1969.
21. *The Cecil King Diary 1965–70* (1972), p. 222.
22. 18 June 1970.
23. Drogheda, op. cit., p. 357.
24. Ibid., p. 215.
25. 27 April 1970.
26. 15 June 1970.
27. 7 January 1972, 21 February 1972.
28. 22 January 1972.
29. 22 March 1972.
30. 30 December 1972.
31. *The Times*, 4 May 1971.
32. *The Cecil King Diary 1970–74* (1975), p. 156.

13. New Horizons, Old Technology: 1973–9

1. *The Times*, 1 January 1971.
2. Parliamentary Papers 1976–7 (6810–14) XL, XLI.
3. 27 December 1973.
4. 6 February 1974.
5. 28 February 1974.
6. 27 March 1974, 23 March 1974.
7. 25 March 1974, 12 June 1974.
8. 10 October 1974.
9. 1 January 1973.
10. 5 June 1975.
11. 12 February 1975.
12. 1 April 1975.
13. *Accountant*, 27 February 1975.
14. 12 July 1975.
15. *Sunday Times*, 13 July 1975.
16. Roderick Martin, *New Technology and Industrial Relations in Fleet Street* (Oxford, 1981), p. 236.
17. *Sunday Times*, 5 September 1976.
18. Martin, op. cit., pp. 198–9.
19. 14 June 1977.
20. Martin, op. cit., p. 212.
21. 26–7 October 1977.
22. Barbara Castle, *The Castle Diaries 1974–76* (1980), p. 559.
23. 29 March 1976.
24. 11 November 1977.
25. 30 September 1976.
26. 5 January 1979.
27. 7 September 1978.
28. 6 September 1978.
29. 3 May 1979.

14. Internationalism: 1979–85

1. 2 January 1979.
2. 2 January 1979.
3. 7 May 1982.
4. 27 March 1980.
5. 16 October 1980.
6. 11 November 1980.

7. 26 April 1980.
8. 3 November 1980.
9. 11 March 1981.
10. 12 October 1981.
11. 24 November 1981.
12. *The Times*, 13 December 1982.
13. *Guardian*, 22 July 1983.
14. *The Times*, 14 July 1983.
15. *Economist*, 30 July 1983.
16. Minutes of the Council of the Newspaper Publishers' Association, 5 July 1983 (not publicly available).
17. 24 January 1984.
18. *World Press Review*, July 1984.
19. 1 July 1985.
20. 4 March 1985.
21. 4 October 1983, 24 October 1984.
22. 3 October 1984, 28 January 1985.
23. 15 November 1983.
24. 30 March 1984.
25. Lord Drogheda, *Double Harness* (1978), p. 171.
26. 25 April 1985.

Postscript: Towards the Second Century

1. Simon Jenkins, *The Market for Glory* (1986), p. 220.
2. *UK Press Gazette*, 2 December 1985.
3. *UK Press Gazette*, 17 March 1986.
4. *New Statesman*, 5 September 1986.
5. 4 January 1986.
6. 22 February 1986.
7. 14 February 1986.
8. *Wall Street Journal*, 17 February 1986.
9. 26 October 1986.
10. 25 June 1986.
11. 19 December 1986.
12. *Time and Tide*, Winter 1986.

INDEX